FOOD PLANTS OF THE WORLD

FOOD PLANTS
OF THE WORLD

An illustrated guide

Ben-Erik van Wyk

Timber Press

Published in North America and the United Kingdom in 2005 by
Timber Press, Inc.
The Haseltine Building
133 S.W. Second Avenue, Suite 450
Portland, Oregon 97204-3527, U.S.A.
www.timberpress.com
For contact information for editorial, marketing, sales, and distribution in the United Kingdom,
see www.timberpress.com/uk.

First edition, first impression, 2005
First edition, second impression 2006

ISBN-13: 978-0-88192-743-6
ISBN-10: 0-88192-743-0

A catalog record for this book is available from the Library of Congress.

Note that some of the terms used in this book may refer to registered trade names even if they are not
indicated as such.

Cover photographs: Clockwise from top left – *Capsicum annuum*; *Linum usitatissimum*; *Brassica rapa* var.
pekinensis; *Hylocereus undatus*; *Phaseolus coccineus*.
Page 37 – TOP LEFT: Pink pepper (*Schinus molle*) TOP RIGHT: Cornelian cherry (*Cornus mas*)
BOTTOM: Pumpkin seeds (*Cucurbita pepo*)

Disclaimer

Although great care has been taken to be as accurate as possible, neither the author nor the
publisher makes any expressed or implied representation as to the accuracy of the information
contained in this book and cannot be held legally responsible or accept liability for any errors or
omissions. Neither the author nor the publisher can be held responsible for claims arising from
the mistaken identity of plants or their inappropriate use. The publisher and author do not assume
responsibility for any sickness, death or other harmful effects resulting from eating or using any
plant described in this book.

Managing editor: Reneé Ferreira
Proofreader: David Pearson
Cover: Sally Whines, The Departure Lounge
Typesetting: Melinda Stark, Lebone Publishing Services, Cape Town
Reproduction: Unifoto, Cape Town
Printed and bound by Tien Wah Press (Pte.) Ltd, Singapore

CONTENTS

PREFACE

As was the case with the companion volume *Medicinal plants of the world* (first published in 2004), this book is aimed at giving the reader a broad overview in a compact, colourful and scientifically accurate reference text (in this case, for all or most of the commercially important food and flavour plants of the world). Each of the 354 plants and their close relatives are treated briefly, giving relevant facts about the plant, its origin and history, the parts that are used, where and how it is cultivated, its main culinary uses and nutritional value. The plants are listed alphabetically by their scientific names but the common names are given in several languages. To make the book more useful to non-botanists, the introductory pages give lists of common names for the plants in each of various categories (cereals, pulses or legumes, nuts and seeds, fruits, vegetables, culinary herbs, sugar plants, beverage plants and spices), with a cross-reference to their scientific names. An overview of the various classes of nutrients found in plants and their relevance to health and diet is also provided, together with a glossary of terms and a list of critical references for suggested further reading. The comprehensive index will hopefully help the reader to quickly find any plant or information of interest.

Plants included in this book are those that will typically be encountered in fresh produce markets and restaurants in various parts of the world. This is not a book on all edible plants, as a comprehensive list alone will require hundreds of pages. There are many plants that are edible and that are occasionally used by rural people but the main emphasis here is on commercially important plants that are regularly cultivated or wild-harvested and traded.

The use of plants for food and flavour is a dynamic and ever-changing activity – new food sources are constantly being found. Hitherto obscure plants may suddenly become well known through active marketing, or new ones are developed by plant breeding and crop development while others go out of fashion. Equally dynamic is the naming of plants – the same plant may have several names or new names may be invented for commercial reasons. An interesting example is the common name for *Camellia sinensis*, best known as *tea* in the English-speaking world but also by the original *chai* in many parts of the world (including China, Russia and Africa). As a result, the common names listed under each plant may be open to criticism and correction. I would greatly appreciate any suggestions or offers of high quality photographs to improve future editions.

People have become more adventurous in their eating habits and are nowadays exploring new cooking styles, both in the home kitchen and in speciality restaurants. Exotic foods, once restricted to particular countries and cultures, are now spreading to remote corners of the earth on an unprecedented scale. The popularity of food and cooking is also evident in the numerous books and magazines (and even television channels) devoted to this important topic. Professional and amateur chefs are confronted with an ever-increasing diversity of food items (unusual vegetables, fruits, spices and beverages). Ingredients from China, India, Indonesia, Malaysia, Africa and South America are becoming widely available and are listed as essential ingredients in recipe books. Most people are curious about what they are eating and will hopefully find this a user-friendly guide that includes essential information about all the major food and flavour plants of the world.

Ben-Erik van Wyk
May 2005

INTRODUCTION

This book is a photographic guide to the best-known and most commonly used food plants of the world. It includes more than 350 different plants that are sources of cereals, nuts, fruits, vegetables, beverages, sugars and starches, cooking herbs, spices and flavours.

The book is intended to provide quick answers to a wide range of questions about food plants – how to identify them, how to use them in cooking and their nutritional value. For each plant, a short, scientifically accurate summary is given of the characteristics of the plant, its origin and history, the parts that are used, brief notes on cultivation and harvesting and especially the culinary uses and nutritional value. The most commonly used vernacular names are given in various languages, including Chinese, French, German, Hindi, Indonesian, Italian, Japanese, Malay, Portuguese and Spanish. For the botanically minded reader, the correct scientific name, main synonyms, author citation and family name are provided. Where possible, the main culinary uses are mentioned, including famous recipes and famous dishes or drinks that have become widely known.

The first part of the book gives a brief historical overview of the geographical origin of various food crops. The main agricultural regions and the famous food plants associated with each of them are highlighted. This is followed by short chapters on the food value and characteristics of each of the main categories of food plants (cereals, nuts, fruits, vegetables, beverages, sugar and starch, culinary herbs and spices). As a quick and easy reference source, the main plants of each category are listed alphabetically by their common names and the botanical names (under which they are listed in the main part) are also given.

Most of the book comprises short treatments of 354 food plants (and their close relatives), including photographs of the plants and the parts that are used. This is followed by a section on the basic principles of diet and health, focusing on the importance of various nutrients, vitamins, minerals and other dietary ingredients. A quick guide and checklist is provided of more than 800 food plants. It gives their scientific names, common names, geographical origin and main nutritional value. A glossary of terms and a list of important references for further reading are also supplied. The comprehensive index allows the reader to quickly find the required information about a particular food plant and its characteristics and uses.

Man has not always been a farmer, but has always relied on plants as the main source of food. When farming started to replace hunting-gathering as the predominant world culture, numerous new crops were developed with improved characteristics (easier to grow, easier to harvest, better looking and better tasting). These "man-made" plants (known as cultigens or cultivars) became the main source of food during the industrial revolution and are increasingly important in our modern world. Biotechnology and sophisticated breeding techniques are applied to create even more productive and attractive food plants. However, the demands of the marketplace often go against real quality – a fruit or vegetable may look perfect but how tasty or healthy is it really? The stresses and strains of the information age and an increased awareness of the importance of a healthy lifestyle have resulted in many people turning to nutritional foods and regular exercise as a way to improve their quality of life. Vegetarian and organic foods have become part of everyday life. More and more people are returning to the ancient art of growing their own food and experiencing the pleasures associated with using fresh and tasty fruits, vegetables and herbs. Many of us are also fascinated with diversity and want to know more about the foods and tastes of other cultures. This book is aimed at providing all food enthusiasts with informative answers to questions and is intended as a convenient guide to the most relevant facts about food plants and their various uses around the world.

REGIONS OF ORIGIN

The origins of agriculture

Until recent times, man was a nomadic hunter-gatherer who obtained food by killing animals and collecting wild fruits, leaves and roots. The earliest evidence of a shift to a sedentary lifestyle (15 000 years ago) was found in Egypt but the domestication of plants and animals only started about 10 000 years ago. Various suggestions have been made as to how this sudden and dramatic change in the cultural development of human societies actually happened but the details seem to have been lost in time.

Evidence of farming activities has been found in Thailand (11000 BC), the Near East (9000 BC) and Mexico (about 6000 BC). These three regions are considered by some authorities to be the primary centres from where domestication of plants spread to several sub-centres. Important contributions to the knowledge of the origin of cultivated plants were made by the famous botanist Alphonse de Candolle in his book *Origine des Plantes Cultivées* (1882) and later by Nicolai Vavilov, who in 1935 proposed seven areas as the places where most crop plants originated, the so-called gene centres. These were China, India, Central Asia, the Near East, the Mediterranean region, Ethiopia, Mexico and Central America, and South America (Peru, Bolivia, Ecuador and Chile). Zeven and de Wet in their *Dictionary of cultivated plants and their regions of diversity* (1982) reviewed the literature and suggested that there were probably three main cradles of agriculture, namely East Asia (China and Myanmar), the Near East (Fertile Crescent) and Central America. They also proposed 12 regions of diversity, as introduced below.

China and Japan

A distinction is sometimes made between northern China, southern China and Japan, as each has contributed a unique diversity of food plants. This region is notable for important fruit crops such as peach, apricot, loquat, kumquat, litchi and many more. Major crops that originated here include tea, soybean, millet and foxtail millet. Agricultural sites in China date back to earlier than 4000 BC.

Indonesia

This area is also known as the tropical Asian centre and is sometimes subdivided into a southern Asian part (Myanmar, Thailand and Indochina) and a southeastern part (Malaysia). Famous food crops of the region include sugar cane, bananas, rice, taro, yam, coconut and numerous tropical fruits. One of the oldest agricultural sites is that of Spirit Cave in northwestern Thailand, inhabited since 10000 BC.

Australia

There are very few domesticated food crops in Australia but the region is well known as the source of numerous species of gum trees (*Eucalyptus*) that are grown for timber and paper production all over the world. Wild food plants played an important role in the hunter-gatherer lifestyle of the aboriginal people and some have been popularised in modern times (called *bush-tucker* in Australia).

India

Agriculture may have originally spread to India from the northeast (Thailand) but there are several archaeological sites dated to 2000 BC or older. Famous food crops originating in the region include mango, aubergine, cucumber, rice (shared with Indonesia), pigeon pea, tree cotton, ginger, cardamom and pepper. India is a secondary centre of diversity for several African and Middle Eastern crops, including Indian finger millet, cowpea, guar (cluster bean) and chickpea.

Rice terraces in Indonesia

Spice market in Jerusalem   Olive tree in Tuscany

Central Asia

This area includes Iran, Afghanistan, the Himalayas, parts of western China, Uzbekistan and the adjoining regions of the former USSR. Agriculture probably reached here from the Near East around 5000 BC. Well-known crops such as onion, garlic, carrot, spinach, broad bean and grass pea originated here.

Near East

This centre includes all of the Arabian Peninsula, Turkey and the eastern shores of the Black Sea. The Fertile Crescent lies within this region, where agriculture is thought to have first started around 9000 BC. A large number of major crops had their origin here, perhaps the most important being wheat, barley, chickpea, cabbage, lentil, quince, pear, medlar and possibly also safflower, pomegranate and citron. A fascinating book by Zohary and Hopf (1994) entitled *Domestication of plants in the Old World* gives detailed archaeological evidence relating to the early history of many well-known food plants that originated here.

Mediterranean region

Many aspects of modern life can be traced back to the areas bordering the Mediterranean Sea, a centre of cultural and scientific developments that have occurred over many centuries. The region includes ancient Greece and Egypt, where the archaeological record indicates farming activities since at least 5000 BC. Important food plants such as olive, grape, oats, beetroot, radish, cabbage, flax and lupin were domesticated in the Mediterranean area.

Africa

Cave deposits in southern Africa show the presence of modern humans some 50 000 to 70 000 years ago. However, it is in East and West Africa that crop domestication is believed to have been initiated at around 5000 BC or possibly earlier. The two earliest archaeological finds were finger millet on the Ethiopian highlands and pearl millet in Mauritania. The Sahara became progressively drier from about 8 000 years ago and African crops moved with a southward migration into the savanna regions. Relatively recent southward migrations also introduced agriculture to southern Africa. Famous African crops include sorghum, finger millet, pearl millet, watermelon, bottle gourd (calabash), West African yams, fonio, African rice, tef, lablab bean, cowpea, Bambara groundnut, okra, cotton, roselle, enset, oil palm, date palm, sesame and kola. Rooibos tea is a recent domesticate from southern Africa.

Europe and Siberia

Many crops cultivated in this region originated from the Near Eastern region and were introduced before 4000 BC. Europe and Siberia can be credited for the development of some important food plants of which fruit trees (apple, pear, plum and cherry) and various berries (currants, strawberries, raspberries and blackberries) are the best known. The region also contributed asparagus, lettuce, corn salad, hops, chicory, hemp, horseradish, sorrel, elderberry, peppermint, spearmint, angelica, chervil, caraway, parsnip, oregano, liquorice, various cabbages and their relatives (kale, seakale, cabbage, rapeseed, rutabaga, turnip and black mustard), fodder legumes (such as lucerne and clover) and grasses (such as millet sanguin and different types of wild wheat). Examples of ancient crops that have declined and become poorly known include orache (*Atriplex hortensis*), gromwell (*Lithospermum officinale*), goosefoot (*Chenopodium album*), Good King Henry (*C. bonus-henricus*), leafy goosefoot (*C. foliosum*), dandelion (*Taraxacum officinale*), winter cress (*Barbarea verna*), groundnut peavine (*Lathyrus tuberosus*) and turnip-rooted chervil (*Chaerophyllum bulbosum*). Some of these interesting plants have seen a revival in recent years as so-called "biofoods" and alternative vegetables.

South America

The Andes region of Bolivia, Ecuador and Peru is remarkable in its exceptional diversity of ancient crop plants that have enriched the lives of people all over the world. We are indeed indebted to the master farmers, the Incas, for important everyday food plants such as potato, tomato, custard apple, babaco, peanut, yam bean, lima bean, banana passion fruit, tree tomato, peppers, Cape gooseberry and pepino. In addition, there are several poorly known Inca crops that have potential for worldwide cultivation. In a fascinating book on the *Lost crops of the Incas* (National Research Council 1989), several plants such as achira, ahipa, arracacha, capuli cherry, kaniwa, kiwicha, maca, mashua, mauka, oca, quinoa, tarwi, ulluco and yacon are described. The tropical parts of South America (especially Brazil and Paraguay) also contributed numerous important food plants. These include cashew, maté, tannia, pineapple, cassava, brazil nut, sapucaia nut, jack bean, Barbados cherry, New World cotton, arrowroot, Surinam cherry, feijoa, jaboticaba, guava, strawberry guava, passion fruit, guaraná and lemon verbena.

Central America and Mexico

The diversity of Aztec and Maya food plants rivals that of the Incas. Many of them became staple foods in other countries and form an important part of modern diets all over the world (consider chocolate, vanilla, popcorn, baked beans, avocado, green peppers and chillies!) Farming has been practised in Mexico at least since 7000 BC. Important and well-known crop plants of Mayan origin include amaranth, grain amaranth, various custard apples, cacao, ceriman, dragon fruit, prickly pear, papaya, sweet potato, various pumpkins, cho-cho, black sapote, corn (maize), pecan, avocado, yam bean, runner bean, common bean, vanilla, winter purslane, white sapote, sapodilla, bell pepper, tabasco pepper and tomatillo.

North America

This region contributed relatively few but important food crops. Noteworthy are sugar maple, sunflower, Jerusalem artichoke, highbush blueberry, cranberry, wild rice, black walnut, potato bean and several species of plums, cherries, grapes, strawberries and raspberries that have been used in the breeding of modern cultivars (or as source of rootstocks).

Harvesting wheat by hand

Winnowing barley in Ethiopia

Harvesting wheat by horse-drawn self-binder

Mexican wild maize (*Zea mays* subsp. *parviglumis*) Fruit of cacao (*Theobroma cacao*)

CEREALS

The collection of wild grasses for food, especially in times of scarcity, is still seen in parts of Africa. Domesticated cereals differ from their wild counterparts mainly in the retention of the grains on the ears at ripening – they are non-shattering. It is not difficult to imagine how this trait was intentionally or inadvertently selected for by the first farmers, perhaps 15 000 years ago. The first cereals were developed independently in three different regions (often called the "Cradles of Agriculture"): rice in east India and Southeast Asia, barley and wheat in Mesopotamia and maize and quinoa in Central America. Also of ancient origin are various millets, still popular in parts of China, Europe and Africa. Numerous other grains soon followed, including oats in central Europe, buckwheat and common millet in southern China, pearl millet, finger millet and sorghum in Africa, and rye and foxtail millet in Europe and Asia.

Practically all cereals belong to the grass family (Poaceae or Gramineae). The grains are actually small, dry, one-seeded fruits (caryopses) in which the seed coat (testa) is fused with the fruit wall (pericarp). These fruits store carbohydrates in a special tissue (endosperm) and also in the single cotyledon. The grains may be free-threshing as in wheat or rye, or they may be enclosed by an inedible husk, as in oats and barley. Only three important cereals are not grasses: grain amaranth (*Amaranthus* species), quinoa (*Chenopodium quinoa*) and buckwheat (*Fagopyrum esculentum*).

Cereals are best eaten as whole, unprocessed grains – cooked like rice or minimally processed as gruels or porridges. Whole grains generally contain 75% starch, about 10–15% protein and 2% fat, together with fibre, vitamins (especially B vitamins) and tocopherols (vitamin E) in the germ. Unfortunately, refined cereal products such as flour have not only the fibre-rich bran removed but also the germ (to avoid spoilage). This may lead to dietary problems such as obesity and gastrointestinal disturbances. Starch is the main energy source – typically giving an energy yield of about 200 to 350 kcal (840 to 1 470 kJ) per 100 g portion. Flour has higher and bread somewhat lower energy values than the raw cereal itself. Starch can be converted to simple sugars during the process of malting (see under Beverages). Because cereals are used as staple foods, the quantity and quality of free and protein-bound amino acids are of the utmost importance. The total proteins vary from low in rice (about 7%), moderate in most cereals (10 to 12%) to high in amaranth and quinoa (about 14%). Some cereals have a low yield of lysine and other important amino acids, which may lead to malnutrition and serious deficiency symptoms if not corrected. Rice has a large percentage available protein and combines perfectly with beans and other legumes. Brown rice is far superior to white rice in nutritional value but is "chewy" and therefore less popular.

Wheat is preferred for baking bread because it is the only cereal with gluten (an elastic protein complex that forms when bread dough is kneaded). Gluten traps the gases produced by yeast and this makes the bread rise. Bread-baking has become a sophisticated art. Variations in the addition of sugar (preferably glucose or fructose and not sucrose, as nutrient source for the yeast), malt and salt (for taste) to the grain flour (various mixtures can be used) all lead to an endless diversity in texture, taste and nutritional value. Modern cultivars of bread wheat (*Triticum aestivum*) have not entirely replaced ancient wheat types such as emmer (*T. turgidum*), einkorn (*T. monococcum*) and spelt (*T. spelta*) which are still grown in some isolated areas and which are even making a comeback as modern "biofoods".

In most societies, cereals are the main staple food and starch source that provides energy. In a balanced diet, cereals should be combined with pulses (beans), nuts (oilseeds), fresh fruits and fresh vegetables, as these will all contribute important amino acids, vitamins and minerals.

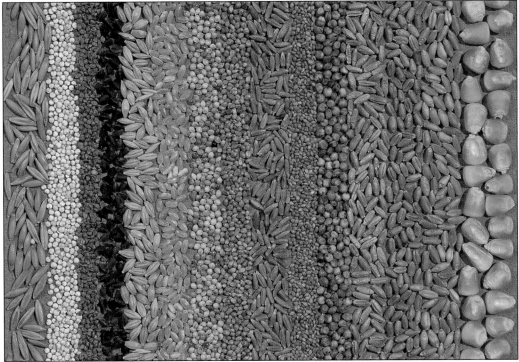

A selection of common cereals: oats, quinoa, Japanese millet, buckwheat, barley, rice, common millet, pearl millet, rye, foxtail millet, sorghum, triticale, bread wheat, pasta wheat and maize (corn)

List of main cereals

adlay (*Coix lachryma-jobi*)
African finger millet (see finger millet)
American wild rice (*Zizania aquatica*)
barley (*Hordeum vulgare*)
bread wheat (*Triticum aestivum*)
buckwheat (*Fagopyrum esculentum*)
Canadian wild rice (*Zizania aquatica*)
Chinese pearl barley (see adlay)
common millet (*Panicum miliaceum*)
corn (*Zea mays*)
durum wheat (*Triticum durum*)
finger millet (*Eleusine coracana*)
fonio (*Digitaria exilis*)
foxtail millet (*Setaria italica*)
grain amaranth (*Amaranthus cruentus*)
Inca wheat (see grain amaranth)

Indian finger millet (see finger millet)
Japanese millet (*Echinochloa frumentacea*)
Job's tears (see adlay)
kaniwa (see under quinoa)
mealies (see maize)
millet (*Panicum miliaceum*)
oats (*Avena sativa*)
pearl millet (*Pennisetum glaucum*)
proso millet (see millet)
quinoa (*Chenopodium quinoa*)
rice (*Oryza sativa*)
rye (*Secale cereale*)
sorghum (*Sorghum bicolor*)
teff (*Eragrostis tef*)
triticale (see under rye)
wild rice (*Zizania aquatica*)

PULSES (legumes)

Pulses and legumes are loosely referred to as "peas" and "beans". They all belong to the legume family (Fabaceae) and have distinctive fruits and seeds. The fruit is a legume or pod – a fruit formed from a single carpel that usually bursts into two halves when it ripens and dries out. Both the upper, seed-bearing suture and lower suture come apart to release the seeds. The seeds are often (but not always) kidney-shaped, with a tough outer seed coat (testa) around the two thick embryonic leaves (cotyledons). These cotyledons store nutrients, which are absorbed by the seedling during germination and early growth.

Plants of the legume family develop root nodules as a result of a symbiotic association with nitrogen-fixing bacteria. These bacteria have the ability to fix atmospheric nitrogen, which becomes available to the host plant. As a result, the seeds tend to have high levels of nitrogen in the form of amino acids and proteins – less than in animal products but nevertheless very important in the diets of vegetarians.

Dried peas, beans and lentils can be variously processed. The most common product is split seeds, known as *dhal* – the seed coat is simply removed and the two cotyledons are split apart. Split peas and split lentils are perhaps the most familiar forms of *dhal*, but practically all pulses can be used in this way. The seeds can also be ground into flour or turned into pastes and various fermented products (even meat and milk substitutes) as in the case of soybean. Sprouted raw legumes can be used fresh in salads or enjoyed on their own as part of a meal. Beans and peas form an important part of most cooking traditions around the world and they add variety, taste and texture to the diet.

Pulses combine well with cereals and are exceptionally nutritious, with 20–25% proteins in the dried, raw seeds and 6–8% in the cooked form (note that the calculation is influenced by the water content). They are an excellent source of the essential amino acid lysine, which is often deficient in cereals. Starch and other carbohydrates represent 50% of the dry seed weight and about 20% after cooking. The fat content is rarely more than 2% (exceptions are soybean and peanuts). The energy yield varies from about 270 kcal (1 144 kJ) per 100 g of dry seeds (lentils and others) to almost 350 kcal per 100 g for soya flour and nearly 400 kcal in the case of winged bean (goa bean) seeds. Pulses are rich in dietary fibre, including soluble fibre. A rich diversity of vitamins and minerals is present, often enriching or complementing those found in cereals.

All pulses except split peas and lentils have to be soaked (in a large volume of water) before cooking to mobilise and leach out anti-nutritional enzymes. Most pulses should be boiled for at least 15 minutes to denature these enzymes. Soaking (and discarding the water) will also reduce the level of indigestible sugars (mainly raffinose and stachyose) that cause flatulence. Humans lack the enzymes needed to digest these carbohydrates, so that they are broken down by bacterial enzymes in the large intestine, leading to the production of gas. Despite these disadvantages, pulses are a versatile and valuable food source that contributes a large part of the protein requirements in a mixed diet.

In many cultures of the world, pulses form one of the three corners of the perfect food triangle – a cereal for energy, a pulse for proteins and vegetables for vitamins and minerals. Examples of such triangles are beans with maize and pumpkin in Mexico, cowpea with sorghum and bottle gourd in Africa, peas or lentils with bread and cabbage in Europe and soybean with rice and mustard leaves in China. The combination of pulse and cereal remains popular in the modern diet, as exemplified by pea soup and bread, beans and tortillas, baked beans on toast or lentils on rice.

A selection of common legumes and pulses: groundnut, pigeonpea, jack bean, chickpea, soybean, lablab bean, lentil, lupin, velvet bean, runner bean, lima bean, common bean, garden pea, fenugreek, broad bean, adzuki bean, urd bean, mung bean, Bambara groundnut and cowpea

List of main pulses and legumes

adzuki bean (*Vigna angularis*)
alfalfa (*Medicago sativa*)
asparagus pea (*Lotus tetragonolobus*)
Bambara groundnut (*Vigna subterranea*)
bean (*Phaseolus vulgaris*)
black-eyed bean (see cowpea)
black gram (see under mung bean)
broad bean (*Vicia faba*)
butter bean (see lima bean)
chickling vetch (see grass pea)
chickpea (*Cicer arietinum*)
cluster bean (*Cyamopsis tetragonoloba*)
common bean (see bean)
cowpea (*Vigna unguiculata*)
fava bean (see broad bean)
fenugreek (*Trigonella foenum-graecum*)
groundnut (*Arachis hypogaea*)
French bean (see bean)
haricot bean (see bean)
garden pea (*Pisum sativum*)
goa bean (see winged bean)
golden gram (see mung bean)
grass pea (*Lathyrus sativus*)
green gram (see mung bean)

groundnut (see peanut)
guar (see cluster bean)
gunga pea (see pigeonpea)
hyacinth bean (see lablab bean)
jack bean (*Canavalia ensiformis*)
jugo bean (*Vigna subterranea*)
lablab bean (*Lablab purpureus*)
lentil (*Lens culinaris*)
lima bean (*Phaseolus lunatus*)
lucerne (*Medicago sativa*)
lupin, lupine (*Lupinus albus*)
mung bean (*Vigna radiata*)
peanut (*Arachis hypogaea*)
pea (*Pisum sativum*)
pigeonpea (*Cajanus cajan*)
runner bean (*Phaseolus coccineus*)
scarlet runner bean (see runner bean)
sieva bean (see lima bean)
soybean (*Glycine max*)
sweet lupin (see lupin)
sword bean (see under jack bean)
urd bean (see under mung bean)
velvet bean (see under jack bean)
winged bean (*Psophocarpus tetragonolobus*)

NUTS AND SEEDS

Nuts are defined as dry, single-seeded fruits with a high oil content, enclosed in a leathery or bony outer layer. Many so-called oilseeds are actually small fruits (achenes) and therefore also fit this definition. Examples are sunflower, niger seed and safflower. On the other hand, some oilseeds are indeed oil-rich seeds and not fruits – these include rapeseed (canola), linseed and poppy seeds. In the list of nuts and seeds given here, some overlap with other categories is unavoidable. Peanuts and soybeans, for example, are both pulses and oilseeds; maize (corn) is a cereal as well as an oilseed (and popcorn is eaten as a snack food in much the same way as nuts).

Nuts are exceptionally nutritious and provide a better combination of nutrients than animal products. Nuts and oilseeds have an exceptionally high energy value (calorific value) due to the high unsaturated fat content. Whereas carbohydrate foods such as cereals yield around 350 kcal per 100 g, most nuts and oilseeds provide between 500 and 700 kcal per 100 g (up to 2 900 kJ). Pure vegetable fats and oils typically yield 900 kcal (3 700 kJ) per 100 g. Fortunately, the nutrient density is very high, so that nuts are not fattening if eaten in moderation. Nuts are rich in proteins and essential amino acids – only 150 g will provide all the daily needs of an average adult. Unlike animal fats, plant fats are unsaturated and therefore considered to be cholesterol lowering and beneficial to the cardiovascular system. The fatty acids are mostly a combination of linoleic acid, oleic acid and palmitic acid. Plant fats and oils contain various natural antioxidants, of which a high concentration of vitamin E is particularly noteworthy.

List of nuts and seeds

almond (*Prunus dulcis*)
argan (*Argania spinosa*)
Bambara groundnut (*Vigna subterranea*)
baobab (*Adansonia digitata*)
ben tree (*Moringa oleifera*)
black cumin (*Nigella sativa*)
black seed (see black cumin)
black walnut (see under walnut)
borage seeds (*Borago officinalis*)
brazil nut (*Bertholletia excelsa*)
broad bean (*Vicia faba*)
candlenut (*Aleurites moluccana*)
canola (see rape)
carob (*Ceratonia siliqua*)
cashew (*Anacardium occidentale*)
chestnut (*Castanea sativa*)
chufa (*Cyperus esculentus*)
cluster bean (*Cyamopsis tetragonoloba*)
cola nut (*Cola acuminata*)
coconut (*Cocos nucifera*)
corn (*Zea mays*)
cotton seeds (*Gossypium hirsutum*)
drumstick tree (*Moringa oleifera*)
fava bean (see broad bean)
fenugreek (*Trigonella foenum-graecum*)
filbert (see hazelnut)
ginkgo nuts (*Ginkgo biloba*)
guar (see cluster bean)
hazelnut (*Corylus avellana*)
jugo bean (*Vigna subterranea*)
linseed (*Linum usitatissimum*)
kalonji (*Nigella sativa*)
lotus (*Nelumbo nucifera*)

macadamia (*Macadamia integrifolia*)
maize (*Zea mays*)
Malabar chestnut (*Pachira aquatica*)
manketti nut (*Schinziophyton rautanenii*)
mongongo (see manketti nut)
monkey bread (see baobab)
niger seed (*Guizotia abyssinica*)
oil palm (*Elaeis guineensis*)
oilseed rape (see rape)
opium poppy (*Papaver somniferum*)
palmyra palm (*Borassus flabellifer*)
peanut (*Arachis hypogaea*)
pecan nut (*Carya illinoinensis*)
Persian walnut (see walnut)
popcorn (*Zea mays*)
pine nuts (*Pinus pinea*)
pistachio (*Pistacia vera*)
poppy seeds (*Papaver somniferum*)
pumpkin seeds (*Cucurbita* species)
rape (*Brassica napus*)
safflower (*Carthamus tinctorius*)
sapucaia nut (see brazil nut)
sesame (*Sesamum indicum*)
soybean (*Glycine max*)
Spanish chestnut (see chestnut)
stone pine (see pine nuts)
sunflower (*Helianthus annuus*)
sweet chestnut (see chestnut)
tiger nut (*Cyperus esculentus*)
turnip rape (see *Brassica rapa* var. *rapa*)
walnut (*Juglans regia*)
West African oil palm (see oil palm)
white nuts (*Ginkgo biloba*)

A selection of common nuts: cashew nut, peanut, brazil nut, pecan nut, hazelnut, pumpkin seeds, walnut, macadamia nut, pine nut, pistachio nut and almond

A selection of oilseeds and various other edible seeds: rapeseed, safflower, niger seed, sunflower, linseed, lotus seed, poppy and sesame

FRUITS

Fruits are the reproductive structures formed by plants, which enclose the seeds and help with their dispersal. Most fruits listed here are fleshy or have fleshy appendages as the edible parts. Fruits can be categorised as stone fruits or drupes (peaches, plums etc., with a single hard stone), pip fruits (apples, pears and quinces, with several pips), berries (fleshy fruits with numerous seeds, such as blueberries, cranberries, gooseberries, melons, tomatoes, bananas, etc.; or compound fruits with numerous small drupelets, such as blackberries, mulberries, strawberries, etc.), citrus fruits (with characteristic fruit segments comprising fleshy juice cells and surrounded by a peel that has an outer zest (*flavedo*) and an inner, white, spongy layer (*albido*)) and aril fruits (large or small, sometimes with inedible seeds but each with an edible, fleshy appendage, e.g. litchi, passion fruit, durian and jackfruit).

There is good evidence that the daily consumption of fresh fruits reduces the risk of diseases, including cancer. However, fruits have a high water content and a relatively low food value (low calories, typically 30 to 70 kcal per 100 g), so that they should always be combined with other foods in order to create a balanced diet. Some exceptions are banana (about 90 kcal), granadilla (95 kcal), avocado (160 kcal) and olives (420 kcal). Fruits are rich sources of important dietary components such as fibre, soluble fibre (pectins and polysaccharides), vitamins (especially vitamins A, C and E), easily digestible sugars (fructose) and minerals. Various organic compounds such as phenols and flavonoids also contribute to the nutritional value by their protective role against cancer and their antioxidant and venotonic effects.

Fruits are variously processed into jams and juices or may be canned or dried. Dried fruits have a high food value because they yield at least four times more calories than fresh fruits. This makes them ideal as a health food and energy source for young children. Sulphur has been used as a preservative for dried fruit but with improved processing methods it is possible to avoid all preservatives. A selection of common dried fruits is shown in the section on sugar plants. Fresh fruit juice, preferably without harmful preservatives, is a fine source of vitamin C and other nutrients. It is important to stress that fruits give their maximum health benefits when combined with other foods in a mixed diet.

List of fruits from cold climates

(Oranges and most other *Citrus* fruits are listed with tropical and subtropical fruits)

American cranberry (*Vaccinium macrocarpon*)
apple (*Malus domestica*)
apricot (*Prunus armeniaca*)
banana passion fruit (*Passiflora mollissima*)
bilberry (*Vaccinium myrtillus*)
bergamot orange (see bitter orange)
blackberry (*Rubus fruticosus*)
black currant (*Ribes nigrum*)
black mulberry (*Morus nigra*)
black nightshade (*Solanum nigrum*)
blueberry (see highbush blueberry, bilberry)
boysenberry (see under loganberry)
bramble (*Rubus fruticosus*)
cantaloupe (see melon)
Cape gooseberry (*Physalis peruviana*)
cherry (see sweet cherry, sour cherry)
cherry guava (see strawberry guava)
cherry plum (see under sloe)
Chinese boxthorn (*Lycium chinense*)
Chinese date (*Ziziphus jujuba*)
Japanese raisin (*Hovenia dulcis*)
jujube (see Chinese date)

Chinese gooseberry (see kiwifruit)
cloudberry (*Rubus chamaemorus*)
common blueberry (see bilberry, highbush blueberry)
cowberry (*Vaccinium vitis-idaea*)
cranberry (see large cranberry, small cranberry)
currant (see blackcurrant, red currant)
curuba (*Passiflora mollissima*)
desert apple (see under Chinese date)
dog rose (*Rosa canina*)
European cranberry (*Vaccinium oxycoccus*)
European plum (see plum)
elderberry (*Sambucus nigra*)
fig (*Ficus carica*)
French jujube (see Chinese date)
gooseberry (*Ribes uva-crispa*)
grape (*Vitis vinifera*)
highbush blueberry (*Vaccinium corymbosum*)
huckleberry (see under black nightshade)
Indian jujube (see under Chinese date)
jamberry (*Physalis ixocarpa*)
raspberry (*Rubus idaeus*)
red currant (*Ribes rubrum*)

A selection of fruits from cold and temperate regions

kiwifruit (*Actinidia deliciosa*)
kumquat (*Fortunella margarita*)
large cranberry (*Vaccinium macrocarpon*)
lemon (*Citrus limon*)
lingonberry (*Vaccinium vitis-idaea*)
loganberry (*Rubus loganobaccus*)
loquat (*Eriobotrya japonica*)
medlar (*Mespilus germanicus*)
melon pear (see pepino)
mirabelle (see under sloe)
mountain ash (*Sorbus aucuparia*)
mulberry (see white mulberry, black mulberry)
nashi (see pear)
olive (*Olea europaea*)
peach (*Prunus persica*)
pear (*Pyrus communis*)
pepino (*Solanum muricatum*)
persimmon (*Diospyros kaki*)
plum (*Prunus domestica*)
prune (see plum)
quince (*Cydonia oblonga*)

red date (see Chinese date)
rose hips (see dog rose)
rose petals (see under dog rose)
rowanberry (see mountain ash)
serviceberry (see mountain ash)
sloe (*Prunus spinosa*)
small cranberry (*Vaccinium oxycoccus*)
sour cherry (*Prunus cerasus*)
strawberry (*Fragaria ananassa*)
strawberry guava (*Psidium littorale*)
strawberry tree (*Arbutus unedo*)
sweet cherry (*Prunus avium*)
table grape (see grape)
tamarillo (see tree tomato)
tayberry (see under loganberry)
tomatillo (*Physalis ixocarpa*)
tree tomato (*Cyphomandra betacea*)
watermelon (*Citrullus lanatus*)
white mulberry (*Morus alba*)
wonderberry (see black nightshade)
youngberry (see under loganberry)

List of fruits from warm climates

acerola (*Malpighia glabra*)
African horned cucumber (see jelly melon)
African mangosteen (see under mangosteen)
African water berry (see under jambolan)
akee (*Blighia sapida*)
ambarella (*Spondias cytherea*)
atemoya (see cherimoya)
avocado (*Persea americana*)
babaco (see under papaya)
banana (*Musa acuminata*)
banana passion fruit (*Passiflora mollissima*)
baobab (*Adansonia digitata*)
Barbados cherry (*Malpighia glabra*)
ber (see under Chinese date)
bilimbi (*Averrhoa bilimbi*)
black persimmon (see black sapote)
black sapote (*Diospyros digyna*)
breadfruit (*Artocarpus altilis*)
brush cherry (see under jambolan)
cactus apple (*Cereus peruvianus*)
canistel (*Pouteria campechiana*)
cantaloupe (see melon)
Cape gooseberry (*Physalis peruviana*)
carambola (*Averrhoa carambola*)
carob (*Ceratonia siliqua*)
ceriman (*Monstera deliciosa*)
Ceylon gooseberry (*Dovyalis hebecarpa*)
cherimoya (*Annona cherimola*)
cherry guava (see strawberry guava)
Chinese boxthorn (*Lycium chinense*)
Chinese date (*Ziziphus jujuba*)
Chinese gooseberry (see kiwifruit)
citron (*Citrus medica*)
clementine (see mandarin)
coconut (*Cocos nucifera*)
Costa Rican guava (see under strawberry guava)
curuba (*Passiflora mollissima*)
custard apple (see cherimoya)
date (*Phoenix dactylifera*)
delicious monster (*Monstera deliciosa*)
dragon fruit (*Hylocereus undatus*)
dragon's eye (see longan)
durian (*Durio zibethinus*)
feijoa (see pineapple guava)
fig (*Ficus carica*)
French jujube (see Chinese date)
gherkin (see West Indian gherkin)
governor's plum (see under kitembilla)
grapefruit (*Citrus paradisi*)

granadilla (*Passiflora edulis*)
guanábana (see sour sop)
guava (*Psidium guajava*)
guavadilla (see granadilla)
hog plum (*Spondias cytherea*)
Indian mulberry (see noni fruit)
jaboticaba (*Myrciaria cauliflora*)
jackfruit (*Artocarpus heterophyllus*)
jamberry (*Physalis ixocarpa*)
jambolan (*Syzygium cumini*)
jambos (*Syzygium jambos*)
Java plum (*Syzygium cumini*)
Java rose apple (*Syzygium samarangense*)
Java wax apple (*Syzygium samarangense*)
jelly melon (*Cucumis metuliferus*)
jujube (see Chinese date)
kei-apple (see under kitembilla)
kitembilla (*Dovyalis hebecarpa*)
kiwifruit (*Actinidia deliciosa*)
kiwano (see jelly melon)
kumquat (*Fortunella margarita*)
lime (*Citrus aurantiifolia*)
litchi (*Litchi chinensis*)
longan (*Dimocarpus longan*)
loquat (*Eriobotrya japonica*)
lychee (*Litchi chinensis*)
Malabar plum (see rose apple)
Malay rose apple (see under Java wax apple)
Malacca rose apple (see under Java wax apple)
mammee (*Mammea americana*)
mandarin (*Citrus reticulata*)
mango (*Mangifera indica*)
mangosteen (*Garcinia mangostana*)
manketti (*Schinziophyton rautanenii*)
maracuja (see passion fruit)
marula (*Sclerocarya birrea*)
melon (*Cucumis melo*)
melon pear (see pepino)
minneola (see mandarin)
mulberry (see white mulberry, black mulberry)
musk melon (see melon)
nartjie (see mandarin)
navel orange (see sweet orange)
noni fruit (*Morinda citrifolia*)
Otaheite gooseberry (*Phyllanthus acidus*)
papaya (*Carica papaya*)
passion fruit (*Passiflora edulis*)
paw paw (see papaya)
pepino (*Solanum muricatum*)

A selection of tropical and subtropical fruits

persimmon (*Diospyros kaki*)
pineapple (*Ananas comosus*)
pineapple guava (*Acca sellowiana*)
pitanga (*Eugenia uniflora*)
pitahaya (see dragon fruit)
pitaya (see cactus apple, dragon fruit)
pomegranate (*Punica granatum*)
pomelo (*Citrus maxima*)
prickly pear (*Opuntia ficus-indica*)
rambutan (*Nephelium lappaceum*)
red date (see Chinese date)
rose apple (*Syzygium jambos*)
rough lemon (see under lemon)
salak (*Salacca edulis*)
sapodilla (*Manilkara zapota*)
sapote (see white sapote, black sapote)
Seville orange (see bitter orange)
shaddock (*Citrus maxima*)
sour fig (*Carpobrotus edulis*)
sour orange (see bitter orange)
soursop (*Annona muricata*)

starfruit (*Averrhoa carambola*)
star gooseberry (*Phyllanthus acidus*)
strawberry guava (*Psidium littorale*)
sugar apple (*Annona squamosa*)
sugar palm (*Arenga pinnata*)
Surinam cherry (*Eugenia uniflora*)
sweet orange (*Citrus sinensis*)
tamarind (*Tamarindus indica*)
tangerine (*Citrus reticulata*)
Tahiti lime (see lime)
tomatillo (*Physalis ixocarpa*)
Valencia orange (see sweet orange)
watermelon (*Citrullus lanatus*)
water apple (see under *Syzygium samarangense*)
watery rose apple (see under *Syzygium samarangense*)
wax jambu (*Syzygium samarangense*)
West Indian gherkin (*Cucumis anguria*)
West Indian lime (see lime)
white mulberry (*Morus alba*)
white sapote (*Casimiroa edulis*)
winter melon (see melon)

VEGETABLES

The term "vegetable" may include almost any part of a plant (roots, stems, leaves, flowers, fruits or even the whole plant). To provide a more useful discussion, vegetables have here been divided into three categories:

- Roots, tubers and bulbs (vegetables used mainly for their underground parts)
- Leaves, stems and flowers (vegetables used mainly for their leaves and stems and/or flowers)
- Fruits and seeds (vegetables used mainly for their unripe or ripe fruits or seeds)

Root, tuber and bulb vegetables (vegetables used mainly for their underground parts)

These plants are known as geophytes – they have fleshy underground parts that originate from roots, stems or leaf bases. The taproot of the plant may become massively swollen and often brightly coloured, as in carrots, beetroots, turnips and radishes. These vegetables usually have a low calorific value (radish: 15 kcal per 100 g, carrots 18 kcal, beetroot 40 kcal and parsnip 59 kcal) but they add important minerals and vitamins to the diet. The pigments are of special dietary significance, especially the carotenoids in the case of carrots, which serve as vitamin A precursors.

The familiar potato is an example of a tuber – rounded, swollen, underground storage structures that are of stem origin (they are not roots). Tubers typically store large amounts of starch that are a valuable food source with a high energy value. Pure starch yields about 340 kcal per 100 g, while the value for potatoes (70 kcal) is lower because of the effect of the high water content of the cooked or boiled vegetable. Cassava roots (134 kcal) and sweet potatoes (108 kcal) resemble tubers in their high starch yield but are true roots and not tubers.

Rhizomes are branching, often fleshy stems that spread below the soil surface and form leaves above and thin roots below. The taro (cocoyam), edible canna and Jerusalem artichoke are examples. Starch is usually the main storage product but in the case of all members of the daisy family (Asteraceae) such as Jerusalem artichoke, chicory, salsify and scorzonera, the storage polysaccharide is inulin and not starch.

Onions and leeks are examples of bulbs – they are practically stemless and have swollen leaf bases that form a fleshy structure below the ground. The true stem is represented by a small, disc-shaped structure to which both the fleshy leaves and the roots are attached (visible when an onion is cut in half). Garlic and shallot plants typically produce numerous bulblets as a result of side shoots that split off from the short main stem. Onions and their relatives are the main bulbous vegetables.

List of common root, tuber and bulb vegetables

achira (*Canna edulis*)
air potato (*Dioscorea bulbifera*)
amicho (see enset)
beetroot (*Beta vulgaris* var. *esculenta*)
black salsify (see scorzonera)
bulb onion (see onion)
burdock (*Arctium lappa*)
canna, edible canna (see achira)
carrot (*Daucus carota*)
cassava (*Manihot esculenta*)
celeriac (*Apium graveolens*)
Chinese water chestnut (*Eleocharis dulcis*)
Chinese yam (see under air potato)
cocoyam (*Colocasia esculenta*)
enset (*Ensete ventricosum*)
garlic (*Allium sativum*)
gobo (see burdock)

Jerusalem artichoke (*Helianthus tuberosus*)
Livingstone potato (*Plectranthus esculentus*)
lotus (*Nelumbo nucifera*)
neeps (see turnip)
New Zealand yam (see oca)
oca (*Oxalis tuberosa*)
onion (*Allium cepa*)
parsnip (*Pastinaca sativa*)
potato (*Solanum tuberosum*)
potato yam (see air potato)
Queensland arrowroot (see achira)
radish (*Raphanus sativus*)
runner bean (*Phaseolus coccineus*)
rutabaga (see swede)
salsify (see under scorzonera)
scarlet runner bean (see runner bean)
scorzonera (*Scorzonera hispanica*)
shallot (see onion)

A selection of vegetables derived from roots, tubers and bulbs

Sudan potato (see under Livingstone potato)	turnip-rooted celery (see celery)
swede (*Brassica napus*)	ulluco (*Ullucus tuberosus*)
sweet potato (*Ipomoea batatas*)	water chestnut (see Chinese water chestnut)
taro (*Colocasia esculenta*)	white yam (*Dioscorea cayenensis*)
tuber nasturtium (*Tropaeolum tuberosum*)	yam (see yellow yam, white yam)
tuberous basella (see ulluco)	yam bean (*Pachyrhizus erosus*)
turnip (*Brassica rapa* var. *rapa*)	yellow yam (*Dioscorea cayenensis*)

Leaf, stem and flower vegetables (vegetables used mainly for their leaves, stems and/or flowers)

Green leaves and stems are an important part of a healthy diet, as they are a good source of several minerals and vitamins. A large part of the diets of our hunter-gatherer forefathers comprised uncooked, green leaves, simply eaten as a snack food. It is therefore no surprise that modern research results emphasise the critical importance of green leaves and their associated nutrients. There is indeed more and more scientific evidence that the regular intake of green vegetables reduces the risk of cancer and lowers cholesterol levels. Anticancer effects are mainly associated with folic acid (common in all green leaves) and sulphur compounds (found mainly in the cabbage family). An important point is that vegetables lose much of their nutrient content when cooked, especially when they are boiled in water. Stir-frying and steaming are therefore recommended, but by far the best way to eat green leaves is raw, in the form of a tasty mixed salad.

The food value of leaf and stem vegetables is linked to their rich supply of minerals (especially calcium, magnesium, iron, phosphorus and sulphur) and also to the high levels of vitamins A, B and C. Folic acid typically exceeds 50 µg and may reach more than 180 µg per 100 g in some vegetables. Green vegetables are amongst the richest sources of vitamin C – often present at a level of 50 to 100 mg per 100 g. Free amino acids are often well supplied, especially in sprouted seeds.

List of common leaf, stem and flower vegetables

amicho (see enset)
artichoke (*Cynara scolymus*)
asparagus (*Asparagus officinalis*)
asparagus bean (see under cowpea)
bamboo shoots (*Dendrocalamus asper*)
beefsteak plant (*Perilla frutescens*)
black-eyed bean (see cowpea)
bok choi (see pak choi)
borekale (see kale)
bottle gourd (*Lagenaria siceraria*)
bracken fern (*Pteridium aquilinum*)
broccoli (*Brassica oleracea* var. *italica*)
brussels sprouts (*Brassica oleracea* var. *gemmifera*)
cabbage (*Brassica oleracea* var. *capitata*)
cabbage leaf mustard
  (see Chinese cabbage mustard)
cabbage mustard (see Chinese cabbage
  mustard)
cabbage turnip (see kohlrabi)
calabrese (see broccoli)
Cape broccoli (see cauliflower)
Cape pondweed (*Aponogeton distachyos*)
cardoon (see under globe artichoke)
cauliflower (*Brassica oleracea* var. *botrytis*)
celery (*Apium graveolens*)
celery cabbage (*Brassica rapa* var. *pekinensis*)
Ceylon spinach (see Malabar spinach)
chard (see Swiss chard)
chicory (*Cichorium intybus*)
Chinese amaranth (see *Chinese spinach*)
Chinese boxthorn (*Lycium chinense*)
Chinese broccoli (see Chinese kale,
Chinese flowering cabbage)
Chinese cabbage (see Chinese
  flowering cabbage, celery cabbage)
Chinese cabbage mustard (*Brassica juncea*
  var. *rugosa*)
Chinese flowering cabbage (*Brassica rapa*
  var. *parachinensis*)
Chinese kale (*Brassica oleracea* var. *alboglabra*)
Chinese leaf (see celery cabbage)
Chinese spinach (*Amaranthus tricolor*)
Chinese white cabbage (see pak choi)
collards (see kale)
corn salad (*Valerianella locusta*)
cowpea (*Vigna unguiculata*)
cress (*Lepidium sativum*)
curly kale (*Brassica oleracea* var. *sabellica*)
dandelion (*Taraxacum officinale*)
endive (*Cichorium endivia*)
enset (*Ensete ventricosum*)
field salad (see corn salad)
Florence fennel (*Foeniculum vulgare*)

garden cress (*Lepidium sativum*)
garland chrysanthemum (*Chrysanthemum
  coronarium*)
globe artichoke (*Cynara scolymus*)
Good King Henry (*Chenopodium bonus-henricus*)
goosefoot (see under Good King Henry)
heading Chinese cabbage (see celery cabbage)
Japanese bunching onion (*Allium fistulosum*)
Jew's mallow (see melokhia)
kale (*Brassica oleracea* var. *acephala*)
kangkong (*Ipomoea aquatica*)
kohlrabi (*Brassica oleracea* var. *gongylodes*)
kurrat (see leek)
laksa leaf (*Persicaria odorata*)
lamb's lettuce (*Valerianella locusta*)
leaf beet (see Swiss chard)
leek (*Allium ameloprasum*)
lettuce (*Lactuca sativa*)
levant garlic (see leek)
Malabar spinach (*Basella rubra*)
melinjo (*Gnetum gnemon*)
melokhia (*Corchorus olitorius*)
mustard greens (see Chinese cabbage mustard)
nasturtium (see watercress, garden nasturtium)
nettle (see stinging nettle)
New Zealand spinach (see under spinach)
orache (*Atriplex hortensis*)
pak choi (*Brassica rapa* var. *chinensis*)
palm hearts (*Bactris gasipaes*)
para cress (*Spilanthes acmella*)
parsley (*Petroselinum crispum*)
pe tsai (see celery cabbage)
peach palm (see palm hearts)
pejibaye (see palm hearts)
Peking cabbage (see celery cabbage)
Portuguese kale (see curly cale)
purslane (*Portulaca oleracea*)
rapunzel (see corn salad)
rau ram (*Persicaria odorata*)
red cabbage (see cabbage)
rhubarb (*Rheum rhabarbarum*)
rocket (*Eruca sativa*)
rosette pak choi (see pak choi)
savoy cabbage (see cabbage)
sawarabi (see bracken fern)
Scotch kale (see curly kale)
seakale (*Crambe maritima*)
shiso (*Perilla frutescens*)
sorrel (*Rumex acetosa*)
sow thistle (see under dandelion)
spilanthes (*Spilanthes acmella*)
spinach (*Spinacea oleracea*)
spinach beet (see Swiss chard)

A selection of vegetables derived from leaves, stems and flowers

Mitsuba (*Cryptotaenia japonica*), a Japanese spinach

Climbing spinach (*Hablitzia tamnoides*) from the Caucasus

spring onion (see onion)
sprouting broccoli (see broccoli)
stinging nettle (*Urtica dioica*)
Swiss chard (*Beta vulgaris* var. *cicla*)
tangho (see garland chrysanthemum)
tat soi (see pak choi)
Vietnamese coriander (see Vietnamese mint)
Vietnamese mint (*Persicaria odorata*)

Warrigal greens (see under spinach)
water spinach (*Ipomoea aquatica*)
waterblommetjie (see Cape pondweed)
watercress (*Rorippa nasturtium-aquaticum*)
Welsh onion (see Japanese bunching onion)
white cabbage (see cabbage)
winter purslane (see under purslane)
wormseed (see under Good King Henry)

Fruit and seed vegetables (vegetables used mainly for their unripe or ripe fruits or seeds)

A large number of fruits and seeds are used as vegetables. The difference between vegetables and fruits is based on the way we use them and not on any scientific principle. In the pumpkin family, for example, sweet melons and watermelons are regarded as fruits, while pumpkins and gourds are used as vegetables.

Raw and cooked vegetables form an essential part of any balanced diet. Fruits and seeds are typically high in proteins, amino acids, vitamins and minerals. Green fruits are similar to leafy vegetables but are generally more nutritious, especially when they are eaten raw. Coloured fruits usually have higher levels of some nutrients than their green counterparts. Red peppers, for example, supply much more vitamin A and vitamin C than green peppers. Orange pumpkin flesh is a rich source of vitamin A, while green pumpkin has much less. Raw is better than cooked, and stir-fried is better than boiled, but the main feature of good nutrition is variety.

List of common fruit and seed vegetables

adzuki bean (*Vigna angularis*)
African horned cucumber (see jelly melon)
angled luffa (*Luffa acutangula*)
asparagus pea (*Lotus tetragonolobus*)
aubergine (*Solanum melongena*)
baby corn (*Zea mays*)
balsam pear (*Momordica charantia*)
bean (*Phaseolus vulgaris*)
bell pepper (see sweet pepper)
ben tree (*Moringa oleifera*)
bitter gourd (see balsam pear)
black-eyed bean (see cowpea)
bottle gourd (*Lagenaria siceraria*)
brinjal (see aubergine)
broad bean (*Vicia faba*)
butternut (*Cucurbita moschata*)
calabash (*Lagenaria siceraria*)
chayote (*Sechium edule*)
cho-cho (see chayote)
cluster bean (*Cyamopsis tetragonoloba*)
cooking banana (see plantain)
corn (see sweetcorn)
cucumber (*Cucumis sativus*)
cushaw (see under butternut)
drumstick tree (*Moringa oleifera*)
egg plant (see aubergine)
fava bean (see broad bean)
fenugreek (*Trigonella foenum-graecum*)
fig-leaf gourd (*Cucurbita ficifolia*)
garden pea (*Pisum sativum*)
gherkin (see cucumber)
goa bean (see winged bean)
green pepper (see sweet pepper)
guar (see cluster bean)
gumbo (see okra)
hairy melon (see wax gourd)

horseradish tree (see drumstick tree)
hyacinth bean (see lablab bean)
jack bean (*Canavalia ensiformis*)
jackfruit (*Artocarpus heterophyllus*)
jelly melon (*Cucumis metuliferus*)
kiwano (see jelly melon)
lablab bean (*Lablab purpureus*)
lady's fingers (see okra)
Malabar gourd (see fig-leaf gourd)
marrow (*Cucurbita pepo*)
musky winter squash (see butternut)
okra (*Abelmoschus esculentus*)
pea (*Pisum sativum*)
peppers (*Capsicum annuum*)
petai (*Parkia speciosa*)
plantain (*Musa paradisiaca*)
pumpkin (*Cucurbita maxima*)
runner bean (*Phaseolus coccineus*)
scarlet runner bean (see runner bean)
snake bean (see under cowpea)
snake gourd (*Trichosanthes cucumerina*)
squash (*Cucurbita pepo*)
summer squash (*Cucurbita pepo*)
sweet pepper (*Capsicum annuum*)
sweetcorn (*Zea mays*)
tamarillo (see tree tomato)
tomatillo (*Physalis ixocarpa*)
tomato (*Lycopersicon esculentum*)
tree tomato (*Cyphomandra betacea*)
vegetable pear (*Sechium edule*)
wax gourd (*Benincasa hispida*)
winged bean (*Psophocarpus tetragonolobus*)
winter squash (*Cucurbita maxima*)
yam bean (*Pachyrhizus erosus*)
yard long bean (see under cowpea)
zucchini (*Cucurbita pepo*)

A selection of vegetables derived from fruits and seeds

Petai (*Parkia speciosa*), a popular Malaysian vegetable

Vegetable fruits on the Singapore market

CULINARY HERBS

Culinary herbs are used to enhance the flavour of a dish and are relatively unimportant as a component of the diet, although they may supply significant amounts of vitamins and minerals when used generously. Sometimes the distinction between green vegetable and cooking herb becomes blurred, especially in oriental cooking. Green leaves used as pot-herbs, however, are here regarded as vegetables and not as herbs.

Many of the flavour herbs used in cooking are derived from the mint family (Lamiaceae) and carrot family (Apiaceae). A feature of both these families is the presence of volatile oil (essential oil) which is formed in specialised glands or ducts in the leaves and fruits. These oils often occur in complex mixtures and are responsible for the characteristic aroma of herbs and spices. Examples of easily recognisable main compounds include menthol (peppermint flavour), limonene (lemon flavour), carvone (spearmint flavour) and anethole (anise flavour). Most of the flavour may evaporate when herbs are dried – a good supply of fresh herbs is therefore important for making an excellent dish.

List of common culinary herbs

angelica (*Angelica archangelica*)
basil (*Ocimum basilicum*)
bay, bay leaf (*Laurus nobilis*)
beefsteak plant (*Perilla frutescens*)
borage (*Borago officinalis*)
caraway (*Carum carvi*)
celery (*Apium graveolens*)
chervil (*Anthriscus cerefolium*)
Chinese chive (see garlic chive)
Chinese parsley (see cilantro)
chives (*Allium schoenoprasum*)
cilantro (*Coriandrum sativum*)
corn mint (see field mint)
daun salam (see salam leaf)
dhania (*Coriandrum sativum*)
dill (*Anethum graveolens*)
fenugreek (*Trigonella foenum-graecum*)
field mint (*Mentha arvensis*)
French tarragon (see tarragon)
garden mint (*Mentha spicata*)
garden nasturtium (*Tropaeolum majus*)
garlic (*Allium sativum*)
garlic chive (*Allium tuberosum*)
horse mint (see under spearmint)
Indian borage (*Plectranthus amboinicus*)
Indian cress (*Tropaeolum majus*)
Indonesian bay leaf (see salam leaf)
Italian parsley (*Petroselinum crispum*)
Japanese bunching onion (*Allium fistulosum*)
Japanese mint (see field mint)
laksa leaf (*Persicaria odorata*)
laurel (see bay)
lemon balm (*Melissa officinalis*)
lemon thyme (see under thyme)
lovage (*Levisticum officinale*)
marjoram (*Origanum majorana*)

mint (*Mentha* species)
onion (*Allium cepa*)
orache (*Atriplex hortensis*)
oregano (*Origanum vulgare*)
pandan (*Pandanus amaryllifolius*)
parsley (*Petroselinum crispum*)
peppermint (*Mentha piperita*)
pineapple mint (see under spearmint)
pot marjoram (see under marjoram)
purslane (*Portulaca oleracea*)
rau ram (*Persicaria odorata*)
rhubarb (*Rheum rhabarbarum*)
rocket (*Eruca sativa*)
rosemary (*Rosmarinus officinalis*)
rue (*Ruta graveolens*)
salad burnet (*Sanguisorba minor*)
salam leaf (*Syzygium polyanthum*)
sage (*Salvia officinalis*)
savory (see summer savory)
shiso (*Perilla frutescens*)
sorrel (*Rumex acetosa*)
spearmint (*Mentha spicata*)
summer savory (*Satureja hortensis*)
sweet balm (see lemon balm)
sweet basil (*Ocimum basilicum*)
sweet bay (see bay)
sweet cicely (*Myrrhis odorata*)
tarragon (*Artemisia dranunculus*)
Thai basil (see under basil)
thyme (*Thymus vulgaris*)
tulsi (see under basil)
Vietnamese coriander (see Vietnamese mint)
Vietnamese mint (*Persicaria odorata*)
Welsh onion (see Japanese bunching onion)
wild thyme (see under thyme)
winter savory (see under summer savory)

A selection of common culinary herbs

Thai basil and sweet basil (*Ocimum basilicum*)

Pandan leaf (*Pandanus amaryllifolius*)

29

SUGARS, GUMS, GELS AND STARCHES

Plant-derived products such as sugar and starch form part of almost every meal but we rarely think about their botanical origin. Sugar is an important energy source – the calorific value ranges from about 300 kcal per 100 g in the case of pure honey, to 399 kcal for pure cane sugar (sucrose). Sugar is widely used in the food industry in canned foods, jams, jellies, juices, sweets and soft drinks. Sugar cane and sugar beet are grown on a large scale and are processed by grinding, pressing out the sap and crystallising to produce molasses (unrefined sugar syrup), brown sugar and finally white sugar (by repeated crystallisation). In addition to these two main industrial sources of sugar, relatively small amounts of palm sugar and maple syrup are produced in rural areas by tapping the sugary sap from sugar palms or sugar maples and concentrating it by boiling or evaporation.

Sweeteners are sometimes used by people who have to restrict their intake of carbohydrates. Artificial sweeteners (aspartame, cyclamate and saccharin) have remained popular despite scientific scrutiny and controversy over the last few decades relating to possible links with cancer. Natural, sugar-free sweeteners such as liquorice root and stevia leaf are therefore preferred, but even they are claimed to present a health risk, especially when used indiscriminately. The most sensible way to satisfy a sweet tooth is to eat dry fruits (raisins, dried figs, dates, apples, apricots, peaches, pears, prunes and others). These are very healthy snack foods because they contain easily digestible sugars and a high density of vitamins, minerals and fibre per unit weight.

Edible gums, mainly from *Acacia* species, are water-soluble polysaccharides that yield simple sugars when digested. Gels (slimy polysaccharides dissolved in water) have become popular for their supposed health properties and are nowadays often included in medicinal products and health tonics. An example is aloe leaf gel, which has become the basis of a very large industry supplying health drinks and food supplements. Agar agar is a flavourless, gelatinous product (polysaccharide) made in Asian countries from red seaweeds. It is a useful replacement for gelatine, an animal product. Pectin, obtained from apple or citrus residues, has similar uses, especially in the making of jams and jellies.

Starch is extracted from pulverised stems or tubers simply by washing with water, straining to remove impurities and drying or concentrating the suspension to recover the pure starch grains. Pure starch has an energy yield of about 340 kcal per 100 g. Several plants in the list below are industrial sources of various starch products known as arrowroot, kudzu, tapioca, sago, salep (from orchid roots), potato flour, water chestnut powder and yam flour. These starches are used as thickening agents for soups and sauces in the same way as maize or wheat flour. Various other starch-rich products (semolina, *couscous*) are manufactured from cereal grains such as maize and wheat.

List of sugar, gum, gel and starch plants

aloe gel (*Aloe vera*)
arrowroot (see under tannia)
breadfruit (*Artocarpus altilis*)
carob seeds (*Ceratonia siliqua*)
cassava (*Manihot esculenta*)
corn (*Zea mays*)
cocoyam (see taro)
enset (*Ensete ventricosum*)
fishtail palm (*Caryota urens*)
gum acacia (see gum arabic)
gum arabic (*Acacia senegal*)
gum senegal (see gum arabic)
kudzu (*Pueraria lobata*)
kuzu (see kudzu)
licorice (see liquorice)
liquorice (*Glycyrrhiza glabra*)
maize (*Zea mays*)

maple sugar (see sugar maple)
mealies (see maize)
melinjo (*Gnetum gnemon*)
new cocoyam (*Xanthosoma sagittifolium*)
sago palm (*Metroxylon sagu*)
stevia (*Stevia rebaudiana*)
sugar beet (*Beta vulgaris* var. *vulgaris*)
sugar cane (*Saccharum officinarum*)
sugar leaf (see stevia)
sugar maple (*Acer saccharum*)
sugar palm (*Arenga pinnata*)
sweet potato (*Ipomoea batatas*)
tannia (*Xanthosoma sagittifolium*)
tapioca (see cassava)
taro (*Colocasia esculenta*)
toddy palm (see fishtail palm)
yam (*Dioscorea cayenensis*)

Various forms of sugar: yellow sugar, sugar cubes, palm sugar, castor sugar, demerara sugar, sugar crystals, Chinese brown sugar, cane sugar, treacle, icing sugar and Chinese lump sugar

A selection of dried fruits: figs, prunes, pears, Chinese dates (*da zao*), apple rings, Chinese sour plums, apricots, Chinese boxthorn (*gou qi zi*), raisins, sultanas, currants, peaches and dates

BEVERAGE PLANTS
(including flavourants)

Plant-derived beverages have been produced in various parts of the world since ancient times and form an interesting and conspicuous part of cultural diversity and local food traditions. Beverages include hot infusions (teas), fruit juices, carbonated drinks, fermented fruit juices (wines), malted and fermented grains (beers) and distilled alcoholic beverages. Hops, cola, quinine, geisho and absinth are examples of flavourants.

Fresh or fermented leaves are used by various cultures as teas. These include black tea or chai, yerba maté, rooibos tea, hibiscus tea and honeybush tea. The process of fermentation is actually an enzymatic oxidation during which phenolic compounds are modified and various flavour components are produced. Green (unfermented) tea has become popular in recent years because it contains higher levels of phenolic compounds and therefore has superior antioxidant properties. Some herbal teas, including hibiscus, rooibos and honeybush, are naturally devoid of stimulants. Tea and maté, in common with coffee, guaraná, cola and cacao, contain substantial quantities of caffeine (an alkaloid with stimulant properties). Caffeine is also the stimulant found in high-energy drinks that have become popular in the rave culture.

Wine is formed when the sugars in fruit juice (typically grape juice) are converted by yeast enzymes to alcohol. Various low alcohol beverages such as white wine, red wine, apple cider, toddy or palm wine, marula beer and *pulque* (fermented agave) are produced in this way. These drinks are similar to traditional beer, produced from fermented malt. Malt is made by germinating and then rapidly drying barley or other cereals. During germination, the starch (storage carbohydrate) is enzymatically converted to sugars. By fermenting the malt, these sugars are converted to alcohol up to a point where the alcohol becomes poisonous to the yeast itself. This natural limitation to the alcohol content of beers can be overcome by distilling the low alcohol beverage to produce various high alcohol drinks such as brandy, whiskey, cane spirit, tequila, vodka, gin, *ouzo*, *sambuca*, *grappa* and numerous others. Liqueurs are made by adding various flavour components (herbs and spices).

List of beverage plants

abata cola (see cola)
absinth (*Artemisia absinthium*)
agave (see tequila plant)
arabica coffee (see coffee)
aronia berry (*Aronia melanocarpa*)
barley (*Hordeum vulgare*)
black chokeberry (see aronia berry)
blue agave (see tequila plant)
cacao (*Theobroma cacao*)
chai (*Camellia sinensis*)
cocoa (*Theobroma cacao*)
coconut milk (*Cocos nucifera*)
chokeberry (see aronia berry)
chicory (*Cichorium intybus*)
chufa (*Cyperus esculentus*)
coffee (*Coffea arabica*)
cola (*Cola acuminata*)
elderberry (*Sambucus nigra*)
fishtail palm (*Caryota urens*)
geisho (*Rhamnus prinoides*)
ginger (*Zingiber officinale*)
ginseng (*Panax ginseng*)
grape (*Vitis vinifera*)

guaraná (*Paullinia cupana*)
hibiscus (*Hibiscus sabdariffa*)
hop(s) (*Humulus lupulus*)
honeybush tea (*Cyclopia genistoides*)
Jamaica sorrel (see hibiscus)
maté (*Ilex paraguariensis*)
mokola palm (*Hyphaene petersiana*)
mountain ash (*Sorbus aucuparia*)
mountain tea (see under honeybush tea)
robusta coffee (see under coffee)
rooibos tea (*Aspalathus linearis*)
roselle (*Hibiscus sabdariffa*)
rowanberry (see mountain ash)
service berry (see mountain ash)
sorb apple (see under mountain ash)
sorghum (*Sorghum bicolor*)
tamarind (*Tamarindus indica*)
tea (*Camellia sinensis*)
tequila plant (*Agave tequilana*)
toddy palm (see fishtail palm)
wine grape (see grape)
yerba maté (*Ilex paraguariensis*)

A selection of common beverages

Vineyards in the Alsace

SPICES AND FLAVOURS

Spices are defined as plant-derived substances that add flavour (and zest, charm or gusto) to a dish. Amongst the well-known spices all parts of plants are represented – roots, rhizomes, stems, leaves, bark, flowers, fruits or seeds. The flavour components are often volatile oils, but can be pungent alkaloids (as in pepper and chilli), pungent mustard oils (as in mustard and horseradish) or sulphur compounds (as in onions and garlic). Spices are used sparingly in dishes and add relatively little to the nutrient content of the diet, but they may have important health effects as digestives, carminatives or stimulants. Many spices are indeed used in traditional medicine as herbal remedies and tonics.

Spices are still an important part of world trade but are no longer the source of fabulous wealth as they once were. The early spice routes were controlled by Arab traders, who cleverly guarded the secret sources of their goods. Countries and city states in the eastern part of the Mediterranean region earned great fortunes in the spice trade. In those days, the poor quality of food (especially meat) called for liberal spicing to make it palatable. Pepper once served as hard currency to pay salaries and bribes (a kilogram was sufficient to pay for freeing a slave). Seafaring nations like Portugal, Spain, Holland and Britain entered the lucrative spice trade and fought wars to maintain or gain commercial control over certain spices. This colonial period was not a happy one, as large numbers of local people were exploited or killed to centralise and monopolise the supply of spices from the famous East Indies (including India, Sri Lanka, Malaysia and Indonesia – and later also the Caribbean and West Indies). These spice monopolies were gradually broken (especially by the French) when plantations of pepper, nutmeg, cinnamon and other valuable spices were established on tropical islands such as French Guiana, French Polynesia, Réunion, Seychelles and Madagascar. In our modern world, spices have become inexpensive and readily available to all. As a result, cooking has become an exciting adventure in which we can explore new tastes and exotic recipes from all corners of the earth.

List of common spices derived from fruits or seeds

ajowan (see under caraway)
allspice (*Pimenta dioica*)
angelica (*Angelica archangelica*)
anise (*Pimpinella anisum*)
annatto (*Bixa orellana*)
bird chilli (*Capsicum frutescens*)
black cumin (*Nigella sativa*)
black mustard (*Brassica nigra*)
black pepper (*Piper nigrum*)
brown mustard (*Brassica juncea* var. *juncea*)
capers (*Capparis spinosa*)
caraway (*Carum carvi*)
cardamom (*Elettaria cardamomum*)
cayenne pepper (*Capsicum annuum, C. frutescens*)
celery (*Apium graveolens*)
chilli (*Capsicum frutescens, C. annuum*)
Chinese anis (*Illicium verum*)
Chinese pepper (see Sichuan pepper)
coriander (*Coriandrum sativum*)
cumin (*Cuminum cyminum*)
dill (*Anethum graveolens*)

fennel (*Foeniculum vulgare*)
fenugreek (*Trigonella foenum-graecum*)
Indian mustard (see brown mustard)
juniper berries (*Juniperus communis*)
lovage (*Levisticum officinale*)
mace (*Myristica fragrans*)
mustard (see black mustard, white mustard)
myrtle (*Myrtus communis*)
nutmeg (*Myristica fragrans*)
papeda (see makrut lime)
paprika (*Capsicum annuum*)
pepper (*Piper nigrum*)
pimento (*Pimenta dioica*)
pink pepper (see under Sichuan pepper)
Sichuan pepper (*Zanthoxylum piperitum*)
star anise (*Illicium verum*)
Tabasco pepper (*Capsicum frutescens*)
tamarind (*Tamarindus indica*)
vanilla (*Vanilla planifolia*)
white mustard (*Sinapis alba*)
white pepper (see pepper)

A selection of common spices: ajowan, allspice, anise, black cumin, black mustard, black pepper, brown mustard, caraway, cardamom seeds, white cardamom, brown cardamom, coriander, cumin, dill, fennel, fenugreek, juniper berries, mace, nutmeg, Sichuan pepper, star anise, vanilla, white mustard, cinnamon, cloves, ginger and turmeric

List of common spices derived from roots, stems, bark, leaves or flowers

absinthe (*Artemisia absinthium*)
allspice (*Pimenta dioica*)
angelica (*Angelica archangelica*)
asafoetida (*Ferula assa-foetida*)
balm (*Melissa officinalis*)
basil (*Ocimum basilicum*)
bay leaf (*Laurus nobilis*)
buchu (*Agathosma betulina*)
capers (*Capparis spinosa*)
cassia (see under cinnamon)
celery (*Apium graveolens*)
Ceylon cinnamon (see cinnamon)
chamomile (*Chamaemelum nobile*)
Chinese keys (*Boesenbergia rotunda*)
cinnamon (*Cinnamomum verum*)
cloves (*Syzygium aromaticum*)
curry leaf (*Murraya koenigii*)
devil's dung (see asafoetida)
Dijon mustard (see brown mustard)
dill (*Anethum graveolens*)
fennel (*Foeniculum vulgare*)

field mint (*Mentha arvensis*)
fragrant pandan (see pandan)
French tarragon (see tarragon)
galangal (*Alpinia galanga*)
garden nasturtium (*Tropaeolum majus*)
ginger (*Zingiber officinale*)
greater galangal (see galangal)
hop(s) (*Humulus lupulus*)
horseradish (*Armoracia rusticana*)
hyssop (*Hyssopus officinalis*)
lemon verbena (*Aloysia triphylla*)
lemongrass (*Cymbopogon citratus*)
licorice (*Glycyrrhiza glabra*)
lime leaf (see makrut lime)
liquorice (*Glycyrrhiza glabra*)
lovage (*Levisticum officinale*)
makrut lime (*Citrus hystrix*)
mint (*Mentha* species)
myrtle (*Myrtus communis*)
oregano (*Origanum vulgare*)

pandan (*Pandanus amaryllifolius*)
papeda (see makrut lime)
peppermint (*Mentha piperita*)
pimento (*Pimenta dioica*)
Roman chamomile (*Chamaemelum nobile*)
round leaf buchu (see buchu)
rue (*Ruta graveolens*)
Russian tarragon (see tarragon)
saffron (*Crocus sativus*)
sage (*Salvia officinalis*)
salam leaf (*Syzygium polyanthum*)
spearmint (*Mentha spicata*)
sweet balm (*Melissa officinalis*)
sweet bay (see bay leaf)
tansy (see under garland chrysanthemum)
tarragon (*Artemisia dracunculus*)
turmeric (*Curcuma longa*)
vervain (see lemon verbena)
wasabi (*Wasabia japonica*)
wormwood (see absinthe)
zedoary (see under turmeric)

Lettuce field in Malaysia

White nuts (*Ginkgo biloba*)

Black soybeans (*Glycine max*)

THE PLANTS
IN ALPHABETICAL ORDER

Energy yield (calorific value) is given in kilocalories (kcal)
per 100 g. For conversion to kilojoules (kJ) the value should
be multiplied by four (for more accurate conversion: × 4.2).

The content of proteins, minerals and vitamins is given
in percentages (%), or in milligrams (mg) or micrograms
(µg) per 100 g fresh or dry weight.

Abelmoschus esculentus

okra • lady's fingers • gumbo

Okra plants

Okra flower and young fruit

Immature okra fruits

DESCRIPTION An erect annual herb of up to 2 m in height with deeply lobed, hairy leaves and attractive yellow flowers, usually with a purple spot in the middle. The fruits are green, finger-like, five-ribbed capsules of about 10–20 cm long. They are mucilaginous inside and contain numerous round seeds. The sepals of *Abelmoschus* species fall off after flowering, while those of the closely related genus *Hibiscus* are persistent. Other crops include rainy season okra (*A. caillei*), the aibika (*A. manihot*) and musk seed or ambrette (*A. moschatus*).

ORIGIN & HISTORY Okra is probably indigenous to tropical West Africa. It has been grown as a crop in rural areas of West Africa and India for centuries and was taken to Central America and North America during the slave trade. The species is today grown in all tropical, subtropical and temperate regions of the world. It is particularly well known as an ingredient of Arabic, West African, Caribbean and eastern Mediterranean cooking.

PARTS USED Immature fruits.

CULTIVATION & HARVESTING Okra is an annual crop grown from seeds. The young fruits are harvested when they are three to five days old.

USES & PROPERTIES Young fruits are used fresh (or canned) as a tasty, gelatinous (slimy) vegetable (typically served with mutton or chicken). They may also be sliced, sun-dried and stored for long periods. Okra is very popular for *tajines* (North African stews), *foutou* (a spicy West African dish based on cassava and bananas) and traditional chicken or seafood gumbos *à la créole* (Creole cookery is a mixture of African, Hindu and West Indian traditions).

NUTRITIONAL VALUE Okra has a relatively high nutritional value as it is rich in minerals (calcium, phosphorus, potassium, magnesium and iron) and vitamin C (20 mg per 100 g in fresh fruits). The energy yield is about 40 kcal per 100 g.

Abelmoschus esculentus (L.) Moench (= *Hibiscus esculentus* L.)   family: Malvaceae

jiao dou, ka fei huang kui (Chinese); *gombo, bamia, bamya* (French); *Okra, Gombo* (German); *bhindi* (Hindi); *ocra* (Italian); *okura* (Japanese); *kachang bendi* (Malay); *quimgombó* (Spanish)

Acacia senegal

gum acacia • gum arabic tree • gum senegal tree

Gum acacia flowers

Gum acacia leaves and fruits

Gum arabic

DESCRIPTION A deciduous, thorny tree of up to 6 m in height, with a rounded or spreading crown, compound leaves and dense, elongated spikes of minute, pale yellow to cream-coloured flowers. The tree is easily identified by the thorns that are arranged in groups of three. *Acacia seyal* and several other *Acacia* species are minor sources of gum. Vegetable gums used in the food industry also include gum tragacanth (*Astragalus* species), gum karaya (*Sterculia urens*) and guar gum (*Cyamopsis tetragonoloba*).

ORIGIN & HISTORY Indigenous to Africa (dry tropical regions, from southern to northern Africa). Gum arabic has been used since 3000 BC (in mummification and as binder for pigments). The main producers are Sudan (about 70%), Chad, Nigeria, Senegal, Mali, Mauritania and Niger.

PARTS USED Gum (the air-dried exudate that flows from the bark under stress conditions).

CULTIVATION & HARVESTING Gum arabic is collected from natural stands or commercial plantations in the dry season. The average yield per tree is around 200–300 g (up to 6 kg in large trees).

USES & PROPERTIES Gum arabic has a bland taste and is highly soluble in water. It is important in the food industry as a bulking agent, emulsifier, thickener, stabiliser and binder of flavours. The gum is used in the manufacture of chewing gum, various types of sweets, lozenges, caramels and toffees. It retards the crystallisation of sugar in gumdrops and other sweets and emulsifies and distributes fat particles. Small amounts are used in confectionery (cakes and muffins) and breakfast cereals as lubricant, oil substitute and binder. It is also widely used in alcoholic and non-alcoholic beverages, frozen dairy products, desserts, puddings, gelatins, imitation dairy products, instant soups, snack foods, candies, fats and oils.

NUTRITIONAL VALUE Gum acacia is highly nutritious and is used as a food source in rural parts of Africa.

Acacia senegal (L.) Willd. family: Fabaceae

acacia gomme arabique (French); *Gummi-Akazie* (German); *acacia del Senegal* (Italian)

Acca sellowiana

feijoa • pineapple guava

Feijoa fruit

Feijoa leaves and flower

Feijoa fruits

DESCRIPTION The feijoa is a large, evergreen shrub or small tree (up to about 5 m) with characteristic leaves that are dark green and smooth above but densely matted with white hairs below. Attractive flowers, each with five whitish petals and several bright red stamens are borne in the upper leaf axils. The fruits are egg-shaped and resemble guavas but they are dull green when ripe, with white flesh.

ORIGIN & HISTORY Feijoa is indigenous to southern Brazil, Paraguay, Uruguay and northeastern Argentina. It is of local importance in South America but reached southern Europe and the USA only around the end of the twentieth century. From here it was distributed to many parts of the world as a popular ornamental shrub for gardens and parks. Commercial cultivation for the fruits is limited to Australia, New Zealand, California, Florida and Cuba. Some cultivars have been developed, including 'Coolidge', 'Mammoth' and 'Triumph'.

PARTS USED Ripe fruits.

CULTIVATION & HARVESTING Plants are propagated from seeds or cuttings. They are tolerant of heat, drought and even light frost, but are prone to fruit fly infestations. Ripe fruits are hand-picked and used locally or packed for export.

USES & PROPERTIES The fruits may be enjoyed fresh – simply cut them in half and scoop out the white, often jelly-like flesh or serve them peeled and sliced as a snack food. They have the taste and flavour of guava mixed with pineapple and strawberries. Ripe fruits are also ideally suited for use in fruit salads or cooked as compote, purées, preserves or jams. They may also be processed and used as ingredient of fruit juices, sorbets and ice creams.

NUTRITIONAL VALUE The fruit flesh contains about 5% carbohydrates and has an energy value of 23 kcal per 100 g. Fresh fruits are rich in niacin (1.8 mg) and vitamin C (19–30 mg).

Acca sellowiana (O. Berg.) Burret (= *Feijoa sellowiana* O. Berg.) family: Myrtaceae

feijoa (French); *Feijoabaum, Ananasguave* (German); *feijão* (Portuguese); *guayabo del pais* (Spanish)

Acer saccharum

sugar maple

Sugar maple leaves

Spout for tapping maple syrup

Sugar maple fruits

Bucket for tapping maple syrup

DESCRIPTION The sugar maple is a large tree of up to 40 m high. It has hand-shaped, lobed leaves that are bright green above and silvery below. Inconspicuous flowers develop into winged fruits (double samaras). The foliage makes a spectacular display in autumn, when the leaves turn yellow and bright red. Several species of maple have been used for syrup tapping, including black maple (*A. nigrum*), but the sugar maple (also known as rock maple or striped maple) is the most important commercial source of maple syrup.

ORIGIN & HISTORY North America (southeastern Canada and northeastern USA). The indigenous people (and later the colonists) utilised the tree as a traditional source of sugar and syrup.

PARTS USED Sap (phloem sap).

CULTIVATION & HARVESTING Tapping is done in plantations and in natural stands. The best sap flow occurs in late winter and early spring before the trees begin to bud. Several tap holes are drilled into the trunk and spouts are inserted into the holes to direct the sap flow into buckets. In modern times, other systems (such as plastic tubing) have partly replaced the traditional harvesting method. The collected sap, which contains 1–3% sugar (sucrose), is concentrated (4:1 ratio) by boiling in kettles (or sometimes by freeze-drying) to produce the well-known maple syrup and a granular residue that can be processed into maple sugar.

USES & PROPERTIES The distinctive taste of maple syrup is due to volatile oils and other natural flavour components. Maple syrup is used in confectionery in the same way as golden syrup. It is popular as a syrup and sweetener with ice cream, pancakes and especially waffles.

NUTRITIONAL VALUE Maple syrup has a high energy value (more than 300 kcal per 100 g).

NOTES The wood is used for furniture and veneers (so-called "bird's eye maple", popular in the Victorian era).

Acer saccharum Marshall   family: Aceraceae

érable à sucre (French); *Zuckerahorn* (German); *acero canadese* (Italian); *arce* (Spanish)

Actinidia deliciosa

kiwifruit • Chinese gooseberry

Kiwifruit plant (young)

Kiwifruit leaves and fruits

Kiwifruits

DESCRIPTION The kiwi or kiwifruit is a vigorous woody climber (vine) with separate female and male plants, easily recognised by the distinctive veins of the large, simple leaves and the attractive white flowers. Female and male flowers are similar (the pollen of female flowers is sterile; the ovary is rudimentary in male flowers). The fruits are large oblong berries with stiff brown bristles and greenish fruit flesh. It was previously considered to be a variety of *A. chinensis* but the two are now considered to be distinct species – *A. chinensis* has smaller, more rounded fruit with soft fur. A third species, *A. arguta*, is of minor importance.

ORIGIN & HISTORY Kiwifruit is indigenous to China: *A. deliciosa* occurs naturally in the hills of southwestern China; *A. chinensis* in the low-lying southeastern region. To this day, thousands of tons of fruits are wild-harvested in China. Kiwifruit is one of the most recently domesticated crop plants. Seeds taken to New Zealand in 1904 formed the basis of several seedling selections, the most important being the cultivar 'Hayward'. The name kiwifruit was coined in New Zealand in 1959.

PARTS USED Fruits.

CULTIVATION & HARVESTING Since the 1970s, commercial cultivation of grafted plants has spread rapidly from New Zealand to Italy, Chile, France, Japan and the USA. Practically all female plants are of the cultivar 'Hayward', while male plants are selected on the basis of flowering time to ensure successful pollination. The annual world production is well over half a million tons.

USES & PROPERTIES The delicious fruits, rich in vitamin C, are eaten fresh or are used in salads. They may also be frozen, canned, or processed into juice, jam, liqueurs and sparkling wine.

NUTRITIONAL VALUE The fruits yield 53 kcal per 100 g and are rich in vitamin C. They can be stored for several months and retain most of their nutritional value.

Actinidia deliciosa (Chev.) A.R. Ferg.   family: Actinidiaceae

yangtao (Chinese); *kiwi* (French); *Kiwi* (German); *kiwi* (Italian); *kiwi* (Spanish)

Adansonia digitata
baobab • monkey bread

Baobab tree

Baobab leaves and flower

Baobab fruits

DESCRIPTION The baobab is an extraordinary tree with a massive trunk of more than 20 m in circumference. Some specimens are thought to be more than 2 000 years old. Compound leaves are borne at the tips of the thick branches, together with large, pendulous, white flowers. These are pollinated by bats and develop into large oblong fruits, each containing a large number of seeds surrounded by fruit pulp that turns powdery when it dries out.

ORIGIN & HISTORY *A. digitata* occurs only in tropical Africa. There are a further six species in Madagascar and one in Australia.

PARTS USED Fruit pulp, seeds and leaves.

CULTIVATION & HARVESTING Trees are occasionally cultivated in gardens and parks but so far no commercial cultivation has been attempted. The fruits are wild-harvested in rural areas.

USES & PROPERTIES The fruit pulp has a pleasant tart taste due to the presence of citric and tartaric acids. It is edible and can be eaten fresh or dried. When dry, the powdery pulp is mixed with water to form a pleasant drink, or it may be prepared in the form of a healthy porridge. The seeds themselves are highly nutritious and may be roasted and eaten like nuts. Leaves are cooked as a vegetable.

NUTRITIONAL VALUE The seeds (nuts) are an excellent food with a high energy value (420 kcal per 100 g) and large quantities of protein (34%), fat (31%) and carbohydrates (5%). Fresh fruit pulp contains more than 200 mg vitamin C and yields 307 kcal per 100 g.

NOTES Baobab trees have numerous uses. The bark provides valuable soft fibres that are traditionally woven into cloth. Beautifully handcrafted mats, handbags and hats are sold along roadsides and in curio shops. Remarkable is the fact that the bark regenerates after it has been stripped.

Adansonia digitata L.   family: Bombacaceae

baobab (French); *Baobab* (German); *baobab* (Italian); *baobab* (Spanish); *muvhuyu* (Venda)

Agathosma betulina
buchu • round leaf buchu

Round leaf buchu

Oval leaf buchu

DESCRIPTION Buchu is a shrub of up to 2 m in height, with small, broad, gland-dotted leaves and white or pale purplish flowers. It is sometimes confused with oval leaf buchu (*Agathosma crenulata*, previously known as *Barosma crenulata*) but the latter has narrower leaves (more than twice as long as broad, while those of *A. betulina* have a length to width ratio of less than 2:1).

ORIGIN & HISTORY Buchu is found only in the high mountains of the Western Cape Province of South Africa. It has a long history as a flavour plant.

PARTS USED Leaves or the essential oil.

CULTIVATION & HARVESTING The plants are relatively difficult to grow commercially but propagation and cultivation protocols are being developed. The buchu trade has become very lucrative and the natural stands are threatened by illegal wild-harvesting. Fortunately, more and more plantations are now being established.

USES & PROPERTIES Buchu leaf and buchu oil are important flavour components. Leaves, leaf extracts or the oil are used in a wide range of beverages, including herbal teas, ice teas and liqueurs. Buchu brandy, for example, is a popular traditional drink in South Africa. The oil is also widely used in the food industry to improve the taste of beverages, sweets and confectionery. The characteristic blackcurrant flavour is partly due to sulphur-containing minor compounds in the essential oil, while the mint-like character is ascribed to diosphenol (so-called buchu camphor) and other volatile oil components. Oval leaf buchu is inferior to round leaf buchu as it lacks some of these ingredients.

NUTRITIONAL VALUE Used in small quantities for flavour only.

NOTES Buchu is an important medicinal plant. It is an excellent tonic and is traditionally used to treat indigestion, as well as ailments of the kidneys and urinary tract. Externally is has been applied (as buchu vinegar) to heal wounds and bruises.

Agathosma betulina (Berg.) Pillans [= *Barosma betulina* (Berg.) Bartl. & H.L. Wendl.]　　　family: Rutaceae

buchu (French); *Duftraute, Bucco* (German); *buchu* (Italian); *buchu* (Spanish)

Agave tequilana
tequila plant • blue agave

Century plants

Tequila plant

Tequila

DESCRIPTION The tequila plant is a robust succulent with firm, bluish-green, persistent leaves. After about 10 to 20 years, an enormous flowering stalk is produced, after which the plant dies. Several species are used to produce alcoholic drinks, including the well-known century plant (*Agave americana*), so named because of the erroneous belief that it lives for 100 years.

ORIGIN & HISTORY *Agave* species are indigenous to the tropical and dry parts of North and South America, and are most abundant in Central America. In Mexico, they have been used as a source of food and alcoholic beverage since antiquity.

PARTS USED Fermented juice from the fleshy "heart" of a plant about to flower (a traditional drink known as *pulque*). The Spanish introduced the practice of distillation to produce *mescal* and *tequila*. The stem "heart" and flowers are traditional food items.

CULTIVATION & HARVESTING Until recently, stems were mostly harvested from the wild but the limited supply is forcing a gradual move to cultivated plants. Massive amounts of a sugary liquid that accumulate in the stem prior to the emergence of the flowering stalk are fermented. For a product to be called *tequila*, it has to originate from *A. tequilana* plants from the Guadalajara region in southwestern Mexico (where the town of Tequila is located). Several other species are also used. In South Africa, for example, a product called *agava* is distilled from naturalised and cultivated *A. americana* plants.

USES & PROPERTIES Tequila is a well-known and popular alcoholic drink. An agave worm (*maguey* worm or *gusano*) is traditionally added to the bottle as proof of quality – it will rot if the alcohol content is too low.

NUTRITIONAL VALUE Tequila has little or no food value.

NOTES *A. sisalana* (the sisal plant) and other species are cultivated in many parts of the world as sources of strong fibre.

Agave tequilana Web.   family: Agavaceae

agave (French); *Tequila-Agave* (German); *agave* (Italian); *maguey* (Spanish)

Aleurites moluccana
candlenut tree

Candlenut tree

Candlenut flowers

Candlenut fruits and seeds

DESCRIPTION The candlenut tree has a rounded crown and grows to a height of about 12 to 15 m. The large leaves are simple or three-lobed, dark green above and silvery below, with two small glands at the point where the stalk is attached. Small white flowers are borne on sparse, much-branched flowering stalks that are characteristically covered in short, rusty brown hairs. These develop into large brownish fruits, each containing two waxy and somewhat warty seeds enclosed in a smooth papery shell that forms within the fleshy part of the fruit.

ORIGIN & HISTORY Southeast Asia (mainly Malaysia and Indonesia). It has been used as a source of illuminating oil for centuries. The ripe, roasted nuts are said to be a traditional food item in Java.

PARTS USED Cooked seeds (known as candle-nuts) or the seed oil.

CULTIVATION & HARVESTING Trees have been cultivated since ancient times (6000 BC?). The nuts are collected by hand when ripe or half ripe.

USES & PROPERTIES The fully ripe, cooked nuts are used in Indonesian and Malaysian cooking – they are a source of cooking oil and are also ground to a paste, which is a popular ingredient of curry dishes. The paste adds texture and flavour. Fresh nuts are poisonous (purgative) and are never eaten raw. Half ripe nuts are a source of candlenut oil (lumbang oil) that is used for illumination. Fully ripe nuts are roasted and then processed to extract the oil for cooking.

NUTRITIONAL VALUE The nuts have a high fat content (65%) and an energy value of 630 kcal per 100 g. They are also a good source of protein and iron.

NOTES Nuts tend to become rancid and are therefore best kept in the refrigerator. The related tung nut tree (*Aleurites fordii*) is a source of tung oil, a drying oil that is included in paints and varnishes.

Aleurites moluccana (L.) Willd. (= *A. triloba* J.R. Forst. & G. Forst.)   family: Euphorbiaceae

Bancoulier (French); *Lichtnussbaum* (German); *kemiri* (Indonesian); *buah keras* (Malaysian); *avellano* (Spanish)

Allium ameloprasum

leek

Leek flowers

Leek plants

Leeks

DESCRIPTION A leafy biennial herb with a cylindrical bulb, broad leaves and small violet flowers borne in a rounded cluster. The cultivated leek is sometimes considered a distinct species (*A. porrum*) but it closely resembles the wild species (*A. ameloprasum*). In addition to the ordinary leek (var. *porrum*), two other types are distinguished: great-headed or Levant garlic (var. *holmense*) and *kurrat* (var. *kurrat*).

ORIGIN & HISTORY Eurasia and North Africa. It is a cultigen and is not known from the wild. Leeks were well known to the ancient Sumerian, Egyptian and Greek civilisations. The Romans introduced them to the British Isles, where they became an important food plant. The leek is the national emblem of Wales, in commemoration of the victory of King Cadwallader over the Saxons in AD 640 – the Welsh soldiers wore leeks on their helmets to distinguish them from the enemy.

PARTS USED Leaf bases (bulb), less often the leaves.

CULTIVATION & HARVESTING Leeks are grown in trenches so that the leaf bases can be covered with soil in order to increase the size of the white portion. They withstand cold temperatures remarkably well and have become an important winter vegetable in large parts of Europe.

USES & PROPERTIES The main use is to make soups – many French *potage* standards (e.g. *vichyssoise*, a leek and potato soup invented in the USA by a French cook) and other famous leek soups (e.g. the Scottish "cock-a-leekie"). Leeks may also be consumed as a vegetable, often boiled, braised or blanched and served with a white sauce or cheese dressing. The bulb of great-headed garlic is used as seasoning ("mild garlic"), while the leaves of *kurrat* are a popular vegetable in Egypt and the Near East.

NUTRITIONAL VALUE Low in calories but rich in sulphur, other minerals and vitamin A.

NOTES Leeks should not be confused with Welsh onion (see *A. fistulosum*).

Allium ameloprasum L. (= *A. porrum* L.)   family: Alliaceae

jiu cong, tai chung (Chinese); *poireau* (French); *Porree, Lauch* (German); *porre* (Italian); *puerro* (Spanish)

Allium cepa
onion • bulb onion

Onion plants

Onion flowers

Onions

Shallots, spring onions and onions

DESCRIPTION The common onion is a biennial with hollow leaves, a fleshy bulb formed by overlapping leaf bases and small white flowers borne in round clusters. Onion bulbs vary considerably in shape, colour and flavour. The closely related shallot (*A. cepa* var. *ascalonicum*) differs in forming clusters of bulbs. It was formerly thought to be a distinct species, *A. ascalonicum*). The potato onion (*A. cepa* var. *aggregatum*) is similarly multiplying, but the small bulbs are included in a common skin. A fourth type is the tree onion or Egyptian onion (of possible hybrid origin), easily distinguished by the small bulbs that develop within the inflorescence. "Scallion" is the original name for the shallot but now often refers to spring onions (young *A. cepa* plants) or to leeks (in the USA).
ORIGIN & HISTORY The onion exists only in cultivation and is thought to be a cultigen derived from wild species in the Middle East (possibly Iran and Afghanistan). It has a recorded history dating back to at least 3000 BC.
PARTS USED Fresh, dried or pickled bulb.
CULTIVATION & HARVESTING It is cultivated as an annual crop in most parts of the world. The total production amounts to several million tons per year.
USES & PROPERTIES Onions have an exceptionally wide range of culinary uses. They are eaten fresh as an ingredient of many dishes (salads, soups, sauces, stews, curries) or variously processed (pickles, chutneys). The main attraction is the distinctive savoury flavour, which is due to a complex mixture of sulphur compounds.
NUTRITIONAL VALUE Onions have a low energy value (27 kcal per 100 g) and are a good source of sulphur and vitamin C.
NOTES Enzymatic breakdown of sulphur-containing substances in damaged tissue gives the pungent volatiles that cause weeping. They inhibit blood-clotting (and hence thrombosis) so that onions are widely used in natural medicine.

Allium cepa L.   family: Alliaceae

cong tou, yang cong (Chinese); *oignon* (French); *Küchenzwiebel* (German); *cipolla* (Italian); *tama negi* (Japanese); *cebola* (Portuguese); *cebolla* (Spanish)

Allium fistulosum
Japanese bunching onion • Welsh onion

Japanese bunching onion plants

Japanese bunching onion plant

Rakkyo bulbs

DESCRIPTION This is a branching perennial tuft with indistinct bulbs bearing hollow leaves and rounded clusters of small white flowers. It is superficially similar to onion (*A. cepa*) but lacks the characteristic bulb. The common name "Welsh onion" is derived from the German *welsche* (meaning foreign) and refers to the non-European origin of the plant. Other common names, Chinese onion or spring onion, are somewhat confusing. The name "Chinese onion" should not be mistaken for "Chinese chives" (see *A. tuberosum*). "Spring onion" may refer to this species or to young onions (*A. cepa*) that are used in the same way.

ORIGIN & HISTORY China. It is known only in cultivation. Domestication is thought to have occurred in central or northwest China and the crop was later introduced into Japan. The plant has long been the main garden onion in China (recorded 100 BC) and Japan (recorded AD 720).

PARTS USED Leaves and fleshy stems.

CULTIVATION & HARVESTING Cultivation is by division of the stems. Various hybrids are cultivated from seeds in the USA, including the cultivar 'Beltsville Bunching' (which is a fertile hybrid between *A. cepa* and *A. fistulosum*).

USES & PROPERTIES Fresh (raw) stems and leaves are added to a variety of oriental dishes and may be used in stir-fries. They are also an important garnish and are shaped into distinctive brushes or tassles.

NUTRITIONAL VALUE Low (the main value is in the flavour).

NOTES Another commercially important crop is the rakkyo (*A. chinense*), a species of Asian origin (known as *chiao tou* in China or *rakkyo* in Japan). The small bulbs are fried or they are pickled in vinegar or brine. At least 18 species of *Allium* are eaten as vegetables, but only seven of them (chive, Chinese chive, garlic, Japanese bunching onion, leek, onion, potato onion and shallot) are of economic importance.

Allium fistulosum L.

family: Alliaceae

cong, da cong (Chinese); *duan bawang* (Indonesian); *ciboule* (French); *Winterzwiebel* (German); *negi* (Japanese); *cipoletta* (Spanish); *ton horm* (Thai)

Allium sativum

garlic

Garlic plants

Garlic bulbs

Elephant garlic and garlic

DESCRIPTION A perennial herb with flat, somewhat silvery leaves and small white flowers in rounded clusters. In common with the closely related leek (*A. ameloprasum*) each flower cluster is covered by a pointed, sheath-like bract that is shed when the flowers open. Some forms produce small bulbs in the inflorescences. The bulb is divided into several segments known as cloves. Elephant garlic, a hybrid between garlic and onion with very large bulbs, has become popular in recent years.

ORIGIN & HISTORY An ancient cultigen of unknown origin (thought to be derived from the wild central Asian species *A. longicuspis*). The recorded history dates back to at least 3000 BC.

PARTS USED Bulb segments (cloves) – used fresh or as garlic powder or garlic oil.

CULTIVATION & HARVESTING Garlic hardly ever produces fertile seeds and is therefore cultivated by planting the cloves (or the bulbils formed in the inflorescences). Unlike other species, the bulbs are formed entirely below the soil surface.

Several million tons are produced each year.

USES & PROPERTIES A well-known and popular flavour ingredient, especially in southern European cuisine. The strong flavour is characteristic of French, Italian, Spanish and Portuguese cooking but garlic is now popular in most parts of the world. It is often pounded and mixed with other ingredients to create a seasoning paste. Roasted garlic (mainly elephant garlic, because of the large cloves and mild flavour) is nowadays eaten as part of a meal. Various suphur-containing compounds are responsible for the flavour and aroma. These are mainly excreted as volatiles via the lungs, hence the noticeable effect on the breath.

NUTRITIONAL VALUE The energy yield is about 130 kcal per 100 g. Garlic contains a fair amount of minerals and vitamins, including vitamin C (14 mg).

NOTES Garlic has numerous medicinal uses – it is strongly antibiotic and has proven lipid-lowering activity.

Allium sativum L.   family: Alliaceae

suan (Chinese); *ail blanc* (French); *Knoblauch* (German); *aglio* (Italian); *gaarikku* (Japanese); *bawang puteh* (Malay); *ajo* (Spanish)

Allium schoenoprasum

chive • chives

Chive plants

Chive flowers

DESCRIPTION The plant is a perennial grass-like tuft with long, thin, tubular (hollow) leaves, white fleshy stem bases and attractive purple flower clusters. It tends to go dormant in the dry or cold season, leaving only the narrow bulbs to grow out again in spring. Chive or onion chive should not be confused with garlic chive or Chinese chive (see *A. tuberosum*). The latter has flat (solid) leaves and white flowers.

ORIGIN & HISTORY Europe and Asia. Domestication is thought to have taken place in the Mediterranean region. Cultivated chive is closely similar to the wild species and has probably been brought into cultivation more than once. The earliest records are relatively recent and date back to sixteenth-century Europe.

PARTS USED Fresh leaves (sometimes freeze-dried).

CULTIVATION & HARVESTING Chives are traditionally grown in home gardens but are also cultivated commercially as a fresh herb. It is propagated from seeds or by dividing the clumps into single stems ("bulbs"). The delicate leaves are harvested before flowering.

USES & PROPERTIES Due to their mild flavour, chive leaves have become popular as a decorative garnish and/or a flavour ingredient of salads, omelettes, scrambled eggs, sauces, mashed potatoes, cream cheese and cottage cheese. They are used to season savoury dishes and dips. The famous *fines herbes* of French cooking are an aromatic mixture of parsley, chervil, tarragon and chives, in various proportions (sometimes with other ingredients added). The mixture is used to flavour omelettes, meat dishes, cream cheese, sautéed vegetables and sauces.

NUTRITIONAL VALUE As is the case with most of its relatives (various *Allium* species), the chive has limited nutritional value in the diet because it is used in small amounts to add flavour.

NOTES Sulphur-containing compounds are responsible for the mild garlic flavour and aroma of chopped chives.

Allium schoenoprasum L.

family: Alliaceae

bei cong (Chinese); *ciboulette, civette* (French); *Schnittlauch* (German); *cipoletta* (Italian); *cebolinha* (Portuguese); *cebollino* (Spanish)

Allium tuberosum

Chinese chive • garlic chive

Garlic chive flowers

Garlic chive plant

Garlic chives

DESCRIPTION This is a clump-forming perennial herb with grass-like, drooping leaves and clusters of white flowers borne on slender stems. It is easily distinguished from other species by the flat leaves (not folded lengthwise as in garlic and leek) that are solid (not hollow as in chive and onion). A range of other common names is sometimes used, including "oriental garlic", "Chinese leeks" and "flowering chives". The characteristic bunches of flower buds are a common sight on oriental markets in Southeast Asia.

ORIGIN & HISTORY East Asia and northeastern India (domesticated since ancient times).

PARTS USED Leaves and young inflorescences (flowering buds, harvested before the buds emerge from the sheaths).

CULTIVATION & HARVESTING The plant is cultivated by seeds or by division of the fleshy rhizomes. It is easy to grow and has become a common sight in herb gardens. Leaves or flowering stalks are harvested just before the flowers open. White or yellow chives are produced by growing the plants in darkness. These are often seen on markets and are much more expensive than the regular green chives.

USES & PROPERTIES Chinese chives have varied uses, both as herb (as a garnish and flavouring) and as vegetable. They are rarely eaten raw and are mostly only briefly cooked, since prolonged cooking makes them bitter. Chopped leaves have a more pungent taste than that of spring onions (young *A. cepa*) and are included in soups, rice dishes and noodle dishes. Flower buds are a popular but expensive vegetable dish, with a taste and flavour resembling that of onions.

NUTRITIONAL VALUE Low energy value with moderate amounts of vitamins and minerals.

NOTES Chinese chive is also used in traditional Chinese medicine and is thought to be a remedy for fatigue. Another species from Southeast Asia, *A. scorodoprasum* (sandleek) has edible bulbs but is rarely used commercially.

Allium tuberosum Rottler ex Sprengel   family: Alliaceae

jiu cai (Chinese); *ciboule de chine à feuilles larges* (French); *Chinesischer Schnittlauch, Schnittknoblauch* (German); *bawang kuchai* (Malay); *cive chino* (Spanish)

Aloysia triphylla

lemon verbena • vervain

Lemon verbena

Lemon verbena leaves and flowers

DESCRIPTION Lemon verbena is a woody, perennial shrub growing to about 1 m high. It has oblong, leathery and markedly fragrant leaves characteristically arranged in groups of three or four at each node. The deciduous leaves have a prominent midrib and are easily recognised by the strong lemon smell that is emitted when they are crushed. Small white or purplish flowers are borne in sparse clusters on the branch ends. The plant is also known as *Lippia citriodora* or *Aloysia citriodora* (sometimes spelled *"citrodora"*) and may be found under these names in some books.

ORIGIN & HISTORY The plant originated in South America and is indigenous to Argentina and Chile. It was introduced into Europe by the Spaniards in the eighteenth century and quickly became popular in southern European cuisine because of the refreshing lemon flavour.

PARTS USED Fresh or dried leaves.

CULTIVATION & HARVESTING Lemon verbena is easily propagated from cuttings and grows well as a garden ornamental in all warm and temperate parts of the world. Harvesting is done by cutting the leafy twigs and drying them in the shade. The leaves are then stripped from the branches and packaged for sale as a dry herb.

USES & PROPERTIES Dried leaves are widely sold for making a relaxing health tea. Fresh or dried leaves are an important ingredient in commercial health teas, tisanes, liqueurs and fruit juice drinks. Fresh leaves are sometimes used in salads. The fresh or dry product often serves as a substitute for lemongrass and is added as a flavour ingredient to soups and stews.

NUTRITIONAL VALUE Unimportant (used for flavour only).

NOTES Lemon verbena is an important traditional medicine and the essential oil is used in aromatherapy. The herb is believed to have digestive and sedative properties. Lemon verbena oil is also used in soaps and cosmetic products.

Aloysia triphylla (L'Herit.) Britton [= *Lippia citriodora* H.B.K.; *L. triphylla* (L'Herit.) Kunze] family: Verbenaceae

verveine odorante (French); *Zitronenstrauch* (German); *limoncina, erba luigia, cedrina* (Italian); *verbena olorosa, hierba luisa* (Spanish)

Alpinia galanga
greater galangal • galangal

Greater galangal plants (*Alpinia galanga*)

Small galangal (*Kaempferia galangal*)

Greater galangal rhizomes

DESCRIPTION Galangal is a leafy perennial herb of nearly 2 m in height with large leaves arising from robust rhizomes below the ground. The attractive flowers are similar to those of the lesser galangal (*Alpinia officinarum*) but the plants rarely flower in cultivation. In growth form it closely resembles ginger and other members of the family. Various English names are known, including galanga, laos and Siamese ginger. It may be confused with the morphologically similar but smaller plant known as lesser galangal (*A. officinarum*) or with the much smaller *Kaempferia galangal* (which is also known as galangal). All these species are popular spices and medicinal plants in Southeast Asia and China but only the greater galangal is widely used and well known.

ORIGIN & HISTORY The plant is indigenous to tropical Asia, mainly Indonesia. It is widely grown in Malaysia, Laos and Thailand. Galangal is particularly popular in Thai cooking. Since the Middle Ages the fresh or dried rhizome has also become known as a spice in eastern Europe and Russia.

PARTS USED The rhizome (without the roots but usually with short pieces of stem and young buds attached). It superficially resembles fresh ginger but can be distinguished by the pinkish colour.

CULTIVATION & HARVESTING Galangal is widely cultivated in tropical regions. The rhizomes are harvested while they are actively growing and are commonly sold on fresh produce markets in Southeast Asia.

USES & PROPERTIES The pungent taste and somewhat peppery fragrance makes this a favourite condiment of Thai cooks, who add bruised chunks or slices of rhizome to curries and soups. Dried and powdered rhizome is also widely used. In Russia it is used in teas, vinegars and alcoholic drinks (e.g. in the liqueur known as *nastoika*).

NUTRITIONAL VALUE Unimportant, as galangal is used in small quantities as a spice (or as an ingredient of digestive bitters).

Alpinia galanga (L.) Sw.

family: Zingiberaceae

dà gao liang jiang (Chinese); *laos* (Indonesian); *lengkuas* (Malay); *kha* (Thai); *galangal* (French); *Großer Galgant* (German); *galanga* (Italian); *galang* (Spanish)

Amaranthus cruentus
grain amaranth • Inca wheat

Amaranthus hypochondriacus

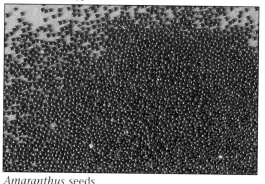

Amaranthus cruentus

Amaranthus seeds

DESCRIPTION Grain amaranths are erect annual herbs of up to 2 m in height, with oblong pointed leaves and clusters of inconspicuous, greenish, wind-pollinated flowers. Domesticated forms characteristically have white seeds (glossy black in wild types). Three species have been domesticated for grain: *A. cruentus, A. hypochondriacus* and *A. caudatus*. The last-mentioned is "Inca wheat" or *kiwicha*, a variable species that includes forms with club-shaped inflorescences, previously known as *A. mantegazzianus* and *A. edulis*.

ORIGIN & HISTORY Domesticated (white-grained) *A. cruentus* can be traced back to 4000 BC (southern Mexico and Central America). It appears that *A. hypochondriacus* was developed in northern Mexico around AD 500. The Central American *A. caudatus* has been found at archaeological sites dating back 2 000 years and is believed to have been domesticated in the Andes. Wild plants are normally green, but purple forms have been selected for ritual purposes.

PARTS USED Seeds (grain).

CULTIVATION & HARVESTING The plants are grown as cereals and the ripe seeds are harvested, popped and milled to produce flour, or boiled and eaten as porridge. Since the seeds of domesticated forms are the same size as those of the wild types, yields have been improved by selecting larger plants with larger inflorescences containing thousands of seeds.

USES & PROPERTIES Grain amaranth is no longer widely used in its regions of origin but has become popular as a health food. *Alegría* is a popular Mexican sweet prepared from popped seeds.

NUTRITIONAL VALUE The health properties are due to the exceptionally nutritious grains, which contain large amounts of high quality protein (14–18%) and especially lysine (800 mg, much higher than conventional cereals). The energy yield is 360 kcal per 100 g.

NOTES Leaves of *Amaranthus* species are popular as pot-herbs (see *A. tricolor*).

Amaranthus cruentus L. (= *A. paniculatus* L.)

family: Amaranthaceae

amarante (French); *Rispenfuchsschwanz, Körneramaranth* (German); *amaranto, trigo inca* (Spanish)

Amaranthus tricolor

Chinese spinach • Chinese amaranth

Chinese spinach (*A. tricolor*)

Common pigweed (*A. hybridus*)

Chinese spinach (*A. tricolor*)

Duck's spinach (*A. viridis*)

DESCRIPTION Chinese spinach is an erect leafy annual with oblong to rounded leaves, sometimes marked with red depending on the variety or cultivar. A large number of different species are cultivated as spinaches in Asia, Africa and Central America (especially the Caribbean region). These include *A. viridis* (duck's spinach or *bayam itek* in Malay), *A. hybridus* (common pigweed, also known as *marog* in Sotho or *imfino* in Zulu), *A. gangeticus*, *A. angustifolius* and others. Young leaves of the grain amaranths (see *A. cruentus*) are also widely used as green vegetables.

ORIGIN & HISTORY *A. tricolor* is an ancient Chinese and Southeast Asian crop plant of uncertain origin. It is widely distributed in tropical regions and is thought to have originated in India.

PARTS USED Young stems and leaves.

CULTIVATION & HARVESTING Various forms of the plant are widely cultivated as a pot-herb. However, *A. tricolor* is only one of several species that are cultivated or wild-harvested for use as spinach. Many species are weeds of agriculture and are often found on rubbish heaps or on roadsides and other disturbed places. *Amaranthus* species are C4 plants (like maize and sugar cane) and make very efficient use of sunlight. Cultivated *A. hybridus* can produce an astounding 30 to 60 tons per hectare. The product is mainly used fresh but can also be dried or canned.

USES & PROPERTIES Chinese spinach and other species are popular as tasty and nutritious green vegetables. Leaves can also be used fresh in salads and are often ingredients of soups (such as *callaloo*, a Caribbean soup made from various green leaves).

NUTRITIONAL VALUE The leaves are very rich in proteins, vitamins (especially vitamin A) and iron.

NOTES Colourful varieties of *A. tricolor*, *A. hybridus* and *A. caudatus* are widely grown as ornamental plants (respectively known as Joseph's coat, prince's feather and love-lies-bleeding).

Amaranthus tricolor L.   family: Amaranthaceae

xiān cài, yin-choi (Chinese); *bayam* (Malay); *amarante* (French); *Dreifarbiger Fuchsschwanz* (German); *amaranto* (Spanish)

Anacardium occidentale

cashew

Cashew flowers and young fruit

Cashew fruits

Cashew nuts

DESCRIPTION An evergreen tree of up to 10 m in height, with broad leaves and clusters of purple flowers. Small kidney-shaped fruits are borne on a yellow to bright red, swollen, juicy fruit stalk, known as the cashew apple. The nuts are surrounded by a thin inner membrane, a layer of irritant oil (known as cashew-nut shell liquid) and a tough, leathery outer shell.

ORIGIN & HISTORY Tropical America (probably northeastern Brazil). It was spread to various parts of the world by the Portuguese and is now cultivated in East Africa, southern Africa (mainly Mozambique), Sri Lanka, India and Malaysia.

PARTS USED The fleshy fruit stalk (cashew apple) and the ripe, roasted seeds (cashew nuts).

CULTIVATION & HARVESTING Cashew-nut trees flourish in the dry tropics but will not tolerate waterlogged or calcareous soils, or frost. A rain-free season is required to ensure flowering and proper fruit set. Harvesting is labour-intensive and the crop is traditionally grown by smallholders in developing countries.

USES & PROPERTIES The main food item is the delicious and nutritious nuts, which have to be roasted to get rid of the irritant and acrid oil. They are usually salted and eaten as a snack, or used in salads or in baking. Despite the astringent taste, the flesh or juice of cashew apples is processed into jams, jellies, chutney, candied fruit, fruit juice, cashew wine, spirits and vinegar. It is used to produce *cajuado*, a popular drink in Brazil.

NUTRITIONAL VALUE Both cashew nuts and cashew apples are very nutritious. The nuts contain up to 25% high quality protein, together with minerals (calcium, phosphorus and iron) and vitamins A, D, K and E. The apples are rich in vitamin A and contain up to five times as much vitamin C (150–400 mg) as citrus juice.

NOTES By-products include cashew-nut shell liquid (CNSL) and stem gum (*acajou* gum).

Anacardium occidentale L.   family: Anacardiaceae

acajou, anacardier (French); *caju* (Portuguese); *Acajubaum, Kaschubaum* (German); *marañon* (Spanish)

Ananas comosus

pineapple

Pineapple plant

Pineapples

DESCRIPTION A perennial herb of about 1 m in height with tough, often spiny leaves. Up to 200 small flowers are borne in dense groups below a characteristic crown of leaves. The compound fruit is formed from the thick axis and fused fleshy flowers, with the bracts and sepals representing the rind. Of the various cultivars that have been developed, 'Smooth Cayenne' is by far the most important, partly because of the non-spiny leaves. Others include 'Pernambuco', 'Queen', 'Red Spanish' and 'Singapore Spanish'.

ORIGIN & HISTORY Pineapple is a pre-Columbian crop that originated in the lowlands of northern South America. It first spread to Central America and was later introduced to other parts of the world by the Portuguese and Spanish. The cultivar 'Smooth Cayenne' originated in French Guiana.

PARTS USED Fruit (a syncarp or *sorosis*).

CULTIVATION & HARVESTING Pineapples are cultivated in the dry tropics. They are remarkably drought-resistant but very sensitive to frost and therefore grown in lowland regions, often near the sea. Plants are propagated from the crowns formed above the fruits and from suckers arising below the fruit. Harvesting can be synchronised by the external application of growth hormones.

USES & PROPERTIES The fruits are used on a large scale for the production of juice, but they are also eaten fresh and are used for a wide range of other culinary purposes – in green salads, fruit salads, pickles, savoury dishes, chutneys and jams.

NUTRITIONAL VALUE Pineapple has a low energy value (55 kcal per 100 g) and is a good source of vitamin C (10–25 mg) and also vitamins A and E.

NOTES The ripe fruit contains a mixture of protein-digesting enzymes (collectively known as bromelain) that is used to treat inflammation and swelling (post-traumatic and post-operative oedemas). The strong, soft and durable leaf fibres (crowa) are used in the textile industry.

Ananas comosus (L.) Merr. [= *A. sativus* (Lindl.) Schult. f.] family: Bromeliaceae

ananas (French); *Ananas* (German); *nanas* (Indonesian); *ananás* (Portuguese); *ananasso* (Italian); *piña* (Spanish)

Anethum graveolens
dill

Dill plantation

Dill plant in flower

Dill fruits

DESCRIPTION Dill is an annual or biennial of up to 1 m in height bearing hairless, finely divided, feathery leaves. The small yellow flowers are borne in characteristic umbels and develop into paired dry fruits (schizocarps). These split into two flat, elliptic, single-seeded parts (mericarps), each with a thin dorsal ridge and distinct yellowish wings along the margins. It is sometimes called false anise or bastard fennel.
ORIGIN & HISTORY Dill is thought to be indigenous to southwestern Asia and southern Europe and has been cultivated in these regions since ancient times. The Romans regarded it as a symbol of vitality. The plant has become naturalised in many parts of Eurasia and North America.
PARTS USED Fresh leaves or the small, dry fruits (sometimes wrongly referred to as seeds).
CULTIVATION & HARVESTING Dill is widely cultivated for culinary purposes and is found in almost every herb or kitchen garden.

USES & PROPERTIES The fresh herb is most famous as a popular seasoning and garnish for fish dishes, potato salad and other salads. The aromatic fruits are used in pickles ("dill pickles", mainly gherkins), butter ("dill butter"), vinegars, bread, cheeses, sauces and vegetables. In North Africa, dill fruits are popular in meat dishes, while the Scandinavians traditionally use them when preparing crayfish or salmon. Dill is more aromatic than fennel and is always used fresh.
NUTRITIONAL VALUE Only small quantities are used as seasoning.
NOTES The fruits (or small quantities of the carvone-rich volatile oil, distilled from the fruits) are traditionally used to treat digestive disorders and flatulence. Dill fruits are also well known as a diuretic medicine and are used as the main ingredient of gripe water to alleviate winds and colic in babies. The word "dill" is indeed derived from the Norse word *dylla* – to soothe – indicating a soothing or calming effect.

Anethum graveolens L.

family: Apiaceae

aneth (French); *Dill* (German); *aneto* (Italian); *eneldo* (Spanish)

Angelica archangelica
angelica

Angelica plant

Angelica flowers

Angelica fruits

DESCRIPTION Angelica is a tall, robust biennial herb, reaching a height of more than 2 m when in flower. The large and distinctly toothed leaves are borne on hollow stems. Typical umbels of green flowers (not yellow or white as in other members of the family) are followed by flat, ribbed, dry fruits (schizocarps). Cultivated angelica is sometimes confused with purple-stemmed angelica or American angelica (*A. atropurpurea*, which has similar uses, with the European wild angelica (*A. sylvestris*) or with Chinese angelica (*A. polymorpha* var. *sinensis*).

ORIGIN & HISTORY *A. archangelica* is indigenous to Europe and Asia but it is widely cultivated in Europe and elsewhere as a culinary and medicinal herb ("angelica" is derived from *angelus*, the Latin word for "angel"). Its spread to central and southern Europe from Iceland, Scandinavia and Russia is ascribed to the Vikings. Monks have cultivated the plant for centuries.

PARTS USED Young stems, leaf stalks, fruits and roots.

CULTIVATION & HARVESTING Commercial cultivation is centred in Europe. The French town of Niort is particularly famous for candied angelica. The stems, stalks, roots or dry fruits (sometimes referred to as "seeds") are harvested.

USES & PROPERTIES The main culinary use is the green leaf stalks that are candied in sugar and used in various types of confectionary (cakes, pastries, desserts), puddings, jams, cassata ice cream and soufflés – the stalks remain bright green when candied and are valued for their colour and flavour. Fresh stems and stalks are eaten with cream cheese or are added to salads. The roots are cooked and eaten as a vegetable. Crushed stems, roots and fruits are used to flavour famous alcoholic beverages such as gin, chartreuse, Bénédictine, vermouth and vespétro.

NUTRITIONAL VALUE Angelica stems and roots are used in small amounts only but they have proven medicinal value as an appetite stimulant, stomachic and spasmolytic.

Angelica archangelica L.

family: Apiaceae

angélique (French); *Engelwurz* (German); *archangelica* (Italian); *angélica* (Spanish)

Annona cherimola
cherimoya • custard apple

Cherimoya

Atemoya

Cherimoya fruits

DESCRIPTION A small tree with broad, oblong to egg-shaped, somewhat hairy leaves that are alternately arranged along the stems. The greenish flowers have three long, narrow sepals and the green, distinctly scaly fruits are relatively small (about 10–12 cm in diameter). They originate from a fleshy axis (receptacle) and numerous fused carpels (segments) that become fleshy. Each segment has a brown or black seed surrounded by delicious, white, custard-like flesh. The term "custard apple" is loosely applied to several different species of *Annona* (see *A. muricata*) but also to a close relative of the cherimoya, *A. squamosa*. This fruit, which is correctly known as "sugar apple" or "sweet sop", is somewhat smaller and less commonly cultivated than the cherimoya. Another "custard apple" is the atemoya, a hybrid between the cherimoya (*A. cherimola*) and the sweet sop (*A. squamosa*). It closely resembles both.

ORIGIN & HISTORY The cherimoya originated in the subtropical highlands of Peru and Ecuador but has long been cultivated for local use in Central America. The sweet sop originated in the Caribbean but is widely grown in Thailand, Malaysia and Indonesia.

PARTS USED Ripe fruits.

CULTIVATION & HARVESTING The cherimoya and atemoya are commonly cultivated in subtropical regions (including the USA, Australia, Israel, Chile, Spain, New Zealand and South Africa), while the sweet sop is most popular in tropical Asia. The fruits are perishable and as a result are mainly sold on local markets.

USES & PROPERTIES The delicious fruit flesh is eaten raw or is used fresh in fruit salad, ice cream, milk shake, jelly, preserves, sherbet and yogurt.

NUTRITIONAL VALUE Fresh fruits contain about 15% sugar (energy yield 60 kcal per 100 g) and some vitamin C (up to 20 mg per 100 g).

NOTES Several other species of "custard apples" are described on the next page.

Annona cherimola Miller   family: Annonaceae

chérimole (French); *Cherimoya* (German); *cherimoya* (Spanish)

Annona muricata

sour sop • guanábana

Sour sop flowers and leaves

Sour sop fruits

Bullock heart flowers and young fruit

DESCRIPTION A small, rounded tree of up to 8 m in height, with glossy, leathery leaves and greenish, bell-shaped flowers that are borne directly on older branches. The fruits, with their distinctive "thorny" surfaces, are very large (up to 3 kg) and usually remain bright green when ripe. They have a somewhat fibrous white fruit flesh surrounding the numerous shiny black seeds. The sour sop is one of numerous species loosely referred to as "custard apples" (see *A. cherimoya*). Well known are the true custard apple or cherimoya (*A. cherimola*), the closely similar sugar apple (*A. squamosa*) and the atemoya (a hybrid between the two). Less well known are the red-skinned bullock heart (*A. reticulata*), the cherimoya-like ilama (*A. diversifolia*), the large-fruited soncoya (*A. purpurea*), the tough-skinned poshte (*A. scleroderma*) and the small-fruited wild custard apple (*A. senegalensis*).

ORIGIN & HISTORY Both sour sop and bullock heart are indigenous to the tropical lowlands of Central America, while the ilama and soncoya originate from Mexico and Central America. The poshte is found in Guatemala, while the wild custard apple occurs in tropical Africa.

PARTS USED Ripe fruits.

CULTIVATION & HARVESTING The sour sop is commonly cultivated in Madeira, India, Jamaica, Indonesia, Thailand and Malaysia. Since the fruits are mostly used fresh, they are mainly sold on local markets.

USES & PROPERTIES Sour sop is sometimes eaten raw (the juicy white flesh is scooped from cut segments with a spoon) but it is mainly processed into fruit juice and soft drinks. The somewhat acidic fruit pulp or juice may be included in fruit salad, mousse, ice cream, jelly and sorbet.

NUTRITIONAL VALUE Similar to the cherimoya, but lower in energy value (55 kcal per 100 g) and higher in minerals and some vitamins.

NOTES The name sour sop (or Indonesian *sirsak*) is derived from the Dutch *zuurzak* meaning "sour sack".

Annona muricata L.   family: Annonaceae

corossol (French); *Sauersack, Stachelannone* (German); *sirsak* (Indonesian); *guanábana* (Spanish)

Anthriscus cerefolium

chervil

Chervil leaves

Chervil flowers and young fruits

Chervil fruits

DESCRIPTION Chervil is an annual herb with bright green, compound leaves that are divided into narrow segments (some forms are similar to parsley). Most parts of the plant (stems, leaves and flower stalks) are sparsely hairy. The inconspicuous white flowers are borne in characteristic umbels, which are followed by oblong, beaked, dry fruits of about 10 mm long. The cultivated form of chervil is also known as garden chervil. Chervil should not be confused with turnip-rooted chervil (*Chaerophyllum bulbosum*), a perennial with thick, edible roots that is a rare vegetable in central and northern Europe.

ORIGIN & HISTORY The plant is indigenous to central Asia, from Iran to southern Russia. It was grown as a culinary herb in ancient times by the Greeks and Romans, who introduced the plant to other parts of Europe. It was mentioned by the Roman writer Pliny the Elder (AD 23–79) in his famous book, *Historia naturalis*.

PARTS USED Fresh or dried leaves.

CULTIVATION & HARVESTING Chervil is widely cultivated in kitchen gardens and also on a commercial scale.

USES & PROPERTIES The aromatic leaves are somewhat reminiscent of parsley and have a delicious, aniseed flavour. Fresh leaves are a popular condiment and seasoning with a wide range of culinary applications. They are used to garnish soups, omelettes and fish dishes. It is one of the components of *fines herbes* (together with parsley, tarragon and chives). French chefs often use it in sauces, such as *béarnaise* (a hot creamy sauce served with meat or fish), *gribiche* (a cold mayonnaise-like sauce served with cold fish or calf's head) and *vinaigrette* (a vinegar-based dressing for salads or cold dishes, also known as "French dressing").

NUTRITIONAL VALUE The herb is used in small amounts only.

NOTES Unlike parsley and dill, chervil is not of much importance in traditional medicine.

Anthriscus cerefolium (L.) Hoffm.   family: Apiaceae

cerfeuil (French); *Gartenkerbel* (German); *perifollo* (Spanish)

Apium graveolens
celery

Celery leaves

Celery flowers

Celeriac

DESCRIPTION A biennial, aromatic herb with bright green, dissected leaves, small yellow flowers and small, dry fruits. Three types are used: Chinese celery (var. *secalinum*), stalk celery (var. *dulce*) and celeriac or turnip-rooted celery (var. *rapaceum*).

ORIGIN & HISTORY Wild celery is widely distributed in Eurasia and was well known to the ancient Chinese, Egyptians, Greeks and Romans who used the bitter-tasting leaves as condiment (not as a vegetable) and for medicine and funeral wreaths. Chinese celery (*qin cài*), derived from the wild Asian form, is still used in this way. The mild-flavoured stalk celery (*sai kan choi* in Chinese) originated in Italy, and celeriac was subsequently developed from it.

PARTS USED Leaf stalks (celery), leaves (Chinese celery), root (celeriac) or the fruits ("celery seeds").

CULTIVATION & HARVESTING Celery is grown all over the world as a vegetable. The leaf stalks are blanched by excluding sunlight (there are also self-blanching forms that spontaneously lose

the chlorophyll in their leaf stalks). Chinese celery is grown only in Southeast Asia and China, while celeriac is a traditional vegetable in central, eastern and northern Europe.

USES & PROPERTIES Chinese celery has a strong bitter taste and is used sparingly as a herb, mainly in soup (the Malay name is *daun sop* or "soup leaf") or in stir-fries, rice dishes and noodle dishes. Celery stalks are eaten raw in salads, added to soups and stews or cooked as a vegetable. Celeriac is a popular vegetable in European cooking – the French call it *céleri rave* and serve the grated root with *rémoulade* sauce.

NUTRITIONAL VALUE Both celery and celeriac have low energy values (respectively 18 and 15 kcal per 100 g). They contain fair amounts of vitamins and folic acid.

NOTES Celery salt (extracted from dried, powdered celeriac) is used in salt-free diets. Celery fruits may be used as a seasoning and sometimes in digestive medicines.

Apium graveolens L.   family: Apiaceae

sai kan choi (Chinese); *céleri* (French); *Sellerie* (German); *sèdano* (Italian); *oranda mitsuba* (Japanese); *apío* (Spanish)

Aponogeton distachyos
Cape pondweed

Cape pondweed plant

Cape pondweed flowers

Canned waterblommetjies

DESCRIPTION This is an aquatic plant that grows in standing or slow-flowing water. It has floating oblong leaves borne on slender stalks. The fragrant, white flower clusters are forked into two parts, each with a double row of pointed, overlapping bracts that protect the small, inconspicuous flowers.

ORIGIN & HISTORY The plant is found only in the Western Cape Province of South Africa where both the flower heads and the starchy rhizomes were traditional food items of the Khoi and San people. Over the last 300 years it has become a popular vegetable in the Cape.

PARTS USED Fresh or canned flower clusters (inflorescences).

CULTIVATION & HARVESTING Plants are commercially cultivated in shallow dams and are picked daily by harvesters in waders towing small rafts. Some prefer young flowers while others insist that older flowers (which have already formed seeds inside) are superior in taste. The product is sold fresh or canned.

USES & PROPERTIES Cape pondweed is almost exclusively used as the main ingredient of a traditional Cape dish known as "waterblommetjie bredie", a delicious stew comprising about one kilogram lamb for each kilogram of flowers, together with two onions, about half a kilogram of young potatoes, a cup of dry white wine, a pinch of sugar and some salt and pepper. A handful of sorrel leaves (*Oxalis pes-caprae*) are traditionally added (or lemon juice) and some cooks also add a few pieces of pork. The flowers are cooked to a pulp and contribute a distinctive fine flavour and thick sauce to the stew. Too much pepper or spice may spoil the dish. Fresh flowers can be used in salads, soups and pickles or steamed and eaten as a vegetable.

NUTRITIONAL VALUE The flowers provide minerals and some vitamins, including folic acid.

NOTES The juice from fresh stems or leaves has been used to treat wounds and burns.

Aponogeton distachyos L.f.   family: Aponogetonaceae

waterblommetjies (Afrikaans); *aponogeton* (French); *Kap-Wasserähre* (German)

Arachis hypogaea
peanut • groundnut

Peanut flowers

Peanut plant

Peanut pods and seeds

DESCRIPTION Peanut is an annual of up to half a metre in height bearing self-pollinated yellow flowers. The stalks elongate after pollination to push the young pods into the ground, where they mature into soft-shelled, up to six-seeded pods. The soft, oily seeds are covered in a reddish brown, membranous seed coat. Four basic types have been described: two prostrate types (Virginia and Peruvian) and two erect types (Valencia and Spanish), botanically known as the varieties *hypogaea, hirsuta, fastigiata* and *vulgaris* respectively.

ORIGIN & HISTORY The plant is a cultigen that was domesticated in northwestern Argentina and southern Bolivia and grown in South and Central America (including Mexico) for at least 3 500 years. From here it spread as an important food plant to Africa, India, China, Southeast Asia and the USA. The annual production is now more than 30 million tons.

PARTS USED The ripe (raw or roasted) seeds, which are not really nuts but legumes.

CULTIVATION & HARVESTING Peanuts are grown in all subtropical and warm temperate regions. Plants are harvested by hand (and collected in stacks to dry out) or mechanically (erect types).

USES & PROPERTIES Peanuts are eaten as a popular snack food, either raw or more often roasted and salted. They are included in a wide range of confectionery, sweetmeats, stews, sauces (including the popular chili sauce used with *satay*), salads, soups and curries. A large part of the annual harvest is processed into peanut butter or cold-pressed to extract the oil (about 50% yield) which is used for cooking oil, salad dressing, margarine and mayonnaise manufacturing and even for packing canned sardines.

NUTRITIONAL VALUE Peanuts are rich in proteins and vitamins and the oil is high in unsaturated oleic and linoleic acids. The energy value is 560 kcal per 100 g.

NOTES Carcinogenic aflatoxins, produced in mouldy peanuts, are a serious health risk.

Arachis hypogaea L.   family: Fabaceae

luo hua sheng (Chinese); *arachide* (French); *Erdnuss* (German); *arachide* (Italian); *nankinmame, piinatsu* (Japanese); *cacahuete* (Spanish)

Arbutus unedo

strawberry tree

Strawberry tree flowers and fruits

DESCRIPTION This is a small tree of up to 10 m in height, with a red flaking bark, glossy green, dentate leaves and small, waxy, white, urn-shaped flowers. The attractive rounded fruits have a red warty skin when ripe. They resemble strawberries in appearance only – the taste is bland and watery. A close relative is the North American *Arbutus menziesii*, commonly known as *madroña* or *madrono* and formerly used for its tanbark and timber.

ORIGIN & HISTORY The strawberry tree is thought to be indigenous to southern Europe, Ireland and the Canary Islands. It is well known as a garden plant and is grown as an evergreen ornamental shrub or small tree in many parts of the world.

PARTS USED Ripe fruits, known as arbutus berries.

CULTIVATION & HARVESTING The tree is cultivated on a small scale (e.g. in the south of France) for fruit production. For this purpose, a cultivar known as the 'Killarney strawberry tree' is most commonly used. The fruits take more than a year to ripen and are harvested by hand.

USES & PROPERTIES Arbutus berries are not eaten raw but are processed into jams, jellies, fruit wine or used as decoration in confectionery. They are an ingredient of several fermented and distilled alcoholic drinks and liqueurs (fruit macerated in *grappa* or *orujo*). *Aguardente de medronho* or *medronho* is a distilled spirit (50% alcohol) unique to the Algarve province in Portugal. In the same region, they make *brandymel* (*medronho* sweetened with honey). Similar drinks include *licor di madrono* (Spain), *liqueur l'arbouse* and a sweeter *crème d'arbouse* (France – Corsica), while *acquavita di corbezzolo* (30% alcohol) and *liquore di corbezzolo* (24% alcohol) are examples from Italy (Sardinia).

NUTRITIONAL VALUE The fruit contains 15% sugar and about 1% malic acid.

NOTES The city of Madrid was once surrounded by strawberry trees and the city's coat of arms shows a bear and a strawberry tree.

Arbutus unedo L. family: Ericaceae

arbousier (French); *Erdbeerbaum* (German); *albatro, corbezollo* (Italian); *medronho, medronheiro* (Portuguese); *madroña* (Spanish)

Arctium lappa
burdock • gobo

Burdock flower heads

Burdock roots

Burdock plantation

DESCRIPTION A robust, weedy, perennial herb with large rounded leaves that are bright green above but covered with a layer of white woolly hairs below. The sturdy flowering stalk is up to 1 m in height and bears thistle-like purple flower heads, each surrounded by layers of bristly, hooked bracts. When the small fruits ripen they are released as burrs that cling to socks and clothing. The taproots are slender, somewhat carrot-like, brown on the outside, white inside and up to 1 m long.

ORIGIN & HISTORY Indigenous to Europe but introduced into Asia and North America. Although burdock has a long history of medicinal use in Europe and Asia, it is mainly the Japanese that grow and use burdock root as a vegetable.

PARTS USED The fresh roots, rarely the young leaves.

CULTIVATION & HARVESTING Burdock is grown as a vegetable crop, mainly in Japan but also to a limited extent in China, Taiwan, Korea and Hawaii. The young roots are harvested before they become fibrous (when they are about 30 cm long and 2 cm in diameter).

USES & PROPERTIES The roots are known as *gobo* in Japanese and are a popular vegetable, similar to carrots. The grated root is added to soups and stews, while slices or slivers are used in stir-fries, mainly for their earthy taste and crunchy texture. Young shoots and leaves are added to soups (or eaten braised) in southern France and Italy.

NUTRITIONAL VALUE The roots are a source of minerals (potassium and magnesium) and also some folic acid.

NOTES As is the case with other members of the daisy family such as chicory (*Cichorium*) and salsify (*Scorzonera*), the roots contain inulin as storage polysaccharide and not starch. Burdock root also contains triterpenoids, polyacetylenes and lignans, to which the medicinal uses (for skin complaints, rheumatism and as diuretic) are ascribed.

Arctium lappa L. (= *A. majus* Bernh.)   family: Asteraceae

bardane (French); *Große Klette* (German); *bardana* (Italian); *gobo* (Japanese); *bardana* (Spanish)

Arenga pinnata

sugar palm

Sugar palm

Sugar palm fruits

Palm sugar

DESCRIPTION The sugar palm (also called *aren* or *gomuti palm*) is a single-stemmed tree of up to 15 m in height, with long dissected leaves, pendulous male or female flower clusters and round fruits. Numerous other palms used for sugar tapping are listed under *Hyphaene petersiana*.

ORIGIN & HISTORY The palm is indigenous to tropical Asia, from India to Indonesia, and has been a source of sugar and palm wine since ancient times.

PARTS USED The sugary sap and the fruits.

CULTIVATION & HARVESTING Sugar palm thrives only in warm climates. Although being commercialised to some extent, sugar-making is still mainly done in villages throughout Southeast Asia. Usually the male (sometimes also the female) flower clusters are cut off and tapped. Sap flow can be maintained for some weeks, yielding several litres in the first few days, after which it steadily declines. The annual yield can be about 1 800 litres of sap per tree (roughly 150 kg sugar). The round fibrous fruits contain three fleshy white seeds that have to be shelled and boiled before they can be eaten, to get rid of the irritant juice.

USES & PROPERTIES Palm sap may be fermented to produce *tuak* (a low alcohol palm wine or toddy), which in turn may be distilled to give *arrack* (palm spirit). The sucrose-rich sap is boiled down to yield the familiar brown palm sugar (known as *gula*, *gula jawa* or *jaggery*). The cooked fruits may be tinned or canned but are usually kept in water by the vendor (*warung*) until they are sold on the roadside – often as part of the popular ice concoction called *es campur* – a mixture of ice, sweet syrup and sliced fruits.

NUTRITIONAL VALUE Similar to sucrose (about 390 kcal per 100 g).

NOTES Fibres at the base of the flower stalks are used for thatching and to make ropes.

Arenga pinnata (Wurb.) Merr. (= *Arenga saccharifera*)   family: Arecaceae (Palmae)

palmier à sucre (French); *Zuckerpalme* (German); *aren* (Indonesian); *kabung* (Malay); *palma della zucchero* (Italian)

Argania spinosa
argan tree

Argan tree

Argan leaves and fruits

Argan flower and fruit

DESCRIPTION This is a shrub or small tree with thorny branches bearing clusters of small, hairless, oblong leaves. Small, yellowish green flowers are produced on the stem tips and on the old wood. The hard, green, olive-like fruits are egg-shaped, somewhat pointed and contain a single oily seed.

ORIGIN & HISTORY The argan tree is indigenous to the northwestern tip of Africa (Morocco and Algeria) where it has been utilised for centuries (especially by the Berber people of southern Morocco). It has been introduced as a crop plant into Israel and Libya and has been naturalised in southern Spain.

PARTS USED Seeds (for extraction of seed oil).

CULTIVATION & HARVESTING The argan tree is a long-lived and drought-hardy plant that is suitable for large-scale commercial cultivation.

USES & PROPERTIES The seed oil, known as argan oil, is cold-pressed from the fruits. Yields of up to 70% are obtained. It is used in much the same way as olive oil and is highly prized for its fine aroma and taste. The oil is popular for cooking and frying and is excellent when used as salad dressing. A thick, chocolate-like paste (known as *amlou*) remains after oil extraction. This is mixed with honey and served as part of the traditional Berber breakfast.

NUTRITIONAL VALUE The oil is very rich in fatty acids (especially oleic and linoleic acid), phytosterols and vitamin E.

NOTES Argan oil has become popular as an ingredient of cosmetics and in aromatherapy, where it is used as carrier oil to dilute precious essential oils or to reduce their concentration (few essential oils can be safely applied in their pure form directly on the skin). The fruit (and fruit cake, after the oil has been extracted) is used as feed for cattle and goats. A useful dark timber is obtained from old trees.

Argania spinosa (L.) Skeels   family: Sapotaceae

bois d'Argan (French); *Arganbaum* (German); *argan* (Italian); *argan* (Spanish)

Armoracia rusticana

horseradish

Horseradish plant

Horseradish flowers

Horseradish roots

DESCRIPTION A perennial herb with numerous large leaves arising directly from a thick taproot. The leaves are bright green with prominent veins and toothed margins. Numerous small white flowers are borne on a slender stalk of up to 1 m in height. The small fruits do not form viable seeds.

ORIGIN & HISTORY Horseradish appears to be an ancient sterile cultigen (possibly of hybrid origin) that is thought to have originated in southeastern Europe. It is now widely distributed and commonly cultivated as a crop all over the world.

PARTS USED Fresh or dried roots.

CULTIVATION & HARVESTING Horseradish plants do not form seeds and are traditionally cultivated from root cuttings.

USES & PROPERTIES The thick, grey or yellowish brown taproot has a pure white flesh with a hot, peppery taste and a sharp smell (due to mustard oil glycosides). It is used (sparingly) as a condiment and is particularly popular in the Alsace, Germany, Russia and Scandinavia. For use with meat and fish dishes, the fresh root is washed, peeled and grated (or thinly sliced). Milk or cream may be added to soften the flavour. In modern times horseradish is mostly used in the form of ready-to-use sauces, prepared by mixing it with various other ingredients, including salt, vinegar, cream and mustard. It is also available as vinegars or powders, and may be used as an ingredient in hot and cold sauces, relishes, dips, salad dressings, mustards, etc. Horseradish is excellent with meat such as beef, pork, sausages and reindeer (traditional in Scandinavia), as well as fish (particularly herring and smoked trout), potato salad and many other dishes.

NUTRITIONAL VALUE Roots are said to contain vitamin C (but use sparingly – large doses are dangerous!).

NOTES Horseradish preparations are taken orally for lung or urinary tract infections or applied on the skin for relief of rheumatic pain or inflammation.

Armoracia rusticana P.Gaertn., Mey. & Scherb. (= *A. lappathifolia* Gilib.; = *Cochlearia armoracia* L.)   family: Brassicaceae

la gen (Chinese); *raifort, grand raifort* (French); *Meerrettich, Kren* (German); *cren* (Italian); *hoosu radiishu, seiyou wasabi* (Japanese); *rábano picante* (Spanish)

Aronia melanocarpa
black chokeberry • aronia berry

Black chokeberry leaves and berries

DESCRIPTION This is a suckering and thicket-forming deciduous shrub of up to 2 m in height, with bright green, smooth leaves that have small black glands along the upper midribs. The beautiful red autumn colours are also characteristic. Small white flowers are borne in clusters, followed by pea-sized berries (about 1 g each) that are glossy violet-black when ripe, with a deep red fruit flesh and small seeds. *Aronia* species are popular garden plants and are sometimes included in the genus *Photinia* in modern classification systems. The North American red chokeberry (*Aronia arbutifolia*) is therefore also known as *Photinia pyrifolia* (= *P. arbutifolia*) and the Japanese chokeberry as *P. glabra*. Black chokeberry differs from red chokeberry in the total absence of hairs.

ORIGIN & HISTORY Indigenous to the eastern part of North America (USA and Canada). It has been cultivated in Europe for over a century. Commercial cultivation has spread to other parts of the world, including Denmark and Russia.

PARTS USED Ripe berries.

CULTIVATION & HARVESTING Plants are easily propagated from seeds or cuttings and grow well in temperate regions. They grow well in acid soils and are drought tolerant. Three cultivars, 'Viking', 'Nero' and 'Aron', are grown commercially.

USES & PROPERTIES The berries are used to produce "Aronia berry juice", a health product that is included in popular soft drinks. The main attraction is the dark purple colour, due to high levels of anthocyanins (natural pigments). Ripe berries can also be used to make tasty jams and jellies that are excellent with meat dishes.

NUTRITIONAL VALUE A good source of minerals (iron) and vitamins (especially vitamin C, at 50–100 mg per 100 g). The health properties are mainly ascribed to the high levels of anthocyanins, polyphenols and flavonoids that act as antioxidants and venotonics (to strengthen arteries and veins).

Aronia melanocarpa (Michx.) Ell.   family: Rosaceae

aronia (French); *Kahle Apfelbeere* (German); *aronia* (Italian); *aronia* (Spanish)

Artemisia absinthium

wormwood • absinthe

Wormwood

Southernwood

Mugwort

DESCRIPTION Wormwood is an aromatic perennial herb of up to 1 m in height, with silky, silvery, pinnately divided leaves and small yellowish flower heads borne in large numbers on the branch ends. Closely related species such as African wormwood (*A. afra*) and the two European species known as southernwood (*A. abrotanum*) and mugwort (*A. vulgaris*) are also used as traditional medicines (bitter tonics).

ORIGIN & HISTORY Wormwood is indigenous to Europe and Asia and has been cultivated as a garden plant since ancient times. In common with other *Artemisia* species, the herb has a long history of medicinal use (mainly as a tonic, febrifuge and especially as a vermifuge, hence the common name) but it is best known as a flavour ingredient of alcoholic beverages.

PARTS USED The leaves (or the essential oil distilled from them).

CULTIVATION & HARVESTING Wormwood thrives in temperate regions and is commonly grown in herb gardens even though it is now mainly of historic interest.

USES & PROPERTIES Wormwood was once an important flavour ingredient of vermouth and other alcoholic beverages such as Pernod and pastis. Most famous (notorious) of all is absinthe, the popular French alcoholic drink (often referred to as "the green Muse") that was banned in 1915 because of its addictive, narcotic, hallucinogenic (and sometimes fatal) effects. Amongst the best-known victims was the Flemish artist Vincent van Gogh. Pernod and pastis are now flavoured with aniseed. Small quantities of the herb, taken sporadically, are probably not harmful but regular ingestion (as is typical in the case of alcoholics) may lead to serious central nervous system disorders.

NUTRITIONAL VALUE Used for flavour only.

NOTES Thujone, a typical component of the essential oil, enhances the effects of alcohol but is a convulsant poison at high doses.

Artemisia absinthium L.   family: Asteraceae

absinthe, herbe d'absinthe (French); *Wermut, Absinth* (German); *assenzio* (Italian); *ajenjo* (Spanish)

Artemisia dracunculus

tarragon • French tarragon

French tarragon

French tarragon in flower

Russian tarragon in flower

DESCRIPTION Tarragon is a sparse perennial herb of about 0.6 m in height with narrowly oblong, bright green leaves and small whitish flower heads borne in loose clusters on the branch ends. Russian or false tarragon (*Artemisia dracunculoides*) is sometimes used as an inferior substitute for real tarragon. It is very similar in appearance (but slightly taller, with sparsely hairy and paler, silvery leaves) but the taste is not as delicate.

ORIGIN & HISTORY The plant is indigenous to Europe and central Asia. The early culinary history of the herb is somewhat obscure and it appears to have become popular only in the sixteenth century.

PARTS USED Fresh, dried or frozen leaves (or leafy stems).

CULTIVATION & HARVESTING French tarragon is commercially cultivated in several countries in central, southern and eastern Europe, as well as the USA. Russian tarragon is easier to grow and is commonly seen in herb gardens. French tarragon is usually sterile (it rarely sets seeds), so that cultivation is by cuttings or division.

USES & PROPERTIES The herb has a fine delicate flavour (reminiscent of liquorice) and is a highly sought after item amongst gourmet chefs. It is best known for the production of tarragon vinegar (leaves added to white wine vinegar), which is mostly used with fish, salads, sauces, pickles and mustard sauces. Fresh leaves may be added to meat dishes, stews and as an ingredient of *fines herbes* (together with parsley, chervil and chives). It is an important ingredient of various sauces ("the honour and glory of French cooking"), including *béarnaise*, *hollandaise*, *tartare* and numerous others that go with vegetables (tarragon cream), poached fowl, meat and soft-boiled or poached eggs.

NUTRITIONAL VALUE The herb is used in small quantities only.

NOTES Tarragon is not used medicinally but was once considered to be a cure for snakebite.

Artemisia dracunculus L.

family: Asteraceae

estragon (French); *Esdragon, Estragon* (German); *estragon* (Italian); *estragon* (Spanish)

Artocarpus altilis
breadfruit

Breadfruit leaves and flowers

Breadfruit

DESCRIPTION A tree (up to 12 m) with very distinctive, deeply lobed leaves (not small and rounded as in jackfruit, see *A. heterophyllus*). The compound fruit, which is formed from an entire flower cluster, is usually rounded in shape (about 2 kg when mature). It has a green, relatively smooth skin that becomes yellowish as the fruit ripens. There are two types: the ordinary seedless type (breadfruit) and one with large, edible seeds (known as breadnut).

ORIGIN & HISTORY The breadfruit is indigenous to the South Pacific region and Southeast Asia, and is a traditional staple food, especially in Polynesia. Breadfruit is famous for its association with Captain William Bligh and the mutiny on the HMS *Bounty* in 1789 (underway from Tahiti to the West Indies with breadfruit plants, intended as a food source for slaves).

PARTS USED Green or ripe fruit (breadfruit) and ripe seeds (breadnut).

CULTIVATION & HARVESTING Breadfruit and breadnut are easily grown from suckers or root cuttings. They are sensitive to cold and thrive only in tropical climates.

USES & PROPERTIES Both breadfruit and breadnut have to be cooked (or boiled, roasted, fried) before they are eaten. They have no distinctive flavour of their own and are mainly a starch source, used to "stretch" a curry or stew (they absorb the flavour of meat and other foods). A common way of preparing breadfruit is to parboil chunks of the peeled fruit before these are added to coconut milk and seasoned to prepare a curry dish. The seeds make a useful snack or vegetable after they are boiled in salt water. The starchy fruit can be cooked, dried and milled to produce flour.

NUTRITIONAL VALUE Breadfruit contains 25% carbohydrates (energy value of 110 kcal per 100 g). It supplies small amounts of minerals (especially potassium and zinc) and vitamins B1 (100 µg) and C (20 mg).

Artocarpus altilis (Parkinson) Fosberg (= *A. communis* J.R. Forst. & G. Forst.; = *A. incisus* L.f.) family: Moraceae

mian bao guo (Chinese); *arbre à pain* (French); *sukun* (Indonesian); *Brotfruchtbaum* (German); *artocarpo* (Italian); *pannoki* (Japanese); *fruta-pão* (Portuguese); *pana, árbor del pan* (Spanish)

Artocarpus heterophyllus
jackfruit

Jackfruits

Jackfruit leaves and flower

Jackfruit seeds

DESCRIPTION Jackfruit or jak is a fast-growing tree of about 10 m in height, with the overall appearance of a wild fig tree. The relatively small, glossy leaves have entire margins (not lobed or toothed). The massive fruits are often borne directly on the trunk. They are oblong in shape, nearly 1 m long (up to 50 kg each), green in colour and have a distinctive surface texture due to regularly spaced, small, soft protuberances. As is typical for the fig family, the compound fruit is formed from an entire flower cluster that becomes fleshy – it contains several hundred individual fruits, each with a large seed surrounded by orange-yellow flesh.

ORIGIN & HISTORY Believed to be indigenous to southern India but cultivated in Southeast Asia since ancient times. From here it spread to all tropical regions of the world.

PARTS USED Fruits.

CULTIVATION & HARVESTING Jackfruit is easily grown from seeds and thrives in warm, tropical areas.

USES & PROPERTIES Immature fruits contain latex but are sliced and cooked as a vegetable. The edible parts of the ripe fruit are the numerous fleshy segments surrounding the seeds – they have a sweet taste reminiscent of pineapple and melon. Small pieces (or loose segments) of the enormous fruit are sold on street markets and eaten fresh or may be pulped and mixed with other fruits. The raw seeds are said to be poisonous but are cooked and eaten like chestnuts. Jackfruit is particularly popular in Java, where a creamy, curry-like dish, known as *gudeg* or *ti-jaque*, is prepared from the cooked fruit.

NUTRITIONAL VALUE Jackfruit is relatively low in carbohydrates (15%) and energy value (70 kcal per 100 g). It is a good source of potassium, iron and nicotinamide.

NOTES The yellow timber is popular for woodcarvings and furniture and was formerly used to dye the robes of Buddhist monks.

Artocarpus heterophyllus Lam. (= *A. integrifolius* auct. non L.f.)   family: Moraceae

bo luo mi (Chinese); *jacquier* (French); *Jackfruchtbaum* (German); *nangka* (Indonesian); *paramitsu* (Japanese); *pane d'Albero* (Italian); *jaca* (Portuguese); *jaca, yaca* (Spanish)

Aspalathus linearis
rooibos tea plant

Rooibos tea leaves and flowers

Rooibos tea plant

Rooibos tea

DESCRIPTION This is a shrub of up to 2 m in height, with bright green, needle-shaped leaves which turn a rich reddish-brown colour when processed. The small, yellow, typically pea-shaped flowers are produced in spring and early summer, followed by single-seeded pods.

ORIGIN & HISTORY Found only in the Western Cape Province of South Africa (commercial cultivation is still centred here). Marketing started in 1904, through the efforts of Benjamin Ginsberg, a Russian immigrant and tea merchant. He bought the tea from the local Khoi people, who traditionally harvested the wild plants and produced tea by a process of cutting (the twigs and leaves) with axes, bruising with wooden hammers, "fermenting" in heaps and finally drying.

PARTS USED Leaves and twigs.

CULTIVATION & HARVESTING *Aspalathus linearis* is grown from seeds (which have to be scarified) and the seedlings are transplanted to deep, acid, sandy soils. The production area has cold wet winters and hot dry summers, with a relatively low rainfall of 300–350 mm per annum. Harvesting is still mostly done by hand (with sickles), but processing has been mechanised. Nowadays, green tea and spray-dried powder (extract) are also produced on a commercial scale.

USES & PROPERTIES Rooibos is popular as a health beverage, prepared and used in the same way as black tea (but unlike the latter, the taste improves after prolonged simmering). The tea contains no harmful stimulants and is totally devoid of caffeine. It has gained popularity as an excellent ice tea (nowadays commonly sold in cans). The product is also used as an ingredient in cosmetics, in slimming products and as a flavouring agent and natural colourant in foods and beverages.

NUTRITIONAL VALUE The tea is a good source of minerals (especially fluoride). The health properties are ascribed to the low tannin content and the antioxidant of unique flavonoid C-glycosides (mainly aspalathin).

Aspalathus linearis (Burm.f.) Dahlg.   family: Fabaceae

rooibos (Afrikaans); *aspalathus* (French); *Rotbusch*, *Rooibos* (German); *aspalathus* (Italian)

Asparagus officinalis

asparagus

Asparagus flowers and fruits

Asparagus (white)

Asparagus plants

Asparagus (green)

DESCRIPTION A perennial herb with an underground rhizome ("crown") from which long slender, bright green, leafless stems emerge in spring and summer. The flowers are small, white to pale yellow in colour and develop into small rounded berries, green at first but turning bright red when they mature. The edible part is the young stem ("spear") that is cut before it emerges (white asparagus) or usually blanched by covering with soil and harvested when about 20–30 cm long. Three varieties are commonly used, namely white, purple and green (the last-mentioned is considered to have the best flavour). Several species of wild asparagus are eaten (or used as medicine) in rural parts of Africa and China.

ORIGIN & HISTORY Indigenous to North Africa, central and southern Europe, and western and central Asia. It was cultivated by the ancient Egyptians, Greeks and Romans but is said to have regained its popularity only in the sixteenth century as a new culinary trend set by Louis XIV of France. Asparagus in season is a speciality dish in the regions of Argenteuil (France), Malines (Belgium) and Heidelberg (Germany).

PARTS USED Young stems (white and blanched, or partly green and not blanched).

CULTIVATION & HARVESTING Plants are grown as a perennial crop in all temperate regions of the world. The harvesting season is relatively short, as the spears are harvested only in late spring up to early summer.

USES & PROPERTIES Asparagus is a very popular vegetable. It is always cooked or steamed and served hot or cold with melted butter or white sauces (or as ingredient of a salad, omelette, savoury tart, stir-fry or soup; it is also used as garnish).

NUTRITIONAL VALUE The energy yield is 18 kcal per 100 g. A good source of minerals and vitamins A, C and E.

NOTES The dried rhizome is a traditional diuretic medicine.

Asparagus officinalis L.   family: Asparagaceae

long xu cài, *lu san* (Chinese); *asperge* (French); *Spargel* (German); *asparago* (Italian); *asuparagasu* (Japanese); *espargo* (Portuguese); *espárrago* (Spanish)

Atriplex hortensis

orache

Orache (green form)

Orache (purple form)

DESCRIPTION Orache is an erect annual herb of up to 2 m in height with bright green, red or yellow foliage. The leaves are relatively large, triangular in shape and have toothed margins. Inconspicuous male and female flowers are borne on the same plant. Various other species of *Atriplex* have been used as wild sources of green leaves for spinach, including the saltbush (*A. canescens*) from North America and sea purslane or seabeach sandwort (*A. halimus* and *A. hastata*) from the Mediterranean region.

ORIGIN & HISTORY Orache was once an important and popular spinach plant in the southeastern parts of Europe and western Asia. Today it is hardly ever used in cooking, even though plants are sometimes cultivated in gardens or found as weeds. *Atriplex* species (commonly known as "saltbushes") are now best known for their value as forage plants for sheep and goats. Species such as *A. nummularia* (old man's saltbush) are utilised as cultivated pastures in dry regions.

PARTS USED Fresh leaves.

CULTIVATION & HARVESTING Orache is easily grown from seed and is commonly seen as a garden ornamental. The fresh leaves are harvested in summer.

USES & PROPERTIES The green or red fleshy leaves are used as a culinary herb or as an ingredient of vegetable soups. They may be served as a vegetable and are cooked like spinach (leaves of the red form turn green after cooking). Cooked leaves make an attractive garnish and are said to be useful for counteracting the bitter taste of sorrel leaves.

NUTRITIONAL VALUE Fresh leaves are a good source of minerals and vitamins (especially vitamin C and folic acid).

NOTES *Atriplex* species are closely related to other "spinach plants" such as *Tetragonia expansa* (New Zealand spinach) and *Chenopodium album* or *C. oahuense* (commonly referred to as "goosefoot").

Atriplex hortensis L.

family: Chenopodiaceae

arroche bonne-dame (French); *Gartenmelde* (German); *armuelle* (Spanish)

Avena sativa

oats

Oats plants

Oats flowers

Oats grains

DESCRIPTION An annual grass of up to 1 m in height with characteristic pendulous spikelets, each comprising two overlapping husks (bracts or glumes) that are dispersed with the grain (a dry, one-seeded fruit). In recently developed naked oats (free threshing oats) the grain is easily removed from the husk.

ORIGIN & HISTORY Oats originated as a weed of other grains (mainly barley and wheat) and represents a hybrid between several wild species, including the European *A. byzantina* and the Ethiopean *A. abyssinica*. Oats appears relatively late in the archaeological record (1000 BC) in central Europe. It has long been used as a staple food for humans (in the gruels of the Gauls, Romans and Teutons) and later also in Scandinavia and Scotland. The straw is an important source of roughage for farm animals. In recent years, the world production of about 40 million tons has declined steadily.

PARTS USED The grain (one-seeded fruit, caryopsis).

CULTIVATION & HARVESTING Oats is sown as an annual crop and is adapted to a wider range of climatic conditions than barley and wheat. It is most commonly grown in Mediterranean climates and in Russia.

USES & PROPERTIES Oats has the highest protein content of all cereals and is important in the human diet as porridge, breakfast foods, baby foods, oatmeal and confectionery (biscuits and cookies). The husks are removed in the milling process, but new cultivars of naked oats have the added advantage of a superior nutritive value while giving the same yield as ordinary oats minus the husks.

NUTRITIONAL VALUE A high quality food. It is rich in proteins (up to 16%), carbohydrates (55%), minerals and vitamins, and in energy (330 kcal per 100 g). Oats is often used as a dietary aid for children and invalids and is claimed to have cholesterol-lowering activity.

Avena sativa L.   family: Poaceae

avoine (French); *Hafer* (German); *avena* (Italian); *avena* (Spanish)

Averrhoa bilimbi

bilimbi

Bilimbi tree

Bilimbi fruits

DESCRIPTION Bilimbi is a small tree, usually about 4 m in height, with attractive pink flowers and small, pale green, smooth fruit. These are borne directly on the older stems in clusters and are often said to look like miniature cucumbers. The bilimbi (also known as camias, *belimbing asam*, *belimbing wuluh*, *bilimbing* or cucumber tree) is closely related to the starfruit, carambola or *belimbing manis* (see *Averrhoa carambola*) but the fruits are smaller and only slightly ribbed.

ORIGIN & HISTORY The plant is indigenous to Southeast Asia and is found throughout Thailand, Malaysia and Indonesia.

PARTS USED Ripe fruits.

CULTIVATION & HARVESTING The tree is rarely cultivated on a commercial scale but is commonly seen in kitchen gardens. It requires a tropical climate and is less drought-tolerant than the starfruit. There is only one cultivated form, which can be propagated from seeds or cuttings. Fruits are produced sporadically throughout the year and are sold fresh on local markets.

USES & PROPERTIES The fruits are extremely sour and are rarely eaten raw. Their main use is as an ingredient of pickles, sambals, chutneys and curries (it is especially popular for fish curries), to which they add a tangy taste. Slices of the fruit may be served with salads or chilli as a side dish. Ripe fruits are suitable for making jam and the juice can be used as a refreshing drink (provided that generous amounts of sugar are added).

NUTRITIONAL VALUE Ripe, fresh fruits are low in calories but rich in malic acid, minerals (especially iron) and vitamin C (about 30 mg per 100 g).

NOTES The fruit is said to have medicinal value in the treatment of fevers and skin ailments. The juice is traditionally used to remove rust and stains from knife blades, weapons, clothing and hands (the stain-removing properties are ascribed to the high levels of potassium oxalate).

Averrhoa bilimbi L.

family: Oxalidaceae

huang gua shu (Chinese); *bilimbi* (French); *Bilimbi* (German); *belimbing wuluh* (Indonesian); *birinbi* (Japanese); *belimbing asam* (Malay); *camia* (Spanish); *ta ling pling* (Thai)

Averrhoa carambola

starfruit • carambola

Starfruit flowers

Starfruit leaves and fruits

Starfruits

DESCRIPTION A small to medium-sized tree that may reach a height of 10 m at maturity. It has compound leaves, small pink flowers and attractive glossy, strongly ribbed fruits that turn orange when they ripen. Starfruit is closely related to the bilimbi but the fruits are quite different. The Malay name *belimbing asam* for the bilimbi (see *Averrhoa bilimbi*) refers to the sour taste (*asam* is the name for the equally sour tamarind fruit), while the much sweeter starfruit is known in Malay as *belimbing manis* (*manis* means "sweet").

ORIGIN & HISTORY Starfruit is indigenous to Southeast Asia but is now cultivated in all tropical regions of the world.

PARTS USED Ripe fruit.

CULTIVATION & HARVESTING Commercial cultivation occurs in many tropical countries (including Brazil, the West Indies, USA, and Malaysia) and fruits are exported to western countries. Trees are grown from seeds but the sweet cultivar (known as "honey starfruit") is sometimes grafted onto the rootstock of the acid type. The fruits are harvested when fully ripe (when the edges of the ribs start to turn brown). They are easily bruised and must be carefully handled to retain the attractive, glossy appearance.

USES & PROPERTIES Fruits of the sweet type have become popular for eating fresh or for adding a beautiful orange colour and a juicy, tart flavour to both green salads and fruit salads. The fruits are eaten skin and all – simply remove the edges of the ribs (they are somewhat fibrous and not so tasty) and cut into lovely star-shaped slices. For a tasty dessert, add cream and sugar. Fruits may also be variously processed and used in fruit tarts, jams, preserves and fruit drinks.

NUTRITIONAL VALUE The energy yield is low (24 kcal per 100 g) and the fruit is rich in potassium, iron, carotenoids, nicotinamide and vitamin C (35 mg per 100 g).

Averrhoa carambola L.   family: Oxalidaceae

yang tao (Chinese); *carambolier vrai* (French); *Karambolabaum, Sternfrucht* (German); *belimbing manis* (Indonesian); *carambola* (Italian); *gorenshi* (Japanese); *caramboleiro* (Portuguese); *carambola* (Spanish)

Bactris gasipaes

pejibaye • peach palm

Pejibaye stem with spines

Pejibaye leaves

Palm hearts

DESCRIPTION The pejibaye is a branched palm with relatively thin stems and long pinnate leaves. A distinct feature is the numerous long, black, brittle spines that cover the stems, leaf bases and leaf midribs. Male and female flowers are borne together and the fruit clusters weigh up to 25 kg. The fruits (10–70 g each) are orange and fibrous outside and starchy and oily inside. Other important sources of palm hearts include the açai (*Euterpe edulis*) and the cabbage palm (*E. oleracea*), both of which are wild-harvested in tropical America.

ORIGIN & HISTORY This is the only New World palm that was ever domesticated. It occurs in the Amazonian region, where cooked fruits are a traditional staple diet (archaeological remains from Costa Rica date back 4 000 years). There is now a renewed interest in the pejibaye as a plantation or agroforestry crop.

PARTS USED Stem tips (apical meristems) known as heart of palm (*coeurs de palmier; Palmherzens*);

to a much lesser extent the fruits.

CULTIVATION & HARVESTING Large plantations have been established for the production of heart of palm, mainly in Costa Rica, Colombia and Brazil. Substantial quantities are exported to Europe and the USA each year. Yields are less than one ton per hectare (heart of palm) and up to 10 tons (fruit).

USES & PROPERTIES Heart of palm is a delicacy that may be thinly sliced and eaten raw, or may be cooked and used in much the same way as artichoke (with a similar taste). Palm hearts are available fresh or canned. Of less commercial importance are the fruits (a source of flour for baking and vegetable oil).

NUTRITIONAL VALUE Palm hearts are low in sugars (1%) and other nutrients. The fruit has commercial potential: the oil is rich in unsaturated fatty acids (up to 78%) and the mesocarp contains high quality protein (about 7%).

Bactris gasipaes Kunth

family: Arecaceae (Palmae)

parepon (French); *Pfirsichpalme* (German); *pejibaye* (Spanish)

Basella alba

Malabar spinach • Ceylon spinach

Malabar spinach (white form)

Malabar spinach (red form)

Madeira vine

DESCRIPTION This is a climbing perennial herb with hairless, somewhat succulent, glossy leaves, inconspicuous flowers and small fruits enclosed by fleshy persistent petals. Two forms are known – the stems and leaf stalks are red in the typical form or green to whitish in another (sometimes referred to as *B. rubra* or *B. rubra* var. *alba*). Other common names for the plant are Indian spinach, red vine spinach and vine spinach. It is sometimes confused with the Madeira vine or mignonette vine (*Anredera cordifolia*) that is also grown to some extent for its edible leaves and rhizomes. The Madeira vine reproduces by aerial tubers that are formed in the leaf axils and later drop down to the ground to form new plants. Another member of the family is the ulluco (*Ullucus tuberosus*), an important Inca food crop, widely grown in the Andes for its edible tubers.

ORIGIN & HISTORY *Basella alba* is a pantropical species that occurs naturally in all tropical parts of the Old World, especially India and Southeast Asia. It is thought not to be indigenous to tropical America. The plant is grown commercially as a leaf vegetable in various parts of the world, including India, Sri Lanka, Malaysia, China, Mexico and the USA.

PARTS USED Fresh leaves.

CULTIVATION & HARVESTING The plant is easily propagated from seeds, cuttings or the fleshy rhizomes and thrives in warm climates, both in tropical and temperate regions.

USES & PROPERTIES Succulent young leaves are boiled as a pot-herb, in much the same way as spinach. They have a distinctive taste and are also included in salads and stir-fries.

NUTRITIONAL VALUE Malabar spinach is often regarded as a functional food because it is rich in minerals (calcium, iron) and vitamins A and C. It also has medicinal properties as a very mild laxative.

Basella alba L. (= *B. rubra* L.)   family: Basellaceae

chán cài (Chinese); *baselle blanche, epinard de Malabar* (French); *Malabarspinat* (German); *remayong, gondola* (Malay); *basella bianca* (Italian); *bacela* (Portuguese); *espinaca de Malabar* (Spanish)

Benincasa hispida
wax gourd

Wax gourd leaves and flower

Wax gourd fruits

Hairy melon fruits

DESCRIPTION A robust annual creeper with long trailing stems bearing shallowly lobed leaves. The yellow flowers resemble those of pumpkins but the lobes are free almost to their bases. Distinctly different fruit types (cultivar groups) are known. The typical wax gourd is very large (more than 2 kg), round or oblong, with a white, waxy surface. The hairy melon or fuzzy melon (known as *mao gua* in Chinese and botanically as *B. hispida* var. *chiehqua*) has much smaller, cucumber-like fruits that are bright green but distinctly hairy, with practically no wax.

ORIGIN & HISTORY Wax gourds and hairy gourds are not known to occur in nature and are ancient cultigens. Circumstantial evidence suggests that they originated in Southeast Asia, possibly Thailand and Java. They were introduced as a crop into China at least 1 500 years ago.

PARTS USED The young or mature fruit (sometimes also the leaves and flowers).

CULTIVATION & HARVESTING The plants are grown all year round in light, well-drained soil. Fruits mature 90 to 110 days after sowing but are often harvested green at various intervals.

USES & PROPERTIES The flesh of the wax gourd is commonly cooked as a vegetable. Various other uses have been recorded, depending on the cultivar and regional customs (e.g. as an ingredient of stews, soups and curries). In China, the wax gourd (sometimes called winter gourd because of its excellent keeping properties) is hollowed out and carved to produce ornamental soup bowls for special occasions. Flowers and leaves can be cooked as a vegetable and may be included in stews and curries. The hairy gourd is mostly eaten raw when young (like a cucumber).

NUTRITIONAL VALUE Wax gourd is rich in minerals (calcium, potassium and silicon) but relatively low in vitamins when compared to pumpkins.

NOTES The fruits have medicinal properties and the surface wax has been used to make candles.

Benincasa hispida (Thunb.) Cogn. (= *B. cerifera* Savi)   family: Cucurbitaceae

dong gua (Chinese); *courge à la cire, courge cireuse* (French); *Wachskürbis* (German); *zucca della cera* (Italian); *tougan* (Japanese); *abóbora d'água* (Portuguese); *calabaza blanca* (Spanish)

Bertholletia excelsa

Brazil nut

Sapucaia nut flowers

Brazil nut flowers

Brazil nuts

DESCRIPTION A large forest tree that reaches 40 m at maturity. It bears simple leaves and attractive white, waxy flowers with a characteristic hood (formed by the stamens) in the centre of the flower. The fruit is an enormous woody capsule (up to 2.5 kg) that contains between 10 and 25 seeds and takes 15 months to mature. Brazil nut and the related sapucaia nut (*Lecythis zabucajo*) have similar flowers and fruits, which are called "monkey-pots" (formerly used as traps: when monkeys grab food placed inside the fruit they are unable to withdraw their extended fists). Sapucaia nuts (also called paradise nuts) are a delicacy but some other species (*L. minor* and *L. ollaria*) have poisonous seeds.

ORIGIN & HISTORY Trees occur naturally in the Amazon jungles of Brazil, Bolivia, Colombia, Guiana, Peru and Venezuela. The wild-harvested nuts are an important source of food and income for local people.

PARTS USED Ripe nuts.

CULTIVATION & HARVESTING The annual production of around 40 000 tons is derived almost entirely from stands of wild trees known as "castanhais" in Brazil or "manchales" in Peru. Harvesting is done by local gatherers, who gather the woody fruits as they fall and then extract the nuts with axes. Some plantations have been established in Brazil, Malaysia and Ghana, using grafted trees. In plantations, commercial yields of 5 kg per tree after 12 years and 10 kg after 18 years are expected.

USES & PROPERTIES Brazil nuts are highly sought after, especially in Europe and the USA. The nuts are eaten raw, roasted or salted, are often included in chocolates, confectionery and ice cream and are used in cooking in the same way as coconut.

NUTRITIONAL VALUE The energy yield is 670 kcal per 100 g. The nuts are rich in minerals (potassium, phosphorus) and contain about 16% protein and 70% oil (mainly linoleic and oleic acid).

Bertholletia excelsa Bonpl.   family: Lecythidaceae

noix du brésil, noyer de pará (French); *Brasilnussbaum, Paranussbaum* (German); *nuez de pará* (Spanish)

Beta vulgaris var. *cicla*

leaf beet • spinach beet • Swiss chard

Swiss chard plants

Swiss chard flowers and fruits

DESCRIPTION This popular vegetable (often misnamed spinach) is an annual or biennial herb with large, fleshy, dark green leaves and broad leaf stalks that are usually white but sometimes red or orange in ornamental forms. The inconspicuous greenish flowers are borne in slender clusters and turn into small, dry, spiny fruits. Swiss chard is the same species as the garden beetroot and sugar beet (these three main beet types are here treated as varieties). Several alternative classification systems are available, none of which can be considered "correct" from a scientific point of view. The same problem arises in kales and cabbages (genus *Brassica*) where there is a bewildering diversity of man-made forms.

ORIGIN & HISTORY Both leaf beets and root beets were developed (possibly by the Romans) from the wild sea-beet, which occurs in coastal regions of Europe and western Asia.

PARTS USED Leaves (leaf beet) and leaf stalks (chard).

CULTIVATION & HARVESTING Seeds are sown from early spring to late summer and leaves can be harvested almost throughout the year in most regions. The largest (lower) leaves are picked at regular intervals, taking care not to remove too many leaves as this may reduce the productivity of the plants.

USES & PROPERTIES The leaves are used in salads or more often prepared and eaten like spinach, usually with a white sauce (cream, cheese, eggs, raisins, pine nuts or other ingredients are often added). They are also a popular ingredient of soups, pastries and savoury tarts. Swiss chard tart (*tourte aux feuilles de bette*), served as dessert, is a speciality of Nice in France. The thick but tender leaf stalks have similar uses to asparagus.

NUTRITIONAL VALUE Cooked leaves yield 20 kcal per 100 g and are very nutritious. They supply good quantities of minerals (calcium, iron, phosphorus, potassium and especially magnesium) and vitamins (especially vitamin A).

Beta vulgaris L. var. *cicla* L.

family: Chenopodiaceae

hou pi cai (Chinese); *bette, bette à couper* (French); *Mangold, Schnittmangold* (German); *bietola* (Italian); *acelga* (Portuguese, Spanish)

Beta vulgaris var. *esculenta*

beetroot

Beetroot plants

Beetroot flowers

Beetroots

DESCRIPTION An annual or biennial herb with succulent, reddish leaves and a fleshy, bright red to dark purple, swollen root. Inconspicuous flowers develop into small, rounded fruits, each containing more than one seed. Beetroot is nowadays grouped with fodder beet and sugar beet in an informal group, the Conditiva group. The old classification system of recognising red beetroot as a distinct entity (var. *esculenta*, meaning edible) is followed here (but var. *esculenta* more correctly falls within the var. *vulgaris*). The numerous cultivars differ in the shape and colour of the root.

ORIGIN & HISTORY Beetroot (and leaf beet or Swiss chard) were developed from wild sea-beet (var. *maritima*) that occurs along the coastlines of southern Europe and western Asia, and is thought to date back to the time of the Assyrians.

PARTS USED The fleshy, swollen root or sometimes the leaves.

CULTIVATION & HARVESTING Beetroot is grown from seeds and harvested when small (for pickles) or fully mature. It may be stored for several months before use.

USES & PROPERTIES The roots are cooked as a vegetable but more often sliced or coarsely grated, soaked in vinegar and eaten as a cold salad. The leaves can be prepared like spinach or added to soup. Beetroot is a feature of Flemish and Slav cooking and is an essential ingredient of bortsch (or borsch), a popular soup originating from Poland and Russia. Bortsch is based on stewed meat (often removed and eaten separately), flour and sour cream, often also potatoes, white cabbage, mushrooms and kidney beans, with beetroot added to give the characteristic bright red colour.

NUTRITIONAL VALUE Cooked beetroot has about 8% sugar and a relatively high energy value (130 kcal per 100 g). It is a rich source of magnesium and manganese and contains some vitamin C.

NOTES The red colour is due to betalains (nitrogen-containing pigments) that are valuable as a natural food colourant.

Beta vulgaris L. var. *esculenta* L.   family: Chenopodiaceae

tian cai (Chinese); *betterave* (French); *Rote Bete, Rote Rübe* (German); *barbabietola rossa* (Italian); *biitsu* (Japanese); *beterraba* (Portuguese); *remolacha* (Spanish)

Beta vulgaris var. *vulgaris*

sugar beet

Sugar beet plantation

Sugar beet plant

Sugar beet root

DESCRIPTION This commercially important beet variety is grown as a biennial crop. It closely resembles beetroot but lacks the typical red pigmentation. Sugar beet and fodder beet are close relatives, differing mainly in the sugar content of the fleshy roots. Fodder beet (var. *rapacea*, called *Rünkelrübe* or *Futterrübe* in German) is grown as cattle fodder.

ORIGIN & HISTORY Sugar beet apparently originated in eighteenth century Europe, at a time when crystalline sugar was a luxury item that had to be imported from warm regions with sugar cane. Large-rooted, garden beets with a high sugar content were selected from fodder beet, resulting in a white-rooted sugar beet ("Weisse Schlesische Rübe") with a sugar concentration of around 6%. Sugar production started in Silesia (today part of Poland) and the first sugar factory was built in 1802. Selection and breeding continues to this day, and the sugar content in modern cultivars now exceeds 18%. Half the current world production of sucrose sugar comes from the former Soviet Union (the biggest producer), Germany, and North America.

PARTS USED The swollen taproot (beetroot).

CULTIVATION & HARVESTING Sugar beet is a crop of temperate regions and all stages of production are highly mechanised. This includes direct sowing (drilling) of modern cultivars with single-seeded (monospermic) fruits to avoid the costly process of thinning. Roots are harvested after two years and the tops are cut off for use as livestock feed. Sugar is extracted in factories using a process similar to that of sugar cane.

USES & PROPERTIES Crystalline sucrose (sugar) has a multitude of domestic and industrial uses as a sweetener and energy source (see also *Saccharum*).

NUTRITIONAL VALUE Beet sugar has an energy value of 399 kcal per 100 g (the same as sucrose).

Beta vulgaris L. var. *vulgaris*

family: Chenopodiaceae

tang tian cai (Chinese); *betterave sucrière* (French); *Zuckerrübe* (German); *barbabietola da zucchero* (Italian); *satou daikon* (Japanese); *betarraga azucarera* (Spanish)

Bixa orellana

annatto tree • lipstick tree

Annatto flowers

Annatto flower and fruits

Annatto capsules and seeds

DESCRIPTION This is a distinctive shrub or small tree with large, heart-shaped leaves and attractive pink flowers borne in clusters on the branch tips. The fruits are pointed spiny capsules, each containing numerous bright red seeds.

ORIGIN & HISTORY Indigenous to tropical America. It is the original source of body paint of the American Indians and has numerous vernacular names, including *achiote*, *bija*, *bijol* and *roucou*. It is still popular in the West Indies, East Indies and also Southeast Asia (especially the Philippines), where the plant was introduced by the Spanish during the seventeenth century.

PARTS USED The bright red seeds.

CULTIVATION & HARVESTING Annatto trees are cultivated commercially in all tropical regions of the world but especially in Africa and Asia. The fruits turn brown when they ripen and are harvested to extract the seeds.

USES & PROPERTIES The seeds contain a bright orange-red natural dye (pigment) known as annatto or *roucou* that is used mainly to colour cheese, butter, oils and smoked fish. Salad oils often become very pale due to deodorisation processes and annatto extracts can be added to improve the colour. Since synthetic food colourings were banned, consumption of annatto has increased. The whole or ground seeds have little flavour but are nevertheless an important spice in Jamaica (e.g. akee-fish-and-rice), in the Philippines (whole seeds are fried in oil and the resulting bright red oil is then used to prepare paella and other rice dishes) and in Mexico (as an ingredient of chilli powders).

NUTRITIONAL VALUE Annatto adds little or no nutrients but in food products it is a valuable natural alternative to tartrazine (an artificial yellow colouring).

NOTES The orange-red pigment is a carotenoid called bixin, which occurs in the seed coat. Annatto extracts are used in soaps and cosmetics. As a textile dye it has been replaced with synthetic dyes.

Bixa orellana L.   family: Bixaceae

yan zhi shu (Chinese); *annatto* (French); *Annattostrauch, Orleanstrauch* (German); *kesumba* (Indonesian); *annatto* (Italian); *jarak belanda, kesumba* (Malay); *achiote, achiotillo* (Spanish); *kam tai* (Thai)

Blighia sapida

akee

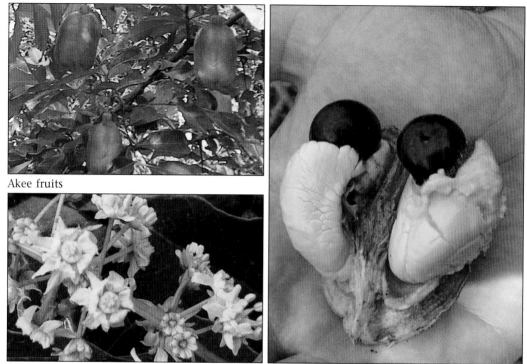

Akee fruits

Akee flowers

Akee seeds with arils

DESCRIPTION An attractive tree (up to 12 m) bearing compound leaves (each with three to five pairs of oblong leaflets) and small white flowers in sparse clusters. The fruit is a yellow to bright red, leathery, three-lobed capsule that splits open at maturity to reveal three shiny black seeds surrounded by cream-coloured, fleshy arils.

ORIGIN & HISTORY Indigenous to West Africa. It reached the West Indies via the slave trade, and became an important food plant. Today it is the national fruit of Jamaica and is widely cultivated in Jamaica and other parts of Central America.

PARTS USED The ripe (mature) seed aril.

CULTIVATION & HARVESTING Trees are grown from seeds or cuttings and thrive in subtropical and tropical climates. Fruits must be allowed to fully ripen and open spontaneously before they are harvested. It is important to note that the unripe or over-ripe aril, the raphe connecting the seed to the aril, the seed itself and the rest of the fruit are all extremely poisonous.

USES & PROPERTIES The fleshy arils are parboiled in salted water and then fried in oil or butter. They resemble scrambled eggs and are widely known as "vegetable brains". In Jamaica, they are considered a delicacy and are used to prepare the famous national dish "akee and saltfish", which is a mixture of cooked akee arils and salted codfish.

NUTRITIONAL VALUE The energy yield is 218 kcal per 100 g. Akee is also a good source of fat (20%), protein (5%), vitamin A (560 µg total carotenoids), vitamin B1 and B2 (130 µg each) and vitamin C (25 mg).

NOTES The poisonous substances are unusual amino acids (hypoglycins, mainly hypoglycin A and hypoglycin B). The symptoms of poisoning include vomiting, convulsions, severe hypoglycaemia, coma and death. Akee was banned in the USA but canned akee is widely available in West Indian shops.

Blighia sapida K.König.   family: Sapindaceae

akée d'Afrique, arbre fricassé (French); *Akipflaume* (German); *castanheiro de Africa* (Portuguese); *arbol de seso, huevo vegetal, seso vegetal* (Spanish)

Boesenbergia rotunda

Chinese keys

Chinese keys flower

Chinese keys plants

Chinese keys roots

DESCRIPTION This member of the ginger family is a perennial herb with large leaves growing from a distinctive, short rhizome that also bears finger-like, fleshy, orange-brown roots. The leaves are elliptic in shape, bright green to bluish green in colour and have prominent veins arising from the midribs. Attractive pink, orchid-like flowers are borne in pairs at the tips of the short stems. They have pale pink outer lobes and a prominent, decorative purplish lip.

ORIGIN & HISTORY Chinese keys are thought to be indigenous to Java and Sumatra but they are now widely cultivated all over Southeast Asia, from India and Sri Lanka to Thailand, Vietnam, Malaysia, Indonesia and Indo-China. It has become an important spice and food plant in Thailand and Vietnam but elsewhere (including central Asian countries, Russia and even Hungary) it is mainly used as traditional medicine and only rarely as a spice. The Vietnamese names include *bong nga truat, cu ngai* and *ngai num kho*.

PARTS USED Rhizomes and roots.

CULTIVATION & HARVESTING Plants grow easily in tropical climates and are propagated by division of the short branching rhizomes. Harvesting can be done at any time of the year and the product is mostly sold as a fresh spice, alongside ginger and galangal.

USES & PROPERTIES The rhizomes and roots are bright yellow inside and have an aromatic, spicy flavour. Small amounts are added to curries, mixed vegetable soups and other dishes. It is nowadays commonly used as an ingredient of instant soups produced in China. In Thailand, fresh rhizomes and roots are eaten raw in salads, or they are added to fish curries, soups and pickles.

NUTRITIONAL VALUE Small quantities are used, mainly as a spice.

NOTES The fresh or dried rhizomes and roots are widely used as aromatic digestive medicine to treat flatulence, colic, indigestion, diarrhoea and dysentery.

Boesenbergia rotunda (L.) Mansf. [= *B. pandurata* (Roxb.) Schltr.]   family: Zingiberaceae

ao chun jiang, suo shi (Chinese); *Tropenkrokus, Fingerwurz, Chinesischer Ingwer* (German); *temu kunchi* (Malay); *kunci* (Indonesian); *krachai* (Thai)

Borago officinalis

borage

Borage flowers

Borage plant

Borage seeds

DESCRIPTION Borage is a robust annual herb of up to 0.5 m in height with large leaves and clusters of drooping, blue (rarely white), star-shaped flowers. All parts are covered with coarse, bristly hairs. Small, black seeds are produced in large numbers.

ORIGIN & HISTORY The plant is thought to be of Middle Eastern origin but occurs naturally in southern Europe and the Mediterranean region. It has been cultivated since ancient times as a pot-herb and medicinal plant.

PARTS USED Leaves, flowers and seeds (as a source of seed oil).

CULTIVATION & HARVESTING Plants are easily grown from seeds and are commonly found as a culinary herb in kitchen gardens. Large-scale cultivation is mainly for the production of seed oil.

USES & PROPERTIES Young leaves were once popular as a pot-herb and are still used to some extent (mainly in France, Italy and Germany) in salads, stews and soups. They have a mild, cucumber-like taste. In China, leaves are stuffed like vine leaves. Leaves and flowers are traditionally added to cold drinks (e.g. in the English gin drink known as Pimm's No 1). The flowers are widely used as garnish and are frequently crystallised (candied) to decorate fruit salads, puddings and pastries. The seed oil, known as "starflower oil", has become a popular dietary supplement.

NUTRITIONAL VALUE The seed oil has very high levels (21%) of unsaturated gamma-linolenic acid (GLA, an essential fatty acid) – higher than in evening primrose oil. Internal use of borage leaves and flowers over long periods may not be safe, as the plant is known to contain trace amounts of pyrrolizidine alkaloids.

NOTES The herb is used medicinally as a traditional tonic, diuretic, diaphoretic, expectorant and mild sedative. Borage seed oil appears to be free of alkaloids and is a modern treatment for eczema and stress-related ailments due to the high GLA content.

Borago officinalis L.

family: Boraginaceae

bourrache (French); *Boretsch* (German); *boragine* (Italian); *borraja* (Spanish)

Borassus flabellifer

palmyra palm

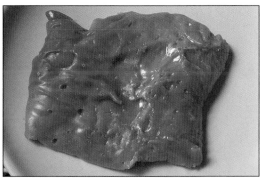
Soft palm sugar (*ghor*)

Palmyra palm

Palm sugar

DESCRIPTION A tall palm with characteristic fan-shaped leaves. Male and female flowers are borne on separate trees. The fruit resembles a small coconut but has three segments, each containing a sap-filled edible nut. African *Hyphaene* species are similar but have single-seeded, inedible nuts ("vegetable ivory").

ORIGIN & HISTORY Indigenous to India and Myanmar. It has a long history of human use and is now an important multi-purpose crop. In addition to its many food uses, the leaf bases yield valuable fibres (known as bassine or Palmyra fibre) and the leaf blades are used as writing paper, thatching and weaving.

PARTS USED The sap and fruits (nuts).

CULTIVATION & HARVESTING The trees are well adapted to dry tropical conditions and do not flourish in wet regions. Propagation is from seeds, and the plants take about 15 years to reach maturity. The inflorescences are cut off and the sugary sap is collected for the production of palm sugar or palm wine. A single palm tree may yield more than 100 000 litres of palm wine during its 40-year lifespan.

USES & PROPERTIES Palm sugar or *jaggery* is a traditional sweetener and energy source in rural areas of India and Myanmar but has become popular in western countries for use in sweets, pastries and confectionery. The sap is also used to make palm wine ("toddy"), which may be turned into vinegar or distilled to produce a strong alcoholic beverage ("arrack"). The liquid inside the nuts resembles coconut milk and is similarly used as a drink. Roasted nuts may be eaten or the fleshy embryos of germinated seeds may be eaten as a vegetable or dried and milled to produce a type of flour known as *odiyal* flour.

NUTRITIONAL VALUE Palm sugar has an energy value of nearly 400 kcal per 100 g (the same as sucrose).

Borassus flabellifer L.   family: Arecaceae (Palmae)

shan ye shu tou zong (Chinese); *borassus, borasse* (French); *Borassuspalme, Palmyrapalme*, (German); *taad* (Hindi); *palma de ferro* (Italian); *parumira yashi* (Japanese); *borassus, palmyra* (Spanish)

Brassica juncea var. *juncea*

brown mustard • Indian mustard • Dijon mustard

Brown mustard plant

Brown mustard (purple form)

Brown mustard seeds

DESCRIPTION This is a perennial herb with lobed leaves, yellow flowers and oblong, beaked, indehiscent (non-shattering) fruit capsules containing several brown or yellowish, spherical seeds. The terms "black", "white" or "brown" are often used interchangeably but mostly refer to *B. nigra*, *Sinapis alba* and *B. juncea*, respectively. In India, the seeds are widely known as *rai*, while Dijon mustard is named after the main production area of mustard paste in France.

ORIGIN & HISTORY Brown mustard originated in the Himalayan region of central Asia, as a hybrid between *B. nigra* and *B. campestris*. From here it spread to India, China and the Caucasus. In China, numerous forms developed, including leaf mustards (see *B. juncea* var. *rugosa*) and a yellow-seeded form. Brown mustard has rapidly replaced black mustard (see *B. nigra*). Together with white mustard, they have become the most important of all spices (160 000 tons sold every year) and second only to black pepper in monetary terms.

PARTS USED Ripe seeds.

CULTIVATION & HARVESTING Brown mustard is grown as an annual crop. The indehiscent seed capsules are mechanically harvested and threshed when ripe.

USES & PROPERTIES Mustard is mainly used as a condiment for cold, grilled or cooked meat dishes. The seeds are mixed with water, vinegar, egg yolk, grape must (*mustum ardens* in Latin or "piquant must", hence "mustard") or various other ingredients depending on local tastes and customs. It is perhaps the most important of all condiments and is particularly popular in European (especially French and English) cooking. Mustard is an ingredient of numerous sauces that are used with sausage, pork, chicken, fish, macaroni, grills and cold meats. Mustard is strongly associated with German *Bratwurst* and the "hot dog" (a USA fast food invention of the 1930s).

NUTRITIONAL VALUE Unimportant, as mustard is used sparingly as a condiment.

Brassica juncea (L) Czern. var. *juncea*   family: Brassicaceae

jie cai (Chinese); *moutarde brune* (French); *Brauner Senf, Indischer Senf, Sareptasenf* (German); *senape indiana* (Italian); *mostarda indiana* (Portuguese); *mostaza de la india* (Spanish)

Brassica juncea var. *rugosa*

cabbage leaf mustard • mustard greens • Chinese mustard

Chinese cabbage mustard

Curly-leaf mustard

DESCRIPTION Perennial herbs with variously shaped leaves – large and rounded to narrow and markedly lobed or crisped. They have small yellow flowers and oblong, beaked fruit capsules. Numerous cultivars and forms of Chinese mustard or mustard greens are known. The typical Chinese cabbage mustard (also known as *kai-choi*, *kai tsoi*, wrapped heart mustard or *swatow* mustard) forms a dense, rounded heart (similar to a head of cabbage). These plants are now considered to be better placed in *B. juncea* subsp. *integrifolia* but for the sake of consistency it is kept here under the older scientific name (var. *rugosa*). Another popular leafy species is *B. juncea* var. *crispifolia*, known as curled mustard or curly-leaf mustard. Several other forms are grown in China and Japan for their leaves or their swollen, edible stems or roots.

ORIGIN & HISTORY Central Asia and the Himalayas, from where it spread to India, the Caucasus and the Orient. In China, numerous types were developed as green vegetables (in addition to a yellow-seeded form of brown mustard – see *B. juncea* var. *juncea*).

PARTS USED Fresh leaves (less commonly the stems or swollen roots).

CULTIVATION & HARVESTING Grown from seeds as annual crops. They are harvested as seedlings or when more mature, depending on the cultivar and the intended use.

USES & PROPERTIES Mustard cabbages can be cooked or stir-fried and eaten as vegetables. They are also variously preserved in salt and vinegar for use as the popular "sour-salt mustards". Forms with a delicate flavour (such as "bamboo mustard") are sometimes eaten fresh as salad. Another popular food item is the preserved stems of some cultivars such as "big stem mustard" (the stems are peeled, pickled and canned).

NUTRITIONAL VALUE Very rich in minerals (especially calcium, 180 mg) and vitamins A and C. The energy value is about 30 kcal per 100 g.

Brassica juncea (L) Czern. var. *rugosa* (Roxb.) N.Tsen & S.N. Lee   family: Brassicaceae

bao xin jie cai, chang jiao jie cai, kai-choi (Chinese); *moutarde chou* (French); *Breitblättriger Senf* (German); *setsuriko* (Japanese); *mostaza de la china* (Spanish)

Brassica napus

rape • oilseed rape • swede • rutabaga

Rape plant

Rape in fruit

Rape seeds

DESCRIPTION Rapes and swedes are annual or biennial herbs with compound leaves and sparse flowering branches bearing yellow flowers in summer. Oilseed rape (var. *napus* or var. *oleifera*) is well known (especially the commercially important 'Canola' or Canadian oilseed), but many others are grown: summer rape (var. *annua*), winter rape (var. *biennis*), the turnip-like rutabaga, also known as swede or Swedish turnip (var. *napobrassica*) and Siberian kale or rape kale (var. *pabularia*). The rutabaga is also known as *chou-navet* (French), *Kohlrübe* (German), *cavolo navone* (Italian) and *colinabo* (Spanish).

ORIGIN & HISTORY *B. napus* is believed to have originated as a hybrid in medieval gardens in Europe, where turnip and cabbage were grown side by side. The original form was probably oilseed rape (in the Middle Ages a source of fodder and oil), from which forage rape and swede were developed. Swedes were introduced into the United Kingdom from Sweden, hence the English common name.

PARTS USED Seeds (rape), the fleshy taproot (swede) or leaves (rape kale).

CULTIVATION & HARVESTING Oilseed rape (especially 'Canola') has become a very important commercial crop and millions of hectares are grown each year. The seeds contain 40% oil and are mechanically harvested. Swedes are hardier than turnips.

USES & PROPERTIES Rapeseed oil (Canola oil) is used as cooking oil and salad oil but the main use is in margarine and mayonnaise manufacture. Swedes or rutabagas are popular root vegetables, used in much the same way as turnip.

NUTRITIONAL VALUE The oil has an energy value of 900 kcal per 100 g and contains oleic acid (52%), linoleic acid (22%) and sterols (250 mg). Roots are rich in minerals and various vitamins, including nicotinamide (850 µg) and vitamin C (30 mg).

NOTES Canola oil is low in erucic acid and glyco-sinolates. It can be esterified to make biodiesel.

Brassica napus L.   family: Brassicaceae

yang you cai (Chinese); *chou colza, navette* (French); *Raps, Ölsaat* (German); *cavolo colza, napo oleifera* (Italian); *colza* (Portuguese), *colza, nabo* (Spanish)

Brassica nigra
black mustard

Black mustard plants

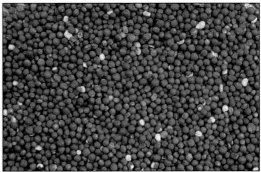

Black mustard seeds

Black mustard flowers and fruit

DESCRIPTION This is an erect annual herb of up to 1 m in height with deeply lobed lower leaves and narrowly oblong upper leaves. Small yellow flowers are followed by smooth, beaked capsules that split open when they ripen to release the black to reddish brown seeds. In addition to black mustard, there are two other main types of mustard, namely brown mustard or Indian mustard (see *Brassica juncea*) and white mustard (see *Sinapis alba*). A third is Ethiopian mustard (*B. carinata*), which is thought to have originated as an ancient hybrid between *B. nigra* and *B. oleracea*. It is locally important in Ethiopia.

ORIGIN & HISTORY Black mustard has been known since ancient times. It originated in the Middle East (probably Iran and Palestine) and soon became popular as a spice crop in most parts of the Old World. Around the 1950s, black mustard was rapidly replaced by brown mustard (*B. juncea*) because the latter has indehiscent capsules (they remain closed at maturity) and is

suitable for mechanical harvesting, while black mustard spontaneously sheds its seeds and therefore has to be hand-harvested.

PARTS USED Ripe seeds.

CULTIVATION & HARVESTING Black mustard is a hardy annual crop. Seeds are harvested by hand at regular intervals or mechanically cut when green but mature and then allowed to ripen and dry on the threshing floor.

USES & PROPERTIES The taste, described as spicy and piquant, develops about 15 minutes after the seeds have been mixed with water ("English mustard") or vinegar ("Continental mustard"). This is due to volatile mustard oil that is released by enzyme action (the mustard-oil glycoside sinigrin is converted to allylisothiocyanate). Culinary uses are many and varied (see brown mustard, *B. juncea* var. *juncea*).

NUTRITIONAL VALUE Used as condiment only.

NOTES Black mustard is an antibacterial agent and is used as counter-irritant to treat rheumatic pain.

Brassica nigra (L.) Koch   family: Brassicaceae

hei jie (Chinese); *moutarde noire* (French); *Schwarzer Senf* (German); *senape nera* (Italian); *kuro garashi* (Japanese); *mostarda negra* (Portuguese); *mostaza negra* (Spanish)

Brassica oleracea var. *acephala*
kale • borecole • collards

Kale plants

Kale leaves and flowers

DESCRIPTION An erect leafy biennial with yellow or white flowers. Wild cabbage (*B. oleracea* var. *oleracea*) is the wild-growing plant of Europe with yellow flowers but it closely resembles some forms of kale. Kale is known in many countries and has common names such as *boerkool* (Afrikaans), *boerenkool* (Dutch), collards (USA), kale, fodder kale or cow cabbage (UK), *chou cavalier* or *chou vert* (French) and *couve forrageira* (Portuguese). A distinctive tall kale known as palm cabbage or Italian kale (*chou palmier* in French, *Palmkohl* in German and *cavolo nero* or *cavolo palmizio* in Italian) is also grouped here. Portuguese kale or curly kale is treated separately below (see *B. oleracea* var. *sabellica*). Another is the tronchuda cabbage or Portuguese cabbage (*chou de Beauvais* in French), known as *couve tronchuda* in Portugal and as *couve-portuguesa* in Brazil. This type has large, partly overlapping leaves that are harvested from the bottom upwards. It is sometimes placed in a group of its own (Costata group or var. *costata*). Tronchuda cabbage has white flowers but differ from kale and Chinese kale in the large, "cabbage-like" leaves borne on a tall stem.

ORIGIN & HISTORY The various kales are believed to have originated during the early Middle Ages from wild *B. oleracea*, most likely in the western (Atlantic and Mediterranean) parts of Europe.

PARTS USED Leaves.

CULTIVATION & HARVESTING Kales are easily grown from seeds and are usually grown as a biennial crop. Leaves are repeatedly harvested until the plants become unproductive.

USES & PROPERTIES Kales are traditionally used for soup but they are also popular as pot-herbs and as a green vegetable. The uses are similar to that of headed cabbage.

NUTRITIONAL VALUE Exceptionally rich in nutrients, including calcium, magnesium, vitamin A and vitamin B6. The energy yield is 37 kcal per 100 g.

Brassica oleracea L. var. *acephala* (DC.) Schübler & Martens   family: Brassicaceae

wu tou gan lai (Chinese); *chou cavalier, chou vert* (French); *Blattkohl, Kuhkohl* (German); *cavolo da foglia* (Italian); *couve forrageira* (Portuguese); *berza, col forrajera* (Spanish)

Brassica oleracea var. *alboglabra*

Chinese kale • Chinese broccoli

Chinese kale in flower

Chinese kale seedlings

Chinese kale at picking stage

DESCRIPTION This is an annual herb with oblong, grey leaves with prominent white midribs. The flower clusters initially resemble small heads of broccoli but then develop into very long, sparse clusters of white flowers and oblong, hairless fruit capsules. In common with cauliflower and broccoli, it is an annual that does not require overwintering to stimulate flowering. The plant is sometimes considered to be a distinct species (*B. alboglabra*) but nowadays usually classified as a variety of *B. oleracea*, or is placed in the Alboglabra group. There are several variations of the Chinese name, including *gai laarn, guy lan, kai laarn, gailarn* and *kalian*.

ORIGIN & HISTORY The origin is shrouded in mystery, as it is not mentioned in the old Chinese texts. It is nevertheless a distinctive plant and is thought to be indigenous to the southern parts of China. The annual growth form and white flowers make it a close relative of the Portuguese cabbages. It is now widely cultivated in Southeast Asia, including Hong Kong, Taiwan and Thailand.

PARTS USED The fleshy young stems (with associated flower buds and some leaves).

CULTIVATION & HARVESTING Plants are easily grown from seeds in temperate areas. It is an annual crop and matures rapidly. Two types are seen on fresh produce markets: very young and tender seedlings, grown in crowded conditions and harvested before bud formation; and more commonly, the young stems and leaves, cut just before the first flower buds open (hence "Chinese broccoli").

USES & PROPERTIES Chinese kale is popular because of its crisp texture, somewhat bitter taste and high mineral (calcium) and vitamin content. It is cooked as a green vegetable, often served in the Cantonese way with oyster sauce. When cut into smaller pieces it can be stir-fried or added to soups and noodle dishes.

NUTRITIONAL VALUE Exceptionally rich in minerals and vitamins A and C.

Brassica oleracea L. var. *alboglabra* (L.H. Bailey) Musil (= *B. alboglabra* L.H. Bailey)   family: Brassicaceae

jie lan, jie lan cai, gai lan (Chinese); *broccoli de Chine* (French); *Chinesischer Brokkoli* (German); *kairan* (Japanese); *bróculi chino* (Spanish)

Brassica oleracea var. *botrytis*

cauliflower • Cape broccoli

Cauliflower (purple Cape broccoli)

Cauliflower (normal type)

Cauliflower (romanesco broccoli)

DESCRIPTION An annual or perennial herb with dense heads of immature or aborted flowers contracted into a single head. Broccoli (more accurately known as sprouting broccoli and calabrese broccoli – see *B. oleracea* var. *italica*) is similar but the heads are partly or completely subdivided into separate small units. The heads are usually white but can also be yellow or purple. The subgroups of cauliflower (some closely resembling broccoli) are nowadays all placed in an informal Botrytis group. Cultivar types include 'Romanesco' or romanesco broccoli – it has characteristic pyramid-shaped flower clusters and is sometimes classified as a broccoli but recently mostly as a cauliflower. Another type is the so-called Cape broccoli, which is also considered to be closer to cauliflower because of the compact, single heads. The cultivars include "green Cape broccoli" with a characteristic green colour, "purple Cape broccoli", "brown Italian broccoli" and "yellow Italian broccoli". The distinction between cauliflower and broccoli is problematic, as both include coloured forms (see *B. oleracea* var. *italica*).

ORIGIN & HISTORY Eastern Mediterranean. It was imported into Italy around the end of the sixteenth century and from there to Germany and France.

PARTS USED The fleshy, aborted flower buds and associated stalks (curds).

CULTIVATION & HARVESTING Cauliflower grows best in temperate regions. The inner leaves are often bent over the head to prevent sun damage and practically the whole plant is cut off at harvesting.

USES & PROPERTIES Cauliflower is easily digested and is sometimes eaten raw (in salad or as a vegetable fondue) but most often cooked with white sauce or cheese sauce. It may be added to soup, soufflés, cold salads, purées and pickles, or variously braised, blanched and fried.

NUTRITIONAL VALUE Cauliflower is less nutritious than broccoli but still provides fair amounts of minerals, biotin and other vitamins.

Brassica oleracea L. var. *botrytis* L.   family: Brassicaceae

cai hua, gai lan hua (Chinese); *chou-fleur* (French); *Blumenkohl* (German); *cavolo broccolo, cavolfiore* (Italian); *couve-flor* (Portuguese); *coliflor* (Spanish)

Brassica oleracea var. *capitata*
cabbage

White cabbage

Field of cabbages

Red cabbage

Savoy cabbage

DESCRIPTION There are three main lines of cultivar development in cabbages but they all share the feature of the large rounded leaves that form a dense crown or head. The various subtypes are: (1) ordinary cabbage or white cabbage; (2) red cabbage, *chou rouge* (French), *Rotkohl* or *Blaukraut* (German), *cavolo rosso* (Italian), *couve roxa* (Portuguese), *repollo colorado* or *repollo rojo* (Spanish) and *zi ye gan lan* (Chinese); (3) savoy cabbage (Subauda group, originally named as a variety of its own – var. *sabauda*) has characteristic wrinkled leaves and was already known in Germany in the sixteenth century. It is believed to have originated in Italy. Savoy cabbage is known as *chou de Milan* or *chou de Savoie* (French), *Wirsingkohl* (German), *cavolo verza* (Italian), *chirimen kanran* (Japanese), *couve crespa* or *couve de Sabóia* (Portuguese) and *col de Saboya*, *col de Milán* or *berza de Saboya* (Spanish).
ORIGIN & HISTORY Mediterranean region. Cabbage developed further in central and southern Europe during the Middle Ages.
PARTS USED The dense head (heart) of leaves with associated thick, fleshy stem.
CULTIVATION & HARVESTING Cabbages are grown from seeds as a popular annual crop of all temperate regions.
USES & PROPERTIES Raw cabbage is sliced and used in salads or with mayonnaise as the familiar coleslaw. It may be cooked as an ingredient of soups, stews and stuffings. Pickled cabbage is a popular food item in Europe. Perhaps most famous of all is *sauerkraut* (*choucroute* in French), which is typical of the German cooking tradition (famous areas include the Alsace, the Black Forest and Bavaria, but there are countless traditional and regional recipes). *Sauerkraut* is sliced, salted and fermented white cabbage, usually served with potatoes, sausage, bacon or a wide variety of other meat dishes.
NUTRITIONAL VALUE Very rich in minerals (calcium, sulphur) and especially vitamin C (up to 150 mg per 100 g).

Brassica oleracea L. var. *capitata* L.

family: Brassicaceae

gan lan, lan cai (Chinese); *chou cabas, chou blanc* (French); *Kopfkohl* (German); *cavolo cappuccino* (Italian); *couve de repolho, couve de cabeça* (Portuguese); *col, repollo, berza común* (Spanish)

Brassica oleracea var. *gemmifera*

Brussels sprouts

Brussels sprouts plants

Brussels sprouts

DESCRIPTION A biennial plant with a single erect stem, a large leafy crown and numerous small heads (axillary buds) produced above the insertion of each leaf stalk. Yellow flowers are formed in the second year, when the small heads open up and develop branched flowering stalks. Green and purple colour forms are available. In modern cultivars, all the sprouts develop and mature at the same time.

ORIGIN & HISTORY Southern Europe. The exact history is not known but the plant is considered to be unrelated to the many-headed cabbages that are illustrated in sixteenth century herbals (for example, the *Brassica capitata polycephala* described by D'Alechamp in 1587). It is thought that the crop may have been introduced into Belgium by the Roman legions and that they always had a rather limited distribution (commonly grown in market gardens around Brussels, hence the common name).

PARTS USED The axillary buds (headed side shoots), resembling tiny cabbages.

CULTIVATION & HARVESTING The crop thrives in colder climates. Seedlings are planted in early spring and are ready for harvesting by late summer to mid winter depending on the region. Sprouts should be picked while young and tender, but old sprouts left over winter will produce edible flowering shoots (like broccoli) in early spring.

USES & PROPERTIES The small heads are blanched, cooked or braised and used as a vegetable. They are served with butter, cream or white sauce, often to accompany meat dishes. Brussels sprouts are particularly popular for gratins and purées. In French cooking they are an important ingredient of *à la bruxelloise* (stewed sprouts, endives and potatoes, served with small joints of meat) or *à la brabançonne* garnishes (made with endives and the young sprouts of hops).

NUTRITIONAL VALUE The nutrients are similar to that of broccoli in composition but lower in concentration.

Brassica oleracea L. var. *gemmifera* DC.　　　　　　　　　　　　family: Brassicaceae

bao zi gan lai (Chinese); *chou de Bruxelles* (French); *Rosenkohl, Kohlsprossen* (German); *cavolo di Bruxelles* (Italian); *couve de Bruxelas* (Portuguese); *col de Bruselas* (Spanish)

Brassica oleracea var. *gongylodes*
kohlrabi • cabbage turnip

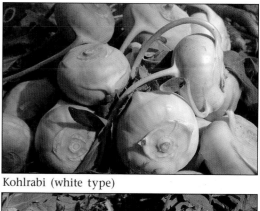

Kohlrabi (white type)

Kohlrabi plant

Kohlrabi (red type)

DESCRIPTION A small biennial plant with slender leaf stalks that are widely spaced on a rounded, turnip-like stem situated above the ground. These edible stems can be green, white, red or purple, depending on the cultivar. If not harvested, the plants will produce yellow flowers in the second year. Two common cultivars are 'Purple Vienna' and 'White Vienna'. The name kohlrabi is derived from the German words *Kohl* (cabbage) and *Rübi* (turnip). Another example of a cabbage that is used for the fleshy stems is marrowstem kale (*chou moellier* in French). This plant is closely related to the kales (see var. *acephala*) but the fleshy stems are the edible part. It was first recorded from the Vendée region of France but is now grown in other parts of Europe and in New Zealand.

ORIGIN & HISTORY The early development of cabbages occurred in the Mediterranean region and the earliest reference to a turnip-like cabbage was by Pliny in the first century AD, who called it a "Pompeian cabbage". Kohlrabi is believed to be of North European origin but the exact history was never recorded.

PARTS USED The swollen stem.

CULTIVATION & HARVESTING These drought-hardy plants are grown from seeds and are now found in all temperate regions of the world. The stems are harvested when young (when they are slightly smaller than a tennis ball), as they get fibrous and bitter with age.

USES & PROPERTIES Kohlrabi is peeled and the crisp, tender interior is commonly used as a cooked vegetable (the water is changed once or twice during the cooking process) but may also be peeled and eaten raw. It is particularly popular as an ingredient of soups and is mostly prepared like turnip or turnip-rooted celeriac.

NUTRITIONAL VALUE Kohlrabi is a rich source of minerals and vitamins. The energy yield is only 24 kcal per 100 g.

Brassica oleracea L. var. *gongylodes* L.

family: Brassicaceae

cai tou, gai lan tou (Chinese); *chou-rave* (French); *Kohlrabi* (German); *cavolo rapa* (Italian); *couve rábano* (Portuguese); *col rábano* (Spanish)

Brassica oleracea var. *italica*

sprouting broccoli • calabrese

Sprouting broccoli (calabrese type)

Sprouting broccoli

DESCRIPTION A biennial with loose heads or sparsely branched groups of flowers on thick, fleshy stalks, usually harvested before the buds open. Previously, two other main types of broccoli were distinguished, namely the so-called "Cape broccoli" and "romanesco" types. Both have dense flower heads, harvested before the buds are clearly distinguishable, and they are nowadays classified under cauliflower – see *B. oleracea* var. *botrytis*. The sprouting types (var. *italica* or the Italica group) are overwintering annuals or perennials that are nowadays considered to be the only "true broccoli". They can be harvested several times (unlike cauliflower or non-sprouting broccoli, where the whole flower head is cut off). The best-known cultivar group is calabrese or green sprouting broccoli, but yellow, purple and even white sprouting broccoli are also available.

ORIGIN & HISTORY Usually associated with Italy but said to be a seventeenth century import from the eastern Mediterranean (possibly Crete or Cyprus). From Italy it spread to other parts of Europe (often known as "Italian asparagus").

PARTS USED Immature flower buds with associated thick fleshy stalks and surrounding leaves.

CULTIVATION & HARVESTING Plants are propagated from seeds and are usually harvested at regular intervals.

USES & PROPERTIES A popular spring vegetable that is prepared in the same way as cauliflower. The stalks may be eaten like asparagus. In Italy it is usually cooked with garlic, olive oil and white wine. Broccoli is stir-fried in China or may be used as a sweet and sour dish (in the same way as Chinese broccoli and Chinese kale).

NUTRITIONAL VALUE One of the most nutritious of all vegetables. It combines a low calorific value (28 kcal per 100 g) with substantial quantities of protein (3%), and a rich diversity of minerals and vitamins at high levels (vitamin C, for example, may exceed 100 mg).

Brassica oleracea L. var. *italica* Plenck

family: Brassicaceae

yang hua ye cai, kai-lan-fa (Chinese); *chou brocoli, brocoli* (French); *Brokkoli* (German); *cavolo broccolo* (Italian); *bróculos* (Portuguese); *brócoli, bróculi* (Spanish)

Brassica oleracea var. *sabellica*
curly kale • Portuguese kale • Scotch kale

Curly kale plant

DESCRIPTION This kale is a short-lived perennial with a single or branched stem that may reach a height of up to 2 m or more. The broad, oblong leaves have characteristically crispy margins. In common with other kales, the flowers are pure white and not yellow as in wild cabbage (var. *oleracea*). Portuguese kale is closely related to other kales and is often included within the kale group (var. *acephala*). It can easily be distinguished by the curly leaf margins and large size. It should not be confused with tronchuda kale (var. *costata*, also known as Portuguese kale, *couve tronchuda*, Madeira cabbage or seakale cabbage), which has thick, white fleshy ribs on the lower surfaces of the leaves. Other well-known kales include collards (popular in southern USA), tree cabbage (*chou cavalier* or giant jersey kale) and palm tree cabbage (*chou palmier*).

ORIGIN & HISTORY Various forms of kales have been cultivated since Greek and Roman times but modern cultivars such as curly kale can be traced back to the Middle Ages.

PARTS USED Leaves.

CULTIVATION & HARVESTING Plants are easily grown from seeds. The lower leaves are regularly harvested, so that the stems of the plants gradually become bare for most of their length. After a few years, the plants get too sparse and unproductive and are replaced with new seedlings. Seeds are sown any time of the year.

USES & PROPERTIES Almost every traditional Portuguese household nurtures a few *couve galega* plants to supply fresh leaves for the traditional kale soup known as *cal do verde* (meaning "green broth"). *Cal do verde* is usually eaten as a vegetarian dish (as is the case with most Portuguese soups) but a few thin slices of *chorizo* (a Spanish or Portuguese sausage made from pork and beef) are often added.

NUTRITIONAL VALUE Exceptionally rich in nutrients (similar to other kales and cabbages).

Brassica oleracea L. var. *sabellica* L.   family: Brassicaceae

chou cavalier frisé, chou frisé (French); *Grünkohl, Braunkohl, Krauskohl* (German); *cavolo riccio* (Italian); *couve frisada, couve galega* (Portuguese); *col crespa* (Spanish)

Brassica rapa var. *chinensis*
pak choi • Chinese white cabbage

Pak choi plant in flower

Shanghai pak choi (left) and bok choi (right)

Tat soi (rosette pak choi)

DESCRIPTION A small, stemless rosette plant with dark green leaves on thick fleshy stalks and yellow flowers. Two basic types are: (1) Chinese white cabbage or *pak choi*, easily recognised on the market as a small rosette with a few thick leaf stalks that make up the bulk of the plant. Cultivars with green leaf stalks are often referred to as Shanghai *pak choi*, while the white-stemmed form is called *bok choi*; (2) Chinese flat cabbage, *tat soi* or rosette *pak choi* (*B. rapa* var. *narinosa*, also known as *B. chinensis* var. *rosularis*), which has distinctive, small, dark green leaves neatly arranged in a multi-leaf spiral rosette. Another close relative is Chinese flowering cabbage or *pak choi sum* (see *B. rapa* var. *parachinensis*). In recent years, a wide range of "Chinese cabbages" has become available on fresh produce markets or at speciality greengrocers throughout the world but their identities and names are a source of much confusion. *Pak choi* or Chinese white cabbage,

for example, is sometimes confused with *pe tsai* or headed Chinese cabbage (see *B. rapa* var. *pekinensis*).

ORIGIN & HISTORY *Pak choi* originated in Southeast Asia and has been grown in China and Japan for centuries. In recent years it has become well known in all temperate parts of the world.

PARTS USED Whole young plants.

CULTIVATION & HARVESTING Plants are easy to grow from seed and should be harvested when young (long before flowering).

USES & PROPERTIES Young plants are boiled as green vegetables (often served with oyster sauce) or they are popular ingredients of stir-fries, noodle dishes and soups. Salted cabbage (*pak choi kan*) is made by a process of pickling in salt for three days, and can be stored for several weeks.

NUTRITIONAL VALUE Similar to cabbage but with a very low calorific value (only 12 kcal per 100 g).

Brassica rapa L. var. *chinensis* (L.) Kitam. (= *Brassica chinensis* L.)   family: Brassicaceae

pak choi, bok choi, bai cai, peh-chai (Chinese); *chou pak choi* (French); *Chinakohl, Chinesischer Senfkohl, Pak-Choi* (German); *cavolo cinese* (Italian); *col chino* (Spanish)

Brassica rapa var. *parachinensis*
Chinese flowering cabbage

Chinese flowering cabbage plant

Chinese flowering cabbage

DESCRIPTION This is a cabbage-like but non-heading plant of up to 1 m in height, with broad, yellowish-green leaves and yellow flowers borne in loose clusters. When young, the plants resemble *pak choi* (see var. *chinensis*) but they soon develop erect flowering stems and never the short, neat and stemless rosettes of the latter. Chinese flowering cabbage is mostly known as *pak choi sum* and was formerly classified as *B. chinensis* var. *parachinensis*. Many of the various forms of "Chinese cabbages" have become popular in recent times but the different types (and cultivars) and their names can be very confusing (see notes under *pak choi*, var. *chinensis*). Chinese flowering cabbage should not be confused with the closely related Chinese cabbage (*pak choi* or *bok choi*) or the more distantly related Peking cabbage or heading Chinese cabbage. Since this variety is grown for the thick flowering shoots, it is often referred to as Chinese broccoli, a name usually given to Chinese kale (*B. oleracea* var. *alboglabra*).

ORIGIN & HISTORY The exact origin of Chinese flowering cabbage is not known, but it probably originated in Southeast Asia and became a popular vegetable in China and Japan. From here it has spread to many other parts of the orient and more recently also the western world.

PARTS USED Flowering stems, with associated small leaves and flower buds.

CULTIVATION & HARVESTING This is an easy and productive vegetable for commercial cultivation and for the home vegetable garden. The stems are cut when the first flowers have opened and are used when still fresh.

USES & PROPERTIES The crispy stems are boiled as green vegetables and served with oyster sauce or various other sauces. As with most Chinese vegetables, they can be stir-fried, used in various noodle dishes and soups or may be pickled.

NUTRITIONAL VALUE Exceptionally rich in minerals and vitamins (similar to broccoli).

Brassica rapa L. var. *parachinensis* (L.H. Bailey) Tsen & Lee (= *Brassica parachinensis* L.H. Bailey)   family: Brassicaceae

pak choi sum, cai xin, choi sam, chai sim (Chinese); *faux pakchoi* (French); *Choi-Sum* (German); *broccoletto cinese* (Italian); *sawi bunga, sawi kembang* (Indonesian); *couve de inflorescència* (Portuguese)

108

Brassica rapa var. *pekinensis*
celery cabbage • pe tsai

Celery cabbage plants

Celery cabbage seedlings

Celery cabbage

DESCRIPTION A robust, leafy annual or biennial herb with toothed leaves, which usually form an oblong head of densely packed, pale yellowish green leaves. Some forms have narrow leaf stalks and never form heads (known as *wong bok*), while others have broad, wing-like leaf stalks and develop into oblong, lettuce-like heads. Several different members of the cabbage family are loosely referred to as "Chinese cabbage", causing uncertainty amongst many non-Chinese vegetable lovers. Chinese white cabbage or *pak choi*, for example, is sometimes mistaken for celery cabbage because of similar nomenclature. To prevent further confusion it is perhaps best to avoid the name "Chinese cabbage" and to call this vegetable celery cabbage (one may also use the Chinese name *pe tsai*, or specify that it is *heading* Chinese cabbage or Peking cabbage). In the USA, it is known as napa cabbage or nappa. The loose (non-heading) forms are often referred to as "Chinese leaf".

ORIGIN & HISTORY An ancient Chinese vegetable that has been grown and used in China, Japan and Korea for centuries. It has recently become known in Europe, the USA and many other parts of the world.

PARTS USED The dense head of leaves (or the loose leaves of the rosette forms).

CULTIVATION & HARVESTING Plants are easily grown from seeds that are usually sown directly. Young plants may be harvested, or more often the pale green (almost white) mature heads. The old and damaged outer leaves are removed.

USES & PROPERTIES Celery cabbage is a crispy, tender vegetable with a mild taste. It is mostly used in soups, mixed vegetable dishes or sometimes as a salad ingredient. The leaves may be chopped and boiled, stir-fried, braised or pickled. The Korean pickle dish known as *kimchee* is made from celery lettuce.

NUTRITIONAL VALUE A low calorific value combined with high levels of minerals and vitamins typical of cabbages.

Brassica rapa L. var. *pekinensis* (Lour.) Hanelt [= *B. pekinensis* (Lour.) Rupr.]   family: Brassicaceae

pe tsai, bai cai, huang ya cai (Chinese); *chou de Pékin, chou pe-tsai* (French); *Pekingkohl* (German); *cavolo sedano* (Italian); *couve petsai* (Portuguese); *col petsai* (Spanish)

Brassica rapa var. *rapa*

turnip • neeps

Japanese tender greens

Turnip plants

Turnips

DESCRIPTION A leafy herb with hairy, compound leaves and a thick, swollen taproot (often purplish near the leaves, and white or yellow inside). There are numerous close relatives that are popular root and leaf vegetables, especially in Japan. Perhaps best known are "Japanese tender greens" which belong to the Komatsuna group of *B. rapa*. They are similar to turnip but do not form thick roots – the young plants are harvested and used as salad or in stir-fries. Turnip is often confused with the similar-looking swede or rutabaga (*B. napus* var. *napobrassica*). Two other turnip types are grown as oilseeds (in the same way as rapeseed or 'Canola' – see *B. napus*). These are biennial turnip rape (usually referred to as *B. rapa* subsp. *oleifera*) and annual turnip rape (*B. rapa* subsp. *campestris*).

ORIGIN & HISTORY One of the oldest root crops, described by Theophrastus (400 BC) and Pliny (about AD 100). The wild plant is *B. rapa* subsp. *sylvestris* which is thought to be of central European origin but is now found all over Europe and Asia (a weed in North America).

PARTS USED Mostly the fleshy taproot (also the young leaves, as "turnip greens" or "Japanese greens"; ripe seeds, in the case of the turnip rapes).

CULTIVATION & HARVESTING Plants are easily grown from seeds as an annual crop and harvested while still young. They may be overwintered and harvested in the spring.

USES & PROPERTIES Turnips are still one of the most popular root vegetables in Europe. They have a wide range of culinary uses (eaten raw and grated, or variously glazed, sautéed in butter or cooked in cream), and have always been an essential ingredient of soups and stews (including the French *pot-au-feu*).

NUTRITIONAL VALUE The calorific value is low (25 kcal per 100 g). A useful source of calcium and vitamin C (about 20 mg).

Brassica rapa L. var. *rapa* (= *B. campestris* L.)   family: Brassicaceae

man jing, wu jing (Chinese); *raap* (Dutch); *navet* (French); *Weiße Rübe* (German); *navone* (Italian); *kabu* (Japanese); *nabo* (Spanish)

Cajanus cajan

pigeonpea • pigeon pea

Pigeonpea flowers and young pods

Pigeonpea plantation

Pigeonpea seeds (three cultivars)

DESCRIPTION An erect, perennial shrub of up to 5 m in height, with trifoliate, hairy leaves, yellow flowers (often streaked with red) and oblong pods containing up to seven seeds (pale grey, brown or often mottled and speckled, depending on the cultivar). The name originated in Barbados, where the seeds were used as pigeon feed. There are at least 350 other vernacular names, including red gram, Congo pea, *arhar* and *gunga* pea.

ORIGIN & HISTORY Almost certainly India, where the greatest diversity of types is found. It spread to Egypt and East Africa many centuries ago and from there further west and south. Pigeonpea reached the Caribbean region via the slave trade, and also spread via Myanmar and Malaysia to Australia. Today it is an important crop in many parts of the dry tropics where it is often grown in subsistence agriculture. Over 90% of the world production (2 million tons) originates in India.

PARTS USED Ripe or green seeds (also leaves, young pods or sprouts).

CULTIVATION & HARVESTING For commercial seed production, pigeonpea is grown as an annual. It ranks fourth after beans, peas and chickpeas in importance as food pulse. In rural areas, the plant is grown as a perennial, multipurpose source of fuel wood, fibre, lac, fodder for animals and as a source of protein-rich seeds for human consumption.

USES & PROPERTIES The main food use is as *dhal*: dry split peas with the seed coat removed. Fresh green seeds are used as a sweet-tasting vegetable. Pigeonpeas are used in soups, stews and many speciality dishes. In Indian cooking, it is mixed with tamarind or green mango to make a tasty side dish.

NUTRITIONAL VALUE Pigeonpeas are very nutritious (rich in vitamins, minerals and amino acids). They have a high energy yield (307 kcal per 100 g) and the protein content is above 20%.

Cajanus cajan (L.) Millsp.   family: Fabaceae

mu do (Chinese); *pois cajun* (French); *arhar, tuur* (Hindi); *Taubenerbse* (German); *caiano* (Italian); *pijonpii* (Japanese); *kacang dal* (Malay); *guandu* (Portuguese); *gandul* (Spanish)

Camellia sinensis

tea • chai

Tea leaves and flower

Tea plantations

Black tea, oolong tea and green tea

DESCRIPTION A woody perennial with glossy leaves and white flowers. The original Chinese tea (var. *sinensis*) is a branched shrub with relatively small, blunt-tipped leaves, while the more southern Assam tea (var. *assamica*) is a tree bearing thin, pointed leaves.

ORIGIN & HISTORY Tea is indigenous to southern China and the adjoining regions of Thailand, Myanmar, Laos and Cambodia. It was originally exported by land from China to Russia and other countries (where tea is still known by the Chinese name *chai*). The name "tea" is based on a southern Chinese dialect and is associated with the more recent shipping trade to England. During the 1830s, both Chinese and Assam tea types were planted in India, from where hybrid seeds reached many parts of the world. Today, about 2.5 million tons are produced each year.

PARTS USED The terminal bud (pekoe) with the two or three leaves immediately below it.

CULTIVATION & HARVESTING Seedlings, cuttings or grafted trees are established in plantations and clipped to a height of 1.5 m to facilitate hand picking. Black tea is produced by a controlled process of withering, rolling (to break cell walls), "fermentation" (enzymatic modification of polyphenols), firing (inactivation of the enzymes and drying) and finally sorting, grading and packing. Green tea is unfermented, while oolong tea is partially fermented.

USES & PROPERTIES Tea is mostly consumed in western countries as black tea (with milk and sugar), while green tea (without milk or sugar) is popular in China and Japan. It is flavoured with essential oils (lemon, bergamot), dried flowers (jasmine) or spices (cinnamon, mint). Ice tea has become important in the cold drink industry. Green tea is used in meat, fish and egg dishes, especially in China and Vietnam.

NUTRITIONAL VALUE Tea (especially green tea) is rich in phenolics with antioxidant effects. It also has stimulant properties (2–4% caffeine).

Camellia sinensis (L.) O. Kuntze (= *Thea sinensis* L.)

family: Theaceae

chai (Chinese); *théier* (French); *Teestrauch* (German); *tè* (Italian); *té* (Spanish)

Canavalia ensiformis
jack bean

Velvet bean (*Mucuna pruriens*)

Jack bean seeds

Jack bean flowers and fruits

DESCRIPTION This is a robust annual climber with compound leaves and clusters of white, pink or purple flowers. The fruits are oblong, somewhat flattened pods that form distinct longitudinal ridges when they mature and dry out. The large seeds are usually white but sometimes greyish or black and mottled. A close relative is the sword bean (*Canavalia gladiata*) from India and Southeast Asia, which is known as *dao dou* (Chinese), *pois sabre* (French), *Schwertbone* (German), *nata mame* (Japanese), *kachang parang* (Malay) and *poroto sable* (Spanish). It is a perennial plant bearing larger and broader pods. Also similar is the velvet bean (*Mucuna pruriens*) but it has dark purple flowers and hairy pods.

ORIGIN & HISTORY The jack bean probably originated in tropical America but it is a cultigen that has never been found in the wild. Seed remains have been found in archaeological sites in Mexico dated to 3000 BC. It is traditionally cultivated mainly in Central America and the Caribbean but is nowadays found as a minor crop plant throughout the tropics.

PARTS USED The young pods or immature seeds (sometimes also the ripe, dried seeds).

CULTIVATION & HARVESTING Jack bean is grown as an annual crop, often to provide fodder and green manure rather than human food.

USES & PROPERTIES Young, green pods (harvested when they are about half their mature size) or the immature seeds are cooked as vegetables. The mature seeds may be dried and stored for use as a pulse, but they have to be thoroughly cooked and leached to remove poisonous substances. Seeds are sometimes used as a coffee substitute.

NUTRITIONAL VALUE Ripe seeds (beans) contain about 25% protein, 2% fat and 50% carbohydrates.

NOTES Jack bean contains canavanine, a non-protein amino acid that mimics arginine in its chemical structure. It is also a commercial source of urease enzymes.

Canavalia ensiformis (L.) DC.

family: Fabaceae

yang dao dou (Chinese); *haricot sabre* (French); *Jackbohne* (German); *tachinata mame* (Japanese); *feijão espada* (Portuguese); *frijol de sabre* (Spanish)

Canna edulis

achira • edible canna • Queensland arrowroot

Achira flower

Achira plant

Achira rhizomes

DESCRIPTION A leafy perennial herb of up to 2.5 m in height with large fleshy leaves arising from edible, underground rhizomes. Attractive bright red to orange flowers are followed by warty seed capsules bearing hard, round, black seeds. The plant is closely related to the well-known ornamental canna (*Canna indica* and *C.* x *generalis*) but the flowers are much smaller.

ORIGIN & HISTORY The crop probably originated in the Andean region (archaeological remains from Peru are said to date from 2500 BC). Nowadays the plant is widely cultivated in Mexico, the West Indies and most parts of South America. In recent times it has also become a commercial starch crop in northern Australia (hence "Queensland arrowroot") and especially in Vietnam.

PARTS USED The rhizomes or young shoots.

CULTIVATION & HARVESTING Achira is exceptionally hardy and easy to cultivate – the rhizome tips are merely stuck into the ground. They thrive in almost any soil and have very few pests and diseases. The rhizomes are harvested (by hand or mechanically) in the early flowering period, about eight to ten months after planting. Yields of 50 tons of rhizomes per hectare (up to 10 tons of starch) are common.

USES & PROPERTIES The rhizomes or young shoots are important food items in Peru and southern Ecuador, where they are cooked or baked (often as part of a traditional feast that includes roasted guinea pig, yacon and quinoa beer). When baked, the rhizomes become translucent, sweet and somewhat slimy. In Vietnam, the crop is grown on a large scale to produce the famous and popular transparent Vietnamese noodles.

NUTRITIONAL VALUE The dried root contains starch (80%), sugar (10%) and protein (1–3%) and is rich in potassium.

NOTES The unique starch granules are the largest ever measured – they are actually visible to the naked eye (twice or three times the size of potato starch grains).

Canna edulis Ker-Gawler   family: Cannaceae

balisier, tous-les-mois (French); *Achira, Essbare Canna* (German); *achira* (Italian); *ganyong* (Malay); *merú, birú manso, araruta bastarda* (Portuguese); *achira* (Spanish); *sakhu chin* (Thai); *dong rieng* (Vietnamese)

114

Capparis spinosa
caper bush

Caper bush flowers

Caper bush

Capers (fruits and buds)

DESCRIPTION A small shrub with trailing, often slightly thorny branches and thick, fleshy leaves. The distinctive flower buds open up into attractive but short-lived, white or pinkish flowers. Each flower has numerous stamens surrounding a single stalked ovary.

ORIGIN & HISTORY Indigenous to Asia Minor and the Mediterranean region, including southern Europe, southeastern Europe and North Africa. Capers were used at least in the time of the ancient Greeks and were popular in Roman times.

PARTS USED The unopened flower buds (less often the fruits), known as capers.

CULTIVATION & HARVESTING Caper bushes are common wild plants in southern Europe and are also cultivated in Mediterranean countries. Italy and Spain are the main producers. The buds are hand-picked before they open (before sunrise) and pickled in white wine vinegar or in brine (Sicilian capers – the salt is washed off before use).

USES & PROPERTIES Capers are an important condiment which are widely used in rice, fish and meat dishes for the strong salty-sour taste. They go well with mustard and horseradish and are a traditional flavour additive in fish sauces (e.g. *tartare*). Capers have become well known all over the world as a garnish for pizzas. In French cooking, capers are an important ingredient of *gribiche* (a cold sauce based on mayonnaise and served with cold fish) and *ravigote* (a spicy sauce served hot or cold with various egg, fish and meat dishes). In Italy, capers are popular as a condiment, garnish (small buds are preferred) or cocktail snack. They are often added to seafood and fish dishes, salads, pizzas and pasta sauces. A famous dish is the Sicilian *pasta colle sarde*, which includes capers with sardines, tomatoes, parsley, pine nuts and raisins.

NUTRITIONAL VALUE Unimportant (used in small amounts).

NOTES Flower buds of other plants (nasturtium, marigold) are used as substitutes for capers.

Capparis spinosa L.   family: Capparidaceae

ci shan gan (Chinese); *câpres, câprier* (French); *Kapernstrauch* (German); *kiari* (Hindi); *cappero* (Italian); *keepaa* (Japanese); *melada* (Malay); *alcaparras* (Portuguese); *alcaparro* (Spanish)

Capsicum annuum

sweet pepper • paprika • chilli

Sweet pepper plant

Sweet peppers

Chilli peppers

DESCRIPTION An annual herb with dark green leaves, solitary milky white flowers and hollow, many-seeded berries. The fruits are extremely variable in size, shape and colour but they are characteristically drooping in most forms. Pungent forms are often confused with chilli pepper or bird chilli (*C. frutescens*, a perennial). There are five main groups: cherry peppers (Cerasiforme group), cone peppers (Conoides group), red cone peppers (Fasciculatum group), bell peppers or sweet peppers (Grossum group) and cayenne peppers or chilli peppers (Longum group). Most familiar is the non-pungent bell pepper, which is rounded (with a depression at the base), thick-skinned, fleshy and green, yellow or orange in colour. The pungent cayenne pepper has long, narrow, drooping fruits.

ORIGIN & HISTORY Indigenous to Central and South America, including Mexico and the Caribbean region. It was developed into a crop plant around 3000 BC or perhaps even earlier.

Columbus introduced *Capsicum* into Europe and it also spread to Africa and Asia.

PARTS USED The green or mature fruit.

CULTIVATION & HARVESTING Sweet pepper is an annual crop, easily grown from seeds.

USES & PROPERTIES The fleshy sweet pepper is very popular as an ingredient of salads and is widely eaten fresh as a tasty and crunchy addition to any meal. The seeds and white membranous placenta inside the fruits are always removed. "Capsicum" means "box" and these hollow fruits are ideal for stuffing. They are particularly popular in Mediterranean cooking – famous dishes include *caponata*, *gazpacho*, *piperade* and *ratatouille*. The paprika pepper is only slightly pungent and is dried and powdered. Paprika powder is widely used to flavour potatoes, cheese and eggs, and is an ingredient of the famous Hungarian *goulash* and many other dishes.

NUTRITIONAL VALUE Green peppers (especially the red types) are very rich in vitamins A and C.

Capsicum annuum L.   family: Solanaceae

tian jiao (Chinese); *poivron* (French); *Gewürzpaprika, Spanischer Pfeffer* (German); *hara mirch* (Hindi); *pimento, pepperone* (Italian); *peppaa* (Japanese); *cabai* (Malay); *pimiento picante* (Spanish); *phrik* (Thai)

Capsicum frutescens

chilli • bird chilli • Tabasco pepper • cayenne pepper

Chilli plant

Chilli flowers and fruits

Habanero chilli

DESCRIPTION A perennial herb with greenish-white flowers, at least some of which are arranged in small groups of two or three. The fruits are small, erect, oblong, orange-red when ripe and extremely pungent. Two cultivar types are grown commercially – 'Tabasco' is used to make the famous Tabasco sauce while 'Habanero' is considered to be the hottest of all. The *habanero* is a small, lantern-shaped chilli (a form of *C. frutescens,* sometimes called *C. chinense*). Two other species are the Bolivian *aji* (*C. baccatum*) and the Andean *rocoto* (*C. pubescens*). Sweet pepper (*C. annuum*) includes many pungent forms that are often confused with the real chilli. Examples are the *jalapeño* (the best known of the Mexican peppers, often used green), *serrano* (a very hot Mexican type, small and oblong in shape) and numerous others (*cascabel, guajillo, pulla, costeño, chilhuacle, de agua, fresno, poblano, pasilla, pequin, catarina* and the New Mexico chillies such as the anaheim).

ORIGIN & HISTORY Central and South America.

In India and Southeast Asia, chilli gradually replaced black pepper, the original pungent principle in Indian food.

PARTS USED The fresh or dried fruit.

CULTIVATION & HARVESTING Chilli fruits are hand-harvested from cultivated plants or from wild plants (bird chilli).

USES & PROPERTIES The hot, spicy flavour is characteristic of most Mexican, West Indian and Indian dishes and has become very popular all over the world. Famous dishes include *chilli con carne* (beef and red beans). Chilli is the main ingredient of numerous spicy sauces, including American Tabasco sauce, North African *harissa* and Chinese *öt*. Cayenne pepper and red pepper (less pungent) are made from powdered dried fruits.

NUTRITIONAL VALUE Fruits contain vitamins A and C but the small quantities used add little nutrients to the diet.

NOTES The pungency is mainly due to capsaicin (an alkaloid-like substance).

Capsicum frutescens L.   family: Solanaceae

la jiao (Chinese); *piment, cayenne* (French); *Chili, Tabasco* (German); *mirch* (Hindi); *peperoncino arbustivo* (Italian); *kidachi tougarashi* (Japanese); *lada merah* (Malay); *guindilla* (Spanish); *phrik kheenuu* (Thai)

Carica papaya

papaya tree • paw paw

Babaco

Papaya trees

Papaya fruits

DESCRIPTION A thick-stemmed giant herb (small tree) with large, hand-shaped leaves, white flowers (male and female flowers are usually borne on separate trees) and large, smooth fruits that turn orange when they ripen. Several other species and hybrids are used. The well-known babaco (*C.* x *pentagona*) is a seedless hybrid between the mountain papaya or *chamburo* (*C. pubescens*) and the *siglalón* (*C. stipulata*). Others are the dwarf Peruvian cooking papaya or *col de monte* (*C. monoica*), the *papayuelo* (*C. goudotiana*) and the *toronchi* (a natural hybrid).

ORIGIN & HISTORY Warm tropical lowlands of Central America. The *chamburo* is widely distributed from Panama to Chile and Argentina. The others are found at higher altitudes – the *papayuelo* is restricted to Colombia while the babaco, *siglalón, col de monte* and *toronchi* are indigenous to Ecuador. The papaya (and later the babaco) became important commercial crops.

PARTS USED Ripe (or rarely unripe) fruits.

CULTIVATION & HARVESTING Papayas are easily cultivated in tropical and subtropical regions. One male tree is planted for every 20 female trees. For commercial harvesting, the green but fully mature fruits are picked (but for home use the ripe fruits).

USES & PROPERTIES Ripe fruits are very popular ingredients of fruit salads (including the Indonesian *rujak* salad) or served as a dessert (with sugar, cream and perhaps a dash of rum added to improve the flavour). They may be used for fruit juice and jam, and are crystallised or dried. In Southeast Asia, unripe fruits are added to salads and are cooked as vegetables.

NUTRITIONAL VALUE A rich source of vitamins and minerals, especially calcium and vitamins A and C. It helps with the digestion of proteins and stimulates the appetite.

NOTES Scarified unripe fruit of papaya is a source of papain, an antibacterial protease enzyme used as meat tenderiser and to clarify beer.

Carica papaya L.   family: Caricaceae

fan mu gua (Chinese); *papayer* (French); *Papayabaum, Melonenbaum* (German); *papiitaa* (Hindi); *papaia* (Italian); *papaiya* (Japanese); *betik* (Malay); *mamao* (Portuguese); *higo de mastuero* (Spanish); *loko* (Thai)

Carpobrotus edulis

sour fig

Sour fig leaves and flower

Sour fig plant

Sour figs

DESCRIPTION The sour fig or pigface is a succulent creeper with thick trailing stems and erect, angular, fleshy leaves. Large solitary flowers with numerous yellow petals are borne near the stem tips and turn into conical orange-brown fruit capsules with slimy fruit pulp containing numerous minute seeds. The common sour fig (*C. edulis*) is easily recognised by the yellow flowers that turn orange with age. The well-known *C. acinaciformis* has pink or purple flowers and is a popular garden succulent.

ORIGIN & HISTORY *Carpobrotus* species are indigenous to southern Africa and Australia, with one species in Chile and California. The edible *C. edulis* is indigenous to the Cape region of South Africa and is an important source of food for rural children, probably since ancient times. The ripe fruits have become popular food items in recent years and are now widely available on markets.

PARTS USED Ripe fruit capsules.

CULTIVATION & HARVESTING Plants are grown commercially on a small scale but most of the fruit are still collected from wild-growing plants. *Carpobrotus* species are commonly used in horticulture as hardy ground covers, often to stabilise sand banks along roads. Fruits are best harvested before they dry out completely and become tough and leathery.

USES & PROPERTIES The fruits are eaten fresh (by chewing off the narrow end and sucking out the slimy sweet-sour pulp). They are also used to make jam and have become a popular ingredient of Indian and Malay dishes. Some cooks prefer to use only soft fruits that have not yet dried out completely, so that the stalk and tough outer layer can easily be removed.

NUTRITIONAL VALUE The fruits supply modest quantities of vitamins, minerals and protein (2%). They are relatively low in energy (110 kcal per 100 g).

NOTES The astringent juice from leaves is gargled to effectively treat a sore throat.

Carpobrotus edulis (L.) L. Bolus   family: Mesembryanthemaceae

suurvy (Afrikaans); *figue marine* (French); *Hottentottenfeige* (German); *carpobrotus* (Italian); *balsamo* (Portuguese); *carpobrotus* (Spanish)

Carthamus tinctorius

safflower

Safflower leaves and flower heads

Safflower dried florets

Safflower seeds

DESCRIPTION An annual, thistle-like herb bearing spiny leaves and attractive flower heads with small, bright yellow, orange or red disc florets surrounded by rows of tough, spiny bracts. The fruits are small one-seeded nuts (achenes) that are pure white in colour and have little or no pappus hairs.

ORIGIN & HISTORY Safflower is not known in nature. It is an ancient crop plant that was probably developed in the Middle East (southern Turkey, Syria, Iran, Iraq, Jordan, Palestine and Israel). From here it spread to ancient India, Egypt, Sudan, Ethiopia and later to Europe and China. The main reason for its early popularity was the valuable red dye obtained from the dried flowers that was used to colour cloth (the pigment is carthamine). When synthetic aniline dyes were developed, the seed oil became the most important product.

PARTS USED Ripe seeds (one-seeded nuts, achenes); on a much smaller scale also the dried florets.

CULTIVATION & HARVESTING Safflower is grown as an annual oilseed crop in many parts of the world, including India, the USA, Mexico, Argentina, Spain, Ethiopia and Australia. The achenes ("seeds") are non-shedding and can be harvested mechanically, in much the same way as sunflower "seeds".

USES & PROPERTIES Edible oil is extracted from the small fruits (by cold pressing or solvent extraction). The oil may be polyunsaturated (used for soft margarines and salad oils) or monounsaturated (high oleic acid, used as cooking oil). The first type is popular in the health food industry because it has the highest linoleic acid content of any known seed oil. Dried flowers are used as a saffron substitute for colouring and flavouring rice dishes. A popular Jamaican spice contains safflower, chilli peppers and cloves.

NUTRITIONAL VALUE Refined oil has a high energy value (900 kcal per 100 g) and contains 75% linoleic acid.

Carthamus tinctorius L.   family: Asteraceae

hong hua (Chinese); *carthame* (French); *Färberdistel, Färbersaflor* (German); *cartamo* (Italian); *cártamo* (Spanish)

Carum carvi

caraway

Caraway flowers

Caraway plant

Ajowan and caraway fruits

DESCRIPTION Caraway is a biennial herb with feathery, bipinnately compound leaves and small white flowers arranged in umbels. The small brown fruits comprise two somewhat sickle-shaped halves (mericarps), each with five ridges, visible as thin, pale brown lines. A closely related herb is ajowan (*Trachylospermum ammi*), which has similar leaves but much smaller, more rounded fruits (usually referred to as "seeds"). This spice is sometimes called *ajwain, carom* or *omam* and is practically unknown outside India, the Middle East and North Africa.

ORIGIN & HISTORY Central Europe, the Mediterranean region and western and central Asia. It has become an important spice crop in many parts of the world. Ajowan is thought to be from southern India but it has been cultivated since ancient times in a broad region that stretches from North Africa and Egypt across Iran and Afghanistan to Pakistan.

PARTS USED The small, ripe fruits ("seeds").

CULTIVATION & HARVESTING Both caraway and ajowan are easily cultivated. In the second year, the ripe fruits are harvested when they turn brown.

USES & PROPERTIES Caraway is a spice with a peppery taste that has been used since ancient times in goulashes, sauerkraut, potatoes, stews, cheeses, breads, cakes and biscuits. In France, it is used to flavour *dragées* (sugar-coated almonds). It is an important ingredient of various alcoholic beverages, including aquavit, kümmel, schnapps and *Vespétro*. Ajowan has a characteristic thyme-like flavour and is widely used in Indian and Middle Eastern cooking, especially in curry dishes, bean dishes, pickles and chutneys. It is added to breads and biscuits, including the crisp Indian bread known as *pappadum*.

NUTRITIONAL VALUE Caraway and ajowan are both used in very small quantities as condiments.

NOTES The fruits and essential oil are used in traditional medicine for their carminative, stomachic, spasmolytic and expectorant properties. Ajowan has similar uses in India.

Carum carvi L.

family: Apiaceae

fang feng, se lu zi (Chinese); *carvi* (French); *shia jira* (Hindi); *Kümmel* (German); *carvi, cumino tedesco* (Italian); *karahe* (Japanese); *alcaravea* (Spanish)

Carya illinoinensis

pecan nut

Pecan nut leaves and fruits

Pecan nuts

Pecan nut male and female flowers

DESCRIPTION A large tree of up to 40 m in height, with pinnately compound leaves and inconspicuous, wind-pollinated flowers. Numerous tiny male flowers are borne in pendulous, three-branched catkins, while the slightly larger female flowers are arranged in small groups of up to ten in erect spikes. When mature, the green, fleshy fruit split open to reveal the smooth, brown, thin-shelled, single-seeded nut inside. Several *Carya* spesies (known as hickories) bear edible nuts but they are of limited commercial interest. Hickory timber is commonly used to flavour smoked fish and meat.

ORIGIN & HISTORY Indigenous to the southern part of North America (southern USA and Mexico). It was an important food item of the indigenous people and was commercialised relatively recently (in the eighteenth century). Several hundreds of cultivars have been developed and they are now grown on a large commercial scale in the USA, Mexico, Brazil,

Israel, South Africa and Australia.

PARTS USED The ripe seed (a bilobed brown nut).

CULTIVATION & HARVESTING Pecan trees are easily cultivated in a wide range of climates, from cold temperate to warm and tropical. Once established (usually as grafted trees) they are surprisingly drought and cold tolerant. Modern cultivars have large fruits with relatively soft shells. Harvesting is done by shaking the trees and sweeping up the nuts from the ground (nowadays mechanical tree shakers, sweepers and vacuum collectors are used).

USES & PROPERTIES The nuts are eaten raw or roasted and salted. They are particularly popular as an ingredient of ice cream, confectionery, biscuits, cakes, breads and especially pecan pie. Pecan nuts are closely related to walnuts (see *Juglans regia*) and resemble them in appearance and taste.

NUTRITIONAL VALUE The nuts have a high fat content (72%) and are relatively low in protein (10%). The energy yield is more than 700 kcal per 100 g.

Carya illinoinensis (Wangenh.) K. Koch   family: Juglandaceae

noix de pacane, pacanier (French); *Pekannuss, Hickorybaum* (German); *pacana, pecán* (Spanish)

Caryota urens
fishtail palm • toddy palm

Fishtail palm leaf

Fishtail palm   Palm sugar

DESCRIPTION A single-stemmed, large, erect tree bearing characteristic compound leaves (the only palm with bipinnate leaves) divided into distinctive fishtail-like leaflets and long drooping clusters of small flowers. The fruits are small, hard and inedible, being filled with irritant crystals. There are 12 species but only *C. urens* is an important and versatile food plant.

ORIGIN & HISTORY The large tropical region that stretches from India eastwards to Malaysia, Indonesia and Australia. It is commonly planted as an ornamental and street tree in most warm parts of the world. The wide diversity of traditional uses shows that this palm was probably of considerable importance to rural people as far back as ancient times.

PARTS USED The stem sap, young leaves and starchy stems.

CULTIVATION & HARVESTING Trees are somewhat weedy and are easily propagated from seeds. They are widely planted but are also wild-harvested on a large scale in rural areas of India, Myanmar and other parts of Malaysia and Indonesia. The flower clusters are cut off and the sugary sap that oozes out is collected – more than 20 litres can be collected per day from a single tree.

USES & PROPERTIES The sap is concentrated to produce palm sugar or it may be fermented to make palm wine or toddy (the latter may be distilled to yield a strong alcoholic beverage known as palm spirit or arrack). The starchy stems have been used as an emergency food and as a source of sago (see sago palm, *Metroxylon sagu*). Young leaves are edible.

NUTRITIONAL VALUE An important source of carbohydrates in rural areas (sugar from the sap and starch from the stems).

NOTES Kitul or kittool fibre (also known as Ceylon piassava) is collected from the leaf bases and is used for making brushes. The stems yield a useful timber and the leaves have become popular in Europe for use as florist greens.

Caryota urens L.   family: Arecaceae (Palmae)

dong zong (Chinese); *caryot brûlant, palmier céleri* (French); *Brennpalme, Fischschwanzpalme* (German); *mari* (Hindi); *palma cariota* (Italian); *palmera de sagú* (Spanish)

Casimiroa edulis

white sapote

White sapote flowers and fruit

White sapote trees

White sapote fruits

DESCRIPTION White sapote is a very variable small tree with trifoliate, gland-dotted leaves and small greenish-yellow flowers. The fruits are bright green and turn yellowish when they ripen. Although "white sapote" is the most commonly used vernacular name, some people call it the Mexican apple or *matasano*. This species should not be confused with black sapote (which is an unrelated plant – see *Diospyros digyna*).

ORIGIN & HISTORY The plant is indigenous to Mexico and Central America. It has become a minor crop and is cultivated in parts of Central America for its edible fruits. In other parts of the world it is practically unknown but experimental plantings have been made in many countries. It is fairly commonly grown as an ornamental tree in gardens and parks.

PARTS USED Ripe fruits.

CULTIVATION & HARVESTING The white sapote is exceptionally hardy and can withstand drought and cold. It is grown from seed or may be grafted onto a suitable rootstock. Several cultivars have been developed, mostly in California and Florida. The fruits are harvested in the period from May to August when they are mature but still hard.

USES & PROPERTIES The fruit flesh is greenish yellow or cream-coloured when ripe and has a delicate, bitter-sweet taste. In the taste and creamy consistency it is somewhat reminiscent of avocado. The fruit is eaten fresh and is used in fruit salads, preserves, milk shakes and various sauces. Peeled, seeded and diced fruit may be added to fruit curries and spicy salsa sauces.

NUTRITIONAL VALUE White sapote fruits contain about 30 mg of vitamin C per 100 g and are a source of niacin and minerals, especially calcium and phosphorus. They are high in sugar (about 20% of wet weight).

NOTES Extracts of the seeds have been used in Mexico as sedatives. The seeds have hypotensive and sleep-inducing effects.

Casimiroa edulis Llave & Lex.　　　　　　　　　　　　　family: Rutaceae

xiang rou guo (Chinese); *matasano, pomme mexicaine* (French); *Weiße Sapote* (German); *zapote* (Italian); *sapoti* (Portuguese); *sapote blanco* (Spanish)

Castanea sativa

chestnut • sweet chestnut • Spanish chestnut

Chestnut fruits and seeds

Chestnut leaves and flowers

Chestnuts

DESCRIPTION A large deciduous tree of up to 30 m in height bearing simple oblong leaves with markedly toothed margins (each tooth ending in a soft spiny tip). Male flowers are borne in slender spikes, while the spinescent female flowers are congested into a few-flowered, short clusters. The fruits contain three large, brown, edible nuts surrounded by a tough spiny capsule that splits open at maturity. Improved cultivars have a single, large nut (called *marrons* in France). Other species of *Castanea* used as commercial sources of edible nuts include Japanese chestnut (*C. crenata*), American chestnut (*C. dentata*), the North American *chinquapin* (*C. pumila*) and Chinese chestnut (*C. mollissima*). Sweet chestnut is sometimes confused with the inedible horse chestnut (*Aesculus hippocastanum*).

ORIGIN & HISTORY The tree occurs naturally from the Mediterranean region to the Caucasus. Chestnuts have a long history as human food and are still roasted and sold on the streets in Europe and the eastern Mediterranean. In Italy, chestnut polenta was made in Roman times before the introduction of maize.

PARTS USED Ripe, roasted or baked seeds (nuts).

CULTIVATION & HARVESTING Chestnuts are wild-harvested and also grown commercially in many parts of southern and central Europe, but France, Italy and Spain are the main producers.

USES & PROPERTIES Chestnuts are roasted and eaten as they are, or they are preserved by freezing, as unsweetened purée (often used in meat stuffings) or in sugar (then eaten as a sweetmeat, known as *marrons glacés* in France). The peeled seeds may also be boiled, grilled, braised or cooked and used as a vegetable or side dish. Chestnuts and chestnut flour are important in confectionery, patisserie and sweet desserts (such as the famous chestnut cream – *crème de marrons*).

NUTRITIONAL VALUE Chestnuts are low in calories and fats and are a good source of vitamins B and C.

Castanea sativa L.   family: Fagaceae

châtaignier (French); *Esskastanie, Edelkastanie* (German); *castagno* (Italian); *castaño* (Spanish)

125

Ceratonia siliqua

carob tree

Carob flowers (male and female)

Carob leaves and flowers

Carob pods

DESCRIPTION This is a medium-sized, evergreen tree of up to 15 m in height. It has a rounded crown and dark green, somewhat leathery, compound leaves. Inconspicuous male and female flowers are borne on separate trees. The oblong pods are flattened, tough and fibrous, with about ten hard seeds embedded in a soft, sugary pulp.

ORIGIN & HISTORY Carob is a cultigen derived somewhere in the Arabian Peninsula. It has been grown (and used as famine food) around the Mediterranean for centuries. The pods are supposedly the "locusts" that sustained John the Baptist in the desert. The seeds are exceptionally uniform in size and weight and are believed to have been the original carat weight that jewellers still use today.

PARTS USED Ripe pods and seeds.

CULTIVATION & HARVESTING Carob is grown from seed in many parts of the world. Ripe pods are harvested by shaking or beating them off onto canvas sheets with long poles.

USES & PROPERTIES Pods are eaten as a sweetmeat or the seeded pods are processed into either a thick molasses (by boiling) or a tasty flour, used as a chocolate substitute for making carob candy bars. The flour can also be enjoyed with hot or cold milk or mixed with wheat flour for baking bread, pancakes and other confectionery. A valuable tragacanth-like gum ('tragasol'), extracted from the seeds, is used as a stabiliser and thickener in ice cream, salad dressings, mustard sauces, processed meats, cheeses and numerous other food products. The seed residue yields a starch-free, sugar-free and high-protein flour for use by diabetics.

NUTRITIONAL VALUE Pods are rich in sugar (up to 50%) and the flour has more minerals and vitamins, less fat and fewer calories (180 kcal per 100 g) than chocolate made from cocoa powder.

NOTES Carob seed gum also has cosmetic, pharmaceutical and industrial uses.

Ceratonia siliqua L.

family: Fabaceae

caroubier (French); *Johannisbrotbaum* (German); *carrubio* (Italian); *algarrobo* (Spanish)

Cereus peruvianus

pitaya • cactus apple

Cactus apple plantation

Cactus apple fruit

Cactus apple plant with flowers

DESCRIPTION This is a large, tree-like (columnar) thorny cactus with thick, ribbed branches and showy white flowers that last for only one day. The fleshy fruit (technically a berry) is usually dark red or purple (rarely yellow) with a soft white flesh and numerous small, black seeds. *Cereus peruvianus* is often confused with *C. jamacaru* from northeastern Brazil. Perhaps the best-known cactus fruit is the prickly pear or Indian pear (see *Opuntia ficus-indica*) but other edible cactus fruits include the Mexican strawberry (*Echinocereus*), the *pitayo dulce* (*Lemaireocereus*) and the *pitahaya* or dragon fruit (see *Hylocereus undatus*). Young stems of *cadushi* (*Cereus repandus*) are despined and eaten as a vegetable.

ORIGIN & HISTORY The cactus apple is indigenous to Mexico and Central America but the exact origin has never been traced. It is a cultigen and traditional food source that has not yet been found in the wild. The plants have been cultivated for ornamental purposes in warm parts of the world since colonial times. Recently there has been renewed interest in cactus apples and they are now grown commercially on a small scale in the southern USA, Israel and Mexico. In Europe they are sometimes called "koubo" to avoid the word *pitaya* (which is close to *pitahaya*, the dragon fruit).

PARTS USED Ripe fruits.

CULTIVATION & HARVESTING Plants are easily propagated from stem cuttings or seeds and are planted in widely spaced rows. There is no need for costly trellising, an advantage over dragon fruit. Fruits are harvested when fully ripe.

USES & PROPERTIES The fruits are eaten fresh or they are variously processed into drinks, jams, preserves, jellies, syrups, frozen pulp, ice cream or dried pulp.

NUTRITIONAL VALUE The fruits contain about 10% carbohydrates and have an energy yield of about 45 kcal per 100 g. They also contain fair amounts of minerals and vitamins, including vitamin C.

Cereus peruvianus (L.) Mill. [= *C. repandus* (L.) Mill.]
family: Cactaceae

pitaya (French); *Apfelkaktus, Pitaya* (German); *pitaya* (Italian); *pitaya* (Spanish)

Chamaemelum nobile
chamomile • Roman chamomile

Roman chamomile plant

Roman chamomile flower heads

German chamomile

DESCRIPTION A perennial herb with much-divided, feathery leaves and large, white, often double flower heads. It is sometimes grown as a fragrant lawn or seat in herb gardens. The name chamomile is confusing as it is also used for the medicinally important *Matricaria recutita*, often referred to as German chamomile. This is an annual plant with slender leaf segments, easily identified by the hollow base of the flower head (solid in Roman chamomile).

ORIGIN & HISTORY Indigenous to the Mediterranean region, as well as southern and western Europe. It has a long history as a herbal tea, taken to alleviate stress and indigestion, and as a gargle for sore throat. Chamomile tea was a popular tonic in the Victorian era.

PARTS USED Dried flower heads or the essential oil.

CULTIVATION & HARVESTING Roman chamomile is commercially cultivated in Europe, the USA and Argentina. The flower heads are harvested and dried, or used as a raw material for the extraction of the essential oil by steam distillation.

USES & PROPERTIES The pale blue essential oil is used to flavour a wide range of beverages (including liqueurs and herbal teas), as well as confectionery and ice cream. The dried flower heads have a pungent, grassy flavour and are popular as herbal infusions, baths and tisanes. Small amounts of chamomile are sometimes added to herbal tea mixtures as a brightening agent.

NUTRITIONAL VALUE Used as flavourant only (large doses or regular consumption may be harmful).

NOTES Both types of chamomile are well known as medicinal plants. Roman chamomile is used as a sedative, antispasmodic and anti-inflammatory (the essential oil is used in aromatherapy), while German chamomile is antispasmodic, anti-inflammatory, carminative and antiseptic. With an annual consumption of 5 000 tons, German chamomile is by far the most important from a medicinal point of view.

Chamaemelum nobile (L.) All. (= *Anthemis nobilis* L.)   family: Asteraceae

camomille romaine (French); *Römische Kamille* (German); *camomilla romana* (Italian); *manzanilla romana* (Spanish)

Chenopodium bonus-henricus
Good King Henry

Good King Henry plant

Goosefoot (*C. album*)

Wormseed (*C. ambrosioides*)

DESCRIPTION This is a perennial herb of up to half a metre in height, with fleshy, triangular leaves and small green flowers. It is also known as "all good" and "blite". Other important *Chenopodium* species used as vegetables include fat hen, goosefoot or lamb's quarters (*C. album*), wormseed, *epazote* or *paiku* (*C. ambrosioides*) and the Mexican *yerba del zorillo* (*C. graveolens*) and *huauzontle* (*C. berlandieri* subsp. *nutalliae*). Another example from the same family is *orache* (see *Atriplex hortensis*). *Chenopodium album*, known as fat hen in Britain and lamb's quarters in the USA, is an important traditional vegetable in many parts of the world (including Europe) and is also a source of grain (pseudocereal) in North India. The common name "pigweed" is confusing, as it is used for both *Chenopodium* and *Amaranthus* species.

ORIGIN & HISTORY The plant is indigenous to Europe and has become naturalised in North America. Good King Henry (or good henry, as it was originally called) is an example of several weedy species of *Chenopodium* (listed above) that have been used for thousands of years as pot-herbs in diverse regions of the world. These herbs are nutritious and valuable as famine foods.

PARTS USED Fresh leaves or young inflorescences.

CULTIVATION & HARVESTING These weedy plants thrive in disturbed places. They are sometimes cultivated but are mostly wild-harvested.

USES & PROPERTIES Fresh leaves are cooked as a vegetable in much the same way as spinach or Swiss chard. Cooking should be brief, to ensure that the flavour and nutritional value are retained.

NUTRITIONAL VALUE Fresh leaves contain fair amounts of vitamins B and C, as well as folic acid. The protein content is about 5%.

NOTES In southern Africa, *C. album* is regularly confused with seedlings of the equally weedy but poisonous wild tobacco (*Nicotiana glauca*), often with fatal results.

Chenopodium bonus-henricus L.   family: Chenopodiaceae

bon henry (French); *Guter Heinrich* (German); *farinello buon-enrico* (Italian); *zurrón* (Spanish)

Chenopodium quinoa
quinoa

Quinoa flowers (white form)

Quinoa plants

Quinoa seeds (grains)

DESCRIPTION Quinoa is a weedy annual herb with an erect stem of up to 2 m in height and toothed, somewhat greyish leaves. Inconspicuous flowers are borne in dense clusters at the top of the plant and also in the axils of the upper leaves. The dry, seed-like fruit (achene) is about 2 mm in diameter and enclosed in a persistent calyx. A hard, shiny fruit wall surrounds each seed, which may be white to pale yellow, pink, orange, red, brown or black. Other important grains include kaniwa or *canihua* (*C. pallidicaule*), a frost- and drought-tolerant semi-weedy crop from high altitudes in southern Peru and northern Bolivia, and the Mexican *huauzontle* (*C. berlandieri* subsp. *nutalliae*) which is used both as a cereal and vegetable.

ORIGIN & HISTORY Quinoa has been the staple grain (pseudocereal) of the Inca people since ancient times. Archaeological remains date back to 5000 BC. It was gradually replaced by modern crops but made a comeback as a health food in the mid-1970s.

PARTS USED Ripe, dehusked seeds.

CULTIVATION & HARVESTING A yield of about one ton per hectare is typical in subsistence agriculture (but five times more with modern methods). Seed heads are harvested by hand, threshed and winnowed to remove the husk.

USES & PROPERTIES The seeds are traditionally cooked to produce a chewy, fluffy meal with a nut-like taste. They are also roasted, ground into flour, or turned into flakes, pastas, breakfast foods, tortillas, pancakes and puffed grains. The flour, mixed with wheat flour, is used for baking. Grains can be fermented into beer (*chicha*), a traditional Inca drink.

NUTRITIONAL VALUE Exceptional. The protein content (14–18%) and fat content are higher than in the major cereals. Quinoa is gluten-free but rich in lysine and methionine. Seeds have to be soaked, washed and rubbed to remove bitter saponins in the seed coat.

Chenopodium quinoa Willd.   family: Chenopodiaceae

quinoa, riz de Pérou (French); *Reismelde, Reisspinat* (German); *quinoa* (Italian); *quinoa, arroz miúdo do Perú* (Portuguese); *quínua, quínoa* (Spanish)

Chrysanthemum coronarium
garland chrysanthemum • tangho

Garland chrysanthemum flower heads

Garland chrysanthemum (Chinese form)

Garland chrysanthemum (Japanese greens)

Tansy leaves and flower heads

DESCRIPTION A strongly aromatic, annual herb with much-branched stems (up to 2 m). The bright green to silvery leaves are toothed in some cultivars or deeply dissected in others. Attractive pale yellow to orange flower heads are borne in large numbers. The numerous common names include *tangho, shungiku,* chopsuey greens, crown daisy, Japanese greens and edible-leaved chrysanthemum. It should not be confused with several other species of *Chrysanthemum* that are also used as food plants. The common or florist chrysanthemum (*C. x morifolium*) is used for herbal teas in China (known there as *ju hua*). Also similar is feverfew (*C. parthenium*), well known as a migraine prophylactic, and alecost (*C. balsamita*), once a flavourant of beer (hence "alecost"). Another relative is tansy (*Chrysanthemum vulgare*, formerly *Tanacetum vulgare*), also known as *tanaise* (French), *Rainfarn* (German) and *tanaceto* (Italian and Spanish). The bitter leaves are still used to some extent to flavour pastries, pies and marinades (especially in Northern Europe and Britain) and sometimes in natural medicine.

ORIGIN & HISTORY Indigenous to the Mediterranean region (once used as a garden ornamental). It has no history of food use in Europe but has become a popular vegetable in China and Japan.

PARTS USED Young plants (seedlings).

CULTIVATION & HARVESTING A hardy annual that can be grown throughout the year in warm regions. Seeds germinate very easily and are sown at regular intervals to ensure a continuous supply of seedlings. Young plants are harvested before they are 20 cm high.

USES & PROPERTIES The young shoots and leaves are cooked and eaten as a vegetable. They are also added to soups and stir-fries. All parts of the plant have a strong distinctive smell that does not appeal to all people.

NUTRITIONAL VALUE Leaves contain 3% protein and are reported to be rich in vitamins A and C.

Chrysanthemum coronarium L.   family: Asteraceae

tong hao, tong-mo (Chinese); *tangho* (French); *Kronenwucherblume* (German); *shungiku, shun giku* (Japanese); *chrysanthemo, tangho* (Italian)

131

Cicer arietinum

chickpea

Chickpea flower and fruit

Chickpea plant

Chickpeas

DESCRIPTION Chickpea is an annual herb with an erect or bushy growth form bearing compound leaves and white or violet-blue flowers. The swollen, oblong pods each contain one or two large seeds. The seeds are rough in texture, with a prominent beak at the tip. They are large and cream-coloured in the erect, white-flowered type (known as the Kabuli type) or smaller and dark-coloured in the bushy, violet-flowered type (Desi type).

ORIGIN & HISTORY This is an ancient cultigen that was domesticated at least 6 000 years ago. It was probably derived from *C. reticulatum*, a wild species that occurs in southeastern Turkey. Seeds have been found in several archaeological sites in the eastern Mediterranean region and the Middle East. It is said to have reached India in about 2000 BC, where it became a staple food (known as *gram*). It was spread to Latin America by Spanish and Portuguese explorers in the sixteenth century.

PARTS USED Ripe dry seeds.

CULTIVATION & HARVESTING Chickpea is the third most important commercial pulse in the world. It is easily cultivated as an annual crop but yields are relatively low.

USES & PROPERTIES The seeds are boiled, roasted or fried and have numerous culinary uses in Mediterranean, Near Eastern, Pakistani and Indian cooking (used in soups, sauces, stews, meat dishes, *couscous* and even salads). They are used as *dhal* or ground to make chickpea flour (*besan*), which has many uses in oriental confectionery (used to make *falafel* – deep-fried croquettes or balls of spiced, ground chickpea, often served inside a pita bread). Chickpeas are the main ingredient of *hummus*, a Middle Eastern dish or dip made from cooked chickpeas and sesame oil.

NUTRITIONAL VALUE Chickpea contains about 17% protein and up to 5% fat. It is used in health food as a meat substitute and to reduce cholesterol.

Cicer arietinum L.

family: Fabaceae

hummus (Arabic); *ying zui dou* (Chinese); *pois chiche* (French); *Kichererbse* (German); *chan* (Hindi); *ceci* (Italian); *hiyoko mame* (Japanese); *grão de bico* (Portuguese); *garbanzo* (Spanish)

Cichorium endivia

endive

Endives

Endive package

Single endive

DESCRIPTION Endive is a robust, lettuce-like, leafy herb with a rosette of green or red leaves that are simple, broad and with a slightly toothed margin, known as *escarole* or broadleaf endive (var. *latifolium*) or variously dissected and ornate, known as curly endive (var. *crispum*). The herb is rarely allowed to flower. The correct names for various species and forms of *Cichorium* are somewhat confused and should not be taken too seriously. Part of the confusion is that a variety of chicory, *C. intybus* var. *foliosum*, is used in the same way as endive. It has elongated, blanched leaves and is usually referred to as Belgium endive. This form is known (somewhat confusingly) as *chicorée* in French, *Salatzichorie or Chicorée* in German, *radicchio* in Italian and *archicoria* in Spanish. In Belgium it is known as *witloof*, and in the USA as blue sailor.

ORIGIN & HISTORY *Cichorium* is indigenous to the Mediterranean region and was developed into three distinct forms. Curly and broadleaf endive were known to the Greeks and were mentioned in the Bible; Belgium endive or *witloof* was developed in the mid-nineteenth century by the discovery that coffee chicory roots left in the dark sprouted white leaves. These blanched forms (*chicons*) resemble "cos" lettuce.

PARTS USED Fresh leaves.

CULTIVATION & HARVESTING Endive is grown in much the same way as lettuce. Belgium endive is blanched to produce an elongated, white, cabbage-like head.

USES & PROPERTIES The slightly bitter curly endive and broadleaf endive are used in the same way as lettuce. They may also be cooked and served as spinach. Belgium endive is served raw and thinly sliced in salads or may be cooked or boiled as a vegetable and served with a topping of cooked ham and cheese sauce.

NUTRITIONAL VALUE Endive is very low in calories but contains a moderate amount of vitamin C.

Cichorium endivia L.   family: Asteraceae

ku ju (Chinese); *endive* (French); *Winterendivie, Escariol* (German); *indiva* (Italian); *kiku jisha* (Japanese); *escarola* (Spanish)

Cichorium intybus

chicory

Chicory flower head

Chicory plant

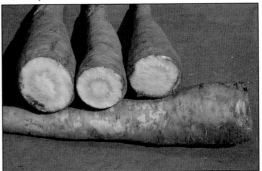
Chicory roots

DESCRIPTION Chicory is a robust perennial herb that produces a rosette of broad leaves in the first year and an erect, branched flowering stalk in the second year. Leaves and stalks have short hairs, while endive has no hairs. The attractive blue flower heads each comprises several small florets. Chicory grown for its roots is known as var. *sativum*, while the var. *foliosum* is used as a salad vegetable in the same way as endive (see *C. endivia*). Wild chicory (var. *intybus*) is used in traditional medicine as a bitter tonic, laxative and diuretic.

ORIGIN & HISTORY The plant is indigenous to Europe and Asia. It has been grown as a coffee substitute since the mid-eighteenth century, first in Italy and later in Germany. It has become a weed in southern Africa. Today, the main producers are in central and eastern Europe (France, Germany, Belgium, Holland and Poland).

PARTS USED The fleshy taproots.

CULTIVATION & HARVESTING The roots are harvested at the end of the first year of growth, in yields of up to 300 tons per hectare. They are washed, sliced, dried, carefully roasted in a controlled process and finally ground to a fine powder or processed to make a liquid extract (which is spray-dried).

USES & PROPERTIES Chicory is used as a coffee additive or coffee substitute. It is often blended with instant coffees but does not have the same aroma or stimulating effects of real coffee.

NUTRITIONAL VALUE Chicory is caffeine-free and is therefore of value as a health drink. The product contains inulin (50–60%) and bitter compounds (lactucin and lactupicrin), all of which are considered to have beneficial properties. Inulin is used as a sucrose substitute for diabetics.

NOTES During the roasting process of the dried roots, the inulin is partly converted to oxymethylfurfurol, which has a coffee-like aroma.

Cichorium intybus L.   family: Asteraceae

ju ju (Chinese); *chicorée* à café (French); *Wurzelzichorie, Kaffeezichorie* (German); *cicoria* (Italian); *kiku nigana* (Japanese); *achicoria* (Spanish)

Cinnamomum verum

cinnamon bark tree • Ceylon cinnamon

Cassia leaves

Cinnamon leaves, flowers and fruits   Cinnamon bark and cassia bark

DESCRIPTION A medium-sized, evergreen tree with bright green, opposite, leathery leaves, each with three prominent veins. Small white flowers are followed by oblong, dark purple fruits resembling small acorns. The tree was previously known as *C. zeylanicum*. It is sometimes confused with cassia (*C. aromaticum*) but this tree has alternate leaves and smaller, more rounded fruits. Cassia originated in Myanmar and the bark is an important commercial spice in China and Vietnam. Other types of cassia include Indonesian cassia (*C. burmanii*), Saigon cassia (*C. loureirii*) and Indian cassia (*C. tamale*).

ORIGIN & HISTORY Cinnamon originated in Sri Lanka (formerly Ceylon) and parts of India. It is one of the oldest of the spices and was popular in ancient Egypt, Rome and the Middle East (mentioned in the Bible and in Sanskrit texts). Today it is cultivated in practically all tropical parts of the world, with Indonesia, Sri Lanka, Seychelles and Madagascar as some of the major producers.

PARTS USED Inner bark (branches, coppice shoots).

CULTIVATION & HARVESTING Bark of cultivated trees is stripped (every two years), scraped to remove the outer bark and dried to produce the familiar tightly rolled, tan-coloured quills of commerce.

USES & PROPERTIES Cinnamon has a sweet aroma and a hot, spicy flavour. It is widely used in confectionery, puddings, custards, desserts and mulled wine. The spice is also added to sauces, meat dishes, stews, poultry, pickles and soups. Ground bark or extracts have numerous applications in bakery and food processing. Cassia bark has a stronger flavour than real cinnamon and is a cheaper substitute with similar culinary uses. In Southeast Asia and the USA, cassia is an everyday spice while true cinnamon is less often used.

NUTRITIONAL VALUE Unimportant, as cinnamon is a spice.

NOTES The flavour is due to cinnamaldehyde, the main component in the essential oil.

Cinnamomum verum J. Presl (= *C. zeylanicum* Blume)   family: Lauraceae

xi lan rou gui (Chinese); *cannellier, canelle de Ceylan* (French); *Ceylon-Zimtbaum* (German); *canella* (Italian); *seiron nikkei* (Japanese); *canela* (Portuguese); *canelo de Ceilán* (Spanish)

Citrullus lanatus

watermelon

Watermelon field

Watermelon plant

Watermelon

DESCRIPTION Watermelon is a climbing annual herb with deeply lobed, hairy leaves, coiled climbing tendrils and yellow, unisexual flowers (male or female). The fruit is a very large, rounded or oblong berry with a dark green to yellow rind (sometimes mottled or striped), yellowish or mostly red fruit flesh and numerous white to black seeds.

ORIGIN & HISTORY Watermelons originated in the subtropical parts of Africa. In the Kalahari Desert region of southern Africa, the San people used wild watermelon (known locally as *tsama* or *tsamma*) as an important water source during the dry season. In earlier times it was only possible to travel through this region during the *tsama* season. The fruit was domesticated in the Mediterranean region and India several centuries ago and later became popular in China, Southeast Asia, Japan and North America.

PARTS USED Ripe fruits (also the ripe seeds).

CULTIVATION & HARVESTING The plant is grown from seed in warm regions. Some of the numerous cultivars are seedless. Fruits are harvested when fully ripe, as they do not ripen further once cut off the vine.

USES & PROPERTIES This is a delicious fruit that is mostly eaten as a dessert. The fruit flesh is simply cut into slices and eaten, or may be variously shaped and added to fruit salads. In Asia, and especially China, ripe seeds are dried, roasted and eaten as a snack. Watermelon juice is nowadays available as a fruit juice (on its own or blended with others) and may be processed into a syrup or even wine.

NUTRITIONAL VALUE Watermelons have a very low energy value (30 kcal per 100 g) and are therefore popular amongst weight watchers. It has relatively low levels of sugar (7%) and moderate quantities of vitamins B and C. The seeds contain about 45% edible oil and 30–40% protein.

Citrullus lanatus (Thunb.) Matsum. & Nakai (= *C. vulgaris* Schrad.)　　　　　family: Cucurbitaceae

xi gua (Chinese); *pastèque* (French); *Wassermelone* (German); *cocomero* (Italian); *suika, shokuyou suika* (Japanese); *melancia* (Portuguese); *scandía* (Spanish)

Citrus aurantiifolia

lime

West Indian lime (*Citrus aurantiifolia*)　　Tahiti lime (*Citrus latifolia*)

West Indian limes　　Seedless limes

DESCRIPTION Lime or West Indian lime is a small tree with strongly aromatic leaves and white flowers. The small, greenish fruits (about 5 cm in diameter) turn yellow when they ripen and contain several seeds. This species is also known as Mexican lime or key lime. A second species (or variety) of lime is commonly found in markets. This is known as the Persian lime, Tahiti lime or seedless lime (*C. latifolia*). It is similar to the West Indian lime but the fruit is slightly larger (8–10 cm in diameter) and the fruit is seedless. See also makrut lime (*C. hystrix*) for further notes on limes and lime-like fruits.

ORIGIN & HISTORY The lime originated somewhere in Southeast Asia and had been grown as a crop in India and China for many centuries before it reached the West Indies and Mexico. Today it is cultivated in the West Indies, Mexico, Peru, Brazil, Egypt, Ivory Coast, India and South Africa.

PARTS USED Unripe or ripe fruits (also the leaves).

CULTIVATION & HARVESTING West Indian lime is one of only two *Citrus* species that are regularly propagated from seed rather than by grafting (the other is bitter orange, *C. aurantium*). The tree requires a tropical climate and is the most frost-tender of all *Citrus* species.

USES & PROPERTIES Limes, lime juice or lime peels are widely used in marmalade, jam, sorbet, chutney, pickles, salad dressings and desserts. Lime is particularly important in sauces, fish and meat dishes. The juice is popular as a drink and in punches and cocktails. The zest is used like lemon zest (see *C. limon*). West Indian lime leaves (dried or preferably fresh) are commonly used in Asian cooking (curries, sambals, chicken soup and fish dishes).

NUTRITIONAL VALUE Lime juice is low in energy and a good source of vitamin C (about 40 mg per 100 g).

Citrus aurantiifolia (Christm.) Swingle　　　　　　　　　　　　　　　　family: Rutaceae

lai meng (Chinese); *limette acide* (French); *Saure Limette* (German); *lima* (Italian); *lima ácida* (Portuguese); *lima, lima ácida* (Spanish)

Citrus aurantium

Seville orange • bitter orange • sour orange

Bitter orange fruits

Bitter orange tree

Bitter orange

DESCRIPTION A thorny tree of up to 10 m bearing gland-dotted leaves with a slightly winged petiole, fragrant white flowers and relatively large, rounded fruits with rough peels. *Citrus bergamia* (sometimes referred to as *C. aurantium* subsp. *bergamia*) is a smaller, thornless tree of up to 5 m in height.

ORIGIN & HISTORY Bitter orange originated in southeastern China and northern Myanmar, from where it spread to India and Japan. It first became popular in the Arabian empire and trees were planted in the Middle East and around the Mediterranean Sea as far west as Spain and Morocco. Sweet orange reached Europe much later. The main production areas are Spain (Seville, Malaga), southern France (Nice), Japan and China. Bergamot is of hybrid origin and is grown in Italy (Calabria) for the production of bergamot oil.

PARTS USED Ripe fruits (also the fruit rind, flowers and leaves for oil distillation).

CULTIVATION & HARVESTING Bitter orange is an attractive ornamental tree (erect growth form, thornier than the sweet orange, more resistant to drought and cold). Trees are grown from seeds (not by grafting) and are commonly used as a rootstock for other *Citrus* species.

USES & PROPERTIES Ripe fruits are mainly processed into marmalade and the peels are candied (crystallised). Extracts from the fruit are also used to flavour soft drinks and aromatic oil from the fruit rind is used in distilling famous liqueurs such as Curaçao, Cointreau and Grand Marnier. French cooks use bitter orange sauce (*sauce bigarade*) with roast duck.

NUTRITIONAL VALUE Unimportant. Fruits are inedible – they are sour (due to the high acid content) and very bitter (high levels of neohesperidin).

NOTES Bergamot oil is famous as ingredient of perfume (*eau de cologne*), developed in Cologne, Germany in 1676, and as flavourant in Earl Grey tea (produced since about 1830).

Citrus aurantium L.   family: Rutaceae

cheng, suan cheng, jin qiu, taitai (Chinese); *orange amère, bigarade* (French); *Bitterorange, Pomeranze* (German); *jeruk manis* (Indonesian); *arancio amaro* (Italian); *daidai* (Japanese); *naranja amargo* (Spanish)

Citrus hystrix
makrut lime • papeda

Calamondin

Makrut lime leaves

Makrut lime leaves

DESCRIPTION This is a small, thorny tree with distinctive leaves (the winged leaf stalk is the same size as the leaf blade itself), fragrant white flowers and small, pear-shaped fruits with a very rough, warty surface and almost no juice inside. Limes can be distinguished from lemons by the white flower buds (not purplish), thin fruit rinds and distinctive flavour. The two best-known limes are the Tahiti lime and West Indian lime (see *Citrus aurantiifolia*). Limes are sometimes confused with kalamansi or calamondin (*Citrus madurensis*) which has very small fruits (only 3–4 cm in diameter). These cumquat-like fruits remain extremely acidic even when ripe and are used to flavour Philippine dishes while the juice is a popular and refreshing drink.

ORIGIN & HISTORY The tree probably originated in Southeast Asia. It is cultivated over a large region that stretches from Sri Lanka through Myanmar, Thailand and Malaysia to the Philippines.

PARTS USED Leaves and green (unripe) fruits.

CULTIVATION & HARVESTING Makrut lime is easily cultivated in warm regions. Leaves and green fruits are harvested and sold fresh on local markets. Dried leaves (or the dried, powdered leaf) have become available in specialist shops all over the world but are considered a poor substitute for the fresh leaves.

USES & PROPERTIES Fresh leaves are used as a herb in Asian cooking, particularly in spicy Thai dishes (such as *tom yam* soup) that are becoming increasingly popular in western countries. In Malaysia, Thailand and Singapore, whole leaves are liberally added to soups and stews (in the same way as bay leaves) or they are finely shredded and mixed into salads, curries, soups and sauces. This lime is valued for its distinctive zest, and grated rind is commonly used in Asian dishes. The fruits have practically no juice and are inedible even when ripe.

NUTRITIONAL VALUE Unimportant (flavour only).

Citrus hystrix DC.   family: Rutaceae

ba bi da (Chinese); *limettier hérissé* (French); *Indische Zitrone* (German); *jeruk purut* (Indonesian); *limau purut* (Malay); *ma kruut* (Thai)

Citrus limon

lemon

Rough lemon (*C. jambhiri*)

Lemon leaves, flowers and fruits

Lemons

DESCRIPTION Lemon is a small, evergreen tree with purplish-white flowers and large, pointed fruits that turn yellow when they ripen. Lemons differ from limes in their purplish flower buds, usually larger fruits with a more pronounced point or nipple, relatively thick fruit rind and a somewhat sweeter taste.

ORIGIN & HISTORY Lemon originated in Asia (possibly the Punjab region of Pakistan and India) and is believed to be a hybrid between lime, citron and pomelo. It spread to China and Southeast Asia many centuries ago, and reached Europe and the New World only in the Middle Ages.

PARTS USED Ripe fruits.

CULTIVATION & HARVESTING Lemon trees (often grafted onto rough lemon, *C. jambhiri*) are grown commercially in practically all warm regions of the world. An advantage is that the tree flowers sporadically for a large part of the year, thus providing a supply of fruits over a long period. Under carefully controlled conditions, lemons can be successfully stored for several months.

USES & PROPERTIES Lemons are amongst the most useful and versatile of all fruits. The juice is used as an antioxidant to prevent browning of fresh fruit and vegetables. Lemon is used in salad dressings, vegetables, meat dishes, marinades, sauces, mayonnaise, and especially in fish and other seafood dishes. Juice (or lemon slices) is essential for various drinks (cocktails, punches, ice teas, alcoholic beverages and the famous lemonade) and also for ice creams and sorbets. The zest (the glandular outer peel, *flavedo*), obtained by peeling or grating, is used to flavour confectionery, tarts, mousses and creams. Candied peel is added to biscuits and cakes.

NUTRITIONAL VALUE Lemons are rich in citric acid (5%) and are one of the best sources of vitamin C (50–60 mg per 100 g). Lemon juice or "lime juice" was once an important remedy for scurvy on ships, hence the name "limey" for British seamen.

Citrus limon (L.) Burm.f.   family: Rutaceae

ning meng, yang ning meng (Chinese); *citron, citronnier commun* (French); *Zitrone, Zitronenbaum* (German); *limone* (Italian); *limão cravo* (Portuguese); *limonero* (Spanish)

Citrus maxima

pomelo • pummelo • shaddock

Pomelo leaves and flowers

Pomelo

Pomelo (shaddock) fruit

DESCRIPTION Pomelo is a medium-sized tree with very large leaves, flowers and fruits (the tree and all other parts are the largest of all *Citrus* species). The enormous, usually thick-skinned fruits (diameter up to 30 cm or more) are borne on drooping branches. The fruit flesh varies from yellow to red. Pomelo is often confused with grapefruit but the juice sacs or vesicles of pomelo are not fused together as in all other *Citrus* species. The leathery membrane of the fruit segment is easily peeled away and the flesh removed and eaten. Grapefruit is typically eaten with a spoon because the juice sacs are fused.

ORIGIN & HISTORY The pomelo is believed to have originated in southern China from where it spread throughout Southeast Asia. The numerous and variable cultivars are usually grouped according to origin: Chinese, Thai and Indonesian. Pomelo has always been popular in Asia but only recently in western countries. Shaddock is said to

be named after Capt. Philip Chaddock who introduced the fruit to the West Indies. It is the parent of several modern *Citrus* types, such as grapefruit (*C. x paradisi*) and tangelo (*C. reticulata*).

PARTS USED Ripe fruits.

CULTIVATION & HARVESTING Since the pomelo is the most tropical of all *Citrus* species, it is mainly grown in tropical and subtropical areas. Some modern cultivars however, are suitable for warm temperate regions as well. The fruits are picked when ripe and they store remarkably well.

USES & PROPERTIES The fruits are eaten raw as a delicious snack or added to fruit salads. In Asia, the peel is sometimes candied and the juice used for fruit juices or for alcoholic beverages.

NUTRITIONAL VALUE Fruits have a high sugar content (12%), contain some vitamin A and are an excellent source of vitamin C (about 50 mg per 100 g).

Citrus maxima (Burm.) Merr. [= *C. grandis* (L.) Osbeck]   family: Rutaceae

you, yu (Chinese); *pamplemousse* (French); *Pampelmuse* (German); *limau* (Indonesian); *pompelmo* (Italian); *buntan* (Japanese); *toronja* (Spanish); *somo, mao* (Thai)

Citrus medica

citron

Citron leaves and fruit

Citron flower and fruit

Citron fruits showing the thick rind

DESCRIPTION Citron is a shrub or small tree, rarely reaching more than 3 m in height. It has distinctive leaves: oblong-elliptic in shape, with prominent veins and small serrations along the margins. The fruit is medium-sized, often pointed, with a very thick, often warty rind, which represents up to 70% of the fruit weight.

ORIGIN & HISTORY The citron is historically interesting, as it is the first *Citrus* species that became known in the western world (around 300 BC). It is indigenous to the foothills of the Himalayas (northeastern India and northern Myanmar). From here it spread to the Middle East (especially the Media region – now part of Iran – after which it was named) and became known to the Greeks and Romans. The citron has religious significance. The 'Etrog' cultivar is used in the Jewish Feast of Tabernacles, while the 'Buddha's Hand' cultivar (a curious fruit divided into finger-like segments) is used in ceremonies in China and Japan (and is a source of medicine and perfume). Citron is one of the parents of the lemon (*C. limon*).

PARTS USED The fruit rind.

CULTIVATION & HARVESTING The tree is grown from seed or cuttings in frost-free regions. It is often grown in private gardens but on a commercial scale mainly in Italy (Calabria), France (Corsica), Greece, and on a small scale in Central America (Puerto Rico) and the USA (California).

USES & PROPERTIES The practically inedible fruits are used mainly to make candied citrus peel but are also popular for making jams and marmalade. The thick peels are soaked in brine to ferment before they are candied. This is an important ingredient of sweets, fruit cake and other confectionery. Citron is used in Corsica to make a liqueur known as *cédratine*.

NUTRITIONAL VALUE Candied citron peel is very high in carbohydrates (the sugar content is about 80%).

Citrus medica L.   family: Rutaceae

cheu yuan (Chinese); *cédrat* (French); *Zitronatzitrone* (German); *cedro, cedrone* (Italian); *bushukan* (Japanese); *cidra, cidrão* (Portuguese); *cidra* (Spanish)

Citrus paradisi
grapefruit

Grapefruits ('Rose' cultivar)

Grapefruit tree

Grapefruits ('Flame' cultivar)

DESCRIPTION Grapefruit is a relatively large tree bearing leaves with markedly winged stalks, fragrant white flowers and large rounded fruit in small bunches like grapes (not single as in pomelo). 'Marsh' is the most famous white cultivar, while 'Ruby', 'Star Ruby' and 'Flame' are examples of the red-pigmented type.

ORIGIN & HISTORY The grapefruit is believed to have originated in the Caribbean region as a hybrid between female pomelo (*C. maxima*) and male sweet orange (*C. sinensis*). It was taken to Central America and from there to the USA where it became an important fruit crop for USA markets. Since World War II it has also been exported to Europe as a breakfast food.

PARTS USED Ripe fruits.

CULTIVATION & HARVESTING Grapefruit requires prolonged periods of high temperature to achieve maximum flavour, sweetness and colour. The choice of rootstock is also important. Grapefruits can be kept on the trees for a considerable period before they are harvested.

USES & PROPERTIES The sweet-sour and slightly bitter fruits are cut in half and served for breakfast or as *hors d'oeuvre* (eaten with a special curved knife or special spoon with a serrated cutting edge). It is a tasty dessert when sprinkled with sugar, briefly grilled and decorated with a glazed cherry. The flesh or juice is also added to cocktails, fruit salads, ice creams and confectionery in the same way as sweet orange. The juice is very popular as a cold drink. Grapefruit may be used in chicken and pork dishes in the same way as pineapple.

NUTRITIONAL VALUE Low in energy (40 kcal per 100 g), rich in potassium and vitamins A and B but relatively low in vitamin C (35 mg per 100 g).

NOTES The red pigment in grapefruit is not anthocyanins (as in blood oranges) but lycopene, the red carotenoid and antioxidant found in tomatoes.

Citrus x paradisi Macfad.   family: Rutaceae

pu tao you, xi you (Chinese); *pamplemoussier* (French); *Grapefruit* (German); *pampelino* (Italian); *gureepufuruushu* (Japanese); *pomelo, toronja* (Spanish)

Citrus reticulata

mandarin • tangerine • naartjie

Mandarin fruiting branches

Mandarin fruits

Minneola (minneola tangelo) fruits

DESCRIPTION This is a small tree with dark green leaves, white fragrant flowers and small, broad fruit. All mandarins are easily recognised by the loose segments and fruit wall that is easily peeled away by hand. The numerous types include the common mandarin or tangerine (*C. reticulata*), the satsuma mandarin or *unshiu mikan* (*C. unshiu*), Mediterranean mandarin (*C. deliciosa*), king mandarin (*C. nobilis*) and various others types. Hybrids include tangors (tangerine × sweet orange) and tangelos (tangerine × grapefruit). One of the best-known tangelos is 'Minneola' or minneola tangelo, while the large-fruited Jamaican 'Ugli' has become popular in Canada and Europe. Amongst the common mandarins, the 'Clementine' type (clementine mandarin) is particularly popular.

ORIGIN & HISTORY Believed to be indigenous to northeastern India or southwestern China, where it has been grown at least since 1000 BC. It spread to other parts of Asia (including Japan, where it became popular as long ago as AD 1000) and reached Europe in the early 1800s.

PARTS USED Ripe fruits.

CULTIVATION & HARVESTING Trees are fairly cold resistant and are cultivated in China, Japan, the Mediterranean region, the USA, and parts of South America and southern Africa. The fruiting season is very short and harvesting has to be well timed to ensure optimum fruit quality.

USES & PROPERTIES Mandarins are mainly eaten raw and are appreciated for their sweet flavour and ease of peeling. The fresh juice has become popular as a cold drink and the fruit is used to some extent for jams, marmalades, preserves, cooking and confectionery in the same way as sweet orange. The peel is used to flavour liqueurs, confectionery and sweet potatoes.

NUTRITIONAL VALUE Rich in vitamin A (400 units per 100 g) and a good source of calcium, potassium and vitamin C (30 mg per 100 g). The sugar content is about 8% (40 kcal per 100 g).

Citrus reticulata Blanco

family: Rutaceae

nartjie (Afrikaans); *chu, ju, chieh* (Chinese); *mandarine, mandarinier* (French); *Mandarine* (German); *santara, suntara* (Indian); *mikan* (Japanese); *mandarino* (Italian); *mandarino* (Spanish)

Citrus sinensis

sweet orange

Sweet orange trees

Sweet orange flowers and fruits

Sweet oranges ('Valencia')

DESCRIPTION The sweet orange is a small tree with fragrant flowers and medium-sized, rounded fruits varying from light to deep orange. Four groups of cultivars are recognised: common oranges such as 'Valencia'; navel oranges such as 'Washington', which have a characteristic "navel" (a rudimentary second fruit visible on the flower side of the fruit); blood oranges such as 'Sanguinello', 'Moro' and 'Tarocco' (red flesh pigmented with anthocyanins); sugar oranges such as 'Succari' (commonly grown in Egypt), which are acidless but with a bland flavour.

ORIGIN & HISTORY Southern China (cultivated for thousands of years). It spread to the Mediterranean region around 1450, and from there to all warm parts of the world. Today the sweet orange is considered to be the most popular of all fruits.

PARTS USED Ripe fruits.

CULTIVATION & HARVESTING Oranges are propagated by grafting them onto a suitable rootstock. Trifoliate orange (the deciduous and cold-hardy *Poncirus trifoliata*) is often used.

USES & PROPERTIES Oranges are mostly eaten fresh or are processed into orange juice (used in a wide range of drinks, syrups, sodas, orangeade, punches, fruit wines and liqueurs). Navel oranges are not suitable for juice due to delayed bitterness. Oranges or candied peel have countless applications in desserts, fruit salads, creams, mousses, sorbets, confectionery, marmalades, jams, filled sponges (including the famous *orangine*), cakes and biscuits. Many famous fish and meat dishes call for oranges as an essential ingredient.

NUTRITIONAL VALUE Exceptional. The low energy value (40 kcal per 100 g) is combined with high levels of vitamin C (50–70 mg per 100 g), vitamin A (200–250 units) and potassium (200 mg).

NOTES The delayed bitterness of navel orange juice is caused by a slow release of limonin, an extremely bitter compound. Bitterness in grapefruit and sour orange is due to respectively naringin and neohesperidin.

Citrus sinensis (L.) Osbeck

family: Rutaceae

tian cheng, guang gan (Chinese); *oranger doux* (French); *Apfelsine, Orange* (German); *arancio dolce, arancio* (Italian); *orenji* (Japanese); *laranjeira* (Portuguese); *naranjo dulce* (Spanish)

Cocos nucifera

coconut

Coconut tree

Coconuts

DESCRIPTION A large palm (30 m in height but 10 m in dwarf cultivars) with a single stem and about 30 large, feathery leaves. Male and female flowers are borne separately in large clusters. The fruits (coconuts) have a smooth outer skin, a fibrous region and an inner hard shell which encloses the nut. Each nut has a white fleshy endosperm with a hollow cavity filled with watery white liquid (coconut milk).

ORIGIN & HISTORY From the Malesian region (between Southeast Asia and the Western Pacific) it spread to the Pacific and Indian Ocean islands some 3 000 years ago. Portuguese and Spanish explorers took coconuts to all tropical regions. Coconut is a major source of oil and countless by-products (including glycerine for explosives).

PARTS USED The nut (oily endosperm, embryo and milk), sugary sap, immature flower and bud (palm heart).

CULTIVATION & HARVESTING The world production of 40 billion nuts comes mainly from Indonesia, the Philippines, India and Sri Lanka. Harvesting and processing is labour intensive.

USES & PROPERTIES Edible coconut oil (coconut butter) is extracted from the dried, oily endosperm (copra) and is used to manufacture ghee, margarine, ice cream, imitation dairy products and chocolate. Dried coconut and coconut flour is used in confectionery (biscuits, cakes); fresh endosperm is used in Indonesian and Polynesian vegetable, fish and meat dishes. Coconut milk (a refreshing drink obtained from unripe nuts) adds flavour to Indian curries, stews and rice. Coconut cream is a marinade for meat and may be added to desserts and pastries. Sugary sap, tapped from flowering stalks, gives palm sugar, palm wine and palm vinegar. Palm heart is a popular vegetable (*ubod* in the Philippines).

NUTRITIONAL VALUE The endosperm is rich in saturated, cholesterol-free fat (370 kcal per 100 g fresh weight) and contains sugars, potassium and phosphorus.

Cocos nucifera L.   family: Arecaceae (Palmae)

cocotier (French); *Kokospalme* (German); *kelapa* (Indonesian); *kelapa* (Malay); *cocotero* (Spanish); *maphrao on* (Thai)

Coffea arabica

coffee tree • Arabian coffee

Coffee tree with fruit

Coffee flowers

Coffee beans

DESCRIPTION A shrub or small tree with shiny green leaves, fragrant white flowers and clusters of round, two-seeded drupes that turn red or purple when they ripen. Two tropical African species of minor commercial importance are *C. canephora* (robusta or Congo coffee), used mainly for instant coffee and *C. liberica* (Liberian or Abeokuta coffee) used to add a bitter flavour to blends.

ORIGIN & HISTORY Arabian coffee is indigenous to Ethiopia. The habit of coffee drinking appears to be a relatively new one. Between AD 1400 and AD 1700 Arabia (Yemen) maintained a monopoly but today coffee is grown in all tropical regions, with Brazil and Colombia as main producers.

PARTS USED Seeds ("coffee beans").

CULTIVATION & HARVESTING Coffee thrives only in tropical climates. Ripe fruits are treated to remove the two seeds from the fleshy outer layer and bony inner layer.

USES & PROPERTIES Roasted beans are ground shortly before the coffee is made (or vacuum-packed). Mocha, Bourbon and Martinique are amongst the most popular types (sometimes flavoured with vanilla or cinnamon). Instant coffee is produced by spray-drying or freeze-drying (since 1930, also decaffeinated coffee). Traditional methods give either Turkish coffee or filter coffee. *Espresso* is strong, black, Italian-style coffee made by passing steam through ground coffee; *cappuccino* is strong black coffee to which frothy cream or milk is added (often served with a sprinkling of cocoa powder). White coffee is made by adding a teaspoon of whipped cream without stirring, while the French *cafe au lait* is coffee made with milk. Coffee is used in desserts, confectionery, ice cream and liqueurs such as Tia Maria.

NUTRITIONAL VALUE Coffee contains some nutrients (niacin and potassium) but is mainly drunk for the taste and stimulating effects (resulting from the 150 mg of caffeine in a typical cup of coffee). Caffeine is addictive and excessive amounts may lead to insomnia and indigestion.

Coffea arabica L.

family: Rubiaceae

ka fei shu (Chinese); *cafeier d'Arabie* (French); *Kaffeestrauch* (German); *caffe* (Italian); *arabika koohii* (Japanese); *café* (Portuguese); *cafeto* (Spanish); *kafae* (Thai)

Coix lachryma-jobi

adlay • Job's tears

Job's tears plant

Job's tears

Job's tears grains

DESCRIPTION This is a grass of up to 2.5 m in height. It has broad leaves and characteristic inflorescences that arise from a bead-like structure (involucre) that encloses a single female spikelet with two fertile flowers. These bead-like structures are hard, shiny and porcelain-like and are usually grey in colour but may vary from white to black. They are used to make necklaces and rosaries. The cultivated form of the species, referred to as adlay (or Chinese pearl barley in the USA), has more papery involucels that are persistent and edible.

ORIGIN & HISTORY The plant is grown as a cereal over a large area in southern Asia and Southeast Asia, from Assam in India to Malaysia and the Philippines. The history of the crop is poorly recorded but domestication may have occurred in the Philippines, where the greatest diversity is found today.

PARTS USED The one-seeded nut (grain).

CULTIVATION & HARVESTING The crop is adapted to tropical climates and is mainly used in subsistence agriculture. The grain is harvested and winnowed in the same way as other cereals. The plants and plant remains are used as animal feed. Under favourable conditions, yields of about 4 tons per hectare can be expected.

USES & PROPERTIES The grain is usually boiled in the same way as rice and is added to soups and stews. It may also be milled to produce flour for bread baking or can be fermented to produce beer and wine. Dehusked grains are sold as a health food in the USA.

NUTRITIONAL VALUE Adlay flour contains more than 50% starch, 14% protein and 6% fat. Fresh seeds have an energy value of 389 kcal per 100 g.

NOTES Seeds (*yi yi jan*) are used in Chinese traditional medicine as a tonic to treat a wide range of ailments. They are claimed to have sedative and painkilling effects.

Coix lachryma-jobi L.   family: Poaceae

chuan gu (Chinese); *larmes de Job, herbe à chapeles* (French); *Hiobsträne* (German); *lacrima di Giobbi, erba da corone* (Italian); *juzudama* (Japanese); *lágrimas de Job* (Spanish)

Cola acuminata

cola nut tree • abata kola

Abata cola leaves

Abata cola fruit

Abata cola seed

DESCRIPTION Cola or kola is a tree of up to 15 m in height bearing large leaves and yellow flowers in clusters. The seeds or nuts are produced in large, multi-seeded pods (technically follicles). A second species of commercial importance is gbanja cola (*C. nitida*, previously known as *C. vera*). This plant has narrower leaves and the flowers are larger, pale yellow and streaked with purple. When the seed coat or testa is removed, the seed of *C. acuminata* splits into about four irregular pieces, while that of *C. nitida* splits in two. Two lesser-known species are bamenda cola (*C. anomala*) and owé cola (*C. verticillata*).

ORIGIN & HISTORY Cola nuts are indigenous to West Africa. *C. acuminata* is indigenous to Congo, Nigeria, and Gabon, while *C. nitida* grows naturally in Ashanti, the Ivory Coast and Sierra Leone. Both species are cultivated in Nigeria, tropical America and Indonesia. Fresh seeds have been used since ancient times for chewing, as they produce a stimulating effect.

PARTS USED Ripe seeds, known as cola nuts.

CULTIVATION & HARVESTING Seeds are harvested from plantations and are also wild-harvested to some extent. After removal of the seed coat, the seeds or seed segments are dried.

USES & PROPERTIES Cola nuts have been used to flavour cola soft drinks but are now largely supplanted by synthetic products. The stimulating effects of the nuts are ascribed to large amounts (1.5–3%) of caffeine and much smaller amounts of theobromine.

NUTRITIONAL VALUE Unimportant, as cola nuts are used in small amounts. They have, however, some health benefits when used in moderation. Seeds or extracts are used to treat mental and physical fatigue and are considered useful as a tonic (mild diuretic effects, secretion of gastric juices is stimulated). People suffering from ulcers or hypertension should restrict their intake of caffeine.

Cola acuminata (Pal.) Schott & Endl.   family: Sterculiaceae

colatier (French); *Kolabaum* (German); *cola* (Italian); *cola* (Spanish)

Colocasia esculenta

taro • cocoyam

Taro plant

Taro tubers (African cultivar)

Taro tubers (Chinese cultivar)

DESCRIPTION Taro is a robust herb with very large, peltate leaves on long stalks, arising from a thick tuber below the ground. The plant rarely flowers as it has been vegetatively propagated for centuries. Various cultivars and forms are known, including some with purple leaves (or purple veins) that are popular as ornamental plants. Other common names include taro potato, eddoe, dasheen, *kalo* (Pacific), *kolkas* (Egypt) and *kolokassi* (Cyprus).

ORIGIN & HISTORY Taro is thought to be indigenous to India but it has been cultivated in Southeast Asia for 10 000 years. It is associated with the ancient irrigation terraces for rice. The crop is also grown in the Pacific region and was distributed to the Middle East, Egypt and Mediterranean region in Greek and Roman times. Spanish and Portuguese explorers carried taro to Africa and the New World.

PARTS USED Tubers (also the young leaves).

CULTIVATION & HARVESTING Plants are easily grown from the tubers by division. They thrive in warm, moist places. The tubers are simply dug up.

USES & PROPERTIES Taro is a staple food in many tropical countries. It is cooked like potatoes or may be processed in various ways (boiled, fried like French fries, cooked *au gratin,* cooked in curries or used in desserts). Taro paste, allowed to ferment, is the well-known *poi* of Hawaii (called *poe* in Tahiti). Grated raw taro is used in Haiti to make various *acras* (savoury fritters with mixed vegetables or fish). Steamed taro balls (stuffed with meat and then fried) are popular in China. The Japanese add taro to vegetable stews. Leaves are used in Asian cooking to wrap other ingredients (known as *pateria*).

NUTRITIONAL VALUE Taro has a high energy value (107 kcal per 100 g). The very small starch grains are easily digested. It is a good source of vitamin C, phosphorus and iron.

Colocasia esculenta (L.) Schott (= *C. antiquorum* Schott)   family: Araceae

yu, yu tou (Chinese); *colocasie* (French); *Taro, Zehrwurz* (German); *aivi* (Indian); *talas* (Indonesian); *taro* (Italian); *sato imo* (Japanese); *daun keladi* (Malay); *malanga, taro* (Spanish); *amadumbe* (Zulu)

Corchorus olitorus
melokhia • Jew's mallow

Melokhia leaves and flower

Corchorus tridens

Corchorus asplenifolius

DESCRIPTION Melokhia is a much-branched, annual or short-lived perennial herb of up to 1.2 m in height. It has distinctive serrated leaves, with the lowermost teeth on either side elongated into slender appendages. The small, pale yellow flowers develop into cylindrical fruit capsules. The plant is better known as a fibre crop (nalta jute, tussa jute or tossa jute). Jute (*C. capsularis*) is a closely related fibre crop of Chinese origin. Several *Corchorus* species (*C. tridens, C. asplenifolius*) are used as vegetables in rural areas in Africa, Asia and China.

ORIGIN & HISTORY Melokhia is thought to be indigenous to India but it is widely distributed in all tropical regions of the world, where it served as a vegetable and pot-herb for centuries. Its use for fibres is a recent development (substitute for hemp).

PARTS USED Young leaves (stems are a source of fibre).

CULTIVATION & HARVESTING In rural areas, the leafy branches are gathered from wild or semi-domesticated plants but the plant is grown as a vegetable crop in Egypt, Syria and Israel. When grown as a fibre crop, the stems are cut and tied into bundles, left for a few days to shed the leaves and then retted in stagnant water to free the fibres.

USES & PROPERTIES Leaves are eaten raw or more often cooked like spinach. Melokhia is best known as an ingredient of a thick soup, *molokhyia*, which is a national dish in Egypt. The soup is made from fatty beef stock with fried onions, garlic, coriander and chopped melokhia leaves. It may be thickened with rice and is sometimes served with lemon juice.

NUTRITIONAL VALUE The herb is very nutritious. It is an excellent source of minerals (especially calcium, magnesium and iron), has high levels of vitamins A and C, as well as moderate quantities of phosphorus and protein.

Corchorus olitorius L.   family: Tiliaceae

mélochie (French); *Langkapseljute* (German); *yute* (Spanish)

Coriandrum sativum

coriander • cilantro

Coriander leaves (cilantro, Chinese parsley)

Coriander leaves and flowers

Coriander fruits (two types)

DESCRIPTION An annual herb with aromatic leaves and pale pink flowers arranged in characteristic umbels (the enlarged outer petals result in a daisy-like appearance). The lower leaves (broad and toothed) are quite different from the upper ones, which are finely divided and feathery. When dry, the small, round fruits (often wrongly referred to as "seeds") split into two halves.

ORIGIN & HISTORY Coriander originated in the eastern Mediterranean region and western Asia. It has been widely grown in all parts of the world as a spice and as a culinary herb for centuries.

PARTS USED Dried fruits as spice (coriander); fresh leaves as herb (cilantro or Chinese parsley).

CULTIVATION & HARVESTING Coriander is easily grown from seed. Young plants are gathered, roots and all, for use as herb. When grown as a spice, the plants are left to mature and are harvested when the fruits are mature but slightly green.

USES & PROPERTIES The distinctive flavour of coriander leaves (known as cilantro in the Americas or as Chinese parsley elsewhere) is an indispensable ingredient in many Asian, Indian, Middle Eastern, Mexican and Spanish American dishes. Leaves are used as a flavour ingredient and garnish (especially in salsas, guacamole and with fish) and have also become popular in western countries. They have a peculiar "bedbug" smell that some people love and others hate. Coriander fruits ("seeds") are a well-known spice used since ancient times in meat dishes, pickles, marinades, vegetable dishes and soups. They are especially important in Asian and Indian cooking and are an indispensable ingredient of curry powder and many other spice mixtures. Coriander is used in confectionery (bread, cakes, biscuits) and to flavour gin and liqueurs such as Chartreuse and Izarra. Coated with sugar, they were once sold as coriander comfits for chewing.

NUTRITIONAL VALUE The fresh herb is rich in calcium, phosphorus and vitamins A and C.

Coriandrum sativum L.   family: Apiaceae

hu sui, xiang sui, yan sui (Chinese); *coriandre, persil arabe* (French); *Koriander* (German); *dhania, dhaanya* (Hindi); *coriandro* (Italian); *ketumbar, daun ketumbar* (Malay); *coriandro, cilantro* (Spanish); *phak chee* (Thai)

Corylus avellana

hazelnut

Hazelnut leaves

Young hazelnuts

Hazelnuts

DESCRIPTION Hazelnut is a shrub or small tree of up to 6 m in height with round, markedly toothed leaves. Male and female flowers are borne on separate trees. The yellowish male flowers are grouped in slender, hanging catkins; the female flowers in small erect groups, each surrounded by a conspicuous leafy husk (involucre) that persists and surrounds the hard brown nuts. The filbert (*C. maxima*) has larger nuts and longer involucres that cover most of the nut and is usually considered to be merely a variety or cultivar of hazelnut. Of less commercial importance are the American hazelnut (*C. americana*) and the Turkish hazelnut (*C. colurna*). Somewhat similar (but unrelated) is the European beechnut (*Fagus sylvatica*), a minor source of good quality oil.

ORIGIN & HISTORY Hazelnuts are indigenous to Europe and Asia (*C. avellana*) or southeastern Europe (*C. maxima*) and have been used as human food since prehistoric times. The nuts were cultivated by the Romans and are now well known all over the world.

PARTS USED Ripe seeds (nuts).

CULTIVATION & HARVESTING Nuts are wild-harvested or are cultivated commercially in temperate countries (mainly Spain, France, Italy and Turkey). Harvesting takes place in the autumn and the nuts are sold either as fresh nuts (with their husks intact) or dried for later use.

USES & PROPERTIES Hazelnuts have become popular dessert nuts that may be roasted and salted. Their main use is in sweetmeats, chocolates and confectionery (cakes, pastries and biscuits). Whole or grated hazelnuts are used to some extent in cooking, especially chicken, fish dishes, stuffings and stews. Ground nuts are used to flavour butter or the extracted oil may be used as salad dressing.

NUTRITIONAL VALUE The nuts have a high energy value (650 kcal per 100 g) and are rich in fat (60%), vitamin E, minerals and amino acids.

Corylus avellana L.   family: Betulaceae

noisetier, coudrier (French); *Haselnuss, Haselstrauch* (German); *nocciola* (Italian); *aveleira* (Portuguese); *avellana* (Spanish)

Crambe maritima

seakale

Seakale flowers

Seakale fruits

Seakale plants

DESCRIPTION A perennial herb with large, cabbage-like, grey leaves arranged in a rosette at ground level. A robust, branched flowering stalk emerges from the centre of each plant. The flowers are typical for the cabbage family – they have four white petals arranged in a cross (hence the old family name, Cruciferae). The rounded (globose), single-seeded, indehiscent fruits are unusual in a family where the fruit capsules normally split open to release the seeds. Species such as *C. hispanica* and *C. abyssinica* are cultivated for their seeds that are cold-pressed to obtain oil with industrial uses.

ORIGIN & HISTORY Seakale is indigenous to the coasts of western Europe and part of western Asia, where it grows along the shoreline close to the sea. The plant is a traditional food in England and Scotland. Cultivation was initiated in the eighteenth century and plants are often grown in botanical gardens in Europe.

PARTS USED Blanched (forced) leaves and flowering stalks.

CULTIVATION & HARVESTING Seakale plants are easily grown from seeds or more often from root cuttings. In early spring, the plants are covered with special seakale forcing pots (made from terracotta) to blanch them. Black polythene, sand or gravel may also be used for this purpose. The white or pale yellow (sometimes reddish) blanched leaves or flowering stalks (not unlike broccoli) are harvested before they unfold.

USES & PROPERTIES Blanched leaf stalks (with unfolded young leaf blades at the top ends) and the flower stalks (about 20 cm in length) are boiled and eaten like asparagus. They are dipped in butter or white sauce. The vegetable may also be enjoyed fresh as salad (with *vinaigrette*) or it may be sautéed with garlic. The flavour is slightly bitter and nut-like.

NUTRITIONAL VALUE Seakale is fairly low in energy value and in nutrients but contains small amounts of vitamin C.

Crambe maritima L.   family: Brassicaceae

chou marin (French); *Meerkohl* (German)

154

Crocus sativus

saffron

Saffron plants

Saffron leaves

Saffron flowers

Saffron (dried styles and stigmas)

DESCRIPTION A small bulbous plant with narrow leaves and funnel-shaped lilac-purple flowers, each with three stamens and three bright red style-branches. The ovary and fruit are borne below the ground. It is similar to *Colchicum* but the latter has six stamens and bears its fruit above the ground.

ORIGIN & HISTORY The species is indigenous to southern Europe and southwestern Asia but the cultivated form is a sterile cultigen believed to have originated in the eastern Mediterranean region. It has been grown as a spice and dye source since ancient times. The name is derived from *zafaran*, the Arabian word for yellow.

PARTS USED Only the stigmas and style branches inside the flower.

CULTIVATION & HARVESTING Saffron is cultivated mainly in Spain (the best product comes from Valencia) and also in Turkey, Greece, Italy, Iran, India and South America. The flowers are picked and processed by hand – about 150 000 flowers

are needed to produce 1 kg of dry spice.

USES & PROPERTIES The main use of saffron is as a reddish-yellow dye and flavourant for cheeses, butter, pastries and confectionery (such as the traditional Swedish saffron bread). It is most famous as an ingredient of French *bouillabaisse* and Spanish *paella*, as well as Indian rice and curry dishes. Saffron is used in *risotto*, mussels, white meats, tripe, stews and tomato sauces. The spice is added to various desserts, such as rice cooked in milk and semolina puddings. It is an ingredient of Chartreuse.

NUTRITIONAL VALUE Saffron is the richest known source of vitamin B2 and has medicinal properties but is used in food in small quantities. It is poisonous: 5 g may cause severe symptoms, while the maximum safe dose is 1 g per day.

NOTES Since saffron is very expensive, adulterants (or substitutes) such as safflower (false saffron) and turmeric (Indian saffron) are sometimes used.

Crocus sativus L.   family: Iridaceae

fan hong hua (Chinese); *safran* (French); *Safran* (German); *zafferano* (Italian); *safuran* (Japanese); *açafrão* (Portuguese); *azafrán* (Spanish); *ya faran* (Thai)

Cucumis anguria

gherkin • West Indian gherkin

Wild gherkin (var. *longipes*)

West Indian gherkin

Gherkin jam

DESCRIPTION West Indian gherkin is an annual with deeply lobed leaves, small yellow male and female flowers that are borne on separate plants (dioecious) and small, oblong fruits with conspicuous soft prickles. It is the only wild cucumber with prickly (aculeate) stems and leaf stalks, and is therefore easily distinguished from other, similar-looking African species. These include two perennials, *C. africanus* and *C. zeyheri* (both monoecious), of which selected non-bitter fruit types are used in the same way as *C. anguria*. Another is *C. kalahariensis*, a food plant of the San people in southern Africa. The fruits are inedible but the fleshy roots are a delicacy when baked or an important water source when eaten raw. The name "gherkin" is mostly used for small (immature) fruits of the common cucumber (*C. sativus*) that are pickled and should not be confused with the real gherkin (*C. anguria*).

ORIGIN & HISTORY Gherkin is a cultigen derived from a wild species that occurs in southwestern Africa. The wild form has bitter fruits with long spines and is known as *C. anguria* var. *longipes*. The West Indian gherkin was once thought to be indigenous to the West Indies but it was probably introduced there from Angola in the days of the slave trade. It has become naturalised in Brazil and is grown on a small scale in Central and South America, the USA and parts of Africa.

PARTS USED Immature or mature fruits.

CULTIVATION & HARVESTING Gherkin requires a warm climate and is easy to cultivate.

USES & PROPERTIES The fruits are pickled when young or are boiled and eaten as a vegetable. Whole, ripe gherkins are commonly preserved as jam and are served with tea or as dessert.

NUTRITIONAL VALUE The gherkin has a low energy value (unless it is preserved in sugar) and is only a modest source of minerals and vitamins.

Cucumis anguria L.

family: Cucurbitaceae

concombre épineux de Antilles (French); *Anguriagurke, Westindische Gurke* (German); *cocomero anguria* (Italian); *pepino-das-Antilhas* (Portuguese); *cohombro espinoso, pepino espinoso* (Spanish)

156

Cucumis melo

melon

Cantaloupe melon ('Pegaso')

Winter melon ('Honeychow')

Musk melon ('Galia')

DESCRIPTION The melon is a creeping or climbing plant with rounded, hairy leaves and small, yellow, male and female flowers borne on the same plant. The fruit is a large berry with a smooth or rough texture and aromatic, green or orange flesh, depending on the cultivar. There are three main cultivar groups: (1) musk melons (netted melons, nutmeg melons) have a characteristic network of pale-coloured, raised ridges on the yellowish or green fruit skin, salmon-orange flesh in many cultivars or green flesh (as in 'Galia' melons); (2) cantaloupe melons (the name derives from Cantalupo, a papal estate near Rome) have a rough or scaly skin but they are never netted. The flesh is usually orange (French 'Charentais' melon) or rarely green (Israeli 'Ogen' melon); (3) winter melons have a smooth, hard, usually white skin and a green flesh that is not so strongly scented. Included here are the popular 'Honey Dew' and the 'Spanish' melon.

ORIGIN & HISTORY The melon is indigenous to sub-Saharan Africa and the Middle Eastern region to Afghanistan. Domestication may have taken place in Asia, as ancient Chinese writings show that melons were an important crop in China at least 2 000 years ago. Cultivation in the Mediterranean region started only at the end of the Roman era. Major producers today are China, France, India, Spain, Turkey and the USA.

PARTS USED Ripe fruits.

CULTIVATION & HARVESTING Melons require a warm climate or are grown under glass.

USES & PROPERTIES Ripe fruits are usually eaten fresh as a snack, at the beginning of a meal (as *hors d'oeuvre* often served with air-dried ham) or as a delicious dessert, served on its own or with ice cream. They may also be cut into cubes and pickled like gherkins.

NUTRITIONAL VALUE Melons have a low energy value (30 kcal per 100 g) and contain some vitamins B and C.

Cucumis melo L.   family: Cucurbitaceae

xiang gua, tian gua (Chinese); *melon* (French); *Melone* (German); *melone* (Italian); *blewah* (Indonesian); *buah semangka* (Malay); *melāo* (Portuguese); *melôn* (Spanish); *taeng lai* (Thai)

Cucumis metuliferus

African horned cucumber • jelly melon • kiwano

Jelly melon fruits

Jelly melon plant

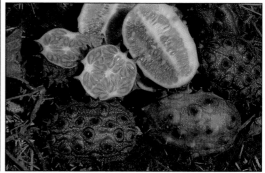

Jelly melons

DESCRIPTION The plant is an annual with creeping or climbing stems radiating from a somewhat woody (non-fleshy) root. Male and female flowers (very small and yellow) are borne on the same plant. The relatively large, ellipsoid fruits are yellow, orange or red in colour and have very distinctive, widely spaced, large conical protuberances (aculei) all over their surfaces. These prickles are blunt, about 10 mm long and 2–5 mm in diameter. The fruit flesh is green, translucent and somewhat mucilaginous, with numerous edible seeds similar to cucumber seeds.

ORIGIN & HISTORY African horned cucumber is indigenous to the woodlands and grasslands of tropical Africa, where it is commonly found as a weed of abandoned fields. It has become a weed in Australia (Queensland). Commercial cultivation of selected (non-bitter) types occurs on a small scale in South Africa and New Zealand. In New Zealand, the African horned cucumber is known as "kiwano", a registered trademark (the same applies to "kiwi fruit" – see *Actinidia*).

PARTS USED Ripe fruits.

CULTIVATION & HARVESTING Plants are easily grown from seed in the same way as cucumbers. They require a hot climate. Fruits are picked when they start to turn orange. They are also wild-harvested to some extent (taking care to select non-bitter types).

USES & PROPERTIES The fruits are used in salads or are eaten as a dessert fruit. They are peeled, sliced and flavoured with lemon juice, salt and black pepper according to taste. Puréed fruit may be served as a chilled soup. These exotic and attractive fruits are often used for table decorations.

NUTRITIONAL VALUE As is the case with other cucumbers and melons, the fruits comprise mainly water (more than 95%), with some minerals and vitamins B and C. They have low levels of sugar and therefore a very low energy value (10–15 kcal per 100 g).

Cucumis metuliferus E. Mey. ex Naudin   family: Cucurbitaceae

concombre africain (French); *Hornmelone, Stachelgurke, Kiwano* (German); *kiwano* (Italian); *kiwano* (Japanese); *pepino africano, kiwano* (Portuguese); *kiwano* (Spanish)

Cucumis sativus

cucumber

Cucumber plant

Cucumbers (Chinese cultivar)

Cucumbers and gherkins

DESCRIPTION The well-known cucumber is a creeping or climbing annual with large, pointed, three- to five-angled leaves, unbranched climbing tendrils and small yellow flowers. Male and female flowers occur on the same plant. The fruits are variable in shape, colour and degree of spininess. They are green when young but turn cream-coloured or brown when ripe. Some cultivars are seedless (parthenocarpic). The term "gherkin" is mostly used for the immature, pickled fruits but confusingly also for the West Indian gherkin (*C. anguria*).

ORIGIN & HISTORY Cucumber is thought to be indigenous to India (southern foothills of the Himalayas) and has been cultivated in western Asia for at least 3 000 years. It was well known to the ancient Greeks and Romans and reached China in the second century BC. It was introduced to the New World by Columbus in 1494.

PARTS USED Immature fruits (gherkins) or near-mature fruits.

CULTIVATION & HARVESTING Cucumbers are grown as a field crop in warm regions or more often under glass. Male flowers of the seedless types are mostly removed to prevent fertilisation (and the development of a bitter taste).

USES & PROPERTIES Cucumbers are eaten raw as a snack food in many parts of the world or are added to green salads, included in sandwiches or used with dips. They are often puréed for use in cold sauces, yogurt dishes and chilled soups. For use in hot dishes, cucumbers are peeled, the seeds are removed and the flesh sliced and blanched in boiling water for a few minutes. They are then cooked, baked, added to stews, sautéed in butter or stuffed, depending on the recipe. Young fruits are pickled in vinegar as gherkins, an important food item in many countries.

NUTRITIONAL VALUE Relatively low (12 kcal per 100 g), with modest amounts of protein, fat, minerals and vitamins B and C.

Cucumis sativus L.   family: Cucurbitaceae

huang gua (Chinese); *concombre* (French); *Gurke* (German); *khira* (Hindi); *ketimun* (Indonesian); *cetriolo* (Italian); *kyu uri* (Japanese); *timun* (Malay); *pepino* (Portuguese); *pepino* (Spanish); *taeng kwaa* (Thai)

Cucurbita ficifolia
fig-leaf gourd • Malabar gourd

Fig-leaf gourd (flowering and fruiting plant)

Various pumpkins and gourds

DESCRIPTION This relatively poorly known gourd is an annual or short-lived perennial with long trailing stems and prickly, deeply lobed leaves resembling the leaves of a fig tree. The flowers are yellow or pale orange, with blunt lobes and the fruits oblong to nearly globular and dark green (often with conspicuous white stripes or blotches). An unusual feature is the black seeds, embedded in white flesh. Other South American cucurbits include the *achocha* or *caihua* (*Cyclanthera pedata*), which is used in the same way as summer squash and the *casabanana* (*Sicana odorifera*) – young fruits are eaten but the inedible mature fruits are used as air fresheners (and to flavour a Nicaraguan drink known as *cojombro*). The Malabar gourd is similar to the West African egusi melon (*Cucumeropsis mannii*; = *C. edulis*), the seeds of which are eaten as a rich source of oil and protein.

ORIGIN & HISTORY Fig-leaf gourd is an ancient crop plant of the Inca people and has been an important and versatile vegetable in Peru, Mexico and other parts of Central America for at least 5 000 years. It has been grown on a small scale in Europe since about 1600 and today it is cultivated in South America, eastern Asia and India.

PARTS USED Immature fruits or seeds (occasionally the young leaves, shoots or flowers).

CULTIVATION & HARVESTING The crop is usually grown as an annual but it is perennial in frost-free areas. Surprisingly, there are no distinct cultivars.

USES & PROPERTIES Immature fruits are eaten like summer squashes. The fruit is used to prepare a kind of marmalade, may be candied and is fermented to produce beer. Seeds are roasted and eaten or are used in cooking. Young leaves, young shoots and flowers are cooked and used as vegetables.

NUTRITIONAL VALUE Similar to that of other pumpkins (see *C. maxima*).

Cucurbita ficifolia Bouché   family: Cucurbitaceae

courge à feuilles de figuier (French); *Feigenblattkürbis* (German); *zucca del Siam, zucca del Malabar* (Italian); *kurodane kabocha* (Japanese); *abóbora-chila* (Portuguese); *lacayote, chilacayote, cidra* (Spanish)

Cucurbita maxima

winter squash • pumpkin

Pumpkin 'Hubbard'

Pumpkin 'Crown Prince'

Pumpkin seeds

DESCRIPTION A trailing annual plant with soft, rounded stems (not angular and bristly to the touch) and rounded leaves (not pointed or deeply lobed). Male and female flowers are yellow, with rounded lobes that flare outwards. The fruit stalk is thick and cylindrical, soft and corky (very distinct from that of *C. pepo*). The fruits are extremely variable and include well-known cultivars like 'Hubbard', 'Golden Hubbard', 'Warted Hubbard', 'Crown Prince', 'Golden Delicious', 'Etamples', 'White Cheesequake', 'Queensland Blue', 'Sweet Dumpling' and numerous others. Pumpkins grown for show purposes (such as 'Show King') may weigh more than 180 kg (the largest of all fruits). The classification of pumpkins and squashes is complicated and is further confused by the terminology used to describe the fruits. For example, the terms winter squash, summer squash and pumpkin have been applied to fruits of different species. A summer squash is usually a fruit that is eaten in its immature state as vegetable, while a winter squash or pumpkin is usually large-fruited and left to mature before it is used.

ORIGIN & HISTORY *C. maxima* appears to have been domesticated in South America (Peru) from where it spread to Mexico and then to all corners of the earth.

PARTS USED Usually the mature fruits.

CULTIVATION & HARVESTING Pumpkins are easily grown from seeds but require exceptionally rich soil (often planted directly into manure or compost).

USES & PROPERTIES The yellow or orange flesh is cooked as a sweet vegetable or enjoyed as a soup. Diced pumpkin may be sprinkled with cheese and olive oil and grilled *au gratin* in a hot oven. Pumpkin is often used as a sweet pie filling (especially popular in the USA).

NUTRITIONAL VALUE The energy value is low (30 kcal per 100 g) but it is a good source of minerals, carotenes and vitamin A, with moderate quantities of vitamins B and C.

Cucurbita maxima Duchesne   family: Cucurbitaceae

sun gua, yang gua (Chinese); *courge d'hiver* (French); *Riesenkürbis* (German); *zucca* (Italian); *seiyou kabotcha* (Japanese); *abóbora-menina, abóbora-moranga* (Portuguese); *calabaza grande* (Spanish)

Cucurbita moschata

butternut • musky winter squash

Musky winter squash flower

Butternuts

Musky winter squash (Chinese cultivar)

DESCRIPTION A trailing or rarely upright annual with hard and angular stems bearing large, soft, shallowly lobed leaves, three- to four-branched climbing tendrils and yellow flowers (often with stalked bracts). The fruit stalk is typically angled and flared out where it joins the fruit. There are several cultivars, of which the butternuts are the best known. Examples are straightnecks such as 'Waltham Butternut', 'Zenith', and 'Ponca' or crooknecks such as 'Early Butternut' (a bush type). Some are also broad and flattened like other pumpkins (e.g. 'Large Cheese', 'Kentucky Field'). These are easily confused with the cushaw (*Cucurbita argyrosperma*, previously known as *C. mixta*). It combines characters of *C. moschata* and *C. maxima* but has a swollen hard corky stalk that is not flared where it meets the fruit and leafy bracts are absent. Both species have white-seeded and black-seeded forms. *C. argyrosperma* is best known for the cushaw and ayote type cultivars (including 'Green Striped Cushaw' and 'Tennessee Sweet Potato').

ORIGIN & HISTORY *C. moschata* was probably domesticated in hot humid lowlands of the southern parts of Central America and in the northern parts of South America, while *C. argyrosperma* seems to be of southern Mexican origin. Archaeological remains of *C. moschata* date back to 4900 BC (southern Mexico) and 3000 BC (coastal Peru).

PARTS USED Mostly the mature fruits.

CULTIVATION & HARVESTING *C. moschata* and *C. argyrosperma* require warm climates and have no cold tolerance. They are usually harvested when fully ripe and can be stored for long periods.

USES & PROPERTIES Butternuts are cooked and eaten as a vegetable (or used in numerous culinary applications – soups, stews, pumpkin pie and pumpkin fritters) in the same way as other squashes and pumpkins. The usually dark orange flesh is considered to be exceptionally tasty.

NUTRITIONAL VALUE See *C. maxima*.

Cucurbita moschata (Duchesne) Poiret   family: Cucurbitaceae

nan gua (Chinese); *courge musquée* (French); *Moschuskürbis* (German); *zucca moscata* (Italian); *nihon kabotcha* (Japanese); *abóbora-rasteira* (Portuguese); *calabaza moscada* (Spanish); *fak thong* (Thai)

Cucurbita pepo

zucchini • marrow • summer squash

Zucchini fruit

Zucchini plant

Summer squashes

DESCRIPTION A trailing or upright annual with angled stems bearing triangular, pointed, markedly lobed leaves. Both stems and leaves are covered in small prickles that make them rough and bristly. Male and female flowers are yellow, with upright (not spreading) lobes. The fruit stalk is typically hard, angular and deeply grooved. Three types can be distinguished: (1) the pumpkins, which are rounded or flattened and often ribbed – hardly distinct from winter squashes (*C. maxima*) but are usually eaten young (note the difference in the fruit stalk); (2) vegetable marrow, zucchini or courgette (oblong fruits, used while young – "baby marrows"); (3) summer squashes, which include numerous ornamental types (some hard-shelled and used as containers – see bottle gourd, *Lagenaria*), scallops (custard squash), straightneck, crookneck and vegetable spaghetti. The vernacular names in various languages listed below attempt to reflect both summer pumpkin and vegetable marrow.

ORIGIN & HISTORY *C. pepo* is one of the oldest known crops (it was found in 10 000-year-old archaeological sites in Mexico). Its cultivation in the southern and eastern USA and some highlands of Central America dates back to at least 2700 BC. The remarkable diversity was already present in pre-Columbian times.

PARTS USED Mostly the young fruits (sometimes mature fruits, seeds, leaves or flowers).

CULTIVATION & HARVESTING Like other cucurbits *C. pepo* is grown from seed in rich soil. It is slightly more tolerant of cold and is therefore the preferred pumpkin in colder temperate regions.

USES & PROPERTIES Squashes and marrows are cooked and eaten as vegetables, often with butter, brown sugar and nutmeg. They may be sautéed, stuffed, boiled, baked, puréed or pickled. Most recipes for pumpkins (see *C. maxima*) generally apply to squashes as well. The seeds are used as nuts (*pepitas*).

NUTRITIONAL VALUE See *C. maxima*. The seeds are nutritious (rich in zinc).

Cucurbita pepo (B) D.   family: Cucurbitaceae

xi hu lu, xi hu gua (Chinese); *potiron, courgette* (French); *Gartenkürbis, Zucchini* (German); *zucca, zucchino* (Italian); *pepo kabotcha, zukkiini* (Japanese); *abóbora, aboborinha* (Portuguese); *calabaza común, calabacín* (Spanish)

Cuminum cyminum
cumin

Cumin flowers

Cumin fruits

Cumin plant

DESCRIPTION A small, annual herb (fennel-like) with slender, dark green leaves divided into narrow segments and white or pinkish flowers arranged in umbels. The small dry fruits are narrowly oblong, about 5 mm long and greenish or greyish-brown. Cumin should not be confused with black cumin (*Nigella sativa*), an unrelated plant.

ORIGIN & HISTORY Cumin is probably indigenous to the Mediterranean region and western Asia. It is a classical spice, mentioned in the Bible and widely used in the Middle Ages to season soups, stews and meat dishes (especially fish and poultry). The ancient French culinary term *cominée* refers to dishes containing cumin. It has been cultivated for many centuries in Egypt, Greece, Turkey, the Middle East and India and today also in northern Europe, Morocco, Russia, Central America, China and Japan.

PARTS USED Ripe dry fruits (often referred to as "seeds").

CULTIVATION & HARVESTING Cumin is pro-pagated by seeds and the young fruits are harvested just before they dry out and are shed.

USES & PROPERTIES The main use of cumin is as a spice – it is one of the essential ingredients of curry powder (and gives it a slightly bitter taste and the distinct spicy aroma). It has numerous other uses in chilli powders and various spice mixtures that are used in Indian and Pakistani cooking. In North African cuisine, cumin is added to traditional lamb dishes, *couscous* and marinades. In eastern European cooking, the spice is added to soups, sauces, fish and meat dishes, as well as cold meats. Cumin is a classical condiment in bread (especially rye bread) and has numerous other uses in salty biscuits and savoury dishes. It is also an important flavourant of cheeses, such as Munster cheese. Cumin is commonly used for pickling.

NUTRITIONAL VALUE Unimportant, as it is used in small amounts as a spice.

Cuminum cyminum L.   family: Apiaceae

zi ran qin (Chinese); *cumin* (French); *Kreuzkümmel, Römischer Kümmel* (German); *jeera, zira* (Hindi); *jinten* (Indonesian); *comino* (Italian); *jintan putih* (Malay); *cominho* (Portuguese); *comino* (Spanish); *yee raa* (Thai)

Curcuma longa

turmeric

Turmeric flowers

Zedoary plants

Turmeric (fresh rhizomes)

DESCRIPTION This is a leafy, stemless, ginger-like plant with oblong, yellowish leaves arising from bright yellow rhizomes. The attractive flowers are borne in oblong clusters. Various species are sources of starch, traditional medicine and dyes. These include Indian arrowroot (*C. angustifolia*), Javanese turmeric (*C. xanthorrhiza*) and zedoary (*C. zedoaria*). Others are used as spices, including mango ginger (*C. amada*) and Indonesian mango ginger (*C. mangga*).

ORIGIN & HISTORY Turmeric is an ancient cultigen that has not yet been found in the wild. It is believed to be indigenous to India, where it has been used as a spice and dye (also in religious rites) for many centuries. From India the plant spread to Southeast Asia and the Far East. India is still by far the most important producer (nearly 350 000 tons per year) but smaller amounts are also produced in Bangladesh, Pakistan and various Southeast Asian countries.

PARTS USED Rhizomes.

CULTIVATION & HARVESTING Turmeric is easily grown in tropical regions by division of the branched rhizomes.

USES & PROPERTIES Fresh roots, powdered root or extracts are an important spice. It is an essential ingredient of curry powders and mustard powders. Turmeric is much used in Indian and Asian cooking –in vegetable, meat, fish and rice dishes for flavour and colour. An example is Malaysian yellow rice (*nasi kunyit*), eaten on ceremonial or festive occasions. Turmeric is a popular natural food dye for dairy products, drinks, confectionery and various ready-made spicy sauces, including mustards and Worcester sauce.

NUTRITIONAL VALUE Unimportant, since very small quantities are used. Turmeric is, however, an important medicinal product that is used for stomach ailments and to stimulate bile secretion – it has proven anti-inflammatory effects.

NOTES The bright yellow colour is due to a pigment known as curcumin.

Curcuma longa L. (= *C. domestica* Valeton)

family: Zingiberaceae

jiang huang, yu jin (Chinese); *curcuma* (French); *Gelbwurzel, Kurkuma* (German); *haldi* (Hindi); *curcuma* (Italian); *taamerikku* (Japanese); *kunyit* (Malay); *curcuma, tumérico* (Spanish); *khamin* (Thai)

Cyamopsis tetragonoloba
cluster bean • guar

Cluster bean plant

Cluster beans

Cluster bean seeds

DESCRIPTION Guar is a large, much-branched annual with broad trifoliate leaves, dense clusters of white, pink or purple flowers and oblong, pointed pods bearing about ten white, grey or black seeds.

ORIGIN & HISTORY The plant is a cultigen that probably originated from a wild West African species, *C. senegalensis*. It was domesticated in India and has been cultivated there for a long time as a vegetable and especially as a fodder plant. Since 1953 it has been grown in the southwestern parts of the USA for the production of guar gum extracted from the seeds.

PARTS USED Young pods, ripe seeds.

CULTIVATION & HARVESTING The plant is grown from seed as an annual crop. It is exceptionally drought-resistant. The young pods or ripe seeds are harvested in subsistence farming for human consumption in India and Pakistan. The commercial interest, however, is in the ripe, pea-like seeds that are milled to flour (guar flour) or extracted to give guar gum.

USES & PROPERTIES The young pods are eaten as a vegetable or the ripe seeds are used as a protein-rich food source. Guar gum, obtained from the endosperm of the ripe seeds, is a high viscosity gum (polysaccharide) that is used as a thickening agent in the food industry. This gum is used in the same way as carob gum, obtained from the seeds of the carob tree (see *Ceratonia siliqua*). It contains 80% gum (guaran, which is a polysaccharide comprising one-third galactose and two-thirds mannose).

NUTRITIONAL VALUE The seeds contain 30% protein, 45% carbohydrates and 2% fat. It is believed that guar gum mixed into bread flour will help reduce cholesterol and blood sugar levels. Guar gum is sometimes used as a bulking agent in slimming products.

NOTES Guar gum has numerous technical applications, not only in the food industry but also in cosmetics and paper-making.

Cyamopsis tetragonoloba (L.) Taubert   family: Fabaceae

guar (French); *Guarbohne, Büschelbohne* (German); *guar, guwar, guar-phali* (Hindii); *guar* (Italian); *guar* (Spanish)

Cyclopia genistoides
honeybush tea

Mountain tea (*C. intermedia*)

Honeybush tea (*C. genistoides*)

Honeybush tea

DESCRIPTION A shrub with yellowish stems bearing trifoliate leaves on very short stalks, each with three oblong leaflets. The attractive, sweet-smelling, yellow flowers develop into oblong, reddish-brown pods. Four species are grown, of which *C. genistoides* (the original honeybush tea) has become the most popular due to its high quality. This species has distinctive narrow leaflets. Until recently, mountain tea(*C. intermedia*) was the most important commercial source of tea, followed by vlei tea (*C. subternata*).

ORIGIN & HISTORY Honeybush tea is a traditional beverage from the Cape region of South Africa. Until recently the product was wild-harvested in the mountains, but plantations are now being established to meet the growing demand.

PARTS USED Leaves and twigs (traditionally also the flowers).

CULTIVATION & HARVESTING Plants are propagated from seeds and are grown in sandy soil. The leafy branches are harvested, cut into short segments, bruised in rubber rollers, dampened with water and allowed to "ferment" at a temperature of about 60 °C (this is actually an enzymatic oxidation process that turns the green material into a rich, aromatic, reddish-brown product). Recently, green ("unfermented") honeybush tea has also become available.

USES & PROPERTIES Honeybush tea is used in much the same way as ordinary tea (enjoyed with milk or a slice of lemon). The flavour improves if it is boiled (as decoction and not merely infused as ordinary tea). It is used pure or variously blended with other herbal teas (often rooibos tea). Honeybush makes an excellent ice tea and is a tasty addition to cold drinks and punches. Strong black honeybush tea may be used in cooking to enhance the colour and flavour of sauces and stews.

NUTRITIONAL VALUE The tea is free from stimulants or harmful substances. It has antioxidant properties and is widely used as a health tea.

Cyclopia genistoides (L.) R. Br.   family: Fabaceae

cyclopia (French); *Honigbusch* (German); *cyclopia* (Italian); *cyclopia* (Spanish)

Cydonia oblonga

quince

Quince young fruits

Quince fruits

Quince leaves and flowers

DESCRIPTION A deciduous small tree (up to 5 m) with rounded leaves that are silver-hairy below, and attractive pink and white flowers. The fruits are yellow when ripe, with persistent sepals on the flower end and a downy surface. Similar-looking fruits known as oriental quinces (*Chaenomeles japonica, C. speciosa*) are grown in China and Japan. They have toothed leaves and deciduous sepals.

ORIGIN & HISTORY The "pear of Cydonia" is indigenous to the Middle East (Caucasus, Turkey and Iran). The cultivated form spread to southern Europe in classical times (part of Greek mythology and traditional Greek cooking) and later to most other parts of the world.

PARTS USED Ripe fruits.

CULTIVATION & HARVESTING Quinces are easily grown from seeds, cuttings or by layering and have a low chilling requirement in order to flower. Fruits produced in warm regions become sweet and palatable, while those grown in cold regions

are hard and not really edible unless cooked.

USES & PROPERTIES Fruits are rarely eaten raw and are mostly cooked as a delicious sweet dessert or side dish. They are popular for making jams, preserves and especially jellies. Due to the exceptionally high pectin content, quince is often added to other fruits, not only to give a nice pink colour but to improve the texture. The Portuguese call the preserve *marmelada*, possibly the origin of the English word "marmalade" (now made from citrus fruits). Quinces are used in Mediterranean cooking in *tajines*, stews and other meat dishes. Quince paste (the famous French *cotignac* or Spanish *dulce de membrillo*) is a pink sweetmeat of ancient origin. *Ratafia* is a home-made liqueur produced by macerating quinces and other fruits in sweetened alcohol.

NUTRITIONAL VALUE Low energy value (30–35 kcal per 100 g) unless sugar is added. Quince is a good source of minerals (especially potassium) and vitamin C (15–40 mg per 100 g).

Cydonia oblonga L.   family: Rosaceae

wen po (Chinese); *coing* (French); *Quitte* (German); *cotogna* (Italian); *marumero* (Japanese); *marmelo* (Portuguese); *membrillo* (Spanish)

Cymbopogon citratus
lemongrass

Lemongrass plant

Lemongrass leaves

Lemongrass

DESCRIPTION A densely tufted perennial with thick stems and broad, aromatic leaves. The plant rarely flowers. Several other species are grown commercially as a source of essential oil. They are distinguished by their characteristic smell and the chemical composition of the oils they produce. The best-known ones are Malabar lemongrass (*C. flexuosus*, sometimes used in Asian cooking in the same way as lemongrass but mainly grown for the essential oil known as East Indian lemongrass oil), ginger grass, palma-rosa or rusha (*C. martini*, yields an oil similar to geranium oil), Ceylon citronella grass (*C. nardus*, sometimes used as a tea) and Java citronella grass (*C. winterianus*).

ORIGIN & HISTORY The origin of lemongrass is unknown. It possibly originated in southern India and Sri Lanka and has become a very important component of Asian cooking. It is mainly used in Sri Lanka, Thailand, Vietnam, Cambodia, Malaysia, Singapore and Indonesia.

PARTS USED The fleshy leaf bases (pseudostems).

CULTIVATION & HARVESTING Propagation is easily done by dividing the clumps. Young stems are broken off by hand and the leaves trimmed and discarded.

USES & PROPERTIES The subtle, never dominating flavour is part of the character of Asian cooking. When lemongrass is eaten raw, only the tender inner parts of the bulbous leaf bases are used (finely sliced, or pounded to a paste). For adding flavour to a dish (typically fish, poultry, seafood, curries and stews), the whole stem may be simply bruised, added to the pot, and later removed again. Lemongrass is often used to make soups ("lemongrass soup") and is an important ingredient of various spice mixtures. The stalks are sometimes used as skewers for prawns or seafood *satay*. Lemongrass may be added to tea for flavour, or mixed with lemon verbena and lemon balm to make lemon tea.

NUTRITIONAL VALUE Lemongrass is used in small amounts only.

Cymbopogon citratus (DC.) Stapf

family: Poaceae

xiang mao coa (Chinese); *verveine de Indes* (French); *Lemongras, Zitronengras* (German); *sereh* (Indonesian); *citronella* (Italian); *remon gurasu* (Japanese); *serai* (Malay); *sontol* (Spanish); *takrai* (Thai); *xa* (Vietnamese)

Cynara scolymus
globe artichoke

Globe artichoke flower head

Globe artichoke field

Globe artichokes

DESCRIPTION A perennial thistle with deeply lobed, grey leaves and sturdy, branched flowering stalks. The large flower heads comprise numerous small, purple florets surrounded by large green bracts with blunt, notched or spiny tips, depending on the cultivar.

ORIGIN & HISTORY Globe artichoke is a cultigen that was probably developed from the wild artichoke or cardoon (*C. cardunculus*). It was known to the Greeks and Romans and has been cultivated in parts of Europe for centuries. Today it has become an important vegetable and is grown mainly in France, Italy, Spain, Belgium and also California in the USA.

PARTS USED Immature flower heads.

CULTIVATION & HARVESTING Artichokes are best grown from sucker shoots that are planted in spring. They are easily grown from seeds but then some flower heads tend to be excessively spiny. The plants are renewed every three or four years. Flower heads are harvested when very young ("baby artichokes") or a little later (before the bracts curl away, indicating that the flower head will open). Artichokes are best used fresh.

USES & PROPERTIES Each head has an edible fleshy base or heart (cooks call it the *fond*; it is the receptacle), which is surrounded by large, scaly bracts, the fleshy bases of which are also edible. The inedible hairy central core (called *choke*, the immature florets) has to be removed. Artichokes may be simply cooked and eaten with a suitable sauce (usually butter or cream) or they are variously stuffed, used in salads or as a garnish for hot or cold dishes. Whole artichokes or hearts are commonly preserved in brine or spicy olive oil.

NUTRITIONAL VALUE Artichoke yields only 60 kcal per 100 g. It is rich in iron and potassium and is said to be diuretic.

NOTES Blanched leaf stalks of cardoon are a popular vegetable in France, Spain and Italy.

Cynara scolymus L.

family: Asteraceae

chao xian ji, yang ji (Chinese); *artichaut* (French); *Artischocke* (German); *carciofo* (Italian); *chousen azami* (Japanese); *alcachofra* (Portuguese); *alcachofera* (Spanish)

Cyperus esculentus

chufa • tiger nut

Tiger nuts

Chufa plant

Tiger nut products

DESCRIPTION Chufa is a grass-like plant with slender, bright green leaves growing from small, brown, tuberous rhizomes below the ground. The flowers are inconspicuous and brownish in colour but the cultivated form of the species (var. *sativa*) rarely flowers. The names "tiger nut" or "rush nut" are not very accurate as the edible part is an underground stem (rhizome) and not really a nut.

ORIGIN & HISTORY The plant is indigenous to western Asia and Africa and the wild form has become a serious weed in many parts of the world. Chufa is an ancient crop (at least 4 000 years old) of the Middle East and Egypt (found in tombs). It is now grown in the Mediterranean region (especially Spain, where it was introduced by the Moors), East India, West Africa (northern Nigeria, Ghana and Togo) and Brazil.

PARTS USED The fleshy tubers (rhizomes), about 15–25 mm in diameter.

CULTIVATION & HARVESTING Seeds are very rarely produced and the plant is grown from the small tubers. Harvesting takes place three to five months after planting. Yields of up to 12 tons per hectare have been recorded.

USES & PROPERTIES The tubers are roasted and eaten in much the same way as potatoes. They have a nut-like (almond-like) taste. Chufa may also be eaten raw or can be processed into flour. A special milk-like drink is made from cooked chufa mixed with water, sugar and cinnamon. This sweet and refreshing cold drink is known as *horchata de chufa* and is commercially available in plastic containers. It is especially popular in Spain (Andalucia, Murcia and Valencia) and nowadays also in Britain and Brazil.

NUTRITIONAL VALUE Chufa is rich in starch (30%), sugar (15%), fat (25%) and protein (4–8%). It is considered healthy because of the high levels of potassium and iron, and the low sodium content.

Cyperus esculentus L.   family: Cyperaceae

amande de terre, choufa (French); *Erdmandel* (German); *doldichini* (Italian); *chufa, juncinha* (Portuguese); *chufa* (Spanish)

Cyphomandra betacea
tree tomato • tamarillo

Tree tomato flowers

Tree tomato fruits

Tree tomato (purple form)

DESCRIPTION Tree tomato is an erect shrub of up to 5 m in height bearing large, soft, heart-shaped leaves and pink flowers. The fruits are egg-shaped, smooth, yellow, bright red or purplish when ripe.

ORIGIN & HISTORY This South American plant is unknown in the wild but is considered to be indigenous to southern Bolivia and northwestern Argentina. It has been grown as a crop in the Andes region for many centuries and is still popular as a garden tree in almost every city and town at higher altitudes in South America. Crop development started in New Zealand about 50 years ago and there is an expanding export trade to Europe, Japan and North America. The name "tamarillo" is a commercial name coined in New Zealand in 1967.

PARTS USED Ripe fruits.

CULTIVATION & HARVESTING The plant is easily propagated from seeds and requires cool but frost-free conditions. It is very productive (20 kg per tree, more than 15 tons per hectare) and may bear fruit all year round. Fruits are hand-picked and can be stored for up to 10 weeks.

USES & PROPERTIES The attractive fruits are eaten fresh – often cut in half and the flesh scooped out. Some people find the taste a little too acidic, but modern cultivars have sweeter fruits. The fruits are used as a dessert in fruit salads and on ice cream. They are included in green salads and in sandwiches in the same way as tomatoes. The whole fruit is liquidised and enjoyed as a fruit juice (sometimes mixed with milk, ice and sugar). Ripe fruits are ideal for jams, jellies, chutneys, syrups and sauces. They are also cooked and added to soups, stews and stuffings.

NUTRITIONAL VALUE The fruit has a low energy value (less than 40 kcal per fruit) and is an excellent source of vitamins A, B6, C and E.

Cyphomandra betacea (Cav.) Sendtn.   family: Solanaceae

shu fan qie (Chinese); *cyphomandre bétacé* (French); *Baumtomate* (German); *tamarillo* (Italian); *tomate de érvore* (Portuguese); *tomate de árbol* (Spanish)

Daucus carota

carrot

Carrot flowers

Carrot plant

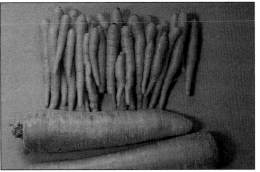

Carrots and baby carrots

DESCRIPTION A biennial plant with compound, feathery leaves and a branched, leafy flowering stalk that appears in the second year. The small white flowers are arranged in umbels surrounded by finely divided bracts. The root is thick, fleshy and tapering in cultivated carrot (subsp. *sativa*), with a bright orange colour in modern cultivars. Wild carrot (subsp. *carota*) has white, fibrous, inedible roots.

ORIGIN & HISTORY Europe and Central Asia. The cultivated form, originally with branched, purple roots, is believed to have originated in Afghanistan. It was taken to the Mediterranean region in the fourteenth century. Yellow colour forms were selected from this original type and from the seventeenth century onwards orange-red types were developed in the Netherlands. They are now a very important vegetable and are grown in all temperate regions.

PARTS USED Fleshy roots.

CULTIVATION & HARVESTING Carrots are easily grown from seeds and are a popular crop in kitchen gardens.

USES & PROPERTIES Coarsely or finely grated carrots are eaten raw as a salad. They are one of the most widely used vegetables and are cut (sliced, diced), cooked, steamed or stir-fried and served with various sauces. Carrots are included in soups and stews and are often an ingredient of sauces and stocks. Commercial products include carrot juice, canned or frozen carrots (either baby carrots or diced carrot, sometimes mixed with other vegetables) and dehydrated carrot. Carrot juice has become popular as a health drink.

NUTRITIONAL VALUE Carrots are the best-known source of beta-carotene (6 mg per 100 g). They yield 25–42 kcal per 100 g and are rich in sugars (5–10%). Beta-carotene (provitamin A) and other carotenoids are converted to vitamin A (retinol) in the liver. Too much can be harmful and too little causes deficiency diseases (ascribed to a lack of pigmented fruits and vegetables in the diet).

Daucus carota L.   family: Apiaceae

hu luo bo (Chinese); *carotte* (French); *Möhre, Karotte* (German); *gajar* (Hindi); *carota* (Italian); *cenoura* (Portuguese); *zanahoria* (Spanish)

Dendrocalamus asper

bamboo

Bamboo shoot (*Dendrocalamus asper*)

Bamboo shoot products

Bamboo shoots

DESCRIPTION Bamboos are tall, woody grasses with underground rhizomes giving rise to erect, hollow stems with distinct nodes and internodes and most of the leaves clustered at the tips. Flowering is highly synchronised, and all mature plants of a particular area may flower and then die at the same time. The edible parts are the buds (young stems) formed at ground level and covered with overlapping scale-like leaves. Other sources include *Dendrocalamus giganteus, D. latifolius, Gigantochloa apus, Phyllostachys edulis* (= *P. pubescens*) and *Bambusa vulgaris*.

ORIGIN & HISTORY *D. asper* is indigenous to Southeast Asia and is widely cultivated for bamboo shoots. *D. giganteus* occurs in Myanmar, while *Bambusa vulgaris* (a cultigen), other *Bambusa* species and *Phyllostachys edulis* are commercial sources of bamboo shoots in China and Taiwan. *Gigantochloa apus* is cultivated in Java.

PARTS USED Young stems (buds, bamboo shoots).

CULTIVATION & HARVESTING Bamboos are easily propagated by division but are also wild-harvested. The young stems may be blanched by covering them with soil before they are cut off, peeled and boiled in salt water to remove poisonous cyanide glycosides.

USES & PROPERTIES The young stems are bland tasting but have a crispy texture and are very popular in oriental and especially Chinese cooking. Bamboo shoots are eaten cooked as a vegetable or added to numerous dishes, especially stir-fries and stews. They may be pickled in vinegar, salted or candied. Canned or preserved bamboo shoots are readily available and are used for *sukiyaki*, a traditional Japanese dish of sliced beef and various vegetables cooked directly at the table. It is served with boiled rice and each mouthful is dipped in raw egg before being eaten.

NUTRITIONAL VALUE Boiled shoots have a low energy value (30 kcal per 100 g) and contain moderate levels of phosphorus, potassium, thiamin and vitamin B.

Dendrocalamus asper (Schultes f.) Heyne   family: Poaceae

zhu sun, tung sun, sun ki (Chinese); *pousses de bambou* (French); *Bambussprossen* (German); *bambú* (Italian); *takenoko* (Japanese); *bambú* (Spanish); *phai tong* (Thai)

Digitaria exilis

fonio

Fonio plant
Fonio ears and grains

DESCRIPTION A small grass (up to 0.8 m) with short leaves and distinctive inflorescences comprising two to four slender racemes of equal length. The small grains of about 1.5 mm in diameter are held in the raceme and are not dispersed as in the wild form of the species. Fonio is also known as white fonio, *achras* or "hungry rice". Several other *Digitaria* species are cultivated as cereals. Black fonio (*D. iburua*) is a slightly taller grass than fonio and has four to ten racemes per inflorescence. It is grown only by the Hausa people of northern Nigeria. Crabgrass (*D. sanguinalis*) is a cereal crop in Russia and Kashmir, while raishan (*D. cruciata*) is grown by the Khasi people of Assam and by hill tribes in Vietnam.

ORIGIN & HISTORY Fonio is indigenous to West Africa. As with other cereals, domestication probably started when this weedy grass was harvested as a wild cereal during times of scarcity. It has been cultivated at least since the fourteenth century and is still a popular cereal in most parts of West Africa where it is the staple food of at least one million people.

PARTS USED Ripe, dry, one-seeded fruits (grains).

CULTIVATION & HARVESTING The plant is very hardy and will give at least some yield under poor soil conditions. Harvesting and processing are still mainly done by hand.

USES & PROPERTIES Fonio is considered to be exceptionally tasty. It can be cooked as porridge, boiled like rice or processed into a high quality *couscous*. The grains may be used to brew beer and can be popped in the same way as popcorn. Fonio may also be ground into excellent flour that can be used for baking bread.

NUTRITIONAL VALUE The nutritional value of fonio is similar to that of other cereals. It contains 8.7% protein, 1% fat and 80% carbohydrates.

Digitaria exilis (Kipp.) Stapf   family: Poaceae

fonio (French); *Foniohirse* (German); *fonio* (Italian); *fônio* (Portuguese); *digitaria* (Spanish)

Dimocarpus longan

longan • dragon's eye

Longan leaves and fruits

Longan fruits

Langsat (duku) fruits

DESCRIPTION A large tree (up to 12 m) with a massive trunk and dense crown of compound leaves. Inconspicuous flowers are borne in large clusters, followed by litchi-like fruits. They are round, pale brown and have a juicy, white flesh surrounding the single, shiny, dark brown seed with an eye-shaped marking (hence dragon's eye). The small-fruited longan or cat's eyes (subsp. *malesianus*) is considered inferior to the larger cultivated longan (subsp. *longan*). Longan may be confused with the similar-looking langsat or duku (*Lansium domesticum*, family Meliaceae) that is occasionally seen on Malaysian markets as clusters of fresh fruits.

ORIGIN & HISTORY Indigenous to India and Sri Lanka (perhaps also southern China). It is grown as a fruit tree in China and Southeast Asia (Thailand, Malaysia and Indonesia).

PARTS USED Ripe fruits (actually the fleshy aril that surrounds the seed).

CULTIVATION & HARVESTING Trees propagated from seeds are used as rootstock or are grown as windbreaks. Commercial cultivars are produced by grafting and are grown in tropical climates. The clusters of fruits, often hidden in the dense foliage, are harvested by hand when ripe but still firm to the touch.

USES & PROPERTIES Fruits are mostly eaten fresh or may be included in fruit salads. They can also be liquidised to make a delicious drink. The flavour is more delicate than that of a litchi, with a distinct fragrance and a sweet-sour taste. Canned longans have become available in supermarkets and are used in the same way as the fresh fruits but the flavour is considered to be inferior. The fruits may also be crystallised or dried (a fruit tea can be made from the dried fruits).

NUTRITIONAL VALUE Fruits have an energy value of 46 kcal per 100 g and a carbohydrate content of around 10%. The pulp contains 64 mg of vitamin C per 100 g.

Dimocarpus longan Lour. [= *Euphoria longan* (Lour.) Steud.; = *Nephelium longan* (Lour.) Hook.] family: Sapindaceae

long yan (Chinese); *longanier* (French); *Longanbaum* (German); *rongan* (Japanese); *mata kucing* (Malay); *longana* (Portuguese); *longán* (Spanish); *lamyai* (Thai)

Dioscorea bulbifera

air potato • potato yam

Air potato (*D. bulbifera*) leaves and tubers

Chinese yam (*D. batatas*)

DESCRIPTION This yam is a perennial creeper (vine) with large, heart-shaped, alternate leaves borne on long stalks. Small bulbils form in the leaf axils, in addition to the much larger underground storage organs. The plant rarely flowers. A similar but commercially less important yam is the Chinese yam (*D. batatas*, sometimes called *D. opposita*), known as *shu yu* in Chinese, *igname de Chine* in French, *Brotwurzel* in German, *ubi* in Indonesian and *naga imo* or *yama imo* in Japanese. It is easily recognised by the opposite leaves (not alternate) and the much shorter leaf stalks. Another Asian yam of commercial importance is *D. esculenta*, often also referred to as potato yam or Chinese yam and frequently confused with *D. batatas*.

ORIGIN & HISTORY *D. bulbifera* occurs naturally in both West Africa and tropical Asia. The species appears to have been developed as a crop plant independently in the two regions. It is now cultivated mainly in Africa, Australia, India, Indonesia and Japan.

PARTS USED Tubers (swollen, underground stems).

CULTIVATION & HARVESTING Both the air potato and Chinese yam are propagated by the bulbils that form on the stems.

USES & PROPERTIES Potato yams are used in much the same way as potatoes or sweet potatoes, but they are usually peeled and then blanched in boiling salt water for about 20 minutes to remove any bitter taste that may be present. They are then boiled, baked or fried. Slices of tuber or puréed tuber may be added to soups, stews, soufflés, fritters and various sweet dishes. Yams also serve as a commercial source of starch that is used in the food industry.

NUTRITIONAL VALUE Yams have a high energy value of 100–120 kcal per 100 g. They are considered to be good sources of vitamin C (10 mg per 100 g), minerals (magnesium, potassium and some iron) and thiamin.

Dioscorea bulbifera L.

family: Dioscoreaceae

huang yao (Chinese); *igname bulbifère* (French); *Yamswurzel, Kartoffelyams* (German); *kashuu imo* (Japanese); *ñame de gunda* (Spanish)

Dioscorea cayenensis

yellow yam • white yam

Yellow yam

White yam

White yam tuber

DESCRIPTION Yellow yam is a perennial geophyte with twining and climbing stems arising from a large, oblong tuber. The lower parts of the stems are spiny, with reduced, bract-like leaves, while the upper parts bear large, heart-shaped leaves arranged alternately. The white yam (*D. rotundata*) is nowadays considered to belong to the same species complex as *D. cayenensis*. However, they differ in the colour of the tubers and in their chromosome numbers. Another yam of considerable commercial importance is the greater yam or water yam (*D. alata*), known as *shen shu* in Chinese, *grande igname* or *igname ailée* in French, *Geflügelter Yam* or *Wasseryam* in German, *daijo* in Japanese and *ñame de agua* in Spanish. It has markedly winged stems and the tubers can be massive, up to 20 kg or more. Only one American yam is cultivated as a staple crop. This is the cush-cush yam or *mapuey* (*D. trifida*), which has trilobed leaves and small, yellow tubers.

ORIGIN & HISTORY *D. cayenensis* and *D. rotundata* are indigenous to West Africa. *D. alata* is an ancient Asian cultigen. *D. trifida* is indigenous to Central America. In West Africa, yams play an important role in the culture and traditions of the local people.

PARTS USED Tubers.

CULTIVATION & HARVESTING Yellow yam and white yam are perennials that are grown commercially as annual crops in Africa (not in Asia). They are mostly propagated by tuber cuttings that grow out and form new tubers.

USES & PROPERTIES The African yams are used to make *fufu*, an important local dish of pounded and steamed yam. White yam is considered to produce the best quality *fufu*. Yams may also be used in the same way as potatoes or sweet potatoes.

NUTRITIONAL VALUE White yam contains about 30% starch and has an energy value of more than 100 kcal per 100 g.

Dioscorea cayenensis Lam. (= *D. rotundata* Poir.)   family: Dioscoreaceae

huang shu yu, bai shy yu (Chinese); *igname blanc, igname de Guinée* (French); *Gelber Yams, Weißer Yams* (German); *ñame blanco, ñame guineo blanco* (Spanish)

Diospyros digyna
black sapote • black persimmon

Lotus plum (*Diospyros lotus*)

Black sapote fruits

Black sapote flowers and fruit

DESCRIPTION A rounded, evergreen tree of up to 10 m in height with simple, pale green leaves and small, greenish yellow flowers. Strongly scented male, female and complete flowers occur on the same tree. The fruit is a large round berry with slight ridges and an olive green skin that turns brownish when the fruit ripens. The fruit pulp is dark brown to blackish and becomes floury and creamy in texture. Black sapote (also called black apple, chocolate pudding fruit or *guayabote*) is related to neither white sapote (see *Casimiroa edulis*) nor sapote (*Pouteria sapota*). In addition to the well-known persimmon (*D. kaki*), there are several other species with edible fruits, loosely referred to as date plums or velvet apples. These include the Malaysian mabola or butterfruit (*D. blancoi*), the Asian lotus plum (*D. lotus*), the North American persimmon (*D. virginiana*), the Pacific *D. major* and the tropical African jackal-berry (*D. mespiliformis*). Ebony (*D. ebenum*) and other species yield valuable timber.

ORIGIN & HISTORY Black sapote is indigenous to Central America (naturalised in Asia). Known since ancient times in Mexico, it is now cultivated in Hawaii, the Philippines, the West Indies, Florida in the USA, Réunion Island and Australia.

PARTS USED Ripe fruits.

CULTIVATION & HARVESTING The tree is usually grown from seeds but can also be grafted. Hot, humid conditions are required.

USES & PROPERTIES The ripe fruit may be cut in half and the pulp eaten with a spoon (often with a little lemon or orange juice). The main use, however, is for various desserts and commercial ice cream. The flesh is puréed and mixed with other fruit purées, mousses, yogurt and a little rum to add flavour.

NUTRITIONAL VALUE The fruit pulp has an energy value of 65 kcal per 100 g and contains significant amounts of vitamin A (45 µg) and vitamin C (20 mg).

Diospyros digyna Jacq.   family: Ebenaceae

hei shi (Chinese); *sapote noire* (French); *Schwarze Sapote* (German); *diosupirosu nigura* (Japanese); *êbano das Antilhas* (Portuguese); *êbeno agrio* (Spanish)

Diospyros kaki

persimmon

Persimmon flowers

Persimmon leaves and fruits

Persimmons

DESCRIPTION A deciduous tree of up to 12 m in height with large, pale green leaves and greenish yellow flowers that have prominent, persistent sepals which enlarge as the fruit develops. The ripe fruit resembles a large tomato in size, shape and colour. The yellow to orange-red, smooth skin surrounds a tannin-rich pulp that becomes sweet and edible when the fruit is fully ripe. Japanese persimmon or oriental persimmon should not be confused with American persimmon (*D. virginiana*).

ORIGIN & HISTORY The tree is indigenous to East Asia and has been cultivated in China and Japan for centuries. The cultivated species is a polyploid derived from a wild species, *D. roxburghii*. A large number of cultivars have been selected, some of which can be eaten when firm (*Fuya*) and others that must be very ripe and soft (*Hachiya*). China and Japan are the main producers, but persimmons are also grown commercially in the Mediterranean region and

the USA. Israel markets a sweet type called "Sharon fruit".

PARTS USED Ripe fruits.

CULTIVATION & HARVESTING Selected cultivars are grafted onto suitable seedlings. Modern persimmons are adapted to temperate climates and can survive moderate frost.

USES & PROPERTIES Persimmons are cut in half and the flesh scooped out with a spoon, leaving the indigestible skin. Slices of peeled fruit may be added to fruit salads or the flesh may be blended to make fresh persimmon juice. It is also processed into jams or sorbets and may be puréed and added to ice cream or cream to create a delicious mousse or fool. Fruits of some varieties are dried in China and used as a source of sugar.

NUTRITIONAL VALUE The energy value is about 65 kcal per 100 g. The fruit is a good source of potassium (200 mg) and vitamin C (6–50 mg) and an excellent source of vitamin A (267 µg).

Diospyros kaki L.f.   family: Ebenaceae

shi, shi zi (Chinese); *kaki* (French); *Kakipflaume* (German); *kaki* (Italian); *kakinoki* (Japanese); *caqui* (Spanish); *phlap chin* (Thai)

Dovyalis hebecarpa

Ceylon gooseberry • kitembilla

Ceylon gooseberry

Kei-apple

Governor's plum

DESCRIPTION Ceylon gooseberry is a large, much-branched shrub with long sharp spines on younger plants and on the older branches of mature plants. The small, yellowish, male and female flowers are borne on separate trees. The fruits are fleshy round berries, the size of small apricots. They are velvety in texture and orange-red to purplish when ripe. A close relative is the kei-apple or wild apricot (*D. caffra*), known as *prune cafre* in French and *umqokolo* in Zulu. It has glossy green leaves and slightly larger fruits that turn orange-yellow. Other relatives are the governor's plum (*Flacourtia indica*), the lovi-lovi (*F. inermis*), the paniala (*F. jangomas*) and the rukam (*F. rukam*).

ORIGIN & HISTORY Ceylon gooseberry is indigenous to Sri Lanka. It is cultivated in India, tropical parts of Asia and on a small scale in the USA. Plants are sometimes seen in botanical gardens and experimental plots in other parts of the world. The kei-apple is indigenous to southern and eastern Africa. It is a popular hedge plant and is grown on a small scale for fruit production in Australia, California, East Africa and Israel. Governor's plum is indigenous to Africa and India and is of local importance as a wild fruit and medicinal plant. The same is true for the Southeast Asian paniala and rukam.

PARTS USED Ripe fruits.

CULTIVATION & HARVESTING Plants are propagated from seeds or cuttings. They are hardy and drought tolerant but require a warm climate. Kei-apple is usually cultivated from seeds and can withstand mild frost.

USES & PROPERTIES Ripe fruits of Ceylon gooseberry, kei-apple and the *Flacourtia* species mentioned above are very popular for making jams and jellies. Their refreshing sweet-sour taste is also ideal for making fruit juices.

NUTRITIONAL VALUE These fruits are rich in vitamin C (in the case of kei-apple, more than 100 mg per 100 g).

Dovyalis hebecarpa (Gardner) Warb.   family: Flacourtiaceae

groseille de Ceylan (French); *Kitembilla* (German); *kitembilla* (Italian, Spanish)

Durio zibethinus

durian

Durian leaves and flower buds

Durians for sale

Durian flower

Durian seeds with edible arils

DESCRIPTION A single-stemmed, tall tree of more than 35 m in height with simple, relatively small leaves. Attractive white or pink flowers are borne directly on the woody branches, followed by very large spiny fruits, each weighing up to 5 kg. The fruit is a capsule, divided into a few large segments, each containing several oblong seeds enclosed in fleshy, cream-coloured arils. The edible arils comprise nearly a third of the total weight of the fruit.

ORIGIN & HISTORY Durian is indigenous to western Malaysia. It is a highly prized and popular traditional food in Southeast Asia and is believed to have aphrodisiac properties. The fruit is commonly cultivated in Thailand, Indonesia, Malaysia and the Philippines.

PARTS USED Ripe fruits; mainly the fleshy pulp (arils), also the seeds.

CULTIVATION & HARVESTING Trees are grown in plantations in hot, humid areas. Fruits ripen towards the end of the dry season (September to December) and fall down by themselves or are harvested by hand. They are eaten soon after they are opened, as the flesh deteriorates rapidly.

USES & PROPERTIES Durian is a controversial fruit because people either love it or hate it. It is the most expensive fruit in Southeast Asia. The taste is a strange mixture of buttery custard mixed with bananas, caramel, vanilla and garlic. The fruits are banned by hotels and airlines because of the overpowering, sulphurous smell. Unripe fruits may be boiled and eaten, and the large seeds are edible when roasted or sliced and fried in oil. Durian can be processed by drying, fermenting, pickling, deep-freezing or salting. It may be eaten with sugar, fresh cream or coconut milk.

NUTRITIONAL VALUE Arils contain carbohydrates (28%) and have an energy value of 140 kcal per 100 g. They also contain proteins (2.7%), vitamin C (32–58 mg) and are rich in potassium, beta-carotene and vitamins B1 and B2.

Durio zibethinus Murray   family: Bombacaceae

liu lian (Chinese); *durio, dourian* (French); *Durianbaum, Zibetbaum* (German); *durian* (Italian); *durian* (Japanese); *durian* (Malay); *durião* (Portuguese); *durian, durión* (Spanish); *thurian* (Thai)

Echinochloa frumentacea
Japanese millet

Japanese millet inflorescence

Japanese millet

Japanese millet grains

DESCRIPTION A robust grass of up to 1.5 m in height with characteristic broad leaves and dense clusters of oblong spikes. The grains are oval in shape and light brown to purplish. Cultivated forms of Japanese millet are classified as *E. frumentacea*, while the wild form is named *E. crus-galli*. Japanese millet is very similar to sawa millet (*E. colona*, the cultivated forms sometimes called *E. utilis*) but the two species are genetically isolated from one another. Sawa is also known as *sama* in Hindi. Another relative is the large cockspur (*E. oryzoides*), a weed of rice cultivation that is harvested as a wild cereal in Russia.

ORIGIN & HISTORY Japanese millet is indigenous to the temperate regions of Asia, while sawa millet is widely distributed in the tropical and subtropical parts of the Old World. *E. frumentacea* is cultivated in China, Japan, Korea and the Philippines but its history is poorly recorded. *E. colona* appears to have been domesticated in Egypt, where wild forms still occur as weeds along the Nile. It is an important cereal in India and Sri Lanka, but has not yet been found in the archaeological record. Sawa often occurs with other cereals as a weed and the two are then harvested together.

PARTS USED Dry, one-seeded fruits (grains).

CULTIVATION & HARVESTING Japanese millet matures in six weeks (the quickest of all millets). It is used as a substitute when the rice crop fails.

USES & PROPERTIES Japanese millet and sawa millet are used as a staple food in much the same way as other millets. It may be cooked like rice or turned into flour.

NUTRITIONAL VALUE Japanese millet and sawa millet are considered to be a high quality staple cereal, similar to real millet (*Panicum miliaceum*) and other millets in their food value.

Echinochloa frumentacea (Roxb.) Link [= *E. crus-galli* (L.) P. Beauv. var. *frumentacea* (Roxb.) W.Wright] family: Poaceae

hu nan ji zi (Chinese); *millet japonais* (French); *Japanische Hirse, Sawahirse, Weizenhirse* (German); *miglio giapponese* (Italian); *hie* (Japanese); *mijo japonés* (Spanish)

Elaeis guineensis
oil palm • West African oil palm

Oil palm tree

Oil palm fruits (with male flowers)

DESCRIPTION A large, single-stemmed palm (15 to 30 m high) with long, feathery leaves. Male and female flowers occur in separate clusters on the same plant. Several hundred fruits are formed in each of two to six bunches per tree. The fruit has three layers: the outer skin (epicarp), a middle layer of fibrous, oil-rich pulp (mesocarp) and a black shell (endocarp) that contains the small embryo with surrounding endosperm. The oil palm is unique in yielding two types of oil: palm oil (from the oil-rich mesocarp containing 50% oil) and palm kernel oil (from the seed endosperm that also contains 50% oil). Of minor importance is the American oil palm (*E. oleifera*) from tropical America.

ORIGIN & HISTORY African oil palm is indigenous to West Africa. The oil has been utilised in rural communities for many centuries. A commercial industry started in West Africa, Sumatra and Malaysia at the beginning of the nineteenth century. The oil palm rapidly became the second most important oil crop (after soybean).

PARTS USED Ripe fruits (mesocarp and endosperm).

CULTIVATION & HARVESTING Young palms are grown from seeds. The thick-shelled Dura type of the past is now replaced with the modern, thin-shelled, higher-yielding Tenera type, giving yields of up to 6.6 tons of palm oil per hectare (the highest yield of all oil crops). The oil is extracted in mechanical presses.

USES & PROPERTIES Palm oil is used mainly to make margarine, cooking oil, snack foods, soap and candles. Palm kernel oil is used in confectionery, ice cream and margarine (also as replacement for cocoa butter).

NUTRITIONAL VALUE In rural areas, unprocessed palm oil is highly nutritious, as it is rich in beta-carotene. Palm oil contains equal proportions of unsaturated and saturated fatty acids, while palm kernel oil is completely saturated.

NOTES Minor food products include palm wine and palm hearts.

Elaeis guineensis Jacq.   family: Arecaceae (Palmae)

you zong (Chinese); *palmier à huile* (French); *Ölpalme* (German); *palma da olio* (Italian); *abura yashi* (Japanese); *kepala sawit* (Malay); *palmera dendém* (Portuguese); *palmera de aceite* (Spanish)

Eleocharis dulcis

Chinese water chestnut

Chinese water chestnut plant

Chinese water chestnuts

Canned Chinese water chestnuts

DESCRIPTION An aquatic plant with a tuft of slender, tubular leaves arising from a rounded tuber or corm that grows below the mud surface. New corms are formed from rhizomes which spread out from older plants. The flattened corm or "chestnut" is dark brown, with a firm white flesh inside. Chinese water chestnut belongs to the sedge family (Cyperaceae) and is often simply called water chestnut. It should therefore not be confused with the common water chestnut, caltrop or ling nut (*Trapa bicornis*), which belongs to the family Trapaceae. The fruits of the ling nut are rich in starch and fat and are used as a staple diet in parts of Asia. The related European water chestnut (*Trapa natans*), also known as water caltrops, saligot, horn nut or Jesuit's nut, is an ancient European food plant but the fruits are no longer used to any extent. Also similar is Chinese arrowroot (*Sagittaria sinensis*) but it has pale brown, more rounded corms.

ORIGIN & HISTORY Old World tropics. It is an ancient Chinese food plant that is nowadays cultivated on a commercial scale in China, Japan, Taiwan and Thailand.

PARTS USED Corms (tuberous stems partly covered with fibrous sheaths).

CULTIVATION & HARVESTING The corms are grown in flooded fields which are drained before harvest. The corms are sold fresh on local markets or are canned for export.

USES & PROPERTIES Chinese water chestnuts have a delicious sweet flavour and crispy texture and may be peeled and eaten raw. This crunchy white vegetable is an important ingredient of Chinese *chop suey* and other dishes. Thin slices are added to soups, fish and meat dishes.

NUTRITIONAL VALUE The corms have a relatively low energy value, with a small amount of starch (5%) and sugars (5%). They also contain fair amounts of minerals and vitamins, especially vitamin B6.

Eleocharis dulcis (Burm. f.) Henschel (= *E. tuberosa* Roem. & Schult.)   family: Cyperaceae

ma ti, ma tai, li zi (Chinese); *macre, madi, châtaigne d'eau* (French); *Chinesische Wassernuss* (German); *singhara* (Hindi); *inu kuro guwai* (Japanese); *nuez china* (Spanish); *haeo* (Thai)

Elettaria cardamomum

cardamom

Cardamom leaves

Cardamom plant with flowers

Cardamom fruits and seeds

DESCRIPTION A perennial herb with broad, pointed, hairless leaves arising from underground rhizomes. It closely resembles ginger but the unique white and pink flowers are borne at ground level on spreading, much-branched flowering clusters bearing scale leaves. The small, three-valved fruit capsules are brown, green or white, depending on the cultivar. Each contains numerous small, angular, highly aromatic, dark brown seeds.

ORIGIN & HISTORY Cardamom is indigenous to peninsular India. Known as the "queen of spices", it was one of the three major spices (with black pepper and dried ginger) of the oriental spice trade as long ago as the third century BC. At first the product was simply wild-harvested but it has become quite rare and is nowadays cultivated on a large scale. Guatemala has become the number one producer, with an annual production of 5 000 tons, closely followed by India with about 4 000 tons. Small amounts are also grown in Sri Lanka, Tanzania and Papua New Guinea.

PARTS USED Ripe fruits and seeds.

CULTIVATION & HARVESTING There are no differences between the wild and cultivated forms of cardamom. The plant is shade loving and is grown under the canopy of trees in tropical climates.

USES & PROPERTIES The spice has a delicious pungent taste. Seeds (alone or with the capsules) are added to Indian curries and curry powders, rice and vegetable dishes, meatballs and sweet desserts. It is very popular as a flavourant of Arabian coffees and is used in Europe and America as an essential ingredient of gingerbread. Scandinavian cooks are amongst the biggest consumers of cardamom – they use it liberally in cooking, confectionery, mulled wines and stewed fruits.

NUTRITIONAL VALUE Used for flavour only.

NOTES Substitutes for true cardamom include the West African melegueta pepper or "grains of paradise" (*Aframomum melegueta*) and several *Amomum* species.

Elettaria cardamomum (L.) Maton   family: Zingiberaceae

bai dou kou, xiao dou kou (Chinese); *cardamomier* (French); *Kardamom* (German); *ilaayacii* (Hindi); *cardamomo* (Italian); *karadamomo* (Japanese); *cardamomo* (Portuguese, Spanish); *luk grawan* (Thai)

Eleusine coracana

Finger millet

African finger millet

Indian goosegrass and African finger millet

African finger millet grains

DESCRIPTION A relatively small, tufted grass, up to 1 m tall, with characteristic finger-like spikes radiating from the tips of the stalks. The grains are small and rounded. Finger millet may be confused with the closely related Indian goosegrass (*E. indica*) but the latter has smaller spikelets and oblong, not rounded, grains.

ORIGIN & HISTORY Wild finger millet (*E. coracana* subsp. *africana*) occurs mainly in Africa, while the cultivated form of the species (*E. coracana* subsp. *coracana*) is widely distributed in Africa and India. The cultivated form has been found in 5 000-year-old archaeological sites in Sudan and Ethiopia, suggesting that finger millet is one of the oldest African crops. Finger millet was carried to India as a cultivated cereal in the first millennium BC. The cultivated form differs mainly in having spikelets that do not shatter when they mature. Five races of cultivated finger millet have been distinguished, based on the size and arrangement of the spikes.

PARTS USED Dry, one-seeded fruits (grains).

CULTIVATION & HARVESTING Finger millet is cultivated along the southern and eastern highlands of Africa and in western Uganda. It is an important cereal in India. The crop is less susceptible to pests and diseases than other grain crops and can be grown in almost any soil, as long as the rainfall is above 800 mm per year. In rural areas, harvesting, threshing and winnowing are often still done by hand. Seed heads may be stored for long periods.

USES & PROPERTIES The grain is ground into flour and used as porridge or for bread. It may also be eaten as gruel. The malted grain has a high sugar content and is popular for brewing traditional beers.

NUTRITIONAL VALUE Finger millet is rich in energy (340 kcal per 100 g) and carbohydrates (75%). The grain contains 6.2% protein and 1.5% fat.

Eleusine coracana (L.) Gaertn.

family: Poaceae

dagussa, tokuso (Amharic, Ethiopia); *tailabon* (Arabic, Sudan); *long zhao ji, ya jiao su* (Chinese); *eleusine cultivée* (French); *Fingerhirse, Ragihirse* (German); *ragi* (Hindi); *coracán, ragi, mijo coracano* (Spanish)

Ensete ventricosum

enset • ensete

Enset plantations

Enset plants

Enset flowers

DESCRIPTION Enset is a single-stemmed, banana-like perennial herb (up to 10 m), with a rounded, underground stem (corm) of up to 1 m in diameter. The large leaves are attached to a short length of true stem but what appears to be the main stem is actually a pseudo-stem formed by the sheathing leaf bases. Numerous flowers and purple bracts form a single flower head of about 1 m long. The fruits resemble small bananas and produce several black, pea-sized seeds.

ORIGIN & HISTORY Enset is widely distributed in southern and eastern Africa. The plant has been domesticated only in Ethiopia, where it is still the staple food of more than 10 million people. It may have been cultivated for at least 5 000 years and more than 50 cultivars or types can be distinguished. Enset is central to the culture of the Sidama, Gurage and other peoples of southern Ethiopia.

PARTS USED Mainly the massive corms (underground stems) and leaf sheaths.

CULTIVATION & HARVESTING Sucker shoots are used for cultivation, rarely seeds. The rural plantations supply not only human food but also fibre for ropes, leaves for wrapping material and animal fodder and dry stems for fuel. The corm and scraped (decorticated) leaf bases are chopped and allowed to ferment for about 20 days. The resultant starch-rich product is called *kocho*. It can be stored (in pits lined with enset leaves) for long periods (even years) without deterioration.

USES & PROPERTIES *Kocho* is mainly used to make flat enset breads (often served with *kitfo* – spiced beef mince). *Bulla* is a more refined, starch-rich, flour-like product that can be used to make various food items such as porridge, pancakes or dumplings. *Amicho* is simply the young corms dug up, chopped into pieces and eaten like potatoes.

NUTRITIONAL VALUE Enset is rich in starch and plays an important role in food security.

Ensete ventricosum (Welw.) Cheesman   family: Musaceae

enset (Amharic); *enset* (French); *Ensete, Zierbanane, Abessinische Banane, Zierbanane* (German); *enset* (Italian, Spanish)

Eragrostis tef

teff • t'ef

Ripe teff

Teff plants

Teff grains

DESCRIPTION A small grass of up to 0.8 m in height bearing relatively narrow leaves and open, much-branched inflorescences with numerous small spikes. The grains are small (about 1 mm in diameter) and vary in colour from reddish brown to white.

ORIGIN & HISTORY Indigenous to the highlands of Ethiopia. It has been grown for centuries to make *injera*, a special Ethiopian bread (see below). White-grained teff was traditionally reserved for royal use. The cereal is also grown on a small scale in Yemen, Kenya, Malawi, India and the USA (and as a cultivated pasture in South Africa and Australia).

PARTS USED The dry, one-seeded fruits (grains).

CULTIVATION & HARVESTING Yields per hectare are relatively low and harvesting is labour intensive, so that the cereal is quite expensive.

USES & PROPERTIES Teff is mainly used for making *injera* – a large, round, flat and somewhat spongy bread with a sour taste. Sieved flour is mixed with a large volume of water (6 litres per 5 kg of flour) and allowed to ferment for two or three days. A little leavening is added and the dough left to rise. A special clay pan (*mitad*) is heated on the fire, greased with oil seeds and the dough poured in a thin layer in concentric circles, from the outside to the centre. A typical meal proceeds with each person breaking off a small piece of the *injera* to first cover and then pick up little bits of various savoury dishes placed in the middle of the bread. Teff is also used with barley in a complicated procedure to make *tella*, a traditional beer.

NUTRITIONAL VALUE Teff contains 9% protein, 2% fat, 74% carbohydrates and is considered a health food, because it is rich in lysine and most of the important minerals. It is also gluten-free and a tasty alternative for persons allergic to wheat.

Eragrostis tef (Zucc.) Trotter (= *E. abyssinica* Link.)   family: Poaceae

tyeff (Amharic); *thaf, t'ef* (Arabic); *mil éthiopien* (French); *Teff, Zwerghirse* (German); *Tefu* (Japanese)

Eriobotrya japonica
loquat

Loquat flowers

Loquat leaves and fruits

Ripe loquats

DESCRIPTION Loquat is a small tree of about 8 m in height with large, leathery leaves that are toothed along the margins. They are glossy, dark green above and white-hairy below. White flowers are borne in clusters on densely woolly stalks. The rounded fruits, the size (and colour) of small apricots, have a downy skin and are borne in clusters, like bunches of grapes (hence *eriobotrya*). The fruits are actually fleshy receptacles (pomes, like apples and pears) with a few large, shiny brown, inedible seeds surrounded by a relatively thin layer of flesh.

ORIGIN & HISTORY Loquat is believed to be indigenous to southeastern China and has been cultivated since ancient times in China and Japan. Numerous cultivars have been developed, differing mainly in colour and texture of the fruit pulp. Loquats are today cultivated in many parts of the world, including Australia, California, India, Israel, the Mediterranean region, South Africa and South America.

PARTS USED Ripe fruits.

CULTIVATION & HARVESTING Loquat is widely grown (as ornamental tree and for fruit) in subtropical and temperate regions. The fruits are picked by hand and sold on local markets. They bruise easily and are therefore not popular for export markets.

USES & PROPERTIES The fruits are delicious to eat raw – they have a slightly acid, refreshing flavour. Loquats may be eaten for dessert, either fresh or as an ingredient of a fruit salad or cooked as compote. They are also processed into conserves (preserved in syrup), jams, jellies, candies and liqueur.

NUTRITIONAL VALUE Loquats have a low energy value (40 kcal per 100 g) and contain about 8% sugars. They are rich in minerals (iron, calcium, selenium), fatty acids, malic acid, as well as vitamin A in the form of beta-carotene (800 µg per 100 g) but are rather low in vitamin C (4 mg per 100 g).

Eriobotrya japonica (Thunb.) Lindley

family: Rosaceae

pi pa (Chinese); *nèfle du japon* (French); *Japanische Wollmispel* (German); *nespola* (Italian); *biwa* (Japanese); *níspero* (Spanish)

Eruca sativa

rocket

Rocket flowers and green fruits

Rocket plant

Rocket leaves

DESCRIPTION A weedy, annual herb with erect stems of up to 0.8 m in height bearing aromatic, lobed leaves (the terminal lobe is larger than the lateral ones, as in turnip and radish). The flowers are white or cream-coloured but marked with dark (reddish) veins. The fruit is an oblong siliqua with a broad, flat tip or beak and contains several small, round, edible, oil-rich seeds.

ORIGIN & HISTORY Rocket is indigenous to the Mediterranean region, where it has been used as an important salad plant for centuries. It is grown as a commercial oilseed in India, Pakistan and Iran (where it replaces rapeseed). The popularity of southern Mediterranean cuisine in the modern world has resulted in rocket becoming universally known.

PARTS USED Fresh leaves (or the seeds).

CULTIVATION & HARVESTING Plants are easily grown from seeds and tend to become weedy. Fresh leaves are produced in market gardens and private kitchen gardens all over the world. As oilseed crop it is handled in the same way as rapeseed and canola.

USES & PROPERTIES Rocket or arugula (*rucola*) is mainly used in fresh salads – the characteristic pungent aroma is often evident when entering French- or Italian-style restaurants. Tender, fresh leaves are used in the traditional salad mixtures known as *mesclun* or *mescladisse* in southern France and *misticanza* in Italy. These often slightly bitter salads typically contain rocket, endive, lettuce, dandelion, purslane, cornsalad, chervil and various other herbs, and are served with *vinaigrette* or olive oil (sometimes with anchovies or walnuts for extra taste). Shredded leaves are used to garnish soup and other dishes. Rocket oil or jamba oil is obtained from the seeds, which contain about 30% oil. This is important as culinary oil (and lubricant) in India.

NUTRITIONAL VALUE Fresh leaves are a rich source of vitamins (especially vitamins A and C), minerals (calcium, iron) and folic acid.

Eruca sativa Mill. [= *E. vesicaria* (L.) Cav. subsp. *sativa* (Miller) Thell.]   family: Brassicaceae

zi ma cai (Chinese); *roquette* (French); *Rauke* (German); *rucola* (Italian); *roketsuto* (Japanese); *rúgula* (Portuguese); *arúgula* (Spanish)

Eugenia uniflora

Surinam cherry • pitanga

Surinam cherry leaves and fruits

Surinam cherry flowers

Surinam cherries

DESCRIPTION A shrub or small tree of up to 6 m in height, with small, dark green leaves in opposite pairs. The young stems and leaves are bright red when they first emerge. Small, white flowers are borne on slender stalks, followed by attractive, bright red, fleshy fruits. Each fruit is markedly ribbed and contains one or two round seeds. *Eugenia* species with edible fruits are loosely referred to as Brazilian cherries, and also include the grumichama (*E. dombeyi*, previously *E. brasiliensis*), the pitomba (*E. luschnathiana*) and the uvalha (*E. uvalha*). The cherry-like fruits on slender stalks are an easy way to tell them from several other fruits (jambolan, water apple, etc.) that have been transferred to the genus *Syzygium* (fruits in branched clusters on short, thick stalks).

ORIGIN & HISTORY The Surinam cherry is indigenous to southern Brazil and northern Argentina. It has been distributed to many warm parts of the world (Africa, southern China, the USA, Central America) but is grown on a commercial scale only in Brazil. The grumichama, pitomba and uvalha all occur naturally in Brazil, where they are of local importance.

PARTS USED Ripe fruits.

CULTIVATION & HARVESTING Surinam cherries are propagated by seeds and are grown in plantations or as an attractive garden shrub or hedge plant. They are pruned to keep the fruits within easy reach. Each tree can produce up to 10 kg of fruit per year.

USES & PROPERTIES Fully ripe fruits are eaten raw – they have a delicious, spicy taste. They also make excellent jams, jellies, candies and sorbets. Various alcoholic and non-alcoholic drinks are prepared from Surinam cherries and other Brazilian cherries, including wine, liqueur and rum punch.

NUTRITIONAL VALUE The fruits are low in sugar (4%) and have an energy value of only 21 kcal. They contain about 25 mg of vitamin C per 100 g.

Eugenia uniflora L.   family: Myrtaceae

hong zi guo (Chinese); *cerise de cayenne* (French); *Pitanga, Surinamkirsche* (German); *ciliegio di cayenna* (Italian); *pitanga da praia* (Portuguese); *pitanga, cereza de cayena* (Spanish); *ma yom farang* (Thai)

Fagopyrum esculentum
buckwheat

Buckwheat leaves and flowers

Buckwheat plants

Buckwheat fruits

DESCRIPTION An annual herb (up to 0.7 m), with soft, heart-shaped leaves and small white or pinkish flowers. The small, dry fruits (achenes) are grey to black and are strongly angular in shape, each with three ribs, a hard shell and a floury endosperm inside. Buckwheat is one of only a few cereals that do not belong to the grass family (it is a pseudocereal). A second species is Siberian buckwheat, Kangra buckwheat or tatary (*F. tataricum*).

ORIGIN & HISTORY Common buckwheat is indigenous to southern China, while tatary occurs naturally from China to northern Pakistan. Buckwheat has been grown in China for at least 1 000 years but is not believed to be an ancient crop. It spread first to Asia and the Middle East and then to Europe and Russia during the Middle Ages, where it became a staple food in some regions. It also reached Africa, the USA and South America (Brazil) relatively recently as a minor crop.

PARTS USED Ripe, dry fruits (achenes).

CULTIVATION & HARVESTING Buckwheat is grown in temperate climates in much the same way as wheat and other cereals. It tolerates poor, sandy soils.

USES & PROPERTIES Dehulled groats are cooked as porridge and form the basis of *kasha* or *kacha*, a traditional Russian dish resembling pilaf. The flour is used for traditional pancakes (in Europe and the USA, and the Russian *blini*), breakfast cereals, Japanese *soba* noodles, certain pastas, biscuits, and various items of confectionery. It is popular as animal and poultry feed.

NUTRITIONAL VALUE Buckwheat is nowadays described as a health food because of the excellent quality of the protein (present at a level of about 9%). It has an energy value of 330–350 kcal per 100 g.

NOTES The name buckwheat comes from the Dutch *boekweit* (*boeke* = beech, *weite* = wheat) – the achenes resemble beechnuts (*Fagus sylvaticus*).

Fagopyrum esculentum Moench

family: Polygonaceae

qiao mai, tian qiao mai (Chinese); *sarrasin* (French); *Buchweizen* (German); *grano saraceno, fagopiro* (Italian); *kyoubaku, soba* (Japanese); *trigo-sarraceno* (Portuguese); *grano sarraceno* (Spanish)

Ferula assa-foetida
asafoetida • devil's dung

Asafoetida plant

Asafoetida fruits

Asafoetida gum (devil's dung)

DESCRIPTION Asafoetida is an erect perennial herb with flowering stems of up to 2 m in height arising from a fleshy taproot. The hairless leaves are finely dissected and dark green in colour. Small yellow flowers are borne in typical compound umbels, followed by small, oblong dry fruits. Gum is mainly obtained from *F. assa-foetida* but also from *F. foetida* and *F. narthex*. The name *assa-foetida* comes from *aza* (Persian for gum) and *foetida* (Latin for foul-smelling).

ORIGIN & HISTORY Asafoetida is indigenous to Iran and Afghanistan. It is one of several plants of the carrot family (Apiaceae or Umbelliferae) that are harvested for various resinous gums used mainly in scents, incenses, perfumes and traditional medicine. Of particular interest is an ancient Roman condiment known as *silphium* or *laserpitium*, obtained from a North African plant that is believed to be extinct as a result of over-exploitation. It was highly prized – said to have fetched the same price as gold. *Silphium*

appears to have been replaced by asafoetida. These gums are produced in a wide region that includes Iran, Afghanistan, Pakistan and India.

PARTS USED Oleoresin gum.

CULTIVATION & HARVESTING Gum is obtained from the upper part of the roots of wild plants by making incisions and collecting the excreted milky latex, which is dried to a waxy, orange-brown gum.

USES & PROPERTIES Asafoetida has a strong, unpleasant, sulphurous smell that earned it the name devil's dung (*Teufelsdreck* in German). It is an important spice in oriental cooking and is used sparingly in meat dishes, stews, gravies, sauces and pickles. The unpleasant odour disappears during cooking but the spice has nevertheless not become popular in western cuisine except as an ingredient of the famous Worcester sauce.

NUTRITIONAL VALUE The gum is used in very small amounts.

NOTES Asafoetida is best known as a carminative and antispasmodic in traditional medicine.

Ferula assa-foetida L.

family: Apiaceae

ferule persique, ase fétide (French); *Stinkasant, Teufelsdreck* (German); *assafetida* (Italian)

Ficus carica

fig tree

Fig tree

Fig leaves and fruits

Dried figs

DESCRIPTION A small deciduous tree (4–7 m high) bearing large, rough-textured, three- to five-lobed leaves. The fig is actually a fleshy, hollow branch modified to bear numerous small flowers and fruits on the inside, with a small hole at the tip (the ostiole) through which the pollinators (small wasps) can enter. This specialised structure, unique to *Ficus*, is called a syconium. Wild figs are dioecious, with male syconia and female syconia on separate trees (known as "caprifigs"). Modern cultivars are female only (known as "true figs"). There are several hundreds of cultivars with green, brown, purple or black skins.

ORIGIN & HISTORY Eastern Mediterranean region. Figs are one of the most ancient of all crops – archaeological evidence indicates that figs have been cultivated since 4000 BC (in Mesopotamia and ancient Egypt). Its present-day cultivation area in the Old World was established in Roman times. Figs are today grown in all temperate regions of the world.

PARTS USED Syconia ("fig fruits").

CULTIVATION & HARVESTING Most fig trees are female and therefore grown from cuttings. Smyrna figs have to be pollinated by suspending twigs of male caprifigs near the female trees to ensure that the fig wasps pollinate the female syconia. Figs are harvested by hand or mechanically and are usually exported in dried or processed form.

USES & PROPERTIES Figs are delicious when eaten fresh (or served as *hors d'oeuvre* with Parma ham or cheese) or dried (perhaps stuffed with almonds or served with pork). Figs are used in cooking, desserts, confectionery, jams, preserves and drinks such as *figuette* (dried figs and juniper berries soaked in water) and to flavour coffee.

NUTRITIONAL VALUE Figs are amongst the sweetest of all fruits – available carbohydrates are 13% in fresh and 55% in dried figs (61 and 250 kcal per 100 g respectively). They are also very rich in minerals and vitamins and have mild laxative effects.

Ficus carica L.   family: Moraceae

wu hua guo (Chinese); *figue* (French); *Feigenbaum* (German); *anjeer* (Hindi); *fico* (Italian); *ichijiku* (Japanese); *figueira* (Portuguese); *higo, higuera* (Spanish)

Foeniculum vulgare

fennel

Florence fennel

Fennel plants

Fennel fruits

DESCRIPTION A perennial herb (up to 1.5 m) with compound leaves that are finely divided into segments, giving them a feathery appearance. Small yellow flowers and the small, dry fruits are borne in distinctive, compound umbels. Two varieties are widely cultivated: the normal sweet fennel, var. *dulce*, grown mainly for the small fruits and var. *azoricum*, known as Florence fennel, a smaller plant grown for the white, bulbous leaf bases.

ORIGIN & HISTORY Mediterranean region. The Greeks called it *marathon* (a symbol of victory over the Persians in 490 BC), the Egyptians used it as a spice and the Romans as a vegetable (Florence fennel is still the most popular vegetable in Italy and Sicily). Today fennel is cultivated worldwide.

PARTS USED Leaves, leaf stalks, swollen stems and the small, dry fruits ("seeds").

CULTIVATION & HARVESTING Fennel is hardy and easily grown from seed – in kitchen gardens and commercial market gardens. The near-ripe fruits are harvested for use as spice or may be steam-distilled to obtain an essential oil rich in anethole. Florence fennel is grown as an annual.

USES & PROPERTIES Leaves are traditionally used with fish dishes, in the same way as dill. They give an anise flavour to soups, stews and meat dishes. Florence fennel is popular as salad ingredient (raw, sliced) or it is cooked as a vegetable, on its own or in a variety of dishes, in much the same way as celery. The fruit oil provides the anise flavour for some liqueurs (see also anise, *Pimpinella anisum*).

NUTRITIONAL VALUE Fennel leaves are rich in minerals (especially potassium) and vitamins A, B, C and E (including 100 μg of folic acid per 100 g). The energy value is low (26 kcal per 100 g). The fruits add few nutrients to the diet as they are used in small amounts, but they are carminative and improve digestion.

NOTES *Foeniculum* is the Latin for "little hay".

Foeniculum vulgare Mill.   family: Apiaceae

hui xiang (Chinese); *fenouil* (French); *Fenchel* (German); *finocchio* (Italian); *fenneru* (Japanese); *funcho* (Portuguese); *hinojo* (Spanish); *phak chi* (Thai)

Fortunella margarita
kumquat • oval kumquat

Kumquat plant

Kumquat flowers and fruits

DESCRIPTION A shrub or small tree of 3–4 m in height bearing small pointed leaves, fragrant white flowers and small, egg-shaped fruits resembling small oranges. The fruit is smooth, bright orange with only four or five segments and two to five seeds. Three species are grown for their fruits: the oval kumquat or 'Nagami' (*F. margarita*), which is the best known of all; the round kumquat or 'Marumi' (*F. japonica*), which has round (globose) fruit with six or seven segments; and the large round kumquat or 'Meiwa' (*F. crassifolia*, known as *neihankinkan* in Japan) which has a thick, sweet rind. Limequats are artificial hybrids between West Indian lime and kumquat.

ORIGIN & HISTORY The kumquat originated in southern or central China and has always been an important fruit crop in China, Vietnam and Japan. It only became known in western countries in the mid-nineteenth century. Today, the oval kumquat is grown commercially in Brazil, California, Florida, Israel and Morocco (round kumquat is less common). An estimated 3 500 tons of large round kumquat are produced in China, Japan and Vietnam each year but it is hardly known elsewhere.

PARTS USED Ripe fruits.

CULTIVATION & HARVESTING Kumquats are exceptionally cold hardy and are easily cultivated (often as ornamental plants). Fruits are left to ripen completely before they are harvested.

USES & PROPERTIES Unlike other citrus types, the kumquat is eaten whole (unpeeled) with seeds and all. The fruit flesh is sour, the outer rind is spicy and the inner rind (albedo) is sweet. The fruits are preserved or processed into jams, marmalades, jellies and chutneys or candied and used in confectionery. The fruits are used as flavourant in meat dishes and stuffings for poultry.

NUTRITIONAL VALUE Kumquat has a relatively high energy value (65 kcal per 100 g) and is rich in calcium, potassium and vitamin A.

Fortunella margarita (Lour.) Swingle   family: Rutaceae

chuikan (Chinese); *kumquat* (French); *Kumquat* (German); *kumquat* (Italian); *kikan* (Japanese); *kumquat* (Spanish)

Fragaria ananassa
strawberry • pineapple strawberry

Strawberry flowers and fruits

Strawberry plant

Strawberries

DESCRIPTION A perennial herb with a very short, woody stem and a rosette of compound leaves. The white flowers are borne in small groups, followed by the reddish false fruits – actually a swollen, edible stalk (receptacle) – bearing numerous tiny little fruits (achenes) on the surface. The plants reproduce by stolons or runners. All of the many known *Fragaria* species are edible (some are dioecious, others monoecious). Cultivated species include the European wild strawberry (*F. vesca*), the Chilean strawberry (*F. chiloensis*), the North American strawberry (*F. virginiana*) and the musk strawberry or hautbois strawberry, *F. moschata*.

ORIGIN & HISTORY Modern strawberry (*F. ananassa*), the so-called pineapple strawberry, is an accidental hybrid that originated in Europe (around 1750) as a cross between cultivated Chilean strawberry and the North American strawberry. The numerous cultivars of *F. ananassa* that now predominate have the large size of the Chilean strawberry combined with a pineapple flavour.

PARTS USED Ripe fruits (false fruits).

CULTIVATION & HARVESTING Strawberries are grown in all temperate and some subtropical regions. Plants are easily produced from runners and are replaced with new plants every few years. Modern cultivars are hermaphroditic and self-compatible, but cross-pollination is advantageous for full fruit set. Strawberry is an important commercial fruit with an estimated annual crop of several million tons.

USES & PROPERTIES Strawberries are delicious to eat fresh (often with a little sugar and cream, or in fruit salads, mousses and ice cream). They may be steeped in wine, champagne, brandy or liqueur (Kirsch) and are used in confectionery (pies, cakes and soufflés). Strawberries are processed into jams, jellies, preserves, sweets and fruit juice.

NUTRITIONAL VALUE Strawberries have a low calorific value (26 kcal per 100 g) and contain 5–6% sugar. They are a rich source of vitamin C (about 60 mg in fresh and 30 mg in canned fruit).

Fragaria ananassa Duchesne ex Rozier

family: Rosaceae

cao mei (Chinese); *fraisier* (French); *Erdbeere* (German); *fragola* (Italian); *ichigo, sutoroberii* (Japanese); *morango* (Portuguese); *fresa* (Spanish)

Garcinia mangostana

mangosteen

African mangosteen fruits

Mangosteen leaves

Mangosteen fruits

DESCRIPTION A medium-sized to large evergreen tree that may reach 20 m at maturity. It has large simple leaves and attractive, scented flowers that develop into round, dark purple fruit with characteristic sepals that persist around the stalk end of the fruit. The thick, purple, relatively soft outer layer surrounds the delicious segmented fruit pulp, which is white or cream-coloured. The imbé or African mangosteen (*G. livingstonei*) also bears delicious orange fruits that are widely used in Africa for eating or brewing beer. Several Southeast Asian and Indian species have sour fruits which are sliced and sun-dried as a tamarind-like spice. These include *asam gelugor* (*G. atroviridis*), wild mangosteen or *assam aur aur* (*G. hombroniana*), the Indian kokam tree (*G. indica*) and malabar tamarind (*G. gummi-guta*, previously *G. cambogia*). Seeds of the West and Central African false kola (*G. kola*) are chewed as stimulant.

ORIGIN & HISTORY Mangosteen is indigenous to Malaysia. It is a cultigen and possibly a hybrid between *G. hombroniana* and *G. malaccensis*. Small-scale cultivation occurs in Southeast Asia, Sri Lanka, and in recent years also in Central America and tropical parts of the USA.

PARTS USED Ripe fruits.

CULTIVATION & HARVESTING The tree is notoriously difficult to propagate (seeds and cuttings are equally problematic) and takes up to 10 years to bear fruit. The fruits bruise easily, so they are only sold on local markets.

USES & PROPERTIES Fruits are eaten fresh (considered by many people to be the most delicious of all tropical fruits – if durian is king, then mangosteen must surely be queen!). It has a delicate sweet-sour taste that goes well with fruit salads, ice creams, sorbets or fruit purées.

NUTRITIONAL VALUE The fruit flesh is relatively rich in sugar (16–18%) and has a high energy value (75 kcal per 100 g). The vitamin C content is low (2–3 mg).

Garcinia mangostana L.

family: Clusiaceae

dao nian zi, shan zhu (Chinese); *mangostanier* (French); *Mangostane* (German); *manggis* (Indonesian); *mangostano* (Italian); *mangosuchin* (Japanese); *manggis* (Malay); *mangostão* (Portuguese); *mangostán* (Spanish); *mangkut* (Thai)

Ginkgo biloba

ginkgo • maidenhair tree

Ginkgo leaves

Ginkgo fruits (female cones)

Ginkgo nuts

DESCRIPTION A large, deciduous tree (up to 35 m) with male and female cones borne on separate trees. The distinctive leaves are fan-shaped, bilobed and have parallel veins. Female cones have a fleshy outer layer that ferments and gives off an unpleasant odour (like rancid butter) but the egg-shaped seed, surrounded by a white, bony layer, is edible and much sought after. They are known as ginkgo nuts or white nuts (*li zi* in Chinese).

ORIGIN & HISTORY Indigenous to eastern China. It is a "living fossil" (identical to fossils that are 200 million years old). The tree has been cultivated in China (especially in temples) since ancient times and was taken to Japan and Korea about 1 000 years ago. Ginkgo has become a popular street tree all over the world. Commercial plantations in China, France and the USA produce leaf extracts that are used in medicine (improvement of age-related circulatory disorders).

PARTS USED Seeds.

CULTIVATION & HARVESTING Propagation by cuttings allows the selective production of male or female plants as required. Trees are exceptionally hardy and withstand pollution and high salinity remarkably well. Flowering starts after 20 years but trees are known to live up to 1 000 years. The cones are collected by hand and cleaned to remove the outer fleshy layer. Seeds are sold fresh or canned (boiled in water).

USES & PROPERTIES Seeds are roasted, boiled, grilled or steamed and eaten as a snack or used as a vegetable or garnish, especially in vegetarian dishes. They accompany various Chinese, Korean and Japanese dishes, including stir-fries, stews and the famous bird's-nest soup (nests built by a type of Chinese swallow, that become gelatinous and sticky when poached in duck or chicken soup).

NUTRITIONAL VALUE The seeds (nuts) are nutritious: they contain 13% protein and 3% fats (comprising linoleic, oleic, palmitic and linolenic acids).

Ginkgo biloba L.   family: Ginkgoaceae

bai guo (Chinese); *ginkgo* (French); *Ginkgo* (German); *ginkgo biloba* (Italian); *pa kewo* (Japanese); *arbol de los escudos* (Spanish)

Glycine max

soybean

Soybean plant

Soybean flower and pod

Soybeans

DESCRIPTION A hairy annual herb of up to 0.5 m in height. The compound leaves each have three broad leaflets. Minute flowers, without stalks, are borne in the leaf axils, followed by broad, flat, hairy pods that each contains up to four seeds. The seeds are very variable in size and colour (from black to white) depending on the cultivar.

ORIGIN & HISTORY Wild soya (*G. soja*) is indigenous to China, Japan, Korea, Taiwan and the former USSR. Domestication probably occurred around the eleventh century BC in northeastern China. It slowly spread to southern China, other parts of Asia and eventually the New World. Soybean is today the most important grain legume crop (100 million tons per year, mainly produced in the USA, Brazil, China and Argentina).

PARTS USED Seeds (also green beans and sprouts).

CULTIVATION & HARVESTING The plant is grown as an annual crop and the ripe pods are harvested mechanically.

USES & PROPERTIES Soybean is a feature of Asian cuisine. Important soy products are soy paste (*miso*), soy sauce (*shoyu*), soy curd (*tofu*), soy milk and fermented soy cakes (*tempeh*). Fresh beans are served as a vegetable with meat dishes, while dry beans are used in soups, salads and sweet dishes. Bean sprouts are commonly added to salads, sweet-and-sour vegetables or spring rolls. Soy flour is used in sauces and confectionery and soy oil is converted to salad oils, mayonnaise and margarine. Processed soybean proteins have become important as meat and milk substitutes.

NUTRITIONAL VALUE A cornerstone of east Asian (and vegetarian) nutrition. The exceptionally high protein content (30–40%) combines with up to 400 kcal per 100 g and many of the essential amino acids, minerals and vitamins required for a healthy diet. Low levels of breast and colon cancer in China and Japan are associated with the high consumption of soybeans.

Glycine max (L.) Merr.   family: Fabaceae

da hou, huang dou (Chinese); *fève de soja, haricot soja* (French); *Sojabohne* (German); *kedelai* (Indonesian); *soia* (Italian); *daizu* (Japanese); *kacang soya* (Malay); *fríjol soya* (Spanish); *thua lueang* (Thai)

Glycyrrhiza glabra

liquorice • licorice

Liquorice flowers

Liquorice plant with fruits

Liquorice roots

DESCRIPTION A perennial herb (up to 1 m) with a network of woody rhizomes below the ground and erect stems above the ground bearing compound leaves. Pale purple or white flowers are borne in elongated clusters in the leaf axils. The bristly pods contain a few small, bean-shaped seeds. Chinese liquorice or *gan cao* (*G. uralensis*) is used in the same way as ordinary liquorice. "Licorice" is the spelling used in the USA and Canada.

ORIGIN & HISTORY Mediterranean region to Central Asia. The plant was known to the ancient Greeks and Romans and has been cultivated for centuries. It was grown extensively around Pontefract in Yorkshire, England in the sixteenth century. Liquorice is grown as a commercial crop mainly in the southern Mediterranean region (Spain, France, Italy), Turkey and Russia.

PARTS USED Dried rhizomes ("liquorice root").

CULTIVATION & HARVESTING Liquorice is propagated from seeds or from rhizome tips kept

for replanting after the harvest. Plants are ready for harvesting after three to five years – the entire plant is dug up and the rhizomes cut in lengths and washed. The rhizomes are sold or more often a syrupy, black juice (a water extract, concentrated by boiling).

USES & PROPERTIES Rhizome pieces may be chewed as a sweet snack, but liquorice juice is mostly used in confectionery, drinks (such as liquorice water), dark beers (stout) and liqueurs. Various types of hard or pliable liquorice sweets are made by mixing the juice (concentrate) with gum arabic, starch or icing sugar and flavouring agents.

NUTRITIONAL VALUE Used as flavourant and sweetener only. Large amounts over long periods may be harmful. Extracts contain 5–10% glycyrrhizine, a mixture of saponins that is 50 times sweeter than sugar. Liquorice is a useful sweetener for diabetics.

NOTES Extracts are used in natural medicine as expectorant, anti-inflammatory and antispasmodic, but also to mask the unpleasant taste of medicine.

Glycyrrhiza glabra L.   family: Fabaceae

gan cao (Chinese); *réglisse* (French); *Süßholz, Lakritzpflanze* (German); *liquirizia* (Italian); *regaliz* (Spanish)

Gnetum gnemon

melinjo

Melinjo leaves

Melinjo cones

Melinjo young fruits

DESCRIPTION An evergreen, medium-sized tree of up to 10 m in height bearing large, simple, glossy leaves. The inflorescences are erect spikes with inconspicuous cones which developed into oblong, green and red, fleshy fruits. Inside the thin, fleshy, outer layer is a hard shell that surrounds the edible seed (nut). Two other species are also minor sources of food, namely the eru (*G. africanum*), a tropical African climber with edible leaves and tubers and the Southeast Asian *G. costatum* which has edible leaves, flowers and seeds.

ORIGIN & HISTORY The melinjo is a poorly known food plant indigenous to Indonesia, Malaysia and Thailand. It is a traditional forest food of Indonesia that has probably been used for many centuries. The plant is now cultivated to a limited extent. Specimens are often seen in botanical gardens in warm regions.

PARTS USED Leaves and seeds (nuts).

CULTIVATION & HARVESTING Trees are mainly propagated from seeds. They require a tropical climate and several years to become productive. Leaves and fruits are also wild-harvested.

USES & PROPERTIES The melinjo is best known as a source of flour (made from the ground seeds) that is used to make *emping*, a flat, crisp, deep-fried wafer biscuit that is very common in Indonesia. It has a slightly bitter, nutty taste and is used as a snack food. *Emping* is often seen in Indonesian restaurants where it is kept in glass jars. The leaves and young flowers are used in Thailand as a vegetable and are an ingredient of vegetable soup. In West Java, a popular vegetable dish known as *sayur asam* contains young leaves and young fruits of melinjo as an essential ingredient. Melinjo fruits can also be boiled, peeled, shelled and the seeds eaten as nuts.

NUTRITIONAL VALUE No information could be found on the nutritional value of the leaves or nuts.

Gnetum gnemon L.   family: Gnetaceae

xian zhou mai ma teng (Chinese); *gnetum à feuilles comestibles* (French); *Gnetumbaum* (German); *melinjo* (Indonesian); *melinjo* (Malay); *pee sae* (Thai)

Gossypium hirsutum

cotton • American cotton

Cotton plant

Cotton plantation

Cotton in fruit

DESCRIPTION *Gossypium* species are shrubs or small trees with simple, hairy leaves and attractive, mostly yellow flowers. The fruits contain several seeds covered with very long seed hairs (these are single cells, 3 000 times longer than wide, commonly known as cotton).

ORIGIN & HISTORY There are four species of commercial cotton: Old World diploids (*G. herbaceum* and *G. arboreum*) and New World tetraploid cottons (*G. hirsutum* and *G. barbadense*). Cotton is an ancient textile crop, independently domesticated in different parts of the world from four different ancestral species. Today there are numerous types of cotton and countless cultivars, each with it own complicated history. So-called Upland cotton, derived from *G. hirsutum*, now accounts for 90% of the world's cotton harvest, produced in 40 countries in temperate and tropical regions. Cotton is second only to soybean as a source of edible seed oil. Cotton oil is a modern innovation (a by-product of the cotton industry).

PARTS USED Seed oil.

CULTIVATION & HARVESTING Modern cultivars of all four species are grown from seed as annuals, but Upland cotton has become predominant. The industry is highly mechanised but in some regions, harvesting and processing are still done by hand. Oil is obtained by solvent extraction after removal of the seed hairs by a process known as ginning.

USES & PROPERTIES Crude cotton oil is dark brown and unsuitable for use as edible oil unless refined. The refined oil is used in the food industry to produce margarine, cooking fats and oils. It solidifies at room temperature and is therefore rarely used as cooking oil. It is used in food processing (sardines, for example, are packed in cotton oil).

NUTRITIONAL VALUE Cotton seeds contain 20–30% oil (predominantly polyunsaturated fat). The refined oil has a high energy value (880 kcal per 100 g) and contains 38 mg of vitamin E per 100 g.

Gossypium hirsutum L.   family: Fabaceae

lu di mian (Chinese); *cotonnier américain* (French); *Amerikanische Baumwolle* (German); *algodoeiro americano* (Portuguese); *algodôn, algodonero americano* (Spanish)

Guizotia abyssinica

niger seed

Niger seed flower heads

Niger seed plant

Niger seed fruits

DESCRIPTION An annual herb (up to 1.5 m), with hairy stems and broad, toothed leaves that are somewhat sandpapery in texture. Attractive yellow flower heads (20–30 mm in diameter) are borne singly or in clusters, each with 40-60 central disc florets surrounded by ligulate florets. The fruit is a small, black, one-seeded achene, often simply referred to as the seed. It resembles a sunflower seed but is much smaller and narrower.

ORIGIN & HISTORY Niger seed is indigenous to Ethiopia, where it has probably served as a rural food source for centuries. The plant has become an important oil crop in Ethiopia and southern India (where respectively about 200 000 and 100 000 tons of oil are produced each year). In Ethiopia, the oil is known as *nehigue* or "noog".

PARTS USED The small, dry fruits.

CULTIVATION & HARVESTING Niger seed is sown in tropical areas, often in rotation with maize or wheat. Flower heads are harvested mechanically or by hand as soon as the florets have wilted. They are then sun-dried, threshed, winnowed and the seeds purified by sieving.

USES & PROPERTIES Niger seed yields a clear, high quality edible oil that can be used as substitute for olive oil or can be mixed with linseed oil, rape oil or sesame oil. The seeds can be fried and eaten (or pressed with honey and made into sweet cakes) or used as a condiment. The oil also has industrial uses in paint, soap and as an illuminant. The seeds have become popular as a food for cage birds and the oil cake (left after oil extraction) is a valuable livestock feed.

NUTRITIONAL VALUE The seeds have an energy value of more than 475 kJ per 100 g and contain about 18% protein, 32% fat and 35% carbohydrates. The main fatty acids are linoleic acid (50%) and oleic acid (35%).

Guizotia abyssinica (L. f.) Cass.   family: Asteraceae

nuk (Amharic); *guizotia oléifere, niger* (French); *Gingellikraut, Nigersaat* (German); *ramtil* (Hindi); *verbesina da India* (Portuguese); *negrillo, ramtilla* (Spanish)

Helianthus annuus

sunflower

Sunflower plant

Sunflower flower heads

Sunflower seeds

DESCRIPTION A tall, robust annual herb (up to 4 m) with sturdy stems and large, coarsely hairy leaves. A single, very large flower head (up to 0.5 m in diameter) is borne at the stem tip. It has numerous, dark brown, fertile disc florets in the middle, with a ring of yellow, sterile ligulate florets around the edge. The fruits are one-seeded achenes (usually referred to as seeds) that are black, brown, grey or striped.

ORIGIN & HISTORY The sunflower is indigenous to the western parts of the USA. It was probably an important food source of the indigenous people and appears to have been domesticated around the second millennium BC. It was taken to Europe in the sixteenth century and became an important oil crop in Russia (where oil-rich cultivars, yielding 50% oil, were developed) and later in other parts of the world (today one of the top three oil crops of the world).

PARTS USED Ripe fruits (achenes).

CULTIVATION & HARVESTING Sunflower is sown as an annual, drought-tolerant crop. Dwarf cultivars that can be mechanically harvested have become popular.

USES & PROPERTIES The main use is for edible oil (suitable for salad oil, mayonnaise and cooking oil) and for the manufacture of margarine. The husked seeds (sometimes roasted or salted) have become a popular snack food, ingredient of breakfast cereals and are used to make sweets and confectionery. Dried seeds can be used to make sunflower seed flour. The seeds are fed to cage birds and the seed cake to stock animals.

NUTRITIONAL VALUE Sunflower seeds are exceptionally nutritious. They have a high energy value (570 kJ per 100 g) and are a rich source of protein (23%), vitamin E, essential amino acids and polyunsaturated fats (50% fat content). In contrast, the consumption of large quantities of the extracted oil is considered to be unhealthy.

Helianthus annuus L.   family: Asteraceae

xiang ri kui (Chinese); *soleil, tournesol* (French); *Sonnenblume* (German); *corona del sole, girasole* (Italian); *himawari, koujitsuki* (Japanese); *girassol* (Portuguese); *girasol* (Spanish)

Helianthus tuberosus

Jerusalem artichoke

Jerusalem artichoke flower heads

Jerusalem artichoke plant

Jerusalem artichokes

DESCRIPTION An erect, robust, deciduous perennial herb of up to 2 m in height. It is similar to the sunflower but the flower heads are much smaller and borne in sparse clusters. The edible part is the fleshy underground rhizomes, which may be white, yellow or reddish in colour and irregular in shape. Unrelated but with very similar uses is the Chinese artichoke (*Stachys sieboldii*), a member of the mint family (Lamiaceae). It is known as *crosne* in French, *gan lu zi* in Chinese, *chorogi* in Japanese and as *tung tung chow* in Malay. The small tubers were once popular as an exotic vegetable but they take a long time to peel (described as "small and fiddly"). They nevertheless have a delicate taste and are cooked in butter or prepared exactly like Jerusalem artichoke.

ORIGIN & HISTORY Indigenous to North America (a cultivated food plant of the Indians). It reached Europe in the sixteenth century and is commonly cultivated in many parts of the world but remains a minor crop.

PARTS USED Rhizomes.

CULTIVATION & HARVESTING Plants are easily grown from rhizomes that can be harvested at any time during the growing season.

USES & PROPERTIES Peeled and sliced (diced) rhizomes are commonly used to make cold salad (like potato salad). They are boiled, braised or steamed and eaten as a vegetable, served with cream, butter or a suitable sauce. The sliced rhizomes are also fried in batter and made into purées and soufflés. The taste is similar to that of artichoke.

NUTRITIONAL VALUE Jerusalem artichoke is considered a health food despite its flatulent properties. It is nutritious, with high levels of potassium and phosphorus and low energy yields (only 32 kcal per 100 g). The storage carbohydrate is not starch but inulin (not digested in the human body) but the presence of fructose makes it suitable for diabetics.

Helianthus tuberosus L.   family: Asteraceae

ju yu (Chinese); *topinambour* (French); *Topinambur, Erdbirne, Jerusalem Artischocke* (German); *topinambur, carciofo di gerusalemme* (Italian); *kiku imo* (Japanese); *pataca* (Spanish)

Hibiscus sabdariffa

hibiscus • roselle • Jamaica sorrel

Hibiscus leaves and flower

Hibiscus fruits with fleshy calyces

Hibiscus flowers (dried calyces)

DESCRIPTION An erect annual herb (usually 2 m in height) with lobed leaves and white or yellow flowers. The petals are surrounded by a single row of fleshy red sepals (the calyx) and an outer row of bracts that resembles a second row of sepals (the epicalyx, typical of the Malvaceae). The sepals (calyces), known as "hibiscus flowers" are dark red, fleshy and edible.

ORIGIN & HISTORY The plant is indigenous to Africa (Angola). It is grown in all warm regions of the world. The main producers are North Africa (Sudan and Egypt), Java, the Philippines, Mexico, India, Thailand and China.

PARTS USED Dried calyces (rarely the leaves).

CULTIVATION & HARVESTING Plants are easily grown from seeds and the ripe fruits are harvested. The persistent calyces are removed by hand and dried.

USES & PROPERTIES The sweet-sour taste and dark red colour of hibiscus flowers make them popular as additive to herbal teas (or "hibiscus tea", a tasty tea in its own right). Hibiscus flowers provide a natural colourant for use in food and especially in alcoholic and non-alcoholic beverages. They are used to make sauces, jellies, jams, chutneys and preserves. The product is used in cooking as a condiment, to flavour meat and fish sauces. *Karkade* is a refreshing, sour drink made from hibiscus that is popular in Egypt. Young leaves can be used like spinach.

NUTRITIONAL VALUE Hibiscus makes a refreshing, caffeine-free drink. It is rich in mucilage polysaccharides (15%), organic acids (including hibiscus, ascorbic, citric, tartaric and malic acids), as well as dark red pigments (anthocyanins, 0.15%) all of which contribute to some extent to the health properties. The mild laxative effect is ascribed to the organic acids.

NOTES Hibiscus tea is a general health tonic used to treat appetite loss, colds, coughs and circulatory ailments. It is a gentle expectorant, laxative and diuretic.

Hibiscus sabdariffa L.

family: Malvaceae

mei gui qie, shan qie zi (Chinese); *karkadé, roselle, oseille de Guinée* (French); *Rosellahanf, Sabdariffa-Eibisch* (German); *karcadè* (Italian); *roozera* (Japanese); *rosela, vinagreira* (Portuguese); *rosa de Jamaica* (Spanish)

Hordeum vulgare

barley

Barley ears

Barley plants

Naked barley and barley

DESCRIPTION A grass of up to 1 m in height with spikelets arranged in threes at each node of the ear. The husk usually adheres to the grain (as in oats) or falls free on threshing in the case of naked barley. Wild barley and some cultivated forms are two-rowed, meaning that only the central spikelet of the three develops into a grain; cultivated types also include six-rowed barley, in which all three spikelets are fertile.

ORIGIN & HISTORY Middle East. Barley is one of the oldest of all crops – domestication occurred in Mesopotamia some 10 000 years ago. It spread to ancient Egypt, Ethiopia and ancient Greece at an early date. Wheat replaced barley as the staple food in classical times. Today, the main uses are animal feed, malt for beer and human food (in order of importance).

PARTS USED Dry one-seeded fruits (grains).

CULTIVATION & HARVESTING Barley is a short-season, early maturing grain tolerant of saline conditions. The grain is germinated (enzymatic conversion of starch to sugars) and then rapidly kiln-dried to produce malt for brewing.

USES & PROPERTIES Barley is a nutritious cereal used as food in the form of flour (it makes flat bread, since gluten is absent), pearl barley (used in soups and stews) or pot barley (polished grains, freed from the husk), barley groats or grits (dehusked, fragmented) and barley flakes. Barley water is made by soaking barley in water and flavouring it with lemon or orange. The massive beer-brewing industry is based on barley malt that is fermented to convert the sugars into alcohol and then flavoured with hops (1 ton barley gives 750 kg malt and 4 000 litres beer). Distillation produces whiskey and other alcoholic drinks.

NUTRITIONAL VALUE Excellent, with high levels of vitamin B5 and lysine. The energy yield is 310–350 kcal per 100 g.

Hordeum vulgare L.

family: Poaceae

mai ya (Chinese); *orge* (French); *Gerste* (German); *orzo* (Italian); *cebada* (Spanish)

Hovenia dulcis

Japanese raisin tree

Raisin tree leaves and green fruits

Raisin tree fruit stalks

Raisin tree health drink

DESCRIPTION This is an attractive, erect, deciduous tree of about 10 m in height. It has simple leaves with prominent lateral veins, each of which has a minute pocket (swelling) where it meets with the midrib. The inconspicuous white flowers develop into small, inedible capsules of about 4 mm in diameter. The branched flower stalks are remarkable in that they swell markedly as the fruit matures and become edible – they end up thick, juicy, reddish in colour and sweet-tasting.

ORIGIN & HISTORY The tree is indigenous to Japan, China, Korea and the Himalayas. It is commonly cultivated as an ornamental tree along streets and in gardens. It is rarely seen outside the natural distribution area except in parks and botanical gardens. It is sometimes also referred to as the Chinese raisin tree.

PARTS USED The fleshy fruit stalks.

CULTIVATION & HARVESTING Trees are mostly propagated from cuttings and can easily be grown in temperate regions. They withstand quite severe frost and grow rapidly in almost any soil. The fleshy stalks are harvested by hand when the small fruit capsules ripen and dry out. They are rarely seen on fresh produce markets and are not commercially cultivated to any extent.

USES & PROPERTIES This unusual food has a delicious, fruity taste that has been compared to that of dried fruits (a combination of raisins, dried figs and jujube). It is widely eaten fresh as a snack food, especially by rural children but can also be dried and stored for several months. The stalks can be crushed in water and fermented to produce an alcoholic drink. It is also used to make a health drink that is said to be helpful against hangovers.

NUTRITIONAL VALUE The stalks are rich in sugars (up to 23%). The seeds contain up to 15% protein and are sometimes eaten with the stalks.

Hovenia dulcis Thunb.

family: Rhamnaceae

kouai tsao (Chinese); *raisin de chine* (French); *Japanischer Rosinenbaum* (German); *ovenia dolce* (Italian); *kemponashi* (Japanese); *uva japonesa* (Spanish)

Humulus lupulus
hop • hops

Hops cones (and male flowers)

Hops (ripe fruits)

Hops plants

DESCRIPTION A perennial, deciduous, wind-pollinated creeper (vine) that may climb up to 10 m high. The stems (called bines) emerge each year from a woody rootstock and bear deeply lobed, toothed leaves. Male and female flowers occur on separate plants – only females are grown (propagated by cuttings) in order to prevent pollination. Hops are the cone-like female flower clusters. Several small flowers are hidden by the leaf-like, overlapping bracts. Towards their bases they have numerous small, glistening lupulin glands which produce essential oils and resins and give the hops its aroma and bitter taste.

ORIGIN & HISTORY Hops is indigenous to the northern temperate regions of Europe, Asia and North America. The first record of wild hops being used in brewing dates back to 3 000 years ago but the first cultivation was recorded in Bavaria in the eighth century. Cultivated hops spread from central Europe to the rest of the world. Modern cultivars, partly based on North American cluster hops, have been selected for their high yields of soft resin, together with resistance against fungal diseases.

PARTS USED The dried, cone-like female flower clusters.

CULTIVATION & HARVESTING Female plants are grown on long poles and can be harvested mechanically or by hand.

USES & PROPERTIES Hops contributes its aroma and bitterness to beer. Essential oils are responsible for the aroma, while the so-called soft resins are responsible for the bitter taste. The resin also has preservative effects (no longer important with modern processing). Shoots with male flowers (*jets de houblon*) are popular in Belgian cooking and are prepared in the same way as asparagus.

NUTRITIONAL VALUE Hops is used for flavour only but the bitter compounds in the beer stimulate appetite and gastric secretions, thereby improving digestion.

Humulus lupulus L.

family: Cannabaceae

houblon (French); *Hopfen* (German); *luppolo* (Italian); *lúpulo* (Spanish)

Hylocereus undatus
pitaya • pithaya • dragon fruit

Pitaya flower

Pitaya plants

Pitaya fruits

DESCRIPTION This cactus is a creeper (vine) with three-angled, thorny stems that climbs by means of fibrous aerial roots. The large, white flowers open at night and last for only one night. They are self-sterile and have to be cross-pollinated (by bats and moths). The attractive fruits are pink or red, thornless on the surface and weigh up to 600 g each. Inside they are white to dark red, with numerous small black seeds embedded in the pulp. The red pitaya (*H. undatus*) has become well known, but several species of *Hylocereus* and *Selenicereus* produce edible fruits. The yellow pitaya (*S. megalanthus*), for example, is similar but the yellow fruit bear spines that fall off when the fruit ripens.

ORIGIN & HISTORY Central America (the exact geographical origin is uncertain). It is widely cultivated in tropical regions of the world. Crop development and commercial production is underway, mainly in Colombia, Nicaragua, Israel and Vietnam.

PARTS USED Ripe fruits.

CULTIVATION & HARVESTING Pitayas are cultivated by cuttings and are planted at wide spacing (3 × 5 m) using trellises or live trees as support. They take six to nine months to start producing fruits. As epiphytes they respond well to compost and to some form of shading. Pollination is usually done by hand to ensure proper fruit set. The ripe fruits are picked by hand.

USES & PROPERTIES The fruits have become popular as attractive and exotic centrepieces in green salads or fruit salads. They are delicious to eat when fresh and chilled – simply cut in half and scoop out the flesh with a spoon. The fruits can also be variously processed to make juice, wine, liqueur and purée for ice cream.

NUTRITIONAL VALUE Ripe fruits contain 10–12% carbohydrates and have an energy yield of 53 kcal per 100 g. The vitamin C content is about 8 mg per 100 g.

Hylocereus undatus (Haw.) Britton & Rose [= *H. triangularis* (L.) BR. & R.]   family: Cactaceae

pitahaya (French); *Pitahaya* (German); *pitahaya roja* (Spanish); *thang loy* (Vietnamese)

Hyphaene petersiana
mokola palm

Mokola palm with fruits

Tapping the mokola palm

DESCRIPTION A large palm with greyish, hand-shaped leaves and clusters of rounded or slightly pear-shaped fruits. The fibrous outer layer has a sweet taste and the inner layer is hard and bony (known as vegetable ivory). The lala palm (*H. coriacea*) is closely related and used in the same way. Examples of other palms that are used for sugar and palm wine include the palmyra or borassus palm (*Borassus flabellifer* from tropical Asia – mainly India), nipa palm (*Nypa fruticans* from India, Southeast Asia to Australia), wild date palms (*Phoenix sylvestris* from India, *P. reclinata* from Africa), buri palm or *gebang* (*Corypha utan* or *C. elata*, widespread in tropical Asia) and the Indomalaysian fishtail or toddy palm (*Caryota urens*).

ORIGIN & HISTORY The mokola palm is indigenous to tropical southern Africa. The history of its use for palm wine (and basket weaving, especially in Botswana) is poorly known.

PARTS USED The stem sap (phloem sap).

CULTIVATION & HARVESTING All the leaves of a young plant are removed and the stem tip cut at an angle to start the sap flow. A gutter of palm leaf directs the flow into a calabash or other suitable container. Regular cutting maintains the flow for up to seven weeks (total yields between 8 and 60 litres, depending on tree size). In other palms, the male inflorescences are often tapped rather than stems (less destructive and more sustainable).

USES & PROPERTIES The sap is usually sufficiently fermented by natural yeasts and converted to palm wine (toddy) within 36 hours. The beverage has a delicious taste (halfway between ginger beer and hops beer). Distillation gives a strong alcoholic drink (*skokiaan* in southern Africa, *arrack* in other parts of the world).

NUTRITIONAL VALUE Palm wine adds important dietary components to traditional starch-rich diets, especially potassium, nicotinic acid and vitamin C. The alcohol content is low (about 3.6%).

Hyphaene petersiana Mart.   family: Arecaceae (Palmae)

palmier à ivoire d'Afrique (French); *Mokolapalme* (German); *omurungu* (Herero); *palma cuci* (Italian); *omulunga* (Ovambo); *mokola* (Tswana)

Hyssopus officinalis

hyssop

Hyssop plant   Hyssop flowers

DESCRIPTION An erect perennial herb of up to 0.6 m in height, with thin, square stems, small, oblong, opposite leaves and bright blue flowers borne in clusters at the stem tips. The flowers may also be pale blue, violet, purple or white in some cultivars.

ORIGIN & HISTORY Hyssop is indigenous to southern and southeastern Europe. It has a long history of use as culinary and medicinal herb in ancient Arabia, Greece and medieval Europe, but the hyssop mentioned several times in the Bible is believed to be the Middle Eastern *Origanum syriacum*, a relative of marjoram and oregano. Hyssop is widely known as a culinary herb and ornamental garden plant. Commercial production occurs mainly in France, Hungary and the Netherlands.

PARTS USED Fresh or dried leaves (or the essential oil distilled from above-ground parts).

CULTIVATION & HARVESTING Hyssop is easily propagated from seeds or cuttings and is grown in herb gardens all over the world. Leafy stems are hand-harvested and used fresh or dried. Steam distillation produces a commercial essential oil (hyssop oil).

USES & PROPERTIES Fresh young leaves have a spicy smell and somewhat bitter taste and are added sparingly to salads, soups, sauces and meat dishes. Fresh or dried leaves are used as seasoning for oily fish dishes and as an ingredient of stuffings and processed pork products (*charcuterie*). The essential oil is used in the distillation of herbal liqueurs such as Chartreuse, produced by Carthusian monks to this day. It is available as a herbal elixir, green Chartreuse or a sweeter yellow Chartreuse. The composition is a closely guarded secret, but hyssop is known to be one of the many ingredients.

NUTRITIONAL VALUE Used for flavour only, but hyssop is thought to aid digestion, especially when eaten with oily foods.

NOTES Hyssop herb and hyssop oil are traditionally used to treat respiratory ailments.

Hyssopus officinalis L.   family: Lamiaceae

hysope (French); *Ysop* (German); *issopo* (Italian); *hisopo* (Spanish)

Ilex paraguariensis

maté • yerba maté

Tree calabash

Maté tea

Maté leaves

DESCRIPTION A large shrub or tree of 6 m or more, with simple, bright green, slightly toothed, leathery leaves. It also bears small white flowers and spherical red berries. It is a relative of the well-known European holly (*Ilex aquifolium*). Both the plant and the tea are also known as Paraguay tea or *yerba maté*.

ORIGIN & HISTORY Brazil and Paraguay. Maté leaves were traditionally chewed as a stimulant by the South American Indians. By the end of the sixteenth century it was brewed as a tea by Jesuit priests who learnt about maté from the Indians. It became a national drink in countries like Argentina, Brazil, Paraguay and Uruguay. The tree was threatened by wild-harvesting but was taken into cultivation during the nineteenth century and is now grown on a commercial scale.

PARTS USED Leaves.

CULTIVATION & HARVESTING The crop requires a high rainfall and subtropical or tropical climate. The leafy twigs are cut off and roasted over fire (in wire baskets) to inactivate enzymes (so that the leaves keep their green colour) and to release volatile aroma compounds. They are then dried and shredded or powdered.

USES & PROPERTIES Maté is drunk in much the same way as ordinary tea. Traditionally it is drunk from a small gourd (fruit of the tree calabash, *Crescentia cujete*) through a silver drinking straw (*bombilla*) with a strainer fitted to the bottom. The gourd is passed around and boiling water is added to the leaf mixture until the brew becomes too weak. Maté may be flavoured with lemon, milk or brandy.

NUTRITIONAL VALUE The infusion has little or no nutritional value. It is rich in caffeine (up to 2%) and is used as a tonic and stimulant to overcome mental and physical fatigue. Very high doses of caffeine can lead to anxiety and sleeplessness.

Ilex paraguariensis A. St.-Hil.   family: Aquifoliaceae

arbre à maté (French); *Matebaum* (German); *matè* (Italian); *yerba maté* (Spanish)

Illicium verum
star anise • Chinese anise

Star anise leaves

Star anise fruits

DESCRIPTION An evergreen tree of up to 10 m in height bearing simple, dark green leaves and solitary, yellow, magnolia-like flowers. The distinctive, star-shaped fruits are brown and woody in texture. The fruit has eight separate follicles, each with a single, pale brown, shiny seed. Star anise should not be confused with the similar-looking fruits of *Illicium anisatum* (known as Japanese anise, bastard anise or *shikimi*). These fruits are poisonous but can be recognised by their smaller size, more irregular shape, yellowish colour and the broader follicles with curved tips.

ORIGIN & HISTORY Indigenous to northeastern Vietnam and southeastern China. The plant is no longer found in the wild but is cultivated in China, Japan, India, Vietnam, Thailand, Malaysia and the Philippines.

PARTS USED Dried fruit.

CULTIVATION & HARVESTING Trees are grown from seeds or cuttings and require a warm, tropical climate. The fruits are harvested by hand when ripe and dried.

USES & PROPERTIES Chinese and Asian cooks add both fruit and seeds whole (often liberally) to meat dishes (pork and duck), curries and gravies. It is an important ingredient in both Chinese and Indian powdered spice mixtures (the fruits with the seeds are ground together). The flavour goes well with sweet desserts (poached fruit and fruit mousses) and confectionery. In Russia and Scandinavian countries, star anise is a common ingredient of biscuits and pastries. The strong anise flavour is located in the fruit wall and not the seeds (the essential oil contains anethole – the same main compound as in real anise and fennel). Star anise oil is used in the same way as anise (*Pimpinella anisum*) in the production of anise liqueurs (anisette) and anise-flavoured sweets.

NUTRITIONAL VALUE Used as a spice only.

NOTES Star anise has antispasmodic effects and is an ingredient of digestive medicines.

Illicium verum Hook.f.　　　　　　　　　　family: Illiciaceae

ba jiao hui xian (Chinese); *badiane de Chine, anis étoilé* (French); *Echter Steranis, Badian* (German); *anice stellato* (Italian); *bunga lawang* (Malay); *anis estallado* (Spanish); *hôi* (Vietnamese)

Ipomoea aquatica
kangkong • water spinach

Kangkong plants (land form)

Kangkong leaves (aquatic form)

Kangkong

DESCRIPTION A perennial, semi-aquatic plant with long, soft, trailing stems bearing fleshy, arrow-shaped leaves and attractive white or pink flowers. It is closely related to sweet potato (*I. batatas*) and morning glory (*Convolvulus* species). Two forms are known: an aquatic form (water kangkong) and a land form (*kangkong puteh*). Other common names include swamp cabbage, kancon and green engtsai.

ORIGIN & HISTORY Kangkong is believed to be indigenous to warm parts of Africa and Asia but the exact origin is uncertain (perhaps southern India). It is a traditional leaf vegetable in many parts of Asia and is harvested from the wild (often as a weed of rice paddies) or cultivated in fields.

PARTS USED Young plants or leafy stems.

CULTIVATION & HARVESTING The two forms of kangkong are cultivated in different ways. The aquatic form (water kangkong) is grown in rice paddies and propagated by cuttings. The land form is grown from seeds and has become popular as a regular vegetable in many warm parts of the world. Leafy stems or young plants (with roots and all) are harvested and sold on local markets.

USES & PROPERTIES Leaves and stems are a very popular salad and vegetable in Asia, used in much the same way as spinach or mustard leaves. Fresh, uncooked young leaves go well with green salads and the leafy stems are cooked as a vegetable or may be added to stir-fries, soups and stews. The land form is considered superior in flavour and texture, but the aquatic form is traditionally used as an important ingredient of cuttlefish-kangkong, a typical Malaysian dish. The vegetable is also popular in Hong Kong, where a white-stemmed form is cultivated.

NUTRITIONAL VALUE Kangkong is said to be rich in folic acid and especially iron, so that it is recommended for people suffering from anaemia.

Ipomoea aquatica Forssk.   family: Convolvulaceae

weng cai (Chinese); *patate aquatique* (French); *Wasserspinat* (German); *kalmi* (Hindi); *kangkong* (Indonesian); *kankon* (Japanese); *patata acquatica* (Italian); *kangkong* (Malay); *batata acuática* (Spanish)

Ipomoea batatas

sweet potato

Sweet potato field

Sweet potato leaves and flowers

Sweet potatoes

DESCRIPTION A trailing herbaceous perennial that spreads along the ground by rooting at the nodes. The leaves are heart-shaped and lobed at their bases. Attractive purple, pink or white flowers are borne on older plants. The tuberous roots are oblong to almost spherical and white, purple, yellow or orange.

ORIGIN & HISTORY Sweet potato is indigenous to the northwestern parts of South America. Archaeological remains from Peru were dated to at least 8000 BC. Domestication probably occurred before 4500 BC in the region that includes Guatemala, Colombia, Ecuador and Peru. From here the crop spread to Polynesia in pre-Columbian times and was later carried by Portuguese and Spanish explorers to Europe, Africa and Asia. In the West Indies and Africa, the starchy *aja* type is preferred, while the sweet *batata* type is popular in most other parts of the world. Sweet potato is the seventh largest food crop, 80% of which is produced in China. It is also a staple food in the Caribbean, Africa, Polynesia and parts of Asia, and an industrial source of starch and ethanol.

PARTS USED Fleshy, tuberous roots.

CULTIVATION & HARVESTING The crop requires subtropical heat and is propagated by pieces of tuber or stem cuttings. Roots are ready for harvesting 60 to 90 days after planting.

USES & PROPERTIES An excellent food source that is eaten cooked as a vegetable or sweet dessert. The roots are prepared like potatoes but are much sweeter. Sweet potatoes are fried, boiled, baked or cooked in their skins, and served with cream or sweet sauces. They may form part of sweet croquettes, soufflés, gratins, sweet desserts and even jams. Young leaves are eaten like spinach.

NUTRITIONAL VALUE Sweet potatoes are exceptionally nutritious, as they contain high quality protein and substantial quantities of vitamins A, B and C. The energy value is high (110 kcal per 100 g).

Ipomoea batatas (L.) Lam.   family: Convolvulaceae

fan shu (Chinese); *patate douce* (French); *Süßkartoffel, Batate* (German); *patata dolce* (Italian); *satsuma imo, kan sho* (Japanese); *ubi keladek* (Malay); *batata doce* (Portuguese); *batata* (Spanish); *man thet* (Thai)

Juglans regia

common walnut • Persian walnut

Black walnut (*Juglans nigra*)

Common walnut (*Juglans regia*)

Walnuts (*Juglans regia*)

DESCRIPTION A large tree of up to 30 m in height bearing compound leaves with 5–11 leaflets and inconspicuous male and female flowers. The fruit has a fleshy layer that peels away at maturity, exposing the hard, brown shell that surrounds the characteristic seed (shaped like two halves of a brain). Common walnut (also known as English walnut or Black Sea walnut) is the most important commercial type but several others are used locally: North American black walnut (*J. nigra*, 11–13 toothed leaflets), North American butternut (*J. cinerea*), Japanese walnut (*J. sieboldiana*) and Manchurian walnut (*J. mandschurica*).

ORIGIN & HISTORY Common walnut is indigenous to southeastern Europe and western and central Asia. It was cultivated by the ancient Persians, Greeks and Romans. The world production is about one million tons, mainly from the USA, China, southern and eastern Europe, the Middle East, Mexico, India and Pakistan.

PARTS USED Ripe fruits (nuts).

CULTIVATION & HARVESTING Trees are propagated by grafting and require a temperate climate with cold winters. The nuts are harvested by hand or mechanically.

USES & PROPERTIES Walnut is an important dessert nut and is widely used in confectionery (biscuits, cakes, sweets, chocolates, pastries and breads) and in ice cream. These are also the main uses for black walnut in the USA. Walnut oil is of exceptional quality and has long been used as a salad oil, especially in France. Chopped or crushed walnuts are added to salads and a wide range of dishes (meat, poultry, fish, stuffings, pastas and patés). Walnut is used to flavour wines and liqueurs (especially *brou de noix*, a French liqueur made from the green husks).

NUTRITIONAL VALUE The nuts are high in energy (650 kcal per 100 g), proteins (3%), fats (15%), linoleic acid (35%), phosphorus and vitamins B and D.

NOTES Walnut yields a high quality furniture and veneer timber.

Juglans regia L.   family: Juglandaceae

hu tao ren (Chinese); *noyer* (French); *Walnuss* (German); *noce* (Italian); *nogal* (Spanish)

Juniperus communis

juniper

Juniper foliage and young cones

Juniper berries

Juniper trees

DESCRIPTION An erect, evergreen shrub or small tree of about 6 m in height. It has densely crowded, small, flat, needle-shaped leaves. Male and female cones are formed on separate plants. The female cones are spherical, fleshy, berry-like, about 10 mm in diameter and blue to black when ripe.

ORIGIN & HISTORY Indigenous to the north temperate region (Asia, Europe and North America). Juniper berries have been used since the Middle Ages as spice and adulterant in pepper. About 200 tons are harvested each year from wild plants in central Europe.

PARTS USED Ripe, fresh or dried female cones (commonly referred to as juniper berries).

CULTIVATION & HARVESTING Trees are rarely cultivated except for ornamental purposes (there are many garden cultivars). The ripe cones (berries) are wild-harvested by hand and air-dried.

USES & PROPERTIES Juniper berries have a pungent, slightly bitter and resinous taste and are widely used to flavour meat dishes. They are particularly popular in Scandinavian cooking. The whole or crushed berries provide a spicy, peppery taste to various types of game (wild boar, reindeer, hare, rabbit, and birds), kidneys, pork dishes, *sauerkraut*, sausages, marinades and sauces. In French cooking, the terms *à la liègeoise* or *à l'ardennaise* refer to dishes (mainly venison or game birds) that contain alcohol and juniper berries (or flamed with gin). Juniper berries are used to flavour gin (from *genever* or *jenever*, the Dutch word for juniper) and related aromatic brandies (*brinjevac, genièvre, péquet* and *schiedam*), as well as wines, herbal liqueurs and Scandinavian beers. The berries contain about 25% sugars that are fermented and distilled to produce various types of schnapps (such as *Steinhäger*).

NUTRITIONAL VALUE Used as a spice in small quantities only.

NOTES Infusions of juniper berries and juniper oil (distilled from the berries) are traditionally used as diuretic and antiseptic medicines.

Juniperus communis L.   family: Cupressaceae

genièvrier (French); *Wacholder* (German); *ginepro* (Italian); *enebro* (Spanish)

Lablab purpureus

hyacinth bean • lablab bean

Hyacinth bean (white form)

Hyacinth bean (purple form)

Hyacinth bean seeds

DESCRIPTION A perennial, twining creeper that may reach 6 m in height (bushy types are also grown). They have trifoliate leaves with broad leaflets and purple or white flowers. The pods have a warty upper suture and each bears up to six distinctive, flat seeds that vary from white to red, brown or black. Other names include lablab dolicho or bonavist bean (previously classified as *Lablab niger* or *Dolichos lablab*). Another species of local importance is the horse gram (*Dolichos biflorus*) – a poor man's pulse in southern India (important for food and fodder) and used in Myanmar to produce a spicy sauce similar to soy sauce.

ORIGIN & HISTORY Tropical East Africa (derived from the wild subsp. *uncinatus*). It is sometimes thought to be indigenous to India. This is an important food plant in rural areas and has been cultivated in warm parts of Africa, India and Southeast Asia for centuries. It reached the West Indies via the slave trade and has also

become popular in the New World.

PARTS USED Young pods, young leaves and ripe seeds.

CULTIVATION & HARVESTING The plant is perennial but is often grown as an annual crop. It thrives in warm, tropical climates and is tolerant of drought and poor soils. Leaves and young pods are picked as green vegetables, or the seeds are left to ripen and are harvested as a pulse.

USES & PROPERTIES Hyacinth bean is a nutritious vegetable, used in the same way as green beans. The ripe seeds are shelled and used as *dhal*, or are added to soups and meat stews. Canned hyacinth beans are available. The beans have to be cooked for at least 10 minutes to remove poisonous substances.

NUTRITIONAL VALUE Dry beans contain 25% protein, 60% carbohydrates and are rich in minerals and vitamins. They have a high energy value (about 340 kcal per 100 g).

Lablab purpureus (L.) Sweet (= *Dolichos lablab* L.)   family: Fabaceae

bian dou (Chinese); *dolic, dolique d'Egypte* (French); *Helmbohne* (German); *fagiolo egiziano* (Italian); *fuji mame* (Japanese); *kacang kara* (Malay); *dólico do Egipto* (Portuguese); *frijol caballero* (Spanish)

Lactuca sativa

lettuce

Cabbage lettuce

Crisphead lettuce

Lettuce flowers

Butterhead lettuce

DESCRIPTION A leafy annual plant with broad, soft leaves that are variously toothed or crisped along the margins and which exude milky latex from the thick white midribs. Much-branched flowering stems appear at the end of the season, with numerous small yellow flower heads and hairy fruits (achenes). A diversity of forms is cultivated, including cabbage lettuce (*Kopfsalat, laitue*), crisphead lettuce (*Schnittsalat*, with red or green, markedly toothed leaves), cos or romaine lettuce (*Römischer Salat, salad romaine*, with loose heads that are tied to blanch the inner leaves), stem lettuce or celtuce (with edible stems) and butterhead lettuce (with soft-textured, yellowish-green leaves).

ORIGIN & HISTORY Mediterranean region and the Near East. Cultivated lettuce is thought to be an ancient cultigen derived from wild lettuce (*L. serriola*). Early types, grown in Egypt as far back as 4500 BC, were probably leafy types with loose heads (like cos or butterhead), while cabbage lettuce appeared only during the

Middle Ages. Lettuce is today the most important of all salad crops and is produced in practically every country around the world, but the major consumers are North America and Europe.

PARTS USED Leaves (rarely stems).

CULTIVATION & HARVESTING Lettuce is easily grown from seed for the fresh market (often chopped or shredded and variously packed).

USES & PROPERTIES Lettuce is always used fresh (except stem lettuce, which is cooked). Leaves are added to green salads and mixed salads and may be served as a *chiffonnade* (chopped strips of lettuce softened in butter, with stock, milk or cream added). It is very popular as a garnish, served with dishes as diverse as roast meat and American hamburgers. Lettuce may also be braised, stuffed, puréed or cooked with cream, often to accompany peas or mange-tout.

NUTRITIONAL VALUE Lettuce contains some minerals and vitamins but has a low food value. The energy yield is a mere 18 kcal per 100 g.

Lactuca sativa L.   family: Asteraceae

sheng cai (Chinese); *laitue* (French); *Kopfsalat, Gartensalat* (German); *lattuga* (Italian); *selada* (Malay); *alface* (Portuguese); *lechuga* (Spanish)

Lagenaria siceraria

bottle gourd • calabash

Bottle gourd flower

Bottle gourd plant

Bottle gourds (Chinese cultivar)

DESCRIPTION An annual, creeping herb with coiling tendrils and large hairy leaves. It resembles the pumpkin but the flowers are white and open at night. The fruits are very variable in size and shape (narrow and oblong to rounded or bottle-shaped) and the seeds are angular and ribbed. Calabash is the only annual species of *Lagenaria* – the other five are all perennials.

ORIGIN & HISTORY This species (the only annual in the genus) is indigenous to Africa. Calabash appears to have been distributed to all tropical parts of the world during ancient times (possibly by means of the buoyant fruits that are able to float on the sea currents for several months without losing viability). Archaeological remains of the distinctive seeds from Mexico date back to 7000 BC. It is not clear if the plant was domesticated for containers (bottles, ladles, cups) or for food. It is a popular crop plant in most parts of Africa and Asia (from India and China to Indonesia).

PARTS USED Unripe fruits.

CULTIVATION & HARVESTING Plants are grown in warm tropical regions in the same way as pumpkins. The young fruits are harvested for vegetables or they are left to ripen for use as containers or ornaments.

USES & PROPERTIES Sliced fruits are used as a vegetable in the same way as squash or zucchini. Calabash is very popular as a food item in India, China, Malaysia, the Philippines and Japan, where it is added to stir-fries, stews, soups and curries. Dried, ribbon-like strips of calabash are used in Japanese cooking as edible string to tie *sushi*. Leaves and stem tips are eaten as vegetables in Africa and in China.

NUTRITIONAL VALUE The fruit flesh has a low energy yield of only 20 kcal per 100 g. It is a moderate source of minerals, especially iron, potassium and zinc. The vitamin C content is about 10 mg per 100 g.

Lagenaria siceraria (Molina) Standley (= *L. vulgaris* Ser.)   family: Cucurbitaceae

hu lu gua (Chinese); *courge bouteille, calebassier* (French); *Flaschenkürbis* (German); *dudhi* (Hindi); *zucca da tabacco* (Italian); *yuugao* (Japanese); *labu botol* (Malay); *cabaco* (Portuguese); *calabaza* (Spanish)

Lathyrus sativus

grass pea • chickling vetch

Ornamental *Lathyrus*

Grass pea seeds

Grass pea

DESCRIPTION A climbing herb with angular, winged stems, branched climbing tendrils and trifoliate leaves with narrow leaflets. The flowers are usually blue but sometimes purplish or white. They develop into small flat pods that contain up to five brown, white or mottled seeds. Several other species of *Lathyrus* are grown in Africa, Europe and Asia as minor pulses, including *L. annuus*, *L. cicera*, *L. clymenum* and *L. ochrus*. Grass pea has numerous other common names such as Indian pea, Riga pea, *khesari*, blue vetchling, *teora*, *guaya* and *gesse blance*.

ORIGIN & HISTORY Eastern Mediterranean. Domestication probably occurred about 8 000 years ago in the Balkan Peninsula and the crop spread to Africa and Asia. It is still an important source of food and fodder in Ethiopia, Bangladesh, India and Pakistan.

PARTS USED Ripe seeds.

CULTIVATION & HARVESTING Grass pea is grown from seeds as an annual crop. It has the advantage that it will give at least some harvest even if all other pulse or grain harvests have failed.

USES & PROPERTIES The seeds are roasted or may be used as *dhal*, included in soups and stews or turned into dried paste balls that can be stored for later use. Grass pea flour is used for cooking or baking bread. A poisonous, non-protein amino acid (ODAP) may cause lathyrism (paralysis of the lower limbs) when grass pea forms a large part of the diet during droughts and famines (often in central India). Over 90% of the substance can be removed by boiling and baking but this unfortunately also reduces the nutritional value of the pulse.

NUTRITIONAL VALUE The seeds are rich in proteins (25–30%) and carbohydrates (60%). The high levels of lysine make it suitable for lysine-poor cereal diets. The use of grass pea continues, despite attempts to discourage it, as there appears to be no alternative for poor people.

Lathyrus sativus L.   family: Fabaceae

ou zhou xiang wan dou (Chinese); *gesse blanche, gesse commune* (French); *Saatplatterbse* (German); *khesari* (Hindi); *cicerchia, circercula* (Italian); *chicharo* (Portuguese); *almorta, gudija* (Spanish)

Laurus nobilis

bay laurel • bay • sweet bay • true laurel

Bay laurel (male plant)

Bay laurel fruits

Bay leaves

DESCRIPTION A shrub or small tree (rarely up to 20 m) with simple, aromatic leaves and small white flowers borne on male or female plants. The fruits resemble small olives. It should not be confused with various other trees and shrubs also called laurel, such as cherry laurel (*Prunus laurocerasus*).

ORIGIN & HISTORY Mediterranean region. The tree is important in Greek mythology and human history. As symbol of honour or victory, a laurel wreath is still given to winners of sport events such as the Olympic Games. It is the basis of expressions such as "resting on your laurels", "nobel laureate" or "baccalaureus scientiae" (bachelor of science). Laurel is widely cultivated as ornamental tree and popular culinary herb.

PARTS USED Fresh or dried leaves (or the essential oil distilled from the leaves).

CULTIVATION & HARVESTING Trees are propagated from seeds or cuttings and are easily grown in temperate and warm regions. Leaves are picked by hand and air-dried (and kept whole or powdered). Commercial production occurs mainly in the southeastern Mediterranean region.

USES & PROPERTIES Bay leaves are one of the most popular of all food flavourants. They are an essential ingredient of a *bouquet garni* (a small bundle of herbs that is removed before the dish is served). One or two leaves are added to stocks, marinades, soups, pickles, pâtés, stews and various chicken, fish and meat dishes (an example is *bobotie*, a traditional South African meat dish of Malay origin). Bay leaves are often used to flavour milk puddings. The leaves and essential oil are commercial flavourants in the food industry.

NUTRITIONAL VALUE Unimportant (used in small amounts for flavour only).

NOTES The leaves and oil have antiseptic activity and are used in traditional medicine as bitter tonic and digestive medicine. Dilute oil is used in aromatherapy to treat inflamed joints or bruised skin.

Laurus nobilis L.   family: Lauraceae

laurier (French); *Lorbeer* (German); *lauro, alloro* (Italian); *laurel* (Spanish)

Lens culinaris
lentil

Lentil flowers and pods

Lentil plant

Lentils

DESCRIPTION A slender, sparsely branched annual with compound leaves and very small flowers that may be white, pink or pale blue. The small pods are broad, flat and contain one or two flat (lens-shaped) seeds that vary in colour from green or yellow to orange, red or brown.

ORIGIN & HISTORY Near East (Turkey to the Arabian Peninsula and eastwards to Afghanistan and Tajikistan). Lentil is one of the oldest of all crops, believed to be a cultigen derived from wild lentil (*L. orientalis*) in the Fertile Crescent between 7000 and 5000 BC. Relatively unchanged by modern agriculture, it has remained one of the most popular of all pulses. It is grown commercially in India (the main producer), Pakistan, Turkey, the Near East, the Mediterranean region and more recently also Argentina, Chile and the USA. The world production is more than a million tons per year.

PARTS USED Ripe seeds.

CULTIVATION & HARVESTING Lentils are grown from seeds as a pulse crop, traditionally with wheat and barley. The plants are too small to be easily harvested by mechanical methods and yields are quite low (500–1 500 kg per ha).

USES & PROPERTIES Lentils are used as *dhal* or flour and are best known for nutritious and tasty soups. The seeds are cooked in the same way as dry beans and eaten as a vegetable, purée or as ingredient of sauces. Lentils are traditionally eaten with pickled pork. Cooked lentils or fresh lentil sprouts are added to salads.

NUTRITIONAL VALUE A nourishing and tasty food, with 25% protein, an energy value of 270–330 kcal per 100 g and substantial quantities of B vitamins. It is used as a meat substitute and dietary supplement for infants, invalids, nursing mothers and vegetarians. Esau – speculated to have been hypoglycaemic – may have lost his birthright in order to save his life.

Lens culinaris Medikus (= *Lens esculenta* Moench)   family: Fabaceae

bing dou (Chinese); *lentille* (French); *Linse* (German); *masur* (Hindi); *lente, lenticchia* (Italian); *aoi mame* (Japanese); *kacang serinding* (Malay); *lentilha* (Portuguese); *lenteja* (Spanish); *thua daeng* (Thai)

Lepidium sativum

garden cress • cress

Land cress plants

Garden cress plant

Garden cress leaves

DESCRIPTION An erect annual of up to 0.6 m in height bearing compound (pinnate or bipinnate) leaves and minute white flowers. The fruits are small, pouch-like capsules of about 5 mm long. Seedlings are easily recognised by the deeply three-lobed seedling leaves (cotyledons). Several other plants are known as cress. Land cress or winter cress (*Barbarea verna*, known as *Wintercresse* in German or *barbarée* in French) has lobed leaves and yellow flowers. Watercress (see *Rorippa nasturtium-aquaticum*, also known as *Nasturtium officinale*) is the best-known and most important cress. Indian cress is *Tropaeolum majus*. Spoonwort or spoon cress (*Cochlearia officinalis*, also known as *Löffelkresse* in German or *cochléaire* in French) grows in salty places and is a minor salad crop.

ORIGIN & HISTORY Garden cress is indigenous to western Asia. It was used by the ancient Egyptians as a food source and became well known in various parts of Europe (including Britain, France, Italy and Germany) where it is still a minor crop.

PARTS USED Fresh leaves or young seedlings.

CULTIVATION & HARVESTING Garden cress is grown as an annual crop and salad source but the seedlings are mostly used. Seeds are germinated in special containers and are marketed as an early spring salad. It is often used for so-called "mustard and cress", a mixture of mustard and cress seedlings (cress takes longer to germinate and is sown four days before the mustard).

USES & PROPERTIES Cress is a popular salad ingredient (especially when used as small seedlings). Young plants are tasty garnishes for salads, sandwiches and various other dishes, to which they give a piquant, somewhat bitter flavour.

NUTRITIONAL VALUE The calorific value is low (33 kcal per 100 g) but the leaves are rich in minerals and vitamins. Especially noteworthy is vitamin C (35–87 mg), together with useful quantities of vitamins A, B and E.

Lepidium sativum L.   family: Brassicaceae

jia du xing cai (Chinese); *cresson alénois* (French); *Gartenkresse* (German); *crescione* (Italian); *agrião, mastruco* (Portuguese); *berro de huerta, berro alenois, mastuerzo* (Spanish)

Levisticum officinale
lovage

Lovage flowers

Lovage plant

Lovage leaf and fruits

DESCRIPTION A robust perennial herb (up to 2 m) with large compound leaves comprising numerous broad, wedge-shaped leaflets that are toothed on their upper margins. The small yellow flowers occur in double umbels and develop into small dry fruits. Lovage may be confused with angelica (*Angelica archangelica*) but this plant has the leaflets finely toothed also along the lower margins. In the northern parts of Britain, Scotch lovage (*Ligusticum scotinum*) is of minor importance as a vegetable. It has the leaflets arranged in threes (ternately pinnate).

ORIGIN & HISTORY Eastern Mediterranean region (possibly Iran and Afghanistan). It was well known to the ancient Greeks and Romans as a culinary and medicinal herb. Lovage spread throughout Europe and North America, where it became naturalised. Today it is commonly grown in private herb gardens and on a commercial scale (for flavour and medicine) in Europe, Latin America and North America.

PARTS USED Leaves, stems, fruit ("seeds") and roots.

CULTIVATION & HARVESTING Plants are easily propagated by division or by seeds for own use. The fresh or dried roots and essential oil, obtained from the roots and fruits by steam distillation, are produced commercially.

USES & PROPERTIES Fresh leaves are popular as a culinary herb in Europe (especially England and Germany). They are added sparingly to salads, soups, sauces, stews (ragouts) and various meat dishes. Blanched stems are eaten in salads (like celery) and are also candied (like angelica). Fresh or cooked roots can be used as a vegetable. Dried and powdered roots have been used as a condiment and to flavour alcoholic herbal tonics. The leaves contain a flavour compound that is said to be an ingredient of the well-known Maggi sauce (made in Switzerland by Julius Maggi in 1885 from processed plant proteins).

NUTRITIONAL VALUE Lovage is used in small amounts for flavour.

Levisticum officinale Koch (= *Ligusticum levisticum* L.)   family: Apiaceae

ou dang gui (Chinese); *livèche* (French); *Liebstöckel, Maggikraut* (German); *levistico* (Italian); *ligústico* (Spanish)

Linum usitatissimum

flax • linseed

Flax plants

Flax flowers and fruits

Linseeds

DESCRIPTION A slender, erect annual herb (up to 1 m) with small, hairless leaves and attractive blue flowers. The rounded capsules contain smooth, oval, compressed, reddish-brown seeds. Some cultivars are grown for their stem fibres (flax), while others are grown for their edible seeds and seed oil.

ORIGIN & HISTORY Western Europe and the Mediterranean region. It is an ancient cultigen derived from wild *L. angustifolium* (sometimes considered to be a subspecies of *L. usitatissimum* and then called subsp. *bienne*). Archaeological remains from Iran and Syria date back to 8000 BC and flax was already a cultivated crop in Mesopotamia by 6000 BC – the earliest crop grown for fibres to weave clothes. Until recently flax was widely cultivated in Europe and Asia but has been replaced by cheaper, imported cotton. Cultivars with large seeds were developed as a source of edible oil.

PARTS USED Ripe, dried seeds.

CULTIVATION & HARVESTING Flax is propagated by seeds and is harvested mechanically or by hand in rural areas. Cooking oil is obtained by cold pressing of the seeds, while lower quality drying oil (for paints and varnishes) is obtained by hot pressing.

USES & PROPERTIES Cold-pressed oil is still important as cooking oil, especially in rural areas of North Africa and the Middle East. Whole or crushed seeds may be eaten and are sometimes added to breads and breakfast cereals. They have little flavour but are used as health food and dietary supplement to improve digestion and elimination (the high mucilage and oil contents add to the bulk laxative effects).

NUTRITIONAL VALUE The seeds have a high energy value (376 kcal per 100 g) and contains up to 25% protein and up to 45% oil (consisting mainly of linoleic and linolenic acid). The oil is rich in fatty acids and vitamin E and has an energy value of 900 kcal per 100 g.

Linum usitatissimum L.

family: Linaceae

ya ma (Chinese); *lin* (French); *Lein, Flachs* (German); *lino* (Italian); *linho* (Portuguese); *lino* (Spanish)

Litchi chinensis

litchi • lychee

Litchi tree

Litchi flowers

Litchis

DESCRIPTION An evergreen tree of up to 30 m in height with a dense rounded crown of simple, glossy leaves that are dark green above and paler below. The inconspicuous yellowish flowers can be male, female or hermaphroditic. Round to slightly oval, reddish fruits with a warty and scaly skin are borne in clusters. The edible part of the fruit is the white, aromatic, fleshy aril that is folded around a large, shiny, inedible seed. It is related to the rambutan (*Nephelium lapaceum*) and has a similar taste but the latter has distinctive hairy fruits.

ORIGIN & HISTORY Tropical China to western Malaysia. The tree has been cultivated in China for thousands of years and is now grown in all tropical parts of the world.

PARTS USED Ripe fruits.

CULTIVATION & HARVESTING Litchi trees are propagated by grafting, using the so-called mountain litchi as rootstock. The trees require cool but frost-free winters and warm, humid summer and produce about 100 kg of fruits per year. Fruits are picked by hand and are an important commercial product.

USES & PROPERTIES After removal of the brittle shell, the translucent white fruits are eaten fresh for their delicious aromatic, somewhat musky and slightly acidic taste. They are processed into fruit juice and may be added to fruit salads. Litchis are also canned (preserved in sugar syrup) or dried whole to produce so-called "litchi nuts" (they turn blackish like prunes and are a delicacy in China). Chinese and Thai cooks sometimes use litchis with meat and fish dishes or as an ingredient of stuffings. Litchis may be preserved in alcohol (especially rum) to make a scented liqueur.

NUTRITIONAL VALUE Fresh fruits contain 17% carbohydrates and have an energy yield of 74 kcal per 100 g. Litchi is an excellent source of vitamin C (25–50 mg per 100 g).

Litchi chinensis Sonn.   family: Sapindaceae

li zhi, li chi (Chinese); *litchier* (French); *Litchipflaume, Chinesische Haselnuss* (German); *litchi* (Italian); *reishi* (Japanese); *litchia* (Portuguese); *litchi* (Spanish)

Lotus tetragonolobus

asparagus pea

Asparagus pea

DESCRIPTION A hairy, trailing annual herb with trifoliate leaves, each with three toothed leaflets and two large stipules. The attractive red flowers are distinctive, as are the oblong, square pods that have four broad, wavy wings (one on each corner of the fruit). Each pod contains six to nine small, reddish brown to reddish grey seeds. The fruits closely resemble those of the winged bean (*Psophocarpus tetragonolobus*) and the two species can easily be confused. The latter has pale purple or pink flowers and large, lobed leaflets.

ORIGIN & HISTORY Asparagus pea is indigenous to southern Europe but has become widely distributed in North Africa and Asia. The plant is a traditional food in the Mediterranean region (mentioned in several medieval text books) and is occasionally grown as a vegetable in many parts of Europe and Asia. It has nothing to do with the legendary lotus-eaters of Greek mythology (described in Homer's *Odyssey*), said to have lived in a drugged, indolent state from feeding on the lotus. The lotus referred to here is the lotus fruit (*Ziziphus lotus*).

PARTS USED Unripe fruits, less often the seeds.

CULTIVATION & HARVESTING The plant is easily propagated from seeds and the young pods are picked by hand when less than 25 mm long (when larger and older they become fibrous). It is not of much commercial importance because the productivity is quite low.

USES & PROPERTIES The young pods are prepared and served in the same way as asparagus (steamed and served with butter or a white sauce). They can be added fresh to salads or may be added to soups and stews. The green seeds or ripe, dry seeds can be used in the same way as peas. Roasted seeds have been used as a coffee substitute.

NUTRITIONAL VALUE The seeds contain 26% protein, 1.7% fat and 50% carbohydrates.

Lotus tetragonolobus L. (= *Tetragonolobus purpureus* Moench.)   family: Fabaceae

chi jia wan dou (Chinese); *lotier rouge, pois asperge* (French); *Rote Spargelerbse* (German); *loto rosso* (Italian); *bocha cultivado, loto cultivado* (Spanish)

Luffa acutangula
angled luffa

Angled luffa plant

Angled luffa flower

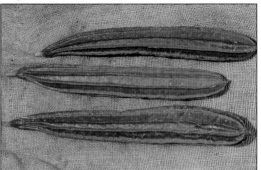

Angled luffas (young fruits)

DESCRIPTION A vigorous annual climber with trailing and climbing stems that may reach 5 m or more in height. It has large, simple, hairy leaves, climbing tendrils and yellow flowers that are usually male or female but perfect (hermaphroditic) in one cultivar ('Satputia'). There are three varieties: var. *acutangula* (the cultivated form), var. *amara* (a wild form with small, bitter fruits) and var. *forskalii* (a poorly known form found in Yemen). The closely related smooth luffa or sponge gourd (*Luffa cylindrica*) has thicker, smooth fruits which are edible when young. The bleached vascular system of the mature fruit is used as bathroom sponges.

ORIGIN & HISTORY The wild form of angled luffa (var. *amara*) is indigenous to India and it is likely that the plant was domesticated in India. The wild form of smooth luffa (var. *leiocarpa*) occurs naturally from Myanmar to the Philippines (also Australia and Tahiti). It has probably been domesticated in Southeast Asia.

Luffas reached China before AD 1000 and are today cultivated in most parts of tropical Asia (and to a limited extent in Africa and America).

PARTS USED Young fruits (sometimes the flowers and young leaves).

CULTIVATION & HARVESTING Luffas grow rapidly from seeds and require warm, tropical conditions. Young fruits are picked by hand for local markets.

USES & PROPERTIES Fruits are peeled, cut into slices and cooked as a vegetable. They can be stir-fried or added to stews and mixed vegetable dishes. The flowers and young leaves of both species can be eaten as vegetables.

NUTRITIONAL VALUE The fruits are low in energy yield (about 20–30 kcal per 100 g) but are rich in minerals, nicotinamide and other vitamins.

NOTES The dry fruit of the smooth luffa (vegetable sponge) has become an important article in export trade, especially for the European and USA markets.

Luffa acutangula (L.) Roxb.   family: Cucurbitaceae

guang dong si gua (Chinese); *courge anguleuse de chine* (French); *Gerippte Schwammgurke, Flügelgurke* (German); *shokuyou hechima* (Japanese); *petola sanding, ketola* (Malay); *lufa riscada* (Portuguese); *calabaza de aristas* (Spanish); *buap* (Thai)

Lupinus albus

white lupin • Egyptian lupin

Yellow lupin

White lupin

Sweet lupin seeds

DESCRIPTION Erect annual herbs with digitate leaves and attractive flower clusters producing hairy pods with large, usually white seeds. Four large-seeded lupins are of direct importance as human and animal food: the white lupin, blue lupin (*L. angustifolius*), yellow lupin (*L. luteus*) and Andean lupin or tarwi (*L. mutabilis*).

ORIGIN & HISTORY Mediterranean region (Andean lupin occurs naturally from Venezuela to northern Chile and Argentina). Domestication in the Old World started with white lupin in Egypt perhaps before 300 BC. Early in the nineteenth century, blue and yellow lupins followed, and sweet lupins (with very low alkaloid levels) were developed in the early twentieth century. Andean lupin has been grown in Peru as an Inca crop since about 2000 BC. Special equipment was introduced to improve on the traditional method of removing alkaloids and more recently, low-alkaloid cultivars have been developed through plant breeding.

PARTS USED Ripe seeds (sweet lupins) or carefully leached, ripe seeds (bitter lupins).

CULTIVATION & HARVESTING Lupin is an annual crop used since ancient times in rotation with cereals to improve soil fertility and to supply fodder and seed protein. Sweet, non-shattering types are harvested mechanically for human use.

USES & PROPERTIES Bitter lupin seeds have to be leached by cooking and soaking. Lupins are still an important source of protein in rural communities (especially in Peru and the Mediterranean region). The seeds are used to some extent as a pulse in soups and stews or may be processed into breakfast cereals and seed flour (which can be used as an alternative to soya). The seed oil is similar to peanut oil and is suitable for kitchen use.

NUTRITIONAL VALUE Very high protein levels (up to 45%) and an oil content of 15–20%. The oil is rich in unsaturated fatty acids, including linoleic acid.

Lupinus albus L. (= *L. termis* Forssk.)

family: Fabaceae

bai yu shan dou (Chinese); *lupin blanc* (French); *Weiße Lupine* (German); *lupino bianco* (Italian); *shiro bana ruupin* (Japanese); *tremoceiro branco* (Portuguese); *altramuz blanco* (Spanish)

Lycium chinense

Chinese boxthorn

Chinese boxthorn flowers and fruit

Chinese boxthorn leaves

Chinese boxthorn plantation

DESCRIPTION A woody shrub of about 1 m in height with thorny stems bearing simple, hairless leaves, small purple flowers and orange-red berries. Closely related and very similar is *L. barbarum*, the so-called Duke of Argyll's tea-tree (previously known as *L. halimifolium*). It is a larger shrub (up to 3 m) with longer flower tubes and larger fruits.

ORIGIN & HISTORY *L. chinense* is widely distributed in eastern Asia, while *L. barbarum* is found mainly in the Ningxia Province of China. The plants are naturalised in North America (both species) and Europe (only *L. barbarum*) and typically occurs in rocky places and on old walls. Chinese boxthorn has been used in China since ancient times as a source of food and medicine and is commonly cultivated in China and Malaysia.

PARTS USED Fresh leaves and ripe berries (fresh or more often dried, known as *gou qi zi*).

CULTIVATION & HARVESTING Cuttings or seedlings are grown in plantations. For the production of leaves, the young leafy stems are cut (giving a hedge-like appearance to the rows). For fruit production, stems are left to flower and fruit. The fruits are picked by hand from plantations or are wild-harvested.

USES & PROPERTIES The leaves are a popular vegetable in Asia, appreciated for the soft texture and slightly bitter taste. They are typically cooked to accompany pork dishes and may also be added to soups. The small, dried fruits are a very important dietary item (a functional food or health food) in China and are eaten like raisins or may be added to soups and stews. A daily dose of 50 g is recommended.

NUTRITIONAL VALUE The leaves are rich in minerals and vitamins (especially folic acid). Of special dietary importance are the berries, which are exceptionally rich in amino acids (up to 5%), polysaccharides and especially carotenoids (converted in the human body to vitamin A).

Lycium chinense Mill.   family: Solanaceae

gou qi cai (Chinese); *lyciet* (French); *Chinesischer Bocksdorn* (German); *licio* (Italian); *frutilla* (Spanish)

234

Lycopersicon esculentum
tomato

Tomato (yellow cherry type)

Tomato plant

Tomatoes

DESCRIPTION A short-lived perennial (usually grown as an annual) with aromatic, compound leaves and small yellow flowers. The bright red or yellow berries vary in shape and size: small (cherry tomatoes), large ("beef tomatoes"), egg-shaped ("jam tomatoes") or oblong (Italian tomatoes).

ORIGIN & HISTORY Wild tomato (var. *cerasiforme*) resembles modern-day cherry tomatoes and occurs naturally as a weed in most parts of South and Central America, so the exact origin is uncertain. Tomatoes were grown as a crop in Mexico and Peru in pre-Columbian times but the early history of domestication is not well known (most probably in Mexico). In Europe, tomatoes were grown as ornaments (thought to be poisonous) and became popular as food only in the eighteenth century. Thousands of cultivars have been developed by modern breeding methods and the tomato today ranks second only to potato in importance as a vegetable.

PARTS USED Ripe fruits.

CULTIVATION & HARVESTING Tomatoes are grown in all parts of the world (in the open or under glass) and are harvested by hand (mostly mechanised in the USA).

USES & PROPERTIES Raw or cooked tomato is one of the most widely used and versatile foods. It is used fresh as a vegetable, a colourful garnish or in salads and spicy salsas. When cooked, it is an indispensable ingredient of sauces, stews and numerous dishes, especially in the southern European cooking tradition (stuffed tomatoes, sauces with pasta, salads with fresh basil, mousses, soups and soufflés). The fruits are also variously processed to make juice, jam, preserves, pickles, sauce, ketchup, purée, paste and powder.

NUTRITIONAL VALUE Tomatoes have a low energy yield (23 kcal per 100 g) and are rich in vitamins A, B and C. The red pigment in tomatoes (lycopene) has been linked to low levels of cancer in people who consume large amounts of cooked or processed tomatoes.

Lycopersicon esculentum Mill.

family: Solanaceae

fan qie (Chinese); *tomate* (French); *Tomate* (German); *tamatar* (Hindi); *pomodoro* (Italian); *tomate* (Portuguese, Spanish)

Macadamia integrifolia

macadamia nut

Macadamia fruits

Macadamia flowers

Macadamia nuts

DESCRIPTION An evergreen tree that grows up to 15 m tall. It has distinctive, toothed, leathery leaves that occur in threes or fours at each node. The small, tubular, cream-coloured flowers are borne in large numbers on slender, pendulous clusters. Up to 10 or more round, shortly stalked fruits are formed on each branch. When mature, the outer, fleshy green peel splits open to reveal a pale brown, thick-shelled nut. The bony shell is smooth in *M. integrifolia* (the main commercial species) and rough in the less important *M. tetraphylla*. Inside is a round, white, somewhat waxy, edible seed.

ORIGIN & HISTORY Australia (southeastern Queensland and the northern parts of New South Wales). It is an important traditional food of the Aborigines. Macadamia was scientifically named only in 1858 (after an Australian, Dr John Macadam) and exported to Hawaii in 1892, where it became (since 1930) an important commercial crop. Production spread to California, Malawi and South Africa, and macadamias became the first major international food plant originating from Australia.

PARTS USED Ripe seeds (nuts).

CULTIVATION & HARVESTING Grafted trees are established in plantations in tropical and subtropical regions. The nuts are sold in their shells or more often shelled (with specialised implements) to produce raw or roasted nuts that fetch a high price.

USES & PROPERTIES Macadamia nuts are considered to be the most delicious of all gourmet nuts. They are mostly eaten as roasted and salted dessert nuts with a crunchy texture and a taste reminiscent of coconut. The nuts may be coated in chocolate and are used in confectionery, baking and ice cream. They are added to Asian curries for taste and texture.

NUTRITIONAL VALUE The nuts have an energy value of more than 700 kcal per 100 g and contain unsaturated fat (70%), protein (8%) and carbohydrates (4–8%).

Macadamia integrifolia Maiden & Betche

family: Proteaceae

noix de macadam, noix de Queensland (French); *Queenslandnuss, Macadamianuss* (German); *macadamia* (Italian); *macadamia* (Spanish)

Malpighia glabra

acerola • Barbados cherry

Acerola leaves, flowers and fruits

DESCRIPTION The acerola is an evergreen shrub that usually grows 2–3 m tall. It has simple, bright green and glossy leaves, attractive pink flowers and red, fleshy, edible fruits. These are slightly grooved, about 20 mm in diameter and contain three relatively large seeds. Acerola is famous for its exceptionally high content of vitamin C. Several other wild fruits are used as sources of vitamin C. The sea buckthorn (*Hippophae rhamnoides*) is a European and Asian shrub bearing clusters of small nuts, each surrounded by yellow, fleshy pulp (used for jams and juice). The cornelian cherry (*Cornus mas*, family Cornaceae) is a small tree indigenous to Europe and Asia with edible fruits containing more than 100 mg vitamin C per 100 g (used for jams, jelly, juice or wine). Acerola is supposedly similar to (and named after) the West Asian azarole (*Crataegus azarolus*) which is cultivated to some extent in southern Europe.

ORIGIN & HISTORY Acerola is indigenous to tropical America (especially the Caribbean region). It is a traditional source of edible fruits and has been distributed to tropical regions all over the world.

PARTS USED Ripe fruits.

CULTIVATION & HARVESTING Plants are grown from seeds or cuttings and require tropical conditions to flourish. Ripe fruits are gathered by hand (often from wild plants).

USES & PROPERTIES The ripe fruits have a pleasant, slightly sour taste but are rarely eaten raw. They are mainly used for jams, jellies, preserves and juice. The fruit pulp or juice is used to increase the level of vitamin C in commercial food products (fruit juices, jams, baby foods and dietary supplements).

NUTRITIONAL VALUE Fresh fruit pulp is one of the richest known sources of vitamin C (1 700–2 000 mg per 100 g – some sources report up to 4 000 mg). The vitamin C content of sea buckthorn is lower (up to 1 200 mg).

Malpighia glabra L. (= *M. punicifolia* L.)   family: Malpighiaceae

acerolier, cerise des Antilles (French); *Acerolakirsche, Barbardoskirsche* (German); *acerola* (Italian); *acerola* (Spanish)

Malus domestica

apple

Apple tree

Apple flowers

Apples ('Granny Smith', 'Golden delicious')

DESCRIPTION A small, deciduous tree with simple leaves, white flowers flushed with pink and fleshy fruits of variable colour and shape (a pome, with a hard core and seeds called pips). Apple differs from pear in the absence of grit in the fruit, the hairy leaves and the yellow pollen (purple in pear flowers). A large number of *Malus* species produce edible fruits. Cultivated apple is a complex hybrid involving several species, including *M. sieversii*, *M. orientalis* and *M. sylvestris*. Various ornamental and small-fruited apples are called crabapples.

ORIGIN & HISTORY Asia Minor. Apples date back to ancient times – the classical Greeks already had named cultivars and practised grafting. 'Golden Delicious' and 'Granny Smith' are only two examples of the thousands of known cultivars. The apple became the most important of all commercial fruits (40 million tons produced each year). China is the main producer, but apples are cultivated in all cool temperate regions.

PARTS USED Ripe fruits.

CULTIVATION & HARVESTING Apples are grafted onto special dwarfing rootstocks and require cross-pollination, winter chilling and careful pruning to regulate fruit production.

USES & PROPERTIES The most popular of all fruits for eating and cooking (both for sweet and savoury dishes). Famous examples are Austrian *strudel* and English apple pie. Apples are also processed into jams, jellies, fresh juice, fermented juice (cider) and dried apple rings. Distilled cider gives apple brandy (Calvados), an age-old speciality of Normandy.

NUTRITIONAL VALUE "An apple a day keeps the doctor away." Apples have moderate levels of a very large number of nutrients (minerals, vitamins, organic acids, sugars and soluble fibre – more than 100 components of dietary significance) and it is this balanced combination that contributes to their nutritional value and popularity. Noteworthy are biotin, vitamin C (3–25 mg), fructose as main sugar and only 50 kcal per 100 g.

Malus x domestica Borkh.   family: Rosaceae

ao zhou (Chinese); *pommelier* (French); *Apfelbaum* (German); *melo* (Italian); *buah apel* (Malay); *manzano* (Spanish); *appoen* (Thai)

Mammea americana
mammee • mamey • mammee apple

Mammee leaves and fruit

DESCRIPTION An evergreen tall tree (up to 25 m), with simple, glossy leaves, white flowers and round to slightly elongated, rough-textured brown fruits containing orange-yellow fruit flesh and up to four seeds. It should not be confused with the mamme zapote or mamey zapote (*Pouteria sapota*). Also similar is the canistel (*P. campechiana*). Less well known are the African mammee apple (*Mammea africana*) and the Indian mammee apple (*M. suriga*), both of which have edible fruits.

ORIGIN & HISTORY *Mammea americana* is indigenous to Central America (mainly the West Indies and Panama). It is an important traditional food source and has been developed as a cultivated crop. Trees are planted in scattered localities over large parts of tropical America (often as wind breaks or street trees). It was introduced to tropical West Africa, Southeast Asia, Java and the Philippines and is commonly seen in botanical gardens and parks in tropical countries.

PARTS USED Ripe fruits.

CULTIVATION & HARVESTING Trees are grown from seeds but cuttings and grafting are also used. They require a warm, tropical climate and are killed by even mild frost. Fruits are picked when ripe and are sold only on local markets.

USES & PROPERTIES The fruits are eaten for their delicious, slightly acid taste (reminiscent of apricots) or added to fruit salads, ice cream and fruit drinks (often served with a little sugar and lime juice). They are processed into jams, jellies, preserves, purées, pastes and sorbets. Flowers are used to produce a liqueur called *au de créole* or *crème de créole*.

NUTRITIONAL VALUE Fresh fruits have an energy yield of about 45 kcal per 100 g. They are rich in carotenoids (converted to vitamin A), other vitamins, minerals and amino acids (including lysine).

NOTES The seeds and other parts of the plant contain an insecticide and are widely used in rural areas for pest control.

Mammea americana L.

family: Clusiaceae

abricotier sauvage, abricot des Antilles (French); *Mammeyapfel* (German); *abricote, abrico do Pará* (Portuguese); *albaricoque de Santo Dominguo* (Spanish)

239

Mangifera indica
mango

Mango flowers

Mangoes (young fruits)

Mangoes

DESCRIPTION A large tropical tree (up to 40 m) with oblong, glossy leaves, small yellow or red flowers and large, oval to kidney-shaped fruits that usually turn yellow, orange or reddish when they ripen. The fruits of modern cultivars lack the fibres and turpentine flavour of the older types. Other species with edible fruit are the bambangan (*M. pajang*), the bauno (*M. caesia*) and the apple mango (*M. odorata*).

ORIGIN & HISTORY All *Mangifera* species are indigenous to Indomalaysia. Mango is a cultigen grown and domesticated since ancient times (perhaps from 4 000 years ago). It was introduced to Africa by about AD 1000 and much later to tropical America. Today, the fruit is of major commercial importance and is cultivated in all tropical and subtropical regions of the world. India, China and Mexico are major contributors to the annual harvest, which exceeds 20 million tons.

PARTS USED Green or ripe fruits.

CULTIVATION & HARVESTING Mangoes are grown from seeds or are grafted. The fruits are usually picked when mature but still green.

USES & PROPERTIES Ripe fruits are eaten for their delicious flesh or they may be added to fruit salads, cold desserts, purées, ice creams, yogurts and soufflés. They are commonly processed for fruit juice. Unripe fruits are widely used in Asian cooking for their sharp, acid, lime-like taste (added to stews, fish dishes, curries, dips and vegetarian dishes). Unripe fruits are popular in Asia and Africa for making chutneys, pickles and hot spicy sauces. They may be dried and powdered to produce *aamchur* or *amchoor*, a spicy condiment used to acidify various dishes, marinades and sauces. Seeds are edible and a source of flour in India.

NUTRITIONAL VALUE Mangoes have an energy yield of about 60 kcal per 100 g (up to 15% sugar) and are a rich source of vitamins A, B and C.

Mangifera indica L.   family: Anacardiaceae

mang guo (Chinese); *mangue, manguier* (French); *Mangobaum* (German); *aam* (Hindi); *mango* (Italian); *mango, mangou* (Japanese); *mangga* (Malay); *manga* (Portuguese); *mango* (Spanish); *mamuang* (Thai)

Manihot esculenta

cassava

Cassava plant

Cassava flowers and fruits

Cassava roots

DESCRIPTION A perennial, woody shrub (up to 5 m) with distinctive, digitately compound leaves and small green flowers (male and female on separate plants). The large, fleshy, starch-rich brown roots are white inside. Two types of cassava are grown – a bitter type (producing about 1 g of cyanide per kg) and a sweet type (with up to 100 mg cyanide). The plant is also referred to as manioc or tapioca.

ORIGIN & HISTORY A cultigen that probably originated in Brazil or Mexico (wild *Manihot* species are all indigenous to the area between Mexico and Argentina). It is an important traditional staple food and elaborate methods of fermentation and heating were developed in various South American cultures to remove the poisonous cyanogenic glycosides. Cassava spread to Africa and India in recent centuries where it became important as staple food (famine food) and as raw material for industrial processing.

PARTS USED Mainly the roots (for starch) and less often the leaves (as a vegetable).

CULTIVATION & HARVESTING Plants are propagated from cuttings and require a warm tropical climate with a pronounced dry season. Roots can be harvested within one to three years after planting. They are sold as vegetables on local markets or to factories for processing.

USES & PROPERTIES Fresh roots are peeled and used in the same way as potatoes. They may also be dried, ground and boiled to produce various starch foods (*fufu*, semolina or flat breads). Slices may be added to soups, stews and meat dishes. Cassava is important in the manufacture of granulated starch, tapioca (pearled starch) and various other products. Tapioca is used as a thickening agent in cooking and is especially popular for making sweet tapioca puddings and milk-based desserts.

NUTRITIONAL VALUE The fresh root yields 134 kcal per 100 g and has a starch content of 30–35%. It is low in proteins (1%), minerals and other nutrients.

Manihot esculenta Crantz   family: Euphorbiaceae

mu shu (Chinese); *manioc, tapioca* (French); *Maniok, Cassava* (German); *maravalli* (Hindi); *manioco* (Italian); *maniokku* (Japanese); *ubi kayu* (Malay); *mandioca* (Portuguese); *yuca* (Spanish); *mansampalang* (Thai)

Manilkara zapota
sapodilla

Mimusops coriacea

Sapodilla flower and young fruits

Sapodilla young fruits (showing latex)

DESCRIPTION A large evergreen tree that may reach 20 m in height. It has simple, glossy leaves, small white flowers and egg-shaped fruits with a rough brown skin and three to five shiny, dark brown or black seeds. The related balata (*M. bidentata*) has edible fruits and non-elastic rubber (used for machine belts and boot soles). Crown gum (*M. chicle*) is a substitute for sapodilla. *Mimusops* species are similar and closely related. The Indian red coondoo (*Mimusops elengi*) has edible fruits but is cultivated mainly for its fragrant flowers, used in perfume. The Mascarene mimusops (*M. coriacea*) has edible fruits and is occasionally grown in gardens and parks.

ORIGIN & HISTORY Indigenous to Mexico and Central America. Sapodilla is a traditional food plant of the Maya and Aztec cultures and the source of chewing gum or *chicle* chewed by the Aztecs in pre-Columbian times. The tree spread to other tropical parts of the world (especially Southeast Asia, Indonesia and Florida in the USA) where it became a minor fruit crop.

PARTS USED Fresh ripe fruits.

CULTIVATION & HARVESTING Trees are easily grown from seeds but sometimes also by grafting and layering. They require tropical conditions. Fruit are harvested when nearly ripe and are mainly sold on local markets. All parts of the tree contain latex or *chicle* and the bark may be tapped every two or three years.

USES & PROPERTIES The fruits are eaten fresh for their sweet, soft, aromatic flesh that has a slightly gritty texture like pears. They are also added to fruit salads, purées, ice creams or iced drinks. The latex was once used as a basis for chewing gum.

NUTRITIONAL VALUE Ripe fruits give an energy yield of 60 kcal per 100 g. They contain about 15% total sugars and the vitamin C content is 10–20 mg per 100 g.

Manilkara zapota (L.) P. Royen (= *Achras zapota* L.)   family: Sapotaceae

ren xin guo (Chinese); *sapotier* (French); *Breiapfelbaum, Kaugummibaum* (German); *sawo manila* (Indonesian); *sapodilla* (Italian); *sapojira* (Japanese); *ciku* (Malay); *zapotillo* (Spanish)

Medicago sativa

lucerne • alfalfa

Lucerne plant

Lucerne flowers

Lucerne seeds and sprouts

DESCRIPTION A perennial herb with a woody root from which flowering branches emerge each year. The small leaves have three leaflets and a pair of small stipules, all with serrated margins. The flowers are usually pale to dark blue and they develop into small, curled and coiled pods, each containing small, pale brown seeds. *Medicago* species are best known for their importance as fodder crops and lucerne has been described as the "queen of forages". It has become a health food in recent years, together with several clover species (genus *Trifolium*), especially *T. pratense* (red clover).

ORIGIN & HISTORY Southwestern Asia. The plant is widely naturalised in Europe, North America and parts of Africa. The earliest archaeological evidence of lucerne as a fodder was found in Turkey and dates back to about 1300 BC.

PARTS USED Seeds, germinated seeds (sprouts) or leaves.

CULTIVATION & HARVESTING Lucerne is esta-blished from seeds and remains productive for several years. It is grown as a fodder crop and the leaves or seeds are mechanically harvested. Seeds or sprouts are often sold on fresh produce markets and in health shops.

USES & PROPERTIES Lucerne sprouts are widely used as a fresh vegetable and salad ingredient in the same way as those of several other species (clovers, grains and mustards). Sprouts can be added to soups, stews, egg dishes and sandwiches as a nutritious garnish. The seeds are eaten to some extent but excessive amounts should be avoided. Dried and ground leaves can be taken as a dietary supplement and tonic because of the high levels of minerals and vitamins.

NUTRITIONAL VALUE Lucerne sprouts have a relatively high energy value (110 kcal per 100 g) and are very rich in proteins, amino acids and minerals. Canavanine (a non-protein amino acid) is potentially harmful in excess but it is largely broken down during seed germination.

Medicago sativa L.   family: Fabaceae

luzerne (French); *Luzerne* (German); *alfa-alfa* (Italian)

Melissa officinalis

lemon balm • balm • sweet balm

Lemon balm flowers

Lemon balm plants

Bee balm

DESCRIPTION An aromatic perennial herb of about half a metre in height, with prominently veined, wrinkled, toothed leaves in opposite pairs and small, two-lipped, white flowers clustered along the stems. The plant should not be confused with the North American bee balm (*Monarda didyma*), that was once used to make a herbal tea called "Oswego tea".

ORIGIN & HISTORY Lemon balm is indigenous to the eastern Mediterranean region and Asia Minor. The herb was well known to the Greeks and Romans, who distributed it throughout Europe. The leaves contain a chemical compound (terpenoid) that acts as a pheromone to attract bees, hence the name *melissa*, the Greek name for honeybees. Commercial production occurs in various parts of southern, central and eastern Europe.

PARTS USED Fresh or dried leaves.

CULTIVATION & HARVESTING Plants grow easily from seeds or cuttings and are seen in almost every herb garden around the world. Fresh leaves are picked for culinary use and to add colour to cocktails.

USES & PROPERTIES The aromatic, lemon-scented leaves are used fresh in salads, fruit salads, desserts, milk puddings, soups, sauces and stuffings. It is an ideal herb for use with eggs, omelettes, stews, white meat and fish, as well as pork dishes and cooked vegetables. Leaves are often used to flavour herbal teas, tisanes, fruit drinks and home-made lemon liqueurs. The sweet-scented flowers are distilled to make *eau de Carmes* and various other lemon drinks and liqueurs such as Bénédictine and Chartreuse.

NUTRITIONAL VALUE The small quantities used for flavouring contribute almost no nutrients to the diet. Nevertheless, the herb has beneficial effects on the digestive system. It is a popular traditional medicine, used for its sedative, carminative and antispasmodic effects, partly ascribed to essential oil components. The lemon flavour is due to the presence of citronellal and citral.

Melissa officinalis L.   family: Lamiaceae

citronnelle, mélisse (French); *Zitronenmelisse* (German); *melissa, cedronella* (Italian); *melissa* (Spanish)

Mentha arvensis

field mint • corn mint • Japanese mint

Four different mint species

Field mint leaves and flowers   Field mint

DESCRIPTION An aromatic herb with creeping stems above and below the ground. The stems are hairy and the leaves are variable in size and shape, depending on the cultivar – pointed or sometimes rounded and then resembling spearmint, but with at least some hairs. Minute pink flowers are borne in dense groups at the nodes. It differs from the similarly flavoured peppermint (see *M. piperita*) also in the axillary flowers (terminal elongated clusters are typical for peppermint). Young leaves of four different mints are shown above: water mint, *M. aquatica* (bottom left); horse mint or longleaf mint, *M. longifolia* (top left); apple mint or woolly mint, *M. suaveolens* (bottom right) and field mint (top right).

ORIGIN & HISTORY Europe and Asia. It differs from other mints in being adapted to warm, tropical conditions (hence its popularity in Asian cooking). It is commercially cultivated in China, Japan, India, Brazil and Paraguay as an industrial source of menthol that is used mainly in toothpaste, oral hygiene products and sweets.

PARTS USED Fresh leaves (or the essential oil).

CULTIVATION & HARVESTING Field mint grows very easily from cuttings and by division and thrives in both Mediterranean and tropical climates. The fresh leaves are harvested by hand (or mechanically, when further processed to extract the valuable, menthol-rich essential oil).

USES & PROPERTIES This mint is a common ingredient of Thai, Malaysian, Japanese and Indian cuisines. Fresh leaves are added to Thai salads and are used to garnish many Indian dishes. In Malaysia, some cooks prefer to use mint as the main ingredient in the spicy noodle soup known as *laksa*. Leaves contain about 60% menthol, which is obtained in crystallised form by cooling the essential oil to near freezing point. Menthol gives the typical peppermint taste ("cooling" sensation) to numerous food products.

NUTRITIONAL VALUE Only small amounts are added to dishes.

Mentha arvensis L. (= *M. arvensis* L. var. *piperascens* Malinv.)   family: Lamiaceae

bo he, xiang hua cai (Chinese); *menthe du Japon, baume de champs* (French); *Ackerminze* (German); *pudina* (Indonesian); *menta selvatica* (Italian); *daun pudina* (Malay); *bai saranae* (Thai)

Mentha piperita

peppermint

Peppermint flowers

Eau de cologne mint

Peppermint leaves

DESCRIPTION An aromatic perennial herb with reddish purple, hairless stems and dark green, pointed leaves. The lilac-pink flowers are borne in elongated clusters on the stem tips. The leaves have a strong, characteristic peppermint smell. Closely related is bergamot mint or eau de cologne mint (*M. x piperita* var. *citrata*), known in French as *menthe citronnée* or *menthe bergamote*. It has a distinct lemon scent and may also be distinguished by the rounded flower clusters and the much broader leaves.

ORIGIN & HISTORY Peppermint is a cultigen derived from three other species. It is a cross between water mint (*M. aquatica*) and spearmint (*M. spicata*). Spearmint itself is a hybrid between apple mint (*M. suaveolens*) and horse mint or longleaf mint (*M. longifolia*). It is a very important crop – the annual production of 3 000 tons essential oil comes mainly from the USA.

PARTS USED Fresh or dried leaves (or the essential oil obtained by steam distillation).

CULTIVATION & HARVESTING Plants are easily grown from cuttings or pieces of rhizome and are often seen in private herb gardens and kitchen gardens.

USES & PROPERTIES Peppermint is well known for the "cooling" sensation in the mouth and throat as a result of the high levels of menthol (which interacts with the mucous membranes). The herb or the essential oil is very popular for flavouring a wide range of sweets (chocolates, peppermints), sweet dishes (jellies, puddings, ice creams), confectionery (cakes, pies, tarts) and drinks (such as *crème de menthe*). Peppermint leaves can be used in cooking but spearmint is usually preferred because of the distinct, non-cooling flavour.

NUTRITIONAL VALUE Used for flavour only.

NOTES Peppermint oil is used in toothpaste for the refreshing taste, cooling effect and proven antimicrobial properties. It is an important component of cough mixtures, cough lozenges and numerous pharmaceutical formulations.

Mentha x piperita L.   family: Lamiaceae

menthe poivrée (French); *Pfefferminze* (German); *menta piperina* (Italian); *la menta* (Spanish)

Mentha spicata
spearmint • garden mint

Horse mint (longleaf mint)

Spearmint (garden mint)

Pineapple mint

DESCRIPTION A perennial herb with creeping rhizomes and erect flowering stems of 0.5 m or more. The leaves are bright green, practically hairless, rather broad, strongly toothed along the margins and can easily be identified by the spearmint smell. It is similar to horse mint or longleaf mint (*M. longifolia*) but the leaves are much broader. Apple mint (*M. suaveolens*) is also similar but much more hairy; a decorative form with variegated leaves is known as pineapple mint.

ORIGIN & HISTORY Spearmint originated somewhere in Europe as a garden hybrid between apple mint and longleaf mint. It became popular in herb gardens and later formed the basis of a large spearmint oil industry in the USA – mainly for sweets, toothpaste and oral hygiene products. Fresh or dried leaves are also produced on a commercial scale in Egypt and eastern Europe.

PARTS USED Fresh or dried leaves (or the essential oil).

CULTIVATION & HARVESTING Plants are very easily propagated from cuttings. Many people have a plant in the garden to supply fresh mint leaves for the kitchen.

USES & PROPERTIES Mint is famous for making mint sauce, a traditional accompaniment for roast leg of lamb in England. It is widely used as a culinary herb to add flavour to sauces, salads and vegetables (especially green peas and boiled potatoes). It is often added to meat dishes and stews. Mint is sometimes used to flavour tea or to make mint tea – an infusion of fresh or dried leaves, sweetened with honey and served hot or cold with a slice of lemon. Mint julep, typical for the southern parts of the USA, is a cocktail made in a tall glass with mint leaves, crushed ice, sugar and bourbon.

NUTRITIONAL VALUE Used for flavour only.

NOTES Spearmint oil is rich in carvone (more than 50%) and is non-cooling because it lacks menthol.

Mentha spicata L.   family: Lamiaceae

menthe verte, menthe douce (French); *Grüne Minze, Ährenminze* (German); *menta ricciuta* (Italian)

Mespilus germanica
medlar

Medlar tree

Medlar flowers

Medlar fruits

DESCRIPTION A shrub or small tree, 2–5 m high, with oblong, slightly hairy leaves and white flowers resembling those of apple or pear. The small, brown, apple-like fruits have five segments around a cup-shaped centre, each with a fleshy base and a single seed. Five persistent sepals around the rim of the fruit are characteristic. Wild forms of medlar have thorny branches but cultivated ones are usually without thorns. A second species, *M. canescens*, occurs in North America (Arkansas).

ORIGIN & HISTORY The medlar is indigenous to an area that stretches from southeastern Europe to Central Asia. It is thought that the Assyrians and Babylonians first cultivated medlars. The fruits were known to the ancient Greeks and the Romans, who developed different cultivars. The medlar occurs sporadically in various parts of Europe and Britain (possibly as a result of Roman influence) and was introduced to North America by the early settlers. Medlars are mainly of historical interest but are still cultivated on a small scale over large parts of North America and Europe.

PARTS USED Over-ripe ("bletted") fruits.

CULTIVATION & HARVESTING Trees are grown from seeds and can be grafted onto rootstocks of hawthorn (*Crataegus*). They require temperate conditions. The fruits become palatable only after being left on the tree, where they are subjected to the first frosts of winter and become partly decayed. The process is known as "bletting", and can also be achieved by leaving the picked fruits on straw to ripen and mature slowly until they become soft and brown.

USES & PROPERTIES Medlars are mainly used to make a high quality jelly and can also be turned into tasty compotes. They have an acidic, wine-like taste and may be eaten raw. The juice makes a tasty drink.

NUTRITIONAL VALUE Ripe fruits are rich in sugars (10%) and yield nearly 100 kcal per 100 g.

Mespilus germanica L.   family: Rosaceae

nèfle (French); *Mispel* (German); *nespola* (Italian); *nispero europeo* (Spanish)

Metroxylon sagu

sago palm

Sago palm leaves

Sago palm

Sago (pearl sago) with tapioca

DESCRIPTION A tree of up to 10 m in height bearing large, pinnate leaves. At maturity (12–15 years) the plant flowers only once and then dies. For about three years before flowering there is a massive accumulation of starch in the stem to allow for the rapid development of the enormous terminal flower cluster. Some forms of the sago palm are spineless, while others (*M. rumphii*) are prickly. Sago can also be made from several other palms and from cocoyam, cassava, sweet potato or potato.

ORIGIN & HISTORY Swamps of Indonesia and Malaysia. Sago palms have been utilised by local people as a starch source for centuries.

PARTS USED Starch (from the stem pith).

CULTIVATION & HARVESTING Sago palms are rarely cultivated but are harvested in the wild on a sustainable basis. When a mature palm is cut (just before flowering), the sucker shoots around it are planted out to ensure a future crop. The stem is cut into sections, the inner pith is pulverised and the starch washed out, collected and dried (up to 200 kg raw starch per stem). To make pearl sago, starch paste is pressed through a sieve and the pieces rapidly dried on a hot plate, resulting in almost perfectly round and gelatinised, somewhat translucent grains.

USES & PROPERTIES Sago is traditionally used in cooking as a thickening agent, especially in chicken broths, stews and soups (also as a garnish and to shorten the cooking time). Another common use is as a sweet dessert, cooked with milk and spices (usually cinnamon). Sago starch is used in Indonesian cooking as a paste (mixed with coconut pulp and milk) to produce desserts and fritters. In India, various sweet dishes are prepared from pearl sago.

NUTRITIONAL VALUE Palm sago contains 80–85% starch and has a high energy value. Proteins and other nutrients are present in small amounts only.

Metroxylon sagu Rottb. [= *M. laeve* Mart.; = *M. rumphii* (Willd.) Mart.]   family: Arecaceae (Palmae)

xi mi zong (Chinese); *sagoutier* (French); *Sagopalme* (German); *pohon sagu* (Indonesian); *sago* (Italian); *sago yashi* (Japanese); *pohon rumbia* (Malay); *palma de sago* (Spanish); *sa khu* (Thai)

Momordica charantia
balsam pear • bitter gourd • bitter melon

Balsam pear flowers

Balsam pear plant

Balsam pear fruits

DESCRIPTION An annual with slender stems that climb by means of coiled tendrils. It has deeply lobed leaves, small yellow flowers and distinctive, warty fruits. Male and female flowers occur on the same plant. The fruits are variable in shape and colour – usually dark green when picked but turning yellow or orange when they ripen. Inside are several black seeds surrounded by bright red arils. A close relative is the balsam apple (*M. balsamina*).

ORIGIN & HISTORY Balsam pear is widely distributed in the Old World tropics (Africa, India and Southeast Asia). It is naturalised in the southeastern parts of the USA. Balsam apple originated in Malaysia but is now present in most tropical parts of the world. Both species are traditional food sources in Pakistan, India, China, Southeast Asia and Indonesia.

PARTS USED Young fruits (also the young leaves).

CULTIVATION & HARVESTING Plants are easily propagated from seeds and grow in both tropical and warm temperate regions. Young fruits are picked by hand and are shipped to local and overseas markets.

USES & PROPERTIES The young fruits are a popular vegetable and are included in curries and pickles. In Chinese cooking it is used as a bitter tonic and vegetable (functional food). Mature fruits are very bitter and purgative – large quantities may be poisonous. They may be steamed or boiled in water to remove or reduce the bitterness. Young stems and leaves are sometimes cooked as a vegetable.

NUTRITIONAL VALUE The fruits are amongst the most nutritious in the pumpkin family. They contain high levels of minerals and vitamins, moderate amounts of vitamin A and quite high levels of vitamin C – up to 50 mg or more in 100 g. The energy yield is low – less than 10 kcal per 100 g.

Momordica charantia L.   family: Cucurbitaceae

ku gua (Chinese); *concombre amer* (French); *Balsambirne* (German); *karela* (Hindi); *pomo meraviglia* (Italian); *niga uri* (Japanese); *peria* (Malay); *bálsamo* (Spanish); *maha* (Thai)

Monstera deliciosa
delicious monster • ceriman

Delicious monster flower cluster

Delicious monster plants

Delicious monster fruits

DESCRIPTION A robust tropical climber that reaches up to 20 m or more. It has thick stems with fleshy, corky aerial roots and large leaves of up to 1 m in diameter. A peculiar feature is the perforated leaves – the holes are created by localised interruptions in growth while the leaf is expanding. Also remarkable is the large, central column (spadix) that bears numerous inconspicuous flowers. It is surrounded by a single large, cream-coloured bract (spatula). The ripe fruit is reminiscent of a slender pineapple – the small, angular "lid" of each individual fruitlet drops off to reveal the fleshy, edible compound fruit. Alternative names are Swiss cheeseplant, cheeseplant or monstera.

ORIGIN & HISTORY Indigenous to Central America (from Mexico to Panama). It is quite rare in the wild but has been distributed to all warm regions of the world within the last two centuries. Delicious monster is a popular houseplant that can be grown out of doors in frost-free areas.

PARTS USED The fleshy columns (compound fruits).

CULTIVATION & HARVESTING Delicious monster is propagated from cuttings – a short piece of the stem will readily take root if planted. The fruits are left on the plant until they are fully ripe – indicated by a fruity smell and the small green peels or lids dropping off.

USES & PROPERTIES The ripe fruit has a delicious flavour often described as a mixture of pineapple and banana. In common with pineapples, numerous sharp crystals are present which irritate the mouth, especially when the fruit is not fully ripe. The fruit can be eaten on its own or added to fruit salads, purées and fools. It can be sliced and served with ice cream as a tasty dessert.

NUTRITIONAL VALUE Ripe fruits contain 16% sugar (70 kcal per 100 g) and are said to be rich in potassium and vitamin C.

Monstera deliciosa Liebm.   family: Araceae

gui bei zhu (Chinese); *cériman, monstera* (French); *Fensterblatt* (German); *monstera* (Italian); *monsutera derishioosa* (Japanese); *balaço, banana de macaco* (Portuguese); *piñanona monstera* (Spanish)

Morinda citrifolia
noni tree • Indian mulberry

Noni flowers

Noni fruit

DESCRIPTION An evergreen shrub or small tree (up to 10 m) with large, simple, glossy leaves and small white flowers arranged in dense, rounded heads. The fruit is a compound drupe, made up of numerous small, fleshy, one-seeded fruitlets. These fruits superficially resemble large mulberries, hence the common name "Indian mulberry". Other common names are canary wood, large-leaved mulberry, noni fruit, nonu or pain killer tree.

ORIGIN & HISTORY The tree is indigenous to India, Southeast Asia and the Pacific region. It is a traditional source of food and medicine in India and especially in Hawaii, where the fruit is known as *noni*. The fruits were used as a famine food on Pacific islands but were also a staple food of choice in Samoa and Fiji.

PARTS USED Ripe fruits or fruit juice.

CULTIVATION & HARVESTING Trees are mostly grown from cuttings and require warm, tropical conditions to thrive. Plantations have been established in Central America and Tahiti and the USA (mainly Florida and Hawaii) and the trees are also wild-harvested to some extent. The ripe fruits are used raw or are subjected to a traditional fermentation process.

USES & PROPERTIES The fruits are traditionally eaten raw (despite their foul smell and taste) or used in chutneys and curries. They have become popular in recent years as a health food, functional food or dietary supplement. Several formulations, often based on fermented or variously processed fruits, are available from health shops.

NUTRITIONAL VALUE The fruits are rich in vitamins B and C and contain substantial quantities of other vitamins and minerals.

NOTES Noni fruit products are said to be beneficial as sexual tonics and useful in treating urinary tract ailments, fever and pain. They contain morindin and other anthraquinones, as well as various proteins and enzymes claimed to be biologically active.

Morinda citrifolia L.

family: Rubiaceae

hai ba ji, wu ning, luo ling (Chinese); *nono* (French); *Indische Maulbeere, Nonibaum* (German); *bengkudu* (Malay); *mora de la India, noni* (Spanish)

Moringa oleifera

ben tree • drumstick tree • horseradish tree

Ben tree leaves and flowers

Ben tree fruits

DESCRIPTION A tree of 5–15 m in height with a short, thick trunk and thick, fleshy roots. Large, two to four times pinnately compound, fern-like leaves are borne on the slender, somewhat drooping branches. The fragrant flowers are small, creamy white, with small spots on the lower petals and are borne in loose clusters. Especially characteristic are the long, slender fruit capsules (up to nearly 1 m long) that contain numerous oil-rich, winged seeds – each seed has three wings and spins around as it falls.

ORIGIN & HISTORY Indigenous to northwestern India. This versatile tree has been valuable to local people for centuries. It is commonly planted in all warm parts of the world but rarely on a commercial scale.

PARTS USED Young leaves, young fruits, roots and seeds.

CULTIVATION & HARVESTING Trees are easily grown from seeds in warm climates. Utilisation is mostly localised in rural areas but leaves and young fruits are often seen on oriental markets and in Asian food stores.

USES & PROPERTIES An important ingredient in Indian cuisine. Leaves are boiled and eaten in curry dishes. The dark green young fruits are scraped to remove the tough skin and are then sliced, boiled and eaten like green beans. Roots are dug up, carefully peeled and used as a seasoning in the same way as horseradish (the roots contain sharp-tasting benzyl mustard oils). The seeds are rich in fat and yield a valuable salad oil ("oil of ben", also used in oil painting).

NUTRITIONAL VALUE The green fruits have an energy yield of about 43 kcal per 100 g. They are known as a rich source of minerals (especially calcium) and vitamins. Vitamin C levels may exceed 100 mg per 100 g.

NOTES Crushed seeds of *M. oleifera* and the related African *M. stenophylla* are important as water purifiers. Both have numerous medicinal uses.

Moringa oleifera Lam. (= *M. pterygosperma* Gaertn.) family: Moringaceae

la mu (Chinese); *ben oléifere* (French); *Pferderettichbaum* (German); *been, bemen* (Italian); *wasabi no ki* (Japanese); *kelor* (Malay); *moringa* (Portuguese); *arbol de las perlas, ben* (Spanish)

Morus alba

white mulberry

White mulberry (black form)

White mulberry (typical form)

DESCRIPTION A medium-sized tree of about 8 m in height with large, soft, glossy, hairless, heart-shaped leaves and inconspicuous male and female flowers which are wind-pollinated. The white or black fruits are juicy syncarps formed from small flowers that become fleshy. The black-fruited form of white mulberry is superficially similar to common mulberry or black mulberry (see *M. nigra*) but the latter is easily recognised by the hairy leaves. A third species is the American red mulberry (*M. rubra*).

ORIGIN & HISTORY Central and eastern China; naturalised in Europe, North America and parts of Africa. It is an ancient crop plant used by the Chinese as food for the silkworm (*Bombyx mori*) and nowadays also in medicine. White mulberry, especially the form with black fruit, is often confused with black mulberry (also by James I of England, who planted four acres of black mulberry in 1610 to start a silk industry in England, unaware that only white mulberry is suitable). There is little or no commercial production of mulberries but the fruits are locally important, especially in rural areas.

PARTS USED Ripe fruits.

CULTIVATION & HARVESTING White mulberry is easily propagated from seeds or cuttings. Fruits are picked when fully ripe but are rarely seen on markets as they do not last long.

USES & PROPERTIES White mulberries are used in the same way as other berries to make jams, jellies, syrups and various other food and dessert items. They are similar to black mulberries but less juicy and not as tasty.

NUTRITIONAL VALUE The black-fruited form has less sugar and a lower calorific value (about 30 kcal per 100 g) than black mulberry but other nutrients are similar (see under *M. nigra*). The anthocyanin pigments are considered valuable in the diet as antioxidants.

NOTES The leaves, bark and fruits are used in Chinese medicine for coughs and colds.

Morus alba L. (= *M. indica* L.)

family: Moraceae

---

sang, sang shu, bai sang (Chinese); *mûrier blanc* (French); *Weißer Maulbeerbaum* (German); *gelso, moro bianco* (Italian); *guwa* (Japanese); *amoreira* (Portuguese); *morera blanca* (Spanish)

Morus nigra

black mulberry

Black mulberry

DESCRIPTION A medium-sized tree (up to 10 m high) with relatively small, somewhat leathery, heart-shaped leaves which are distinctly hairy on the lower surfaces and on the stalks. The inconspicuous male and female flowers occur in hanging catkins and are wind-pollinated. The black compound fruits are made up of numerous small flowers that become fleshy. Some forms of white mulberry (*M. alba*) also have black fruits but they are easily distinguished by the soft, glossy, completely hairless leaves.

ORIGIN & HISTORY The black mulberry or common mulberry is an ancient cultigen of unknown origin (possibly the Middle East) that is widely planted in all temperate regions as a source of delicious fruits.

PARTS USED Ripe fruits.

CULTIVATION & HARVESTING Black mulberry is traditionally grown from cuttings or truncheons (thick branches, up to 2.5 m long). Mulberries are unimportant in world trade as they do not transport well. They have to be harvested when ripe, as the unripe fruit can be harmful and unhealthy. In the Middle East (Iran) they are dried and used like raisins.

USES & PROPERTIES Black mulberries are superior to white mulberries in taste and juiciness. They have a delicious sweet-sour taste and dark purple colour due to anthocyanin pigments. Ripe mulberries are popular for making jams, jellies, syrups, cold drinks and mulberry wine. Mulberries are also used in fruit salads, various cold desserts, pies and puddings.

NUTRITIONAL VALUE Ripe black mulberries have a calorific value of 57 kcal per 100 g. They contain about 8% sugar and are rich in minerals such as potassium (more than 200 mg per 100 g) and vitamin C (15 mg per 100 g). The sour taste is due mainly to citric acid. Anthocyanins are known to have antioxidant and venotonic effects so that their presence in high concentrations no doubt adds to the nutritional value.

Morus nigra L.   family: Moraceae

hei sang (Chinese), *mûrier noir* (French), *Schwarzer Maulbeerbaum* (German), *moro nero* (Italian), *kuro guwa* (Japanese), *amoreira nigra* (Portuguese); *morera negra* (Spanish)

Murraya koenigii
curry leaf

Curry leaf flowers

Curry leaf fruits

Curry leaf leaves

DESCRIPTION A small, aromatic, evergreen tree, 3–6 m in height. The compound leaves comprise about ten pairs of small, pointed, toothed and gland-dotted leaflets. Small white flowers are borne in clusters, followed by round berries that turn red when they ripen. Curry leaf is related to the East Asian mock orange (*M. paniculata*, previously *M. exotica*) that is widely grown in gardens as an ornamental plant.

ORIGIN & HISTORY India and Sri Lanka. The tree is an important part of Indian culture, used as traditional medicine and for food flavouring for centuries. It was introduced to many parts of the world over the last few centuries by Indian immigrants, who use it daily as an important part of Indian cuisine. Curry leaf is well known in Thailand, Malaysia and Indonesia, where it has also become part of local cooking.

PARTS USED Fresh or dried leaves.

CULTIVATION & HARVESTING Trees are easily grown from seeds or cuttings. Leafy twigs are picked and sold on local markets or the leaves are air-dried, sieved to remove the stalks and the leaflets packed as a spice.

USES & PROPERTIES Curry leaf is an indispensable ingredient of Indian curries and the leaves are always added when the dish is cooked. It has become popular in Malaysia and Indonesia for fish curries. Curry leaf may be fried in a little oil (with brown mustard and chilli powder) and added to southern Indian lentil dishes. Curry is of Indian origin and refers to any dish flavoured with curry powder. There is much regional variation but curry powder typically contains pepper, cumin and chilli pepper as essential ingredients, but usually also brown mustard, cardamom, cloves, coriander, ginger, tamarind and turmeric.

NUTRITIONAL VALUE The leaflets are used in small quantities for flavour only.

NOTES The leaves contain 2.6% essential oil that is used in the soap industry.

Murraya koenigii (L.) Spreng.   family: Rutaceae

Ma jiao ye, ka li cai, duo ye jiu li xiang (Chinese); *arbre à feuilles de curry* (French); *Curryblattbaum, Curry-Orangeraute* (German); *karipatta* (Hindi); *duan kari* (Indonesian, Malay); *bai karee* (Thai)

Musa acuminata

banana

Banana flower cluster

Banana plantation

Cooking banana

DESCRIPTION A robust, leafy perennial herb with fleshy underground rhizomes and large leaves (the stalks form pseudostems) and massive flower clusters with deciduous male flowers at the tip and numerous female flowers at the base. Cultivated bananas are sterile and develop the typical seedless fruits without the need for pollination. The plantain or cooking banana (*M. paradisiaca*) has a green skin when ripe.

ORIGIN & HISTORY Southeast Asia (still a centre of tremendous diversity in shape, colour, texture, flavour and fragrance). An ancient cultigen (derived from wild *M. acuminata* and *M. balbisiana*), banana reached Africa via Indo-Malaysian immigrants who colonised Madagascar long before European intervention. At the same time (around AD 1000) the crop spread to the Pacific region and much later to the New World. Bananas are important as the staple diet of millions of people in Asia and Africa. They are cultivated on a large scale in tropical regions.

PARTS USED Ripe fruits (fresh or dried).

CULTIVATION & HARVESTING Propagation is by division (nowadays also tissue culture). The fruit bunches are harvested when still green and are carefully ripened during shipping or storage.

USES & PROPERTIES Normal eating bananas have a delicious, soft, sugary flesh and are eaten raw or baked in many different ways in both savoury and sweet dishes. Examples are fruit salads, purées, juices, yogurts, omelettes, pancakes, fritters and breads. The famous banana split is a USA invention – a banana cut lengthwise served with three balls of ice cream, chocolate or strawberry sauce, glacé cherries and sprinkled with crushed walnuts. Plantains (low in sugar, rich in starch) are cooked as a vegetable, especially in African and West Indian cuisine.

NUTRITIONAL VALUE Exceptional. The energy yield is 88–100 kcal per 100 g and the ripe fruit is well supplied with a wide diversity of important minerals and vitamins.

Musa acuminata Colla

family: Musaceae

jiao (Chinese); *bananier* (French); *Bananenstaude* (German); *kelaa* (Hindi); *banano* (Italian); *banana* (Japanese); *pisang* (Malay); *bananeira* (Portuguese); *banano* (Spanish); *kluai* (Thai)

Myrciaria cauliflora
jaboticaba

Jaboticaba flower

Jaboticaba green fruits

Jaboticaba ripe fruits

DESCRIPTION A small to medium sized tree (up to 10 m) with a distinctive smooth and peeling bark resembling that of gum trees (*Eucalyptus* species). The leaves are simple, dark green and borne towards the branch tips. Flowers and fruits are borne directly on the trunk and older branches (an unusual and distinctive feature). The small, white flowers develop into small, rounded, grape-like fruits that turn dark purple to black when they ripen. *Myrciaria* differs from the closely related *Eugenia* in the calyx tube that is fused for some length above the ovary (persistent and sometimes still visible on the ripe fruits). The fruit has a white to pale pink flesh, contains up to four small seeds and is sometimes referred to as Brazilian grape.

ORIGIN & HISTORY Jaboticaba is indigenous to southern Brazil, where it is a traditional food source and much appreciated by local people. The tree has become an important crop plant in Brazil and is grown on an experimental scale in other tropical regions of the world.

PARTS USED Ripe fruits.

CULTIVATION & HARVESTING Trees are easily grown from seeds or cuttings. They require tropical or subtropical conditions and are killed by frost. Ripe fruits are picked by hand.

USES & PROPERTIES The small fruits (the size of medium-sized grapes) are eaten raw for their delicious taste, considered by some people to resemble a mixture of grape, litchi and blackcurrant. The tough skins are usually discarded. The fruits can be added to fruit salads or served with ice cream. They may also be processed into jams, jellies, sauces, compotes, fruit juices, ice drinks or may be fermented to produce a dark red wine. A sweet sauce made with jaboticabas and onions goes well with chicken or duck.

NUTRITIONAL VALUE The fruits are rich in vitamin C and anthocyanins but accurate details are not available.

Myrciaria cauliflora (C. Martius) O. Berg.   family: Myrtaceae

jaboticaba (French); *Jaboticaba* (German); *jaboticaba* (Portuguese, Spanish)

Myristica fragrans

nutmeg tree

Nutmeg leaves and fruit

Nutmeg flower

Nutmeg and mace

DESCRIPTION An evergreen tree (up to 20 m) with simple, leathery leaves and small white flowers. Female trees produce a yellowish brown, fleshy fruit that splits open to reveal the large, single seed surrounded by a bright red, fleshy, net-like aril. Adulterants and alternatives include Bombay nutmeg (*M. malabarica* and *M. beddomii*), Brazilian nutmeg (*Cryptocarya moschato*) and Madagascar nutmeg (*Ravensara aromatica*).

ORIGIN & HISTORY Indigenous to Southeast Asia (specifically Amboine Island, one of the Molucca islands). The tree was distributed to India, Brazil, Mauritius, Malaysia, Sri Lanka, Sumatra and the Caribbean Islands. Nutmeg has been used as a spice (especially in southern India) for centuries. It was introduced into Europe in AD 540 and became popular around AD 1100. The Portuguese, French and British competed for the monopoly in the nutmeg trade during the colonial period. Today, most of the annual production of 10 000 tons comes from Indonesia, New Guinea and Granada.

PARTS USED Ripe, dried, shelled seeds (nutmeg) or the dried aril around the seed (mace).

CULTIVATION & HARVESTING Trees are grown from seeds and require very specific conditions.

USES & PROPERTIES The main use of nutmeg is as a spice in cooking. It is always grated and used for the spicy flavour and aroma in potato dishes, omelettes, soufflés, cakes and custards. French cooks use it in snail dishes, mincemeat, onion soup and *béchamel* sauces. Grated nutmeg has traditional uses in flavouring fortified wines and other alcoholic drinks. Mace is included in spice mixtures and may be used in the same way as nutmeg in sauces, fish and meat dishes (especially pork).

NUTRITIONAL VALUE Both nutmeg and mace are used in small quantities for flavour and not for nutrition (large amounts are indeed dangerous).

NOTES Nutmeg and mace are traditional medicines used to treat digestive complaints.

Myristica fragrans L.   family: Myristicaceae

rou dou kou (Chinese); *muscadier* (French); *Muskatnussbaum* (German); *pala* (Indonesian); *nikuzuku* (Japanese); *noce moscata* (Italian); *buah pala* (Malay); *nuez moscada* (Spanish); *chan thet* (Thai)

Myrrhis odorata

sweet cicely

Sweet cicely leaves and fruits

DESCRIPTION A robust, aromatic, herbaceous perennial of up to 1 m in height. It has erect, grooved, hairy stems and large, compound, dentate leaves of up to 0.5 m long. The inconspicuous white flowers are borne in typical umbels, followed by small, narrowly beaked, dry fruits that typically turn dark brown when they ripen. The plant is quite similar to chervil (*Anthriscus cerefolium*) and can easily be confused with it. It is, however, much larger and easily recognised by the aroma, the large, fern-like leaves and the dark brown fruits. Sweet cicely is also known as cicely, anise chervil or garden myrrh. The term myrrh refers to aromatic resins, of which the most famous are true myrrh (*Commiphora myrrha*), an Afro-Arabian tree, the bark of which exudes an aromatic resin and the eastern Mediterranean myrrh shrub (*Cistus creticus*), with an aromatic resin obtained by boiling the branches in water and skimming off the resin. The latter is believed to be the "myrrh" referred to in the Bible (in Genesis).

ORIGIN & HISTORY The plant is indigenous to Europe. It has a long history of use as pot-herb and for strewing on medieval church floors. Roots were once eaten as a vegetable. It is still occasionally wild-harvested but is also commonly grown in herb gardens as an attractive decoration for shady corners.

PARTS USED Leaves and fruits.

CULTIVATION & HARVESTING Plants are grown from seeds or by division and grow best in shady places. Leaves are used fresh, while the young fruits are collected when still green and then dried.

USES & PROPERTIES Leaves and fruits are used as a culinary herb to give a pleasant, sweet, aniseed or liquorice taste to salads, soups, omelettes, stewed fruits, drinks and liqueurs. The fruits can be used to give a sweet spicy taste to meat dishes.

NUTRITIONAL VALUE Used for flavour only.

Myrrhis odorata (L.) Scop.   family: Apiaceae

cerfeuil odorant, cerfeuil musqué (French); *Süßdolde, Myrrhenkerbel* (German); *finocchio dei boschi* (Italian)

Myrtus communis

myrtle

Myrtle flowers

Myrtle tree

Myrtle fruits

DESCRIPTION An evergreen, aromatic shrub of 2–3 m high. It bears small, dark green, simple leaves in opposite pairs, small white flowers with numerous stamens and dark purple to black edible berries that look like miniature guavas. The typical form of the species has relatively large, dark green leaves. Ornamental cultivars with very small leaves or with variegated leaves are grown in gardens.

ORIGIN & HISTORY The exact origin of myrtle is not known. It is now found from the Mediterranean area to southern Asia, and has been cultivated in this region for centuries. Myrtle has a long history and features in Greek mythology, rituals and ceremonies. It is a symbol of purity.

PARTS USED Leaves and berries.

CULTIVATION & HARVESTING Myrtle is usually grown from cuttings. It thrives in almost any climate and is tolerant of mild frost. Plants are not grown for food but for the valuable essential oil ("eau d'Ange", used in the perfume industry), which is distilled from the leaves. Fresh leaves and berries are picked when needed – the latter may be dried and stored for future use as spice.

USES & PROPERTIES Leaves were used by the Romans to flavour stews and wines and are still important in the cuisine of Corsica and Sardinia. On these islands they are added to *bouillabaisse* and dishes of pork and wild boar. Myrtle leaves are also used to flavour a liqueur known as *nerto*. Leaves and berries can be used in stuffings or as a wrapping added to a roast or game bird for five to ten minutes before serving. Dried berries can be ground in a pepper mill to add a spicy flavour to stews and meat dishes.

NUTRITIONAL VALUE Myrtle is used in small amounts for flavour and not as food.

NOTES Myrtle is still important in medicine, as expectorant, astringent and urinary tract disinfectant.

Myrtus communis L.

family: Myrtaceae

myrte (French); *Echte Myrte, Brautmyrte* (German); *mirto* (Italian)

Nelumbo nucifera
lotus

Lotus flower and fruit

Lotus rhizomes

Lotus fruits (one-seeded nuts)

DESCRIPTION A type of water lily with large round leaves of up to 1 m in diameter growing from a long, fleshy rhizome below the mud. The large, attractive flowers may be red, pink or white. The one-seeded fruits (nuts) occur together in a characteristic flat-topped, compound fruit.

ORIGIN & HISTORY Southern and eastern Asia (Iran to Southeast Asia to tropical Australia). Lotus is very important in Asian mythology and religion – it is sacred in India, Tibet and China. The plant has been cultivated in China and other tropical parts of Asia for thousands of years. It was introduced to the Nile valley in Egypt around 500 BC but is no longer found there. Lotus is today an important commercial food crop.

PARTS USED Young rhizomes, fruits (one-seeded nuts) or rarely the leaves.

CULTIVATION & HARVESTING Plants are easily grown in shallow water in tropical regions. The rhizomes are said to grow up to 20 m in one season. They are dug up and sold fresh (for food) or dried (for medicine).

USES & PROPERTIES Rhizomes are boiled or roasted and eaten as a vegetable or may be fried like chips. Sliced rhizomes (with their distinctive perforations) are commonly sold in canned form. They are used to garnish meat or poultry dishes. The roots may also be pickled or candied. Seeds are eaten raw (after removal of the bitter embryo) or boiled, grilled, pickled in vinegar or candied in syrup. They have an almond-like taste and are added to soups and stews. Young leaves may be eaten like spinach or stuffed with rice, prawns or meat fillings.

NUTRITIONAL VALUE Canned rhizomes yield about 15 kcal per 100 g. They contain 6% starch, 2% protein and are rich in minerals and vitamins. The nuts are very nutritious, with 60% starch, 15% protein and only 2% fat.

Nelumbo nucifera Gaertn.   family: Nymphaeaceae

lian (Chinese); *nelumbo* (French); *Lotosblume* (German); *kanwal* (Hindi); *nelumbo* (Italian); *bunga telpok*, *teratai* (Malay); *kamala* (Sanskrit); *loto* (Spanish)

Nephelium lappaceum
rambutan

Rambutan leaves and fruit

Rambutan flowers

Rambutan fruits

DESCRIPTION An evergreen tree of up to 15 m in height with large leaves and small, yellowish flowers that develop into clusters of about ten distinctive, red or yellow fruits covered with thick, soft hairs. Each fruit has a single large seed surrounded by a soft, white, fleshy aril (the sarcotesta). Rambutan is also called hairy litchi ("rambutan" is derived from *rambut*, the Malay word for hair). A close relative and minor commercial fruit is the West Malaysian pulasan (*N. ramboutan-ake*, previously known as *N. mutabile*). Other relatives with edible arils are real litchi (*Litchi chinensis*), longan (*Dimocarpus longan*) and akee (*Blighia sapida*).

ORIGIN & HISTORY Rambutan originated in Malaysia and has been grown in this region since ancient times for the fruit (and a black dye obtained from the fruit peels). Commercial cultivation in the form of small plantations has spread throughout Southeast Asia (from Myanmar and Vietnam to Indonesia) and more recently also Zanzibar, Madagascar, Central America and Australia. The fruit is still relatively poorly known outside Southeast Asia.

PARTS USED Ripe fruits (fleshy seed arils).

CULTIVATION & HARVESTING Trees are grown from seeds or cuttings and thrive only under moist, tropical conditions. Fruits are harvested by hand when ripe and are sold fresh (they last for about a week in the refrigerator) or canned in syrup.

USES & PROPERTIES The tough skin is easily removed by hand to reveal the white, aromatic, fragrant, litchi-like flesh that is delicious to eat on its own or as part of fruit salads or sweet desserts. Rambutans may also be processed into stews and jams and are readily available in canned form. They are sometimes used in cooking to accompany meat dishes.

NUTRITIONAL VALUE The fresh arils contain about 15% sugar (energy yield of 66 kcal per 100 g) and are rich in vitamin C (35–70 mg per 100 g).

Nephelium lappaceum L.   family: Sapindaceae

Hong mao dan (Chinese); *ramboutanier* (French); *Rambutan* (German); *ramboostan* (Hindi); *nefelio* (Italian); *ranbuutan* (Japanese); *rambutan* (Malay); *rambután* (Spanish); *ngoh* (Thai)

Nigella sativa

black cumin • black seed • kalonji

Love-in-a-mist

Black cumin leaves and flowers

Black cumin seeds

DESCRIPTION Black cumin is an erect annual herb of about 0.4 m in height with finely dissected, compound leaves, attractive white flowers with distinctive erect styles and many-seeded, segmented fruit capsules. A close relative is the attractive blue-flowered *N. damascena*, called love-in-a-mist or *chernushka* in Russian. It is a popular ornamental plant in gardens.

ORIGIN & HISTORY Indigenous to southern Europe, North Africa and western Asia. The plant was probably domesticated in the Fertile Crescent (Assyria and Mesopotamia) and was cultivated in ancient Egypt – seeds were found in Tutankhamen's tomb. The plant is still an important condiment in Arabia, Egypt, India and Pakistan (formerly also in southern and central Europe). The Indian name *kala jeera* means "black cumin".

PARTS USED Ripe seeds, sometimes called "onion seed" or *quatre-épices* ("four spices") in French.

CULTIVATION & HARVESTING Plants are easily grown from seeds in temperate regions. The ripe seed capsules are harvested and the purified seeds supplied to spice markets.

USES & PROPERTIES The aromatic and pungent seeds are widely used in Indian and Middle Eastern cuisine as a condiment and pepper substitute to flavour spicy dishes. They are also sprinkled over cakes and breads, especially the traditional *naan* bread. The Indian *panch phora* ("five spices") is a mixture of black cumin with real cumin, fennel, fenugreek and mustard. In eastern Europe (Russia, Poland) the seeds of *N. damascena* are sprinkled over cakes and breads.

NUTRITIONAL VALUE Seeds are used sparingly for flavour only. However, they are commonly used as a tonic, claimed to have immune-stimulating properties. A typical dose is one teaspoon of crushed seeds taken twice a day.

NOTES The seeds contain a fixed oil (up to 40% of dry weight) rich in phytosterols, as well as an essential oil with thymoquinone as main ingredient, to which beneficial effects are ascribed.

Nigella sativa L.   family: Ranunculaceae

pei hei zhong cao (Chinese); *nigelle, poivrette, cumin noire* (French); *Schwarzkümmel* (German); *kalonji, kala jeera* (Hindi); *cuminella* (Italian); *nigela* (Portuguese); *niguiella, ajenuz común* (Spanish)

Ocimum basilicum

basil • sweet basil

Sweet basil

Flowers of Thai basil

Sacred basil (*tulsi*)

DESCRIPTION Sweet basil is an erect, robust annual of up to 0.7 m in height with soft, hairless leaves and flower clusters with widely spaced, stalkless white flowers. Sacred basil or holy basil (*O. tenuiflorum*, previously known as *O. sanctum*) is a short-lived perennial with hairy stems and sparsely hairy leaves. It is known as *tulsi* in Hindi. A form with brightly coloured (usually purple) bracts below the flowers is known as Thai basil. Hairy basil (*O. canum*) is an African species with smooth leaves but hairy calyces. Numerous basil cultivars have been developed, some with strong lemon or cinnamon flavours.

ORIGIN & HISTORY Basil species are widely distributed throughout Africa, the Middle East, India and Southeast Asia. The exact origin of sweet basil and other cultivated forms is not clear, as these plants have been used as culinary herbs for centuries – first in India, the Near East and North Africa, later in southern and central Europe.

PARTS USED Fresh or dried leaves.

CULTIVATION & HARVESTING Plants are easily grown from seeds or cuttings but require warm conditions and rich soil. Fresh leaves are best – drying results in a loss of flavour – but preservation in olive oil can be recommended.

USES & PROPERTIES Sweet basil is strongly associated with Italian cooking. The flavour complements any tomato salad or tomato dish exceptionally well. Basil is used in salads, soups, sauces, stuffings, meat dishes and especially pastas. The most famous of all basil dishes is *pesto*, a sauce originating in Genoa that calls for liberal quantities of fresh basil crushed with garlic, Parmesan cheese, pine nuts and olive oil. Thai basil is popular in Vietnamese and Thai cooking (stir-fries, curries and salads). Holy basil is rarely used fresh but mostly cooked to release the flavours (as an ingredient of fish, poultry and meat dishes).

NUTRITIONAL VALUE Used in small amounts only.

Ocimum basilicum L. family: Lamiaceae

luo le, yu xiang cai (Chinese); *basilic* (French); *Basilikum* (German); *babui tulsi* (Hindi); *basilico* (Italian); *bajiru* (Japanese); *kemangi, selaseh* (Malay); *alfavaca* (Portuguese); *albahaca* (Spanish); *horapha* (Thai)

Olea europaea

olive

Green olive fruits

Olive flowers

Black and green olives

DESCRIPTION Long-lived, evergreen trees (up to 10 m) with narrow leaves in opposite pairs (dark green above, pale below). The small white flowers have only two stamens and the oval, one-seeded fruits (olives) are distinctive.

ORIGIN & HISTORY Mediterranean region and western Asia. Olive is an ancient cultigen with a long history of use by the Assyrians, Egyptians, Greeks, Romans and Palestinians (with several Biblical references – the leaves are an ancient sign of peace and goodwill). The production of olives and especially olive oil is a massive industry, still centred in the Mediterranean region but rapidly expanding to other temperate parts of the world (Africa, Australia, South America and California in the USA).

PARTS USED The green or ripe fruits (table olives) or the oil obtained from the fruit pulp (olive oil).

CULTIVATION & HARVESTING Olives are propagated from seeds or by grafting. The fruits are too bitter to eat and have to be processed (pickled in brine) to make them edible. Green (unripe) olives are first treated with lye to neutralise the bitter taste, while black (ripe) olives require no such pretreatment. Fruits of oil cultivars contain up to 40% oil and are cold pressed. The first pressing is referred to as "extra virgin" or "virgin" – these oils retain the flavour of the olives, while refined oils have all the smells and flavours removed.

USES & PROPERTIES Olives can be stuffed with red peppers, onions or nuts and have numerous uses as snack food and ingredient of savoury dishes. Olive oil is typical of southern European cooking but has become popular all over the world as premier cooking oil and salad oil.

NUTRITIONAL VALUE Olives have the highest energy yield of all fruits (up to 200 kcal per 100 g) and are rich in minerals (calcium, potassium) and vitamins. The oil is monounsaturated, with high levels of oleic acid.

Olea europaea L.   family: Oleaceae

olivier (French); *Olivenbaum* (German); *olivo, ulivo* (Italian); *olivo* (Spanish)

Opuntia ficus-indica

prickly pear

Prickly pear plant

Prickly pears

Peeled prickly pears

DESCRIPTION A leafless, succulent, spiny shrub of about 3 m in height. The stems are represented by large flat joints or pads with scattered groups of spines (glochids). Large yellow or orange flowers are followed by greenish orange to purple, pear-shaped fruit covered with minute spines. Prickly pears are usually orange or red inside, with numerous hard, edible seeds dispersed in the sweet fruit flesh. A close relative is the Mexican nopalea cactus or cochineal plant (*O. cochenillifera*). It is the host plant of cochineal, a type of mealy bug that produces a valuable red vegetable dye known as carmine (carminic acid). Immature young stems are called *nopales* or *nopalitos* and are sold as vegetables or pickles.

ORIGIN & HISTORY Indigenous to Mexico and an important food source since prehistoric times. It spread around the world in post-Columbian times, sometimes becoming troublesome weeds. Today, prickly pears are grown on a commercial scale in various countries, including Australia, South Africa and the USA.

PARTS USED Ripe fruits.

CULTIVATION & HARVESTING Stem pads are simply broken off and planted. The crop adapts to a wide range of climatic conditions. Protective clothing and gloves are needed to harvest the fruits, which are packed after most of the thorns have been removed.

USES & PROPERTIES Prickly pears are eaten raw for their delicious taste, sometimes with a little lemon or lime juice to add flavour. They can be included in fruit salads or compotes some Indian and Mexican savoury dishes. The fruit flesh can be cooked and puréed for jams, preserves, cold desserts, ice creams and milk shakes.

NUTRITIONAL VALUE Ripe fruits are an excellent source of minerals (especially calcium and magnesium), as well as vitamins (up to 40 mg vitamin C and 380 µg nicotinamide). The energy yield is low (36 kcal per 100 g).

Opuntia ficus-indica (L.) Mill.

family: Cactaceae

ci li, xian tao (Chinese); *oponce, figue de barbarie* (French); *Feigenkaktus* (German); *fico d'India* (Italian); *opunchia* (Japanese); *figo de cacto* (Portuguese); *tuna* (Spanish)

Origanum majorana

marjoram

Marjoram plant

Field of marjoram

Marjoram leaves

DESCRIPTION A perennial herb (up to 0.5 m) with small, hairy leaves borne on square stems in opposite pairs. The purple, pink or white flowers are borne in terminal clusters. Marjoram is very similar to wild marjoram, better known as oregano, but it has a milder flavour. Pot marjoram (*O. onites*) is used as substitute (or even an adulterant) for marjoram and oregano but the quality is inferior. It is similar to marjoram but the flowers are borne in small, cone-like flower clusters.

ORIGIN & HISTORY The Mediterranean region (especially Turkey). Marjoram has been a popular culinary herb since ancient times (used by the Egyptians, Greeks and Romans). It is very important in European cooking and is especially common in Britain, Germany, France, Hungary, northern Italy and Spain.

PARTS USED Fresh leaves (or the essential oil obtained by steam distillation).

CULTIVATION & HARVESTING Marjoram is easily propagated by seeds or cuttings. Plants are commonly seen in private herb gardens to ensure a reliable supply of fresh leaves. Fresh or dried product is nowadays readily available from supermarkets.

USES & PROPERTIES Marjoram is an essential part of European cooking. The strong, aromatic scent is widely used to flavour meat, sausages, poultry, beans, carrots and cucumber. It is sparingly added to fresh salads, fish dishes, omelettes, sauces and stuffings. The herb is added towards the end of the cooking period to ensure that the volatile flavour is not lost. Marjoram oil is used in the food industry to flavour tinned meats and sausages. The main ingredient is methyl chavicol. Marjoram is combined with bay leaves, parsley and thyme in the classic *bouquet garni*. Dried leaves are incorporated in herb mixtures. Drying tends to concentrate the flavour so that dried leaves are used sparingly.

NUTRITIONAL VALUE Not significant at the small quantities that are typically used.

Origanum majorana L. (= *Majorana hortensis* Moench)   family: Lamiaceae

marjolaine (French); *Majoran* (German); *maggiorana* (Italian); *amàraco* (Spanish)

Origanum vulgare

oregano

Oregano flowers

Oregano plant

Oregano with marjoram

DESCRIPTION A perennial herb (up to 0.6 m) with square reddish stems and dark green, hairy leaves. The flowers are typically reddish purple and are borne amongst purplish bracts. Oregano is also called wild marjoram and the two species are used almost interchangeably. However, oregano is easily recognised by the much more pungent flavour. Pot marjoram (*O. onites*) is an inferior substitute. Of historical interest are the dittany of Crete and Greece (*O. dictamnus*) and the Middle Eastern "hyssop" of the Bible (*O. syriacum*).

ORIGIN & HISTORY Europe to Central Asia. Oregano is a common wild plant that has been used since prehistoric times as a culinary herb and medicinal plant. It was known to the ancient Greeks and Romans and is especially important in the culinary traditions of the Mediterranean region. It was introduced to North America, where it became naturalised in the eastern parts. Oregano is today of major importance as a crop plant – not only in southern Europe but also in the USA, where it is strongly associated with the enormously popular pizza industry.

PARTS USED Fresh or dried leaves.

CULTIVATION & HARVESTING Oregano is exceptionally easy to cultivate from seeds or cuttings. It does best in alkaline soil in a warm Mediterranean climate. The leafy branches are harvested and sold fresh or in dried form. To retain the flavour, the dried leaves are not powdered but broken into small fragments.

USES & PROPERTIES Oregano is the classical flavour of pizza, so that the pungent flavour has become known to many people around the world. It is also an essential ingredient of tomato dishes and roast meats, especially in southern Italy (but not in the north, where marjoram is preferred). A wild form with white flowers (*rigani*) is popular in Greek cuisine, especially for roast lamb.

NUTRITIONAL VALUE Used in small amounts for flavour only.

Origanum vulgare L.

family: Lamiaceae

origan (French); *Echter Dost* (German); *origano* (Italian); *orégano* (Spanish)

Oryza sativa

rice

Rice ears

Rice plants

Various types of rice

DESCRIPTION A perennial grass of wet places, mostly grown as an annual. It has erect, leafy culms bearing sparse clusters of oblong spikelets, each containing a single grain. Asian rice (*O. sativa*) is very similar to African rice (*O. glaberrima*), which it is rapidly replacing. There are thousands of rice cultivars of two main groups: long-grained *indica* and short-grained *japonica*. Popular types include basmati (aromatic, long-grained), glutinous (short-grained, white, red or black, becomes sweet and sticky when boiled), Italian (very short-grained, traditionally used for *risotto*) and Thai rice or jasmine rice (long-grained, highly perfumed).

ORIGIN & HISTORY India, southern China to Thailand. The exact date and area of domestication of this ancient crop are unknown. Rice rivals wheat as the most important cereal and is the staple food in China, India, Indonesia, Bangladesh and parts of Africa and Latin America. Only 5% of the annual harvest (500 million tons) enters world trade (mainly from Thailand, the USA, Pakistan, India, China and the Piedmont region of Italy).

PARTS USED Ripe, one-seeded fruits (grains).

CULTIVATION & HARVESTING Seedlings are evenly spaced in shallow dams (paddies) and irrigated by flooding. Brown rice is dehusked and beige in colour, while the more popular white rice is polished (rubbed against abrasive discs) to remove all outer layers. Rice is often parboiled.

USES & PROPERTIES Rice is eaten cooked, as hot or cold and sweet or savoury dishes. Rice absorbs water, milk, oil or stock during cooking. There is a remarkable diversity of rice dishes, e.g. Italian *risotto*, Spanish *paella*, Dutch/Indonesian *rijstafel* and Japanese/Thai sticky rice. Rice-based alcoholic drinks include Chinese *chao xing*, Japanese *sake*, Malaysian *samau* and Vietnamese *choum*.

NUTRITIONAL VALUE Very high in energy (350 kcal per 100 g), digestible starch (75%) and B vitamins (outer layers of brown rice). Low in some amino acids (so it combines perfectly with beans).

Oryza sativa L.   family: Poaceae

dao (Chinese); *riz* (French); *Reis* (German); *chawal* (Hindi); *riso* (Italian); *kome* (Japanese); *arroz* (Portuguese, Spanish); *kao* (Thai)

Oxalis tuberosa

oca

Oca plant (white type)

Oca plant (red type)

Oca tuber

DESCRIPTION A hardy perennial herb with fleshy stems and clover-like leaves. The plants bear oblong, segmented tubers that are white, yellow or red in colour. The plant rarely flowers (only the white type; the yellow and red ones never flower).

ORIGIN & HISTORY Indigenous to the Andean highlands in South America. It is an ancient Inca crop, second only to potato in importance. Oca is still a staple food in the high altitude region of South America (Venezuela to Argentina) and has also become an important crop in Mexico (referred to as *papa roja* or "red potato"). In recent years it has also been introduced to New Zealand (so-called "New Zealand yam"). Oca is still practically unknown outside South America, Mexico and New Zealand but has potential for commercial cultivation in cool temperate regions.

PARTS USED Tubers (fleshy underground stems).

CULTIVATION & HARVESTING Oca is easily grown from tubers or cuttings and is exceptionally hardy and tolerant of poor soils, drought and cold (but not heat).

USES & PROPERTIES The tubers are boiled, baked or fried and used in much the same way as potatoes or are added to soups and stews. Unlike potatoes, some sweet types can be eaten raw in salads or pickled in vinegar. Bitter types are processed or dried to remove bitterness and to improve the storage life (the dry product is known as *cavi* or *caya*). Oca tubers may also be sweetened by placing them in the sun for a few days (the glucose level may nearly double).

NUTRITIONAL VALUE Oca is variable in its nutrient content. The tubers contain 70–80% water, 11–22% easily digestible carbohydrates and up to 9% proteins. The amino acids are fairly balanced (only valine and tryptophan are in short supply). It is an excellent source of iron and calcium. Sour types contain oxalic acid but sweet types have only trace amounts.

Oxalis tuberosa Molina   family: Oxalidaceae

oca d'Amérique, trufette acide (French); *Knollen-Sauerklee* (German); *acetosella crenata* (Italian); *oca* (Spanish)

Pachira aquatica

Malabar chestnut

Malabar chestnut leaves and fruits

Malabar chestnut flower

Malabar chestnut seeds

DESCRIPTION The Malabar chestnut is a fast-growing, medium-sized tree of up to 18 m in height with a spreading crown and smooth, greenish bark. It has glossy compound leaves comprising five to nine leaflets and attractive, creamy white flowers, each with five narrow petals that surround a showy tuft of stamens. The fruit is a five-valved, green, woody pod containing several rounded, brown seeds. Several other common names have been recorded, including Malabar nut, Guiana chestnut, Guyana chestnut, saba nut, provision tree and French peanut. It is often grown in gardens, parks and experimental plantings under the older name *Bombax glabrum*.

ORIGIN & HISTORY The tree occurs naturally in the tropical parts of Central America, from southern Mexico to Guyana, Ecuador, Peru and northern Brazil. It is found along the margins of estuaries. Although relatively poorly known, the tree is an important traditional food source.

PARTS USED The ripe seeds (nuts) or more rarely the young leaves and flowers.

CULTIVATION & HARVESTING Trees grow easily in frost-free regions and are propagated from seeds or cuttings. They are tolerant of poor soils and will even survive short periods of drought. As a result, the Malabar chestnut has become a popular ornamental tree in home gardens. The seeds are released from the fruits when they ripen and are easily collected.

USES & PROPERTIES When eaten raw, the seeds taste like peanuts. They can be roasted or fried, in which case the taste is said to be reminiscent of chestnuts. The nuts are also ground into flour for baking bread. Young leaves and flowers are sometimes cooked as vegetables. Malabar chestnut is relatively poorly known as a food plant.

NUTRITIONAL VALUE Seeds have 10% starch, 16% protein and 40–50% fat but are said to also contain poisonous (cyclopropenic) fatty acids.

Pachira aquatica Aublet [= *Bombax glabrum* (Pasq.) A. Robyns]   family: Bombacaceae

pachira, châtaignier de Guyane, noix de Malabar, noisette de Cayenne (French); *Sumpf-Rasierpinselbaum* (German); *pachira acuática* (Italian); *catanho de agua* (Spanish)

Pachyrhizus erosus

yam bean

Yam bean plant

Yam bean leaf

Yam bean tubers

DESCRIPTION A twining, herbaceous, annual climber with a single, thick, fleshy tuber and very large, trifoliate leaves with three-lobed leaflets. The erect, axillary flower clusters develop into edible pods of about 10 cm long. Three species of *Pachyrhizus* have been domesticated. The Mexican *P. erosus* (also known as the *jícima*, Mexican potato or potato bean) is the best known and most widely cultivated. The others are the Andean yam bean or *ahipa* (*P. ahipa*) and the Amazonian yam bean (*P. tuberosus*).

ORIGIN & HISTORY Mexican yam bean has been cultivated since ancient times by the Mexicans, Aztecs and Mayas. In the sixteenth century, the Spaniards introduced it to the Philippines, from where it spread further into Indonesia, the Far East, Mauritius, Réunion and West Africa. It is still an important crop in Mexico, but has become a common sight on markets in many parts of the world, including China and the southern USA (sold as "chop suey bean").

PARTS USED The fleshy tuber or more rarely the young pods.

CULTIVATION & HARVESTING Unlike all other tuber crops, the yam bean is cultivated from seeds. The plants are regularly pruned to promote tuber development (yields of up to 100 tons per hectare).

USES & PROPERTIES The tuber is white inside and has a bland, sweetish taste but refreshingly crisp texture. It is thinly sliced and eaten raw in salads or as a popular snack food with lime juice. The tubers may be boiled, baked or steamed and used like potatoes. In Asian cooking it is pickled or used as a substitute for water chestnuts. In Thailand, young pods are eaten as a vegetable.

NUTRITIONAL VALUE The tuber is regarded as a health food because it contains 10–15% highly digestible carbohydrates, up to 2.5% protein and only 0.1% fats.

NOTES Ripe seeds are poisonous – they contain high levels of rotenone.

Pachyrhizus erosus (L.) Urban   family: Fabaceae

sha ge (Chinese); *pachyrrhize* (French); *Yamsbohne, Knollenbohne* (German); *ubi sengkung* (Malay); *jícima de agua, jícima de leche* (Spanish)

Panax ginseng

ginseng

Ginseng plants

Ginseng fruits

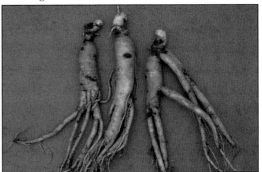

Ginseng roots

DESCRIPTION Ginseng is a perennial herb with a single stem arising from a short rhizome attached to a fleshy, carrot-like root. The leaves are compound, each with three to five pointed leaflets. Inconspicuous white flowers are borne in a single cluster, followed by bright red, fleshy fruits. The most famous species is *P. ginseng* (also known as Asian ginseng, Korean ginseng or *sang*), but the closely related American ginseng (*P. quinquefolius*) has become an equally important commercial source of ginseng root. Of lesser importance are the southern Asian *sanchi* (*P. pseudoginseng*) and the North American dwarf ginseng (*P. trifolius*).

ORIGIN & HISTORY The plant occurs naturally in the mountain forests of Korea and northeastern China. Ginseng has been used as a dietary supplement since ancient times. It is grown commercially in China, Japan, Korea and Russia. American ginseng is found in eastern North America (USA and Canada) where it is also cultivated on a large scale for export to China and for local use in the health food industry.

PARTS USED The fleshy roots.

CULTIVATION & HARVESTING Ginseng is propagated from seeds. The plants are cultivated in partial shade and reach maturity in three to four years. The roots are used fresh or dried.

USES & PROPERTIES Ginseng is nowadays commonly used as a food supplement and is added to a wide range of health food products (including tonic drinks and food supplement bars). It is not aimed at any particular disease, but is considered to be an adaptogenic tonic to treat fatigue, weakness and lack of concentration. Clinical studies have indeed shown that ginseng has a positive effect on physical and intellectual performance, mood, immune response and convalescence.

NUTRITIONAL VALUE The beneficial effects are ascribed to a mixture of triterpenoid saponins, known as ginsenosides, which are thought to affect membrane transport of steroids.

Panax ginseng C.A. Mey.   family: Araliaceae

ren shen (Chinese); *ginseng* (French); *Ginseng* (German); *ginseng* (Italian); *yakuyou ninjin* (Japanese); *ginseng da China* (Portuguese); *ginseng chino* (Spanish); *som* (Thai)

Pandanus amaryllifolius
pandan • fragrant pandan

Pandan plants

Wilted pandan leaves

DESCRIPTION Pandan is a leafy, palm-like plant of up to 1.5 m in height bearing erect stems with long, bright green, sword-shaped leaves and occasional clusters of aerial roots. The plant is sterile and hardly ever flowers. Various *Pandanus* species ("screw-pines") are local sources of fibre, perfume (from male flowers) and edible fruits, including *P. julianettii, P. leram* and *P. tectorius* (= *P. odoratissimus*).

ORIGIN & HISTORY This species (the only one with fragrant leaves) is an ancient cultigen that is now commonly cultivated in most parts of Southeast Asia (from southern India to New Guinea). Rare occurrences of male flowers on the Moluccas indicate a possible origin on these islands.

PARTS USED Fresh but wilted leaves.

CULTIVATION & HARVESTING Stem cuttings grow easily in tropical regions. Leafy branches are simply cut off and tied in bundles.

USES & PROPERTIES Wilted leaves have a distinctive nutty or hay-like aroma similar to that found in Thai jasmine rice. In Thai, Malay and Indonesian cooking, pandan is therefore used to enhance the flavour of rice or rice dishes (often cooked in coconut milk, e.g. *nasi lemak* and *nasi kuning*). In Indonesia, rice is steamed in little baskets woven from pandan leaves. One of the most famous Thai dishes is pandan chicken or *gai ob bai toey* (marinated chicken pieces wrapped in pandan leaves and deep-fried in a wok). The most important culinary use is in various sweet snacks, desserts and iced drinks (based on ice cream or coconut milk). Sweet puddings that turn semi-solid on cooling are cooked from glutinous rice, palm sugar, pandan leaves and coconut milk. Pandan essence (*pandan* or *toey*) is often used as a substitute for leaves – green food dye gives the popular and characteristic bright green colour. It is possible to substitute pandan essence with vanilla essence.

NUTRITIONAL VALUE Unimportant (flavouring only).

Pandanus amaryllifolius Roxb.   family: Pandanaceae

ban lan ye (Chinese); *pandanus* (French); *Schraubenpalme* (German); *duan pandan* (Indonesian); *pandano* (Italian); *pandan rampeh, pandan wangi* (Malay); *pandano* (Portuguese, Spanish); *bai toey hom* (Thai)

Panicum miliaceum

millet • common millet • proso millet

Millet plants

Millet ears

Millet grains

DESCRIPTION Common millet is an annual grass of about 1 m in height, with characteristic much-branched seed heads. The grains (small, one-seeded dry fruits) vary from pale brown to reddish brown. This is the original millet that is also known as broomcorn millet, Russian millet or Indian millet. It should not be confused with various other millets such as pearl millet (see *Pennisetum glaucum*), Italian millet (see *Setaria italica*), Japanese millet (see *Echinochloa frumentacea*) and finger millet (see *Eleusine coracana*).

ORIGIN & HISTORY Millet is one of the most ancient of all cereals. It is a cultigen believed to be of central Asian or perhaps Chinese origin (the wild ancestor has not yet been identified). Millet has been grown since the beginnings of agriculture (possibly as a companion to wheat and barley) in central and eastern Asia and in central and eastern Europe. It is the true millet (the Roman *milium* and Hebrew *dokhan*). Today

millet is grown in central and eastern Asia, India and parts of the Middle East.

PARTS USED The ripe grains (one-seeded dry fruits).

CULTIVATION & HARVESTING Millet is one of the hardiest of all cereals and can withstand severe drought, heat and poor soils. The harvest is ready in 60 to 90 days.

USES & PROPERTIES Millet with its nutty taste is used as a cereal for human consumption. It is sold in the form of grain or may be variously processed into flakes and flour. It is ready for eating as porridge after boiling in twice its volume of water or milk for 20 minutes.

NUTRITIONAL VALUE The absence of gluten and high levels of magnesium, iron and vitamins A and B make it a health food (e.g. in wheat-free diets) but also means that it cannot be used for raised breads except when mixed with other types of flour. The energy yield is 350 kcal.

Panicum miliaceum L.   family: Poaceae

ji, shu (Chinese); *millet commun, mil* (French); *Echte Hirse, Rispenhirse* (German); *chenaa* (Hindi); *miglio* (Italian); *kibi* (Japanese); *milho miúdo* (Portuguese); *mijo* (Spanish)

Papaver somniferum

opium poppy

Opium poppy plant with flower

Opium poppy fruits

Poppy seeds

DESCRIPTION This is an erect annual herb of up to 1.5 m in height with hairless, greyish leaves and large white, red or purple flowers borne on slender stalks. The distinctive fruit capsules act like salt shakers – they have several small holes around the top through which the numerous blue-grey or whitish seeds are dispersed.

ORIGIN & HISTORY Opium poppy is another cultigen of unknown origin that is believed to be indigenous to southwestern Asia. It has been grown as a crop in Europe, Asia, China and North Africa for many centuries. Opium is legally produced in India and Turkey, while poppy seeds and seed oil originate mainly from Europe, the Middle East and India.

PARTS USED The ripe seeds (or seed oil).

CULTIVATION & HARVESTING The plant is grown from seeds as an annual crop. Ripe seed capsules are harvested mechanically. Black poppy seeds are most commonly produced, but white poppy seeds (originating in India) have also become popular, mainly in Southeast Asia.

USES & PROPERTIES The seeds are used in baking and pastries – originally in Turkey, Egypt, central Europe and Britain, but nowadays in practically all parts of the world. Most people have seen them sprinkled over bread rolls. They are also used as a condiment for various cheeses and as flavour ingredient in Chinese rice-flour noodles. The seeds (often the white form) are ground to a paste and added to Indian and Malay-style curries to give a thicker texture and better flavour (but only when previously fried to bring out the nutty taste). Poppy-seed oil is extracted from various cultivars – it has a pale colour and pleasant taste and is used in cooking in the same way as olive oil.

NUTRITIONAL VALUE Unimportant (eaten in small quantities).

NOTES Opium is made from the latex of the green fruit capsule – the seeds contain no alkaloids.

Papaver somniferum L.   family: Papaveraceae

ying su, ya pian (Chinese); *oeillette, pavot somnifere* (French); *Schlafmohn* (German); *aphim* (Hindi); *papavero domestico* (Italian); *keshi* (Japanese); *kas kas* (Malay); *adormidera* (Spanish)

Parkia speciosa
petai

Petai tree

Petai flower and fruit

DESCRIPTION This is a large tree of up to 40 m in height bearing very large, twice pinnate leaves, each with 10 to 19 pairs of pinnate leaflets. The minute, cream-coloured to slightly pinkish flowers occur in dense heads borne on slender pendulous stalks (an adaptation to bat pollination). About five to ten very large pods are borne in a loose cluster. Each pod is half a metre long, straight or usually slightly twisted, with up to 18 flat, green seeds. In addition to *P. speciosa*, two other species are of local importance as food plants. In the West Indies, the pods of the African *P. biglobosa* (locust bean) are an important food source, while in West Africa the seeds of the local *P. filicoidea* (African locust) are boiled, fermented and eaten.

ORIGIN & HISTORY Petai is a Malaysian species of lowland forests that has been an important jungle food source for centuries. It is still very popular in Myanmar, southern Thailand, Malaysia and Indonesia, where it is cultivated in villages and kitchen gardens.

PARTS USED Mainly the pods and seeds.

CULTIVATION & HARVESTING The trees are easily grown from seeds and the young pods are harvested when half ripe.

USES & PROPERTIES The young pods and seeds (and sometimes also the young leaves and flower stalks) are eaten raw. The distinctive taste is strong and garlic-like (definitely an acquired one) with a bitter after-taste and imparts a garlic scent on the breath of eaters. The pods and seeds may also be fried and pickled and are exported in jars and cans. They combine well with garlic, chillies, dried shrimp and strongly flavoured food such as Thai curries.

NUTRITIONAL VALUE The pods and seeds are rich in proteins. The green seeds are viewed as a functional food as it is believed that they alleviate the symptoms of diabetes.

Parkia speciosa Hassk.   family: Fabaceae

cong dou, chou dou (Chinese); *petai* (French); *Petai* (German); *peteh* (Indonesian); *petai* (Italian); *nejire-fusamame* (Japanese); *petai, petah* (Malaysian); *sataw*, "sator" (Thai)

Passiflora edulis
passion fruit • granadilla

Passion fruit leaf and flower

Passion fruits (purple form)

Passion fruits (yellow form)

DESCRIPTION A vigorous climber (vine) with smooth, deeply lobed, toothed leaves and spiralling climbing tendrils. The attractive white flowers have numerous stamens and characteristic curved styles. The fruit is an egg-shaped berry with a tough skin (purple or yellow, and somewhat wrinkled at maturity) containing numerous seeds with fleshy, sweet or sour arils. Two types are grown: the common purple-fruited, sweet, black-seeded type (forma *edulis*, which has the flowers open in the morning) and the yellow-fruited sour, brown-seeded type (forma *flavicarpa*, which has the flowers open in the afternoon). The latter is also referred to as yellow passion fruit, golden passion fruit or guavadilla. Some other types of passion fruits are described under banana passion fruit (see *P. mollissima*).

ORIGIN & HISTORY Indigenous to southern Brazil, Paraguay and northern Argentina. It was introduced to the rest of the world by the Spaniards and has become an important commercial fruit crop on all continents.

PARTS USED Ripe fruits.

CULTIVATION & HARVESTING Plants are usually propagated from seeds. The purple passion fruit is subtropical but can withstand mild frost. The yellow passion fruit is more tropical and does not thrive in cold regions. Fruits are picked when they ripen but are best left to turn purple and wrinkled before they are used.

USES & PROPERTIES Passion fruit is mainly eaten fresh or the fruit pulp is used in drinks, yogurts and desserts. The fruit pulp is processed and combined with sauces, jams, candies, ice cream, sorbet, cake icing, cake fillings, jellies and cocktails. Purple fruits are preferred for eating, while the more acidic yellow type has become an important commercial source of juice for the beverage industry.

NUTRITIONAL VALUE The fruit pulp yields about 60 kcal and contains fair amounts of vitamin C (20–30 mg), carotenes, vitamin A, niacin, riboflavin, phosphorus and potassium.

Passiflora edulis (Aubl.) Schum.   family: Passifloraceae

ji dan guo (Chinese); *grenadille* (French); *Purpurgrenadille, Passionsblume* (German); *granadiglia* (Italian); *kudamonotokeiso* (Japan); *markisa* (Malay); *granadilho, maracujá* (Portuguese); *granadilla, maracuya* (Spanish)

Passiflora mollissima

curuba • banana passion fruit

Curuba flowers and fruits

Sweet passion fruit (*P. ligularis*)

Wingstem passion fruit (*P. alata*)

DESCRIPTION This species is similar to the common passion fruit but the flowers and fruits are very distinctive. The flowers are tubular and pendulous, with pink petals and the soft-walled fruits that are narrowly oblong, smooth and yellow (rarely green) when ripe. It is one of at least ten species that have become commercialised to some extent. The sweet passion fruit (*P. ligularis*) has large, simple leaves and purple-tinged fruits that turn orange when they ripen, with translucent, white, sweet pulp. The wingstem passion fruit (*P. alata*) is almost indistinguishable from the giant granadilla (*P. quadrangularis*) but the fruits of the former are smaller and elliptic in shape, while those of *P. quadrangularis* are much larger (up to 30 cm long). The chulupa (*P. maliformis*) bears green or yellow, apple-shaped fruits with a white-dotted, tough skin and orange-yellow, aromatic pulp (said to be grape-flavoured; served with sugar and wine in Jamaica).

ORIGIN & HISTORY The curuba is indigenous to the Andes region (Bolivia, Peru, Colombia and Venezuela). Over the last few hundred years it has become domesticated and is now commonly cultivated in home gardens and commercial plantations (especially in Colombia).

PARTS USED Ripe fruits.

CULTIVATION & HARVESTING The plant is grown mainly from seeds. It is more frost tolerant than the common passion fruit and can withstand brief exposure to temperatures of –5°C. Up to 300 fruits can be produced on a single vine.

USES & PROPERTIES Curuba is popular for making jams, jellies, ice creams, gelatin desserts, cocktail drinks and even wine (the juice is considered to be the best of all passion fruit juices). Equal amounts of pulp and sugar, together with four to five parts of chilled milk are blended and then strained to remove the pips. This popular and delicious drink is known as *sorbete de curuba*.

NUTRITIONAL VALUE Similar to passion fruit.

Passiflora mollissima (Kunth) L. Bailey   family: Passifloraceae

tacso, taxo (French); *Curuba* (German); *curuba* (Italian); *curuba* (Spanish)

Pastinaca sativa

parsnip

Parsnip plant

Parsnip flowers and fruits

Parsnips

DESCRIPTION An erect, biennial herb of up to 2 m in height, with hollow, furrowed stems, large compound leaves and small yellow flowers borne in umbels. The fleshy, white, carrot-like taproots may reach more than 3 m in length. The plant superficially resembles celery (see *Apium graveolens*) but the leaf segments are more sharply pointed and dull green in colour. Peruvian parsnip (*Arracacia xanthorrhiza*), also called arracache or Peruvian celery is an ancient Inca root crop that is still important in Peru and Colombia.

ORIGIN & HISTORY Temperate Europe and Western Asia. It was cultivated in Roman times and was once an important food item in Germany and other parts of central and northern Europe. Parsnip root was added to bread, eaten with salt fish and used to produce wine, but the popularity declined when the potato was introduced. The crop spread to western Europe, the West Indies and North America, where it is still a popular vegetable.

PARTS USED The root.

CULTIVATION & HARVESTING Parsnip is cultivated from fresh seeds sown in spring. Roots are harvested in autumn and winter. The flavour is thought to be improved by exposure to frost.

USES & PROPERTIES Parsnip is used as a cooked vegetable in much the same way as turnip. It is boiled, fried or baked, sometimes mashed or puréed, and often added to soups and stews (especially beef stew, as the relatively strong flavour goes well with this dish). Roots may be cooked or baked like carrots. The high sugar content was formerly exploited to produce jam, sweet flour for cakes and even parsnip wine (by fermentation of the juice). Candied parsnip is still a popular snack in North America.

NUTRITIONAL VALUE Cooked parsnip is a moderate source of vitamins C and E. It yields 59 kcal.

NOTES Parsnip leaves contain furanocoumarins which may cause severe irritation after skin contact but not after eating normal quantities.

Pastinaca sativa L.   family: Apiaceae

panais, patenais (French); *Hammelmöhre, Pastinak* (German); *pastinaca* (Italian); *pastinaca, chirivia* (Portuguese); *chirivía* (Spanish)

Paullinia cupana

guaraná

Guaraná leaves

Guaraná fruits

Guaraná seeds

DESCRIPTION This is a woody climber (vine) with irregularly compound leaves and coiled tendrils by which the plant supports itself. The inconspicuous yellow flowers develop into small, bright red fruits containing shiny, dark brown seeds. Another species is *P. yoco*, the source of a South American caffeine-rich drink (especially popular in Colombia), called *yoco*.

ORIGIN & HISTORY The plant is indigenous to the lower Amazon region of South America and is now widely cultivated in Brazil. The traditional uses of guaraná are linked to the Maués Indians of Brazil.

PARTS USED The ripe seeds (or a dried paste prepared from roasted, powdered seeds mixed with water).

CULTIVATION & HARVESTING Propagation is mostly from seeds and the plants are grown in full sun on acid soils. Yields are very low (less than 140 kg of seeds per hectare).

USES & PROPERTIES Guaraná is the basis of an extremely popular, non-alcoholic, fizzy soft drink known as *guaraná* or *cupana*. It has a fruity taste and pleasant aftertaste. Millions of bottles are sold each day in Brazil. The drink is known as *Tai* in the USA and has also become popular in other parts of the world. Major soft drink companies have started to produce imitation brands but the original Brazilian brands are still the most popular. These fashionable "energy drinks" are rich in caffeine and are therefore used as general tonics and to counteract fatigue. Guaraná is also available in the form of chocolate bars, chewing gums, syrups, powders and tablets. The product allegedly has aphrodisiac properties and is widely used to help with weight loss programmes (claims are often exaggerated). Guaraná is nevertheless listed as a functional food.

NUTRITIONAL VALUE Limited. Caffeine is a central nervous system stimulant that may cause sleeplessness, lack of concentration and heart palpitations when taken at high doses.

Paullinia cupana Kunth   family: Sapindaceae

guarana (French); *Guarana-Strauch* (German); *cupana* (Spanish)

Pennisetum glaucum

pearl millet

Pearl millet ears

Pearl millet in flower

Pearl millet grains

DESCRIPTION Pearl millet is a tall, robust grass of up to 4 m or more in height, with thick stems, broad leaves and characteristic oblong flower heads resembling bulrushes (hence the common name bulrush millet). The fruits (grains) are small and more or less rounded, with a shiny, greyish colour (not unlike small pearls, hence "pearl millet"). Four different cultivar groups are distinguished, based on the shape of the grains. Pearl millet should not be confused with various other types of millet such as the true millet (see *Panicum miliaceum*).

ORIGIN & HISTORY Pearl millet was domesticated in West Africa about 4 000 years ago. From there it spread across the Sahel to the savanna regions of Africa, from Sudan to eastern and southern Africa, including northern Namibia and adjacent Angola. It reached India at least 3 000 years ago where it became an important staple food in the state of Rajasthan. Today, pearl millet is grown on about 16 million hectares in Africa and about 11 million hectares in India and southeastern Pakistan. As a human staple food, pearl millet is by far the most important of the millet species.

PARTS USED The ripe grains (dry, one-seeded fruits).

CULTIVATION & HARVESTING The success of pearl millet is due to its extreme tolerance of high temperatures and drought. It will produce a crop even under the most severe conditions and is therefore very important for food security in rural areas. The seed heads are harvested (mostly by hand) when ripe.

USES & PROPERTIES Pearl millet is an important staple cereal in parts of Africa and India and is variously prepared as porridge, bread, popcorn or couscous. The relatively high sugar content makes it an important source of malt for brewing traditional beer.

NUTRITIONAL VALUE The grains contain 8–20% protein, 5% fat and 67% carbohydrates (370 kcal per 100 g).

Pennisetum glaucum (L.) R. Br.   family: Poaceae

yu gu (Chinese); *millet perlé* (French); *Rohrkolbenhirse* (German); *bajra* (Hindi); *miglio perla* (Italian); *toujin kibi* (Japanese); *milhete, milho africano* (Portuguese); *mijo perla* (Spanish); *mawele* (Swahili)

Perilla frutescens
perilla • beefsteak plant • shiso

Perilla plant in flower

Purple perilla leaves

Green perilla plants

DESCRIPTION An annual herb with square stems, rounded, often crisped leaves (either green or dark purple) and minute pink flowers borne in terminal spikes. Various cultivars have been developed as ornamental plants and for the production of essential oils as well as seed oil (a drying oil with many industrial uses). Two varieties are distinguished: var. *frutescens* is used for seed oil production, while var. *crispa* is used as garnish and vegetable (both colour forms). In Japan, the green form is known as *ao-shiso* or *aojiso*, the purple form as *aka-shiso* or *akajiso*.

ORIGIN & HISTORY The species is indigenous to a wide region stretching from the Himalayas to East Asia. It has been cultivated for many centuries in China (once a popular vegetable there) but only in Japan and Korea is it still an important food plant.

PARTS USED Fresh or pickled leaves (rarely the seed oil).

CULTIVATION & HARVESTING Perilla is similar to basil in its horticultural requirements. It is easily grown from seeds and thrives in light, slightly acid soil in a warm position.

USES & PROPERTIES The plant is an important garnish and vegetable in Japanese and Korean cooking, and is used in much the same way as parsley. There are several traditional uses. The leaves are added as a garnish to a raw fish dish known as *sashimi* or they are sometimes served with a popular battered dish called *tempura* (either as garnish or battered and deep-fried in sesame oil). The purple leaves add flavour and colour to the traditional *umeboshi*, prepared from pickled sour plums derived from *Prunus mume*. They are also an ingredient in *beni shoga* (a kind of pickled ginger that is eaten with *sushi*).

NUTRITIONAL VALUE The seed oil is rich in linolenic acid. Fresh leaves are a good source of folic acid and minerals.

Perilla frutescens (L.) Britton (= *Perilla arguta* Benth.)   family: Lamiaceae

zhou bai su, ri ben bai su (Chinese); *pérille verte cultivée, pérille rouge cultivée* (French); *Perilla, Chinesische Melisse* (German); *shiso* (Japanese); *kkaennip* (Korean)

Persea americana

avocado

Avocado flowers

Avocado fruits

Avocado pears

DESCRIPTION A large, evergreen tree with oblong, simple leaves that are bright green above and distinctly paler beneath. Small yellowish flowers are followed by pear-shaped, green or purplish fruits with a greenish yellow, butter-textured flesh around the single, very large seed. There are three ecotypes or horticultural races, namely the Mexican, Guatemalan and Lowland (= West Indian) types. Popular cultivars include 'Fuerte' (smooth, green skin) and 'Hass' (warty skin that turns purplish black).

ORIGIN & HISTORY Central America. These strange fruits may be adapted for dispersal by some large animals that are now extinct. Evidence of human use in Mexico dates back 8 000 years. The original Aztec name *ahuacatl* has been corrupted to the Spanish *ahuacate* or *aguacate,* and then to avocado in English.

PARTS USED Mature fruits.

CULTIVATION & HARVESTING Trees are easily grown from seeds but from about 100 years ago,

grafted trees have been cultivated in Central America, southern USA, Southeast Asia, South Africa, Israel and Australia. Fruits become edible only after removal from the tree.

USES & PROPERTIES Avocado is one of the most delicious of all salad vegetables and sandwich fillings. The fruit is unusual in being oily rather than sweet (it contains up to 25 % monounsaturated fat). It may be eaten on its own, with some salt, pepper or lime juice added. Some people prefer to add sugar or condensed milk and the flesh may be puréed to make milk shakes and ice creams. The most famous spread or dip is *guacamole* (of Aztec origin), made from mashed avocado mixed with spices.

NUTRITIONAL VALUE Avocado is considered to be the most nutritious of all fruits. It is high in calories (220 kcal per 100 g) and is a good source of folic acid, vitamin C, vitamin A, riboflavin, niacin, thiamin, iron and potassium.

NOTES The flesh contains a valuable oil similar to olive oil.

Persea americana L (= *P. gratissima* Gaertn.)   family: Lauraceae

you li (Chinese); *avocatier* (French); *Avocado* (German); *avocato* (Italian); *abokado* (Japanese); *buah apukado* (Malay); *abacate, abacateiro* (Portuguese); *ahuacate, aguacate* (Spanish)

Persicaria odorata

laksa plant • Vietnamese mint • Vietnamese coriander

Vietnamese mint plants

Vietnamese mint leaves

Laksa leaf

DESCRIPTION The laksa plant is a spreading perennial herb with soft stems, characteristic sheathing stipules and pointed leaves, often with a reddish brown patch near the middle. The minute pink flowers are rarely seen in cultivated plants. It is very similar to water pepper (*Persicaria hydropiper*) but the latter is a more erect plant with dark green leaves. Another species used as a pot-herb is Sikkim knotweed (*P. mollis*).

ORIGIN & HISTORY The laksa plant is indigenous to Southeast Asia and is a traditional food of the region.

PARTS USED Fresh leaves.

CULTIVATION & HARVESTING Plants are very easily grown from cuttings rooted in a glass of water and then planted out into a container or directly into the kitchen garden. They survive light frost but are best grown in a warm, sunny spot.

USES & PROPERTIES The leaves are an indispensable ingredient and garnish of the famous Singaporean and Malaysian seafood noodle soup known as *laksa* (hence the common names laksa plant and laksa leaf). This dish is sometimes made with boiled chicken (instead of fish or crab) and includes a variety of vegetables, together with a spice paste (*bumbu*) made from chillies, galangal, garlic, lemongrass and turmeric, to which shrimp paste is added. A generous handful of chopped laksa leaf is added to the bowl when the dish is served. The leaves are eaten fresh in Vietnamese and Thai salads (that often include coriander and mint leaves) and also with the popular Vietnamese spring rolls. Fresh herbs such as laksa are indeed a feature of Vietnamese cuisine and are responsible for the distinctive taste of many meals. Large heaps are served with almost any dish, but particularly with various types of noodle soups (*pho*) into which the leaves are dipped (using chopsticks) and eaten.

NUTRITIONAL VALUE The leaves are a good source of folic acid and iron.

Persicaria odorata (Lour.) Soják (= *Polygonum odoratum* Lour.)　　　　　　　　　　　　　family: Polygonaceae

la liao, laksa-yip (Chinese); *coriandre du Vietnam* (French); *Laksa Blatt, Vietnamesische Mintze* (German); *daun kesum, daun laksa* (Malay); *phak phai* (Thai); *rau ram* (Vietnamese)

Petroselinum crispum

parsley

Parsley (common crisped type)

Parsley leaf with flowers

Italian parsley and common parsley

DESCRIPTION Parsley is a biennial herb that forms a rosette of leaves in the first year and a branched flowering stalk with inconspicuous yellow flowers and small dry fruits in the second year. The compound leaves are finely divided – crisped in the common variety or flat in the cultivated Italian- or celery-leaved parsley (var. *neapolitanum*). The fleshy roots of Hamburg- or turnip-rooted parsley (var. *tuberosum*) are cooked and eaten like celeriac.

ORIGIN & HISTORY Parsley is indigenous to the Mediterranean parts of southern Europe and western Asia (some say Sardinia is the original home). The plant was well known to the Greeks and Romans and is nowadays one of the most popular of all culinary herbs.

PARTS USED Fresh leaves (rarely the dried leaves, the small dry fruits or the fleshy roots).

CULTIVATION & HARVESTING Parsley is propagated from seeds and is cultivated in most parts of the world. The leaves are picked throughout the first growing season and the plants may be left to flower and fruit in the second season.

USES & PROPERTIES The fresh leaves are popular as a garnish and flavour ingredient of soups, salads, sauces, omelettes, stews and stuffings. Chopped parsley is often added to cooked dishes just before serving or is sprinkled over the food. It is commonly used to flavour butter, cheese or sauces. The *persillade* of French cooking is a mixture of chopped parsley and garlic that is added to certain dishes at the end of the cooking time (e.g. beef *persillade*). The word *persillé* is used for veined cheeses but also for dishes that are finished with *persillade* or with large amounts of chopped parsley (e.g. ham with parsley or *jambon persillé*).

NUTRITIONAL VALUE Fresh parsley is rich in vitamin C and is also a good source of iron and vitamins A and B. It yields 50 kcal per 100 g.

Petroselinum crispum (Mill.) A.W. Hill   family: Apiaceae

fan yan sui (Chinese); *persil* (French); *Petersilie* (German); *prezzemolo* (Italian); *perejil* (Spanish)

Phaseolus coccineus

runner bean • scarlet runner bean

Runner bean flowers

Runner bean plant

Runner bean seeds

DESCRIPTION Runner beans are robust perennial climbers (vines) with twining stems that grow from fleshy roots, large pinnately compound leaves and clusters of attractive, orange-red flowers. The very large pods bear several beans that are usually purple mottled with black, or rarely white. Modern cultivars are sometimes dwarf and bushy, may have variegated or white flowers and produce seeds of various colours and sizes. Two lesser known *Phaseolus* species of commercial interest are the year bean (*P. polyanthus*) and tepary bean (*P. acutifolius*).

ORIGIN & HISTORY Scarlet runner bean occurs naturally in cool mountainous areas, from Mexico to Panama. It is believed to have been domesticated in Mexico at least 2 000 years ago and was introduced into Europe and Africa in the sixteenth century.

PARTS USED Mostly the green pods, sometimes also the seeds or tuberous roots.

CULTIVATION & HARVESTING The plant is a perennial in frost-free areas but in Europe and other temperate regions it is cultivated as an annual crop – directly sown and grown on trellises for support. It is popular both as garden ornamental and vegetable. The young pods are harvested just before they are fully developed and turn stringy (when they are about 20 to 30 cm long). Pods may be left for the seed to ripen.

USES & PROPERTIES Young pods are cooked as green vegetables, in the same way as common beans. They have a similar flavour and taste. In Japan, the dry seeds are boiled and sweetened with sugar or molasses (the dishes are known as *nimame* and *ama-nattoh*). They have to be cooked in water for a considerable period to destroy harmful substances. In Mexico, the fleshy roots are also an important food item.

NUTRITIONAL VALUE Pods contain about 2% protein (seeds much higher, about 15–18%) and are a good source of vitamins B, C and E.

Phaseolus coccineus L. (= *P. multiflorus* Lam.)   family: Fabaceae

hong hua cai dou (Chinese); *haricot d'Espagne* (French); *Feuerbohne, Prunkbohne* (German); *fagioli rampicante di Spagna* (Italian); *hana mame* (Japanese); *feijão-da-Espanha* (Portuguese); *frijol chamborote* (Spanish)

Phaseolus lunatus

lima bean

Lima bean plant

Lima bean leaf and flowers

Lima beans

DESCRIPTION Perennial leafy herbs with pinnately trifoliate leaves, white flowers and broad flat pods containing several pale green or white seeds. Large-seeded forms are known as butter beans, white butter beans and Madagascar beans, while small-seeded forms are referred to as *sieva*, sieva beans or Burma beans. Climbing or bushy cultivars of both types are available.

ORIGIN & HISTORY Central America, from Mexico to Ecuador, Peru and Argentina. The common name refers to Lima, the capital city of Peru. Large-seeded types were domesticated in Peru, perhaps 8 000 years ago. The small-seeded (*sieva*) type appears to have been developed in Central America and Mexico at least 500 years ago. The Spaniards introduced small-seeded types to the Philippines and other parts of Asia, while large-seeded limas reached Africa and Madagascar via Brazil. Both types found their way to the USA, where they have become important crops.

PARTS USED Mostly the ripe seeds (dry beans) but also the green pods.

CULTIVATION & HARVESTING Lima beans are grown in the same way as other beans but they require a hotter climate. As a result, the main areas of production (southern USA, Myanmar, tropical Africa, Madagascar) are in warm, subtropical regions of the world. Most of the annual production of more than 100 000 tons is in the form of dry beans.

USES & PROPERTIES The uses of lima beans are the same as those of the common bean (haricot bean). They are soaked in water for several hours and are then cooked in a variety of sauces (butter, cream or tomato) or added to stews, soups, salads or other dishes. Cooked lima beans often accompany meat dishes.

NUTRITIONAL VALUE The dry beans must be cooked for ten minutes to remove poisonous cyanogenic glycosides. As in other beans, the protein and mineral content are exceptional.

Phaseolus lunatus L.   family: Fabaceae

cai dou, *li ma dou* (Chinese); *haricot de Lima* (French); *Limabohne* (German); *fagiolo di Lima* (Italian); *rai mame* (Japanese); *feijão de Lima* (Portuguese); *frijol de Lima* (Spanish)

Phaseolus vulgaris
common bean • French bean • kidney bean

Common bean

Common bean flowers

Common beans (various cultivars)

DESCRIPTION An annual plant with long, twining stems in climbing forms and short, erect stems in bushy types. It has trifoliate leaves, white or pink flowers (with tightly coiled styles) and narrowly oblong pods. The seeds are oblong to kidney-shaped and vary in colour, shape and size, depending on the cultivar.

ORIGIN & HISTORY Central America, from Mexico to Peru, Bolivia and Argentina. At least two separate domestication events have been proposed: small-seeded beans were developed in Mexico about 7 000 years ago, while large-seeded types were cultivated in Peru about 8 000 years ago. Beans formed part of the classical American Indian food plant triangle that comprised bean, maize and pumpkin. Since about AD 1500, the same trio has become established in the Old World.

PARTS USED The dry, ripe seeds (as a pulse) or the young green pods (as a vegetable).

CULTIVATION & HARVESTING Beans are easily grown from the non-dormant seeds and a multitude of cultivars have been developed.

USES & PROPERTIES Green beans (string beans) are a popular vegetable that may also be canned and frozen. Fresh young pods are cooked by plunging them into boiling water and cooking until they are still slightly crisp. They are then variously prepared with sauces or as salad ingredient. Dry beans are soaked in water and boiled until soft or added to soups and stews as a nourishing ingredient. Famous bean dishes include the French *cassoulet* and Mexican *chilli con carne*. Beans are often prepared with sweet or savoury sauces. Beans with tomato sauce are the popular baked beans or navy beans of which more than a million tins are consumed each day. In Japan, China and other parts of Asia, beans are eaten as a sweet dish.

NUTRITIONAL VALUE Beans have a very high food value, with about 20% protein and 50% carbohydrates. Green beans yield 33 kcal per 100 g; dry beans 237 kcal per 100 g.

Phaseolus vulgaris L.   family: Fabaceae

si ji dou, cai dou (Chinese); *haricot* (French); *Gartenbohne, Stangenbohne, Fasiole* (German); *fagiolo* (Italian); *ingen mame* (Japanese); *kachang bunchis* (Malay); *judia* (Spanish)

Phoenix dactylifera
date palm

Date palm

Bunches of dates

Dates

DESCRIPTION The date palm has an erect stem of up to 25 m and a cluster of feather-shaped, greyish leaves. Young trees form suckers at their bases. The yellowish flowers turn into clusters of oblong, brownish fruits of up to 50 g each.

ORIGIN & HISTORY Date is an ancient cultigen developed in the Near East (probably lower Mesopotamia). Today, wild and cultivated date palms occur over the large desert region that stretches from Morocco to Egypt, Arabia and Pakistan. Archaeological excavations and Sumerian cuneiform texts indicate that dates were domesticated by at least 4000 BC.

PARTS USED The ripe fruits.

CULTIVATION & HARVESTING Date palms require hot, dry conditions to produce good quality fruits in high yields but water must be available to the roots at all times. Thousands of cultivars (all of them female) are propagated by suckering or tissue culture. One male tree is grown for every 50 female trees, and artificial pollination is practised to ensure proper fruit set. The annual production is 2 million tons.

USES & PROPERTIES Dates are classified as soft, semi-dry or dry, depending on the moisture content. They are consumed as a staple food in many parts of the Middle East, North Africa and Western Asia. The very high sugar content and low moisture content ensure that dates keep well for long periods. Dates are eaten as sweetmeats and have countless uses in jams, desserts, confectionery, sauces, curries, fish dishes and stews (especially the *tajines* of North Africa and the *ragouts* of French cooking).

NUTRITIONAL VALUE Dates are rich in sugar (60 to 70% of dry weight, 276 kcal per 100 g) and very nutritious, as they contain niacin, folic acid, magnesium and numerous vitamins and minerals.

NOTES *Phoenix* is the Greek word for red or purple (the colour of the fruit), while *dactylifera* ("finger-bearing") refers to the finger-like fruits.

Phoenix dactylifera L.　　　　　　　　　　　family: Arecaceae (Palmae)

tamar (Arabic); *hai zao, ye zao* (Chinese); *dattier* (French); *Dattelpalme* (German); *dattero* (Italian); *natsume yashi* (Japanese); *tâmara, tamareira* (Portuguese); *dátilera* (Spanish)

Phyllanthus acidus

Otaheite gooseberry • star gooseberry

Otaheite gooseberry

Emblic leaves and fruits

DESCRIPTION The Otaheite gooseberry is a large shrub or small tree of up to 9 m in height. It bears neatly arranged rows of simple leaves and clusters of small, pinkish flowers that are formed on the trunk and main branches. The small, yellowish, waxy, 6- to 8-ribbed fruits are formed in large numbers. Despite the common name Otaheite gooseberry (also Malay, Indian, Sri Lankan, West Indian, country or star gooseberry), the plant is not related to gooseberries but merely resembles them in the acid taste of the fruits.

ORIGIN & HISTORY The exact origin of the plant is not clear (possibly South America, but some authors consider it to be African and South Asian). Today it is found in practically all tropical and subtropical regions of the world.

PARTS USED The ripe fruits.

CULTIVATION & HARVESTING Trees are not really cultivated on a commercial scale but are widely grown in villages and on farms. Propagation is from seeds, less often cuttings and air-layers. Seedlings produce the first substantial crop after about four years.

USES & PROPERTIES The fruits are too acidic to be eaten fresh, so that they are processed into cold drinks, jellies, vinegars, sauces, syrups, chutneys, jams, pickles and even wine (in Thailand). In Indonesian cooking, the fresh fruit flesh may be added to dishes as flavouring agent. Malay cooks use the ripe or unripe fruits to produce syrups, sweet preserves and relishes. The fruits and juice turn bright red when cooked in sugar. **NUTRITIONAL VALUE** The fruits contain moderate amounts of phosphorus, calcium, iron and vitamin C.

NOTES This species, the closely related emblic or *ambal* (*P. emblica*) and *bhumi amalaki* (*P. amarus*) are used as medicinal plants in India and Southeast Asia. Emblic also bears edible fruits and is a traditional source of dyes, tans and fuel.

Phyllanthus acidus (L.) Skeels (= *P. distichus* Muell. Arg.)   family: Euphorbiaceae

grosella, groseille étoilée (French); *Grosella, Stachelbeerbaum* (German); *cermai* (Indonesian); *cermai, cheremai* (Malay); *groselha* (Portuguese); *grosella* (Spanish); *mayom* (Thai)

Physalis ixocarpa
tomatillo • jamberry

Tomatillo

Bladder cherry

DESCRIPTION This is an annual or short-lived perennial with prostrate branches that may reach a metre or more in height. The oval, pointed leaves are smooth, not downy as in Cape gooseberry. A single yellow flower with brown or purplish spots is borne in each leaf axil. A tight-fitting, papery husk formed from the calyx encloses the yellow, green or purple berry, which is typically wider than long. It is also known as Mexican husk tomato or Mayan husk tomato. Cultivars include the green-fruited 'Rendidora' and the yellow-fruited 'New Sugar Giant'.

ORIGIN & HISTORY The tomatillo was an important staple food in the Mayan and Aztec cultures and has been cultivated in Mexico and Guatemala for many centuries. In recent times, it has been distributed to many parts of the world as a new fruit crop.

PARTS USED The ripe fruit.

CULTIVATION & HARVESTING Plants are usually grown from seeds and thrive in temperate and subtropical regions. Fruits fall to the ground when nearly ripe and should be collected every day. They are kept for up to four weeks for the husk to dry out and the berry to fully ripen. Yields of about 1 kg per plant (20 tons per hectare) can be achieved.

USES & PROPERTIES The tomatillo is often eaten raw, but the main use is as a vegetable and not a fruit. In Mexico, the popular *salsa verde*, a meat sauce, is made from the ripe fruits (with or without green chillies). The fruits are widely used as a vegetable in stews, curries, cooked meat dishes and soups; less often for marmalade, jams and dessert sauces.

NUTRITIONAL VALUE Fruits are rich in minerals and are a fairly good source of vitamins A and C.

NOTES The ornamental bladder cherry or Chinese lantern plant (*Physalis alkekengi*) has edible red berries but the husks are poisonous.

Physalis ixocarpa Brot. (= *P. philadelphica* Lam.; *P. aequata* Jacq.)   family: Solanaceae

alkékenge du Mexique (French); *Tomatillo* (German); *tomatillo, tomate de fresadilla, tomate verde* (Spanish)

Physalis peruviana
Cape gooseberry

Cape gooseberry leaves, flower and young fruit

Cape gooseberry flowers and fruit

Cape gooseberries

DESCRIPTION A scrambling perennial herb of about 1 m high with downy, symmetrical leaves, yellow flowers that have brown spots in the throat and characteristic bladdery fruits. The berry is rounded in shape and bright orange when ripe. A feature of all *Physalis* species is the large, persistent calyx that surrounds the fruit and which becomes papery in the ripe fruit. Cape gooseberry is very similar to the North American ground cherry or dwarf Cape gooseberry (*P. pruinosa*, also known as the husk tomato or strawberry tomato) but the latter has asymmetrical leaves – one basal lobe of the leaf is larger than the other.

ORIGIN & HISTORY Tropical South America; cultivated as a crop in many parts of the world, including Australia, New Zealand, California, the United Kingdom, southern Europe and East Africa. It has been particularly popular in South Africa, hence the name "Cape gooseberry". Some sources suggest that the original name was

"caped gooseberry", in reference to the lantern-like cape, calyx or husk.

PARTS USED The ripe fruit.

CULTIVATION & HARVESTING Plants grow easily from seeds and adapt to a wide range of climatic conditions and soil types. Fruits fall to the ground when they ripen and are collected every day. Annual yields of more than 25 tons per hectare can be achieved.

USES & PROPERTIES Cape gooseberries have a delicious sweet-sour taste and may be eaten fresh or as part of a fruit salad. They are very popular for making excellent jams, jellies and tarts. In French confectionery, the ripe fruits are sugared or glazed and served as *petit fours*. The tart flavour also makes Cape gooseberry a popular ingredient of syrups, sorbets and ice creams.

NUTRITIONAL VALUE The fruits are rich in minerals (especially potassium), carotenoids and vitamins C (10–40 mg), B and E. The energy yield is 70 kcal per 100 g.

Physalis peruviana L.   family: Solanaceae

xiao guo suan jiang (Chinese); *alkékenge, coqueret du Perou* (French); *Kapstachelbeere* (German); *alchechenge giallo* (Italian); *ke hòzuki* (Japanese); *alquequenje amarelo* (Portuguese); *alchechengi del Perú* (Spanish)

Pimenta dioica

allspice • pimento

Allspice flowers

Allspice leaves and fruits

Allspice (dried fruits)

DESCRIPTION A large, evergreen shrub or small tree with an erect growth form and dark, glossy green leaves with prominent, pale midribs. The small, white flowers with their numerous stamens are similar to those of myrtle but they are smaller and are borne in sparse clusters. Male and female flowers occur on different plants (hence the Latin name *dioica*). The small fruits are crowned by persistent calyx lobes and resemble miniature guava fruits. They turn purplish black at maturity. Berries of the closely related bay rum tree (*Pimenta racemosa*) are sometimes used to adulterate allspice.

ORIGIN & HISTORY The tree is indigenous to Central America and the West Indies. Spanish explorers introduced the spice to Europe in the sixteenth century, from where it spread to most parts of the world. Jamaica remains the main exporter (also Mexico, Honduras and Réunion).

PARTS USED Dried, unripe berries (or the essential oil distilled from the leaves).

CULTIVATION & HARVESTING Plants are grown in plantations but the berries are also wild-harvested to some extent.

USES & PROPERTIES The English name "allspice" reflects the complex aroma, which is said to combine the flavours of cinnamon, cloves and nutmeg. It is widely used to flavour meat dishes, including sausages, salted beef and pork, meat pastries, pickles, sauces and stuffings. Scandinavians use it with *smorgasbord*, fish (herring), cheese and vegetable dishes. Mexicans produce allspice mainly for use in their famous *mole* sauces. Ethiopians use it in *berbere* (a spice mixture). In Great Britain, allspice is an ingredient of the traditional Christmas cake. Famous French liqueurs such as Bénédictine and Chartreuse are said to contain allspice in their secret formulas.

NUTRITIONAL VALUE Unimportant, as allspice is used in small amounts as a spice.

NOTES The flavour is due mainly to eugenol, a volatile oil.

Pimenta dioica (L.) Merr. (= *P. officinalis* Lindl.)   family: Myrtaceae

piment, poivre de la jamaïque (French); *Piment, Nelkenpfeffer* (German); *pimento* (Italian); *pimenta-da-jamaica* (Portuguese); *pimienta de Jamaica* (Spanish)

Pimpinella anisum

anise

Anise plant

Anise flowers

Anise fruits

DESCRIPTION Anise is an erect annual herb of about half a metre in height with rounded, simple leaves at the base of the plant becoming progressively more divided and lobed higher up on the stems. The small white flowers are borne in compound umbels and are followed by very small, greyish brown, dry fruits. Anise is sometimes confused with star anise (see *Illicium verum*) or even fennel (see *Foeniculum vulgare*), as the flavour of these plants strongly resembles that of anise.

ORIGIN & HISTORY Anise is believed to be indigenous to the eastern Mediterranean region and the Middle East but is historically mainly associated with the Greek and Egyptian cultures. Today it is an important crop plant in temperate regions of the world.

PARTS USED The ripe, dry fruits (often loosely referred to as seeds).

CULTIVATION & HARVESTING Anise is an annual crop, commonly grown in Turkey, Spain, Italy and India. Fruits are harvested when they start to ripen and are then dried in the shade.

USES & PROPERTIES Fruits are commonly included in biscuits, breads and cakes, to which they give a distinctive anise flavour. They are used to some extent as a spice in soufflés, meat dishes (stews, sausages) and vegetables (cabbage, carrots, turnips). Chopped fresh leaves are used to season salads, pickled vegetables and fish soups. Anise is best known for its use in various anise liqueurs such as the French *anisette*, *pastis* and *pernod*, Italian *sambuca*, Greek *ouzo*, Turkish *raki* and Middle Eastern *arrack*. These are diluted with water (or drunk with water in a separate glass).

NUTRITIONAL VALUE The spice is rich in iron but is unimportant as a dietary ingredient.

NOTES Aniseed oil or aniseed extracts are used to treat indigestion and flatulence and are added to cough mixtures for both the taste and the medicinal (expectorant) properties.

Pimpinella anisum L.   family: Apiaceae

yan kok, pa chio (Chinese); *anis vert* (French); *Anis* (German); *anice verde* (Italian); *anis, erva-doce* (Portuguese), *anis* (Spanish)

Pinus pinea

stone pine

Stone pine tree

Stone pine cones

Stone pine seeds

DESCRIPTION The stone pine is a large tree with orange-brown, scaly bark and a characteristic rounded, umbrella-shaped crown. Leaves are present in the form of small clusters of needles. The female cones have large overlapping scales each bearing two oblong, wingless seeds on their upper side. The stone pine is the best-known source of pine nuts, but several other pine trees are harvested to some extent. These include the Siberian cedar (*Pinus cembra*), the Mexican pine (*P. cembroides*), the piñon (*P. edulis*) and Korean pine (*P. koraiensis*). Several other cone-bearing trees produce edible nuts, such as the monkey-puzzle (*Araucaria araucana*) and bunya-bunya pine (*A. bidwillii*).

ORIGIN & HISTORY The use of pine nuts in the Mediterranean region (especially Italy and North Africa) and the Middle East dates back to ancient times.

PARTS USED The ripe seeds, known as pine nuts (*pignon* or *pignoles* in French; *pignolia* in Italian).

CULTIVATION & HARVESTING Stone pines are cultivated to some extent but the seeds are also wild-harvested from trees that occur naturally in the wild (especially in Spain, Italy and Greece).

USES & PROPERTIES Pine nuts are eaten raw or roasted as a snack and as dessert nuts. They have a characteristic resinous, spicy taste and are an essential ingredient of *pesto* sauce. The nuts are also included in numerous meat, pasta, fish, poultry and egg dishes in southern Europe, as well as various types of confectionery, including *croissants*, biscuits, tarts and pastries. In Turkey, the Middle East and India, the nuts are a popular garnish for rice and rice dishes. They add a delicious flavour to fresh salads dressed with olive oil.

NUTRITIONAL VALUE Pine nuts have a very high energy value (670 kcal per 100 g) and are rich in protein, thiamin, phosphorus and iron. The oil is high in unsaturated fat (about 80%).

Pinus pinea L.   family: Pinaceae

pin (French); *Pinie, Schirmkiefer* (German); *pino* (Italian); *piña* (Spanish)

297

Piper nigrum

pepper • black pepper

Pepper leaves and fruits

Pepper plant

Green, black and white pepper

DESCRIPTION A perennial climber (vine) that grows up to a height of 4 m. It has large, heart-shaped leaves, small flowers and rounded fruits (about 5 mm in diameter) borne in long, hanging spikes. *Piper* species of lesser importance are Indian long pepper (*P. longum*), tailed pepper or *cubeb* (*P. cubeba*) and Javanese long pepper (*P. retrofractum*). Other "peppers" include the South American pink pepper (*Schinus molle*), African Guinea pepper (*Xylopia aethiopica*), Asian Szechuan pepper (*Zanthoxylum piperitum*) and West African melegueta pepper (*Aframomum melegueta*).

ORIGIN & HISTORY Pepper originated in the Malabar region of southwestern India. It featured prominently in the spice trade of the Middle Ages. With an annual production of 80 000 tons (mainly in India, Sarawak, Indonesia and Brazil) it remains one of the most important of all spices.

PARTS USED The unripe or ripe fruits.

CULTIVATION & HARVESTING Pepper has been cultivated for at least 3 000 years. Black pepper is unripe peppercorns dried in the sun – the green skin becomes black and shrivelled. White pepper is made by removing the red skins from ripe peppercorns, after which they are bleached and dried in the sun. Green pepper is made by pickling or freeze-drying the fresh green fruits.

USES & PROPERTIES Pepper was the original spicy ingredient of Indian and oriental cooking until it was replaced by chilli peppers from Mexico. White pepper is preferred by Chinese cooks and by the French for white sauces. Black pepper is used in practically all savoury dishes. Names such as pepper steak, *poivrade* sauce and *Pfefferkuchen* testify to the culinary importance of pepper. Whole peppercorns add flavour to pickles and marinades, freshly ground pepper adds a spicy character while a pinch of pepper gives a more subtle flavour.

NUTRITIONAL VALUE Pepper is rich in mineral salts and stimulates the appetite but large amounts may cause irritation.

Piper nigrum L.   family: Piperaceae

hu jiao (Chinese); *poivre* (French); *Pfeffer* (German); *kaalii mirch* (Hindi); *merica* (Indonesian); *pepe nero* (Italian); *pappaa* (Japanese); *lada hitam* (Malay); *pimenta negra* (Portuguese); *pimienta* (Spanish); *phrik thai* (Thai)

Pistacia vera

pistachio

Pistachio leaves and fruits

Pistachio female and male flowers

Pistachio nuts

DESCRIPTION Pistachio is a small, deciduous tree of 3 to 10 m in height. It has compound leaves, each with three to seven leaflets. Male and female flowers are borne on different trees. They are inconspicuous but occur in large clusters on one-year-old stems. The egg-shaped drupes take several months to mature. Each one has a fleshy outer layer with a single green seed (nut) enclosed in a white bony shell. Several species produce small edible nuts (*P. atlantica*, *P. mutica* and *P. terebinthus*) but only *P. vera*, with its spontaneously splitting husks, is grown commercially.

ORIGIN & HISTORY Pistachio is indigenous to Afghanistan, Iran, Baluchistan, parts of the former USSR and Turkey. It is commonly found in ancient archaeological sites and has been planted as a crop for centuries (especially in Iran, Syria, Palestine and Turkey). Several different cultivars have been developed. In recent times the production areas have expanded to include California (now the second largest producer, next

to Iran), Mexico, Israel, Australia, Italy, Greece, North Africa and South Africa.

PARTS USED The ripe seeds (nuts).

CULTIVATION & HARVESTING Pistachios are wind-pollinated so that five to eight female trees are planted for each male tree. The crop requires long, dry summers and cold winters. Fruits are harvested (by hand or mechanically), the outer skins are removed and the bony husks are dried until they split open.

USES & PROPERTIES Pistachios are eaten raw or roasted and salted as a delicious snack. They are included in desserts, ice creams, confectionery, nougat, cakes, biscuits and pastries. Pistachio nuts are an essential ingredient in many Mediterranean and Indian dishes (including lamb, poultry, cheese and rice dishes).

NUTRITIONAL VALUE The nuts have a very high food value, with about 630 kcal per 100 g, more than 20% protein and more than 50% oil, of which 80% is unsaturated.

Pistacia vera L.   family: Anacardiaceae

pistache (French); *Echte Pistazie* (German); *pistachio* (Italian); *pistachio* (Spanish)

Pisum sativum
pea • garden pea

Pea cultivar (for dry peas)

Garden pea flowers and fruit

Pea pods and seeds

DESCRIPTION An annual, herbaceous climber with compound leaves ending in branched tendrils. The flowers are pink and purple in cultivars used for the production of dry peas (split peas) and usually white in garden pea cultivars that are eaten as green vegetables. The oblong pods contain up to eight round seeds.

ORIGIN & HISTORY This ancient crop – perhaps as old as wheat and barley – originated somewhere in the eastern Mediterranean region, northeast Africa and the Middle East. Dry peas have been eaten for at least 7 000 years, while green peas and "edible-podded" peas are more recent developments.

PARTS USED Green or ripe (dry) seeds or the young green pods.

CULTIVATION & HARVESTING Peas are grown commercially in cool temperate regions of the world. The annual production is about 20 million tons.

USES & PROPERTIES Dry (mature) seeds are cooked whole or split, and can be ground into flour for use in soups, stews and a variety of dishes. Green (immature) peas are cooked as a vegetable (often to accompany veal, lamb and poultry). Fresh peas are delicious (especially the small type known as *petit pois*) but frozen or canned peas are also very tasty. Modern cultivars with edible, non-fibrous pods include *mange-tout* or sugar pea (developed in Europe) and the closely similar snow pea that has become popular in Asia. Young shoots of the latter (known as *tou mio*) are used as a vegetable in stir-fries.

NUTRITIONAL VALUE Peas are exceptionally nutritious, with significant amounts of vitamins B and C, phosphorus and potassium. Ripe seeds (split peas) have a high energy value (up to 120 kcal per 100 g), with high levels of proteins and amino acids. Green peas have somewhat lower levels of proteins but are higher in sugar (about 16%), with an energy value of about 75 kcal per 100 g.

Pisum sativum L.   family: Fabaceae

he lan dou, tian wan dou (Chinese); *pois* (French); *Gartenerbse* (German); *pisello* (Italian); *piisu* (Japanese); *ervilha* (Portuguese); *guisante* (Spanish)

Plectranthus amboinicus

Indian borage

Indian borage plant

Indian borage leaves

DESCRIPTION This species is a robust, somewhat succulent perennial herb that may reach 0.7 m in height. It has very large, fleshy leaves with prominently toothed margins that are borne in opposite pairs. The plant rarely produces pale violet flowers. Various forms (cultivars) with coloured foliage have been developed as popular garden ornamentals.

ORIGIN & HISTORY Indian borage, despite its common name, is believed to be indigenous to tropical Africa, from where it first reached India and later also various parts of Southeast Asia. In recent times, the plant has become well known in Australia, South America and the West Indies. The leaves appear to be highly sought after in many rural parts of the world (including parts of Brazil) where they are grown in subsistence agriculture. The common names are quite confusing and inaccurate: real borage is *Borago officinalis*; the Filipinos call it "oregano" (real oregano is *Oreganum vulgare*); in the West Indies it is known as "broad-leaf thyme" (thyme is *Thymus vulgaris*).

PARTS USED Fresh leaves.

CULTIVATION & HARVESTING Plants are commonly grown in containers and in kitchen gardens to ensure a reliable supply of fresh leaves. It is rarely seen on fresh produce markets.

USES & PROPERTIES The aromatic leaves are used in much the same way as thyme or sage. Chopped leaves are popular for flavouring meat dishes and to replace sage in stuffings and poultry dishes. In Malaysia and Java, it is added to fish and goat meat curries with the aim of reducing the strong smell.

NUTRITIONAL VALUE Rich in some minerals, vitamins and folic acid; verly low in calories.

NOTES The aromatic leaves are used in India as a traditional cough medicine. In parts of Indonesia, nursing mothers eat the leaves with the aim of increasing milk flow. Essential oil distilled from the leaves is used in shampoos.

Plectranthus amboinicus (Lour.) Sprengel (= *Coleus ambonicus* Lour.)   family: Lamiaceae

yin dub bo he, pok-hor (Chinese); *coleus* (French); *Jamaikathymian* (German); *daun kambing* (Indonesian); *coleus* (Italian); *daun bangun-bangun* (Malaysian); *oregano* (Tagalog)

Plectranthus esculentus

Livingstone potato

Sudan potato tubers

Livingstone potato

Livingstone potato tubers

DESCRIPTION A perennial herb with somewhat fleshy, opposite leaves borne on angular stems. Some of the basal branches bend down and grow into the ground to form oblong tubers. The plant has yellow flowers but these are rarely seen, as vegetative propagation predominates. Additional common names include African potato and Hausa potato but the latter name is often used for another minor African tuber crop, the Sudan potato or Zulu round potato (*Plectranthus rotundifolius*, previously known as *Solenostemon rotundifolius*). Also belonging to the mint family (and similar in taste and uses) is the Chinese artichoke (*Stachys sieboldii*) – see Notes under *Helianthus tuberosus* (Jerusalem artichoke).

ORIGIN & HISTORY Livingstone potato is indigenous to southern tropical Africa. It is regarded as one of the "lost crops" of Africa, cultivated since pre-historic times and occasionally still seen in rural parts of southern Africa. There have been recent attempts at reintroducing the crop.

PARTS USED The fleshy underground stems (tubers).

CULTIVATION & HARVESTING *P. esculentus* is exceptionally hardy and is easily grown in frost-free regions. The tubers are harvested as required in subsistence agriculture and the crop has only been commercialised to a limited extent.

USES & PROPERTIES Tubers are used in much the same way as potatoes but have a more distinctive, somewhat aromatic taste. They can be eaten raw or are boiled and eaten as a vegetable, staple food or as an ingredient of soups and stews.

NUTRITIONAL VALUE Livingstone potato is considered to be superior to other tuber crops in terms of its food value and especially the high content of essential amino acids. In a 100 g portion, the crude protein level is about 13 g, the total lipids 0.6 g and the total carbohydrates 80 g. In addition, significant levels of calcium (140 mg), iron (50 mg) and vitamin A (0.17 mg) have been reported.

Plectranthus esculentus N.E. Br.   family: Lamiaceae

plectranthus, *pomme de terre d'Afrique* (French); *Plectranthus* (German); *plectranthus* (Italian); *plectranthus* (Spanish)

Portulaca oleracea

purslane

Purslane plant

Purslane flowers

Winter purslane

DESCRIPTION A weedy annual herb with thick red stems, fleshy leaves and small yellow flowers. Two forms are recognised: the wild plant (subsp. *oleracea*) with spreading stems and a cultivated selection (subsp. *sativa*), which has an erect growth form. A related plant with similar culinary uses is the so-called winter purslane, miner's lettuce or Cuban spinach (*Montia perfoliata*), a North American species. It has distinctive broad leaves that completely surround the stems. Another purslane relative is talinum, flameflower or waterleaf (*Talinum triangulare*), a traditional North American spinach plant that is rarely cultivated in Africa and Asia. Several wild talinums are eaten in Africa.

ORIGIN & HISTORY A cosmopolitan weed. The use of purslane is said to date back to Roman times and the herb was commonly used for pickles in the Middle Ages. The cultivated form has been selected in Europe.

PARTS USED Fresh leaves.

CULTIVATION & HARVESTING Purslane is usually wild-harvested but modern varieties are cultivated as vegetables. They have become popular in parts of Europe.

USES & PROPERTIES The spicy flavour makes it a popular food item that can be included in stews and early season salads or cooked on its own like spinach (with butter, gravy or cream added). It has the ability to thicken dishes in which it is cooked. The leaves are useful as a garnish for soups, omelettes and meat dishes. French cooks sometimes use the leaves of purslane or winter purslane to flavour *béarnaise* sauce (a hot creamy sauce made from egg yolks, vinegar and butter) and a version thereof, known as *paloise* sauce.

NUTRITIONAL VALUE The energy yield is a mere 11 kcal per 100 g. Purslane is considered to be exceptionally nutritious as it contains high levels of omega-3-hepta-linoleic acid. It is an excellent source of vitamins B and C, nicotinamide and minerals (magnesium, potassium and nitrate).

Portulaca oleracea L.   family: Portulacaceae

pourpier (French); *Portulak, Sauburtzel* (German); *verdolaga* (Spanish)

Pouteria campechiana

canistel

Canistel leaves and fruits

Canistel leaves and fruits

Canistel fruits

DESCRIPTION A tree that may reach a height of up to 30 m and gradually develops a thick trunk and spreading crown. The oblong, glossy leaves are crowded towards the tips of the velvety brown stems. Small, fragrant, cream-coloured flowers develop into large, green, usually egg-shaped and pointed fruits that turn orange yellow when they ripen. It is also known as egg-fruit or yellow sapote. Another locally important fruit is the Central American sapote or marmalade plum (*P. sapota*).

ORIGIN & HISTORY Indigenous to the extreme southern parts of North America (southern Mexico, Belize, El Salvador and Guatemala). It has spread to Florida and Central America, including the Bahamas, Costa Rica, Panama, Puerto Rico, Jamaica and Cuba (where it has become particularly popular). Nowadays experimental plantings are found in almost all tropical regions of the world.

PARTS USED Ripe fruits.

CULTIVATION & HARVESTING Trees are easily grown from fresh seeds but various forms of grafting and air-layering are used to speed up fruit-bearing. Mature but firm fruits are harvested and allowed to ripen indoors at room temperature. They turn soft and orange yellow after a few days.

USES & PROPERTIES The fruits are not crisp and juicy like most other fruits but the flesh is mealy and pasty, with the texture of baked sweet potato or the yolk of a hard-boiled egg. It may be eaten as is, but is often mixed with salt and pepper or lime juice. The pulp, mixed with milk, sugar and vanilla, makes a delicious drink, or can be added to custard or ice cream. It may be used to prepare pies, pancakes, jams and marmalade.

NUTRITIONAL VALUE Canistels are nutritious, as they contain significant amounts of calcium, phosphorus, niacin, carotene, ascorbic acid and amino acids (notably tryptophane and lysine). The energy yield is 160 kcal per 100 g.

Pouteria campechiana (Kunth) Baehni
family: Sapotaceae

canistel (French); *Canistel* (German); *canistel* (Italian); *canistel, zapote amarillo* (Spanish)

Prunus armeniaca

apricot

Apricot flowers

Apricot leaves and fruits

Apricots

DESCRIPTION Apricot is a deciduous tree of up to 10 m in height. It bears round leaves, white flowers and rounded fruits with a yellow to orange, velvety skin.

ORIGIN & HISTORY Apricot originated in northern China and first spread to Armenia and western Asia, where it was already cultivated a few centuries BC. From here it was introduced into Europe during the Roman period.

PARTS USED Ripe fruits (also the seed oil).

CULTIVATION & HARVESTING Numerous cultivars are grown in all temperate regions. They require some chilling in winter and the flowers are self-fertile. Fruits are picked by hand – mature and firm for fresh consumption or canning, fully ripe when used for drying.

USES & PROPERTIES Apricots are delicious to eat fresh or to drink as fruit juice. It is one of the most widely used fruits for hot or cold sweet dishes and is commonly included in fruit salads,
desserts, cakes and pastries. Apricots are popular for canning and especially for jam (a few edible kernels may be added for flavour). Dried apricots are eaten as they are or soaked in water for a few hours when used in baking and cooking (in meat dishes or stewed as a side dish). Sweets or cakes are given a glossy appearance by spreading a thin layer of apricot jam over them (a process known as apricoting). *Barack* is an alcoholic spirit distilled from fermented apricots. Amaretto, an Italian almond liqueur, is said to be flavoured with apricot kernels.

NUTRITIONAL VALUE Apricots are low in calories (less than 50 kcal per 100 g), rich in carotene (vitamin A) and contain fair amounts of vitamin C. They are also rich in minerals such as calcium, phosphorus and iron.

NOTES The kernels inside the loose stones are edible but only in small quantities – those of some cultivars contain laetrile, a cyanide compound.

Prunus armeniaca L.   family: Rosaceae

xing (Chinese); *abricotier* (French); *Aprikosenbaum* (German); *albicocca* (Italian); *apurikotto* (Japanese); *aberikos* (Malay); *abricô* (Portuguese); *albericoque* (Spanish); *aprikhot* (Thai)

Prunus avium

sweet cherry

Sweet cherry fruits

Sweet cherry tree

Sweet cherries

DESCRIPTION Sweet cherry is an erect deciduous tree (up to 18 m high) with relatively large, elliptic leaves. The white flowers occur in clusters of up to five. The smooth, shiny fruits are borne on slender stalks and vary in colour from pale yellow to red, dark purple or black.

ORIGIN & HISTORY Sweet cherries are closely related to the wild cherries that grow naturally over large parts of temperate Europe and western Asia. Cherries were already a cultivated crop in the time of Theophrastus (300 BC) and became very popular in Roman times. After a decline in interest during the Middle Ages, cherries became popular again in Europe and later in North America.

PARTS USED Ripe fruits (technically a stone fruit or drupe – a fleshy fruit with a single stone that contains one seed).

CULTIVATION & HARVESTING A large number of cultivars and hybrids are grown. Sweet cherry (unlike sour cherry) requires cross-pollination to set fruit so that two (or more) cultivars are planted in a stand. Fruits are hand-picked when ripe.

USES & PROPERTIES Sweet cherries are eaten in large amounts during the short cherry season. The soft sweet cherries known as geans in England (*guignes* in French) are especially popular for tarts and as dessert fruit (on their own or in fruit salad). They may be frozen but are more often candied or preserved in jams, liqueurs and syrups. Candied cherries (*glacé* cherries) are commonly used in cakes and puddings – as ingredient and for decoration, especially on various ice cream dishes. Cherries are used for pickles, sweet and sour dishes and as condiment to go with duck and game. Various alcoholic drinks are prepared from cherries (see *Prunus cerasus*).

NUTRITIONAL VALUE Sweet cherries have a relatively high energy value (62 kcal per 100 g) and are rich in sugar, minerals and vitamin C but fairly low in organic acids.

Prunus avium L. family: Rosaceae

ou zhou tian ying tao (Chinese); *cerise douce* (French); *Süßkirsche, Vogelkirsche* (German); *ciliegia dolce* (Italian); *kanka outou* (Japanese); *cerejeira* (Portuguese); *cerezo* (Spanish)

Prunus cerasus

sour cherry

Sour cherry (red form)

Sour cherry (black form)

Sour cherries

DESCRIPTION A deciduous shrub or small tree with a spreading growth form. The leaves are somewhat smaller than those of the sweet cherry but the flowers and fruits are similar in appearance. Sour cherry is quite variable. Two varieties are well known. The amarelle cherry (var. *cerasus*) has light to medium-red fruits with light-coloured or clear juice and a relatively low acid content. The morello or morelle cherry (var. *austera*) has rounded, dark red fruits yielding red juice with a high acid content.

ORIGIN & HISTORY The sour cherry (a tetraploid) is believed to have originated in southeast Europe and western Asia as a hybrid between the diploid sweet cherry (*P. avium*) and a tetraploid wild cherry (*P. fruticosa*). Both sour and sweet cherries were cultivated in Asia Minor and southeastern Europe in ancient times and were spread throughout Europe by the Romans. Sour cherries are grown commercially in all cold temperate parts of the world.

PARTS USED Ripe fruit.

CULTIVATION & HARVESTING Sour cherries are self-compatible (they do not need cross-pollination). The fruit is mostly used for processing and is often mechanically harvested by shaking. The cherries are washed, pitted and processed within hours from being harvested.

USES & PROPERTIES Sour or bitter cherries are used in much the same way as sweet cherries. They are less often eaten fresh but are mainly candied (crystallised), preserved in syrup or brandy or processed into jam. Sour cherries are popular for making alcoholic beverages such as cherry wine or cherry liqueur. Especially famous are cherry brandy from England, Kirsch from Alsace (where they also make savoury cherry soup on Christmas Eve), Maraschino from Italy and various cherry liqueurs (such as the French *guignolet* made in Anjou).

NUTRITIONAL VALUE Sour cherries have less sugar (53 kcal per 100 g) and much higher levels of malic acid and vitamin A than sweet cherries.

Prunus cerasus L.

family: Rosaceae

suan guo ying tao (Chinese); *griotte, cerise aigre* (French); *Sauerkirsche, Weichsel* (German); *ciliegia acida* (Italian); *sanka outou* (Japanese); *ginja garrafal* (Portuguese); *cereza ácida* (Spanish)

Prunus domestica

European plum

Plum tree with fruits

Plum flowers

Plums

DESCRIPTION The European plum or common plum is a small deciduous tree with simple leaves, white flowers and round fruits (drupes) that may be green, yellow, red, purple or black. Japanese plum (*P. salicina*) and American plum (*P. americana*) or their hybrids have also become popular as dessert fruits. Several species of plum that are mainly used for cooking and processing are discussed elsewhere (see *P. spinosa*).

ORIGIN & HISTORY The European plum is considered to be an ancient cultigen derived from the cherry plum (*P. cerasifera*) and possibly the sloe (see *P. spinosa*) and / or the damson plum (*P. insititia*). Plums were grown by the Syrians and Romans and later taken to western Europe by the Crusaders.

PARTS USED Fresh or dried ripe fruits.

CULTIVATION & HARVESTING Plums are usually propagated by grafting (often on cherry plum as stock) and are produced in all temperate regions. Numerous cultivars of eating plums are available, including 'Czar', 'Burbank', 'D'Agen', 'Kirke's Blue', 'Pershore', 'Santa Rosa' and 'Victoria'. Last-mentioned is the most popular plum in the United Kingdom.

USES & PROPERTIES Plums are eaten for their sweet or somewhat tart and fragrant flesh. Prunes are red or purple plums that have been carefully dried to keep for a long time. The fresh, dried or preserved fruits have numerous culinary uses. They can be cooked to make the famous English plum pudding or variously used in jams, tarts and in other confectionery. Plums are also preserved in brandy or fermented and distilled to produce alcoholic drinks. Prunes are eaten as such, used in tarts and puddings, cooked as a side dish or more commonly used as a condiment or ingredient of meat dishes or cocktail snacks (such as prunes with bacon).

NUTRITIONAL VALUE Plums and prunes are high in sugar content (energy yield of 48 kcal per 100 g) and are rich in calcium, potassium and vitamins.

Prunus domestica L.   family: Rosaceae

ou zhou li, li zi (Chinese); *prune commune* (French); *Pflaumenbaum, Zwetschge* (German); *susina* (Italian); *seiyou sumomo* (Japanese); *abrunheiro* (Portuguese); *ciruela, prunero* (Spanish)

Prunus dulcis

almond

Almond flowers

Almond fruits

Almonds

DESCRIPTION A small to medium-sized tree with oblong leaves and pale pink to white flowers. The velvety fruits resemble those of the peach but the outer layer does not become fleshy and later cracks open to reveal the papery or bony shell that contains the edible seed. Sweet almond (var. *dulcis*) is edible; bitter almond (var. *amara*) produces hydrocyanic acid and is poisonous.

ORIGIN & HISTORY Central to western Asia. Almonds have been cultivated for at least 3 000 years in the Near East, North Africa and southern Europe and much later in other parts of the world such as Australia and California in the USA.

PARTS USED The seeds (nuts).

CULTIVATION & HARVESTING Almonds are self-incompatible, so that carefully chosen pollinating cultivars are planted in separate rows to ensure adequate fruit set. Fruits are harvested when the husks dry out (by hand or mechanical shakers).

USES & PROPERTIES This important nut may be salted and eaten but is dried, flaked, ground and pulverised as a widely used ingredient of confectionery. Ground sweet almonds, together with sugar and egg whites are used to make marzipan, an indispensable item for the icing on wedding cakes, as well as numerous types of sweets, sweetmeats (the French *massepains*) and confectionery. Almond paste is similar and has much the same uses. Almonds are used for almond soup, almond milk, almond milk jelly and sweet desserts, such as *blancmange*. Dried bitter almonds are sometimes added in small quantities for flavour. Amaretto is an almond-flavoured Italian liqueur.

NUTRITIONAL VALUE Almonds have a high energy value (583 kcal per 100 g) and are rich in protein, sugar, fat and vitamins.

NOTES Cold-pressed sweet almond oil is valuable as carrier oil in aromatherapy, cosmetics and creams. Bitter almond yields an essential oil that contains benzaldehyde and is used to flavour food and perfume.

Prunus dulcis (Mill.) D.A. Webb [= *Amygdalis communis* L., *P. amygdalis* (L.) Batsch]   family: Rosaceae

bian tou, xing ren (Chinese); *amandier* (French); *Mandelbaum* (German); *mandoria* (Italian); *aamondo, kara momo* (Japanese); *amendoeira* (Portuguese); *almendro* (Spanish)

Prunus persica

peach

Peach flowers

Peaches (nectarines and clingstones)

Peach leaves and fruits

DESCRIPTION A small tree with oblong leaves, dark pink flowers and fleshy stone fruits. Three groups of cultivars can be distinguished: nectarines (fruit hairless); freestone peaches (fruit velvety, with a free stone and soft flesh); clingstone peaches (fruit velvety, with firm flesh clinging to the stone).

ORIGIN & HISTORY Peach is believed to be an ancient cultigen derived from the Chinese wild peach (*P. davidiana*). It spread from China to Iran (Persia) and then Europe in the last 2 000 years. During the last three or four centuries, peach became a major crop in other temperate parts of the world – especially North America, South Africa and Australia.

PARTS USED Fresh or dried fruit.

CULTIVATION & HARVESTING Peach is self-fertile, so that a single cultivar is usually planted. Trees are pruned and trellised to ensure even light exposure and productivity. Firm, mature fruits are harvested by hand.

USES & PROPERTIES Peach is a popular fruit for eating – those with white flesh are usually considered tastier than those with yellow flesh. Peaches are used fresh or canned, for a wide range of desserts, fruit salads, pastries, tarts, fritters, jams, juices, ices, sorbets and drinks, including peach liqueur and peach brandy. The famous Peach Melba (created in 1892 and named after the Australian opera singer Nellie Melba) is made from poached peach halves on vanilla ice cream and topped with raspberry purée or redcurrant jelly. In Italian cooking, peaches are often served with *amaretti* or macaroons (biscuits made from ground almonds) and Amaretto liqueur. Canned peaches or cooked, dried peaches are often used to complement savoury meat dishes, especially mutton, duck and crab.

NUTRITIONAL VALUE Peaches are relatively low in calories (10% sugar, 40–45 kcal per 100 g) but contain high levels of potassium, iron and vitamins A, B1, B2 and C.

Prunus persica (L.) Batsch   family: Rosaceae

tao, tao zi (Chinese); *pêcher* (French); *Pfirsichbaum* (German); *aaruu* (Hindi); *persico* (Italian); *piichi, ke momo* (Japanese); *persik* (Malay); *melocotôn, pérsico duraznero* (Spanish)

Prunus spinosa

sloe • blackthorn

Sloe leaves and fruit

DESCRIPTION This is a thorny shrub with white flowers and small bluish black fruits the size of a small cherry. It is one of several wild plums that are used as food items. Others include the cherry plum (*P. cerasifera*) that is also known as myrobalan plum (*Kirschpflaume* in German, *cerisette* in French). It is possibly the wild ancestor of the European plum (see *P. domestica*). The damsons and bullaces (*P. insititia*) are another type of widely used cooking plums. A group of cultivars known as gages (e.g. 'Green Gage') is popular in Europe and has been crossed with several other plums.

ORIGIN & HISTORY Sloe is indigenous to Europe and western Asia. The fruits have undoubtedly been collected from the wild since ancient times. The cherry plum occurs naturally in western and central Asia and is mostly cultivated as a rootstock for other plums. The damson plum and bullace originated in western Asia and have

been developed into several modern cultivars.

PARTS USED Fresh or dried fruit.

CULTIVATION & HARVESTING Sloe and other cooking plums are not commonly cultivated and are mostly harvested from wild trees. They require cold temperate conditions with chilling in winter.

USES & PROPERTIES Sloe fruits are very acidic and are mainly used for jams, jellies, sloe wine or sloe gin. Wild and domesticated plums are eaten fresh or are similarly used for canning, bottling, jellies and jams and as ingredient of various tarts, pastries and puddings. They are used to make prune juice and plum purée and are commonly distilled to produce smooth and fruity brandies such as *mirabelle* brandy and *quetsche*.

NUTRITIONAL VALUE Sloe and other plums contain about 10 % sugar and are high in minerals (especially potassium) but relatively low in vitamin C.

Prunus spinosa L.   family: Rosaceae

ci li, hei ci li (Chinese); *épine noire, prunellier* (French); *Schlehdorn, Schwarzdorn* (German); *prugnolo, prunello* (Italian); *abrunheiro* (Portuguese); *endrino* (Spanish)

Psidium guajava

guava

Guava fruits

Guava leaves and flowers

Guavas

DESCRIPTION A shrub or small tree with a characteristic smooth, pale bark and opposite leaves showing prominent, parallel veins. The flowers are white, with numerous stamens. The fruit is rounded or pear-shaped with persistent sepals at the tip and numerous small seeds embedded in soft, yellow or pink, fragrant fruit flesh. Other species are discussed under *P. littorale*.

ORIGIN & HISTORY Guava is indigenous to Central America. It became naturalised in many parts of the world and is now an important commercial fruit crop in Central America, India, Asia, Africa and Australia.

PARTS USED Ripe fruits.

CULTIVATION & HARVESTING Propagation is mainly by seeds and less often by air-layering, grafting and root cuttings. The trees are drought-tolerant but sensitive to frost. Fruits for eating are hand-picked when yellow-green, while those intended for processing may be mechanically harvested.

USES & PROPERTIES Guavas are eaten raw or used in desserts and fruit salads. The delicious sour taste of the fresh fruit may be complemented with a little sugar or rum. Cooked (canned) fruits are popular, as are guava jelly, jam, paste (cheese), juice and nectar. Processing often involves boiling the sliced fruit and removal of the seeds from the pulp or juice by filtering. Guavas are used in jams, marmalade, jelly, chutney, relish, confectionery (tarts, cakes, pies), desserts (puddings, sauces, ice cream), breakfast foods and baby-food.

NUTRITIONAL VALUE One of the best sources of vitamin C, which is concentrated in the skin and outer layers of the fruit. The levels are quite variable: 50–600 mg per 100 g portion, depending on ripeness, age and heat processing. They are also a good source of phosphorus, niacin and vitamin A but are low in energy (34 kcal per 100 g).

NOTES Roots, bark, leaves and immature fruits are used in traditional medicine (treatment of diarrhoea and diabetes).

Psidium guajava L.   family: Myrtaceae

fan shi liu, fan tao (Chinese); *goyave, goyavier* (French); *Guajavenbaum* (German); *guava* (Italian); *banjirou* (Japanese); *araçá* (Portuguese); *arazá, guayabo* (Spanish)

Psidium littorale

strawberry guava

Strawberry guava (yellow variety)

Strawberry guava leaves and fruits

Costa Rican guava leaves and fruits

DESCRIPTION Strawberry guava (also called cattley guava) is a shrub or small tree that may eventually reach 12 m in height. The leaves are small, with a prominent midrib and somewhat waxy in texture. The small white flowers develop into small, rounded fruits (about the size of a walnut) tipped with the remains of the calyx. They have a thin, reddish-purple or yellow skin with white or cream-coloured flesh. The yellow type is a distinct botanical variety (var. *lucidum*). Strawberry guava is often listed under the older name, *P. cattleianum*. Two other guavas are of some commercial interest. These are the Costa Rican guava (*P. friedrichsthalianum*) which is similar to the common guava (and has similar uses) and the Guinea guava or *guisaro* (*P. guineense*) which is used for jelly.

ORIGIN & HISTORY The tree originated in the lowlands of eastern Brazil but has been distributed to most parts of the world as a fruit tree and ornamental plant. It has become a serious weed in some regions.

PARTS USED Ripe fruits.

CULTIVATION & HARVESTING Trees are usually grown from seeds but may also be propagated by root or stem cuttings and by layering and grafting. The plant is tolerant of drought and poor soils and (unlike the common guava) survives moderate frost.

USES & PROPERTIES Fruits are eaten for their delicious, sour taste. They are also processed into jam, jelly, guava paste and sherbet. Various drinks are prepared from the juice, obtained by boiling and straining. Pulp or purée made from ripe fruits cooked with water and sugar makes a delicious filling for tarts, pastries and pancakes.

NUTRITIONAL VALUE The fruits have a relatively low energy value (about 25 kcal per 100 g; the sugar content is 4–10%). They are also a good source of vitamin C (20–50 mg).

Psidium littorale Raddi (= *P. cattleianum* Sabine)
family: Myrtaceae

cao mei fan shi liu (Chinese); *gouyave fraise, goyavier-fraise* (French); *Erdbeerguave* (German); *araçá-amarelo* (Portuguese); *guayaba de fresa* (Spanish)

Psophocarpus tetragonolobus

winged bean

Winged bean plant

Winged bean with flowers and fruits

Winged bean fruits

DESCRIPTION The winged bean is a twining and climbing herbaceous perennial with a large tuberous root. The compound leaves resemble those of the common bean. Pale purple or rarely white flowers develop into the characteristic four-angled pods that have four prominent wings with wavy margins. This bean is also known as winged pea, Goa bean, asparagus pea, prince's pea or *dambala*. It should not be confused with the superficially similar *Lotus tetragonolobus* (asparagus pea), which has red flowers.

ORIGIN & HISTORY It is a cultigen that originated in tropical Africa but it was domesticated in tropical Asia many centuries ago. It is cultivated, mainly in subsistence agriculture, in India, Myanmar, Thailand, New Guinea, Malaysia and Indonesia.

PARTS USED Mainly the green pods but also the tuberous roots, ripe seeds, flowers and young leaves.

CULTIVATION & HARVESTING Winged bean is an underutilised annual or perennial crop with considerable potential. It is grown from seeds. Young pods are hand-harvested at regular intervals. The plant is grown commercially for the tuberous, potato-like roots in New Guinea and Myanmar.

USES & PROPERTIES The immature pods (and less often also the flowers and leaves) are used as vegetables. The pods are cooked and eaten like green beans. Tubers are enjoyed fresh or are boiled in the same way as potatoes. The ripe seeds are also used as an energy-rich, nutritious food or as a source of seed oil (similar to soybean oil).

NUTRITIONAL VALUE Green pods are a good source of protein (2.5% of fresh weight), calcium, iron and vitamin A. Ripe seeds are comparable to soybeans in nutritional value and contain 35% protein, 15–20% oil and 5–10% carbohydrates. The seed oil is chemically similar to peanut oil (high in linoleic, oleic and behenic fatty acids). Tubers contain 14% protein (ten times more than cassava or sweet potato).

Psophocarpus tetragonolobus (L.) DC.   family: Fabaceae

si jiao dou (Chinese); *pois asperge* (French); *Goabohne, Flügelbohne* (German); *fagiolo quadrato* (Italian); *sikaku mame* (Japanese); *kachang botol* (Malay); *fava de cavalo* (Portuguese); *dôlico de Goa* (Spanish)

Pteridium aquilinum
bracken fern

Bracken fern

DESCRIPTION Bracken fern (or simply called bracken) is a perennial plant with compound, feathery leaves arising from creeping, underground rhizomes. The young leaf is curled like a fiddlehead before it unfolds and matures into a sturdy, firm-textured frond.

ORIGIN & HISTORY The bracken fern is one of the most cosmopolitan of all plants. It has been widely used as a source of food in different parts of the world and is still an important commercial food source in Japan and Korea.

PARTS USED The young fronds and rhizomes.

CULTIVATION & HARVESTING Bracken is not cultivated but simply wild-harvested. The young leaves are picked before they unfold.

USES & PROPERTIES The New Zealand Maoris and the North American Indians used the pounded rhizomes as a source of starch (it is said to have been a staple food). On the Canary Islands, rhizomes are ground with oats to make a traditional dish known as *goflo*. In Japan, Korea,

Thailand, the Philippines and also Canada and the northeastern parts of North America, young fronds are blanched and eaten as a salad or cooked as a vegetable. They are available on local fresh produce markets and also in canned form (known as *sawarabi* in Japan; *warabi-ko* is the edible starch obtained from the rhizomes). The main attractions of *sawarabi* are the mild taste (reminiscent of asparagus and artichoke) and especially the crisp texture.

NUTRITIONAL VALUE Bracken is said to be a high fibre and low calorie food that contains minerals such as iron and zinc. However, it contains a carcinogenic substance (terpenoid) known as ptaquiloside. It is claimed that blanching or cooking removes the poison but there is a high incidence of certain forms of cancer in areas where young fronds are regularly consumed as human food. Most experts strongly advise against eating bracken fern.

Pteridium aquilinum (L.) Kuhn   family: Dennstaedtiaceae

fougère aigle (French); *Adlerfarn* (German); *felce aquilina* (Italian); *sawarabi, pako shida, zenmai* (Japanese); *pako* (Philippines); *phak kuut* (Thai)

Punica granatum
pomegranate

Pomegranate flowers

Pomegranates

Pomegranate fruits

Pomegranate seeds

DESCRIPTION This is a thorny shrub with bright green leaves, attractive orange flowers and distinctive rounded fruits crowned with persistent calyx teeth. The fruit contains numerous seeds, each surrounded by a bright red to whitish juice sac (aril).

ORIGIN & HISTORY Pomegranate is an ancient cultigen of Middle Eastern (Persian) origin that is perhaps indigenous to parts of Turkey and the adjoining Caspian region. The plant is steeped in history: it is a symbol of fertility and is believed to be the "Tree of Knowledge" of the Bible. The persistent calyx is thought to have inspired the crown of King Solomon and hence the typical crown of European kings. The fruit gave its name to the Spanish city of Granada and even the deadly hand grenade. *Punica* refers to the Roman name for Carthage, from where pomegranates were once imported to Italy, and *granatum* means "with many seed grains".

PARTS USED Ripe fruits.

CULTIVATION & HARVESTING Pomegranate is widely cultivated as a crop (mostly from seeds), especially in the Middle East, Mediterranean region and India. Fruits are picked when fully ripe.

USES & PROPERTIES The fleshy seeds are eaten fresh and the extracted juice is a popular beverage in the Middle East. Pomegranate is best known as the source of grenadine, a bright red concentrate that is used for mixed drinks. Pomegranate concentrate is also used in cooking and especially in Middle Eastern (Lebanese) and Mediterranean sauces, soups, meat dishes, salads and sweet *couscous*. Dried seeds are an important spice (*anardana*) for sweet-sour dishes in northwestern India (especially in Punjab and Gujarat).

NUTRITIONAL VALUE Pomegranate is low in calories (30–60 kcal per 100 g) and rich in phosphorus and potassium.

NOTES All parts of the plant have been used in traditional medicine. The bark and fruit rind are important sources of tans and dyes.

Punica granatum L.   family: Punicaceae

shi liu, shi liu pi (Chinese); *grenade* (French); *Granatapfelbaum* (German); *melograna* (Italian); *zakuro* (Japanese); *romãzeira* (Portuguese); *granado* (Spanish)

316

Pyrus communis

pear

Pear flowers

Pear tree with pears

Asian pear (*nashi*)

DESCRIPTION A medium-sized tree with elliptic leaves and white flowers in small clusters of up to seven. The fruit is the receptacle of the flower that becomes fleshy. Unlike the apple, all pears contain grit cells in the fruit flesh. Two main species are the common or European pear, which is always pear-shaped and the Asian pear or *nashi*, *Pyrus pyrifolia* (= *P. serotina*) which is usually apple-like with a crisp, granular texture and a somewhat bland flavour.

ORIGIN & HISTORY Pears originated in Europe and western Asia. They have been cultivated in China for at least 4 000 years and were known to the Romans, who spread them throughout Europe. Today there are more than 1 000 cultivars.

PARTS USED Ripe fruits.

CULTIVATION & HARVESTING Pears are propagated by grafting. They are mostly self-infertile, so that more than one cultivar must be grown together. European pears are picked when still hard and green, while the fruit of the Asian pear are allowed to ripen on the tree.

USES & PROPERTIES Dessert pears are eaten raw as a popular table fruit or in fruit salads. When used as a garnish, the fruits are sprinkled with lemon juice to prevent oxidisation and discolouration. Cooking pears are no longer very common, as normal dessert pears are used instead. Fresh or canned pears are included in numerous desserts, such as pies, tarts, mousses, compotes, jellies, ice creams and sorbets. They are often served in wine sauce. Pears are also cooked with meat dishes, especially chicken, hare and duck. Dried pears are eaten as snacks or cooked to accompany savoury dishes. Fermented juice, called pear cider or perry, may be distilled to make pear brandy or pear liqueur.

NUTRITIONAL VALUE Pears are relatively low in calories (about 60 kcal per 100 g) and contain fair amounts of minerals (especially potassium and iron) and vitamins B and C.

Pyrus communis L.

family: Rosaceae

poire (French); *Birne* (German); *peral* (Italian); *nashi* (Japanese); *peral* (Spanish)

Raphanus sativus

radish

Radish plants

Radishes (small European type)

Giant radish (daikon or mouli type)

DESCRIPTION A biennial plant with a rosette of lobed and irregularly toothed leaves that produces a leafy flowering stalk in the second year, bearing white or pink flowers, each with four petals. The swollen roots are exceptionally variable. There are five basic types: (1) small-rooted, short-season European radishes – usually red or red and white; (2) large-rooted Asian types – exceptionally variable in shape, size and colour; (3) black-rooted European type suitable for winter storage; (4) rat-tail radish, grown in Southeast Asia for the leaves and extraordinarily long fruits; (5) fodder radish.

ORIGIN & HISTORY Radish is indigenous to Europe and Asia. Domestication is believed to have occurred independently in the eastern Mediterranean region and China. Records date back to 5 000 years ago in Egypt, and at least 2 000 years ago in China. Radishes were well known to the Greeks and Romans. Today, radishes are grown in all parts of the world and they are a staple food in many Asian countries (especially China, Japan and Korea).

PARTS USED The fleshy roots (less often the leaves or fruits).

CULTIVATION & HARVESTING The crop is easily grown from seeds and matures very rapidly.

USES & PROPERTIES Radishes are mostly eaten fresh for their sharp taste, on their own as a *hors d'oeuvre* or in green salads. They are eaten whole, with or without the peel, or may be sliced. Radishes have a very diverse application in Asian cooking. They are eaten raw or may be cooked, steamed or stir-fried. They may be mashed and mixed with flour to make Chinese dough cake, or grated and sliced as a common flavour ingredient of Japanese dishes.

NUTRITIONAL VALUE Radishes have a low energy value (only about 20 kcal per 100 g). They contain fair amounts of minerals and vitamin C (7–27 mg per 100 g). The sharp taste is due to mustard oils (glucosinolates).

Raphanus sativus L.   family: Brassicaceae

luo bo (Chinese); *radis* (French); *Rettich, Radieschen* (German); *ravanello* (Italian); *radeisshu* (Japanese); *lobak* (Malay); *rabanete* (Portuguese); *rabanito* (Spanish)

Rhamnus prinoides
geisho

Geisho leaves and flowers

DESCRIPTION A shrub or small tree of up to 6 m in height with glossy, hairless, serrated, alternately arranged leaves (often alternately larger and smaller). The small flowers are yellowish green and are solitary or in small clusters. The fruits are small berries that turn red to purple when they mature.

ORIGIN & HISTORY Indigenous to sub-Saharan Africa, from southern Africa to Ethiopia. It has been grown as a crop in Ethiopia for centuries and is still important in the rural economy.

PARTS USED Dried leaves.

CULTIVATION & HARVESTING Plants are propagated from seeds; seedlings germinating spontaneously under existing plants are merely transplanted. Harvesting is done three times a year by stripping off all the leaves except the growing tips. Plants should be at least three years old before they are first harvested. The productive lifespan of a plant is very long and they can be continually harvested for up to 50 years or more, depending on local conditions. The leaves are air-dried, packed in bags and sold on local markets.

USES & PROPERTIES Geisho is used to flavour traditional alcoholic beverages produced and sold locally in Ethiopia. These include the traditional beer known as *tella* (called *sewa* in some regions). It is brewed from finger millet, maize or sorghum, using germinated barley to start the fermentation process. Geisho is used as bitter flavourant for the delicious traditional Ethiopean honey beer, known as *tej* in Amharic (sometimes called *mies*). A traditional home-brewed spirit drink called *areki* or *katikala* is flavoured with geisho. These drinks are on sale at rural beer houses throughout Ethiopia.

NUTRITIONAL VALUE The leaves are used for their flavour only but beneficial effects are claimed for the herb against skin infections, sore throat and intestinal parasites.

NOTES Leaves are a source of pigments for dyeing.

Rhamnus prinoides L.'Herit.   family: Rhamnaceae

geisho (Amharic); *geisho* (French); *Afrikanischer Faulbaum* (German)

Rheum rhabarbarum
rhubarb

Rhubarb plants

Rhubarb plants

Rhubarb leaf stalks

DESCRIPTION Rhubarb is a perennial herb with very large leaves and tall inflorescences growing from a rootstock of short rhizomes. A large number of cultivars have been developed, differing mainly in the colour of the stalks (bright red to green).

ORIGIN & HISTORY *R. rhabarbarum* is indigenous to Mongolia. The garden rhubarb is sometimes considered to be a hybrid, with *R. rhabarbarum* as one parent (then called *R. x hybridum* or *R. x cultorum*). Rhizomes of various species have been used as traditional laxative medicine in northern Asia for centuries, especially Chinese rhubarb (*R. palmatum* and *R. officinalis*) and rhapontic rhubarb (*R. rhaponticum*). Rhubarb was first planted for medicinal purposes in Europe in the sixteenth century. The use of rhubarb stalks for eating started in England or France in the eighteenth century and spread to North America and many other parts of the world.

PARTS USED Only the leaf stalks. The leaf itself is not edible (contains large amounts of oxalic acid).

CULTIVATION & HARVESTING Rhubarb is a hardy perennial that requires a cool temperate climate with mild summers. It can be grown from seed or by division. Plants are sometimes brought indoors in winter and forced to produce an early crop and they are often blanched with pots in early spring.

USES & PROPERTIES The stalks are used in the same way as fruit but they are very sour and have to be sweetened with sugar. The main uses are for pie fillings, compotes and jams. Rhubarb can also be made into wine and chutney.

NUTRITIONAL VALUE Rhubarb contains some minerals and vitamin C (10 mg per 100 g). It has a very low energy value (16 kcal per 100 g). The high levels of acids (especially oxalic acid, nearly 0.5%) give the sharp taste but excessive consumption can lead to poisoning (interference with the absorption of calcium and iron).

Rheum rhabarbarum L. (= *R. x hybridum* Murray)   family: Polygonaceae

da huang (Chinese); *rhubarbe* (French); *Rhabarber* (German); *rabarbaro* (Italian); *ruibarbo* (Portuguese, Spanish)

Ribes nigrum
blackcurrant

Blackcurrant plant

Jostaberry

Blackcurrant

DESCRIPTION A multi-stemmed shrub with toothed leaves and clusters of greenish flowers that develop into attractive, black, juicy berries. The similar-looking jostaberry (*R. x nidigrolaria*) is a three-way hybrid between blackcurrant, gooseberry (*R. uva-crispa*) and Worcesterberry (*R. divaricatum*).

ORIGIN & HISTORY Indigenous to northern Europe and northern Asia, where it was developed as a crop over several centuries by crossing with wild Asian species and later with North American species such as the Californian blackcurrant (*R. bracteosum*) and western blackcurrant (*R. petiolare*). Production (mostly in Europe) amounts to nearly half a million tons per year.

PARTS USED Ripe fruit.

CULTIVATION & HARVESTING Blackcurrant requires at least ten weeks of subzero temperatures during winter. Optimal ripeness is critical, so that harvesting has become mechanised.

USES & PROPERTIES Blackcurrants are used for jams, jellies, fruit juice, syrups and iced purée with many applications in confectionery, desserts and cooking (served with meat dishes). *Crème de cassis* is blackcurrant liqueur, made from macerated berries soaked in alcohol and later sweetened. Double crème or super-cassis has 20% alcohol and twice as much fruit as the normal liqueur with 16% alcohol. The liqueur is used in cooking but is mostly enjoyed as *kir* (a spoonful of liqueur topped up with dry white wine), *kir royale* (topped up with *champagne brut*) or *communard* (topped up with dry red wine). *Kir* is named after Canon Félix Kir, the mayor of Dijon and a hero of the French Resistance, who popularised the drink after the war at a time when liqueur-makers were fighting for survival.

NUTRITIONAL VALUE As one of the richest known sources of vitamin C (70–180 mg per 100 g), the fruit or juice may serve as a dietary supplement during the cold and flu season. The seed oil is rich in gamma-linolenic acid (15%) and is an alternative to evening primrose oil.

Ribes nigrum L.   family: Grossulariaceae

hei sui cu li (Chinese); *cassis* (French); *Schwarze Johannisbeere* (German); *ribes nero* (Italian); *kuro fusa suguri* (Japanese); *casis, grosella negra* (Spanish)

Ribes rubrum

redcurrant

Redcurrant (pale form)

Redcurrant

Redcurrants

DESCRIPTION Redcurrant is a deciduous shrub with woody branches bearing broad, three-lobed, toothed leaves. The small, greenish flowers are borne in pendulous clusters. They develop into slender clusters of about 6 to 20 small, red, glistening berries, each about 5–10 mm in diameter. A form with white berries is also known (it lacks the red pigment and is known as white currant). There are several other wild or cultivated species of redcurrants, including the large-fruited cherry currants (*R. sativum*), the red- or black-fruited *R. petraeum* and two multi-flowered species *R. multiflorum* and *R. longeracemosum*.

ORIGIN & HISTORY *R. rubrum* occurs naturally in Europe and North Asia. Redcurrants were developed as a crop over a period of 500 years in Europe. The first species to be planted was the western European *R. sativum* and the more widely distributed *R. petraeum*, followed much later by *R. rubrum*. It is thought that the present-day redcurrant is the product of hybridisation and back crossing with *R. sativum*, *R. petraeum* and possibly other species as well.

PARTS USED Ripe berries.

CULTIVATION & HARVESTING The plants are mostly grown from cuttings and require a cold temperate climate. Berries are harvested by hand when ripe.

USES & PROPERTIES Redcurrants are eaten raw (often with sugar added to counteract the sour taste) or they are used for jams, jellies or fruit juice. The berries are included in fruit salads, cold desserts, sorbets, syrups and in confectionery (pastries and tarts). A speciality in France is *Bar-le-Duc* jelly, made from red and white currants.

NUTRITIONAL VALUE The berries contain vitamin C (35–40 mg per 100 g) and are rich in organic acids (about 2.5%), of which citric acid is the main component. The acid level is double that of gooseberry but similar to the level found in blackcurrant.

Ribes rubrum L.   family: Grossulariaceae

ru hong cu li (Chinese); *groseille rouge* (French); *Rote Johannisbeere* (German); *ribes rosso* (Italian); *aka fusa suguri* (Japanese); *grosella roja* (Spanish)

Ribes uva-crispa

gooseberry

Gooseberry leaves and fruit

Gooseberries (red cultivar)

Gooseberries (green cultivar)

DESCRIPTION A spiny, long-lived, deciduous shrub with broad, toothed leaves and small, greenish red flowers. The glossy, sparsely hairy berries are translucent so that the veins (vascular tissue) are clearly visible. Also distinctive are the remains of the sepals. These large berries are borne singly or in pairs and are green or sometimes yellow, red or purple, depending on the cultivar. There are numerous other species, including the North American Worcesterberry (*R. divaricatum*) and currant gooseberry (*R. hirtellum*). Closely related are blackcurrant (*R. nigrum*) and redcurrant (*R. rubrum*).

ORIGIN & HISTORY Gooseberry is widely distributed throughout Europe and Asia. Cultivation started in the fifteenth century, and became very popular during the eighteenth century, when many cultivars were developed. Commercial production is centred in western, central and eastern Europe, with Germany as the leading producer.

PARTS USED Unripe or ripe berries.

CULTIVATION & HARVESTING Gooseberries are usually grown from cuttings. They require a temperate climate and cold winters. Mildew-resistant cultivars are available.

USES & PROPERTIES Ripe berries are enjoyed fresh or are variously processed into juice, jam, desserts and puddings, including fruit salads, sorbets, syrups and fools (a fool is a chilled, sweetened fruit purée mixed with whipped cream). Unripe berries are used to make jams and jellies. Gooseberries can be used to garnish fish and poultry or made into chutneys and sauces to accompany various dishes. The French name for gooseberry means "gooseberry of mackerel" because it is used to make a sauce traditionally served with mackerel.

NUTRITIONAL VALUE Gooseberries have a low energy value (30 kcal per 100 g) and are a fairly good source of vitamin C (15–35 mg per 100 g). They are also rich in dietary fibre, iron and potassium.

Ribes uva-crispa L. (= *R. grossularia* L.)   family: Grossulariaceae

cu li (Chinese); *groseille à maquereau* (French); *Stachelbeere* (German); *uva spina* (Italian); *maru suguri* (Japanese); *grosella blanca* (Spanish)

Rorippa nasturtium-aquaticum

watercress

Watercress flowers

Watercress plants

Watercress

DESCRIPTION A spreading perennial herb with irregularly compound leaves, rounded, smooth leaflets and oblong clusters of white flowers, each with only four petals (as is typical of the cabbage family). The seeds are borne in oblong capsules. Brown watercress or winter watercress (*R. microphylla*) is a plant of hybrid origin with larger flowers and leaves that turn brown to purplish in winter. Closely related are garden cress (*Lepidium sativum*) and land cress (*Barbarea verna*).

ORIGIN & HISTORY Watercress is indigenous to Europe. It has become a cosmopolitan weed of wet places. Watercress was known to the Persians, Greeks and Romans, who ate it as a medicine or health food. Cultivation only started in the nineteenth century. Watercress and brown watercress are now important crop plants in all parts of the world.

PARTS USED Fresh leafy stems.

CULTIVATION & HARVESTING The crop is grown in large inundated beds. A reliable supply of clean running water is necessary to maintain the irrigation system. Stems are cut by hand, washed and packed.

USES & PROPERTIES Watercress has a distinctive peppery taste and is the most popular type of cress. The leaves are removed from the stems and eaten raw in salads and on sandwiches. It makes a tasty soup – this is the only way in which watercress is eaten in Southeast Asia and other parts of the world. Other typical dishes include cooked watercress (made in the same way as spinach) and watercress purée (mixed with purée of potato or split peas). The French term for dishes containing watercress is *à la cressonnière*.

NUTRITIONAL VALUE Watercress has a low energy value (17 kcal per 100 g) and is a rich source of minerals (potassium, magnesium, iron), nicotinic acid and vitamin C (25–187 mg per 100 g). Watercress collected in the wild can transmit parasites.

Rorippa nasturtium-aquaticum (L.) Hayek (= *Nasturtium officinale* R. Br.)   family: Brassicaceae

xi yang cai, dou ban cai (Chinese); *cresson de fontaine* (French); *Brunnenkresse* (German); *crescione acquatico* (Italian); *mizu garashi* (Japanese); *selada air* (Malay); *agrião* (Portuguese); *berro* (Spanish)

Rosa canina

dog rose

Dog rose plant

Dog rose flowers and dry hips

Rosa rugosa with hips

DESCRIPTION A woody creeper with thorny stems, compound leaves and attractive pink flowers. The fleshy red fruits are actually berry-like receptacles that surround the seeds. Several species provide hips and petals (see below).

ORIGIN & HISTORY *R. canina* is indigenous to Europe and Asia, while *R. rugosa* occurs naturally in China, Japan and Korea. Rose-hips have a long history of food use in Europe, China and Japan. The hips of *R. rugosa*, for example, are a traditional food of the indigenous Ainu people of Japan. Vitamin-rich extracts of the hips of *R. roxburghii* are a nutritional supplement in China.

PARTS USED The hips and petals.

CULTIVATION & HARVESTING Rose-hips are collected from wild plants of *R. canina* and wild or cultivated *R. rugosa*. Rose petals are collected from the common rose (*R. gallica*), cabbage rose (*R. x centifolia*) and damask rose (*R. x damascena*).

USES & PROPERTIES Rose-hips are widely used to make jams, preserves, jellies and sauces. Hips of the Japanese rose are used to flavour Chinese wine. Rose petals add flavour to confectionery and creams, may be candied or turned into rose-petal jam, a delicacy of the Balkan region and the Middle East. Petals also yield rose water and rose essence, used to flavour rose wines, jellies, creams, sorbets, sweets, ices, pastries and cakes (such as *loukoum*). Rosebuds are boiled in honey to make rose honey. The petals are crushed in wine vinegar and steeped in the sun to make rose vinegar. Dried and powdered rosebuds are an ingredient of *ras al-hanout*, a spice mixture containing cinnamon, cloves and black pepper, which is used for Moroccan and Tunisian ragouts and other North African dishes.

NUTRITIONAL VALUE Rose-hips are exceptionally rich in vitamin C (250–2 900 mg per 100 g), lycopene and other carotenoids and gamma-linolenic acid (in the seeds).

Rosa canina L.   family: Rosaceae

églantier (French); *Hundsrose, Gemeine Heckenrose* (German); *rosa canina* (Italian); *escaramujo* (Spanish)

Rosmarinus officinalis

rosemary

Rosemary leaves and flowers

DESCRIPTION An aromatic, evergreen shrub with narrow leaves that are bright green above, with rolled in margins and white hairs below. The small, two-lipped flowers are various shades of blue and purple (rarely pink or white).

ORIGIN & HISTORY Indigenous to the Mediterranean region. Rosemary was well known to the Greeks and Romans, who used it for ritual purposes during weddings and funerals. It has a long history of use as medicinal plant and only later became important as a culinary herb.

PARTS USED Fresh or dried leaves.

CULTIVATION & HARVESTING Rosemary is widely cultivated in kitchen gardens and market gardens. The leaves are harvested and sold fresh or may be dried and packed. Commercial cultivation is often aimed at the production of essential oil, which is widely used in cosmetics, perfumery and aromatherapy.

USES & PROPERTIES Leaves are used sparingly to flavour meat dishes, especially game, grills, sausage meat, ragouts, stews, marinades, sauces, soups, salads and salad dressings. It goes well with lamb, pork, veal, fish and poultry. The sharp, spicy flavour makes it a popular addition to patés and pasta sauces (especially tomato sauces). It adds a subtle flavour to herb butter or to milk used for desserts. Fresh flowers make a fine garnish for salads and candied (crystallised) flowers are used to decorate confectionery. Rosemary is one of 27 flavour ingredients of Bénédictine, a famous French liqueur used as a digestive.

NUTRITIONAL VALUE Unimportant (used sparingly for flavour).

NOTES Rosemary is used in general tonics and antimicrobial and spasmolytic preparations. Rosemary oil is used externally in ointments and baths to stimulate blood circulation and to give relief from muscle aches and joint pains. The related lavender (*Lavandula* species) has similar uses but is rarely used in cooking (to flavour jellies and tisanes).

Rosmarinus officinalis L.   family: Lamiaceae

romarin (French); *Rosmarin* (German); *rosmarino* (Italian); *roméro* (Spanish)

Rubus chamaemorus

cloudberry

Cloudberry plants

Cloudberry fruit

Cloudberry flower

Cloudberry product

DESCRIPTION A small creeping perennial with slender branches of up to 0.2 m in height bearing a few simple, three- to five-lobed, slightly hairy leaves. Male and female flowers occur on separate plants. They are small, with five white petals and five persistent green sepals (similar to strawberry flowers). The fruit is an attractive, yellow to bright orange, compound berry with 20 or more small, fleshy segments (drupelets). The above-ground parts die back after fruiting.

ORIGIN & HISTORY Cloudberry is restricted to the Arctic polar region and adjoining cold temperate parts of northern Europe, Asia and America. The fruits have been wild-harvested by indigenous people such as the Sami (previously known as Lapps) and Inuit since ancient times. In recent years cloudberry has become a minor commercial product, especially popular in Sweden, Norway and Denmark.

PARTS USED Ripe fruits.

CULTIVATION & HARVESTING Cloudberry thrives in the boreal region with its short but intensive growing season when it receives sunshine virtually 24 hours per day. It is not cultivated but is wild-harvested just before winter. Ripe fruits are carefully hand-picked – a very labour-intensive activity.

USES & PROPERTIES Cloudberries are a delicacy that may be eaten raw or preserved by cooking in sugar syrup. They may also be frozen and used for many months. The fruits make a delicious jam and in recent times have become a popular addition to fruit yogurts and fruit juices. They are also used in fruit salads and as a side dish with various meat dishes. Fresh or preserved fruits make a tasty ingredient and attractive decoration for desserts, pastries, tarts and cakes.

NUTRITIONAL VALUE Cloudberries are very rich in vitamin C (105 mg per 100 g) and are still an important source of this vitamin in an area where fresh fruits are relatively scarce.

Rubus chamaemorus L.   family: Rosaceae

Moltebeere, Arktische Brombeere (German); *hjortron* (Swedish)

327

Rubus fruticosus

blackberry • bramble

Blackberry flowers and fruits

Blackberry plant

Thornless blackberry

DESCRIPTION A prickly shrub of up to 3 m in height bearing compound leaves with small thorns along the midribs and sparse hairs on the lower surfaces. The flowers are white or pale pink and the fruits are initially bright red but turn dark reddish purplish to black when they ripen. They are produced on side shoots in the second year of growth. Blackberry is a complex of numerous species and hybrids, some of which are listed under loganberry (see *R. loganobaccus*).

ORIGIN & HISTORY Blackberry is indigenous to Europe and the Mediterranean region and has become naturalised in many parts of the world, where it often hybridises with local species. Blackberries have always been gathered in the wild. Cultivation and cultivar development started relatively recently (about 150 years ago) both in Europe and North America. Related species that are significant in the development of commercial crops include the European *R. laciniatus* and *R. ulmifolius*, as well as the North American *R. allegheniensis*. Thornless cultivars, usually derived from *R. laciniatus*, have become quite popular.

PARTS USED Ripe fruits.

CULTIVATION & HARVESTING Commercial cultivation is mainly centred in the USA, New Zealand and parts of Europe. Large quantities of blackberries are also harvested in the wild, especially in Europe.

USES & PROPERTIES Fruits are eaten fresh, often with sugar and cream, as a delicious dessert. They are processed into jams, preserves, jellies, purées, syrups, juice, blackberry wine, *ratafia*, *schnapps* and liqueur. Fresh or preserved berries are used in tarts, pie fillings, cakes and other confectionery.

NUTRITIONAL VALUE The fruits have a low energy value (37 kcal per 100 g) because of the rather low sugar content (5%). They are rich in organic acids (citric and malic acid), with moderate amounts of vitamins B and C (15–17 mg per 100 g).

Rubus fruticosus L.

family: Rosaceae

ronce noire, mûre sauvage (French); *Brombeere* (German); *rovo* (Italian); *zarzamora* (Spanish)

Rubus idaeus

raspberry

Raspberry leaves and fruits

Raspberry plants

Raspberries

DESCRIPTION A lax shrub with sparsely thorny stems and compound leaves with white, densely hairy lower surfaces. The flowers are pale pink or white and the reddish pink fruits are unique as they come free from the stalk (receptacle) at maturity.

ORIGIN & HISTORY Raspberry is indigenous to Europe, Asia and North America. Although wild forms have been used since ancient times, raspberry only became a crop during the Middle Ages and cultivars only made their appearance late in the eighteenth century. The black-fruited American raspberry (*R. occidentalis*) first gave rise to cultivated forms with purple fruits, which were later used to produce modern cultivars through hybridisation and backcrossing. Raspberry is today an important commercial crop, with an annual production of nearly 300 000 tons. The main production areas are Russia, Europe (especially central and eastern Europe, but also France and England), the USA and Canada.

PARTS USED Ripe fruits.

CULTIVATION & HARVESTING Raspberries are relatively easy to grow in temperate regions. Fruits are normally produced on one-year-old stems (canes) but modern cultivars also give fruits in the first year of growth.

USES & PROPERTIES Raspberries are eaten fresh and are used in fruit salads and desserts, often served with sugar and cream. They are considered to be one of the most delicious of all dessert fruits. Raspberries are an important source of juice for the fruit juice industry and an equally important flavouring agent for a wide range of food products and beverages. Other uses include jams, jellies, purées, compotes, syrups, fermented drinks, liqueurs and brandies.

NUTRITIONAL VALUE Raspberries have a low energy value (25 kcal per 100 g) but are rich in minerals (especially calcium, phosphorus and iron), dietary fibre and vitamin C (25 mg per 100 g).

NOTES Fermented and dried raspberry leaves are used in traditional medicine as an astringent.

Rubus idaeus L.   family: Rosaceae

fu pen zi, shan mei (Chinese); *framboise* (French); *Himbeere* (German); *lampone* (Italian); *yezo ichigo* (Japanese); *frambuesa* (Spanish)

Rubus loganobaccus
loganberry

Wild bramble

Loganberry flowers and fruits

Loganberries

DESCRIPTION Loganberry is a scrambling shrub with relatively large, soft, compound leaves, white flowers and oblong, dull red fruit. Loganberry is just one of a large number of species, hybrids and cultivars with edible berries, often loosely referred to as brambles. Wineberry (*R. phoenicolasius*) is a Chinese and Japanese species with thornless stems and orange berries. The Japanese strawberry-raspberry (*R. illecebrosus*) is a creeping plant with red berries. Youngberry is a hybrid between *R. vitifolius* and *R. caesius* and is sometimes called "South African loganberry". Boysenberry is a large black berry thought to have originated as a loganberry backcrossed with one of its two parents (blackberry and raspberry) and is similar to loganberry. Some forms of boysenberry have no thorns. Tayberry is a complex hybrid involving veitchberry (*R. ulmifolius*), sunberry (a hybrid with *R. vitifolius*) and an American blackberry. Hildaberry is a hybrid between tayberry and boysenberry.

ORIGIN & HISTORY Loganberry originated as a cross between a blackberry (see *R. fruticosus*) and a raspberry (see *R. idaeus*). It was named after James H. Logan, who produced it in California in 1881.

PARTS USED Ripe fruits.

CULTIVATION & HARVESTING Loganberry is one of many hybrids and cultivars that are grown commercially for fruit production. Modern hybrids (such as tayberry and hildaberry) are more resistant to diseases and are nowadays preferred for commercial production.

USES & PROPERTIES Loganberries have a delicious, tart taste and are eaten fresh or are used in fruit salads, desserts, jams, jellies, sauces, syrups and juices. It is used in much the same way as raspberry and blackberry.

NUTRITIONAL VALUE Loganberry and boysenberry are low in energy (33 kcal per 100 g) but rich in minerals and organic acids. They contain moderate levels of vitamin C (15–25 mg per 100 g).

Rubus loganobaccus L. Bailey

family: Rosaceae

Loganbeere (German)

Rumex acetosa

sorrel

Sorrel plants

Sorrel flowers

Sorrel leaves

DESCRIPTION Sorrel is a weedy perennial herb with soft, hairless, spear-shaped leaves with distinct pointed lobes or ears on either side of the attachment of the leaf stalk. Inconspicuous flowers are borne in slender clusters. A second popular species is French sorrel (*R. scutatus*), easily distinguished by the crispy or wavy leaf margins. It is available in green and purple forms.

ORIGIN & HISTORY The plant is indigenous to Europe and northern Asia. Sorrel is a common wild plant that has been used since ancient times as a pot-herb (also by the Egyptians, Greeks and Romans) and for making an early spring soup. The cultivated form is sometimes considered to be a separate species, *R. rugosus*.

PARTS USED Fresh leaves.

CULTIVATION & HARVESTING Sorrel is easily grown from seeds or by cuttings or division. It is common in kitchen gardens but is also available on fresh produce markets. In many parts of Europe, sorrel leaves are wild-harvested.

USES & PROPERTIES Sorrel leaves have a sour and bitter taste due to the presence of oxalic acid. They have numerous culinary uses, especially in the French tradition. The leaves, usually with the stalks removed, are cooked in the same way as spinach. They may be shredded or puréed, often enhanced with cream, a white sauce or a white *roux*. Fresh, young and tender leaves are added to salads. Sorrel is traditionally served with fish, veal and egg dishes. It may be used as a filling for omelettes and for *velouté* soup.

NUTRITIONAL VALUE Sorrel leaves have a low energy value (only 25 kcal per 100 g) but are very nutritious. They have high levels of vitamins A (3.5 mg) and C (47 mg) and are rich in potassium and magnesium.

NOTES Sorrel juice is said to have been used to remove stains from linen.

Rumex acetosa L. (= *R. rugosus* Campd.)   family: Polygonaceae

oseille (French); *Sauerampfer* (German); *acetosa* (Italian); *acedera* (Spanish)

Ruta graveolens

rue • herb of grace

Rue flowering plant

Rue fruiting plant

Rue flowers and fruits

DESCRIPTION A strong-smelling perennial shrub with woody branches and irregularly divided, compound, grey-green leaves covered with minute, translucent glands. The small flowers have four or five bright yellow petals with hairy margins and the fruits are gland-dotted, four-lobed capsules. A second species, the Mediterranean Aleppo rue (*R. chalepensis*) is used in the same way.

ORIGIN & HISTORY Rue is indigenous to southern Europe and has been grown since ancient times as pot-herb and traditional herbal tonic. It is mentioned in the Bible and was known to the famous Roman writer Pliny the Elder (AD 23–79). Rue was used in church ceremonies in England and became known as "herb of grace".

PARTS USED Fresh leaves.

CULTIVATION & HARVESTING Rue is easily grown from seeds or cuttings. It is not commercially available but is grown in kitchen gardens and herb gardens in most parts of the world.

USES & PROPERTIES Rue leaves have a bitter and pungent taste but are used sparingly as a pot-herb in Europe, North America, Malaysia and China. In Singapore, Chinese cooks use it with green beans. It is traditionally used to flavour sausage meat and meat stuffings. In Eastern Europe it is used in marinades (especially for game) and cream cheeses. Italians use it to flavour *grappa della ruta* (a marc brandy) by putting a small bunch of leaves into the bottle. Rue is especially well known for its use in hippocras – a medieval homemade spicy drink produced from red or white wine mixed with various fruits, herbs and spices. It is sweetened, filtered and served cool or iced before or after a meal.

NUTRITIONAL VALUE Unimportant, as rue is used only in small amounts. It should be noted that rue is poisonous in high doses and that it may cause severe skin irritation in sensitive people. Commercial use is banned in France.

Ruta graveolens L.   family: Rutaceae

chou cao (Chinese); *rue* (French); *Weinraute* (German); *ruta* (Italian); *duan aroda* (Malay); *ruda común* (Spanish)

Saccharum officinarum

sugar cane

Sugar cane plants

Sugar cane plantations

Sugar cane (Malaysian cultivar)

DESCRIPTION Sugar cane is a large perennial grass of 3 to 6 m in height. It has thick, hard, juicy stems that may be green, yellow or purple and occasionally bear plumes of small pink flowers.

ORIGIN & HISTORY *S. officinarum* is a cultigen selected in New Guinea as a chewing cane. It has a long and complicated history of domestication, involving hybridisation with species such as *S. spontaneum*, *S. sinense* and *S. barberi*. Since at least 2500 BC the crop has radiated out to the Pacific region, Southeast Asia and India, where crude sugar (*gur, jaggery*) was first produced. Later it spread to China, North Africa, Madagascar and the Mediterranean region, where it was first cultivated on a commercial scale. Plantations were established in the West Indies, Caribbean, Brazil and the USA. Several countries around the world (especially Brazil and India) now produce more than 1 billion tons per year. An additional 250 million tons come from sugar beet.

PARTS USED Stems.

CULTIVATION & HARVESTING Stem cuttings are planted in frost-free areas with high rainfall and fertile soil. The cut canes are crushed and the sugary juice (15% sucrose) concentrated by evaporation and centrifuged to separate the brown syrupy molasses from the crude sugar, which is purified by repeated crystallisation.

USES & PROPERTIES Various forms of cane sugar are used in large quantities in the food industry to manufacture confectionery, jams, ice creams, tinned fruits, carbonated drinks, syrups, sweet wines, liqueurs and many other products. Syrup and molasses are fermented to produce rum and other cane spirits. Sugar has countless uses in cookery and confectionery to preserve, sweeten and to enhance flavour.

NUTRITIONAL VALUE Cane sugar yields 375 kcal per 100 g. It is digested to glucose (essential for healthy living, has to be maintained at 1 g per litre blood).

Saccharum officinale L.   family: Poaceae

hong gan zhe (Chinese); *canne à sucre* (French); *Zuckerrohr* (German); *tebu* (Indonesian); *canna da zucchero* (Italian); *satou kibi* (Japanese); *cana de açúcar* (Portuguese); *caña de azúcar* (Spanish)

Salacca zalacca
salak

Salak fruits

Salak palm

Salak fruits showing fleshy segments

DESCRIPTION A nearly stemless palm with large, feathery leaves and clothed with many sharp spines. Male and female flowers are borne on separate trees. Bunches of fruits are formed in the crown of the female palms. They are pear-shaped, with a smooth and conspicuously scaly skin that peels away easily to reveal three or four yellowish-white, fleshy segments, each containing a single, shiny, brown seed. Another species with edible fruits is the rakum palm (*S. wallichiana*) that is grown in Thailand. It is known as *rekam* in Malay and *sala* or *rakam* in Thai and several cultivars have been developed. Palm hearts are obtained from *S. zalacca* (also known as *salak* in Malay and Indonesian), *S. conferta* (*kelubi* in Malay) and *S. vermicularis* (*kepela* in Malay).

ORIGIN & HISTORY *S. zalacca* is indigenous to Malaysia and is widely cultivated in Southeast Asia (for example on Bali and other parts of Indonesia).

PARTS USED Ripe fruits.

CULTIVATION & HARVESTING Salak palms are usually grown from seeds but in *S. flabellata* the flower cluster will develop roots and form new plants. The ripe fruits are carefully harvested to avoid the sharp spines. Unripe fruits are astringent (they contain high levels of tannins) and are not edible. The fruits are sometimes called snake fruit because of the remarkable shiny, scaly skin. They are commonly seen on fresh produce markets in Malaysia and Indonesia.

USES & PROPERTIES The ripe fruit flesh has a somewhat dry but crisp texture (like a raw carrot) and a slightly nutty taste but is neither sweet nor sour. Fruits are usually eaten fresh and may also be added to fruit salads.

NUTRITIONAL VALUE No reliable information could be found on the nutritional properties of salak fruits.

NOTES The leaf stalks of *Salacca* species are often used to construct walls and partitions.

Salacca zalacca (Gaertner) Voss (= *Salacca edulis* Reinw.)   family: Arecaceae (Palmae)

ke shi sa la ka zong (Chinese); *palmier à peau de serpent* (French); *Salakpalme* (German); *sarakka yashi* (Japanese); *salak* (Malay); *fruta cobra* (Portuguese); *salaca* (Spanish); *sala, rakam* (Thai)

Salvia officinalis

sage

Sage leaves and flowers

Clary sage plant

DESCRIPTION Sage is a perennial shrublet (up to 0.6 m) with square stems and opposite, coarsely textured, grey leaves. Attractive purplish blue flowers are borne in elongated clusters. A close relative with similar culinary uses is Greek sage (*S. fruticosa*), with characteristic lobed leaf bases. It is a common adulterant of dried sage and is used in local drinks in Cyprus. Another is clary sage (*S. sclarea*), which has large green leaves, violet bracts and white and blue flowers. The essential oil is used to flavour vermouth and liqueurs.

ORIGIN & HISTORY Sage is indigenous to southern Europe and the eastern Mediterranean region. Greek sage grows naturally in the eastern Mediterranean region (Italy and Greece to Syria), while clary sage occurs from southern Europe to central Asia. Sage has a long history as a medicinal plant (*salvus* is Latin for healthy). Commercial cultivation occurs in the Mediterranean region, eastern Europe, Asia and the USA.

PARTS USED Fresh or dried leaves.

CULTIVATION & HARVESTING Plants are easily propagated from seeds or cuttings. They prefer alkaline (lime-rich) soils.

USES & PROPERTIES Sage has a strong, aromatic and slightly bitter flavour and is traditionally used to season roast meats, game, liver, poultry, stuffings, fish, marinades, omelettes, vegetables, salads, sauces, soups and some cheeses. The herb is especially popular in Italian cooking and is an essential ingredient of *osso bucco* (unboned veal knuckle braised in white wine with onion and tomato), *piccata* (small, round veal slices fried in butter and served with lemon or *marsala* – a Sicilian fortified wine) and *saltimbocca alla romana* (veal slices and ham topped with sage leaves). In Tuscany, sage is used to flavour white haricot beans (*fagioli*).

NUTRITIONAL VALUE Used for flavour only. Large doses taken for prolonged periods may be harmful due to the presence of thujone (a known neurotoxin).

Salvia officinalis L.   family: Lamiaceae

sauge officinale, sauge commune (French); *Echter Salbei, Gartensalbei* (German); *salvia* (Italian); *salvia official* (Spanish)

Sambucus nigra

elderberry

Elderberry leaves and flowers

Elderberry plantation

Elderberry fruits

DESCRIPTION A shrub or small tree (up to 6 m) with sparsely branched, pithy stems, compound leaves and small white flowers in flat-topped clusters. The fruits are shiny, fleshy, black drupes, each with three seeds. It is similar to the American elder (*S. canadensis*), an ornamental shrub that also produces edible fruits. The berries of grape elder (*S. racemosa*) are gathered and processed into juice, jellies or jams.

ORIGIN & HISTORY Common elderberry is indigenous to North Africa, Europe and Asia. Grape elder is Eurasian, while American elder occurs naturally in the eastern parts of North America.

PARTS USED Ripe fruits or flowers (rarely the stems).

CULTIVATION & HARVESTING Berries and flowers are often wild-harvested but elderberries are grown in plantations in Europe. The flowers are harvested and sieved to remove the stalks from the fused petals (corollas), which is the part mostly used. The berries are hand-picked when ripe.

USES & PROPERTIES The aromatic flowers (actually only the petals) are made into fritters (mixed with egg and flour) or they are used to flavour jams, vinegars and fermented drinks. The ripe berries, or flowers soaked in sugar water, are fermented to make wine and distilled for alcoholic drinks such as *sambuca*. This strong, sweet, colourless, Italian anise liqueur is usually served *con la mosca* – "with the fly" – meaning with a coffee bean. The bitterness of the coffee bean perfectly counteracts the sweet taste of the *sambuca*. Ripe elderberries, with seeds removed, are used in jams, jellies and apple pies. They are sometimes used to add colour to port wine. Young shoots contain a soft, edible core (*moelle de sureau*) that is served like asparagus by French cooks.

NUTRITIONAL VALUE Elderberries are low in sugar (about 6%) and energy value (64 kcal per 100 g) and contain some vitamin C (18 mg per 100 g).

Sambucus nigra L.

family: Caprifoliaceae

grand sureau (French); *Schwarzer Holunder* (German); *sambuco* (Italian); *sabuco* (Spanish)

Sanguisorba minor
salad burnet

Salad burnet leaf and flower heads

Salad burnet plant

Burnet (greater burnet)

DESCRIPTION This is a small, perennial, rosette-forming herb with compound, fern-like leaves comprising several pairs of toothed leaflets. The inconspicuous reddish flowers are wind-pollinated. They are grouped into dense rounded heads borne on slender stalks that arise from the middle of the rosette. Salad burnet may be confused with burnet (also called garden burnet or greater burnet), *S. officinalis*. This is a much taller plant with oblong, purplish flower heads. Both species are sometimes included in the genus *Poterium*.

ORIGIN & HISTORY Salad burnet is indigenous to central and southern Europe. It was once a very popular culinary herb and is still commonly seen in herb gardens. *S. officinalis* is indigenous to Europe and Asia, and is naturalised in North America.

PARTS USED Fresh leaves.

CULTIVATION & HARVESTING The fresh or dried herb is not readily available and usually has to be grown for own use. It is easily propagated from seeds.

USES & PROPERTIES Fresh leaves are said to have a cucumber-like or nutty taste and are added to salads, cheeses and herb butter. In French cooking, they are used in soups, cold sauces, marinades and omelettes, as well as in fresh salads, in the same way as watercress. The herb is also used to flavour vinegar and may be added to cold drinks in the same way as borage. The leaves can be pickled for use throughout the year.

NUTRITIONAL VALUE As is the case with most leafy vegetables, the herb is low in energy value but rich in minerals and folic acid.

NOTES The dried roots and rhizomes of *S. minor* have been used in traditional medicine (in Europe and China) in much the same way as those of *S. officinalis*, namely to stop bleeding. The generic name *sanguis* (blood) and *sorbeo* (absorb) refers to this traditional use.

Sanguisorba minor Scop. (= *Poterium sanguisorba* L.)   family: Rosaceae

pimprenelle (French); *Bibernelle, Pimpernell, Kleiner Wiesenknopf* (German); *pimpinella* (Italian)

Satureja hortensis

summer savory

Summer savory leaves

Summer savory leaves and flowers

Winter savory leaves and flowers

DESCRIPTION Summer savory is an annual herb that forms a small, erect bush bearing narrow leaves in opposite pairs. Small pink flowers are borne along the stem tips. It is similar to winter savory (*S. montana*) but the latter is a perennial with a spreading growth form. Winter savory is also easily recognised by the smaller, stiffer, more sharply pointed leaves and the white flowers.

ORIGIN & HISTORY Summer savory is indigenous to southeastern Europe, while winter savory occurs in the Mediterranean region (southern Europe and North Africa).

PARTS USED Fresh or dried stem tips with leaves.

CULTIVATION & HARVESTING Both species are easily cultivated from seeds sown in spring (*S. montana* is often grown from cuttings). The stem tips are harvested and used fresh (the best way) or are dried.

USES & PROPERTIES Fresh summer savory is traditionally used to flavour beans and bean dishes (pulses), especially broad beans. It is a popular addition to salads, mushroom dishes, ragouts, grilled veal, roast lamb and loin of pork. When dried, the herb can be used to flavour peas, stews, ragouts, soups, patés and stuffings (forcemeats). The dried herb is commonly added to spice mixtures and dried herbal mixtures. Winter savory is said to have an inferior flavour but is nevertheless traditionally used to flavour certain marinades and soft cheeses made from goats' milk or sheep's milk. The flavour of summer savory is similar to that of mint and thyme.

NUTRITIONAL VALUE The small quantities used do not contribute much to nutrition.

NOTES The Latin *satureia* (meaning satyr's herb) refers to the alleged aphrodisiac properties the herb was once thought to have. Summer savory is mixed with honey and taken as tea to treat coughs and asthma. Winter savory is used to alleviate stomach disorders. The essential oil of both species has application in cosmetics, soaps and washing powders.

Satureja hortensis L.   family: Lamiaceae

sarriette (French); *Bohnenkraut* (German); *santoreggia* (Italian); *ajedrea* (Spanish)

Schinziophyton rautanenii
manketti tree • mongongo

Manketti tree

Manketti fruits and nuts

Manketti leaves and fruit

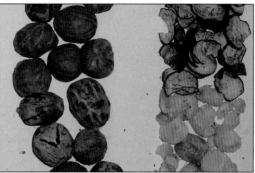

Manketti seeds (with and without seed coat)

DESCRIPTION A large, summer-deciduous tree with a rounded crown and hand-shaped leaves (each with five to seven large stalked leaflets). Male and female flowers, yellow in colour, are borne on separate trees. The fruits are egg-shaped, velvety in texture and have a thin layer of flesh around the hard pitted shell that covers the nutritious nut.

ORIGIN & HISTORY The tree is indigenous to southern Africa (Namibia, Botswana, Zimbabwe and Mozambique). It has been a staple food of the indigenous people for at least 7 000 years. Attempts at cultivating the tree have so far not been very successful.

PARTS USED Ripe fruits (mainly the oily nut, also the fruit flesh).

CULTIVATION & HARVESTING The manketti tree requires a hot subtropical climate to thrive. It is not cultivated except on an experimental scale.

USES & PROPERTIES The fruits are cooked to remove the maroon-coloured flesh from the hard inner nuts, which is eaten on its own or as a relish with other dishes. The roasted nuts are very tasty and are consumed in large numbers as a staple food. They are pounded and mixed with other ingredients to make a variety of traditional dishes. Both fruit and nut are nutritious and valuable because they dry out and remain edible for a large part of the year.

NUTRITIONAL VALUE The fruits and especially the nuts are highly nutritious. The energy value of the nuts is 645 kcal per 100 g (the fruit pulp 336 kcal per 100 g). The protein content of the nuts is 26% and the fat content 58%. Both the nuts and the fruit pulp are rich in minerals and thiamin, while the vitamin C content of the fruit pulp is 27 mg per 100 g.

NOTES The oil of the nuts is used as a traditional cosmetic to soften and moisten the skin.

Schinziophyton rautanenii (Schinz) Radcliffe-Sm. (= *Ricinodendron rautanenii* Schinz)family: Euphorbiaceae

manketti (Afrikaans); *Mankettibaum* (German); *mokongwa, monghònghò* (Tswana)

Sclerocarya birrea
marula tree

Marula flowers

Marula fruits

Marula leaves and fruits

DESCRIPTION A large tree of up to 15 m tall with a rounded crown and compound leaves comprising ten or more pairs of sharply pointed leaflets. Male and female flowers usually occur on separate trees. The large, rounded and slightly flattened fruits are greenish-yellow when ripe, with a juicy layer of flesh surrounding the single, large bony seed. Each seed or stone contains three oblong nuts that are covered by a small, round bony "lid" that becomes detached when the stone is cracked.

ORIGIN & HISTORY Widely distributed in tropical and subtropical Africa. This important fruit tree has been used as a food source by local people since ancient times. Experimental plantings indicate that the marula has potential to become a cultivated, multi-purpose fruit crop.

PARTS USED Ripe fruits and seeds (nuts).

CULTIVATION & HARVESTING Marula is still mainly wild-harvested but grafted trees have yielded 500 kg of fruit per year and selected types bear large fruits (nearly 100 g each). The fruits are never picked but simply gathered as they fall to the ground in large numbers when they ripen.

USES & PROPERTIES Marula fruits are delicious to eat raw and may be processed into traditional beer or marula wine (known locally as *mokhope* or *ubuganu*), jellies, jams, preserves, syrups, sweets and vinegar. Marula fruit pulp is used to flavour Amarula, a cream liqueur. The nuts are difficult to extract but they are very tasty and yield valuable oil.

NUTRITIONAL VALUE The fresh fruits have an energy value of 54 kcal per 100 g. The pulp is exceptionally rich in vitamin C (194 mg per 100 g; after fermentation, the beer or wine still contains 49 mg per 100 g). The nuts have a high energy value of 643 kcal per 100 g and comprise 28% protein and 57% fat.

Sclerocarya birrea (A. Rich.) Hochst. (= *S. caffra* Sond.)   family: Anacardiaceae

marula (French); *Marulabaum* (German); *marula* (Italian, Spanish); *morula* (Sotho); *umganu* (Zulu)

Scorzonera hispanica
scorzonera • black salsify

Scorzonera flowers

Scorzonera leaves and flowers

Scorzonera roots

DESCRIPTION Scorzonera is a hardy perennial plant with a rosette of oblong, hairy leaves growing from a cylindrical, fleshy, black taproot. A long, thin, sparsely leafy flowering stalk emerges in summer. It bears yellow flower heads on slender stalks that closely resemble dandelions. A close relative with similar uses is salsify or oyster plant (*Tragopogon porrifolius*; *Haferwurzel* in German, *salsifis* in French and *salsifi blanco* in Italian and Spanish). It differs in the purple flower heads and whitish roots.

ORIGIN & HISTORY Indigenous to southern Europe, salsify to the Mediterranean region. Both have been brought into cultivation relatively recently, perhaps in the sixteenth century. These plants are occasionally grown for commercial use but are more often seen in kitchen gardens.

PARTS USED Mainly the carrot-like roots (sometimes the leaves).

CULTIVATION & HARVESTING Scorzonera and salsify are grown from seed sown in spring. The roots may be harvested at the end of the first season but can also be left for winter use. Both these root vegetables are in season between October and March.

USES & PROPERTIES Salsify and scorzonera (black salsify) have a similar slightly bitter taste and are prepared in exactly the same way. The roots are scraped or peeled, sliced into sections and then cooked, steamed or sautéed and served with white meat dishes. Cooked and puréed root may be coated with flour and deep-fried in oil to make salsify fritters. The cooked roots and fresh leaves may be added to salads. Roasted roots have been used as coffee substitute, in the same way as chicory.

NUTRITIONAL VALUE The roots contain inulin instead of starch as storage carbohydrate. When digested, it yields fructose and not glucose and is therefore ideally suited for use by diabetics. The roots are also rich in dietary fibre and contain small amounts of minerals and vitamins A and C.

Scorzonera hispanica L. family: Asteraceae

ou zhou ya cong (Chinese); *scorsonère* (French); *Schwarzwurzel* (German); *scorzonera* (Italian); *kiku gobou* (Japanese); *escorcioneira* (Portuguese); *salsifi negro* (Spanish)

Secale cereale

rye

Rye ears

Rye plants

Rye grains (left), *triticale* and bread wheat

DESCRIPTION A tall annual grass (up to 2 m) with blue-green leaves and long angular spikes that are typically curved (arched) at maturity. Each of the dry, one-seeded fruits is enclosed in a bract (lemma) with a long awn. *Triticale* is an artificial hybrid between *Triticum* (wheat) and *Secale* (rye) that combines the hardiness of rye with the nutritional value and baking qualities of wheat.

ORIGIN & HISTORY Rye is derived from the perennial *S. montanum*, a weed of wheat and barley. *S. montanum* is distributed from the Mediterranean region to Iran, Iraq and eastern Turkey, where is it believed that *S. cereale* was selected from several weedy annual forms that occur in the Middle Eastern region. It spread to northern Europe and northwestern Asia before the Iron Age and became an important staple food.

PARTS USED Ripe grains (dry, one-seeded fruits).

CULTIVATION & HARVESTING Rye is more cold tolerant and drought resistant than other cereals and can be grown on poor sandy soils.

USES & PROPERTIES Rye is traditionally used to bake dark bread (*Schwarzbrot*, pumpernickel) that has a slightly sour taste and a heavy but friable texture. The flour is usually mixed with wheat flour to improve the baking properties (rye has no gluten) and is used in some types of bread, rye rolls, gingerbread and certain cakes and confectionery. Rye is used to make the popular Scandinavian crispbreads (*knäckebrot*) with their delicious flavour, crisp texture and excellent storage properties. It is also used in breakfast cereals and in muesli. Malted or non-malted rye is used to make American rye whisky, Dutch gin and Russian beer and vodka.

NUTRITIONAL VALUE Rye has less protein than other cereals but is rich in minerals and vitamin B. The energy value is 335 kcal per 100 g.

NOTES Ergot poisoning is due to a fungus that grows on rye.

Secale cereale L.　　　　　　　　　　　　　　　　　　family: Poaceae

seigle (French); *Roggen* (German); *segale* (Italian); *centeno* (Spanish)

Sechium edule

chayote • vegetable pear

Chayote plant

Chayote flower

Chayote fruits

DESCRIPTION A vigorous climber with long stems arising from a tuberous root and bearing large, soft leaves, small yellow flowers and distinctive pear-shaped fruits that vary from smooth to spiny or warty and green to white. The plant resembles pumpkin and cucumber but the one-seeded fruit is unique. Many vernacular names exist in various parts of the world, including custard marrow, Madeira marrow, *choko, mirliton, choco, cho-cho, chow chow, shu-shu, huisquil* and *guisqil.*

ORIGIN & HISTORY The crop developed in Central America (probably Mexico, where seemingly wild plants with bitter fruits are still found). The plant was known to the Aztecs in pre-Columbian times but its exact age and history are poorly recorded.

PARTS USED Ripe or unripe fruits, tubers and young stems.

CULTIVATION & HARVESTING Chayote is easily grown in tropical and subtropical regions throughout the world. The large seed germinates while the fruit is still attached to the vine (viviparous) and the whole fruit is planted.

USES & PROPERTIES All parts of the plant are eaten, but the fruits, with their bland, sweetish taste are best known in cookery (especially in Caribbean and Malaysian dishes). Raw, slightly unripe fruits may be thinly sliced and added to salads or they are cooked and eaten as a vegetable. Fruits may be hollowed out and stuffed with various spicy ingredients, after which they are baked in the oven. They may also be chopped, boiled, sautéed or puréed and are especially popular as an ingredient of *acras* (spicy fritters), soufflés, pork curries, vegetable stews (ragouts) and gratins. Chayote is considered an essential ingredient of a dish known as *mange-mèle* (*ratatouille* with bacon and coconut milk).

NUTRITIONAL VALUE Fruits have a low energy value (12–15 kcal per 100 g). They add modest quantities of proteins (0.1%), minerals (0.3%), fat (6%) and vitamin C (6–17 mg) to the diet.

Sechium edule (Jacq.) Sw.

family: Cucurbitaceae

fo shou gua, sun ren gua, li gua (Chinese); *chayote, christophine* (French); *Chayote* (German); *saiotta* (Italian); *hayato uri* (Japanese); *alcaiota, chuchú* (Portuguese); *chayote, chayotera* (Spanish)

343

Sesamum indicum

sesame

Sesame seed capsules

Sesame leaves and flowers

Sesame seeds

DESCRIPTION An erect annual plant (up to 2 m) bearing oblong leaves and pale pink to purple flowers in the axils of the leaves, close to the stem. The oval seeds are black, red, brown or white and are borne in oblong seed capsules.

ORIGIN & HISTORY Sesame is an ancient cultigen of unknown origin. Archaeological and linguistic evidence suggest that the origin was in East Africa or India. It was recorded on Assyrian clay tablets and in early Greek writings. Sesame is an important oilseed, with more than 2 million tons produced each year, mainly in India, China, Sudan and Myanmar.

PARTS USED Ripe seeds.

CULTIVATION & HARVESTING Plants are grown from seeds in all warm climatic regions. They do not tolerate frost or being waterlogged. Mechanical harvesting is problematic, as the capsules progressively mature from the bottom up.

USES & PROPERTIES The seeds are eaten raw or roasted, or used for cooking oil (especially in Arab, Chinese and Japanese cooking) or in confectionery (sprinkled on bread and cakes like poppy seeds, and the flour used to make pancakes and biscuits). The oil can be stored for long periods without going rancid. *Halva* is a delicious sweet with a unique texture made from ground sesame seeds, almonds and sugar. *Tahini*, a thick paste used in Lebanese cooking, is made from ground sesame seeds, lemon juice, pepper, garlic and various spices. It is served with savoury or sweet dishes (salads, vegetables, meat and poultry dishes, and beans and peas). The well-known condiment *hummus* is a mixture of *tahini* and chickpeas. Delicious sesame sauces are made in Japan and Africa (e.g. to accompany the traditional *injera* of Ethiopia).

NUTRITIONAL VALUE Seeds yield 588 kcal per 100 g and contain 50% fat (80% unsaturated), more than 20% protein, 10% carbohydrates and very high levels of minerals (especially iron and calcium). The oil lowers cholesterol.

Sesamum indicum L.   family: Pedaliaceae

sim sim (Arabic); *hu ma* (Chinese); *sésame* (French); *gingli* (Hindi); *Sesam* (German); *sesamo* (Italian); *goma, shiro goma* (Japanese); *sésamo* (Portuguese, Spanish); *susam* (Turkish)

Setaria italica

foxtail millet

Foxtail millet plant

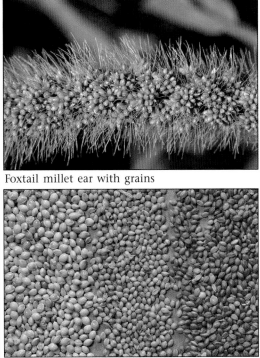

Foxtail millet ear with grains

Foxtail millet (white, yellow and red types)

DESCRIPTION An annual grass of up to 2 m in height with leafy stalks and arching, spike-like panicles, each comprising dense groups of short side branches surrounded by bristles. The single-seeded fruits (grains) are about 2 mm in diameter and are variable in colour (yellow, white, red, brown or black). Several wild species are wild-harvested for food: *S. sphacelata* in Africa, *S. pallidifusca* in Burkina Faso and *S. palmifolia* in the Philippines. A minor cereal known as korali (*S. pumila*) is cultivated in southern India.

ORIGIN & HISTORY Foxtail millet is indigenous to temperate Europe and Asia. It is believed to be derived from green foxtail millet (*S. viridis*), which is indigenous to temperate Asia. It is not clear exactly where domestication took place but it has been recorded as a crop in China about 5 000 years ago. Archaeological sites in Europe date back to Neolithic times and foxtail millet was widely cultivated in Europe during the Bronze Age. Today, three cultivar groups or races are grown: race *Moharia* in Europe and southwestern Asia, race *Maxima* in Russia and the Far East and race *Indica* in India and southeastern Asia. Foxtail millet is still an important grain in traditional agriculture, and is cultivated for home consumption in China (4 million hectares) and India (1 million hectares).

PARTS USED The dry, one-seeded fruits (grains).

CULTIVATION & HARVESTING Modern cultivars mature early and are resistant to diseases. It is no longer cultivated to any extent in Europe.

USES & PROPERTIES The grain is an important staple food in China and India where it is turned into flour or cooked in water or milk. In Russia it is used to make beer and in Europe and the USA it is best known as a birdseed.

NUTRITIONAL VALUE The grain is very nutritious and contains 11% protein, 4% fat and 60% carbohydrates.

Setaria italica (L.) P. Beauv.   family: Poaceae

liang, huang liang mi (Chinese); *millet d'Italie* (French); *Borstenhirse, Kolbenhirse* (German); *panico* (Italian); *awa* (Japanese); *milho painço* (Portuguese); *mijo de Italia* (Spanish)

Sinapis alba

white mustard

White mustard plant

White mustard flowers and fruits

White mustard seeds

DESCRIPTION An erect annual with lobed leaves and yellow flowers. White mustard can easily be distinguished from both black and brown mustard by the flat (not rounded) beaks and hairy surfaces of the seed capsules (smooth in black and brown mustard). Some wild forms originally had black or brown seeds but modern cultivars all have white to yellowish seeds.

ORIGIN & HISTORY White mustard originated in the eastern Mediterranean region and spread to other parts of Europe during the Middle Ages. In northern Europe (especially Sweden), taller and leafier forms were developed as green manure crops; others specifically for oil production. The main production areas today are the USA, Canada, the UK and parts of Europe.

PARTS USED Ripe seeds.

CULTIVATION & HARVESTING Plants are grown as an annual crop and seeds are mechanically harvested. More than 160 000 tons of seeds (white and brown combined) are sold each year, making mustard the most important of all spices.

USES & PROPERTIES The typical sharp taste (due to mustard oils) develops only after crushed seeds (or mustard powder) are mixed with water or wine. White mustard has a "hot" (bitter and pungent) taste, while black and brown mustard give a more spicy and piquant taste. In France, a distinction is made between the pastes made from black or brown mustard (called "mustard") and those made from white mustard (referred to merely as "condiments"). A single exception is the famous Alsace mustard from the Rhine and Moselle regions, made from white mustard but also called "mustard" or *moutarde*.

NUTRITIONAL VALUE Unimportant, but mustard oils stimulate the circulation and digestive system and are believed to have anticancer activity.

NOTES White mustard contains sinalbin as the main mustard-oil glycoside. When hydrolysed by the enzyme myrosinase it produces a pungent, non-volatile isothiocyanate.

Sinapis alba L.   family: Brassicaceae

bai jie (Chinese); *moutarde blanche* (French); *Weißer Senf* (German); *senape bianca* (Italian); *shiro garashi* (Japanese); *mostarda branca* (Portuguese); *mostaza blanca* (Spanish); *senap* (Swedish)

Solanum melongena
aubergine • eggplant • brinjal

Aubergine flower and fruits

Aubergine flower and fruits

Aubergines (Asian cultivar)

DESCRIPTION A perennial herb of up to 1.5 m in height with hairy stems bearing large, lobed leaves and violet flowers borne on slightly spiny stalks. The fruits are very variable, from egg-shaped and white (hence the name eggplant) to oblong or sausage-shaped and bright to dark purple. The spongy flesh contains numerous small seeds.

ORIGIN & HISTORY Wild aubergine is a spiny plant with bitter fruits, indigenous to India. The cultivated form is believed to have been selected in India, with a secondary centre in China (known there since 500 BC). It reached Africa and Europe via Arabia and Persia but only became popular in southern Europe from the seventeenth century onwards. Aubergines are today cultivated in many parts of the world.

PARTS USED Ripe fruits.

CULTIVATION & HARVESTING The plants require a warm climate and are grown as an annual crop. The fruits are harvested by hand when ripe.

USES & PROPERTIES Aubergines are used as vegetables in a variety of dishes, especially in Eastern and Mediterranean cooking. They are fried, boiled, baked, stuffed or stewed and go well with Indian, Malaysian or Thai curries, as well as mutton and white meat dishes. Their mushroom-like texture makes them a good substitute for meat in vegetarian diets. Particularly well known is *moussaka* (aubergine slices cooked with chopped mutton, onions and garlic, and served with tomato sauce), a popular dish in the Balkan region, Turkey and Greece. Perhaps the most famous Italian aubergine dishes are *melanzane alla parmigiani* (aubergine baked with tomato sauce and Parmesan cheese) and the Sicilian *caponata* (aubergines, celery, olives and capers with a sweet and sour sauce).

NUTRITIONAL VALUE The fruits have a low energy value (30 kcal per 100 g), are rich in potassium and calcium but have only a modest quantity of proteins (1.2%) and vitamin C (5 mg per 100 g).

Solanum melongena L.

family: Solanaceae

qie zi, ai gua (Chinese); *aubergine, melongène* (French); *Eierfrucht, Eierpflanz, Aubergine* (German); *baigan, brinjal* (Hindi); *melanzane* (Italian); *daimaru nasu* (Japanese); *berenjena* (Spanish); *makhua* (Thai)

Solanum muricatum

pepino • melon-pear

Pepino flower and fruit

Pepino fruits

DESCRIPTION A perennial herb with spreading branches that may root where they touch the ground. The leaves are usually simple but sometimes compound, with three to seven leaflets. It has white to pale purple flowers and smooth, round to egg-shaped fruits that are cream-coloured to pale orange, with distinctive purple streaks. Another South American *Solanum* is the *naranjilla* or *lulo* (*S. quitoense*), a perennial with pale lilac flowers and rounded, yellowish-orange, conspicuously hairy fruits. Inside it closely resembles a tomato but the pulp is sweet and is eaten raw or used to make drinks.

ORIGIN & HISTORY Indigenous to the Andes region of South America. The exact place of origin is unknown, but it is an ancient crop that has been depicted on Peruvian pottery of the pre-Columbian period. Fruits are commonly sold on local markets in Bolivia, Chile, Colombia, Ecuador and Peru. It is now grown on a commercial scale in Chile, California and New Zealand for export to Europe, Japan and the USA. The original name was *pepino dulce* (Spanish for "sweet cucumber") so that the shortening to pepino may be confusing as it also relates to cucumber.

PARTS USED Ripe fruits.

CULTIVATION & HARVESTING The plant is easily propagated from cuttings and is usually grown as an annual. It requires a relatively cool climate for optimal production. The fruits are hand-picked when ripe and can be stored for several weeks.

USES & PROPERTIES Pepinos are eaten fresh as a dessert fruit or sliced and included in fruit salads. They have many potential uses in soups, seafood, meats, sauces and desserts. The fruits can be frozen, preserved or jellied.

NUTRITIONAL VALUE The pepino has a low energy value (21 kcal per 100 g; only 7% carbohydrates) and is a very good source of vitamin C (30–35 mg per 100 g). It supplies a fair amount of minerals and vitamin A.

Solanum muricatum Ait.   family: Solanaceae

poire melon (French); *Birnenmelone, Kachuma* (German); *pepino* (Italian); *pepino dulce* (Spanish)

Solanum nigrum

black nightshade • wonderberry

Black nightshade flowers

Black nightshade plant

Black nightshade fruits

DESCRIPTION This is an erect annual of up to 1 m in height, with oval, lobed leaves, small white flowers and small, rounded, black berries (about 5 mm in diameter) borne in small clusters. Closely related is the huckleberry or garden huckleberry, *S. melanocerasum*, usually listed as *S. intrusum* or sometimes as *S. nigrum* (or *S. nigrum* var. *guineense*). It is a slightly taller plant with larger leaves, smooth leaf margins and slightly larger fruits. In southern Africa, *S. retroflexum* (*umsoba* or *msoba*) is wild-harvested and cultivated on a small scale for jam. It can be distinguished by the spreading hairs on the stems and the lobed leaves. Another species, *S. chenopodioides*, is similar and is used in the same way.

ORIGIN & HISTORY Black nightshade (*S. nigrum*) is a variable species complex believed to be indigenous to Europe. It is widely cultivated on a small scale and has become naturalised in many parts of the world. Huckleberry (*S. melanocerasum*) is a cultigen of unknown origin.

It is cultivated in West Africa.

PARTS USED Ripe berries (or the leaves as pot-herb).

CULTIVATION & HARVESTING Black nightshade, huckleberry and various other species are weedy plants that are cultivated to some extent. Berries are often gathered from wild plants. Care should be taken to only pick ripe berries, because the unripe (green) fruits may contain toxic levels of alkaloids (6-8 unripe berries may kill a child).

USES & PROPERTIES The dark purple to black berries are delicious to eat raw and make excellent jams. The juicy pulp may be used for pie fillings, jellies and drinks. Young leaves are commonly used as pot-herb in rural parts of Africa and Asia.

NUTRITIONAL VALUE The berries have an energy value of 46 kcal per 100 g, with 5.3% carbohydrates and 5.3% protein. They are very rich in minerals, especially calcium, magnesium and phosphorus.

Solanum nigrum L.

family: Solanaceae

long kui (Chinese); *morelle des jardins, morelle noire* (French); *Schwarzer Nachtschatten* (German); *morella, solano nero* (Italian); *inu hôzuki* (Japanese); *yerba mora* (Spanish)

Solanum tuberosum

potato

Potato plants

Potato plant with flowers

Potatoes

DESCRIPTION A perennial herb with weak, annual stems that emerge from underground tubers. The leaves are compound, slightly hairy and the flowers range from white to purple. The tubers are the tips of greatly enlarged underground stems that store starch.

ORIGIN & HISTORY Indigenous to Central and South America. It was developed as a crop in the region of Lake Titicaca in Bolivia and Peru, at least 7 000 years ago. Hundreds of different wild and semi-domesticated types are still found there. The Spanish explorers took potatoes to Europe, where they became popular, first amongst hungry peasants only and later as a general food source. Large numbers of Irish people migrated to the USA around 1850 as a result of widespread famine due to potato crop failure caused by the potato blight fungus. Potatoes are a major staple food in all temperate regions – the annual consumption (mostly local) is more than 300 million tons (up to 200 kg per capita).

PARTS USED Tubers.

CULTIVATION & HARVESTING Cultivation is very easy and there are numerous cultivars, each suited to particular uses. Harvesting is done mechanically.

USES & PROPERTIES Potato is one of the most versatile of all vegetables. It is used in a wide range of recipes and may be boiled, baked, roasted, steamed, deep-fried or sautéed and has become very popular for making chips (French fries) and mashed potato. Potatoes are used industrially as a source of starch, for distilling of alcohol (especially vodka) and in the manufacture of cracker biscuits.

NUTRITIONAL VALUE The energy value is 86 kcal per 100 g. Potatoes are rich in carbohydrates but low in proteins. They have a fair amount of mineral salts (calcium, potassium and iron), vitamin B, nicotinamid and vitamin C (17 mg per 100 g). The use of too much fat (as in chips) can lead to dietary problems.

Solanum tuberosum L.   family: Solanaceae

ma ling shu (Chinese); *pommes de terre* (French); *Kartoffel* (German); *patate* (Italian); *ubi kenteng* (Malay); *batata* (Portuguese); *papa* (Spanish)

Sorbus aucuparia

mountain ash

Mountain ash leaves and fruits

Mountain ash tree

Mountain ash cultivar

DESCRIPTION A small tree (up to 10 m) bearing compound leaves with toothed leaflets, small, white, smelly flowers and clusters of small, orange fruits looking like miniature apples. The tree is also known as quickbeam or rowan (rowanberry). Other species with edible fruits include *S. aria* (whitebeam berry), as well as *S. domestica* and *S. torminalis*, both of which are known as service tree (serviceberry, sorb apple).

ORIGIN & HISTORY *S. aucuparia* is indigenous to Europe and southwestern Asia. *S. domestica* occurs naturally in the same area but extends to North Africa, while *S. torminalis* is indigenous to the Mediterranean region. Fruits from wild trees have been used since ancient times.

PARTS USED Ripe fruits (a fleshy receptacle).

CULTIVATION & HARVESTING Trees are occasionally cultivated for the fruits (but more often as ornamental trees). Fruits are hand-picked (often wild-harvested) and stored until they almost start to decompose (a process known as bletting).

USES & PROPERTIES The fruits are eaten when bletted or they are used to make syrups, jams, vinegar, brandy and other alcoholic drinks. They are sometimes cooked and dried. Sorb apple (*S. domestica*) is cultivated in France, Germany and Italy for the production of a fermented, cider-like drink (*Apfelwein*, *cormé*). *S. torminalis* is similarly used in a drink called checkers or chequers.

NUTRITIONAL VALUE Fruits have an energy value of 85 kcal per 100 g and a very high vitamin C content (around 100 mg per 100 g). *Sorbus* fruits contain sorbitol (10%), which is about half as sweet as sucrose (nowadays produced synthetically). It is used as a sweetener by diabetics because it is converted to fructose in the liver but no glucose is released into the bloodstream. Also present is an irritant acid, parasorbic acid, which is broken down during bletting and cooking. The seeds contain cyanogenic glycosides and should be avoided.

Sorbus aucuparia L. family: Rosaceae

sorbier des oiseleurs (French); *Eberesche* (German); *sorbo degli uccellatori* (Italian); *serbal de cazadores* (Spanish)

Sorghum bicolor

sorghum

Sorghum plants

Sorghum field

Sorghum grains (yellow and red types)

DESCRIPTION A robust grass of up to 3 m in height bearing branching clusters of grains, each about 4 mm in diameter, rounded in shape and yellowish to reddish brown in colour. Sorghum is mainly grown for the edible grain, and several cultivated races or cultivar groups have been described. They are all classified as subsp. *bicolor*, while the wild types are included in subsp. *arundinaceum*. Sweet-stemmed forms are used for chewing like sugar cane, while others serve as livestock and poultry feed, forage, fencing and even brooms.

ORIGIN & HISTORY Sorghum is indigenous to Africa (domesticated in Ethiopia at least 5 000 years ago). From here it spread to India (around 3 000 years ago) and then to Southeast Asia and China. It is still a staple food in Africa, India, Southeast Asia and China and is the fourth most important cereal, after wheat, rice and maize. Nearly 1 000 cultivars are distinguished in China for food, industrial uses and sugar. In the last

century it has become an important crop in the New World.

PARTS USED The ripe, one-seeded fruits (grain or caryopsis); less often the sweet stems.

CULTIVATION & HARVESTING Sorghum will produce at least some grain even under severe drought conditions.

USES & PROPERTIES Sorghum flour is used to make thin or thick porridges and may be fermented to make unleavened breads (such as *kisra* in Sudan), low-alcohol beer (e.g. *pombé* in Sudan) or alcoholic beverages (*caoliang* in China). Malted sorghum is used to make porridge and sorghum beer (*chibuku* in southern Africa). The grain may also be boiled whole and eaten like rice. It is used for a type of *couscous* in Mali or *sohleb*, a kind of porridge made with ginger and sold in the streets in Tunisia.

NUTRITIONAL VALUE Sorghum is very nutritious as it contains 60–75% carbohydrates (350 kcal per 100 g) and 8–13% proteins.

Sorghum bicolor (L.) Moench (= *S. vulgare* Pers.)

family: Poaceae

gao liang (Chinese); *sorgho* (French); *Mohrenhirse* (German); *jowar* (Hindi); *sorgo coltivato* (Italian); *morokoshi*, *sorugamu* (Japanese); *millo*, *sorgo comun* (Spanish)

Spilanthes acmella

spilanthes • pará cress

Spilanthes plant with flower heads

DESCRIPTION A weedy annual of up to 0.4 m in height, with soft, green or purple-flushed leaves and solitary flower heads, each with numerous yellow and maroon-red disc florets (and no ligulate florets). The cultivar most commonly grown as salad plant is known as Brazilian cress, *S. acmella* var. *oleracea* or *S. acmella* 'Oleracea' (formerly *S. oleracea*). In a new classification system it is listed as *Acmella oleracea*.

ORIGIN & HISTORY The plant is indigenous to South America and is believed to be an ancient cultigen of Peruvian origin. It spread to various parts of South America and from there to most tropical parts of the world. Spilanthes is well known as a food plant in Southeast Asia and China.

PARTS USED Fresh leaves.

CULTIVATION & HARVESTING Propagation is by seeds. The crop is easily grown in warm regions and the leaves are picked by hand on a regular basis.

USES & PROPERTIES Fresh young leaves are used in salads and can also be added to soups and stews. Experiments are underway to include extracts in soft drinks to create a tingling effect, similar to sorbet. Several forms of cress are used in salads and as purées for their sharp-tasting leaves, resulting from the presence of mustard oils. Pará cress is not related to these plants. They all belong to the cabbage or mustard family (Brassicaceae) and include garden cress (*Lepidium sativum*), land cress (*Barbarea verna*) and watercress (*Rorippa nasturtium-aquaticum*).

NUTRITIONAL VALUE Fresh leaves are rich in minerals and are a useful source of folic acid and vitamin C.

NOTES Spilanthes has been used as a medicinal plant to alleviate toothache, to stimulate the flow of saliva and for its antibiotic effects. The tingling and anaesthetic activity is due to spilanthol, a compound present at a level of 1.2% in the flower heads (much lower in leaves).

Spilanthes acmella (L.) Murr. [= *Spilanthes oleracea* L., = *Acmella oleracea* (L.) R.K. Jansen] family: Asteraceae

qian ri ju (Chinese); *cresson de Para, spilanthe des potagers* (French); *Parakresse* (German); *spilante* (Italian); *agrião do Brasil, agrião do Pará* (Portuguese)

Spinacea oleracea

spinach

Spinach plant

New Zealand spinach

DESCRIPTION An annual herb with toothed, fleshy leaves that form a rosette when young. Small, unisexual flowers are borne on erect, leafy stalks, followed by small fruits with smooth or prickly surfaces. Two basic types are grown – a crinkle-leaved 'Savoy' type and a smooth-leaved type. Several other plants are loosely referred to as spinach. New Zealand spinach or Warrigal greens (*Tetragonia tetragonioides*, family Aizoaceae) is used in exactly the same way as real spinach. It has small, yellow flowers and conical capsules and occurs from Australia to China and Japan.

ORIGIN & HISTORY Spinach is indigenous to southwestern Asia (mainly Persia, now Iraq). It reached China around AD 600 and spread further to Japan and Korea. The Moors took it to Spain in the eleventh century and it slowly spread to the rest of Europe during the Middle Ages. Today, spinach is a popular crop in all temperate regions of the world.

PARTS USED Fresh leaves.

CULTIVATION & HARVESTING Spinach is easily cultivated from seeds. Whole young plants are usually harvested.

USES & PROPERTIES Leaves are eaten fresh in salads or are cooked and served with butter as a vegetable to accompany meat and egg dishes. Spinach can be used in soups, quiches, tarts, patés, stuffings, soufflés, purées and gratins. It is particularly famous for Italian Florentine dishes (the term *alla florentina* is used), in which spinach and a *béchamel* or mornay sauce are combined with eggs, fish or white meat dishes. Spinach is also available in frozen and canned form.

NUTRITIONAL VALUE Both real spinach and New Zealand spinach have low energy values (20–30 kcal per 100 g) and are rich in minerals (especially iron), folic acid and vitamins A, B and C. Cook only briefly to retain the nutritional value. New Zealand spinach needs to be boiled to leach out saponins and oxalates that reduce the uptake of iron.

Spinacea oleracea L.   family: Chenopodiaceae

bo cai (Chinese); *épinard* (French); *Spinat* (German); *paalak* (Hindi); *spinacio* (Italian); *hourensou* (Japanese); *espinafre* (Portuguese); *espinaca* (Spanish)

Spondias cytherea

ambarella • hog plum

Ambarella flowers and fruits

Ambarella leaves and fruits

Ambarella ripe fruits

DESCRIPTION A deciduous tree of up to 10 m in height, with compound leaves comprising seven to nine pairs of pointed leaflets that turn yellow before they fall. Small, white flowers are arranged in loose clusters, followed by yellow, mango-like fruits the size and shape of large eggs, with indistinct longitudinal grooves and a single, large stone inside. The fruit flesh is crisp and tangy when unripe, turning sweet and somewhat fibrous when the fruit ripens. Several species of *Spondias* bear edible fruits that are used in the same way as those of ambarella (see below). These include yellow mombin, *cajá* or *taperebá* (*S. mombin*, previously known as *S. lutea*), Spanish plum or Jamaican plum (*S. purpurea*), and *imbú* (*S. tuberosa*).

ORIGIN & HISTORY The tree is indigenous to Tahiti and the surrounding Polynesian region. The fruit is often called golden apple or Otaheiti apple (Otaheiti is the old name for Tahiti). It is cultivated on a small scale in the West Indies and in other tropical regions of the world (Southeast Asia, Indonesia, Réunion).

PARTS USED The ripe or unripe fruits.

CULTIVATION & HARVESTING Ambarella is grown from seeds that take about two months to germinate. The tree is quite hardy and adapts to any soil type but it is sensitive to frost. The fruits are usually harvested when unripe and green and are sold on local markets.

USES & PROPERTIES The fruits are eaten raw (sometimes with a little salt) or the ripe fruits are turned into jams, jellies, pickles and chutney. They are used in salads in Thailand and Indonesia. The fruits are also included in tropical iced fruit mixes and can be blended with milk, ice cream or liqueurs to create delicious, sweet cold drinks.

NUTRITIONAL VALUE The fruits contribute small amounts of minerals, carotenoids and vitamins to the diet.

Spondias cytherea Sonn. (= *S. dulcis* Sol. ex Parkinson)   family: Anacardiaceae

gway (Burmese); *pommier de cythère* (French); *Goldpflaume, Tahitiapfel* (German); *ambarella* (Italian, Spanish); *kedongdong* (Malay); *makok farang* (Thai)

Stevia rebaudiana

stevia • sugar-leaf

Stevia plant

Stevia flower heads

Miracle fruit berries

DESCRIPTION A perennial herb with erect branches (up to 0.6 m) bearing small, oblong, toothed leaves. Large clusters of small, white flower heads are borne on the stem tips. The minute, one-seeded fruits are borne on feathery plumes that assist in their dispersal.

ORIGIN & HISTORY Stevia is indigenous to South America (Paraguay). It is traditionally used by local people to sweeten drinks. The local common name is *caa-ehe*. In recent years, stevia has become popular as a replacement for artificial sweeteners.

PARTS USED Fresh or dried leaves (or extracts).

CULTIVATION & HARVESTING Seeds are difficult to germinate and plants are usually grown from root or stem cuttings. Once established, they are fairly hardy and survive dry or cold conditions. For commercial use, the leafy twigs are harvested and dried.

USES & PROPERTIES The fresh leaves, dried leaves or extracts are exceptionally sweet and are used as natural sweeteners.

NUTRITIONAL VALUE Stevia adds little or no calories to the diet, since the active ingredient (stevioside) is not absorbed.

NOTES Stevioside is a diterpene glycoside said to be 300 times sweeter than sucrose, and more than half as effective as saccharine as a sweetener. Stevioside is classified with artificial sweeteners such as cyclamate and saccharin as an intense sweetener because the sweetness greatly exceeds that of sucrose. Bulk sweeteners like mannitol and sorbitol are sweet like sucrose but they are not metabolised in the same way. Cyclamates and saccharin have become controversial because there is some evidence that they may be teratogenic and carcinogenic. Stevia is used in Japan but has been banned as a sweetener in the USA. Another natural sweetener is the miracle fruit or miraculous berry (*Synsepalum dulcificum*), which contains a glycoprotein (miraculin) that affects the taste buds so that salty and sour foods taste sweet.

Stevia rebaudiana (Bertoni) Bertoni   family: Asteraceae

stevia (French); *Stevia* (German); *stevia* (Italian); *stevia* (Spanish)

Syzygium aromaticum

clove

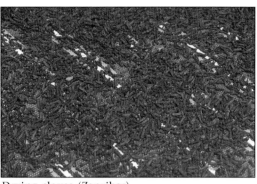

Drying cloves (Zanzibar)

Clove leaves and flower buds

Cloves

DESCRIPTION An evergreen tree of up to 12 m in height, with glossy leaves in opposite pairs and small, white flowers bearing numerous stamens.

ORIGIN & HISTORY The plant is indigenous to five small islands in Indonesia (North Molucca island group). Wild cloves still occur on these islands. The tree has been cultivated for at least 2 000 years and has a rich history of colonial exploitation and intrigue. Around 200 BC, the Chinese first used cloves and exported them to other countries. The Portuguese dominated the clove trade until the Dutch established a monopoly in the seventeenth century. Around 1770, the French took plants from the Moluccas to Réunion and Mauritius, from where it reached Madagascar and Zanzibar, and later the Caribbean. In 1932, the Dutch secretly reintroduced cloves from Zanzibar to Indonesia. The reason was that the smokers of *kretek* cigarettes (made from 60% tobacco and 40% cloves) preferred Zanzibar cloves. The use of cloves in Indonesia (for *kretek* cigarettes) is currently estimated to be around 100 000 tons.

PARTS USED Unopened, dried flower buds.

CULTIVATION & HARVESTING Trees are grown from seeds (or seedlings gathered in existing plantations). Commercial harvesting of the clusters of flower buds (by hand-picking) starts after about six to ten years. Trees remain productive for up to 60 years. The buds are spread out in the sun to dry.

USES & PROPERTIES Cloves are an important spice with many culinary applications. They are an essential component of oriental spice mixtures. Cloves are used in meat dishes (especially game and poultry), marinades, gherkins and pickles, some sweet pastries, fruits in brandy, and mulled wines (usually referred to as bishop, *gluhwein*, grog or punch).

NUTRITIONAL VALUE Unimportant (spice only). Excessive use may cause allergies.

NOTES Cloves or clove oil is important in dentistry (as pain killer and disinfectant).

Syzygium aromaticum (L.) Merr. & Perry [= *Eugenia caryophyllus* (C. Spreng.) Bull. & Harr.]family: Myrtaceae

ding xiang (Chinese); *giroflier* (French); *Gewürznelkenbaum* (German); *chiodi di garofano* (Italian); *kuroobu, shouji* (Japanese); *bunga cingkeh* (Malay); *clavero, arbol del clavo* (Spanish); *garn ploo* (Thai)

Syzygium cumini

jambolan • Java plum

Brush cherry (*S. paniculatum*)

Jambolan leaves and fruits

African water berry (*S. cordatum*)

DESCRIPTION A large tree of up to 12 m or more, with a rounded crown and a thick trunk. Large, leathery leaves are borne in opposite pairs on slender, pale-coloured stems. The small, white flowers have many stamens and occur in sparse clusters. The relatively small, oblong, olive-like fruits are pinkish purple but turn dark purple to almost black when they mature. These fruits are almost indistinguishable from those of three African species, the water berry (*S. cordatum*), the forest water berry (*S. gerrardii*) and water pear (*S. guineense*). They all grow in wet places and all have edible but rather bland-tasting fruits. These species are also similar to the garden eugenia or brush cherry (*S. paniculatum*), a popular ornamental shrub or small tree that produces small, oblong, reddish-purplish fruits that are sometimes used for jams and jellies.

ORIGIN & HISTORY The jambolan is indigenous to India, Malaysia and Indonesia. It is commonly cultivated in India and Java and has been distributed to botanical gardens in all tropical parts of the world. It is often grown as an ornamental tree but rarely in commercial plantations.

PARTS USED Ripe or unripe fruits.

CULTIVATION & HARVESTING The trees prefer relatively dry, tropical conditions. Fruits do not travel well and are sold on local markets during the rather brief harvesting period.

USES & PROPERTIES The fruit has a large oblong seed surrounded by white flesh. It should be eaten when ripe and sweet, but some people prefer the sour and tangy taste of the near-ripe fruit. The fruits are often dipped in salt or in salt water before they are eaten. They are also used for juice and can be turned into wine and vinegar.

NUTRITIONAL VALUE The fruits have a low energy value (around 48 kcal per 100 g) and contain some vitamin C (10–15 mg per 100 g).

Syzygium cumini (L.) Skeels [= *Eugenia cumini* (L.) Druce]   family: Myrtaceae

hai nan pu tao (Chinese); *jambolanier* (French); *Wachsjambuse, Jambolanapflaume* (German); *jamun* (Hindi); *jamblang, duwet* (Indonesian); *aceituna dulce* (Italian); *janboran* (Japanese); *jambolan* (Malay); *jambolana* (Spanish); *look hwa* (Thai)

Syzygium jambos

rose apple • Malabar plum • jambos

Rose apple tree

Rose apple flower

Rose apple ripe fruits

DESCRIPTION A large, much-branched shrub or small tree of up to 10 m in height with opposite, leathery, hairless, narrowly elliptic leaves. Flowers are present in the form of large, powder-puffs, comprised almost entirely of numerous (about 300) cream-coloured to pale yellow stamens of up to 40 mm long. The fruits are strikingly similar to guava fruits in shape and size – they have prominent, persistent sepals and turn yellow when ripe. In many parts of the world, the plant is known as *jambos*. The common names rose apple, wax apple and water apple can be very confusing, as they are sometimes used indiscriminately for different species of *Syzygium*. Species with pear-shaped fruits are discussed and illustrated under wax apple (*S. samarangense*).

ORIGIN & HISTORY Widely distributed in India and Southeast Asia. The trees have been grown as a source of fruits for centuries. It is frequently encountered in botanical gardens and private gardens in all warm regions of the world.

PARTS USED Ripe fruits.

CULTIVATION & HARVESTING Rose apple can be grown successfully even in temperate regions provided there is no frost. The large fruits are hand-picked when ripe but are rarely seen on fresh produce markets, as they do not last very long.

USES & PROPERTIES The fruits have a rather bland taste but can be processed into delicious jams, jellies and preserves. They are rarely eaten but have a pleasant aroma (like roses). Brandy distilled from fermented ripe fruits is said to also smell of roses.

NUTRITIONAL VALUE The total carbohydrate content of ripe fruits is 7–12 g per 100 g and the energy yield is fairly low (30–50 kcal per 100 g). The fruits also provide reasonable quantities of minerals, amino acids (1.2 mg nicotinic acid per 100 g) and vitamin C (about 15–30 mg per 100 g).

Syzygium jambos (L.) Alston (= *Eugenia jambos* L.)   family: Myrtaceae

pu tao (Chinese); *jambosier* (French); *Rosenjambuse, Rosenapfel* (German); *futo momo* (Japanese); *jambu kelampok* (Malay); *jambo amarelo* (Portuguese); *jambo amarillo* (Spanish); *chomphuu namdokmai* (Thai)

Syzygium polyanthum

salam leaf • daun salam • Indonesian bay leaf

Salam leaf in flower

DESCRIPTION A tall, evergreen tree with simple, oval leaves in opposite pairs. The tree bears small, cream-coloured flowers in clusters, followed by small fleshy fruits. Young leaves are aromatic.

ORIGIN & HISTORY The plant is indigenous to southern Asia, and is widely distributed from Myanmar to Malaysia and Indonesia. Leaves of the tree are a traditional source of flavour and considered to be one of the essential ingredients of Indonesian cooking, together with chillies, coconut, coriander, garlic, galangal, ginger, lime, noodles, palm sugar, peanuts, rice, shallots, shrimp paste, tamarind and *tempeh* (cooked, fermented soybean).

PARTS USED Young leaves (fresh or dry).

CULTIVATION & HARVESTING Trees are not cultivated commercially to any extent. Twigs with leaves are simply wild-harvested and sold on local fresh produce markets or the leaves are dried and sold in packets as a spice.

USES & PROPERTIES The leaves are used as a vegetable – whole, fresh leaves are cooked with pieces of meat. Indonesian cooks add a few fresh or dried leaves to various curries (fish, chicken), stews (chicken, beef) and sauces. Regular visitors to Bali would know the popularity and importance of this spice in almost every dish, from coconut milk to lobster curry. The flavour is mild, slightly sour and astringent – quite unlike that of bay leaf (*Laurus nobilis*) with which it is sometimes confused (or substituted). The use of bay leaf in some Malay and Indonesian dishes may have resulted from salam leaf not being available to cooks in Europe and other parts of the world. Bay leaf is considered to be unsuitable as a substitute by those in the know.

NUTRITIONAL VALUE The leaves are mostly used as a spice only. The flavour may be partly ascribed to the small amount (0.2%) of essential oil that is present (said to contain eugenol and citral).

Syzygium polyanthum (Wight) Walpers (= *Eugenia polyantha* Wight)   family: Myrtaceae

duo hua pu tao (Chinese); *daun salam, laurier indonésien* (French); *Indonesisches Lorbeerblatt* (German); *daun salam* (Indonesian, Malay); *daeng klua* (Thai)

Syzygium samarangense

Java wax apple • wax jambu • Java rose apple

Java wax apple flowers and fruit

Java wax apple fruits

Water apple (*S. aqueum*) fruits

Malay rose apple (*S. malaccense*) fruits

DESCRIPTION A large, evergreen shrub or small tree with leathery leaves and showy white or pinkish flowers borne in small clusters. The attractive fruits are waxy in appearance, pear-shaped and yellowish-green to pink. Differences between various species with pear-shaped fruits known as wax apples, rose apples and water apples are rather subtle, and they are often confused. They can, however, easily be distinguished from jambolan or java plum (*S. cumini*) and related species that have small, dark purple, oblong fruits. The rose apple or Malabar plum (*S. jambos*) has rounded, guava-like fruits. Java wax apple (*S. samarangense*) has white flowers and rounded leaf bases, water apple or watery rose apple (*S. aqueum*) has large, usually green but sometimes pink fruits with a spongy texture and Malacca apple or Malay rose apple (*S. malaccense*) has reddish flowers and dark red fruit.

ORIGIN & HISTORY *S. samarangense*, *S. malaccense* and *S. aqueum* are all indigenous to Malaysia. The fruits have been collected for human use since ancient times, but details are poorly recorded.

PARTS USED Ripe fruits.

CULTIVATION & HARVESTING Trees are usually grown for ornamental purposes along streets and in gardens and parks (rarely in commercial plantations). Fruits are harvested (and wild-harvested) for local markets in Malaysia, where they are a common sight.

USES & PROPERTIES These fruits are enjoyed more for their crisp texture than for their flavour, which tends to be watery and only slightly sweet. Java wax apple and water apple are usually eaten fresh, while Malay rose apple may also be cooked. All of them are suitable for jams, jellies and preserves.

NUTRITIONAL VALUE Wax apples have a low energy value of only 17 kcal per 100 g. The carbohydrate level in ripe fruits is about 4 g per 100 g and there is a fair amount of vitamin C (about 15 mg per 100 g).

Syzygium samarangense (Blume) Merr. & Perry (= *Eugenia javanica* Lam.)   family: Myrtaceae

jin shan pu tao (Chinese); *pomme de Java* (French); *Java-Apfel* (German); *renbu* (Japanese); *jambu air mawar* (Malay); *manzana de Java* (Spanish); *chom phuu* (Thai)

Tamarindus indica

tamarind

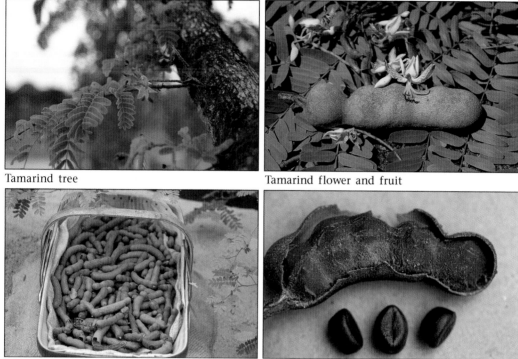

Tamarind tree

Tamarind flower and fruit

Tamarind fruits

Tamarind pulp and seeds

DESCRIPTION A large, graceful tree (up to 25 m) with feathery, compound leaves that fold in at night (sleep movements). Clusters of white and yellow flowers are formed on the branches and a few of them develop into oblong pods of about 10 cm long and 2 cm wide. They contain about 6–10 brown seeds surrounded by an edible, reddish brown pulp (part of the fruit wall).

ORIGIN & HISTORY Tamarind is a cultigen believed to be of North African origin. It was distributed to the Middle East and India centuries ago, from where it spread into Malaysia and Indonesia. Tamarind trees are today found in almost all warm parts of the world, but are commercially cultivated mainly in India, Puerto Rico and Thailand. Tamarind means "Indian date", from the Arabic *tamar* (date) and *hindi* (from India).

PARTS USED The fleshy fruit wall (mesocarp), rarely the seeds.

CULTIVATION & HARVESTING Trees are easily propagated from seeds and thrive in a warm, frost-free climate. The ripe pods are hand-picked and processed to remove the outer skin (peel) and seeds from the pulp. The yield is about 90 kg of purified pulp per large tree.

USES & PROPERTIES Tamarind has a delicious sweet-sour taste that is widely used in cooking, when sourness is required in a dish. It is processed to make chutneys, condiments, spice mixtures, drinks, jams, sorbets, fruit purées and vegetable purées. It is an ingredient of commercial chutneys and the famous Worcester sauce. Chinese chefs garnish sweet and sour soup with crystallised (candied) tamarind. In India, tamarind water (*imli panni*) is a refreshing drink made by soaking the pulp in hot water. It is also added to curries.

NUTRITIONAL VALUE Fruit pulp contains 2% protein, 30–40% sugar and 12% organic acids (mainly tartaric acid) and only 3 mg vitamin C per 100 g. It has a mild laxative action.

Tamarindus indica L.

family: Fabaceae

tamar hindi (Arabic); *suan dou* (Chinese); *tamarinier* (French); *Tamarinde, Sauerdattel* (German); *ambli* (Hindi); *tamarindo* (Italian, Japanese); *asam* (Malay); *tamarindeiro* (Portuguese); *tamaŕindo* (Spanish); *ma khaam* (Thai)

Taraxacum officinale
dandelion

Dandelion plant

Dandelion leaves and flower head

Sow thistle

DESCRIPTION A common, weedy herb with a rosette of oblong, markedly toothed leaves and solitary, yellow flower heads borne on slender, hollow stalks. The small fruits are wind-dispersed. Numerous species have been described, but they are usually collectively referred to as *T. officinale* in the broad sense. A related weed used in the same way as dandelion is the sow thistle (*Sonchus oleraceus*). In common with lettuce and dandelion, the leaves contain milky latex. Young leaves are cooked as a pot-herb or are included in salads. It is said to contain a fair amount of vitamin C.

ORIGIN & HISTORY Originally Europe and Asia, but now a cosmopolitan weed. The roots were once burnt as a coffee substitute and the leaves eaten as a pot-herb and wild salad for centuries. Cultivars of dandelion (giant, curly-leaved) are grown commercially to a limited extent in southern Europe (Italy and France).

PARTS USED Young leaves (rarely the roots or flower heads).

CULTIVATION & HARVESTING Plants may be grown from seeds and the leaves harvested while still young. They may also be blanched by covering the plants with straw or plastic sheeting.

USES & PROPERTIES Young leaves are added to fresh salads and eaten raw (they have a slightly bitter taste), or they may be cooked and used like spinach. A traditional French dandelion salad contains garlic-flavoured croutons, pieces of bacon, walnuts and hard-boiled eggs. The open flower heads are dried and used to make dandelion wine.

NUTRITIONAL VALUE Leaves have a low energy value (27 kcal per 100 g) and contain 2.5% protein. They are a rich source of minerals (especially iron) and vitamins (especially vitamins A, B1, B2 and C).

NOTES The herb is claimed to have diuretic properties – hence the French name *pissenlit*. The common name is derived from the French *dent-de-lion* ("lion's tooth") and refers to the toothed leaf edges.

Taraxacum officinale Weber ex Wigg. family: Asteraceae

pissenlit (French); *Löwenzahn* (German); *taraxaco* (Italian); *diente de león* (Spanish)

Theobroma cacao

cacao • cocoa tree

Cacao leaves

Cacao trees

Cacao flower, fruit and fruit pulp

DESCRIPTION A small tree (up to 8 m) with large, simple leaves and white flowers borne directly on the trunk and branches. The large fruit may be green, yellow, red or purplish and contains a fleshy white pulp in which up to 60 seeds are embedded. Three main types of cacao are *Forastero* (with flattened seeds), the high-quality *Criollo* (rounded seeds) and hybrids (*Trinitario*).

ORIGIN & HISTORY Central America (upper Amazon basin). Grown commercially in West Africa, Central America and Southeast Asia. It was used by the Maya people in ancient times and cultivated for at least 2 000 years. The original drink was a mixture of cacao beans, maize and hot chilli peppers boiled in water. The Spaniards preferred to add sugar and vanilla, and these chocolate drinks soon became fashionable in Europe, long before coffee and tea. Cocoa powder and slab chocolate are recent inventions that date back to the early eighteenth century.

PARTS USED Ripe seeds (cacao beans).

CULTIVATION & HARVESTING Cacao trees are grown from seeds and require high humidity, temperature and rainfall. The fruits are fermented in boxes for about six days to oxidise and release aroma compounds in the beans. The pulp is washed away and the processed beans are dried and packed.

USES & PROPERTIES Cacao beans are roasted, pulverised and half of the fat (cocoa butter) is extracted, while the remaining material is powdered as cocoa powder. Chocolate is a mixture of cocoa powder, milk powder and sugar. Cocoa drinks are chocolate or cocoa powder mixed with water or milk. Various delicious desserts, confectionery and truffles are made from chocolate.

NUTRITIONAL VALUE Unlike tea and coffee, cacao has considerable food value. Cocoa powder contains 25% fat, 15% protein and 10% carbohydrates. Chocolate is addictive; cocoa contains the stimulating alkaloids theobromine (2%), caffeine (0.2%) and other stimulants.

Theobroma cacao L.

family: Sterculiaceae

cacaotier, cacaoyer (French); *Kakaobaum* (German); *cacao* (Italian); *cacao real* (Spanish)

Thymus vulgaris

common thyme • garden thyme

Wild thyme

Common thyme

Lemon thyme

DESCRIPTION An aromatic, perennial shrublet with small, opposite, greyish leaves borne on slender stems. The small flowers are typically two-lipped and usually pale mauve or sometimes white or purple. Many species and cultivars are grown as ornamental plants and culinary or medicinal herbs, including lemon thyme (*T. x citriodora*, a hybrid between *T. pulegioides* and *T. vulgaris*), wild thyme (*T. serpyllum*) and caraway thyme (*T. herbabarona*). Lemon thyme is a smaller, more spreading plant with rounded leaves (often variegated) and a distinct lemon smell.

ORIGIN & HISTORY Western Mediterranean to southeastern Italy. Thyme appears to have been burnt like incense by the ancient Greeks. It has a long history of use as medicinal and culinary herb and is cultivated in many parts of the world.

PARTS USED Fresh or dried leaves.

CULTIVATION & HARVESTING Plants are easily grown from seeds or cuttings. It prefers alkaline soil.

USES & PROPERTIES Thyme is one of the basic herbs used in cooking and is an essential ingredient of stuffings, sausages, meat, poultry and fish dishes. It is added to soups, stews, lentils, scrambled eggs, tomato dishes and salads. It is traditionally included, together with parsley, bay leaves and rosemary, in a *bouquet garni* (a small bundle of herbs used to flavour a sauce or stock and tied together so that it can easily be removed before serving). So-called "mixed herbs" always include thyme. It is used to flavour Benedictine and other liqueurs. Wild thyme, known as *serpolet* in French, is a feature of Provençal cooking (the *farigoule* of Provence, used in mutton, rabbit and trout). Lemon thyme goes well with chicken, veal, potatoes and seafood.

NUTRITIONAL VALUE Used in small quantities (for flavour only).

NOTES The essential oil contains thymol, an antiseptic compound that is used medicinally against lung infections (to expel phlegm from the lungs).

Thymus vulgaris L.   family: Lamiaceae

thym (French); *Gartenthymian* (German); *timo* (Italian); *tomillo* (Spanish)

Trichosanthes cucumerina

snake gourd

Snake gourd flower

Snake gourd plant with fruits

Snake gourd leaves

Snake gourds

DESCRIPTION An annual climber with rounded leaves and white flowers with a fringe of hairs along the margins. Male and female flowers are borne on the same plant and open at night. The fruit is a long, narrow, often slightly coiling, snake-like gourd of up to 1 m long with irregular green stripes on a whitish surface. The cultivated form is known as *T. cucumerina* var. *anguina* (previously *T. anguina*). It is one of several species grown for their fruits or fleshy roots that are used as a starch source. These include the Japanese snake gourd (*T. cucumeroides*), the pointed gourd (*T. dioica*) and Mongolian snake gourd (*T. kirilowii*).

ORIGIN & HISTORY *T. cucumerina* is of Indian and Malaysian origin. It has been grown as a vegetable for centuries but is poorly known in western countries.

PARTS USED Unripe or ripe fruits.

CULTIVATION & HARVESTING Snake gourd is easily grown from seeds in the same way as squashes and pumpkins. Tying a stone to the end of the young developing fruit is believed to keep it from coiling and to induce it to grow longer.

USES & PROPERTIES Immature fruit is cut into slices and cooked as a vegetable. It is said to be a good substitute for French beans and is often added to curries. The red pulp from the mature fruit is used like tomato paste but the fruit flesh becomes fibrous and bitter. Fruits and leaves of the pointed gourd (*T. dioica*) are eaten as vegetables in India while the roots of Japanese and Mongolian snake gourds are used as starch sources in China and Japan.

NUTRITIONAL VALUE Snake gourd has a relatively low food value but is a good source of minerals and some vitamins. Older fruits are used in traditional medicine as bitter tonic to stimulate appetite and improve digestion.

Trichosanthes cucumerina L. var. **anguina** (L.) Haines (= *T. anguina* L.)   family: Cucurbitaceae

she gua (Chinese); *courge serpent cultivée* (French); *Schlangengurke* (German); *chachinda* (Hindi); *serpente vegetale* (Italian); *ebi uri* (Japanese); *ketola ular* (Malay); *abobora-serpente* (Portuguese); *calabaza anguina* (Spanish)

Trigonella foenum-graecum
fenugreek

Fenugreek flower and fruit

Fenugreek plant

Fenugreek seeds

DESCRIPTION A sparse annual herb of up to 0.8 m in height bearing compound leaves with three markedly toothed leaflets. The small white flowers have no stalks and are clustered in the leaf axils. They develop into slender, slightly curved pods that are prominently beaked, each containing up to 20 angular, yellowish brown seeds.

ORIGIN & HISTORY Indigenous to southern Europe and Western Asia. Fenugreek has been grown since ancient times (e.g. by the Assyrians) as food (used like lentils), for medicinal purposes and as a fodder plant (*foenum-graecum* means "Greek hay"). Seeds have been found in Tutankhamen's grave (1325 BC). It is an important food crop in rural parts of Ethiopia, the Middle East and India, where it is also grown commercially as a pulse.

PARTS USED Ripe seeds (more rarely the fresh or dried leaves).

CULTIVATION & HARVESTING Fenugreek is easily grown from seeds in dry temperate and subtropical regions. Harvesting is done mechanically or by hand.

USES & PROPERTIES Seeds are soaked and cooked as a protein-rich food in the same way as beans and lentils. They are used to make a milk substitute for babies and a high quality traditional food for women (the flour is mixed with olive oil and castor sugar). Fenugreek is also used as a spice – the powdered seeds are an ingredient of curry powders and may be added to fish curries, pickles and chutneys. *Panch phora* is an Indian spice mixture containing fenugreek, brown mustard, cumin, black cumin and fennel. Cooking or roasting the seeds converts the strange smell into a pleasant aroma that is used to flavour artificial maple syrup. Fresh or dried leaves are used as a vegetable and culinary herb in Turkey, India and Arabian countries.

NUTRITIONAL VALUE The seeds are very high in protein, carbohydrates, mucilages (about 35%) and B vitamins.

Trigonella foenum-graecum L.   family: Fabaceae

ku tou (Chinese); *fenugrec* (French); *Bockshornklee* (German); *methi* (Hindi); *fieno greco* (Italian); *alholva* (Spanish)

Triticum aestivum
bread wheat

Wheat plants

Wheat ears

Wheat grains (with durum wheat)

DESCRIPTION An annual grass with bright green leaves and terminal spikes of awned or awnless flowers. It is superficially similar to barley but the husks fall off during threshing.

ORIGIN & HISTORY Middle East. The use of wild wheats with brittle spikes dates back to around 28000 BC, while domesticated emmer wheat (*T. turgidum* var. *dicoccum*) and einkorn wheat (*T. monococcum*) appeared at about 7000 BC. Modern wheat is the result of introgression and hybridisation between emmer wheat and wild *Aegilops squarrosa*. Modern hulled, hexaploid wheats were grown in Turkey, Iran, Mesopotamia and Egypt by 7000 to 5000 BC. From here wheat spread to Europe, central Asia, China and elsewhere to become one of the top three cereals (with rice and maize), on its own responsible for feeding more than a billion people. There are more than 25 000 cultivars.

PARTS USED Ripe, dry, one-seeded fruits (grains).

CULTIVATION & HARVESTING Wheat is an annual crop adapted to a wet winter and rain-free summer. Growing and harvesting are highly mechanised.

USES & PROPERTIES Bread wheat forms gluten when the dough is kneaded. The sticky gluten proteins trap the carbon dioxide that is released by the yeast during fermentation, thus causing the leavened dough to rise. If no yeast is added, a flat bread is produced. Hard wheats give flour suitable for bread, while soft wheat flour is used in confectionery (cakes, biscuits, pastries, etc.). Wheat is a raw material for the extraction of starch and wheatgerm oil. Wheat is used to make wheat beer (*Weizenbier* or *Weißbier*), a Bavarian speciality and schnapps (*Korn, Kornbranntwein*).

NUTRITIONAL VALUE Wheat has a very high nutritive value and contains 60–80% carbohydrates (mainly starch), 8–15% protein (all the essential amino acids except lysine, tryptophane and methionine) and various vitamins (especially B and E). The energy yield is 330 kcal per 100 g.

Triticum aestivum L.

family: Poaceae

xiao mai (Chinese); *blé* (French); *Saatweizen, Weichweizen, Brotweizen* (German); *frumento* (Italian); *trigo* (Spanish)

Triticum durum

durum wheat

Durum wheat plants

Wild emmer (*Triticum turgidum*)

Durum wheat (with bread wheat)

DESCRIPTION An annual grass very similar to bread wheat but differing in the larger, harder grains, higher protein content and different chromosome number.

ORIGIN & HISTORY Middle East. Durum wheat is derived from wild emmer or kamut (*T. turgidum*) through a series of mutations and selections that led to a free-threshing wheat. Cultivated forms date back to 8000 BC. Today it is grown commercially in all temperate parts of the world.

PARTS USED Ripe, dry, one-seeded fruits (grains).

CULTIVATION & HARVESTING It is cultivated in relatively dry regions and harvested in the same way as wheat and other cereals.

USES & PROPERTIES Durum wheat has a very hard grain with a low gluten content that makes it unsuitable for bread but ideal for pasta, semolina, *couscous* and *bulgar*. The wheat is milled in such a way that the grain is separated into bran, germ and semolina. *Bulgar* (a staple food in Turkey and Mediterranean countries, normally prepared like rice) is made by pre-boiling, drying and then cracking the grain. Semolina is made from a hard cereal like durum, maize or rice, which is ground into small granules (yellow semolina is made from wheat, white semolina from rice). *Couscous* (the national dish of Algeria, Morocco and Tunisia) is made by skilfully rolling semolina and flour in the hands to make tiny pellets. Commercial *couscous* is made with special machines. Authentic pasta is simply durum semolina to which various liquids (water, milk or eggs) are added. The shape varies from small (soup pastas) to long and thin (spaghetti and numerous others, used for boiling), flat (e.g. lasagna, *tortiglioni*, used for baking) or filled (e.g. *cannelloni, ravioli, tortellini, tortelloni*). The correct degree of cooking is known as *al dente*. A wide range of sauces is served with pasta.

NUTRITIONAL VALUE Durum wheat has a slightly lower food value than bread wheat.

Triticum durum Desf. [= *T. turgidum* L. subsp. *durum* (Desf.) Thell.]   family: Poaceae

ying li xiao mai (Chinese); *blé dur* (French); *Durum Weizen, Hartweizen* (German); *grano duro* (Italian); *trio duro* (Spanish)

369

Tropaeolum tuberosum
tuber nasturtium

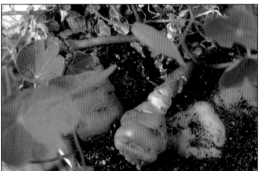

Tuber nasturtium flowers

Tuber nasturtium plant

Tuber nasturtium tubers

DESCRIPTION A creeper with fleshy stems, lobed leaves and attractive, orange-red, spurred flowers. The fleshy, edible tubers are whitish with purple spots. A close relative is the garden nasturtium or Indian cress (*T. majus*). It is an annual creeper with umbrella-like leaves and attractive red to yellow, spurred, edible flowers. This popular salad plant is also known as *Kapuzinerkresse* (German), *capucine* (French) and *capuchina* (Spanish).

ORIGIN & HISTORY Both species are indigenous to the Andes region (Peru and Bolivia). They were cultivated by the Inca people as food plants for centuries. The tuber nasturtium is an important staple food in high altitude areas where potatoes cannot be grown. Garden nasturtium was introduced to Europe in the late seventeenth century and became popular as ornamental plant. The tuber nasturtium is not well known outside of South America.

PARTS USED Tubers (*T. tuberosum*) or the leaves, flowers, buds and seeds (*T. majus*).

CULTIVATION & HARVESTING The plant is propagated from the tubers (*T. majus* is grown from seeds as an annual). Tubers are dug up and cured in the sun, after which they are dried for long-term storage.

USES & PROPERTIES The tubers are not eaten fresh but are always dried and eaten like potatoes. Pickled tubers have been used in Europe to garnish *hors d'oeuvres* and cold meats. Leaves of the garden nasturtium are added to salads for their sharp, spicy taste and the flowers as an attractive, edible garnish. Flower buds or seeds are pickled in tarragon vinegar and can be used as a substitute for capers.

NUTRITIONAL VALUE The tubers contain 10% carbohydrates, 1–2% protein and vitamin C (about 60 mg per 100 g). Garden nasturtium is also known to be rich in vitamin C.

NOTES *Tropaeolum* species contain sharp-tasting mustard oils that are also found in mustard and horseradish (family Brassicaceae).

Tropaeolum tuberosum Ruíz & Pavón   family: Tropaeolaceae

capucine tubéreuse (French); *Knollige Kapuzinerkresse* (German); *nasturzio tuberoso* (Italian); *añu, ysaño, mashua* (Spanish)

Ullucus tuberosus

ulluco • tuberous basella

Ulluco leaves

Ulluco plant

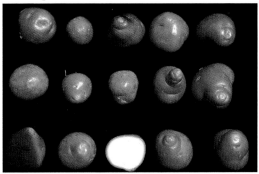

Ulluco tubers

DESCRIPTION Ulluco (pronounced oo-yoo-koh) is a perennial, prostrate herb with heart-shaped fleshy, hairless leaves, inconspicuous flowers and small berries as fruits. The stem tubers are 6–8 cm long, variously shaped and may be white, yellow, pink, red or purple, depending on the cultivar. Ulluco (also known as *ullucu* or *ullucus*) is closely related to *Basella rubra* (Malabar spinach) and other edible members of the family Basellaceae.

ORIGIN & HISTORY Indigenous to the Andes mountains (Ecuador, Peru, Bolivia and northern Argentina). The plant is an ancient Inca food source and has been cultivated at high altitudes for centuries. Ulluco has become commercialised to some extent and the area under cultivation has extended to include Chile, Venezuela and parts of Argentina. In Peru alone, some 30 000 tons are sold on local markets each year. Unsuccessful attempts have been made to introduce ulluco into Europe as a substitute for potato.

PARTS USED Stem tubers (less often the leaves).

CULTIVATION & HARVESTING The plant is grown from tubers like a potato. It is frost resistant and forms tubers above and below the ground (5–9 tons per hectare, harvested by hand).

USES & PROPERTIES The fleshy tubers are boiled or roasted (rarely baked) and eaten like potatoes. They are added to soups and stews as thickening agent or boiled and served as a cold salad. Processed and dried tubers form a product known as *lingli* that may be stored for long periods. Leaves are boiled to make soups or are used in the same way as spinach. Ulluco is sometimes sold in supermarkets in South America and canned ulluco has become an export product from Peru.

NUTRITIONAL VALUE Fresh tubers contain 12–14% starch, 1–2% protein and vitamin C (23 mg per 100 g). On a dry weight basis, leaves contain 12% protein and the tubers yield about 370 kcal per 100 g.

Ullucus tuberosus Caldas   family: Basellaceae

baselle tubéreuse, ulluque (French); *Knollenbaselle, Basellkartoffel, Ulluco, Ulluma, Melloca* (German); *papa lisa* (Spanish)

Urtica dioica

stinging nettle

Perennial stinging nettle

Annual stinging nettle

DESCRIPTION An erect perennial herb with toothed, opposite leaves bearing stinging hairs. The green, inconspicuous male and female flowers are borne in separate clusters. The annual stinging nettle (*U. urens*) has dark green leaves and is a smaller plant.

ORIGIN & HISTORY The perennial stinging nettle occurs naturally in Europe and Asia, while the annual stinging nettle is indigenous to the northern temperate region (but it has become a cosmopolitan weed). Nettles were probably gathered in ancient times as a source of nutrients and especially vitamin C.

PARTS USED Young leaves.

CULTIVATION & HARVESTING Nettles are not cultivated but are wild-harvested. Only the young tops are used, as the older parts become fibrous and bitter.

USES & PROPERTIES Nettles are widely used as pot-herb and cooked like spinach. Perennial stinging nettle is used in soups (on its own or combined with other vegetables such as leeks, cabbage or watercress). It is a popular vegetable in Scotland, often served with butter or gravy and used with haggis, leeks, onions, rice and oatmeal. The leaves of annual stinging nettle are chopped and used in salads. Scandinavian cooks dry the leaves of both species in the oven and add the crushed and powdered leaves to flour used for baking bread and other confectionery. Nettles have been used to make herbal teas and even beer.

NUTRITIONAL VALUE Nettles are similar to or surpass spinach in their nutritional value and have an energy yield of 40 kcal per 100 g. They are very high in protein (7%) and minerals (more than 2%, especially potassium, magnesium, calcium, copper, phosphorus and iron). The leaves have significant quantities of vitamins A and C (respectively 742 mg and 333 mg per 100 g).

NOTES Nettle roots are rich in phytosterols and are an important traditional medicine, used to treat arthritis.

Urtica dioica L.   family: Urticaceae

grande ortie, ortie brulante (French); *Große Brennessel* (German); *ortico maschio* (Italian); *ortiga mayor* (Spanish)

372

Vaccinium corymbosum

highbush blueberry

Highbush blueberry plant

Highbush blueberry leaves and fruits

Highbush blueberries

DESCRIPTION A perennial shrub of up to 1.5 m in height bearing simple leaves and clusters of attractive, white, tubular flowers. The fruits are bluish-black and up to 12 mm in diameter. It is similar to bilberry (*V. myrtillus*) but both the plant and the fruits are larger. The related lowbush blueberry (*V. angustifolium*) is about 30 cm high and has greenish white flowers and berries very similar to those of highbush blueberry. Also of commercial value is the rabbiteye blueberry (*V. ashei*).

ORIGIN & HISTORY *V. corymbosum* and *V. ashei* are indigenous to the eastern parts of the USA (*V. angustifolium* in the northeast). Local people have used these berries as a food source for centuries. Highbush blueberry was domesticated only towards the end of the nineteenth century and has become the most important blueberry crop in North America, Canada, parts of Europe, Australia and New Zealand. The annual production exceeds 40 000 tons. Rabbiteye blueberry is grown in southeastern USA, while lowbush blueberry is wild-harvested from wild stands in Canada that are specially managed for this purpose.

PARTS USED Ripe fruits.

CULTIVATION & HARVESTING Modern highbush blueberries share some genes with other species and are propagated only from cuttings or by tissue culture. They are planted on acid soils, require temperate conditions and are mechanically harvested to some extent.

USES & PROPERTIES Blueberries are eaten as a dessert fruit and as an ingredient of fruit salads, sorbets, ices, juices, yogurts, purées, jellies, syrups and compotes. They are used to make jams and are a popular ingredient of tarts, muffins and cakes. Blueberries can be successfully frozen.

NUTRITIONAL VALUE The energy value is about 50 kcal per 100 g (higher than bilberry due to the higher sugar content of about 15%). The fresh berries contain 15–22 mg of vitamin C and 1–2% citric acid.

Vaccinium corymbosum L.   family: Ericaceae

airelle d'Amérique, myrtille d'Amérique (French); *Kulturheidelbeere, Amerikanische Heidelbeere, Amerikanische, Blaubeere* (German); *arándano americano* (Spanish)

Vaccinium macrocarpon
large cranberry • American cranberry

Cranberry flowers and fruits

Cranberry field in flower

Cranberries

DESCRIPTION A creeping perennial shrub that grows in marshy places. It has attractive pink, beak-like flowers on gracefully curved, slender stalks resembling a crane's neck (hence the common name "craneberry", which became cranberry). The fruit is a bright red berry of about 12–20 mm in diameter. It is practically identical to the European cranberry or small cranberry (*V. oxycoccus*) but the fruits of the latter are much smaller (6–8 mm in diameter).

ORIGIN & HISTORY American cranberry is indigenous to North Asia and North America (USA and Canada) while the small or common cranberry is found in Northern Europe, Northern Asia and North America. Cranberry has been wild-harvested in Europe for centuries. The closely related but larger American cranberry became an important crop plant in the early part of the twentieth century (currently about 9 000 ha are under cultivation with an annual yield of more than 150 000 tons).

PARTS USED Ripe fruits.

CULTIVATION & HARVESTING Cranberry is wild-harvested and of local importance but commercial cranberry is now almost entirely derived from the American cranberry. Plants are grown in sandy marshes (flooded for the harvest) and are harvested by loosening the berries so that they float on the surface of the water. Ripe berries are selectively scooped into the processing machines, as the unripe ones float deeper in the water.

USES & PROPERTIES Cranberries have a tart flavour and are best known for cranberry sauce, traditionally served with roast turkey. The fresh or frozen fruits are used for jams, jellies, compotes and preserves and can be included in tarts and puddings. Cranberry juice became a popular fruit juice in the late 1950s.

NUTRITIONAL VALUE The ripe fruit is relatively low in sugars (3–4%) and low in energy (60 kcal per 100 g). It contains fair amounts of vitamin C (12 mg), organic acids and minerals (especially iron).

Vaccinium macrocarpon Aiton   family: Ericaceae

da guo yue jie (Chinese); *airelle à gros fruits* (French); *Große Moosbeere, Kranbeere* (German); *mirtillo palustre* (Italian); *arándo trepador* (Spanish)

Vaccinium myrtillus

bilberry • common blueberry

Bilberry shrubs

Bilberry fruits

Bilberry leaves and fruits

DESCRIPTION Bilberry (sometimes called blueberry or wortleberry) is a low shrub of about 0.2 to 0.6 m in height that occurs in dense stands. The simple, toothed leaves are borne on angular stems. Small, greenish pink, waxy flowers occur alone or in pairs and are followed by small, pale red berries of about 6 mm in diameter that turn bluish-black when they ripen. Several other closely related species (see *V. corymbosum*) have similar (but slightly larger) fruits and larger, differently shaped flowers.

ORIGIN & HISTORY Bilberry is indigenous to Europe, Asia and North America. It has been wild-harvested in the open woodlands and moors of the northern temperate region for centuries. Small quantities are sometimes exported from Austria and the Balkan region.

PARTS USED Ripe berries.

CULTIVATION & HARVESTING The plant is not cultivated commercially but is wild-harvested on a large scale. Harvesting is a labour-intensive operation because of the small size of both the berries and the shrubs on which they grow. Blueberries available in shops are cultivated *V. corymbosum* and not *V. myrtillus* as people may think. Bilberries are harvested locally for own use and are rarely available on markets.

USES & PROPERTIES The fresh or frozen fruits have a wide range of culinary uses. They have an acid flavour and may be eaten as a dessert fruit (often with cream or ice cream) or used in confectionery as an ingredient and garnish for tarts. They are used for fruit salads, ices, sorbets, syrups, jams, jellies and liqueurs.

NUTRITIONAL VALUE Bilberries have an energy value of around 16 kcal per 100 g. They are rich in vitamin A and in purple pigments (anthocyanins) that act as antioxidants and free-radical scavengers. The vitamin C content is about 15 mg per 100 g.

NOTES The berries are used in traditional medicine to treat diarrhoea.

Vaccinium myrtillus L.   family: Ericaceae

hei guo yue jie (Chinese); *myrtille* (French); *Heidelbeere, Blaubeere, Waldbeere* (German); *mirtillo* (Italian); *biruberii* (Japanese); *arándano commun, mirtillo* (Spanish)

Vaccinium vitis-idaea
lingonberry • cowberry

Lingonberry flowers and fruits

Lingonberry plant with ripe fruits

Lingonberry juice

DESCRIPTION A prostrate and mat-forming, evergreen shrublet with woody, horizontal branches below the ground giving rise to short, erect shoots of up to 30 cm long. These bear small, dark green leaves, small but attractive, bell-shaped, waxy white flowers (sometimes flushed with pink) and rounded berries (6–8 mm in diameter) that turn red when they ripen. The berries are sometimes referred to as mountain cranberries, lingberries or foxberries.

ORIGIN & HISTORY Indigenous to northern parts of Europe, Asia and North America. It is locally dominant in pine forest and open woodland and dry heathland. The berries have served as a wild fruit and food source for centuries and are an important part of Scandinavian cuisine. They are mainly wild-harvested (in Scandinavia, the former USSR, Europe and eastern Canada) and have become very popular in recent years. Production varies greatly and is influenced by local conditions. Domestication started only a few decades ago and

new lingonberry cultivars are being developed.
PARTS USED Ripe berries.
CULTIVATION & HARVESTING Fruits are mainly collected in the wild – picked by hand (a labour-intensive operation) and are variously processed.
USES & PROPERTIES Lingon or cowberry is mainly used to make sour sauces that accompany savoury dishes. It is particularly popular in Norway, Sweden, Denmark and Germany where it is stewed and used as a sauce with roasted goose, game and boiled meat. The fruit is used in iced mousse (*kissel*), jams, jellies, compotes, preserves and pastries. It is now possible to buy lingonberry yogurt and lingonberry juice.
NUTRITIONAL VALUE Lingonberries are rich in vitamin C (22 mg per 100 g) and are a good source of minerals (calcium, phosphorus, iron and silicon), some other vitamins and organic acids.
NOTES Leaves are rich in tannins and anthocyanins and are traditional urinary tract antiseptics and diuretics.

Vaccinium vitis-idaea L.   family: Ericaceae

hong dou yue ju (Chinese); *airelle rouge* (French); *Preiselbeere, Kronsbeere* (German); *mirtillo rosso* (Italian); *arándano rojo* (Spanish); *lingon* (Swedish)

Valerianella locusta

corn salad • lamb's lettuce

Corn salad plants

Corn salad field

DESCRIPTION A small annual plant with a rosette of rounded leaves. Stalks with inconspicuous flowers are produced in early spring and they give rise to numerous small seeds. The plant is also known as field salad, hog salad and marsh salad or as *Feldsalad* and *Rapunzel* (German), *mâche, doucette, oreille-de-lièvre, raiponce* and *valérianelle potagère* (French). A second species, *V. olitoria*, is used in the same way.

ORIGIN & HISTORY Indigenous to Europe and the Mediterranean region. The plant is a traditional winter salad mainly in France, Italy and Germany. Several cultivars have been developed since the seventeenth century, of which those with very small, rounded rosettes are considered to be the more juicy and tasty.

PARTS USED Whole plant (rosette).

CULTIVATION & HARVESTING Corn salad is grown from seeds that are planted in carefully spaced rows. The plants are resistant to frost and are grown during the European winter months (October to March). The small heads are harvested by hand and must be carefully washed and dried leaf by leaf.

USES & PROPERTIES The leaves are eaten raw in salads and are very popular because of their delicious taste. They are used in mixed salads with beetroot, potatoes or walnuts. Some salad recipes call for a little Roquefort cheese, *vinaigrette,* bits of fried bacon or *croutons.* Corn salad can be added to poultry stuffings and may also be cooked like spinach.

NUTRITIONAL VALUE The energy value is very low (only 36 kcal per 100 g) but the leaves are mostly valued for their dietary fibre (1.5%), vitamins (especially vitamin C, which may be as high as 35 mg per 100 g), and minerals (0.8%). Small amounts of protein (2%), fat (less than 0.5%) and carbohydrates (0.7%) are present.

NOTES *Valerianella* is related to valerian (*Valeriana officinalis*), the roots of which are used in traditional medicine as a tranquilliser.

Valerianella locusta (L.) Laterr.   family: Valerianaceae

mâche (French); *Feldsalad, Rapunzel, Ackersalat* (German); *Vogerlsalat* (Austria); *Nüsslisalat* (Switzerland); *valeriana* (Italian)

Vanilla planifolia
vanilla

Vanilla flower and young fruits

Vanilla plant

Vanilla fruits

DESCRIPTION An epiphytic orchid with long stems that climb into trees (up to 10 m). It has oblong, fleshy leaves and greenish yellow flowers. They open in the morning and have to be pollinated (in nature by hummingbirds or bumblebees) to produce the valuable orchid fruits – long, thin and smooth, with thousands of tiny seeds inside.
ORIGIN & HISTORY Indigenous to tropical America (mainly Mexico). Mexicans of the Vera Cruz region used vanilla to flavour their cacao drinks. For many years, Mexico held a monopoly until vanilla plants were successfully grown by the Dutch on Java and by the French on Réunion. Today, vanilla is cultivated in Central America, Indonesia, Madagascar, the Comoros and Uganda. The annual harvest is several thousand tons.
PARTS USED The near-ripe fruits ("vanilla beans").
CULTIVATION & HARVESTING Plants grow from cuttings and require moist, tropical conditions. The flowers are pollinated by hand to ensure proper fruit set. The near-ripe beans are subjected

to a lengthy curing process that involves "killing" the fruits with steam, heating them in the sun for several hours and then fermenting them overnight in air-tight containers. The process is repeated several times, during which the characteristic vanilla flavour develops (vanillin-glycoside is converted to glucose and vanillin, which becomes visible on the surface of the now dark brown and pliable fruits as white crystals).
USES & PROPERTIES Whole fruits are widely used to flavour chocolate, ice cream, milk shakes, custards, puddings, sweets, sugar, soft drinks, liqueurs, confectionery, various sweet dishes and preserved fruits. The whole vanilla bean is added (and repeatedly used) or it is split lengthwise and the soft interior scraped out.
NUTRITIONAL VALUE Used for flavour only.
NOTES Vanilla contains about 3% vanillin but there are at least 35 other flavour components. Synthetic vanillin (produced from eugenol or wood pulp) is a cheap but inferior substitute.

Vanilla planifolia Andr.   family: Orchidaceae

vanille (French); *Echte Vanille* (German); *vaniglia* (Italian); *vainilla* (Spanish)

Vicia faba

broad bean • fava bean

Broad bean plant

Broad bean pods and seeds

Broad beans (ripe seeds)

DESCRIPTION An erect, annual herb with thick, four-ribbed stems, compound leaves with large leaflets and clusters of white (rarely red) flowers in the leaf axils, each with a distinctive black blotch. The large pods have up to eight seeds. Broad bean is known as fava bean in the USA.

ORIGIN & HISTORY The crop is believed to have originated in the Fertile Crescent (the oldest remains of cultivated broad bean date back to 5000 BC in Jericho). From here it spread to Europe, Asia and North Africa. It was known to the ancient Greeks and Romans and became an important food source in China some time after AD 1200. Today, broad bean is cultivated in all temperate parts of the world, with China as the major producer. Some countries in Africa, Asia and the Mediterranean region rely on broad bean for a large part of their protein requirements.

PARTS USED Ripe or unripe seeds (less often the green pods).

CULTIVATION & HARVESTING Plants are easily grown from seeds. Flowers have to be cross-pollinated by insects to ensure proper seed set. The unripe or mostly the ripe pods are harvested for the large flat seeds.

USES & PROPERTIES The tough outer skin of the ripe seed is removed before it is cooked and eaten, often as a purée or as part of soups and stews. It may be added to various traditional dishes such as the Spanish *fabada* or the Egyptian *foul*. Seed flour can be mixed with bread flour. Unripe pods are eaten as a vegetable.

NUTRITIONAL VALUE Dry seeds contain 25% protein, 55% carbohydrates and 2% fat (energy value of 340 kcal per 100 g). Substantial quantities of amino acids, minerals and vitamins B and E are present.

NOTES Favism is a rare, inherited allergic reaction triggered by broad beans which results in severe anaemia.

Vicia faba L.   family: Fabaceae

can dou (Chinese); *feve* (French); *Dicke Bohne, Saubohne* (German); *anhuri* (Hindi); *fave* (Italian); *sora mame* (Japanese); *fava, faveira* (Portuguese); *haba* (Spanish)

Vigna angularis
adzuki bean

Adzuki bean plants

Adzuki bean leaf and flower

Adzuki beans

DESCRIPTION An annual, bushy herb with compound leaves (each with three leaflets), pale yellow flowers and long, narrow pods. The seeds are variable in colour (usually red but also white, yellow, green, brown, black or variously mottled, depending on the cultivar). In addition to adzuki bean, various other *Vigna* species are of regional importance in Asia: mung bean (*V. radiata*), urd bean or black gram (*V. mungo*), rice bean (*V. umbellata*), moth bean (*V. aconitifolia*) and pillipesara bean or jungle mat bean (*V. trilobata*). Rice bean is also known as *haricot riz* (French), *Reisbohne* (German), *shima tsuru azuki* (Japanese), *kacang uci* (Malay) and *frijol de arroz* (Spanish).

ORIGIN & HISTORY Eastern Asia. Adzuki bean is believed to be of relatively recent origin. It appears to be a selection of the wild adzuki bean (*V. angularis* var. *nipponensis*) that grows in China, Japan, Korea, Nepal and Taiwan. Adzuki bean is today mostly produced in China, Japan (Hokkaido) and Taiwan but increasingly also in other parts of the world, for export to Japan (the main consumer of adzuki beans).

PARTS USED Ripe, dry seeds (rarely the green pods).

CULTIVATION & HARVESTING Adzuki bean is grown as a pulse crop. Harvesting has been mechanised to a large extent.

USES & PROPERTIES Seeds of the red type are mainly used in Japan and China as a sweetened confection (often eaten as a sweet, porridge-like dessert). It is used in the form of bean paste (*sarashi-an*) or can be cooked on its own and served with rice. The dry bean may be ground into flour for pastries. Adzuki beans are sometimes germinated for sprouts (also outside Japan and China).

NUTRITIONAL VALUE Seeds contain 20% protein, 50–60% carbohydrate, 1.5% fat and 1.8% minerals. They are a good source of the amino acid lysine and are therefore a valuable addition to cereal-based and vegetarian diets.

Vigna angularis (Willd.) Ohwi & Ohashi [= *Phaseolus angularis* (Willd.) W.F. Wright]   family: Fabaceae

chi dou (Chinese); *haricot anguleux, haricot adzuki* (French); *Adzukibohne* (German); *guruns* (Hindi); *fagiolo adzuki* (Italian); *azuki* (Japanese); *feijão adzuki* (Portuguese); *frijol adzuki* (Spanish)

Vigna radiata

mung bean • green gram

Mung bean flowers and fruits

Mung bean plant

Mung beans and urd beans

DESCRIPTION A bushy annual with compound leaves, yellow flowers and long, narrow pods that turn dark brown, each containing numerous small, usually green or yellow seeds. The main types are var. *chlorospermum* (green gram), var. *radiata* (golden gram) and var. *sublobata* (wild mung bean). A similar and equally important Indian pulse is the urd bean or black gram (*V. mungo*), also called *hei lu dou* (Chinese), *haricot mung* (French), *Urdbohne* (German), *ke tsuru azuki* (Japanese) and *frijol mungo* (Spanish).

ORIGIN & HISTORY Mung bean was domesticated in India, where it has been used for at least 3 500 years. It was selected from the wild mung bean (subsp. *sublobata*), which is widely distributed in Asia and Africa. Urd bean or black gram was developed more recently from a wild form (var. *silvestris*) restricted to the foothills of the Himalayas in India. Mung bean and urd bean are produced on a large scale in southern and eastern Asia. China, Australia, the USA and other countries have started growing these crops.

PARTS USED Mainly the dry, ripe seeds.

CULTIVATION & HARVESTING Both species are important annual pulse crops.

USES & PROPERTIES Mung bean and urd bean are used in many different ways but mostly as *dhal* (split pea) and for sprouts. They are eaten fresh or fermented, whole or split or milled into flour. They are often cooked and eaten as a sweet, soup-like dish. The flour is used to make pastries, bread, biscuits and starch noodles. In most countries, mung beans have become the most important source of bean sprouts – eaten raw or in salads and widely used in oriental cooking.

NUTRITIONAL VALUE Mung bean and urd bean are almost identical: good sources of energy, proteins (23%), minerals (3–4%) and amino acids (such as lysine). The sprouts have a lower calorific value but have more vitamins B and C.

Vigna radiata (L.) R. Wilczek [= *Vigna aureus* (Roxb.) Hepper]   family: Fabaceae

lü dou (Chinese); *haricot mung à grain vert* (French); *Mungbohne, Lunjabohne* (German); *bundou, fundou* (Japanese); *kacang hijau* (Malay); *thua thong* (Thai)

Vigna subterranea
jugo bean • Bambara groundnut

Jugo bean fruits

Jugo bean plant

Jugo bean seeds

DESCRIPTION An annual herb with numerous thin stems bearing trifoliate leaves on slender stalks. The minute flowers grow into the ground after fertilisation and the rounded, single-seeded, slightly wrinkled pods are formed underground (in the same way as the groundnut or peanut, *Arachis hypogaea*). The seeds are variable in size and colour (yellow, red, brown or black, depending on the cultivar). Another (lesser known) African groundnut is the Hausa groundnut or Kersting's groundnut (*Macrotyloma geocarpum*, previously called *Kerstingiella geocarpa*).

ORIGIN & HISTORY Indigenous to tropical Africa, from West Africa to southern Africa. Domestication is believed to have taken place in West Africa. The plant is an ancient African crop that is still of local importance in rural parts of Africa and Madagascar. It is grown on a small scale in the USA, Australia, central Asia and Southeast Asia.

PARTS USED Ripe or near-ripe seeds.

CULTIVATION & HARVESTING The jugo bean is a promising crop for semi-arid areas, as it is remarkably tolerant of drought and poor soil. Pods are usually harvested just before the seeds ripen (when they are still soft).

USES & PROPERTIES The beans are eaten as a delicious snack food. They are boiled in salted water and eaten by popping them out of the soft pods into the mouth, one by one. Various recipes exist for adding the boiled nuts to stews and other dishes. Fully ripe seeds may be dried and ground into flour, which can be used for baking. Ripe seeds may be cooked and used in the same way as ordinary beans or lentils but they require a long period of boiling to soften.

NUTRITIONAL VALUE Similar to other pulses. The ripe seeds contain 23% high quality protein, 7% fat, 55% carbohydrates and 3% minerals. They are an important source of amino acids for rural people who live on cereal-rich diets.

Vigna subterranea (L.) Verdc. [*Voandzeia subterranea* (L.) Thouars]   family: Fabaceae

pois bambara (French); *Angola-Erbse, Erderbse, Bambarra-erdnuss* (German); *pisello di terra* (Italian); *banbara mame* (Japanese); *kacang bogor* (Malay); *jinguba-de-cabambe* (Portuguese); *guisante de tierra, maní africano* (Spanish)

Vigna unguiculata

cowpea • black-eyed bean

Cowpea flowers and pods

Cowpea field

Asparagus bean (subsp. *sesquipedalis*)

Cowpea seeds

DESCRIPTION An annual bushy or climbing herb with compound leaves, white or pale purple flowers and pods resembling those of the common bean. The seeds are variable in colour but often white with a black spot (hence "black-eyed bean"). Various types include the common cowpea (subsp. *unguiculata*), the vernacular names of which are given below. A type with oblong seeds (subsp. *cylindrica*) is known as catjang pea or Indian cowpea in English and *duan jia jiang dou* (Chinese), *dolique catjan* (French), *Catjangbohne* (German), *fagiolo del occhio* (Italian), *hata sasage* (Japanese) and *judía catjang* (Spanish). A distinctive type with exceptionally long pods (subsp. *sesquipedalis*, previously *Vigna sesquipedalis*) has numerous common names, including asparagus bean, snake bean or yard long bean; also *dolique asperge* (French), *Spargelbohne* (German), *fagiolo asparago* (Italian), *juuroku sasage* (Japanese), *kacang panjang* (Malay) and *judía espárrago* (Spanish). Wild cowpea (*Vigna vexillata*) is sometimes grown for its seeds and edible fleshy roots.

ORIGIN & HISTORY Indigenous to Africa. Cowpea was developed as a crop in West Africa or perhaps Ethiopia. It has been used in subsistence agriculture since ancient times (as a pulse, leaf vegetable and fodder for cattle). The crop spread to Europe, India and Asia more than 2 000 years ago. In southern China, a form with slender pods (asparagus bean) was developed as a vegetable. Cowpea is today also grown in South America and southern parts of the USA.

PARTS USED Ripe seeds (or green pods and leaves).

CULTIVATION & HARVESTING An extremely drought tolerant, annual crop that is used in mixed systems in Africa.

USES & PROPERTIES The mature seeds, young pods and leaves are eaten as vegetables and are added to numerous traditional dishes (soups, stews, curries). Seeds are popular in India for *dhal* soup (made from dehusked, split beans). Immature seeds are canned or frozen.

NUTRITIONAL VALUE Very similar to mung bean.

Vigna unguiculata (L.) Walp.   family: Fabaceae

jiang dou (Chinese); *dolique à oeil noir, niébé* (French); *Kuerbse, Augenbohne* (German); *fagiolo dall'occhio nero* (Italian); *sasage* (Japanese); *kacang merah* (Malay); *frijol de vaca* (Spanish)

Vitis vinifera
grapevine

Grapevine flowers

Grapevine with fruits

Grapes

DESCRIPTION A woody, deciduous, perennial climber with coiled tendrils, large, toothed leaves and clusters of inconspicuous flowers that develop into bunches of juicy berries. The North American muscadine grape (*V. rotundifolia*) and slip skin grape (*V. labrusca*) are of minor importance.

ORIGIN & HISTORY Wild grape (subsp. *sylvestris*) occurs naturally in Middle Asia. The cultivated form (subsp. *vinifera*) is hardly different but has become much diversified (10 000 cultivars, red or white, small-berried wine grapes, large, oval-berried table grapes). Cultivation in the Near East dates from 8000 BC. The Egyptians, Greeks and Romans spread the wine culture to the west and east. Europe is still the main producer (France, Italy, Spain, and many others) but now also Australia, Argentine, Chile, South Africa and California in the USA.

PARTS USED Ripe fruits.

CULTIVATION & HARVESTING Modern cultivars are grafted onto a suitable rootstock and are grown in all regions with hot, dry summers and cold, wet winters. The plants are carefully supported and pruned to regulate fruiting.

USES & PROPERTIES Grapes are eaten as table grapes, enjoyed as juice or fermented to make wine, sparkling wine, brandy and vinegar. Dried grapes give raisins, white sultanas or small, black currants (produced in Greece; named after Corinth). Red wine results from contact between the skins of red grapes and their white juice during fermentation but white wine can also be made from red grapes (*blanc de noir*) and not only from white grapes (*blanc de blanc*). Short exposure to the red skins gives rosé wine. The diversity of wine and its complexity is a feature of western culture. Wine is important in cooking (sauces, *coq au vin*, etc.). Grape leaves stuffed with rice and mince are the *dolmades* of Greek cooking. A by-product is grapeseed oil.

NUTRITIONAL VALUE Grapes contain sugar (15–25%), tartaric and malic acids, minerals and modest amounts of vitamin C.

Vitis vinifera L.   family: Vitaceae

vigne (French); *Weinrebe* (German); *vino* (Italian); *vid* (Spanish)

Wasabia japonica

wasabi

Wasabi plants

Wasabi flowers

Wasabi stem

Wasabi products

DESCRIPTION A perennial herb with thick stems, large, round leaves (like a pumpkin) and white flowers similar to those of horseradish.

ORIGIN & HISTORY Indigenous to Japan. The plant is wild-harvested but several cultivars are grown commercially in Japan and in recent times also in North America and New Zealand.

PARTS USED The root and stem base.

CULTIVATION & HARVESTING Plants are propagated mainly from seeds and are said to be rather difficult to grow. There are two forms: one cultivated in normal soil, and the other grown in running water. The stems and roots are harvested and sold on fresh produce markets or are processed into powders and pastes.

USES & PROPERTIES Wasabi is available as an expensive green powder or green paste. Beware of fake wasabi (which is horseradish that is coloured green). It is very pungent (and lachrymatory!) and is a popular condiment in Japan, where it is used like horseradish. The most important use is with raw fish (*sashimi*), but it is added to numerous other dishes, including *tempura* (deep-fried, battered vegetables, such as perilla), noodle dishes and various versions of *sushi*. *Sashimi* is fresh fish dipped in soy sauce and wasabi paste. It is less well known than *sushi*, which is short grain rice cooked in sugar and vinegar and served with salmon, tuna, shrimp, scrambled egg, pickled ginger or rolled in seaweed (*nori*). Like *sushi* (the Japanese version of the sandwich, using rice instead of bread), wasabi is becoming popular in western countries.

NUTRITIONAL VALUE Wasabi is used in small amounts only.

NOTES As with other members of the cabbage family such as mustard and horseradish, the pungent taste is due to isothiocyanates. The main compound in wasabi is sinigrin (also present in black mustard and horseradish). It is tasteless and only becomes pungent after enzymatic conversion to "mustard oils".

Wasabia japonica (Miq.) Matsum. [= *Wasabia wasabi* (Siebold) Makino]   family: Brassicaceae

shan yu cai (Chinese); *raifort du japon* (French); *Wasabi, Japanischer Kren, Japanischer Meerrettich* (German); *wasabi* (Japanese); *wasábia* (Spanish)

385

Xanthosoma sagittifolium

tannia • new cocoyam

Tannia leaves

Tannia plant

Tannia tubers

DESCRIPTION A robust perennial herb with fleshy tubers and large leaves shaped like arrowheads. There are several species of *Xanthosoma* and the same names used for other starch roots such as cocoyam, taro and dasheen are also applied to these plants. Tannia is known as white malanga, while yellow malanga is *X. atrovirens*. Several other sources of starch are known as arrowroots (used by American Indians to treat arrow wounds). These unrelated plants include the West Indian arrowroot (*Maranta arundinacea*, Marantaceae), Chinese arrowroot (*Nelumbo nucifera*, Nymphaeaceae), Guinea arrowroot (*Calathea allouia*, Marantaceae), Indian arrowroot (*Curcuma angustifolia*, Zingiberaceae), Queensland arrowroot (*Canna edulis*, Cannaceae) and Tahiti arrowroot (*Tacca leontopetaloides*, Taccaceae). Arrowroot should not be confused with arrowhead or Chinese arrowhead (*Sagittaria sinensis*, Alismataceae). This is a water plant grown in China and Japan for its onion-like corms that are cooked in stews, fried like potatoes or dried for flour.

ORIGIN & HISTORY Tropical America (original distribution unknown). It has been cultivated in Central America and the Caribbean region since pre-Columbian times and is associated with the slave trade from West Africa, where it has become an important crop.

PARTS USED Tubers, stems and young leaves.

CULTIVATION & HARVESTING Plants are grown from tubers and thrive in tropical conditions.

USES & PROPERTIES Stems and leaves are used as vegetables, while the tuber is a source of starch. They are used like taro in West Africa to prepare *fufu*. Yellow malanga (*X. atrovirens*) is considered to be an even more important commercial source of starch. Starch is an easily digestible white powder that is used in cooking to thicken sauces, soups and stews and to prepare desserts, gruels and porridges.

NUTRITIONAL VALUE Mainly a source of energy (starch has an energy value of about 340 kcal per 100 g); yellow malanga contains some vitamin A.

Xanthosoma sagittifolium (L.) Schott   family: Araceae

qian nian yu (Chinese); *tannia* (French); *Tannia, Goldnarbe* (German); *keladi* (Malay); *yautia, malanga* (Spanish)

Zanthoxylum piperitum

Sichuan pepper

Sichuan pepper leaves

Zanthoxylum simulans

Sichuan pepper

DESCRIPTION A small, deciduous tree (up to 4 m) with thorny stems, bright green, compound leaves, tiny whitish flowers and small, brown capsules each with one or two small, shiny black seeds. Another species cultivated and used in a similar way is *Z. simulans* (= *Z. bungei*) from China. The original, real pepper is an unrelated plant (*Piper nigrum*) but there are several trees that provide pepper-like condiments. These include the West African tree known as Guinea pepper (*Xylopia aethiopica*, family Annonaceae) and the South American pepper tree (*Schinus molle*, Anacardiaceae). Ripe fruits of the latter are known as "pink pepper" and have become popular as a pepper substitute.

ORIGIN & HISTORY Indigenous to East Asia. The plant is a traditional source of spice in China and Japan – Sichuan pepper or Japanese pepper was used long before black peppercorns became known.

PARTS USED Ripe seed capsules with the seeds (or less often the leaves).

CULTIVATION & HARVESTING Trees are grown from seeds or cuttings. The small capsules are picked by hand when nearly ripe and allowed to dry in the sun until they split open. Leaves may be dried and powdered to make a Japanese spice known as *sansho*.

USES & PROPERTIES Sichuan pepper is used in much the same way as pepper (Chinese cooks prefer white pepper and rarely use black pepper). It adds a sharp, spicy flavour when ground and sprinkled on chicken, noodle dishes, soups and other Chinese and Japanese dishes. It is one of very few condiments used in Japanese cooking, where the natural flavours of fresh ingredients are typically allowed to dominate in a dish. Leaf powder or *sansho* is milder in flavour than the fruits and more citrus-like because of the essential oils that are contained in the leaves.

NUTRITIONAL VALUE Used in small quantities for flavour only.

Zanthoxylum piperitum (L.) DC.   family: Rutaceae

hu chiao, chin chiao, shu chiao, hua jiao (Chinese); *poivre du Setchuan* (French); *Japanischer Pfeffer, Szechuan-pfeffer, Chinesischer Pfeffer* (German); *sansho* (Japanese)

Zea mays

corn • maize • mealies

White maize cob

Maize field

Sweetcorn and baby corn

Yellow maize, white maize and popcorn

DESCRIPTION A robust annual grass (up to 4 m) with male flowers in plumes (tassels) at the tips and female flowers with silky styles forming ears lower down, turning into yellow or white grains. The endosperm is soft in dent types and hard in flint types and popcorn (which puff up when heated). Sweetcorn has a high sugar content in the endosperm.

ORIGIN & HISTORY Central America (Mexico). Maize is a cultigen derived from wild maize or teosinte (subsp. *mexicana*) and has been cultivated in Mexico for at least 7 500 years. It is one of the three top cereals (with rice and wheat). Nearly half the world production comes from the Corn Belt in the USA but many temperate and tropical countries produce maize for own consumption.

PARTS USED Dry, one-seeded fruits (grains).

CULTIVATION & HARVESTING Highly mechanised except in rural parts of Africa and Latin America.

USES & PROPERTIES The grain is used as human food in the form of semolina, flour and porridge (Africa and South America), polenta in Italy, hominy (crushed grain or grits) in North America and various items of confectionery such as muffins, cookies and pancakes. Cornflour or cornstarch is used as thickening agent. Maize is also eaten as cornflakes and other breakfast cereals, tortillas, corn on the cob and the famous USA snack food, popcorn. Sweetcorn and babycorn are used as vegetables and can be frozen, dehydrated or canned. The endosperm contains up to 50% oil, rich in polyunsaturated fats (60% linoleic acid). Maize is fermented to produce beer and bourbon whisky, the national spirits of the USA. Most maize is used as livestock feed.

NUTRITIONAL VALUE Maize has a high energy value (350 kcal per 100 g) and is rich in vitamins A and E but as staple diet the low levels of lysine and niacin have to be supplemented.

Zea mays L.   family: Poaceae

yu mi, yu shu shu (Chinese); *mäis* (French); *Körnermais* (German); *anaaj* (Hindi); *granoturco* (Italian); *toumorokoshi* (Japanese); *jagung* (Malay); *milho* (Portuguese); *maíz* (Spanish)

Zingiber officinale

ginger

Ginger flower

Ginger plants

Mature and young ginger

DESCRIPTION A perennial, aromatic herb (up to 1 m) with large leaves arising from creeping, branching rhizomes below the ground. Yellow flowers are borne in cone-like clusters (but plants rarely flower).

ORIGIN & HISTORY Ginger is a cultigen that has not yet been found in the wild. It is believed to originate from northeastern India or southern China and has been grown since ancient times as a spice and medicine. India is the largest producer but most countries in tropical regions of Asia, Africa and America now grow the crop on a large commercial scale.

PARTS USED Young or mature rhizomes.

CULTIVATION & HARVESTING Plants are easily propagated from rhizomes. Ginger is sold young (green ginger), mature, preserved (China and Hong Kong) or dried and powdered.

USES & PROPERTIES Ginger is an important spice that is much used in Asian cooking to flavour meat dishes, marinades, fish, curries, soups, sauces, rice dishes and stir-fries. The fresh, pickled or candied root is eaten in China and Japan. It is widely used in confectionery such as biscuits, cakes and sweets, and especially the famous British gingerbread or its French equivalent, *pain d'épice*. Pieces of fresh or preserved ginger are added to preserves and jams. Ginger is important in the beverage industry. Ginger beer is a frothy, low-alcohol drink (particularly popular in Britain), which is made from water, sugar, ginger and cream of tartar, and allowed to ferment. Ginger ale is carbonised water to which ginger essence and colouring are added. It is used in the same way as club soda in long drinks made from gin or whisky. Ginger extracts or ginger oil are also used in ginger wine, liqueur, brandy and flavoured teas.

NUTRITIONAL VALUE Limited, as ginger is used in small amounts for flavour.

NOTES Ginger is widely used to counteract nausea and to improve digestion.

Zingiber officinale Rosc.   family: Zingiberaceae

jiang (Chinese); *gingembre* (French); *Ingwer* (German); *zénzero* (Italian); *jinjaa, shouga* (Japanese); *haliya* (Malay); *jengibre* (Spanish); *khing* (Thai)

Zizania aquatica

American wild rice • Canadian wild rice

American wild rice flowers

American wild rice leaves

American wild rice grains

DESCRIPTION A tall, annual grass of up to 2 m in height that grows in the shallow water of lakes. It has a sparse panicle bearing a single female spikelet above six male spikelets. The grains are elongated and dark brown to almost black. Another species, *Z. palustris*, is sometimes confused with *Z. aquatica*. Chinese wild rice, also known as Manchurian wild rice (*Z. latifolia*) has served as a traditional food source in East Asia since ancient times (both as a wild cereal and for the crispy, succulent stems, eaten as a vegetable).

ORIGIN & HISTORY Indigenous to the Great Lakes region (eastern Canada and northeastern USA). The ripe grains were traditionally collected by the North American Indians for whom it served as staple food. Wild supplies were exhausted during the 1970s and the plant became the only cereal to be domesticated in historical times.

PARTS USED Dry, one-seeded fruits (grains).

CULTIVATION & HARVESTING Wild rice is still wild-harvested to some extent. Historically this was done from a canoe by bending the stalks over and beating them with sticks so that the grains accumulated in the canoe. Today, wild rice is grown commercially as a new crop, mainly in Massachusetts and California in the USA. Non-shattering cultivars are being developed. Seedlings are planted in paddies and the crop is mechanically harvested.

USES & PROPERTIES The dark, shiny grains have become a common sight in health shops all over the world. They are heated during processing to release the husks and this gives them a delicious nutty flavour. Wild rice is used in the same way as ordinary rice.

NUTRITIONAL VALUE Considered a health food because of the high protein content (up to 15%) that includes important amino acids such as lysine and methionine. Also noteworthy are the high levels of B vitamins (including thiamin, riboflavin and niacin).

Zizania aquatica L.   family: Poaceae

gu, mei zhou ye hei dao (Chinese); *riz sauvage américain* (French); *Wildreis, Kanadischer Wildreis, Indianerreis, Tuscarorareis* (German); *amerika makomo* (Japanese)

Ziziphus jujuba
Chinese date • jujube tree • French jujube

Chinese date leaves and fruits

Chinese date flowers

Chinese dates

DESCRIPTION A spiny shrub or small tree (sometimes reaching 15 m) with zigzag stems bearing sharp thorns and glossy, three-nerved leaves. The flowers are yellowish green and inconspicuous and the oblong, fleshy fruits are plum-like, reddish-brown in colour, with one or two hard seeds. Several other *Ziziphus* species bear edible fruits that are of local importance. Indian jujube, desert apple or *ber* (*Z. mauritiana*) is commonly cultivated in the dry regions of India (and parts of Southeast Asia) for the small fruits that are eaten raw, preserved or dried. In the Near East (eastern Mediterranean to Arabia), the Christ's-thorn or *ilb* (*Z. spina-christi*) bears small, oblong fruits with the taste and texture of apple. Christ's crown of thorns is believed to have been made from this tree. *Ziziphus lotus* bears the "lotus fruits" of ancient mythology. *Ziziphus mistol* from the Andes yields edible fruits that are used for alcoholic beverages. The African buffalo thorn (*Z. mucronata*) is an important source of fruits

and traditional medicine in rural areas.

ORIGIN & HISTORY Southeastern Europe to China. The plant has a long history of human use and is still widely cultivated in southern Europe and Asia.

PARTS USED Ripe fruits (fresh or dried).

CULTIVATION & HARVESTING Trees are grown from seeds and cuttings. Ripe, hand-picked fruits are used fresh but are usually sold in the international trade as dried fruits ("Chinese dates" or "red dates").

USES & PROPERTIES The delicious and nutritious fruits are eaten fresh, dried or candied. They are also used in pastry-making and in savoury dishes, and as ingredient of stuffings, sauces and soups.

NUTRITIONAL VALUE The dried fruit has a high calorific value (315 kcal per 100 g) and the fresh fruit contains up to 70 mg vitamin C. This is an important functional food in China, used to improve general health, gain weight and alleviate respiratory disorders.

Ziziphus jujuba Mill. (= *Z. vulgaris* Lam.)

family: Rhamnaceae

da zao (Chinese); *jujubier* (French); *Brustbeerbaum* (German); *badara*, *ber* (Hindi); *giuggiolo* (Italian); *sanebuto natsume* (Japanese); *azufaifo chino* (Spanish); *phutsaa cheen* (Thai)

NUTRIENTS, DIET AND HEALTH

Diversity and balance

Good nutrition and healthy living require diversity and balance. By eating a wide range of different foods, we improve the probability that all the essential ingredients are present in the diet. Balance is equally important, as too much proteins or too much fat can be as detrimental as too little. It is the combination of food in our diet that keeps us healthy, and plants provide a large proportion of our daily energy and nutritional needs. The proportion of plant foods in human diets varies from about 96% in poor countries to as low as 50% in affluent societies. The main nutrients are carbohydrates, fats and proteins – these three provide all our energy needs. Vitamins and minerals are present in small amounts – they give no energy but are important for maintaining specific functions of the body.

Energy

The energy value of food depends on the water content and the combination of carbohydrate, fat and protein. Energy is measured in kilocalories (abbreviated as kcal or sometimes Cal) or in kilojoules (abbreviated as kJ). To convert kcal to kJ simply multiply by 4.18 (1 kcal = 4.18 kJ). Adults require about 1 500 to 3 000 kilocalories per day. The main sources of energy are carbohydrates (simple and compound sugars), fat and protein. The energy yields are about 400 kcal per 100 g of carbohydrate, 900 kcal per 100 g of fat and 400 kcal per 100 g protein (corresponding to 1 700, 3 700 and 1 700 kJ respectively). The alcohol (ethanol) in alcoholic beverages also gives energy (700 kcal or 2 900 kJ per 100 g). The water content of food has an important influence on the calorific value – nuts and grains have a low water content (5 to 10 %) and therefore have a very high energy value, while starch tubers and fruits have a high water content (80 to 90%) and therefore a relatively low energy yield per 100 g. When the energy value is calculated on a dry weight basis, then the values would be similar.

Carbohydrates

Carbohydrates are the main energy source utilised by our bodies. Practically all carbohydrates in the human diet are derived from plants (lactose or milk sugar is the only exception). Green plants have the unique ability to produce sugars through a miracle process known as photosynthesis – the chlorophyll in leaves creates simple sugars using carbon dioxide, water and sunlight, and yields oxygen as a "waste" product. We are therefore indebted to plants not only for our food, but also for the air we breathe – without plants no animal life would be possible.

The sugars are variously combined to produce disaccharides (two simple sugars joined together), sugar alcohols (modified sugars found naturally in plants), oligosaccharides (short chains of sugars), polysaccharides (long chains of sugar molecules such as starch, cellulose and gums) and dietary fibre (polysaccharide materials which are resistant to digestion but which have important effects on health – see below). Carbohydrates are best consumed in the form of fruits and especially dried fruit, where they are combined with other nutritional elements. The ingestion of pure sugar (so-called "empty calories") in the form of refined sugars, sweets and soft drinks is considered unhealthy as it may lead to obesity, high blood pressure, tooth decay and other symptoms of poor health. It has been suggested that a diet of 60 to 70% carbohydrates is ideal for athletes. For endurance events, "carbo-loading" is sometimes done to increase the glycogen stored in muscle tissue.

Simple sugars (monosaccharides)

These sugars are very common in nature, often forming a component of more complex sugars. The most important monosaccharides are hexose sugars (with six carbon atoms), which include glucose, fructose and galactose. Less common in plants are pentose sugars (with five carbon atoms) such as xylose, ribose and deoxyribose. Glucose is a component of honey and various fruits and vegetables and is the main building block of most carbohydrates in human food (such as sucrose and starch). Fructose is less common but occurs in honey and in many fruits and vegetables. Galactose is relatively rare but is a component of some legume polysaccharides (and lactose or milk sugar). A healthy person has to maintain a blood glucose level of around 1 g per litre of blood.

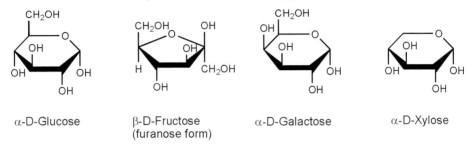

α-D-Glucose   β-D-Fructose (furanose form)   α-D-Galactose   α-D-Xylose

Chemical structures of common monosaccharides

Disaccharides

These are sugars with two monosaccharides joined together. Sucrose (one glucose linked to one fructose molecule) is by far the most common example – it occurs in many fruits and vegetables and often accumulates to high levels, as in sugar cane and sugar beet. Another common disaccharide is maltose or malt sugar (two glucose molecules joined together). It is formed when starch is broken down during the process of malting. Malting is the controlled germination of grains such as barley or wheat, during which the stored starch reserve is enzymatically converted to maltose to serve as an energy source for the young seedling. Malting or sprouting is commonly employed to produce malted food products and alcoholic beverages such as beer and whiskey.

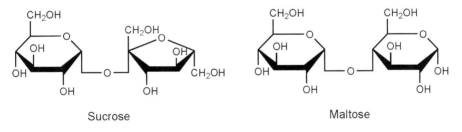

Sucrose   Maltose

Chemical structures of common disaccharides

Sugar alcohols, alcohol and sweeteners

Sugar alcohols commonly occur in various fruits and are structurally related to monosaccharides and disaccharides but with an alcohol (-OH) group attached. The most common ones are sorbitol, mannitol and inositol (also known as pinitol). Sorbitol is widely used in foods and sweets (especially for diabetics), as it is less sweet than sucrose and more slowly absorbed into the bloodstream. It also slows down tooth decay and is therefore added to sweets and chewing gum. Mannitol and pinitol are both considered useful in lowering blood sugar levels in diabetics. Sweeteners of this type are known as bulk sweeteners. Intense sweeteners are chemical compounds with a sweetness that greatly exceeds the sweetness of sucrose. They are often artificial and include alitame, aspartame, acesulfam-K, thaumatin, cyclamate, saccharin and stevioside. Saccharin, cyclamate (various salts of cyclamic acid) and aspartame are banned in some countries because of suspected negative side effects (including neurotoxic, teratogenic and carcinogenic effects). Alcohol is produced by yeast fermentation of various carbohydrate sources such as grape juice, palm sap, fruit juice, sugar cane, malted barley or potato. The sugar is simply converted into alcohol, which contributes about 5% of the total energy in the diet of people who regularly drink beer, wine or other alcoholic beverages.

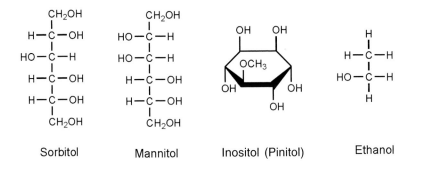

Sorbitol   Mannitol   Inositol (Pinitol)   Ethanol

Chemical structures of common sugar alcohols and ethanol

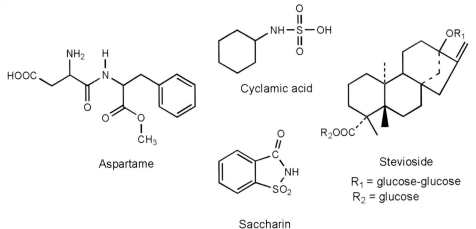

Aspartame   Cyclamic acid   Stevioside

R₁ = glucose-glucose
R₂ = glucose

Saccharin

Chemical structures of intense sweeteners (three artificial sweeteners and one natural sweetener, stevioside)

Oligosaccharides

Most of these short chain sugars are not digested by enzymes in the human digestive system but by bacterial fermentation in the large intestine, causing flatulence. The best-known oligosaccharides are raffinose and stachyose (found in legume seeds), fructans (in some vegetables) and inulin (the main storage carbohydrate of Asteraceae, such as Jerusalem artichoke).

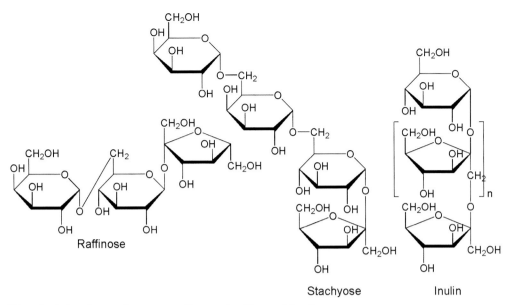

Chemical structures of common oligosaccharides and inulin

Polysaccharides

Simple sugars may be joined together into long chains to form polysaccharides. The best-known and most important polysaccharides are starch and cellulose. Starch is the most important storage carbohydrate found in plant tissues (roots, stems and cereals). It is broken down in the human body by special enzymes (amylases), secreted by the salivary glands and the pancreas. The first step in the digestion of starch occurs in the mouth, hence the importance of chewing food properly. Some starches are more easily digested than others, depending on the way in which the glucose molecules are linked together.

Cellulose is the building material of cell walls but the human digestive system is incapable of digesting it. Micro-organisms in the gut of herbivores such as sheep and cattle produce the enzyme cellulase, which breaks down the cellulose into glucose molecules. In the human diet, cellulose nevertheless plays an important part as dietary fibre – it speeds up the bulk movement of food through the intestines and regulates the rate of absorption of nutrients.

Dietary fibre (also called non-starch polysaccharide or NSP) is defined as that part of plant material that is resistant to digestion. It can be insoluble (mainly cellulose) or non-cellulose and water-soluble. The latter includes pectin (the gelling agent found in fruits and jams), α-glucans (found in cereals), various gums (exudates or extracts from legume seeds used as emulsifiers and stabilisers in food products), mucilages and agar (thickeners obtained from algae). The soluble and insoluble fractions of dietary fibre can occur in roughly equal proportions in vegetable and legume seeds but the ratio varies greatly in cereals, fruits and other types of food. One of the interesting effects of soluble NSP is that it reduces cholesterol by preventing the reabsorption of bile acids in the intestine. Bile acids are formed from cholesterol, so that the formation of new bile acids reduces blood cholesterol levels.

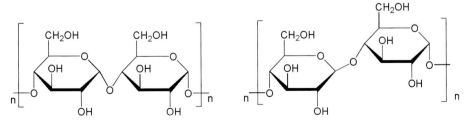

Starch (linked α-D-Glucose)   Cellulose (linked β-D-Glucose)

Chemical structures of starch and cellulose

395

Fats and oils (lipids)

Fat is an important energy source in the human diet and is also important for normal growth and development. The essential fatty acids that form part of the chemical structure of fats and oils are essential for the structure of cell membranes and prostaglandins. Fats and oils are the solvents and carriers of vitamins A, D, E and K – these are not soluble in water. Although fat is an important dietary component, too much of it can lead to cardiovascular diseases and some forms of cancer. The excessive intake of fat in the Western world (especially the USA) is a source of concern. Fat contributes to the texture and taste of food, hence its popularity.

Most dietary fats occur in nature as triglycerides – these comprise three fatty acids combined with glycerol. Fatty acids consist of a chain of carbon atoms with a carboxyl group (-COOH) at the one end. In saturated fatty acids, all the additional bonds of the carbon atoms are occupied by hydrogen atoms. This means that there are no double bonds in the carbon chain of saturated fatty acids. Animal fats contain mainly palmitic acid and stearic acid – both saturated fatty acids.

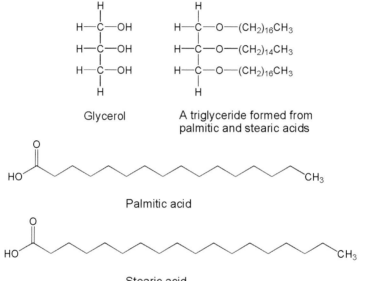

Chemical structures of palmitic and stearic acids and a triglyceride

Unsaturated fatty acids have one or more double bonds between the carbon atoms in the carbon chain. They are commonly found in plant foods. Monounsaturated fatty acids have only one double bond, while polyunsaturated fatty acids have two or more double bonds. Monounsaturated fatty acids are further distinguished by the position of the double bond – omega-3 (on the third carbon), omega-6 on the sixth carbon, and so on. Oleic acid, the main fatty acid in olive oil, is a monounsaturated fatty acid as it has a single double bond.

Common polyunsaturated fatty acids found in plant foods are linoleic and linolenic acids. Because of the double bonds, plant fats usually occur as oils, while animal fats tend to be solid. Most vegetable oils are rich in monounsaturated fatty acids, while the percentage of saturated fatty acids is typically between 10 and 20% of the total. Some plant fats, however, have quite high levels of saturated fatty acids: cottonseed oil (25%), palm oil (45%) and coconut oil (nearly 90%). Essential fatty acids are those that cannot be made within the human body and have to be obtained from the diet. Humans are unable to insert double bonds in positions three and six of the carbon chain. Since linoleic acid and linolenic acid have double bonds in these positions, they have to be obtained directly from food and cannot be manufactured from other fatty acids. These two essential fatty acids form part of cell membranes and are the precursors of prostaglandins.

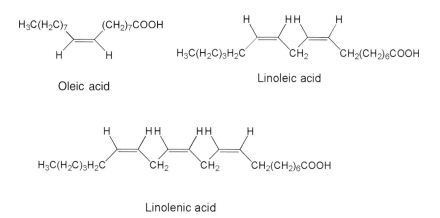

Chemical structures of three common fatty acids found in plant food

Cholesterol belongs to a type of fat commonly referred to as steroids. It is present in animal foods but totally absent from plant foods. Cholesterol is also produced by the human body, so that a high consumption of animal products may lead to excessive amounts which may block arterial walls. Cholesterol is bound by two types of protein which act as carriers, so-called HDL (high-density lipoprotein) and LDL (low-density lipoprotein). LDL is considered bad because it tends to attach to arterial walls, while HDL is considered good because it promotes the removal of cholesterol from arteries and its transport to the liver, where it is broken down. A large proportion of animal fats in the diet will lead to an increase in the harmful LDL cholesterol.

Fats are insoluble in water and therefore have to be emulsified (dispersed as small droplets) before they can be digested. In the digestive system, bile salts and lecithin are added to promote emulsification (lecithin is an emulsifier that occurs naturally in legume seeds and other plant foods). The fat droplets are then digested by lipases (enzymes secreted by the pancreas) and bile into fatty acids and glycerol. After absorption, these components are reassembled again to form triglycerides. Modern techniques to stabilise and preserve oils and fats include hydrogenation, a process that converts natural *cis* fatty acids into less fluid *trans* fatty acids. These *trans* fatty acids are associated with numerous detrimental effects on health. Natural fats and oils with high levels of monounsaturated fatty acids (such as olive oil) are healthier than margarine and are also more stable when used as cooking oil.

Proteins

The word "protein" means "first" or "primary" (derived from Greek) and proteins are indeed very important in nutrition. Proteins consist of several peptide chains which may be linked and folded in various ways. The peptide chains comprise numerous amino acids – these are the basic building blocks of proteins. Amino acids have an amino group (-NH2) on the one end and an acid carboxyl group (-COOH) on the other end. The amino group of one amino acid can be linked to the carboxyl group of another amino acid and in this way long peptide chains are formed.

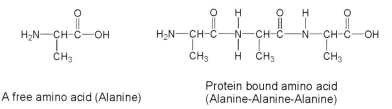

A free amino acid (Alanine)

Protein bound amino acid
(Alanine-Alanine-Alanine)

Chemical structures of free and protein-bound amino acids

Twenty common amino acids are found in proteins. They differ in the structure of the R group (there are 20 different R groups). Some amino acids can be manufactured in the human body – they are called non-essential amino acids. The essential amino acids are those that have to be obtained from food – isoleucine, leucine, lysine, methionine, phenylalanine, threonine, tryptophan, valine and histidine (essential for infants only). The non-essential amino acids are glycine, glutamic acid, arginine, aspartic acid, proline, alanine, serine, tyrosine, cysteine, asparagine and glutamine. There are literally millions of different combinations in which these 20 amino acids can be linked to form polypeptides and proteins. Plant proteins are more easily digested than animal proteins but are called incomplete proteins because they lack one or more essential amino acids – only animal proteins have all. It is therefore important to include mixtures of different plant proteins in a vegetarian diet – different types of grains, legumes (pulses) and nuts – in order to ensure that all the essential amino acids are supplied. The daily requirement of proteins in the diet of adults is considered to be about 0.8 g per kg body weight per day. Infants require about 1.8 g per kg per day, while the elderly need 1 g per kg per day. From these figures it is clear that too much protein is consumed in Western countries, leading to detrimental effects such as obesity, cardiovascular disease, diabetes and cancer.

Vitamins

The term "vitamin" derives from "vital amine" – originally based on the idea that the essential factors in food were amines. Vitamin A, known to be fat-soluble, was later identified as retinol. Vitamin B turned out to be a mixture of different compounds. Not all letters were used to name the vitamins, as some were already known by other names.

The vitamins of relevance to plant foods are divided into two main groups: fat-soluble vitamins (A, D, E and K) and water-soluble vitamins (B_1, B_2, B_6, B_{12}, biotin, C, folic acid, niacin and pantothenic acid). The recommended daily allowance (RDA) – the quantity needed to prevent deficiency – varies from country to country. RDAs allowed for labelling purposes in the European Union (EU) are given below.

Vitamin A

The chemical name for vitamin A is retinol. The original source of all retinol is provitamin A, better known as ß-carotene, and is found in plant pigments. Vitamin A offers protection against cancer and infectious diseases and is essential for the formation of eye pigment. Deficiencies cause night blindness or in severe cases, complete blindness. The units of vitamin A are given in retinol equivalents or RE (1 RE = 1 µg of retinol = 6 µg of β-carotene = 12 µg of other carotenoids). The recommended daily allowance (RDA) for vitamin A is 800 µg or RE (about 0.8 mg of retinol or nearly 5 mg of β-carotene per day). Overdoses resulting from the inappropriate or excessive use of vitamin supplements can be dangerous. Pigmented fruits (red and yellow) and green or yellow vegetables are the best natural sources of vitamin A. A 100 g portion of carrots supplies nearly three times the RDA.

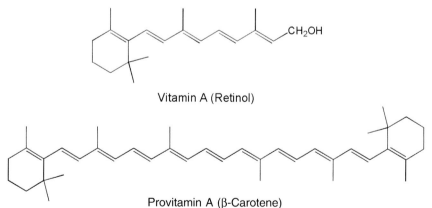

Vitamin A (Retinol)

Provitamin A (β-Carotene)

Chemical structures of vitamin A (retinol) and provitamin A (β-carotene)

Vitamin D

Calciferol or vitamin D is found only in animal foods but its absorption may be impaired in people with a diet very high in phytate. Phytate is a common ingredient of plant foods – it is a cyclic complex formed by inositol linked to six phosphate molecules. Due to its ability to bind to minerals, phytate prevents the absorption of these minerals into the bloodstream. Deficiency symptoms are common in people deprived from sunlight. The RDA is 5 µg.

Vitamin E

This is the name given to a group of eight tocopherols and tocotrienols that are powerful antioxidants. They protect fatty acids and other membrane components from oxidation by free radicals. Vitamin E is fat-soluble and vegetable oils are the major source of this vitamin. The RDA is 10 mg of α-tocopherol.

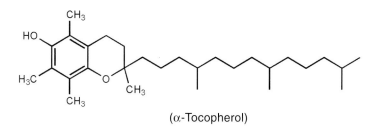

(α-Tocopherol)

Chemical structure of vitamin E (α-tocopherol)

Vitamin K

The chemical names of this vitamin are phytomenadione (=α-phylloquinone, K_1), menaquinone (=β-phylloquinone, K_2) and menadione (K_3). It occurs in green leafy vegetables but deficiencies (resulting in impaired blood clotting) are rare. In food tables the level of phylloquinone (vitamin K_1) is usually given – a daily dose of 1 mg is considered safe.

Vitamin B$_1$

Also known as thiamin, this vitamin occurs mainly in cereal grains (but not in refined products). Thiamin deficiency causes a disease known as beriberi, which is nowadays rare but still occurs sporadically in Asian countries where people eat polished rice. The symptoms are muscle weakness and nerve damage. The RDA is 1.4 mg.

Vitamin B$_2$

This vitamin is better known by its chemical name riboflavin. It is present in many plant foods (and milk) – unrefined cereals and cereal bran are good sources. Deficiencies are still quite common and lead to skin eruptions and sores in the mouth. The RDA is 1.6 mg per day.

Vitamin B$_6$

This is a generic name for three chemical compounds that have the same function – pyridoxine, pyridoxal and pyridoxamine. Nuts, vegetables and unrefined cereals (as well as meat) are good sources of vitamin B$_6$, so that deficiencies are extremely rare. The most common compound is pyridoxine, with a RDA of 2 mg.

Vitamin B₁₂

The chemical name for this vitamin is cobalamin. It is not present in plant foods but occurs in animal foods and yeast products. A deficiency of vitamin B_{12} may lead to inadequate absorption of folic acid.

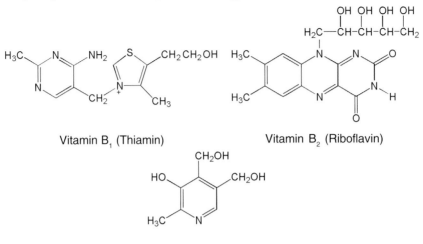

Vitamin B₁ (Thiamin)

Vitamin B₂ (Riboflavin)

Vitamin B₆ (Pyridoxine)

Chemical structures of important B vitamins

Biotin (vitamin H)

Biotin seldom causes deficiency symptoms. It is found in a large variety of foods. The RDA is 150 µg.

Vitamin C

Vitamin C is also known as ascorbic acid, and may sometimes occur with dehydroascorbic acid, which has the same activity. Ascorbic acid is found in fresh fruits and vegetables. In the past, deficiencies were quite common as fresh fruits were unavailable during long winters (and long voyages on ships). A shortage in the diet leads to scurvy, poor wound healing and various other symptoms – in severe cases, the condition may be fatal. The discovery that citrus fruits can reverse the symptoms of scurvy saved the lives of many sailors – the nickname "limey" comes from the daily ration of lime juice introduced by the British navy. Deficiencies are still fairly common, especially in alcoholics, smokers and the elderly. Vitamin C is water-soluble and is rapidly excreted, so that a regular supply is important. The RDA is 60 mg. Vitamin C acts as an antioxidant (in the same way as β-carotene) and plays a role in preventing heart disease and some cancers.

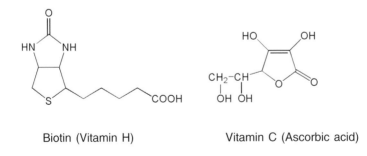

Biotin (Vitamin H)

Vitamin C (Ascorbic acid)

Chemical structures of biotin (vitamin H) and vitamin C (ascorbic acid)

Folic acid (folate)

Folate is a term used for the various derivatives of pteroylglutamic acid (PGA or folic acid, the most stable form of this group of vitamins). Folic acid is a vitamin that occurs in most fresh foods but not in processed cereals. It is also easily oxidised. As a result, deficiencies are fairly common, and staple foods are nowadays often fortified with folic acid. A shortage in the diet leads to a condition known as megaloblastic anaemia, characterised by large, immature red blood cells. Deficiencies during pregnancy have been linked to birth defects such as spina bifida. The RDA is 200 µg and the upper safe limit is considered to be 1 000 µg.

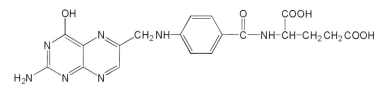

Folic acid (Pteroylglutamic acid, PGA)

Chemical structure of folic acid (the main compound of folate)

Niacin

Niacin is the generic term used for two different compounds, namely nicotinic acid and nicotinamide, which both have the same activity. Niacin can be formed in the human body from the amino acid tryptophan. Cereals (especially whole grains) are a good source of preformed niacin. The RDA is 18 mg.

Pantothenic acid

This vitamin occurs in a wide range of foods so that deficiencies are very rare. The RDA is 6 mg.

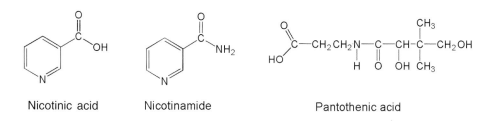

Nicotinic acid   Nicotinamide   Pantothenic acid

Chemical structures of niacin (nicotinic acid, nicotinamide) and pantothenic acid

Special biologically active compounds

In addition to vitamins, numerous other components (phytochemicals) in the diet are known to have positive health effects. The main classes of compounds are alkaloids, antioxidants, flavonoids, sulphur-containing substances and tannins. Alkaloids such as caffeine (found in tea and coffee) and quinine (found in tonic water) are bitter substances that stimulate the flow of gastric juices (the so-called *amarum* effect), thereby improving digestion. They are also stimulants that increase the heart rate and enhance the production of urine. Antioxidants comprise a wide diversity of compounds, including several vitamins as discussed above (mainly vitamins A, C and E). Phenolic compounds such as flavonoids and phenolic acids contribute to antioxidant activity. They reduce the rate of oxidation of food components (such as polyunsaturated fatty acids) by their ability to capture free radicals (active oxygen molecules). One of the most common dietary flavonoids is quercetin, a flavonol found in onions and black tea. Sulphur-containing compounds include the alliins found in garlic and glucosinolates in various members of the cabbage and mustard family. Alliins are known to lower blood cholesterol levels and are believed to protect the body against cancer, as there is a low incidence of cancer in people with a high consumption of garlic. The glucosinolates are a group of compounds that are enzymatically converted to volatile and pungent isothiocyanates when chewed or processed. There is evidence that regular consumption of glucosinolates may offer protection against cancer. Tannins are astringent substances that are considered to be detrimental to good digestion, at least in animals. However, it has been suggested that the high levels of tannins (mainly catechins) in red wine are responsible for the low incidence of coronary heart disease in Mediterranean countries despite the popularity of smoking and the high fat consumption in this region (the so-called "Mediterranean paradox"). It is clear that some foods have significant health properties, not only due to nutritional components but also to other biologically active substances. In recent years, so-called "functional foods" have become a popular concept in Western countries. The concept is an ancient tradition in China and Japan, where some foods are eaten as much for their medicinal value as for their nutritional benefits.

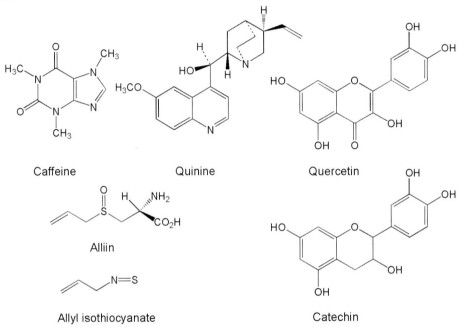

Chemical structures of some biologically active dietary components

Minerals

Some minerals are needed in relatively large quantities per day to build or support the structure of bones and teeth (calcium, magnesium and phosphorus) and to maintain a normal composition of fluids (chloride, sodium and potassium). Others are mainly involved in the structure and function of various enzymes and are required in very small amounts (iron, copper, molybdenum, selenium, zinc, chromium, iodine, magnesium, manganese). Essential minerals of which the exact functions are as yet unknown include nickel, silicon, tin and vanadium. Fluoride is not considered essential but is beneficial in protecting teeth from dental decay.

Calcium is important for healthy bones and teeth and for muscle contraction. Dark green leafy vegetables, brown bread and various pulses are good sources of this mineral. The RDA is 800 mg. Magnesium is involved in healthy bones and teeth, energy metabolism and muscle movement. The best plant sources are unrefined cereals, peanuts and vegetables. The RDA is 300 mg. Phosphorus is important in the calcification process. It has a recorded RDA of 800 mg in the EU.

Several minerals are required in small amounts and are mainly involved in enzyme systems. Iron is important for the formation of haemoglobin and the transport of oxygen (RDA = 14 mg). It is found in unrefined cereals, spinach and other green vegetables. Copper is involved in growth processes and nerve functioning. It occurs mainly in liver but also in plant sources such as cereals and dried beans. There is insufficient information to support an RDA value, but the upper safe limit is considered to be

5 mg per day. Molybdenum is important in enzymes that regulate carbohydrate and fat metabolism. It occurs in cereals, brown rice, peas, beans and dark green leafy vegetables. The upper safe limit is 200 µg. Selenium occurs in cereals and nuts and in vegetables grown in selenium-rich soils. Selenium is important in various enzymes and is part of the body's defence system. The upper safe limit in supplementation is set at 200 µg. Zinc has numerous functions in several enzyme systems. It is abundant in animal foods but also occurs in cereals and pulses. Both the RDA and suggested upper safe limit is 15 mg. Chromium is important in the metabolism of glucose, amino acids and fats. Plant food sources include nuts, pulses and wholegrain cereals. An upper safe limit is considered to be 200 µg per day for adults. Iodine is used to form thyroid hormones and is found in foods derived from the sea (fish, shellfish and kelp). The RDA is 150 µg. Manganese is mainly derived from plant food sources (green vegetables, cereals, nuts and pulses). It is associated with numerous enzyme systems but is not considered to be an essential mineral. The upper safe limit is 15 mg per day.

QUICK GUIDE TO COMMERCIALISED FOOD PLANTS

Regions of Origin: China (Chin); Tropical Asia (Indonesia) (TrAs); Australia (Aus); India (Ind); Central Asia (Himalayan region) (CAs); Near East (NE); Mediterranean (Med); Africa (Afr); Europe-Siberia (Eu); South America (SAm); Central America (including Mexico) (CAm); North America (NAm).

Data on nutritional value are cited mainly from Souci *et al.* (2000) but also from Wehmeyer (1986), Royal Society of Chemistry, Ministry of Agriculture, Fisheries and Food (1991) and United States Department of Agriculture (1992). Average values are given.

Species; family; common name(s) (**bold and underlined** scientific name: treated and illustrated species; **bold** only: illustrated species)	Region of origin	Edible plant part(s)	Nutritional value				
			Energy (kcal)	Protein	Fat	Minerals	Vitamins (very high levels in **bold**); Bio = biotin, Fol = Folic acid, Nic = Nicotinic acid, Pan = Pantothenic acid
			(g per 100 g)				
Abelmoschus esculentus; Malvaceae; okra, lady's fingers, gumbo	Afr	young fruit	19	2.10	0.20	0.90	A, B1, B2, C, Nic
Abelmoschus moschatus; Malvaceae; musk mallow, ambrette	Ind	seeds (spice)					
Abutilon indicum; Malvaceae; country mallow, Indian abutilon	TrAs	leaves, seeds					
Acacia senegal; Fabaceae; gum Arabic, gum acacia	Afr	gum					
Acanthosicyos horridus; Cucurbitaceae; nara	Afr Namibia	fruit seeds	55 **648**	1.40 **30.7**	0.30 57.0	1.60 3.40	A, B1, B2, Nic Nic
Acca sellowiana; Myrtaceae; feijoa, pineapple guava	SAm	fruit					
Acer saccharum; Aceraceae; sugar maple	NAm	stem sap					
Acmella oleracea – see *Spilanthes acmella*							
Actinidia arguta; Actinidiaceae; tara vine	Chin	fruit					
Actinidia chinensis; Actinidiaceae; kiwi, Cinese gooseberry, yang tao	Chin	fruit					
Actinidia deliciosa; Actinidiaceae; kiwi fruit	Chin	fruit	51	1.00	0.63	0.72	A, K, B1, B2, C, Nic
Actinidia kolomicta; Actinidiaceae; kolomicta	Chin	fruit					
Actinidia polygama; Actinidiaceae; silver vine	Chin	leaves					
Adansonia digitata; Bombacaceae; baobab	Afr	fruit pulp (leaves) seeds	309 431	2.70 **33.7**	0.20 30.6	5.80 5.90	B1, B2, C, Nic B1, B2, Nic

Aegilops squarrosa; Poaceae	CAs	fruit (grains)					
Aegopodium podagraria; Apiaceae; gout weed, ground elder	Eu	leaves	39	8.37	0.42	1.52	A, C
Aframomum melegueta; Zingiberaceae; grains of paradise, melegueta pepper	Afr	seeds					
Agathosma betulina; Rutaceae; buchu, round leaf buchu	Afr (South)	leaves					
Agathosma crenulata; Rutaceae; oval leaf buchu	Afr (South)	leaves					
Agave americana; Agavaceae; century plant, blue agave	CAm	stem base					
Agave tequilana; Agavaceae; tequila plant, blue agave	CAm	stem base					
Aleurites moluccana; Euphorbiaceae; candlenut tree	TrAs	seeds					
Allium ameloprasum var. *porrum*; Alliaceae; leek	NE, Med	leaf bases (bulb)	24	2.21	0.29	0.86	A, E, K, B1, B2, B6, Bio, C, Fol, Nic, Pan
Allium ameloprasum var. *holmense*; Alliaceae; great-headed garlic; Levant garlic	NE, Med	leaf bases (bulb)					
Allium ameloprasum var. *kurrat*; Alliaceae; kurrat	NE, Med	leaf bases (bulb)					
Allium cepa; Alliaceae; onion, bulb onion	CAs, NE	bulb	27	1.18	0.25	0.51	A, E, K, B1, B2, B6, Bio, C, Fol, Nic, Pan
Allium cepa var. *aggregatum*; Alliaceae; potato onion	CAs, NE	bulb					
Allium cepa var. **ascalonicum**; Alliaceae; shallot	CAs	bulb					
Allium chinense; Alliaceae; rakkyo, chiao tou	Chin	bulb					
Allium fistulosum; Alliaceae; Welsh onion, Japanese bunching onion	Chin	bulb					
Allium sativum; Alliaceae; garlic	CAs, NE	bulb	139	6.05	0.12	1.42	E, K, B1, B2, C, Nic
Allium schoenoprasum; Alliaceae; chive	Eu, Asia, Med	leaves	27	3.58	0.74	1.70	A, K, B1, B2, B6, C, Nic
Allium scorodoprasum; Alliaceae; sandleek	Eu, Asia	bulb					
Allium tuberosum; Alliaceae; Chinese chive, garlic chives	Chin	leaves, buds					
Allium ursinum; Alliaceae; bear's garlic	Eu, Asia	leaf	12	–	–	0.85	C
Alocasia macrorrhizos; Araceae; giant taro	TrAs	rhizomes					
Aloysia triphylla; Verbenaceae; lemon verbena	SAm	leaves					
Alpinia galanga; Zingiberaceae; greater galangal, galangal, Siamese ginger	TrAs	rhizomes					
Alpinia officinarum; Zingiberaceae; lesser galangal , small galangal	Chin	rhizomes					

Amaranthus angustifolius; Amaranthaceae; wild spinach	Ind	leaves					
Amaranthus caudatus; Amaranthaceae; *kiwicha*, Inca wheat	SAm	seeds leaves					
Amaranthus cruentus; Amaranthaceae; grain amaranth, Inca wheat	CAm, SAm	seeds leaves					
Amaranthus gangeticus; Amaranthaceae; wild spinach	Ind	leaves					
Amaranthus hybridus; Amaranthaceae; common pigweed	CAm, SAm	leaves	45	3.50	0.30	2.00	B1, B2, C, Nic
Amaranthus hypochondriacus; Amaranthaceae; grain amaranth, Inca wheat	CAm, SAm	seeds	365	15.8	8.81	3.25	B1, B2, Nic
Amaranthus tricolor; Amaranthaceae; Chinese spinach, Chinese amaranth	Chin, TrAs	leaves					
Amaranthus viridis; Amaranthaceae; duck's spinach	Eu, Med	leaves					
Amomum aromaticum; Zingiberaceae; Bengal cardamom	Ind	fruits & seeds					
Amomum globosum; Zingiberaceae; round Chinese cardamon	Chin	fruits & seeds					
Amomum kepulaga; Zingiberaceae; round cardamom	TrAs	fruits & seeds					
Amomum krervanh; Zingiberaceae; krervanh	TrAs	fruits & seeds					
Amomum maximum; Zingiberaceae; Java cardamom	TrAs	fruits & seeds					
Amorphophallus campanulatus – see *A. paeoniifolius*							
Amorphophallus konjac; Araceae; konjaku	Chin, TrAs	tuber					
Amorphophallus paeoniifolius; Araceae; elephant yam, whitespot giant arum	TrAs	tuber					
Amorphophallus rivieri – see *A. konjac*							
Anacardium occidentale; Anacardiaceae; cashew nut	SAm	seeds	**572**	20.6	42.2	2.90	A, E, K, B1, B2, Nic, Pan
		fruit (apple)	53	1.00	0.70	0.40	A, B1, B2, Bio, C, Nic, Pan
Ananas comosus; Bromeliaceae; pineapple	SAm	fruit	55	0.46	0.15	0.39	A, E, K, B1, B2, B6, C, Fol, Nic, Pan
Anethum graveolens; Apiaceae; dill	Ind, NE	fruit "seeds"					
Anethum sowa – see *A. graveolens*							
Angelica archangelica; Apiaceae; angelica	Eu, Asia	leaf stalks, roots, fruit					
Annona cherimola; Annonaceae; cherimoya, custard apple	SAm	fruit	62	1.50	0.30	0.80	B1, B2, C, Nic
Annona cherimola x **_A. squamosa;_** Annonaceae; atemoya	SAm	fruit					

Annona diversifolia; Annonaceae; ilama	CAm	fruit					
Annona muricata; Annonaceae; sour sop, guanábana	CAm	fruit					
Annona purpurea; Annonaceae; soncoya	SAm	fruit					
Annona reticulata; Annonaceae; bullock('s) heart, custard apple	CAm	fruit					
Annona scleroderma; Annonaceae; poshte	CAm	fruit					
Annona squamosa; Annonaceae; sugar apple, sweet sop	SAm	fruit					
Anredera cordifolia; Basellaceae; Maderia vine, mignonette vine	SAm	leaves, rhizomes					
Anthriscus cerefolium; Apiaceae; chervil	NE, Asia	leaves					
Apium graveolens var. dulce; Apiaceae; celery	Eu, Asia	leaves & leaf stalks	15	1.20	0.20	1.10	A, K, B1, B2, B6, C, Fol, Nic, Pan
Apium graveolens var. rapaceum; Apiaceae; celeriac, turnip-rooted celery	Eu, Asia	stem & root	18	1.55	0.33	0.94	E, K, B1, B2, B6, C, Fol, Nic, Pan
Apium graveolens var. secalinum; Apiaceae; Chinese celery	Asia	leaves					
Aponogeton distachyos; Aponogetonaceae; Cape pondweed	Afr (South)	flowers & fruits					
Arachis hypogaea; Fabaceae; peanut, groundnut	SAm	seeds	**564**	**29.8**	48.1	2.22	A, **E**, B1, B2, B6, Bio, C, Fol, Nic, Pan
Aralia cordata; Araliaceae; udo, Japanese spikenard	Chin	young leaves					
Araucaria araucana; Araucariaceae; chile nuts	SAm (Chile)	seeds					
Araucaria angustifolia; Araucariaceae; Paraná pine	SAm	seeds					
Araucaria bidwillii; Araucariaceae; bunya-bunya pine	Aus	seeds					
Arbutus unedo; Ericaceae; strawberry tree, arbutus	Med	fruit					
Arctium lappa; Asteraceae; burdock, gobo	Eu (Japan)	roots					
Arenga pinnata; Palmae; sugar palm	TrAs, Ind	leaf stem sap, fruit	28	6.17	–	–	C
Argania spinosa; Sapotaceae; argan tree	Afr (North)	seeds (oil)					
Armoracia rusticana; Brassicaceae; horseradish	Eu	roots	63	2.8	0.30	2.20	A, B1, B2, B6, C, Nic
Aronia melanocarpa; Rosaceae; black chokeberry, aronia berry	NAm	fruit					
Arracacia xanthorrhiza; Apiaceae; arracache. Peruvian parsnip	SAm (Peru)	roots					
Artemisia abrotanum; Asteraceae; southernwood	Eu?	leaves					
Artemisia absinthium; Asteraceae; wormwood, absinthe	Eu, Asia	leaves					

Artemisia dracunculus; Asteraceae; tarragon, French tarragon, estragon	Eu, Asia	leaves						
Artemisia dracunculoides; Asteraceae; Russian tarragon, false tarragon	Eu, Asia	leaves						
Artemisia pontica; Asteraceae; Roman wormwood	Eu	leaves						
Artemisia vulgaris; Asteraceae; mugwort	Eu, Asia	leaves						
Artocarpus altilis; Moraceae; breadfruit, breadnut	TrAs	fruits, seeds	110	1.50	0.30	0.90	A, B1, B2, C, Nic
Artocarpus camansi; Moraceae; kamansi	TrAs	fruits						
Artocarpus heterophyllus; Moraceae; jackfruit	Ind	fruits	70	1.10	0.45	1.00	A, B1, B2, C, Nic
Artocarpus integer; Moraceae; champedak, chempedak	TrAs	fruits, seeds						
Artocarpus lacucha; Moraceae; lacoocha	TrAs	fruits, seeds						
Artocarpus nobilis; Moraceae	Ind (Sri Lanka)	fruits, seeds						
Artocarpus odoratissimus; Moraceae; marang, terap	TrAs	fruits						
Artocarpus rigidus; Moraceae; monkey jack	TrAs	fruits						
Aspalathus linearis; Fabaceae; rooibos tea	Afr (South)	leaves & twigs	202	6.30	0.50	2.10	B1, B2, Nic
Asparagus officinalis; Asparagaceae; asparagus	Afr, Eu, Asia	young stems	18	1.91	0.16	0.57	A, E, K, B1, B2, B6, Bio, C, **Fol**, Nic, Pan
Atriplex canescens; Chenopodiaceae; saltbush	NAm	leaves						
Atriplex halimus; Chenopodiaceae; sea purslane, seabeach sandwort	Med	leaves						
Atriplex hortensis; Chenopodiaceae; orache	Eu, Asia	leaves	20	3.20	0.26	2.08	A, C
Avena sativa; Poaceae; oats	NE, Med	fruit (grains)	333	12.6	7.09	2.85	E, K, Bio, B1, B2, B6, Fol
Averrhoa bilimbi; Oxalidaceae; bilimbi	TrAs	fruit						
Averrhoa carambola; Oxalidaceae; starfruit, carambola	TrAs	fruit	24	1.2	0.50	0.40	A, B1, B2, C, Nic
Baccaurea dulcis; Euphorbiaceae; tjoopa	TrAs	fruit						
Baccaurea motleyana; Euphorbiaceae; rambai	TrAs	fruit						
Baccaurea ramiflora (=B. sapida); Euphorbiaceae; rambai, lutqua	TrAs	fruit						
Bactris gasipes; Arecaceae; pejibaye, peach palm	SAm	stem tips, fruits						
Balanites aegyptiaca; Zygophyllaceae; betu, dessert date	Med, Afr	leaves, fruit						

Bambusa bambos (=*B. arundinacea*); Poaceae; spiny bamboo, male bamboo	Ind, TrAs	shoots					
Bambusa beecheyana; Poaceae	Chin	shoots					
Bambusa cornuta; Poaceae	TrAs	shoots					
Bambusa spinosa; Poaceae	TrAs	shoots					
Bambusa vulgaris; Poaceae; common bamboo	TrAs	shoots	17	2.5	0.30	0.90	A, B1, B2, C, Nic
Barbarea verna; Brassicaceae; land cress, winter cress	Med, NE	leaves	21	5.14	–	1.49	C
Basella alba (=*B. rubra*); Basellaceae; Malabar spinach, Ceylon spinach	Ind, TrAs	leaves					
Bauhinia esculenta (=*Tylosema esculenta*); Fabaceae; marama bean	Afr (South)	seeds	**539**	**32.9**	37.8	3.00	B1, B2, Nic
Benincasa hispida; Curcubitaceae; wax gourd, white gourd	TrAs	fruit					
Benincasa hispida var. **chiehqua**; Curcubitaceae; hairy melon, fuzzy melon, mao gua	TrAs	fruit					
Bertholletia excelsa; Lecythidaceae; Brazil nut	SAm	seeds	**670**	16	66.8	3.65	A, E, B1, B2, B6, C, Fol, Nic, Pan
Beta vulgaris var. **cicla**; Chenopodiaceae; leaf beet, spinach beet, Swiss chard	NE, Eu	leaves	14	2.13	0.28	1.68	A, B1, B2, C, Fol, Nic, Pan
Beta vulgaris var. **esculenta**; Chenopodiaceae; beetroot	NE, Eu	roots (leaves)	41	1.53	0.10	1.00	A, E, B1, B2, B6, C, Fol, Pan, Nic
Beta vulgaris var. **vulgaris**; Chenopodiaceae; sugarbeet	Eu	roots					
Bixa orellana; Bixaceae; annatto, lipstick tree	SAm	seeds					
Blighia sapida; Sapindaceae; akee, vegetable brains	Afr (West)	seed aril	218	5.00	20.0	1.20	A, B1, B2, C, Nic
Boesenbergia rotunda; Zingiberaceae; Chinese keys	TrAs	rhizome					
Borago officinalis; Boraginaceae; borage	NE, Med, Eu	flowers, seeds (oil)					
Borassus flabellifer; Arecaceae; borassus palm, palmyra palm	Ind, TrAs	stem sap, seeds					
Brasenia schreberi; Cabombaceae; watershield, junsai	Chin	leaves					
Brassica campestris – see *Brassica rapa* var. *rapa*							
Brassica carinata; Brassicaceae; Ethiopean mustard, Texsel greens	Afr	leaves, seeds					
Brassica hirta – see *Sinapis alba*							
Brassica chinensis – see *B. rapa* var. *chinensis*							
Brassica juncea var. **juncea**; Brassicaceae; brown mustard, Indian mustard, Dijon mustard	CAs	seeds					

Brassica juncea var. *rugosa*; Brassicaceae; cabbage leaf mustard, mustard greens	CAs	leaves					
Brassica juncea var. *crispifolia*; Brassicaceae; curly-leaf mustard	CAs	leaves					
Brassica napus var. *napobrassica*; Brassicaceae; swede, rutabaga, Swedish turnip	Eu	roots	29	1.16	0.16	0.77	A, B1, B2, B6, Bio, C, Fol, Nic, Pan
Brassica napus var. *napus*; Brassicaceae; rape, oilseed rape	Eu	seeds					
Brassica napus var. *pabularia*; Brassicaceae; rape cale	Eu	leaves					
Brassica narinosa – see *B. rapa* var. *narinosa*							
Brassica nigra; Brassicaceae; black mustard	NE	seeds (leaves)					
Brassica oleracea var. *acephala*; Brassicaceae; kale, borecole, collards	Med	leaves	37	4.3	0.90	1.70	**A**, E, K, B1, B2, B6, Bio, C, Fol, Nic
Brassica oleracea var. *alboglabra*; Brassicaceae; Chinese kale, Chinese broccoli	Chin?	leaves					
Brassica oleracea var. *oleracea*; Brassicaceae; wild cabbage	Med	leaves					
Brassica oleracea var. *botryris*; Brassicaceae; cauliflower, Cape broccoli	Med	flower buds	22	2.46	0.28	0.80	A, E, K, B1, B2, B6, Bio, C, Fol, Nic, Pan
Brassica oleracea var. *capitata*; Brassicaceae; cabbage	Med	leaves	25	1.37	0.20	0.60	A, E, K, B1, B2, B6, Bio, C, Fol, Nic, Pan
Brassica oleracea var. *costata*; Brassicaceae; tronchuda cabbage	Med	leaves					
Brassica oleracea var. *gemmifera*; Brassicaceae; Brussels sprouts	Eu	axillary buds	36	4.45	0.34	1.40	A, E, K, B1, B2, B6, Bio, C, Fol, Nic, Pan
Brassica oleracea var. *gongylodes*; Brassicaceae; kohlrabi, cabbage turnip	Eu	stems	24	1.94	0.16	0.95	A, K, B1, B2, B6, Bio, C, Fol, Pan
Brassica oleracea var. *italica*; Brassicaceae; sprouting broccoli, calabrese	Med	flower buds	28	3.54	0.20	1.10	**A**, E, K, B1, B2, B6, Bio, C, Fol, Nic, Pan
Brassica oleracea var. *sabellica*; Brassicaceae; curly kale, Portuguese kale, Scotch kale	Med	leaves					
Brassica rapa var. *chinensis*; Brassicaceae; pak choi, Chinese white cabbage	TrAs, Chin	young plants	12	1.07	0.30	0.58	A, E, K, B1, B2, B6, C, Fol, Nic, Pan
Brassica rapa var. *narinosa*; Brassicaceae; tat soi, rosette pak choi, Chinese flat cabbage	TrAs, Chin	young plants					
Brassica rapa var. *parachinensis*; Brassicaceae; Chinese flowering cabbage	TrAs, Chin	flowering stems					
Brassica rapa var. *pekinensis*; Brassicaceae; celery cabbage; *pe tsai*	Chin	leaves	12	1.00	0.20	–	A, B1, B2, C, Fol
Brassica rapa var. *rapa*; Brassicaceae; turnip, neeps	Eu	roots	25	0.99	0.22	0.73	A, B1, B2, B6, Bio, C, Fol, Nic, Pan

Brassica rapa subsp. *campestris*; Brassicaceae; annual turnip rape	Eu	seeds (oil)				
Brassica rapa subsp. *oleifera*; Brassicaceae; biennial turnip rape	Eu	seeds (oil)				
Cajanus cajan; Fabaceae; pigeonpea, pigeon pea	Ind	seeds (leaves)	281	20.2	1.40	3.60	A, B1, B2, B6, C, Fol, Nic, Pan
Calophyllum calaba; Clusiaceae; (Guttiferae); calaba	TrAs	fruit, seeds (oil)				
Calystegia sepium; Convolvulaceae; bindweed	Chin	roots (leaves)				
Camellia sinensis; Theaceae; tea, chai	Chin, Ind	leaves (for tea)	147	25.4	4.73	5.60	K, B1, B2, B6, C, Nic, Pan
Canarium album; Burseraceae; white Chinese olive, pili nut	TrAs	fruits, seeds				
Canarium commune; Burseraceae; Java almond	TrAs	seeds				
Canarium harvei; Burseraceae; Polynesian pili nut	TrAs	fruit				
Canarium ovatum; Burseraceae; pili, pili nut	TrAs	seeds (oil)				
Canarium pimela; Burseraceae; black Chinese olive	TrAs	fruit				
Canavalia ensiformis; Fabaceae; jack bean	SAm, CAm?	young fruit, seeds				
Canavalia gladiata; Fabaceae; sword bean	Chin	young fruit, seeds				
Canavalia polystacha; Fabaceae	TrAs	leaves, seeds				
Canna edulis; Cannaceae; achira, edible canna, Queensland arrowroot	SAm	rhizomes				
Cannabis sativa; Cannabaceae; hemp	Chin, Ind	seeds (oil)				
Capparis spinosa; Capparidaceae; caper bush, capers	Med	buds (fruit)				
Capsella bursa-pastoris; Brassicaceae; shepherd's purse	Med	leaves				
Capsicum annuum; Solanaceae; bell pepper, sweet pepper, paprika, chilli	CAm, SAm	fruit	19	1.08	0.24	0.50	A, E, K, B1, B2, B6, Bio, C, Fol, Nic, Pan
Capsicum baccatum; Solanaceae; aji	SAm (Bolivia)	fruit				
Capsicum frutescens; Solanaceae; chilli, bird chilli, Tabasco- or cayenne pepper	CAm, SAm	fruit				
Capsicum pubescens; Solanaceae; rocoto	SAm (Andes)	fruit				
Carica goudotiana; Caricaceae; papayuelo	SAm	fruit				
Carica monoica; Caricaceae; col de monte, dwarf cooking papapaya	SAm	fruit				
Carica papaya; Caricaceae; papaya, paw paw	CAm	fruit	32	0.52	0.09	0.55	A, B1, B2, C, Nic
Carica x pentagona; Caricaceae; babaco	CAm, SAm	fruit				

Carica pubescens; Caricaceae; chamburo, mountain papaya	CAm, SAm	fruit					
Carica stipulata; Caricaceae; siglalón	SAm	fruit					
Carissa macrocarpa (= *C. grandiflora*); Apocynaceae; Natal plum	Afr	fruit	78	0.45	1.10	0.40	A, B1, B2, C, Nic
Carpobrotus edulis; Mesembryanthemaceae; sour fig	Afr (South)	fruit	109	2.40	0.30	2.40	B1, B2, C, Nic
Carthamus tinctorius; Asteraceae; safflower	NE, CAs	fruit (oilseeds)					
Carum carvi; Apiaceae; caraway	Eu, CAs, NE	fruit (seeds)					
		leaves	26	4.90	–	–	C
		roots	106	–	–	–	–
Carya illinoinensis; Juglandaceae; pecan nut	NAm, CAm	seeds	**703**	11.0	72.0	1.60	A, E, K, B1, B2, C, Nic
Caryota urens; Arecaceae; fishtail palm, toddy palm	TrAs, Ind, Aus	stem sap, leaves					
Casimiroa edulis; Rutaceae; white sapote	CAm	fruit					
Castanea crenata; Fagaceae; Japanese chestnut	Chin	seeds					
Castanea dentata; Fagaceae; American chestnut	NAm	seeds					
Castanea mollissima; Fagaceae; Chinese chestnut	Chin	seeds					
Castanea pumila; Fagaceae; chinquapin	NAm	seeds					
Castanea sativa; Fagaceae; chestnut, sweet chestnut, Spanish chestnut	CAs	seeds	192	2.93	1.90	1.18	A, E, B1, B2, B6, Bio, C, Nic, Pan
Celosia argentea; Amaranthaceae; quail grass, mfungu	Ind, Afr	leaves					
Ceratonia siliqua; Fabaceae; carob tree	NE, Med	fruit, seeds					
Cereus peruvianus; Cactaceae; pitaya, cactus apple	CAm	fruit					
Cereus repandus; Cactaceae; cadushi	CAm	young stems					
Chaenomeles sinensis; Rosaceae; Chinese quince, Japanese quince	Chin	fruit					
Chaerophyllum bulbosum; Apiaceae; turnip-rooted chervil	Eu	roots					
Chamaemelum nobile; Asteraceae; chamomile, Roman chamomile	Med, Eu	flower heads					
Chenopodium album; Chenopodiaceae; goosefoot, fat hen, lamb's quarters	Eu, Asia, NAm	leaves	38	4.4	0.30	4.4	A, B1, B2, C, Nic
Chenopodium ambrosioides; Chenopodiaceae; wormseed, epazote, paiku	SAm, CAm	leaves, seeds					
Chenopodium berlandieri subsp. *nutalliae*; Chenopodiaceae; huauzontle	CAm	leaves, seeds					

Chenopodium bonus-henricus; Chenopodiaceae; Good King Henry	Eu	leaves, stems	38	6.53	0.49	1.96	A, C
Chenopodium foliosum; Chenopodiaceae; leafy goosefoot	Eu	leaves	44	3.0	0.30	3.20	B1, B2, Nic
Chenopodium graveolens; Chenopodiaceae; yerba del zorillo	CAm	leaves					
Chenopodium pallidicaule; Chenopodiaceae; kaniwa, canihua	SAm	seeds					
Chenopodium quinoa; Chenopodiaceae; quinoa	SAm	seeds	334	14.8	5.04	3.33	B1, Nic
Chloranthus erectus (=*C officinalis*); Chloranthaceae	TrAs	leaves (tea)					
Chloranthus spicatus; Chloranthaceae	TrAs	flowers (tea spice)					
Chrozophora tinctoria; Euphorbiaceae; tournesol plant, *bezetta rubra*	Med	leaves (food dye)					
Chrysanthemum balsamita; Asteraceae; alecost	Eu	leaves					
Chrysanthemum coronarium; Asteraceae; garland chrysanthemum, tangho, shungiku	Med	seedlings					
Chrysanthemum x *morifolium*; Asteraceae; common or florist chrysanthemum, *ju hua*	Chin	flower heads					
Chrysanthemum parthenium; Asteraceae; feverfew	Med	leaves					
Chrysanthemum segetum; Asteraceae; corn marigold	Eu, NE	leaves					
Chrysanthemum vulgare; Asteraceae; tansy	Eu	leaves					
Cicer arietinum; Fabaceae; chickpea	NE, Med	seeds	**307**	**19.0**	5.92	2.88	A, K, B1, B2, B6, C, Fol, Nic, Pan
Cichorium endivia; Asteraceae; endive	Med	leaves	14	1.75	0.20	0.90	A, B1, B2, C, Fol, Nic
Cichorium intybus **var.** *sativum*; Asteraceae; chicory, root chicory	Eu, Asia	roots (powder)	42	6.80	1.60	4.40	–
Cichorium intybus var. *foliosum*; Asteraceae; chicory, salad chicory	Eu, Asia	leaves	16	1.27	0.18	0.79	A, B1, B2, B6, Bio, C, Fol, Nic
Cinnamomum aromaticum (=*C. cassia*); Lauraceae; cassia, cassia cinnamon, Chinese cinnamon	TrAs	bark (buds, leaves)					
Cinnamomum burmanii; Lauraceae; Indonesian cassia, Indonesian cinnamon	TrAs	bark					
Cinnamomum loureirii; Lauraceae; Saigon cassia	TrAs	bark					
Cinnamomum tamala; Lauraceae; Indian cassia	Ind	bark					
Cinnamomum verum (=*C. zeylanicum*); Lauraceae; cinnamon, Ceylon cinnamon	Chin	bark					
Citrullus lanatus; Cucurbitaceae; watermelon	Afr	fruit	37	0.60	0.20	0.40	A, K, B1, B2, B6, C, Fol, Nic, Pan

Citrus aurantiifolia; Rutaceae; lime, West Indian lime	TrAs	fruit	31	0.50	2.40	0.20	A, B1, B2, C, Nic
Citrus aurantium; Rutaceae; Seville orange, bitter orange, sour orange	TrAs	fruit					
Citrus aurantium subsp. *bergamia*; Rutaceae; bergamot	Med	fruit (oil)					
Citrus deliciosa; Rutaceae; Mediterranean mandarin	TrAs	fruit					
Citrus grandis – see *C. maxima*							
Citrus hystrix; Rutaceae; makrut lime, papeda	TrAs	leaves, fruit					
Citrus jambhiri; Rutaceae; rough lemon	TrAs	fruit					
Citrus latifolia; Rutaceae; Tahiti lime, Persian lime, seedless lime	TrAs	fruit					
Citrus limetta; Rutaceae; sweet lemon	TrAs	fruit					
Citrus limon; Rutaceae; lemon	TrAs	fruit					
Citus madurensis; Rutaceae; calamondin	TrAs	fruit					
Citrus maxima; Rutaceae; pomelo, pummelo, shaddock	TrAs	fruit					
Citrus medica; Rutaceae; citron	TrAs, CAs	fruit	35	0.70	0.60	0.50	A, K, B1, B2, B6, C, Nic, Pan
Citrus nobilis; Rutaceae; king mandarin	TrAs	fruit					
Citrus paradisi; Rutaceae; grapefruit	TrAs (CAm)	fruit	38	0.60	0.15	0.35	A, E, B1, B2, B6, Bio, C, Fol, Nic, Pan
Citrus reticulata; Rutaceae; mandarin, tangerine, nartjie	Chin, TrAs	fruit	46	0.70	0.30	0.70	A, E, B1, B2, B6, Bio, C, Fol, Nic
Citrus sinensis; Rutaceae; sweet orange	TrAs	fruit	42	1.00	0.20	0.48	A, E, K, B1, B2, B6, Bio, C, Fol, Nic, Pan
Citrus unshiu; Rutaceae; satsuma mandarin	Chin, TrAs	fruit					
Clausena dentata; Rutaceae	Ind	fruit					
Clausena lansium; Rutaceae; wampi	Chin	fruit					
Cleome gynandra; Capparaceae; cleome	Afr	leaves	42	4.60	0.90	3.2	B1, B2, Nic
Cochlearia officinalis; Brassicaceae; spoonwort, spoon cress, scurvy grass	Eu	leaves					
Cocos nucifera; Arecaceae; coconut	TrAs	seed, (stem)	363	4.63	36.5	1.18	E, B1, B2, B6, C, Fol, Nic, Pan
Coffea arabica; Rubiaceae; coffee, Arabian coffee	Afr Ethiopia	seeds	190	11.2	13.1	4.00	B1, B2, B6, Fol, Nic, Pan
Coffea canephora; Rubiaceae; robusta coffee, Congo coffee	Afr	seeds					
Coffea liberica; Rubiaceae; Liberian coffee, Abeokuta coffee	Afr	seeds					

Species; Family; common names	Origin	Part used					Vitamins
Coix lachryma-jobi; Poaceae; adlay, Job's tears, Chinese pearl barley	TrAs	fruit (grain)					
Cola acuminata; Sterculiaceae; cola nut, abata kola	Afr	seed	228	6.28	1.75	2.90	B1
Cola nitida; Sterculiaceae; gbanja cola	Afr	seed					
Colocasia esculenta; Araceae; taro, taro potato, cocoyam, eddoe, dasheen	Chin, Ind	tubers (leaves)	107	2.00	0.25	1.00	A, B1, B2, C
Corchorus olitorus; Tiliaceae; melokhia, Jew's-mallow	Ind	leaves	76	4.30	0.70	3.00	B1, B2, Nic
Coriandrum sativum; Apiaceae; coriander, cilantro	NE, Ind, Med	fruits, leaves					
Cornus mas; Cornaceae; Cornelian cherry	Eu, Asia	fruits	68	2.04	–	0.73	C
Corylus americana; Betulaceae; American hazelnut	NAm	seed					
Corylus avellana; Betulaceae; hazelnut, Europaean hazelnut	Eu, CAs	seed	**644**	14.1	61.6	2.44	A, E, K, B1, B2, B6, C, Fol, Nic, Pan
Corylus colurna; Betulaceae; Turkish hazelnut	NE	seed					
Corylus manshurica; Betulaceae; Manchurian hazelnut	Chin	seed					
Corylus maxima; Betulaceae; filbert, red filbert, white filbert	Eu, CAs, NE	seed					
Corylus sieboldiana; Betulaceae; Siebold's hazelnut	Chin	seed					
Corypha utan (=*C. elata*); Arecaceae; buri palm, gebang	TrAs	stem sap, stem, fruit					
Crambe maritima; Brassicaceae; seakale	Eu, NE	leaves					
Crataegus azarolus; Rosaceae; azarole	Eu, NE	fruit					
Crataegus douglasii; Rosaceae; black haw	NAm	fruit					
Crataegus hupehensis; Rosaceae; hupen	Chin	fruit					
Crataegus pentagyna; Rosaceae; Chinese hawthorn	Eu, NE	fruit					
Crataegus stipulosa; Rosaceae; manzanilla	CAm	fruit					
Crocus sativus; Iridaceae; saffron, saffron crocus	Med, NE	styles					
Cryptotaenia japonica; Apiaceae; mitsuba, mitzuba, Japanese parsley	Chin	leaves, roots					
Cucumis anguria; Cucurbitaceae; gherkin, West Indian gherkin	Afr	fruit					
Cucumis melo; Cucurbitaceae; melon, musk melon, cantaloupe melon	Afr, NE, CAs	fruit	54	0.90	0.10	0.40	A, E, K, B1, B2, C, Fol, Nic
Cucumis metuliferus; Cucurbitaceae; African horned cucumber, kiwano	Afr	fruit	32	1.10	0.70	0.90	B1, B2, C, Nic

Cucumis sativus; Cucurbitaceae; cucumber, gherkin	Ind, CAs	fruit	12	0.60	0.20	0.60	A, E, K, B1, B2, B6, Bio, C, Fol, Nic, Pan
Cucurbita argyrosperma; Cucurbitaceae; cushaw	CAm	fruit					
Cucurbita ficifolia; Cucurbitaceae; fig-leaf gourd, Malabar gourd	CAm, SAm	fruit, seeds					
Cucurbita maxima; Cucurbitaceae; winter squash, pumpkin	SAm	fruit, seeds	26	1.40	0.20	0.70	A, E, B1, B2, C, Nic
Cucurbita moschata; Cucurbitaceae; butternut, musky winter squash	CAm, SAm	fruit, seeds					
Cucurbita pepo; Cucurbitaceae; zucchini, marrow, summer squash	CAm	fruit, seeds	25	1.10	0.13	0.77	A, E, K, B1, B2, B6, Bio, C, Fol, Nic, Pan
Cuminum cyminum; Apiaceae; cumin	NE, Ind, CAs	fruit ("seeds")					
Curcuma amada; Zingiberaceae; mango ginger	Ind	rhizome					
Curcuma angustifolia; Zingiberaceae; Indian arrowroot	Ind	rhizome					
Curcuma heyneana; Zingiberaceae; arrowroot	TrAs	rhizome					
Curcuma longa (=*C. domestica*); Zingiberaceae; turmeric, curcuma	Ind	rhizome					
Curcuma mangga; Zingiberaceae; Indonesian mango ginger	TrAs	rhizome					
Curcuma xanthorrhiza; Zingiberaceae; Javanese turmeric	TrAs	rhizome					
Curcuma zedoaria; Zingiberaceae; zedoary	Ind	rhizome					
Cyamopsis tetragonoloba; Fabaceae; cluster bean, guar	Afr, Ind	young fruit, seeds					
Cyclanthera pedata; Cucurbitaceae; achocha	SAm	fruit					
Cyclopia genistoides; Fabaceae; honeybush tea	Afr (South)	leaves (tea)	241	6.50	1.20	1.90	B1, B2, Nic2
Cyclopia intermedia; Fabaceae; mountain tea, honeybush tea	Afr (South)	leaves (tea)					
Cyclopia subternata; Fabaceae; vlei tea, honeybush tea	Afr (South)	leaves (tea)					
Cydonia oblonga (=*Cydonia vulgaris*); Rosaceae; quince	NE	fruit	38	0.42	0.50	0.44	A, B1, B2, B6, C, Nic
Cymbopogon citratus; Poaceae; lemongrass	Ind, TrAs	leaf bases					
Cymbopogon flexuosus; Poaceae; East Indian lemongrass, Malabar lemongrass	TrAs	leaf bases					
Cymbopogon martinii; Poaceae; ginger grass, rosha, rusha, palma-rosa	Ind	leaves					
Cymbopogon nardus; Poaceae; citronella grass, mana grass	TrAs	leaves					
Cynara cardunculus; Asteraceae; cardoon, wild artichoke	Med	leaf stalks					

Cynara scolymus; Asteraceae; globe artichoke	Med	flower heads	22	2.40	0.12	1.29	A, E, B1, B2, C, Nic
Cyperus esculentus; Cyperaceae; chufa, tiger nut, earth almond	Afr, NE	rhizome ("tuber")	82	0.90	0.10	1.30	B1, C, Nic
Cyphomandra betacea; Solanaceae; tree tomato, tamarillo	SAm	fruit	56	1.70	0.80	0.90	A, B1, B2, C, Nic
Daucus carota; Apiaceae; carrot	Eu, CAs	roots	26	0.98	0.20	0.86	**A**, E, K, B1, B2, B6, Bio, C, Fol, Nic, Pan
Dendrocalamus asper; Poaceae; bamboo	TrAs	shoots	17	2.5	0.30	0.90	A, B1, B2, C, Nic
Dendrocalamus giganteus; Poaceae; bamboo	TrAs	shoots					
Dendrocalamus latifolius; Poaceae; bamboo	TrAs	shoots					
Digitaria cruciata; Poaceae	TrAs	fruit (grains)					
Digitaria exilis; Poaceae; fonio, white fonio	Afr (West)	fruit (grains)					
Digitaria iburua; Poaceae; black fonio, iburu	Afr (West)	fruit (grains)					
Digitaria sanguinalis; Poaceae; crabgrass	Ind	fruit (grains)					
Dimocarpus longan; (=*Nephelium longanum*); Sapindaceae; longan	Ind	seed aril ("fruit")	70	1.00	0.75	0.85	B1, B2, C, Nic
Dioscorea alata; Dioscoreaceae; greater yam, water yam, winged yam	TrAs	tuber					
Dioscorea batatas (=*D. opposita*); Dioscoreaceae; Chinese yam, *shu yu*	Chin	tuber	99	2.00	0.13	1.00	A, B1, B2, C, Nic
Dioscorea bulbifera; Dioscoreaceae; air potato, potato yam, aerial yam	TrAs, Afr	tuber	118	3.30	0.40	1.30	B1, B2, C, Nic
Dioscorea cayenensis (=*D. rotundata*); Dioscoreaceae; yellow yam , white yam	Afr	tuber					
Dioscorea dumetorum; Dioscoreaceae	Afr	tuber					
Dioscorea esculenta; Dioscoreaceae; lesser yam, potato yam, Chinese yam	TrAs	tuber					
Dioscorea trifida; Dioscoreaceae; cush-cush yam, mapuey	CAm, SAm	tuber					
Diospyros blanchoi (=*D. discolor*); Ebenaceae; mabola, velvet fruit, velvet apple	TrAs	fruit					
Diospyros digyna; Ebenaceae; black sapote	CAm	fruit					
Diospyros kaki; Ebenaceae; persimmon, Japanese persimmon, kaki	Chin	fruit	70	0.64	0.30	0.67	A, B1, B2, C, Nic
Diospyros lotus; Ebenaceae; lotus plum, Caucasian persimmon	Chin, CAs	fruit					
Diospyros major; Ebenaceae; Tonga persimmon	East Asia	fruit, seeds (oil)					
Diospyros mespiliformis; Ebenaceae; jackal-berry	Afr	fruit	97	1.10	0.40	1.30	B1, B2, C, Nic
Diospyros virginiana; Ebenaceae; American persimmon	NAm	fruit					

Dolichos biflorus; Fabaceae; horse gram	Ind, TrAs	seeds					
Dovalis caffra; Flacourtiaceae; kei-apple, wild apricot	Afr	fruit	56	0.40	0.40	0.30	**A**, B1, B2, C, Nic
Dovyalis hebecarpa; Flacourtiaceae; kitembilla, Ceylon gooseberry	Ind (Sri Lanka)	fruit					
Durio zibethinus; Bombacaceae; durian	TrAs	seeds, seed arils	141	2.70	1.80	1.10	A, B1, B2, C, Nic
Echinochloa colona (=*E. utilis*); Poaceae; sawa millet, sama, jungle rice	Ind, Afr, Asia	fruit (grains)					
Echinochloa frumentacea; Poaceae; Japanese millet	Chin	fruit (grains)					
Echinochloa oryzoides; Poaceae; large cockspur	un-known	fruit (grains)					
Elaeagnus multiflora; Elaeagnaceae; cherry eleagnus	Chin	fruit (nuts)					
Elaeocarpus serratus; Elaeocarpaceae; Ceylon olive	TrAs	fruit					
Elaeocarpus sphaericus; Elaeocarpaceae; olive nut	Ind, TrAs	fruit					
Elaeocarpus tectorius; Elaeocarpaceae	TrAs	fruit					
Elaeis guineensis; Arecaceae; oil palm, West African oil palm	Afr	fruit					
Elaeis oleifera; Arecaceae; American oil palm	SAm	fruit					
Eleocharis dulcis (=*E. tuberosa*); Cyperaceae; water chestnut	Chin, TrAs	corms	64	1.40	0.30	1.10	B1, B2, C, Nic
Elettaria cardamomum; Zingiberaceae; cardamom	Ind	seeds					
Eleusine coracana; Poaceae; African finger millet	Afr	fruit (grains)	340	6.20	1.50	5.10	B1, B2, Nic
Eleusine indica; Poaceae; Indian goosegrass	Ind	fruit (grains)					
Englerophytum magalismontanum Apocynaceae; milkplum, *stamvrug*	Afr	fruit	95	0.90	0.60	0.70	A, B1, B2, C, Nic
Ensete ventricosa; Musaceae; enset, ensete	Afr	rhizome, leaves					
Eragrostis tef; Poaceae; teff, t'ef	Afr Ethiopia	fruit (grains)					
Eriobotrya japonica; Rosaceae; loquat	Chin	fruit	40	0.55	0.20	0.48	A, B1, B2, C, Nic
Erioglossum fruticosum –see *Lepisanthes fruticosa*							
Eruca sativa (=*E. vesicaria*); Brassicaceae; rocket, salad rocket	Med	leaves, seeds (oil)	15	2.60	0.70	–	A, B1, B2, B6, Nic
Erythrina edulis; Fabaceae; basul	SAm	seeds					
Etlingera elatior (=*Phaeomeria magnifica*) ; Zingiberaceae; torch ginger	TrAs	flower buds					

Eugenia dombeya (=*E. brasiliensis*); Myrtaceae; grumichama, Brazilian cherry	SAm	fruit					
Eugenia luschnathiana; Myrtaceae; pitomba, Brazilian cherry	SAm	fruit					
Eugenia uvalha; Myrtaceae; uvalha, Brazilian cherry	SAm	fruit					
Eugenia uniflora; Myrtaceae; Surinam cherry, pitanga	SAm	fruit					
Euryale ferox; Euryalaceae; euryale nuts	Chin	seeds, rhizomes					
Euterpe edulis; Arecaceae; açaí, assai	SAm	stem tips					
Euterpe oleracea; Arecaceae; cabbage palm	SAm	stem tips					
Fagopyrum esculentum; Polygonaceae; buckwheat	CAs	fruit	336	9.78	1.73	1.72	E, B1, B2, Nic, Pan
Fagopyrum tataricum; Polygonaceae; Siberian buckwheat, Kangra buckwheat, tatary	Chin, Asia	fruit					
Fagus sylvatica; Fagaceae; beech tree	Eu	seeds (nuts)					
Feijoa sellowiana – see *Acca sellowiana*							
Ferula assa-foetida; Apiaceae; asafoetida, devil's dung	NE, CAs	gum					
Ficus carica; Moraceae; fig tree	NE, Med	fruit	61	1.3	0.50	0.70	A, B1, B2, B6, C, Fol, Nic, Pan
Ficus sycomorus; Moraceae; sycamore fig	CAs	fruit					
Flacourtia indica (=*F. ramontchi*); Flacourtiaceae; governor's plum, Madagascar plum	Afr, Ind	fruit	33	0.90	1.00	0.60	A, B1, B2, C, Nic
Flacourtia inermis; Flacourtiaceae; lovi-lovi	un-known	fruit					
Flacourtia jangomas; Flacourtiaceae; paniala	un-known	fruit					
Flacourtia rukam; Flacourtaceae; rukam	TrAs	fruit					
Flemingia vestita; Fabaceae; souphlong	CAs, Ind	tubers					
Foeniculum vulgare* var. *dulce; Apiaceae; fennel	Med	fruits, leaves	24	2.43	0.30	1.70	A, K, B1, B2, B6, Bio, C, Fol, Nic, Pan
Foeniculum vulgare* var. *azoricum; Apiaceae; Florence fennel	Med	leaf bases	19	1.4	0.20	1.00	A, B1, B2, B6, C, Fol, Nic
Fortunella crassifolia; Rutaceae; large round kumquat, Meiwa kumquat	Chin	fruit					
Fortunella japonica; Rutaceae, round kumquat, Marumi kumquat	Chin	fruit					
Fortunella margarita; Rutaceace; kumquat, oval kumquat, Nagami kumquat	Chin	fruit	64	0.65	0.30	0.55	A, B1, B2, C, Nic

Fragaria ananassa; Rosaceae; strawberry	Eu	fruit	32	0.82	0.40	0.50	A, E, K, B1, B2, B6, Bio, C, Fol, Nic, Pan
Fragaria chiloensis; Rosaceae; Chilean strawberry	SAm	fruit					
Fragaria muricata (=*F. moschata*); Rosaceae; musk strawberry, hautbois strawberry	Eu	fruit					
Fragaria vesca; Rosaceae; wild strawberry	Eu, NAm, Asia	fruit					
Fragaria virginiana; Rosaceae; American strawberry	NAm	fruit					
Fritillaria imperialis; Liliaceae; crown imperial	CAs	bulb (starch)					
Galinsoga parviflora (=*G. ciliata*); Asteraceae; galinsoga	SAm, CAm	leaves	19	3.29	–	2.06	A, C
Garcinia brasiliensis; Clusiaceae; (Guttiferae); bakupari	SAm	fruit					
Garcinia cowa; Clusiaceae; (Guttiferae); cowa	TrAs	fruit					
Garcinia dulcis; Clusiaceae; (Guttiferae); baniti	TrAs	fruits					
Garcinia gummi-guta (=*G. cambogia*); Clusiaceae; Malabar tamarind	Ind	fruit (dried)					
Garcinia indica; Clusiaceae; (Guttiferae); kokum, kokam, ktambi, wild mangosteen	TrAs, Ind	fruits, seeds (oil)					
Garcinia livingstonei; Clusiaceae; (Guttiferae); imbé, African mangosteen	Afr	fruits	62	0.80	0.30	0.40	B2, C, Nic
Garcinia mangostana; Clusiaceae; (Guttiferae); mangosteen	TrAs	fruits	71	0.60	0.60	0.20	B1, B2, C, Nic
Garcinia multiflora; Clusiaceae; (Guttiferae); Cây giôc, Bira tai	TrAs	fruits					
Garcinia pedunculata; Clusiaceae; (Guttiferae); tikul	TrAs	fruits					
Gigantochloa apus; Poaceae	TrAs	shoots					
Gigantochloa ligulata; Poaceae	TrAs	shoots					
Ginkgo biloba; Ginkgoaceae; ginkgo, maidenhair tree, white nuts	Chin	seeds					
Glechoma hederacea; Lamiaceae; ground ivy, alehoof	Eu	leaves	27	6.11	–	1.51	C
Glycine max; Fabaceae; soybean, soya	Chin	seeds	327	37.6	18.3	4.69	A, E, K, B1, B2, B6, Bio, C, Fol, Nic, Pan
Glycyrrhiza glabra; Fabaceae; liquorice, licorice	Med, NE, CAs	rhizomes					
Glycyrrhiza uralensis; Fabaceae; Chinese liquorice	Chin	rhizomes					
Gnetum gnemon; Gnetaceae; gnetum, melinjo	TrAs	leaves, seeds					
Gossypium arboreum; Malvaceae; tree cotton	TrAs, Ind NE	seed (oil)					
Gossypium barbadense; Malvaceae; sea island cotton	SAm	seed (oil)					

Gossypium herbaceum; Malvaceae; short staple cotton	Afr, NE, Ind	seed (oil)					
Gossypium hirsutum; Malvaceae; Upland cotton, American cotton	CAm	seed (oil)					
Grewia asiatica; Tiliaceae; phassa	CAs	fruit					
Grewia flava; Tiliaceae; bushman raisin bush	Afr	fruit	264	5.00	0.50	3.00	B1, B2, Nic
Guizotia abyssinica; Asteraceae; niger seed	Afr Ethiopia	fruit					
Hablitzia tamnoides; Chenopodiaceae; climbing spinach	CAs	leaves					
Harpephyllum caffrum; Anacardiaceae; sour plum	Afr	fruit	41	0.70	0.20	0.80	B1, C
Helianthus annuus; Asteraceae; sunflower	NAm	fruit	**580**	**26.5**	49.0	3.30	B1, B2, B6, C, Nic
Helianthus tuberosus; Asteraceae; Jerusalem artichoke	NAm	rhizomes	31	2.44	0.41	1.74	A, B1, B2, C, Nic
Hibiscus esculentus – see *Abelmoschus esculentus*							
Hibiscus sabdariffa; Malvaceae; roselle, red sorrel, hibiscus	Afr (Angola)	calyces					
Hippophae rhamnoides; Eleagnaceae; sea buckthorn	Eu, Asia, Chin	fruit	89	1.42	7.10	0.45	A, E, B1, B2, B6, Bio, C, Fol, Nic, Pan
Hodgsonia macrocarpa; Cucurbitaceae; lard fruit	Chin	seeds (oil)					
Hordeum vulgare; Poaceae; barley	NE	fruit (grains)	311	10.6	2.10	2.25	A, E, B1, B2, B6, Fol
Houttuynia cordata; Saururaceae;	Chin, CAs	leaves					
Hovenia dulcis; Rhamnaceae; Japanese raisin tree	Chin	flower stalks					
Humulus lupulus; Cannabaceae; hop, hops	Chin	cones					
Hydrolea zeylanica; Hydrophyllaceae	TrAs	leaves					
Hylocereus undatus; Cactaceae; pitaya, pithaya, dragon fruit	CAm	fruit					
Hyphaene coriacea; Arecaceae; lala palm	Afr	stem sap, fruit					
Hyphaene petersiana; Arecaceae; mokola palm	Afr	stem sap, fruit					
Hyssopus officinalis; Lamiaceae; hyssop	Med	leaves					
Ilex paraguariensis; Aquifoliaceae; maté, yerba maté	SAm	leaves					
Illicium verum; Illiciaceae; star anise, Chinese anise	Chin	fruit					
Inga feuillei; Fabaceae; ice-cream bean, pacay	SAm	fruit					
Inga vera; Fabaceae; ice-cream bean, guaba	CAm, SAm	fruit					
Inocarpus fagifer (=*I. edulis*); Fabaceae; Tahiti chestnut, O'taheite chestnut	TrAs	seeds					

Ipomoea aquatica; Convolvulaceae; kangkong, water spinach	Afr, Asia	leaves					
Ipomoea batatas; Convolvulaceae; sweet potato	SAm	tubers	108	1.63	0.60	1.12	A, B1, B2, B6, Bio, C, Fol, Nic, Pan
Jasiminum grandiflorus; Oleaceae; Catalonian jasmin, Italian jasmine	Ind	flowers (tea scent)					
Jasminum officinale; Oleaceae; common white jasmine	CAs, Chin	flowers (tea scent)					
Jasminum sambac; Oleaceae; Arabian jasmine	Ind?	flowers (tea scent)					
Juglans cinerea; Juglandaceae; butternut	NAm	seeds					
Juglans mandschurica; Juglandaceae; Manchurian walnut	Chin	seeds					
Juglans nigra; Juglandaceae; black walnut	NAm	seeds					
Juglans regia; Juglandaceae; common walnut, Persian walnut	CAs	seeds	663	17.0	62.5	1.98	A, E, K, B1, B2, B6, Bio, C, Fol, Nic, Pan
Juglans sieboldiana (=J. ailantifolia); Juglandaceae; Japanese walnut, Siebold's walnut	Chin	seeds					
Juniperus communis; Cupressaceae; juniper	Asia, Eu, NAm	female cones					
Kaempferia galanga; Zingiberaceae; galangal	TrAs	rhizome					
Kaempferia rotunda; Zingiberaceae	TrAs	rhizome					
Lablab purpureus; Fabaceae; hyacinth bean, lablab bean	Afr	seeds, fruit, leaves	322	19.70	1.00	3.40	B1, B2, Nic
Lactuca indica; Asteraceae; Indian lettuce	Chin	leaves					
Lactuca sativa; Asteraceae; lettuce	Med	leaves	11	1.22	0.22	0.72	A, E, K, B1, B2, B6, Bio, C, Fol, Nic, Pan
Lactuca serriola; Asteraceae; prickly lettuce	Med, NE	seeds (oil)					
Lagenaria siceraria; Cucurbitaceae; bottle gourd, calabash	Afr	fruit	43	1.20	0.10	0.90	B1, B2, C, Nic
Lallemantia iberica; Lamiaceae; lallemantia	NE, CAs	seeds (oil)					
Lallemantia royleana; Lamiaceae; lallemantia	NE, CAs	seeds (oil)					
Lamium album; Lamiaceae; dead nettle, white dead nettle	Eu, Asia	leaves	30	5.34	0.62	1.64	A, C
Landolphia kirkii; Anacardiaceae; wild peach	Afr	fruit					
Lansium domesticum; Meliaceae; langsat, duku	TrAs	fruit					
Lathyrus annuus; Fabaceae	Med	seeds					
Lathyrus cicera; Fabaceae	Med	seeds					
Lathyrus clymenum; Fabaceae	Med	seeds					
Lathyrus linifolius; Fabaceae	Eu	tubers					
Lathyrus sativus; Fabaceae; grass pea, chickling vetch	Med	seeds					

Species; Family; common names	Origin	Part used					Vitamins
Lathyrus tuberosus; Fabaceae; earth chestnut, groundnut peavine	Eu, Asia, Med	tubers					
Laurus nobilis; Lauraceae; bay leaf, true laurel	Med	leaves					
Lavandula officinalis; Lamiaceae; lavender	Med	leaves (flavour)					
Lecythis zabucajo; Lecythidaceae; sapucaia nut, paradise nut	SAm	seeds					
Lens culinaris (=*L. esculenta*); Fabaceae; lentil	NE, CAs	seeds	270	**23.4**	1.53	2.67	A, K, B1, B2, B6, C, Fol, Nic, Pan
Lepisanthes fruticosa; Sapindaceae; luna nut	TrAs	fruit					
Lepidium draba; Cruciferae; hoary cress	Eu, Asia Med	seeds					
Lepidium latifolium; Cruciferae; dittander	Eu, Afr Med	leaves					
Lepididium meyenii; Brassicaceae; maca	SAm	roots					
Lepidium sativum; Brassicaceae; garden cress, cress	NE, CAs	leaves	33	4.2	0.70	1.90	A, E, B1, B2, B6, C, Nic
Levisticum officinale; Apiaceae; lovage	NE, CAs	leaves, fruits, root					
Ligusticum scotinum; Apiaceae; Scotch lovage	Eu	leaves					
Lilium auratum; Liliaceae; golden-rayed lily, *yama-yuri*	Chin	bulbs					
Lilium cordifolium; Liliaceae	Chin	bulbs					
Lilium lancifolium (=*L. tigrinum*); Liliaceae; tiger lily, *oni-yuri*	Chin	bulbs					
Lilium martagon; Liliaceae; Turk's cap lily	Eu, Asia	bulbs					
Lilium maximowiczii; Liliaceae; *ko-oni-yuri*	Chin	bulbs					
Limnocharis flava; Alismataceae; vegetable waterlettuce	TrAs	leaves					
Limonia acidissima (=*Feronia elephantum*); Rutaceae; elephant apple, Indian wood apple	Ind	fruit					
Linum usitatissimum; Linaceae; flax, linseed	Eu, Med	seeds	376	**28.8**	30.9	–	K, B1, B2, Nic
Lippia citriodora – see Aloysia triphylla							
Litchi chinensis; Sapindaceae; litchi, lychee	Chin, TrAs	fruit	74	0.90	0.30	0.45	B1, B2, C, Nic
Lithospermum officinale; Boraginaceae; gromwell	Eu	leaves					
Litsea cubeba; Lauraceae	CAs, TrAs	fruit					
Lotus tetragonolobus (=*L. edulis*); Fabaceae; asparagus pea, winged pea	Med	fruit					
Luffa acutangula; Cucurbitaceae; angled luffa, angled loofah, sing-kwa	Ind	young fruit					

Luffa cylindrica (=*L. aegyptiaca*); Cucurbitaceae; sponge gourd, smooth luffa, vegetable sponge	TrAs	young fruit					
Lupinus albus (=*L. termis*); Fabaceae; white lupin, Egyptian lupin	Med	seeds					
Lupinus angustifolius; Fabaceae; narrow-leaved lupin, blue lupin	Med	seeds					
Lupinus luteus; Fabaceae; yellow lupin	Med	seeds					
Lupinus mutabilis; Fabaceae; tarwi, tarhui, Andean lupin, pearl lupin	SAm	seeds					
Lycium barbarum; Solanaceae; Duke of Argyll's tea-tree	Chin	fruit, leaves					
Lycium chinense; Solanaceae; Chinese boxthorn, Chinese wolfberry	Chin, TrAs	fruit, leaves					
Lycopersicon esculentum; Solanaceae; tomato	SAm, CAm	fruit	17	0.95	0.21	0.61	A, E, K, B1, B2, B6, Bio, C, Fol, Nic, Pan
Macadamia integrifolia; Proteaceae; macadamia nut, Queensland nut	Aus	seed	**703**	8.80	73.0	1.60	B1, B2, C, Nic
Macadamia tetraphylla; Proteaceae; macadamia nut	Aus	seed					
Macrotyloma geocarpum; Fabaceae; hausa groundnut, Kerstingiella groundnut	Afr	seed					
Madhuca indica; Sapotaceae; moa tree	Ind	flowers (nectar)					
Madhuca longifolia; Sapotaceae; mahwa, mahua, mowra butter tree	Ind	seed					
Malabaila secacul; Apiaceae; sekakul	CAs	roots					
Malpighia glabra; (= *M. punicifolia*); Malpighiaceae; acerola, Barbados cherry	CAm	fruit	16	0.21	0.23	0.45	A, B1, B2, B6, Bio, C (1-2%), Nic, Pan
Malus baccata; Rosaceae; Manchurian crab apple	Chin	roots					
Malus x domestica; Rosaceae; apple	NE	fruit	54	0.34	0.58	0.32	A, E, K, B1, B2, B6, Bio, C, Fol, Nic, Pan
Malus hupehensis (=*M. theifera*); Rosaceae; Chinese crab apple, tea crab apple	Chin	leaves (tea)					
Malus prunifolia; Rosaceae; Chinese apple	CAs	fruit					
Malva parviflora; Malvaceae; Egyptian mallow	Med, CAs	leaves					
Malva sylvestris; Malvaceae; common mallow, high mallow	Eu, Med	leaves, fruit	37	7.29	–	2.40	A, C
Malva verticillata; Malvaceae; mallow	Eu, Asia, Chin	leaves					
Mammea africana; Clusiaceae; (Guttiferae); African mammee apple	Afr	fruit					

Mammea americana; Clusiaceae; (Guttiferae); mammee, mamey, mammee apple	CAm	fruit	55	0.50	0.35	0.30	**A**, B1, B2, C, Nic
Mammea suriga; Clusiaceae; (Guttiferae); Indian mammee apple	Ind	fruit					
Mangifera caesia; Anacardiaceae; bauno, binjai	TrAs	fruit					
Mangifera indica; Anacardiaceae; mango	Ind, TrAs	fruit	57	0.60	0.45	0.50	**A**, E, B1, B2, C, Fol, Nic
Mangifera pajang; Anacardiaceae; bambangan	TrAs (Borneo)	fruit					
Mangifera odorata; Anacardiaceae; apple mango	TrAs	fruit					
Manihot esculenta; Euphorbiaceae; cassava	CAm, SAm	roots (leaves)	134	1.00	0.23	0.70	**A**, B1, B2, C, Nic
Manilkara bidentata; Sapotaceae; balata	CAm, SAm	fruit					
Manilkara cicle; Sapotaceae; crown gum	CAm, SAm	fruit					
Manilkara hexandra; Sapotaceae; palu	Ind	fruit					
Manilkara obovata; Sapotaceae; African pear	Afr	fruit					
Manilkara zapota (=*Achras zapota*); Sapotaceae; sapodilla, chiku, chicle	CAm	fruit (latex)	86	0.50	0.90	0.50	**A**, B1, B2, C, Nic
Maranta arundinacea; Marantaceae; arrowroot, Bermuda or St. Vincent arrowroot	CAm	rhizome					
Matricaria recutita; Asteraceae; German chamomile	Eu	flower heads					
Medicago sativa; Fabaceae; lucerne, alfalfa	NE, CAs	seeds, sprouts					
Melaleuca cajuputi; Myrtaceae; cajéput tree	TrAs, Aus	leaves (oil, flavour)					
Melaleuca quinquenervia; Myrtaceae; niaouli tree	TrAs, Aus	leaves (oil, flavour)					
Melicoccus bijugatus; Sapindaceae; genip, mamoncillo	SAm	fruit, seed					
Melilotus macrocarpa; Fabaceae; large-fruited melilotus	Med	fruit (spice)					
Melissa officinalis; Lamiaceae; lemon balm	Med, NE	leaves					
Mentha aquatica; Lamiaceae; water mint	Eu, Asia	leaves (oil)					
Mentha arvensis; Lamiaceae; field mint, corn mint, Japanese mint	Eu, Asia	leaves (oil)					
Mentha longifolia; Lamiaceae; horse mint, long-leaf mint	Eu, Afr, Asia, Ind	leaves (oil)					
Mentha x *piperita*; Lamiaceae; peppermint	Eu	leaves (oil)					
Mentha x *piperita* var. *citrata*; Lamiaceae; eau de cologne mint	Eu	leaves (oil)					

425

Mentha spicata; Lamiaceae; spearmint, garden mint	Eu	leaves (oil)					
Mentha suaveolens; Lamiaceae; apple mint, pineapple mint	Eu, Med	leaves (oil)					
Mespilus germanica; Rosaceae; medlar	Eu, CAs	fruit	43	0.5	–	–	C
Metroxylon sagu (=*M. rumphii*); Arecaceae; sago palm	TrAs	stems (starch)					
Mimusops coriacea; Sapotaceae; Madagascar mimusops	Afr (Madagas.)	fruit					
Mimusops elengi; Sapotaceae; red coondoo	Ind	fruit					
Mirabilis expansa; Nyctaginaceae; mauka	SAm	roots (stems)					
Momordica balsamina; Cucurbitaceae; balsam apple	TrAs	fruit	29	2.00	0.10	1.60	B1, B2, C, Nic
Momordica charantia; Cucurbitaceae; balsam pear, bitter gourd, bitter melon, karela	Afr, Ind, TrAs	fruit (leaves)					
Monarda didyma; Lamiaceae; bee balm, Oswego tea	NAm	leaves (tea)					
Monstera deliciosa; Araceae; delicious monster, ceriman	CAm	fruit					
Montia perfoliata; Portulacaceae; winter purslane, miner's lettuce, Cuban spinach	NAm	leaves					
Morinda citrifolia; Rubiaceae; noni tree, Indian mulberry	Ind, TrAs	fruit					
Moringa oleifera; Moringaceae; ben tree, drumstick tree, horse-radish tree	Ind	fruit, seeds leaves, root					
Morus alba; Moraceae; white mulberry	Chin	fruit					
Morus nigra; Moraceae; black mulberry	NE	fruit	36	1.3	–	–	B1, B2, C, Fol
Mucuna pruriens, Fabaceae; velvet bean	TrAs	seeds					
Murraya koenigii; Rutaeae; curry leaf	Ind	leaves					
Musa acuminata; (= *M. sapientum*); Musaceae; banana	TrAs	fruit	88	1.15	0.18	0.83	A, E, K, B1, B2, B6, Bio, C, Fol, Nic, Pan
Musa paradisiaca; Musaceae; plaintain, cooking banana	TrAs	fruit					
Myrica rubra; Myricaceae; Chinese strawberry tree, ioobai, yama momo	Chin	fruit					
Myrciaria cauliflora; Myrtaceae; jaboticaba	SAm	fruit	73	0.50	1.80	0.40	B1, B2, C, Nic
Myristica fragrans; Myristicaceae; nutmeg, mace	TrAs	seeds, aril					
Myrrhis odorata; Apiaceae; sweet cicely	Eu	leaves, fruit					
Myrtus communis; Myrtaceae; myrtle	Eu, NE	leaves, fruit					

Myrtus ugni; Myrtaceae; ugni	SAm (Chile)	fruit					
Nasturtium officinale – see *Rorippa nasturtium-aquaticum*							
Nelumbo nucifera; Nymphaeaceae; lotus	Asia, Aus	fruits, rhizomes					
Nephelium lappaceum; Sapindaceae; rambutan	TrAs	fruit	65	1.00	0.10	0.40	B1, B2, C, Nic
Nephelium mutabile (=*N. ramboutan-ake*); Sapindaceae; pulasan	TrAs	fruit					
Neptunia prostrata (=*N. aquatica*, *N. oleracea*); Fabaceae	TrAs	leaves					
Nigella sativa; Ranunculaceae; black cumin, black seed, kalonji	Eu, NE, Afr, Asia	seeds					
Nypa fruticans; Palmae; nipa palm	TrAs	stem sap, stem tips					
Ocimum basilicum; Lamiaceae; basil	Afr, NE, Asia	leaves					
Ocimum canum; Lamiaceae; hairy basil, African basil	Afr	leaves					
Ocimum gratissimum; Lamiaceae;	Asia, Ind, Afr	leaves					
Ocimum tenuiflorum (=*O. sanctum*); Lamiaceae; sacred basil, holy basil, tulsi, **Thai basil** (form)	TrAs	leaves					
Olea europaea; Oleaceae; olive	Med, Afr, NE	fruit (fruit oil)	138	1.38	13.9	5.80	A, B1, B2, B6, C, Nic, Pan
Opuntia cochenillifera; Cactaceae; nopalea cactus, cochineal plant	CAm (Mexico)	young stems					
Opuntia ficus-indica; Cactaceae; prickly pear	CAm (Mexico)	fruit	36	1.00	0.40	0.30	A, B1, B2, C, Nic
Origanum majorana; Lamiaceae; marjoram	Med, NE	leaves					
Origanum onites; Lamiaceae; pot marjoram	Med, NE	leaves					
Origanum vulgare; Lamiaceae; oregano	Med, NE	leaves					
Oryza glaberrima; Poaceae; African rice	Afr	fruit (grains)					
Oryza sativa; Poaceae; rice, Asian rice	Chin, Ind	fruit (grains)	345	7.78	2.20	1.20	E, B1, B2, B6, Bio, Fol
Osmanthus fragrans; Oleaceae; kwei	Chin	flowers, tea flavour					
Oxalis tuberosa; Oxalidaceae; oca	SAm (Andes)	tubers					
Pachira aquatica (= *Bombax glabrum*); Bombacaceae; Malabar chestnut, saba nut	CAm, SAm	seeds					
Pachyrhizus ahipa; Fabaceae; ahipa, Andean yam bean	SAm (Andes)	tubers, fruit					

Pachyrhizus erosus; Fabaceae; yam bean, Mexican potato, potato bean, jicima	CAm	tubers, fruit					
Pachyrhizus tuberosus; Fabaceae; Amazonian yam bean	SAm	tubers, fruit					
Panax ginseng; Araliaceae; ginseng, Asian ginseng, Korean ginseng	Chin	roots					
Panax pseudoginseng; Araliaceae; sanchi	Asia	roots					
Panax quinquefolius; Araliaceae; American ginseng	NAm	roots					
Pandanus amaryllifolius; Pandanaceae; pandan, fragrant pandan	TrAs, Ind	leaves					
Pandanus leram; Pandanaceae; Nicobar breadfruit	TrAs	fruits					
Pandanus tectorius; Pandanaceae; ketaki	TrAs	fruit					
Pangium edule; Flacourtaceae; pangium	TrAs	fruit					
Panicum miliaceum; Poaceae; millet, common millet, proso millet	CAs, Chin	fruit (grains)	349	10.6	3.90	1.60	E, B1, B2, B6, Nic
Panicum sonorum; Poaceae; sauwi	Afr	fruit (grains)					
Panicum sumatrense; Poaceae; little millet, sama	TrAs	fruit (grains)					
Papaver somniferum; Papaveraceae; opium poppy	NE, Med	seeds	**477**	**23.8**	42.2	6.8	B1, B2, B6, Nic
Parinari curatellifolia; Chrysobalanaceae; mobola	Afr	fruit seeds (nuts)	128 **655**	1.60 **28.7**	0.50 58.0	1.50 2.70	B1, B2, C, Nic B1, B2
Parkia biglobosa; Fabaceae; locust bean	CAm	fruit					
Parkia filicoidea; Fabaceae; African locust	Afr	fruit					
Parkia speciosa; Fabaceae; petai	TrAs	fruit, seeds					
Paspalum scrobiculatum; Poaceae; kodo millet, ricegrass	Ind	fruit (grains)					
Passiflora alata; Passifloraceae; wingstem passion fruit	SAm	fruit					
Passiflora edulis; Passifloraceae; passion fruit, granadilla	SAm	fruit	63	2.40	0.40	0.90	A, B1, B2, C, Nic
Passiflora incarnata; Passifloraceae; apricot vine	SAm	fruit					
Passiflora laurifolia; Passifloraceae; yellow granadilla	SAm	fruit					
Passiflora ligularis; Passifloraceae; sweet passion fruit	SAm	fruit					
Passiflora maliformis; Passifloraceae; chulupa	SAm	fruit					
Passiflora mollissima; Passifloraceae; curuba, banana passion fruit	SAm	fruit					

Passiflora quadrangularis; Passifloraceae; giant passion fruit	SAm	fruit					
Pastinaca sativa; Apiaceae; parsnip	Eu, WAs	roots	59	1.31	0.43	1.18	A, E, B1, B2, B6, C, Bio, Fol, Nic, Pan
Paullinia cupana; Sapindaceae; guaraná	SAm	seeds					
Paullinia yoco; Sapindaceae; yoco	SAm	seeds					
Pennisetum glaucum; Poaceae; pearl millet, bulrush millet	Afr	fruit (grains)					
Pentaphragma begoniaefolium; Pentaphragmaceae	TrAs	leaves					
Perilla frutescens (=*Perilla arguta*); Lamiaceae; perilla, beefsteak plant, *shiso*	CAs, Chin	leaves, seeds					
Persea americana (= *P. gratissima*); Lauraceae; avocado	CAm	fruit	**221**	1.90	23.5	1.36	A, E, K, B1, B2, B6, Bio, C, Fol, Nic, Pan
Persicaria hydropiper; Polygonaceae; water pepper	TrAs	leaves					
Persicaria mollis; Polygonaceae; Sikkim knotweed	TrAs	leaves					
Persicaria odorata; Polygonaceae; laksa plant, Vietnamese mint	TrAs	leaves					
Petasites japonicus; Asteraceae; fuhi	Chin	flower buds, leaf stalks					
Petroselinum crispum; Apiaceae; parsley	Med, NE	leaves, fruit	50	4.43	0.36	1.68	**A**, E, K, B1, B2, B6, Bio, **C**, **Fol**, Nic, Pan
Petroselinum crispum* var. *neapolitanum; Apiaceae; Italian parsley, celery-leaved parsley	Med, NE	leaves, fruit					
Petroselinum crispum var. *tuberosum*; Apiaceae; parsley	Med, NE	root	40	2.88	0.47	1.62	A, B1, B2, B6, C, Nic
Phaeomeria magnifica – see *Etlingera elatior*							
Phaseolus coccineus; Fabaceae; runner bean, scarlet runner bean	CAm	fruit, seeds (roots)					
Phaseolus angularis – see *Vigna angularis*							
Phaseolus lunatus; Fabaceae; lima bean	CAm, SAm	seeds (fruit)	**275**	20.6	1.40	3.70	K, B1, B2, B6, Bio, C, Fol, Nic, Pan
Phaseolus polyanthus; Fabaceae; year bean	CAm, SAm	seeds, fruit					
Phaseolus vulgaris; Fabaceae; asparagus bean, common bean, French bean	Chin	seeds	237	21.1	1.60	3.85	A, E, B1, B2, B6, C, Fol, Nic, Pan
		fruit	33	2.39	0.24	0.70	A, E, K, B1, B2, B6, Bio, C, Fol, Nic, Pan
Phoenix dactylifera; Arecaeae; date palm	NE	fruit	**276**	1.85	0.53	1.82	A, B1, B2, B6, C, Fol, Nic, Pan
Phoenix reclinata; Arecaceae; African wild date palm	Afr	stem sap, fruit					
Phoenix sylvestris; Arecaceae; Indian wild date palm	Ind	stem sap, fruit					

Phyllanthus acidus; Euphorbiaceae; Otaheite gooseberry, star gooseberry	SAm?	fruit					
Phyllanthus emblica; Euphorbiaceae; emblic, ambal	TrAs	fruit					
Phyllostachys aurea; Poaceae; fish-pole bamboo	Chin	shoots					
Phyllostachys bambusoides; Poaceae; madake bamboo	Chin	shoots					
Phyllostachys dulcis; Poaceae; sweetshoot bamboo	Chin	shoots					
Phyllostachys edulis; Poaceae; bamboo shoots bamboo	Chin	shoots					
Physalis alkekengi; Solanaceae; bladder cherry, Chinese lantern plant	Eu, Asia	fruit					
Physalis ixocarpa; Solanaceae; tomatillo, jamberry	CAm	fruit					
Physalis peruviana; Solanaceae; Cape gooseberry	SAm	fruit	72	2.30	1.10	0.80	A, B1, B2, C, Nic
Physalis pruinosa; Solanaceae; ground cherry, dwarf Cape gooseberry	NAm	fruit					
Phytolacca acinosa; Phytolacaceae; vegetable phytolacca	TrAs, Chin	leaves					
Pimento dioica; Myrtaceae; allspice, pimento, Jamaica pepper	CAm	fruit, leaves					
Pimenta racemosa (=*P. acris*); Myrtaceae; bay rum tree	CAm	fruit, leaves					
Pimpinella anisum; Apiaceae; anise	Med, NE	fruit					
Pinus cembra; Pinaceae; Siberian cedar	Eu, Asia	seeds					
Pinus cembroides; Pinaceae; Mexican pine	NAm	seeds					
Pinus edulis; Pinaceae; *piñon*	NAm	seeds					
Pinus koraiensis; Pinaceae; Korean pine	Chin	seeds					
Pinus pinea; Pinaceae; stone pine	Med	seeds	679	14.0	68.6	–	A, E, B1, B2,
Piper clusii; Piperaceae; West African black pepper, African cubebs	TrAs	fruits					
Piper cubeba; Piperaceae; cubeb, cubebe, tailed pepper, Java pepper	TrAs	fruits					
Piper longum; Piperaceae; Indian long pepper, Jaborandi pepper	CAs, Ind	fruits					
Piper methysticum; Piperaceae; kava pepper, kava kava	TrAs	rhizomes, roots					
Piper nigrum; Piperaceae; black pepper, pepper	Ind	fruits					

Piper retrofractum; Piperaceae; Javanese long pepper	TrAs	flowers				
Pisonia grandis (=*P. alba*); Nyctaginaceae; lettuce tree, Moluccan cabbage	TrAs	leaves				
Pistacia vera; Anacardiaceae; pistachio	NE, CAs	seeds	**581**	20.8	51.6	2.70	A, E, K, B1, B2, C, Fol, Nic
Pisum sativum; Fabaceae; pea, garden pea	NE, Med	fruit and seeds (green)	81	6.55	0.48	0.92	A, E, K, B1, B2, B6, Bio, C, Fol, Nic, Pan
		seeds (dry)	**271**	22.9	1.44	2.68	A, K, B1, B2, B6, Bio, C, Fol, Nic, Pan
Pithecellobium dulce; Fabaceae; Manila tamarind, opiuma	CAm	fruit				
Pithecellobium lobatum; Fabaceae	TrAs	fruits, leaves				
Plantago lanceolata; Plantaginaceae; plantain, ribwort plantain	Eu, As	leaves	19	2.23	0.42	1.43	C
Plantago major; Plantaginaceae; broadleaf plantain	Eu, As	leaves	24	3.41	0.42	1.72	C
Plectranthus amboinicus; (=*Coleus amboinicus*); Lamiaceae; Indian borage	Afr	leaves				
Plectranthus esculentus; Lamiaceae; Livingstone potato, Hausa potato	Afr	tubers				
Plectranthus rotundifolius; Lamiaceae; Sudan potato, Zulu round potato	Afr	tubers				
Pluchea indica; Asteraceae	TrAs, Ind	leaves				
Plukenetia conophora; Euphorbiaceae; owusa nut	Afr	seeds				
Plukenetia corniculata; Euphorbiaceae; painapaina	TrAs	seeds				
Pogostemon mutamba; Lamiaceae; mutamba	Afr	tubers				
Polygonum hydropiper – see *Persicaria hydropiper*						
Polygonum odoratum – see *Persicaria odorata*						
Polymnia sonchifolia; Asteraceae; yacon	SAm	tubers				
Pometia pinnata; Sapindaceae	TrAs	fruit				
Poncirus trifoliata; Rutaceae; trifoliate orange	Chin	fruit				
Portulaca oleracea; Portulacaceae; purslane	cosmo-politan	leaves	11	1.48	0.34	1.41	A, K, B1, B2, B6, C, Fol, Nic
Pouteria cainito; Sapotaceae; abiu	CAm	fruit				
Pouteria campechiana; Sapotaceae; canistel	CAm	fruit				
Pouteria lucuma; Sapotaceae; lucuma	SAm	fruit				
Pouteria sapota; Sapotaceae; sapote, mamme zapote, marmalade plum	CAm	fruit	94	1.40	0.50	0.90	A, B1, B2, C, Nic

Prunus americana; Rosaceae; American plum	NAm	fruit					
Prunus armeniaca; Rosaceae; apricot	Chin	fruit	43	0.90	0.13	0.66	**A**, E, K, B1, B2, B6, C, Fol, Nic, Pan
Prunus avium; Rosaceae; sweet cherry	Eu, Asia	fruit	62	0.90	0.31	0.49	A, E, K, B1, B2, B6, Bio, C, Fol, Nic, Pan
Prunus cantabrigiensis; Rosaceae; Chinese sour cherry, yingtao cherry	Chin	fruit					
Prunus capuli; Rosaceae; capuli	CAm	fruit					
Prunus cerasifera; Rosaceae; cherry plum, myrobalan	CAs	fruit					
Prunus cerasus; Rosaceae; sour cherry	CAs	fruit	53	0.90	0.50	0.50	A, E, B1, B2, C, Fol, Nic
Prunus domestica; Rosaceae; European plum, garden plum	CAs	fruit	48	0.60	0.17	0.49	A, E, K, B1, B2, B6, Bio, C, Fol, Nic, Pan
Prunus dulcis; Rosaceae; almond	CAs, NE	fruit	**583**	**22.1**	54.1	2.65	A, E, B1, B2, B6, Bio, C, Fol, Nic, Pan
Prunus institia; Rosaceae; damson plum, greengage	Eu	fruit	56	0.79	–	0.60	A, C
Prunus maritima; Rosaceae; beach plum	NAm	fruit					
Prunus mume; Rosaceae; mume, Japanese apricot	Chin	fruit					
Prunus munsoniana; Rosaceae; wild goose plum	NAm	fruit					
Prunus nigra; Rosaceae; Canada plum	NAm	fruit					
Prunus persica; Rosaceae; peach	Chin	fruit	41	0.76	0.11	0.45	A, E, K, B1, B2, B6, Bio, C, Fol, Nic, Pan
Prunus persica* var. *nectarina; Rosaceae; nectarine	Chin	fruit					
Prunus salicina; Rosaceae Japanese plum, Chinese plum	Chin	fruit					
Prunus sargentii; Rosaceae; sergeant cherry, mountain cherry	Chin	fruit					
Prunus simonii; Rosaceae; apricot plum	Chin	fruit					
Prunus spinosa; Rosaceae; sloe, blackthorn	CAs	fruit	47	0.75	–	1.05	–
Prunus tomentosa; Rosaceae; Nanking cherry, Chinese bush cherry	Chin	fruit					
Prunus virginiana; Rosaceae; chokecherry	NAm	fruit					
Psidium friedrichsthalianum; Myrtaceae; Costa Rican guava	CAm	fruit					
Psidium guajava; Myrtaceae; guava	CAm	fruit	34	0.90	0.50	0.68	A, B1, B2, **C**, Nic
Psidium guineense; Myrtaceae; Guinea guava, guisaro	CAm, SAm	fruit					

Psidium littorale; Myrtaceae; strawberry guava	SAm	fruit					
Psidium littorale var. *lucidum*; Myrtaceae; yellow strawberry guava	SAm	fruit					
Psophocarpus tetragonolobus; Fabaceae; winged bean, asparagus bean, Goa bean	Afr	seeds (fruit, root)	401	33.1	16.2	3.8	–
Pteridium aquilinum; Dennstaedtiaceae; bracken, sawarabi	cosmo-politan	fronds, rhizome					
Pueraria montana var. *lobata*; Fabaceae; kudzu vine, Japanese arrowroot	Chin, Ind	tuber					
Pugionum cornutum; Brassicaceae	CAs	leaves					
Punica granatum; Punicaceae; pomegranate	NE	fruit	74	0.70	0.60	0.70	A, B1, B2, C, Nic
Pyrus communis; Rosaceae; pear	Eu, WAsia	fruit	55	0.47	0.29	0.33	A, E, K, B1, B2, B6, Bio, C, Fol, Nic, Pan
Pyrus pyrifolia; Rosaceae; Asian pear, nashi, sand pear	Chin	fruit					
Ranunculus ficaria; Ranunculaceae; figwort, pilewort, celandine	Eu, NE	leaves	15	2.53	–	1.29	A, C
Raphanus sativus; Brassicaceae; radish, small radish	Eu, Asia	roots	14	1.05	0.14	0.90	A, B1, B2, B6, C, Fol, Nic, Pan
Raphanus sativus var. *oleiformis*; Brassicaceae; oil-seed radish, fodder radish	Eu, Asia	seeds					
Rhamnus prinoides; Rhamnaceae; geisho	Afr Ethiopia	leaves					
Rheum rhabarbarum; Polygonaceae; rhubarb	CAs	leaf stalks	13	0.60	0.14	0.64	A, E, K, B1, B2, B6, C, Fol, Nic, Pan
Rhodomyrtus macrocarpa; Myrtaceae; finger cherry	Aus	fruit					
Rhodomyrtus tormentosa; Myrtaceae; downy rose-myrtle	TrAs	fruit					
Ribes americanum; Grossulariaceae; American blackcurrant	NAm	fruit					
Ribes cynosbati; Gossulariaceae; American wild gooseberry	NAm	fruit					
Ribes divaricatum; Gossulariaceae; Worcesterberry	NAm	fruit					
Ribes hirtellum; Gossulariaceae; currant gooseberry	NAm	fruit					
Ribes longeracemosum; Gossulariaceae	Chin	fruit					
Ribes multiflorum; Grossulariaceae	Med	fruit					
Ribes rubrum; Gossulariaceae; red currant	Eu, Asia	fruit	33	1.13	0.20	0.63	A, E, K, B1, B2, B6, Bio, C, Fol, Nic, Pan
Ribes x *nidigrolaria*; Gossulariaceae; jostaberry	Eu	fruit					
Ribes nigrum; Gossulariaceae; black currant	Eu, Asia	fruit	39	1.28	0.22	0.80	A, E, K, B1, B2, B6, Bio, C, Fol, Nic, Pan
Ribes ussuriense; Grossulariaceae	Chin	fruit					

Ribes uva-crispa (=*R. grossularia*); Gossulariaceae; gooseberry	Eu, Asia	fruit	37	0.80	0.15	0.45	A, E, B1, B2, B6, Bio, C, Fol, Nic, Pan
Rorippa microphylla; Brassicaceae; brown watercress, winter watercress	Eu	leaves					
Rorippa nasturtium-aquaticum; Brassicaceae; watercress	Eu	leaves	17	1.60	0.30	1.10	A, K, B1, B2, C, Nic
Rosa canina; Rosaceae; dog rose	Eu, Asia	fruit (hips)	94	3.60	0.60	2.60	A, E, K, B1, B2, B6, C, Nic
Rosa roxburghii; Rosaceae; Chinese rose	Chin	fruit (hips)					
Rosa rugosa; Rosaceae; Japanese rose	Chin	fruit (hips)					
Rosmarinus officinalis; Lamiaceae; rosemary	Med	leaves					
Rubus caesius; Rosaceae; European dewberry	Eu, Asia	fruit					
Rubus chamaemorus; Rosaceae; cloudberry	Eu, Asia, NAm	fruit					
Rubus flaggelaris; Rosaceae; American dewberry	NAm	fruit					
Rubus fruticosus; Rosaceae; blackberry, bramble	Eu, Med	fruit	44	1.20	1.00	0.51	A, E, B1, B2, B6, C, Nic, Pan
Rubus glaucus; Rosaceae; South American raspberry, mora de Castilla	CAm,	fruit					
Rubus idaeus, Rosaceae; raspberry	Eu, Asia, NAm	fruit	34	1.30	0.30	0.51	A, E, K, B1, B2, B6, C, Fol, Nic, Pan
Rubus illecebrosus; Rosaceae; strawberry raspberry, balloon berry	Chin	fruit					
Rubus laciniatus; Rosaceae; cut-leaved bramble	Eu	fruit					
Rubus loganobaccus; Rosaceae; loganberry, Boysenberry	NAm	fruit	33	0.50	0.30	0.90	A, B1, B2, C, Nic
Rubus phoenicolasius; Rosaceae; wineberry, wine raspberry	Chin	fruit					
Rubus rosifolius; Rosaceae; Mauritius raspberry	TrAs	fruit					
Rubus ulmifolius; Rosaceae; blackberry	Eu	fruit					
Rubus vitifolius; Rosaceae; dewberry	NAm	fruit					
Rumex acetosa; Polygonaceae; sorrel	Eu, Asia	leaves	21	3.19	0.36	0.80	A, C
Rumex scutatus; Polygonaceae; French sorrel	Eu, Asia	leaves					
Ruta chalepensis; Rutaceae; Aleppo rue	Med	leaves					
Ruta graveolens; Rutaceae; rue, herb of grace	Eu	leaves					
Saccharum edule; Poaceae; lowland sugar, pit pit sugar	TrAs	stems					

Saccharum officinarum; Poaceae; sugar-cane	TrAs	stems (sap)	**399**	–	–	0.04	–
Saccharum spontaneum; Poaceae; wild sugar cane	TrAs	stems					
Sagittaria sagittifolia; Alismataceae; arrowhead, Chinese arrowhead	Eu, Chin	corms					
Salacca conferta; Arecaceae; kelubi	TrAs	stem tip					
Salacca vermicularis; Arecaceae; kepela	TrAs	stem tip					
Salacca wallichiana; Arecaceae; rakum palm, rekum, sala	TrAs	fruit, stem tip					
Salacca zalacca (=*S. edulis*); Arecaceae; salak	TrAs	fruit, stem tip					
Salsola komarovii; Chenopodiaceae; *oka-hijiki*	Chin	leaves					
Salvia fruticosa; Lamiaceae; Greek sage	Med	leaves					
Salvia officinalis; Lamiaceae; sage	Med, Eu	leaves					
Salvia sclarea; Lamiaceae; clary sage	Eu, Asia	leaves					
Sambucus canadensis; Caprifoliaceae; American elderberry	NAm	fruit					
Sambucus nigra; Caprifoliaceae; elderberry	Afr, Eu, Asia	fruit	54	2.53	1.70	0.69	A, B1, B2, B6, Bio, C, Fol, Nic, Pan
Sambucus racemosa; Caprifoliaceae; grape elder	Eu, Asia	fruit					
Sandoricum koetjape; Meliaceae; santol, sentul	TrAs	fruits					
Sanguisorba minor (= *Poterium sanguisorba*); Rosaceae; burnet, salad burnet	Eu	leaves					
Satureja hortensis; Lamiaceae; summer savory	Eu	leaves					
Satureja montana; Lamiaceae; winter savory	Med	leaves					
Schinus molle; Anacardiaceae; pepper tree, pink pepper	SAm (Andes)	fruit					
Schinziophyton rautanenii; Euphorbiaceae; manketti tree, mongongo nut tree	Afr	fruit	337	7.80	0.50	5.2	B1, B2, C, Nic
		seeds (nuts)	**650**	**26.3**	58.1	4.10	B1, B2, Nic
Sclerocarya birrea; Anacardiaceae; marula tree	Afr	fruit	54	0.50	0.40	0.90	B1, B2, C, Nic
		seeds (nuts)	**647**	**28.3**	57.3	3.80	B1, B2, Nic
Scolymus hispanicus; Asteraceae; golden thistle, Spanish oyster plant	Med	root					
Scorzonera hispanica; Asteraceae; scorzonera, black salsify	Med	root	18	1.39	0.43	0.99	A, E, B1, B2, C, Nic
Secale cereale; Poaceae; rye	NE	fruit (grains)	294	9.51	1.70	1.90	E, B1, B2, B6, Bio, Fol
Sechium edule; Cucurbitaceae; chayote, vegetable pear	CAm	fruit, tubers	27	0.75	0.10	0.30	A, B1, B2, C, Nic
Selenicereus megalanthus; Cactaceae; yellow pitahaya	CAm	fruit					

Sesamum indicum; Pedaliaceae; sesame	Afr, NE, Ind	seeds	**565**	**20.9**	50.4	5.3	K, B1, B2, B6, Nic
Sesbania grandiflora; Fabaceae; bakphul, Agati sesbania, sesban	TrAs	flowers, seeds					
Setaria italica; Poaceae; foxtail millet	Eu	fruit (grains)	347	14.3	4.90	3.10	B1, B2, Nic
Setaria palmifolia; Poaceae	TrAs	young stems					
Setaria pumila; Poaceae; yellow foxtail, pigeon grass	Asia, Ind	fruit (grains)					
Shorea macrophylla; Dipterocarpaceae; illipe nut	TrAs	seeds (oil)					
Sicana odorifera; Cucurbitaceae; casabanana	SAm	fruit					
Sinapis alba (=*Brassica hirta*); Brassicaceae; white mustard	Med	seeds, (leaves)					
Smilax bona-nox; Smilacaceae; Chinese briar	NAm	rhizome					
Smilax regelii; Smilacaceae; Jamaica sarsaparilla	CAm	rhizome					
Solanum melanocerasum (=*S. intrusum*); Solanaceae; garden huckleberry	un-known	fruit					
Solanum melongena; Solanaceae; aubergine, eggplant, brinjal	Ind	fruit	17	1.24	0.18	0.50	A, E, K, B1, B2, B6, C, Fol, Nic, Pan
Solanum muricatum; Solanaceae; pepino	SAm (Andes)	fruit					
Solanum nigrum; Solanaceae; black nightshade, wonderberry	Eu	fruit					
Solanum quitoense; Solanaceae; naranjilla, lulo	SAm	fruit	44	1.00	0.15	0.64	A, B1, B2, C, Nic
Solanum retroflexum; Solanaceae; msoba, umsoba	Afr	fruit					
Solanum tuberosum; Solanaceae; potato	SAm (Andes)	fruit	70	2.04	0.11	1.02	A, E, K, B1, B2, B6, Bio, C, Fol, Pan
Solanum uporo; Solanaceae; uporo	TrAs	fruit					
Solenostemon rotundifolius – see *Plectranthus rotundifolius*							
Sonchus oleraceus; Asteraceae; sow thistle	Eu, Asia Med	leaves					
Sorbus aria; Rosaceae; whitebeam berry	Eu	fruit					
Sorbus aucuparia; Rosaceae; mountain ash, rowan	Eu, NE	fruit	85	1.50	–	0.68	A, C
Sorbus domestica; Rosaceae; service tree, sorb apple	Eu, NE, Afr	fruit					
Sorbus torminalis; Rosaceae; service tree, sorb apple	Med	fruit					
Sorghum bicolor; Poaceae; sorghum, broomcorn	Afr	fruit (grains)	349	11.1	3.2	1.75	A, E, B1, B2, Nic
Sauropus androgynus; Euphorbiaceae; sweet-shoot, chekur manis	TrAs	leaves					

Spilanthes acmella (=*Acmella oleracea*); Asteraceae; spilanthes, pará cress	SAm	leaves				
Spinacea oleracea; Chenopodiaceae; spinach	NE	leaves	16	2.65	0.30	1.69	A, E, K, B1, B2, B6, Bio, C, **Fol**, Nic, Pan
Spondias cytherea (=*S. dulcis*); Anacardiaceae; ambarella, hog plum	TrAs	fruit				
Spondias mombin (=*S. lutea*); Anacardiaceae; yellow mombin, caja fuit, jobo	CAm, SAm	fruit				
Spondias purpurea; Anacardiaceae; Spanish plum, red mombin, Jamacaica plum	CAm, SAm	fruit				
Stachys sieboldii; Lamiaceae; Chinese artichoke	Chin	tuber				
Stellaria media; Caryophyllaceae; chickweed, common chickweed	Eu, Med	leaves	7	1.79	–	1.62	A, C
Stevia rebaudiana; Asteraceae; stevia, sugar-leaf	SAm	leaves				
Strychnos spinosa; Strychnaceae; monkey orange	Afr	fruit	73	2.70	0.10	1.90	B1, B2, C, Nic
Synsepalum dulcificum; Sapotaceae; miraculous berry, miracle fruit	Afr	fruit				
Syzygium aromaticum; Myrtaceae; clove	TrAs	flower buds				
Syzygium aqueum; Myrtaceae; water apple, watery rose apple	TrAs	fruit				
Syzygium cumini; Myrtaceae; jambolan, Java plum	TrAs	fruit				
Syzygium jambos; Myrtaceae; rose apple, Malabar plum, jambos	TrAs	fruits	32	0.60	0.30	0.40	A, B1, B2, C, Nic
Syzygium malaccensis; Myrtaceae; Malay rose apple, pomerac	TrAs	fruits				
Syzygium paniculatum; Myrtaceae; garden eugenia, brush cherry	Aus	fruits				
Syzygium polyantha; Myrtaceae; salam leaf, duan salam, Indonesian bay leaf	TrAs	leaves				
Syzygium samarangense; Myrtaceae; Java wax apple, wax jambu, Java rose apple	TrAs	fruits				
Talinum triangulare; Portulacaeae; talinum, flameflower, waterleaf	NAm	leaves				
Tamarindus indica; Fabaceae; tamarind	Afr	fruit	**238**	2.30	0.20	2.10	A, B1, B2, C, Nic
Tanacetum parthenium – see *Chrysanthemum parthenium*						
Tanacetum vulgare – see *Chrysanthemum vulgare*						
Taraxacum officinale; Asteraceae; dandelion	Eu, Asia	leaves	27	2.87	0.62	1.65	A, E, K, B1, B2, C, Nic
Terminalia catappa; Combretaceae: Indian almond	TrAs	fruit, seed				

Terminalia kaernbachii; Combretaceae; okari	TrAs	fruit, seed					
Tetragonia tetragonioides; Aizoaceae; New Zealand spinach, Warrigal greens	Chin, TrAs	leaves					
Theobroma cacao; Sterculiaceae; cacao, cocoa tree	SAm	seeds (powder)	343	19.8	24.5	6.53	B1, B2, B6, Bio, Fol, Nic, Pan
Thymus x citriodorus; Lamiaceae; lemon thyme	Eu	leaves					
Thymus vulgaris; Lamiaceae; common thyme, garden thyme	Med	leaves					
Tournefortia argentea; Boraginaceae; velvet leaf	TrAs	leaves					
Trachyspermum ammi (=*T. copticum*); Apiaceae; ajowan, ajwain, carom, omam	NE, Ind, Asia, Afr	fruit ("seeds")					
Tragopogon porrifolius; Asteraceae; salsify, oyster plant	Med	roots					
Tragopogon pratensis; Asteraceae; goat's beard	Eu	leaves	17	2.85	–	1.45	C
Trapa bicornis; Trapaceae; water chestnut, caltrop, ling nut	Chin	corms					
Trapa bispinosa; Trapaceae; singara nut	Eu, AS	seeds					
Trapa natans; Trapaceae; European water chestnut, water caltrops	Chin	seeds					
Trichosanthes cucumerina (=*T. anguina*); Cucurbitaceae; snake gourd	TrAs, Ind	fruit					
Trichosanthes dioica; Cucurbitaceae; pointed gourd	TrAs	roots					
Trichosanthes kirilowii (=*T. japonica*); Cucurbitaceae; Mongolian gourd	Chin	roots					
Trichosanthes ovigera (=*T. cucumeroides*); Cucurbitaceae; Japanese snake gourd	Chin	roots					
Trifolium pratense; Fabaceae; red clover	Eu, CAs	seeds (sprouts)					
Trigonella foenum-graecum; Fabaceae; fenugreek	Med, NE	seeds					
Triphasia trifolia; Rutaceae; lime berry, trifoliate lime berry	TrAs, Chin	fruits					
Triticale (Triticum x Secale); Poaceae; triticale	Cult.	fruit (grains)	329	13.9	2.48	1.87	B1, B2, Fol, Nic, Pan
Triticum aestivum; Poaceae; bread wheat	NE	fruit (grains)	298	11.7	1.83	1.67	A, E, B1, B2, B6, Fol, Nic
Triticum durum; Poaceae; durum wheat	NE	fruit (grains)	339	13.7	2.50	–	B1, B2
Triticum monococcum; Poaceae; einkorn wheat	Med, NE	fruit (grains)					
Triticum spelta; Poaceae; spelt (spelt wheat)	Eu, NE	fruit (grains)	332	14.4	2.55	1.89	E, B1, B2, B6

Triticum turgidum var. *dicoccum*; Poaceae; emmer wheat	Med, NE	fruit (grains)					
Tropaeolum majus; Tropaeolaceae; garden nasturtium, Indian cress	SAm (Andes)	flowers, seeds					
Tropaeolum tuberosum; Tropaeolaceae; tuber nasturtium, ysaño, mashua, añu	SAm (Andes)	tubers					
Uapaca kirkiana; Euphorbiaceae; wild loquat, mahobohobo	Afr	fruit	66	0.60	0.20	0.50	B1, B2, C, Nic
Ullucus tuberosus; Basellaceae; ulluco, tuberous basella	SAm (Andes)	tubers (leaves)					
Urtica dioica; Urticaceae; perennial stinging nettle	Eu, Asia	leaves	40	7.37	0.61	2.26	A, **C**
Urtica urens; Urticaceae; annual stinging nettle	Eu, Asia, NAm	leaves	55	5.40	0.70	4.90	A, B1, B2, Nic
Vaccinium angustifolium; Ericaceae; lowbush blueberry	NAm	fruit					
Vaccinium ashei; Ericaceae; rabbiteye blueberry	NAm	fruit					
Vaccinium corymbosum; Ericaceae; highbush blueberry	NAm	fruit					
Vaccinium floribundum; Ericaceae; mortiño, Andes blueberry	SAm	fruit					
Vaccinium macrocarpon; Ericaceae; large cranberry, American cranberry	NAm, Asia	fruit					
Vaccinium myrtillus; Ericaceae; bilberry, common blueberry	Eu, Asia, NAm	fruit	36	0.60	0.60	0.30	A, E, K, B1, B2, B6, Bio, C, Fol, Nic, Pan
Vaccinium oxycoccus; Ericaceae; small cranberry, European cranberry	Eu, Asia, NAm	fruit	35	0.35	0.70	0.24	A, B1, B2, C, Nic
Vaccinium vitis-idaea; Ericaceae; lingonberry, cowberry C, Fol, Nic, Pan	Eu, Asia, NAm	fruit	35	0.28	0.53	0.26	A, E, K, B1, B2, B6,
Valerianella locusta; Valerianaceae; corn salad, lamb's lettuce	Eu, Med	whole plant					
Valerianella olitoria; Valerianaceae; corn salad, lamb's lettuce	Eu, Med	whole plant	14	1.84	0.36	0.80	A, E, B1, B2, B6, C, Fol, Nic
Vanilla planifolia; Orchidaceae; vanilla	CAm (Mexico)	fruit					
Vicia faba; Fabaceae; broad bean, fava bean	NE	seeds (fresh)	82	7.90	0.60	–	A, E, B1, B2, C, Fol
Vigna aconitifolia; Fabaceae, moth bean	Ind, TrAs	seeds					
Vigna angularis; Fabaceae; adzuki bean	Chin	seeds					
Vigna mungo; Fabaceae; urd bean, black gram	CAs, Ind TrAs	seeds	269	**23.1**	1.2	3.5	A, K, B1, B2, B6, Bio, C, Fol, Nic, Pan
Vigna radiata; Fabaceae; mung bean, green gram, golden gram, moong	Ind	seeds	281	**23.8**	1.31	3.29	K, B1, B2, B6, C, Fol, Nic, Pan

Vigna subterranea; Fabaceae; Bambara groundnut, jugo bean	Afr	seeds	**376**	18.4	6.90	3.60	B1, B2, Nic
Vigna umbellata, Fabaceae; rice bean	TrAs	seeds					
Vigna unguiculata; Fabaceae; cowpea , black-eyed bean	Afr	seeds	239	**23.5**	1.40	3.50	A, B1, B2, B6, C, Fol, Nic, Pan
Vigna unguiculata subsp. *sesquipedalis*; Fabaceae; asparagus bean, yard long bean	China	seeds, fruit (green)					
Vigna vexillata; Fabaceae	Afr	roots					
Vitis labrusca; Vitaceae; slip skin grape, fox grape	NAm	fruit					
Vitis rotundifolia; Vitaceae; muscadine grape, bullace grape	NAm	fruit					
Vitis vinifera; Vitaceae; grapevine, common grape, European grape	CAs, NE	fruit	67	0.68	0.28	0.48	A, E, K, B1, B2, B6, Bio, C, Fol, Nic, Pan
Wasabia japonica; Brassicaceae; wasabi, Japanese horseradish	Chin	rhizome, stem					
Xanthosoma atrovirens; Araceae; yellow malanga	CAm	tubers, leaves					
Xanthosoma sagittifolium; Araceae; tannia, new cocyam, white malanga	CAm	tubers, leaves					
Ximenia americana; Olacaceae; sour plum, monkey plum	Afr	fruit (seed)	133	2.80	0.80	1.90	A, C
Xylopia aethiopica; Annonaceae; Guinea pepper	Afr	fruit					
Zanthoxylum piperitum; Rutaceae; Sichuan pepper, Japan pepper	Chin	fruit					
Zanthoxylum simulans (=*Z. bungei*); Rutaceae	Chin	fruit					
Zea mays; Poaceae; corn, maize, mealies	CAm (Mexico)	fruit (grains)	325	9.20	3.80	1.30	A, E, K, B1, B2, B6, Bio
		sweetcorn	87	3.28	1.23	0.80	A, E, K, B1, B2, B6, Bio, C, Fol, Nic, Pan
Zingiber officinale; Zingiberaceae; ginger	Ind	rhizome					
Zizania aquatica; Poaceae; American wild rice, Canadian wild rice	NAm	fruit (grains)	357	14.7	1.10	–	B1, B2, Fol
Zizania latifolia; Poaceae; Chinese wild rice, Manchurian wild rice	Chin	fruit, leaves					
Ziziphus jujuba; Rhamnaceae; Chinese date, jujube tree, French jujube	Eu, Asia	fruit	105	1.40	0.30	0.70	A, B1, B2, C, Nic
Ziziphus lotus; Rhamnaceae; lotus fruit	Med	fruit					
Ziziphus mauritiana; Rhamnaceae; desert apple, Indian jujube, ber	Ind, NE	fruit					
Ziziphus mistol; Rhamnaceae; mistol	SAm	fruit (Andes)					
Ziziphus mucronata; Rhamnaceae; buffalo thorn	Afr	fruit	**287**	3.20	0.60	2.60	B1, B2, Nic
Ziziphus spina-christi; Rhamnaceae; Christ's crown of thorns, ilb	NE	fruit					

GLOSSARY

Achene – a small, dry, indehiscent, one-seeded fruit

Aflatoxin – a poison produced by a fungus that grows on peanuts or maize that causes cancer

Agroforestry – a farming system that integrates the use of trees with other crops

Amarum – a bitter substance that stimulates the secretion of gastric juices

Anthocyanins – the most common red or purple pigments found in leaves and flowers

Antibiotic – a substance that kills or inhibits the growth of micro-organisms

Antioxidant – a substance that protects cells or counteracts the damage caused by oxidation and oxygen free radicals

Aperitif – a drink that stimulates the appetite

Appetite suppressant – a substance that inhibits the desire for food

Aril – a fleshy layer around a seed, derived from the funicle (seed stalk)

Aromatherapy – the medicinal use of aroma substances, mainly by inhalation, bath and massage

Artificial sweetener – a non-carbohydrate (non-sugar) substance with a sweet taste

Aztec – a member of the Mexican Indian people who established an empire in Mexico

Berber – a member of a Caucasoid Muslim people of North Africa

Berry – a fleshy fruit with numerous small seeds

Biodiversity – the variety of plants and animals in their natural environments, including the species, genes and communities

Biofoods – foods that are used in the same form as they occur in nature (see whole food), without refining, processing or addition of any substances

Biotechnology – the manipulation of living organisms (usually micro-organisms) for beneficial effects (such as production of nutrients, hormones, enzymes, etc.)

Bitter – a substance that stimulates the secretion of digestive juices

Blanch – (1) removal of colour (chlorophyll) from vegetables such as celery and chicory by the exclusion of sunlight; (2) preparing vegetables and other food by plunging it in boiling water

Bract – a leaf-like structure found at the base of a flower

Bran – the husks of cereal grain

Bulb – a rounded or elongated structure formed from fleshy overlapping leaf bases borne on a very small underground stem

Bush-tucker – an Australian term for food obtained in the bush (in the wild)

C4-plants – plants such as sugar cane and maize that has a more efficient system of photosynthesis and therefore use sunlight more efficiently than normal C3 plants

Calcification – the formation of bone tissue by addition of calcium

Calorie – a calorie is a unit of heat (energy) equal to 4.1868 joules (also called a small calorie); a Calorie (capital C, also written as kcal) is a kilogram calorie or large calorie, equal to one thousand calories

Calyx – the outer (usually green) leaf-like structures in a flower that surround the petals

Capsule – a dry, dehiscent fruit formed from several carpels that splits open along more than one suture

Caramel – burnt sugar

Carcinogenic – cancer-causing

Cardiovascular disease – a disease of the heart and the blood vessels that may lead to a heart attack

Carminative – a substance that reduces flatulence

Carpels – the leaf-like structures from which a fruit is formed (often fused into a single unit)

Carrier oil – oil that is used to dilute another oil (typically a vegetable oil used to dilute an essential oil)

Caryopsis – the technical term for a grain fruit of the family Gramineae or Poaceae (a small, dry, starch-rich, single-seeded fruit that has the seed coat and fruit wall fused)

Catkin – a pendulous (hanging), elongated flower cluster comprising numerous inconspicuous, sessile flowers

Chlorophyll – the green pigment in leaves that is able to convert sun energy into sugars through the process of photosynthesis

Climber – a plant that grows upwards by twining or using tendrils (see creeper, vine)

Compote – a dish of fruit stewed in sugar water or syrup

Corolla – a collective term describing the structure formed by the petals of a flower (see petals)

Cotyledon – the embryonic leaves found in a seed (one in monocotyledons such as maize, two in dicotyledons such as bean)

Couscous – a dish of Algeria, Morocco and Tunisia, traditionally hand-made by skilfully rolling semolina in flour so that the flour progressively binds to the semolina particles to form evenly-sized grains

Creeper – a plant that grows upwards by twining or using tendrils (see climber, vine)

Culinary herb – a plant with aromatic leaves used in cooking to add flavour to a dish

Cultigen – a form of a plant (usually a mutation) originating from human selection that is not found in nature

Cultivar – a **culti**vated **var**iety (a form of a plant that originated from human selection or plant breeding that is maintained in cultivation and not found in nature)

Deciduous – a term used to describe the annual shedding of leaves (see evergreen)

Dhal – a food made from several types of pulses (dry peas, beans, etc.) by removing the seed coat and splitting the two cotyledons

Diabetic – abnormally high blood sugar levels caused by a lack of insulin

Digestive – a substance that aids digestion

Diuretic – a substance that increases the volume of urine

Domestication – the process of converting a wild plant into a crop

Drupe – a fleshy fruit containing a single seed

Ears (of grains) – the part of a cereal plant that contains the grains (seeds)

Emulsifier – a food additive that prevents the separation of the components of processed food

Endosperm – a nutrient-rich tissue found within the seed of flowering plants that nourishes the embryo

Entire – a smooth leaf margin, not lobed or toothed

Essential oil – a mixture of volatile terpenoids with the flavour and odour of the plant from which is was extracted

Evergreen – a term used to describe plants that retain their leaves during the dormant season

Febrifuge – a substance that reduces fever

Fertile Crescent – an ancient agricultural region in the Middle East (around the rivers Tigris and Euphrates) where several crop plants originated

Fixed oil – a mixture of non-volatile, liquid fats extracted from oily seeds

Flatulence – an accumulation of gas in the intestines

Follicle – a dehiscent fruit that splits open along a single suture

Food triangle – a combination of the three main elements of balanced nutrition (a cereal for energy, a pulse for protein and coloured vegetable or fruit for vitamins)

Free radical – an unstable form of oxygen molecule that can damage cells

Freeze-dry – a method to dry and preserve food by freezing and removal of water under vacuum

Functional food – a food containing nutritional elements or additives that are aimed at maintaining or improving health

Garnish – an edible decoration added to a dish to improve the appearance and flavour

Gel – a jelly-like colloid in which a liquid is dispersed in a solid

Gene centre – a locality or region with a high concentration of different (indigenous) plant species

Geophytes – plants that have their permanent stems underground

Germ (of grain) – the embryo (rudimentary plant) in a cereal seed that is usually removed during milling and processing in order to increase the shelf life of the flour

Glumes – a pair of dry, membranous bracts at the base of the spikelets of grasses and cereals

Gluten – a glue-like mixture of proteins that is formed when the dough of some cereals (especially bread wheat) is kneaded

Glycogen – a polysaccharide of glucose units (the storage form of carbohydrates in animals and humans)

Gourmet – a person with a well-developed palate for enjoying and evaluating good food and drink

Grafting – the process of propagation in horticulture by which a small piece of plant tissue of the desired plant (scion) is made to unite with an established plant (the stock or rootstock)

Green tea – a tea that is specially dried without the usual fermentation process in order to retain the green colour, phenolic substances and antioxidant effects found in the fresh plant

Gum – a sticky plant excretion that forms a viscous mass when dissolved in water

Hallucinogenic – a substance that induces the perception of objects or sensations that are not actually present

Health food – a food used for its real or imagined benefits to health, often with a high level of nutrients and dietary fibre and often produced organically

Heartburn – an uncomfortable burning sensation in the chest due to an upwelling of stomach acid into the oesophagus

Herb – a non-woody, annual or perennial plant

Hunter-gatherer – a human culture in which all food is collected from nature through hunting and gathering (and not from crops or domestic animals)

Husks – the membranous outer covering of fruits or seeds that are normally removed by winnowing

Hyperlipidemia – an abnormally high triglyceride and cholesterol content in blood (above 160 mg and 260 mg per 100 ml respectively)

Hypoglycaemic – an abnormally low glucose level in blood

Immune stimulant – a substance capable of improving the immune system

Inca – a member of a South American Indian people of expert farmers who established an empire in Peru and other parts of the Andes

Indigestion – difficulty in digesting food, often accompanied by stomach pain and heartburn

Inflorescence – the system of stalks of a plant on which the flowers are borne

Insoluble fibre – the insoluble, bulk-forming part of plant food (mostly cellulose)

Inuit – a member of the indigenous people of Greenland and other parts of the Arctic region (hunter-gatherers previously referred to as Eskimos)

Joule – the standard unit of work or energy (the work required to move a force of 1 newton over a distance of 1 m in the direction of the force)

Khoi (also Khoikhoi) – a member of a Southern African people indigenous to the Cape region and Namibia (traditional herders with a distinctive language of clicking sounds)

Kilocalories (kcal) – a unit of heat (energy) equal to one thousand calories or 4.1868 kilojoules (kJ) (see calorie)

Kilojoules – a unit of energy (see kilocalories)

Laxative – a substance that loosens the bowels

Lecithin – a phospholipid produced by the liver that helps with the emulsification of dietary fats in the duodenum

Legume – a fruit (of the family Leguminosae or Fabaceae) that is formed from a single carpel that splits open along two sutures

Lozenge – a medicated tablet that slowly dissolves in the mouth

Lysine – an essential amino acid that is in short supply in some cereals

Malic acid – one of several organic acids found in fruits

Malt – a product made by soaking cereal grains (especially barley) in water and then drying the germinated grains in a kiln

Maple syrup – a sugary syrup made by collecting and concentrating the phloem sap of certain maple trees

Maya – a member of an American Indian people indigenous to the region of the Yucatán, Belize and northern Guatemala

Mediterranean paradox – the relatively low incidence of cardiovascular diseases in the Mediterranean region despite the popularity of smoking, drinking and eating a fat-rich diet

Mericarps – the two parts of a schizocarp (the fruit of coriander, fennel and other members of the family Umbelliferae or Apiaceae)

Microgram (µg) – the standard small unit of weight or mass (1 000 µg = 1 mg)

Milligram (mg) – the standard unit of weight or mass (1 000 mg = 1 g)

Molasses – a thick brown syrup obtained during the processing and refining of sugar

Mousse – a light creamy dish usually made from eggs, cream and various other ingredients (fruits, chocolate, fish or meat) and set with gelatine

Natural sweetener – a plant-derived substance (usually a carbohydrate) with a sweet taste

Neurotoxin – a poisonous substance that affects the brain or central nervous system

Nut – a dry, one-seeded, indehiscent fruit with an oily seed surrounded by a woody or leathery wall

Nutrient density – the amount of nutrients per unit weight of food (influenced mainly by water content)

Obesity – the excessive accumulation of fat

Oedema (edema) – the swelling of tissue due to an accumulation of fluids (usually caused by kidney or heart failure)

Oilseed – a dry fruit or seed that is used as a source of vegetable oil

Omega-3 fatty acid – an essential fatty acid with a double bond in position 3 of the carbon chain that cannot be manufactured by the human body and has to be obtained through the diet

Omega-6 fatty acid – an essential fatty acid (see omega-3 fatty acid)

Organic – relating to a substance or food produced without the use of chemical fertilisers or chemical pesticides

Osteoporosis – a reduction in bone mass, resulting in fractures

Pectin – acidic polysaccharides occurring in ripe fruits and vegetables that solidify into a gel (often used in jams)

Persistent – a term used to describe any plant structure that does not fall off (dehisce) at maturity

Petals – the inner, usually brightly coloured, leaf-like structures in a flower

Phloem – the conducting tissue in higher plants that distributes nutrients from the leaves to other parts

Phloem sap – the sugary fluid in phloem tissue

Phytochemicals – chemical compounds found in plants

Pinnate – compound leaf with the leaflets in two rows along the length of the communal stem (rachis) of the leaf

Plant breeding – the processes of selection, hybridisation or genetic manipulation through which new plant cultivars are developed

Pod – a fruit from the family Leguminosae or Fabaceae that contains peas or beans (see legume)

Pot-herb – a plant with leaves and/or stems that are cooked as a vegetable

Preserve – to treat food (by salting, drying or through addition of sugar and other preservatives) so that it will resist decomposition or chemical change

Prostaglandins – a group of physiologically active, hormone-like substances within tissues that is important in various metabolic processes (stimulation of muscles, blood vessels, inflammation)

Pulse – edible dry seeds derived from a member of the family Leguminosae or Fabaceae such as beans, peas and lentils

Purée – a food substance processed into a thick, smooth pulp

Raceme – a flower cluster with stalked flowers arranged along a single axis and opening from the bottom up

Recommended daily allowance (RDA) – the amount of essential nutrients required each day to prevent deficiency

Rémoulade sauce – a sauce made by adding mustard, capers, gherkins, chopped herbs and various other ingredients to mayonnaise

Rheumatoid arthritis – a chronic disease characterised by inflammation and swelling of the joints

Rhizome – a stem (often fleshy) that grows horizontally below or partly above the ground

Rootstock – (1) an alternative name for a rhizome; (2) a rooted plant used as stock in grafting

Samara (key fruit) – a dry, winged, one-seeded fruit

Sambal – a spicy Indonesian condiment made with chilli peppers, onions, oil, vinegar and various chopped fruits

Sami – a member of the indigenous people of Lapland

San – a member of a southern African indigenous people (traditional hunter-gatherers with a distinctive language of clicking sounds, sometimes referred to as Bushmen)

Satay (kebab) – a dish of small pieces of meat, onions and various vegetables grilled on a skewer

Schizocarp – a small dry fruit that splits into two halves (two mericarps), often referred to as "seeds" (typical of coriander, fennel and other members of the family Umbelliferae or Apiaceae)

Scurvy – a disease caused by a deficiency of vitamin C (symptoms include spongy gums, anaemia and bleeding beneath the skin)

Semolina – a granular food obtained by coarsely grinding a hard cereal (durum wheat, rice, etc.) into small, evenly sized particles

Sepals – the outer leaf-like structures (usually green) that surround the petals

Sessile – without a stalk (used to describe leaves or flowers)

Sherbet – a fruit-flavoured, slightly effervescent powder eaten as a sweet or used to make drinks (see sorbet)

Soluble fibre – water-soluble fibres in the diet

such as polysaccharides, pectins and gums

Sorbet – (1) a soft ice made from fruit juices or fruit purées with various flavour ingredients added; (2) the word used in the USA and Canada for sherbet

Sorosis – technical term for a compound fruit in which the whole inflorescence becomes fleshy (such as a pineapple)

Soufflé – a sweet or savoury oven dish cooked in a mould and served hot from the oven

Spasmolytic – a substance that causes relief of spasms

Spice – an aromatic plant substance used to add flavour to a dish

Spike – a type of flower cluster with sessile (stalkless) flowers along an elongated axis

Spikelet – one of several groups of floret(s) that make up the ear of a grass cereal

Spina bifida – a congenital condition in which the meninges (spinal membrane) of the spinal cord protrude through a gap in the backbone

Sprouts – germinated seeds or very small seedlings that are eaten fresh in salads

Stabiliser – a substance used to preserve the texture of food

Stamen – the male reproductive organ in a flower consisting of a stalk (filament) with a head (anther) in which the pollen is formed

Staple food – the principal food of a region

Stigma – the terminal part of the style on the ovary of a flower where the pollen is deposited during pollination

Stimulant – a substance that increases physiological activity

Stomachic – a substance that promotes appetite and digestion

Style – the structure in a flower that connects the stigma(s) to the ovary

Sweetener – a sugar or non-sugar substance added for its sweet taste

Syncarp – a fleshy compound fruit formed from the fused carpels of one or several flowers

Taproot – the main root of the plant that grows vertically downwards (often bearing smaller lateral roots)

Teratogenic – a substance or process that causes malformation in a foetus

Thickener – a substance added to a liquid to thicken it

Tisane – an (often weak) infusion made from leaves or flowers

Toffee – a sweet made from sugar boiled with butter (often with nuts or dry fruits added)

Tonic – a medicinal preparation that improves the functioning of the body or increases the feeling of wellbeing

Treacle – the term for molasses in the USA and Canada

Tuber – swollen underground part of a stem or root

Umbel – a flower cluster that has all the flowers arising at the same point (typical for the family Umbelliferae or Apiaceae)

Unsaturated fat – a fat with one or more double bonds (unsaturated carbon atoms) in the carbon chain

Vegan – a person who uses no animal products

Vegetarian – a person who uses no meat or fish (sometimes also no eggs, milk or cheese)

Venotonic – a substance that strengthens the arteries and veins

Vermifuge – a substance that kills or expels intestinal worms

Vine – a plant that grows upwards by twining or using tendrils (see climber, creeper)

Volatile oil – a mixture of aromatic and volatile terpenoids obtained from plants

Whole food – a food of which the nutrient composition is the same as is found in nature

Winnow – the process to separate grains from chaff using the wind or an air current

Yeast – various single-celled fungi which are able to ferment sugars (used to brew beer or to raise dough for bread)

FURTHER READING

Borget M (1992) Food Legumes. The Tropical Agriculturalist Series. Macmillan, London

Borget M (1993) Spice Plants. The Tropical Agriculturalist Series. Macmillan, London

Bostid A (1979) Tropical Legumes: Resources for the Future. National Academy of Sciences, Washington

Brouk B (1975) Plants Consumed by Man. Academic Press, London

Brücher H (1977) Tropische Nutzpflanzen. Ursprung, Evolution und Domestikation. Springer Verlag, Berlin

Brücher H (1989) Useful Plants of Neotropical Origin. Springer Verlag, Berlin

Cabbalero B (ed) (1993) Encyclopedia of Food Sciences and Nutrition. 2nd edn. Academic Press (Elsevier), Kent

Chrispeels MJ, Sadava DE (1994) Plants, Genes, and Agriculture. Jones and Bartlett Publishers, Boston and London

Couplan F, Duke J (1998) The Encyclopedia of Edible Plants of North America. McGraw-Hill, New York

Davidson A (1999) The Oxford Companion to Food. Oxford University Press, Oxford

De Candolle ALPP (1882) Origine des Plantes Cultivées. Germer Bailliere et Cie, Paris

De Guzman CC, Siemonsma JS (eds) (1999) PROSEA Handbook 13. Spices. PROSEA, Bogor

Densmore F (1974) How Indians Use Wild Plants for Food, Medicine and Crafts. Dover Publications, New York

Economic Botany (1946-), Journal of the Society for Economic Botany at the New York Botanical Garden, New York

Esdorn J, Pirson H (1973) Die Nutzpflanzen der Tropen und Subtropen in der Weltwirtschaft. 2nd edn. Fischer Verlag, Stuttgart

Expert Group on Vitamins and Minerals (2003) Safe Upper Levels for Vitamins and Minerals. Food Standards Agency, London

FAO (1999) FAO Production Yearbook 1998, Vol. 52. FAO Statistics Series No. 148. FAO, Rome

Flach M, Rumawas F (eds) (1996) PROSEA Handbook 9. Plants Yielding Non-seed Carbohydrates. PROSEA, Bogor

Fox FW, Norwood Young ME (1982) Food from the Veld. Edible Wild Plants of Southern Africa. Delta Books, Johannesburg

Franke W (1997) Nutzpflanzenkunde. Nutzbare Gewächse der gemäßigten Breiten, Subtropen und Tropen. George Thieme Verlag, Stuttgart

Gibbon D, Pain A (1980) Crops of the Drier Regions of the Tropics. Intermediate Tropical Agriculture Series. Longman, Harlow, Essex

Grubben GJH, Partohardjono S (eds) (1996) PROSEA Handbook 10. Cereals. PROSEA, Bogor

Heiser CB (1985) Of Plants and People. University of Oklahoma Press, Norman, Oklahoma

Huxley A (1992) Green Inheritance. Four Walls Eight Windows, New York

Janick J, Schery RW, Woods FW, Ruttan VW (1981) Plant Science. An Introduction to World Crops. WH Freeman and Company, San Francisco

Kiple KF, Ornelas KC (eds) (2000) The Cambridge World History of Food. Cambridge University Press, Cambridge

Langer RHM, Hill GD (1991) Agricultural Plants. 2nd edn. Cambridge University Press, Cambridge

Larousse (1999) The Concise Larousse Gastronomique. The World's Greatest Cookery Encyclopedia. Hamlyn, London

Le Bellec F, Renard V (1999) Tropical Fruits. The Compendium. Editions Orphie, Cirad, Montpellier

Lewington A (1990) Plants for People. The Natural History Museum, London

Low T (1991) Wild Food Plants of Australia. Angus & Robertson, Sydney

Mabberley DJ (1997) The Plant-Book. A Portable Dictionary of the Vascular Plants. 2nd edn. Cambridge University Press, Cambridge

McMahon, MJ, Kofranek AM, Rubatzky VE (2002) Hartmann's Plant Science. Growth, Development and Utilization of Cultivated Plants. Prentice Hall, New Jersey

Morton JF (1987) Fruits of Warm Climates. JF Morton, Miami, Florida

National Research Council (1989) Lost Crops of the Incas: Little-Known Plants of the Andes with Promise for Worldwide Cultivation. National Academy Press, Washington

Peters CR, O'Brien EM, Drummond RB (1992) Edible Wild Plants of sub-Saharan Africa. Royal Botanic Gardens, Kew

Peterson LA (1977) Edible Wild Plants of Eastern and Central North America. Houghton Mifflin Company, Boston

Phillips R, Rix M (1993) Vegetables. The Pan Garden Plant Series. Pan Books, London

Purseglove JW (1975) Tropical Crops. 2nd edn. Longman, London

Rehm S, Espig G (1984) Die Kulturpflanzen der Tropen und Subtropen. 2nd edn. Ulmer, Stuttgart

Rogers J (1990) What Food is That? and How Healthy is It? Weldon Publishing, Sydney

Royal Society of Chemistry, Ministry of Agriculture, Fisheries and Food (1991) McCance and Widdowson's The Composition of Foods. 5th edn. Royal Society of Chemistry and Ministry of Agriculture, Fisheries and Food, Cambridge

Saunt J (2000) Citrus Varieties of the World. Sinclair International, Norwich

Shiu-ying H (2005) Food Plants of China. The Chinese University Press, Hong Kong

Siemonsma JS, Piluek K (eds) (1993) PROSEA Handbook 8. Vegetables. PROSEA, Bogor

Simpson BB, Ogorzaly MC (2001) Economic Botany: Plants in Our World. 3rd edn. McGraw-Hill International Edition. New York

Smartt J, Simmonds NW (eds) (1995) Evolution of Crop Plants. 2nd edn. Longman Scientific and Technical Publishers, London

Souci SW, Fachmann W, Kraut H (2000) Food Composition and Nutrition Tables. 6th edn. Medpharm Scientific Publishers, Stuttgart

Swahn JO (1999) The Lore of Spices. Their History, Nature and Uses around the World. Senate Publishing, London

United States Department of Agriculture (1992) Composition of Foods. Agriculture Handbook no 8. USDA, Washington

Van der Maesen LJG, Somaatmadja S (eds) (1989) PROSEA Handbook 1. Pulses. PROSEA, Bogor

Van der Vossen HAM, Umali BE (eds) (2001) PROSEA Handbook 14. Vegetable Oils and Fats. PROSEA, Bogor

Van Wyk B-E, Gericke N (2000) People's Plants. A Guide to Useful Plants of Southern Africa. Briza Publications, Pretoria

Vaughan JG, Geissler CA (1997) The New Oxford Book of Food Plants. Oxford University Press, Oxford

Veith WJ (1998) Diet and Health. Scientific Perspectives. Medpharm Scientific Publishers, Stuttgart

Verheij EWM, Coronel RE (eds) (1991) PROSEA Handbook 2. Edible Fruits and Nuts. PROSEA, Bogor

Wehmeyer AS (1986) Edible Wild Plants of Southern Africa. Data on the Nutrient Contents of over 300 Species. Unpublished report, August 1986

Williams CN, Chew WY, Rajaratnam JA (1980) Tree and Field Crops of the Wetter Regions of the Tropics. Intermediate Tropical Agriculture Series. Longman Scientific & Technical, Harlow, Essex

Zander (1994) Zander, Handwörterbuch der Pflanzennamen. 15th edn. Ulmer, Stuttgart

Zeven AC, De Wet JMJ (1982) Dictionary of Cultivated Plants and their Regions of Diversity. 2nd edn. Centre for Agricultural Publishing and Documentation, Wageningen

Zohary D, Hopf M (1994) Domestication of Plants in the Old World. 2nd edn. Clarendon Press, Oxford

ACKNOWLEDGEMENTS

The author wishes to thank Briza Publications and the production team, especially Reneé Ferreira, David Pearson and Melinda Stark, for their professionalism. Eben van Wyk is thanked for his inspiration and support ever since our first photo sessions in Singapore and Malaysia in 1998.

Thank you to Friedel Herrmann for translating the book into German and to Susanne Warmuth for editing the German text and for valuable comments, corrections and suggestions. A word of thanks is also due to Siegmar Bauer (Wissenschaftliche Verlagsgesellschaft, Stuttgart) for support and friendship over many years.

Without the help and encouragement of my family (Mariana, Teodor and Signe), this project would not have been possible. I also thank Frits van Oudtshoorn, Michael Wink and Coralie Wink for their enthusiasm and valued companionship during several photo trips.

The University of Johannesburg (formerly Rand Afrikaans University) provided institutional support. The interest and assistance of staff and students of the Botany and Chemistry Departments (some are listed individually below) are much appreciated. A special thanks to Pat Tilney, Chantal O'Brien and Bernard de Villiers for help with field work, Lisa Timmerman for drawing chemical structures and Marianne le Roux for help with the checklist of food plants.

Several persons and institutions have supplied photographs, samples or literature; some helped with field work and photo sessions or simply gave support and encouragement:

The Agricultural Research Council of South Africa (Research Institutes at Burgershall, Nelspruit and Roodeplaat); James Alleman (Roodeplaat, Pretoria); Torbjørn Alm (University of Tromsø, Norway); June Rodrigues Alves (São Paulo, Brazil); Tatiana Anderson (TopTropicals Botanical Centre, Davie, Florida, USA); Dr David Arkcoll (Stellenbosch); Botanical Gardens of Durban, Frankfurt, Heidelberg, Johannesburg, Kew, Kirstenbosch, Mainz, Missouri, Oxford, Padua, Pisa, Singapore, Stockholm (Bergius Foundation), Sydney and Zurich; Joreth Duvenhage (Du Roi Nursery, Letsitele, South Africa); Siegmar Bauer (Wissenschaftliche Verlagsgesellschaft, Stuttgart); Stephen Boatwright (University of Johannesburg); Daniel Carrión (Tigernuts Traders, Valencia, Spain); Johnny Chia (Pasir Pajang Market, Singapore); Boo Chin Min (National Parks Board, Singapore); Jean-françois Cruz (Montpellier, France); Prof Ermias Dagne (Addis Ababa, Ethiopia); Tony de Castro (Johannesburg); Bernard de Villiers (University of Johannesburg); Pierre du Plessis (CRIAA-DC, Windhoek, Namibia); Rosemary du Preez (Nelspruit, South Africa); Leon Esselen (Esselen Nursery, Malelane, South Africa); Thinus Fourie (University of Johannesburg); Craig Gardner (Johannesburg); Prof David Fankhauser (Batavia, USA); Mr Subraya Gounden (Durban); Mike Gray (Palm and Cycad Societies of Australia); Dr Roland and Andrea Greinwald (Kensingen, Germany); Paul Griffiths (Chicory SA, Alexandria, South Africa); Jamilah Hassan (Marshall Cavendish International, Singapore); Prof W. John Hayden (University of Richmond, Virginia, USA); Armin Jagel (Botanical Garden Bochum, Germany); Dr Stanley J Kays (The University of Georgia, Athens, Georgia, USA); Johan Koekemoer (Nelspruit, South Africa); S. Tugrul Körüklü (University of Ankara, Turkey); Tihomir Kostadinov (University of Richmond, Virginia, USA); Dr Klaus Kramer (University of Heidelberg, Germany); At Kruger (Roodeplaat, Pretoria); Sree Latha (National Parks Board, Singapore); Marianne le Roux (University of Johannesburg); Andre Lezar (National Gene Bank, Roodeplaat, Pretoria); Mei (Rebecca) Liu (Harbin, China); Flip Lochner (Clanwilliam Hotel, Clanwilliam, South Africa); Kent Loeffler (Cornell University, Ithaca, New York, USA); Harri Lorenzi (Instituto Plantarum de Estudos da Flora, Nova Odessa, Brazil); Ken Love (University of Hawaii, Hawaii, USA); Leidulf Lund (University of Tromsø, Norway); Anthony Magee (University of Johannesburg); Jip Margadant (Wood Solutions, The Hague, Netherlands); Inger Martinussen (Tromsø, Norway); Prof Yosef Mizrahi (Ben Gurion University, Beer-Sheva, Israel); Thomas Mulcaire (São Paulo, Brazil); Anton Muller (Green Valley Nuts, Prieska, South Africa); Dr Robbie Nel (Tzaneen, South Africa); Lieveke Noyons (Randburg, South Africa); Dr Brian Oates (President, Pacific Coast Wasabi Ltd, Vancouver, Canada); Chantal O'Brien (University of Johannesburg); Dr Daryl O'Connor (Queensland, Australia); Patricia Ong (Marshall Cavendish International, Singapore); Violet Phoon (Marshall Cavendish International, Singapore); Gretha Quinlan (Durban); Dr CF Quiros (University of Davis,

California, USA); Ramón Rautenstrauch (Tigernuts Traders, Valencia, Spain); Maria Marcela Reynoso (Johannesburg); Veronica Rood (Botswana); Donnette Ross (Johannesburg); Christo Smit (Citrusdal, South Africa); Shu Suehiro (Osaka, Japan); Dr H. David Thurston (Cornell University, New York, USA); Dr Patricia M. Tilney (University of Johannesburg); Lisa Timmerman (University of Johannesburg); Marike Trytsman (Roodeplaat, Pretoria); Erika van den Heever (Roodeplaat, Pretoria); Prof Fanie R. van Heerden (University of KwaZulu-Natal, Pietermaritzburg, South Africa); Prof Bosch van Oudtshoorn (Pretoria); Frits van Oudtshoorn (Nylstroom, South Africa); James van Putten (Lamberts Bay, South Africa); Pieter and Corli van Rensburg (Lagos, Nigeria); Abraham van Rooyen (Du Roi Nursery, Letsitele, South Africa); Mariana van Wyk (Johannesburg); Signe van Wyk (Johannesburg); Teodor van Wyk (Johannesburg); Susanne Vetter (University of Cape Town, South Africa); Prof Alvaro Viljoen (University of the Witwatersrand, Johannesburg); Jan-Adriaan Viljoen (Kyushu, Japan); Chris Welgemoed (Nelspruit, South Africa); Prof Michael Wink (University of Heidelberg, Germany); Dr Coralie Wink (Romneya Press, Dossenheim, Germany); Prof Charles Whitehead (University of Johannesburg); Chris Wong (Marshall Cavendish International, Singapore)

PHOTOGRAPHIC CONTRIBUTIONS

All photographs were taken by **Ben-Erik van Wyk** except those listed below. These are arranged alphabetically from top to bottom and from left to right, according to photographer and page number:

Torbjørn Alm (Tromsø museum, University of Tromsø, Norway): 327a (*Rubus chamaemorus*); **Tatiana Anderson** (TopTropicals.com): 91b (*Blighia sapida*); **Dr Thomas Brendler** (PlantaPhile, Berlin, Germany; http://www.plantaphile.com): 282c (*Paullinia cupana*); **Jean-françois Cruz** (Cirad – UR Qualité des aliments tropicaux, Montpellier, France): 175a-e (*Digitaria exilis*); **Pierre du Plessis** (CRIAA-DC, Windhoek, Namibia): 339bd (*Schinziophyton rautanenii*); **Joreth Duvenhage** (Du Roi Nursery, Letsitele, South Africa): 378a (*Vanilla planifolia*); **Prof David B. Fankhauser** (University of Cincinnati Clermont College, Batavia, USA): 41bd (*Acer saccharum* – maple syrup tapping); **Brett Gardner** (Johannesburg, South Africa): 9b (rice paddies in Indonesia); **Mike Gray** (Palm and Cycad Societies of Australia; http://www.pacsoa.org.au/ ; mikeg@pacsoa.org.au): 334a (*Salacca zalacca*); **Kerim Güney** (Herbarium ANK, Department of Biology, University of Ankara, Turkey): 155ac (*Crocus sativus*); **Armin Jagel** (Botanical Garden Bochum, Germany): 366ac (*Trichosanthes cucumerina*); **Dr Stanley J Kays** (Department of Horticulture, The University of Georgia, Athens, Georgia, USA): 271c, 370c, 371b (*Oxalis tuberosa, Tropaeolum tuberosum, Ullucus tuberosus*); **Tihomir Kostadinov** (University of Richmond, Virginia, USA): 41c (*Acer saccharum*); **Dr Klaus Kramer** (University of Heidelberg, Germany): 374c (*Vaccinium oxycoccus*); **Harri Lorenzi** (Instituto Plantarum de Estudos da Flora, Nova Odessa, Brazil): 86a (*Bertholletia excelsa*); **Ken Love** (University of Hawaii, PO Box 1242, Captain Cook, Hi. 96704, Hawaii, USA; kenlove@hawaii.edu; http://www.hawaiifruit.net): 176ac, 181c, 182c, 258c, 282b, 292a, 356c (*Dimocarpus longan, Lansium domesticum, Flacourtia indica, Durio zibethinus, Myrciaria cauliflora, Paullinia cupana, Phyllanthus acidus, Synsepalum dulcificum*); **Leidulf Lund** (Institute of Biology, University of Tromsø, Norway): 327bc (*Rubus chamaemorus*); **Jip Margadant** (Wood Solutions, The Hague, Netherlands): 133abc, 341c (*Cichorium endivia, Scorzonera hispanica*); **Marshall Cavendish International (Asia) Pte Ltd** (A member of Times Publishing Limited, Times Centre, 1 New Industrial Road, Singapore 536196; email: te@sg.marshallcavendish.com): 92c (*Boesenbergia rotunda*); **National Parks Board, Singapore:** 91ac (*Blighia sapida*); **Dr Daryl O'Connor** (Queensland, Australia; http://www.geocities.com): 94a (*Borassus flabellifer*); **Pacific Coast Wasabi Ltd** (Vancouver, Canada, www.wasabia.ca): 385abc (*Wasabia japonica*); **Dr CF Quiros** (Dept. of Plant Sciences, University of Davis, California, USA): 370b (*Tropaeolum tubersum*); **Shu Suehiro** (Shijonawate-City, Osaka-Prefecture, Japan): 366b (*Trichosanthes cucumerina*); **Dr H. David Thurston** (Cornell University, USA, http://www.tropag-fieldtrip.cornell.edu): 371c (*Ullucus tuberosus*); **Dr Patricia Tilney** (University of Johannesburg, South Africa): 364d (*Theobroma cacao*); **Tigernuts Traders, S.L.** (Valencia, Spain - www.tigernuts.com): 171bc (*Cyperus esculentus*); **Frits van Oudtshoorn** (Nylstroom, South Africa): 75b (*Artocarpus altilis*); **Eben van Wyk** (Sannieshof, South Africa): 11e, 36b, 37c, 52c, 54c, 75a, 76ab, 85a, 113a, 149c, 152b, 178c, 180c, 206b, 212c, 234ac, 250b, 226bc, 285c, 324c, 334c, 343a, 359a, 362a, 364abc, 383ab, 388b; **Dr Piet van Wyk** (Pretoria, South Africa): 39b, 339ac (*Acacia senegal, Schinziophyton rautanenii*); **Jan-Adriaan Viljoen** (Kyushu, Japan): 49c, 68ac, 270b, 284c (rakkyo bulbs, *Arctium lappa, Oryza sativa, Perilla frutescens*); **Prof Dr Michael Wink** (University of Heidelberg, Germany): 233a (*Lupinus albus*); **Liang De Zhang** (Wandashan Ginseng Farm, Hulin, Heilongjiang Province, China): 274ab (*Panax ginseng*).

Names and page numbers in **bold print** indicate main entries and illustrations.

451

456

462

471

480